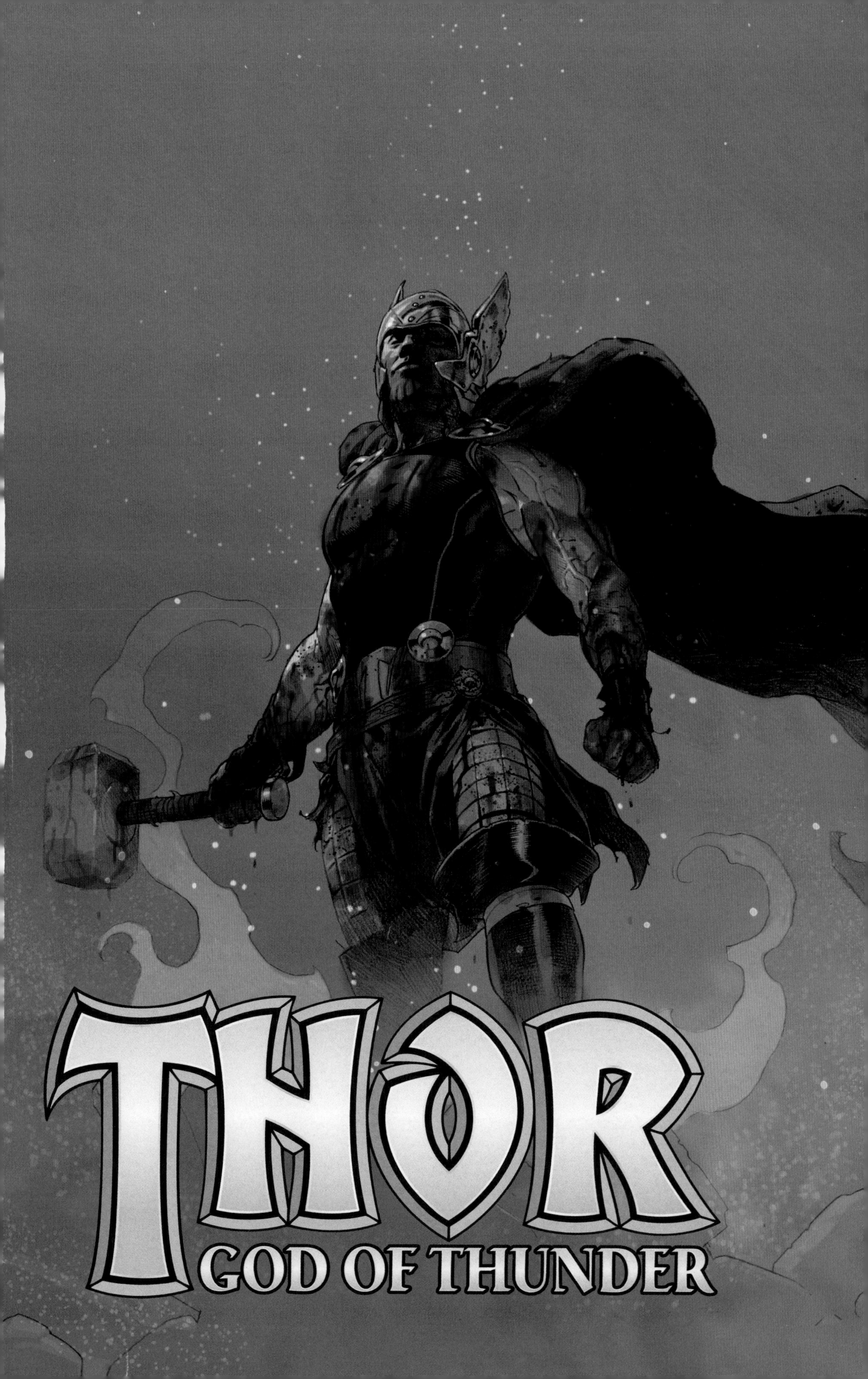
THOR
GOD OF THUNDER

Collection Editor: **Jennifer Grünwald**

Assistant Editor: **Sarah Brunstad**

Associate Managing Editor: **Alex Starbuck**

Editor, Special Projects: **Mark D. Beazley**

Senior Editor, Special Projects: **Jeff Youngquist**

SVP Print, Sales & Marketing: **David Gabriel**

Book Design: **Jeff Powell**

Editor in Chief: **Axel Alonso**

Chief Creative Officer: **Joe Quesada**

Publisher: **Dan Buckley**

Executive Producer: **Alan Fine**

THOR: GOD OF THUNDER VOL. 1. Contains material originally published in magazine form as THOR: GOD OF THUNDER #1-11. First printing 2014. ISBN# 978-0-7851-9113-1. Published by MARVEL WORLDWIDE, INC., a subsidiary of MARVEL ENTERTAINMENT, LLC. OFFICE OF PUBLICATION: 135 West 50th Street, New York, NY 10020. Copyright © 2012, 2013 and 2014 Marvel Characters, Inc. All rights reserved. All characters featured in this issue and the distinctive names and likenesses thereof, and all related indicia are trademarks of Marvel Characters, Inc. No similarity between any of the names, characters, persons, and/or institutions in this magazine with those of any living or dead person or institution is intended, and any such similarity which may exist is purely coincidental. **Printed in China.** ALAN FINE, EVP - Office of the President, Marvel Worldwide, Inc. and EVP & CMO Marvel Characters B.V.; DAN BUCKLEY, Publisher & President - Print, Animation & Digital Divisions; JOE QUESADA, Chief Creative Officer; TOM BREVOORT, SVP of Publishing; DAVID BOGART, SVP of Operations & Procurement, Publishing; C.B. CEBULSKI, SVP of Creator & Content Development; DAVID GABRIEL, SVP Print, Sales & Marketing; JIM O'KEEFE, VP of Operations & Logistics; DAN CARR, Executive Director of Publishing Technology; SUSAN CRESPI, Editorial Operations Manager; ALEX MORALES, Publishing Operations Manager; STAN LEE, Chairman Emeritus. For information regarding advertising in Marvel Comics or on Marvel.com, please contact Niza Disla, Director of Marvel Partnerships, at ndisla@marvel.com. For Marvel subscription inquiries, please call 800-217-9158. **Manufactured between 7/18/2014 and 9/15/2014 by R.R. DONNELLEY ASIA PRINTING SOLUTIONS, CHINA.**

10 9 8 7 6 5 4 3 2 1

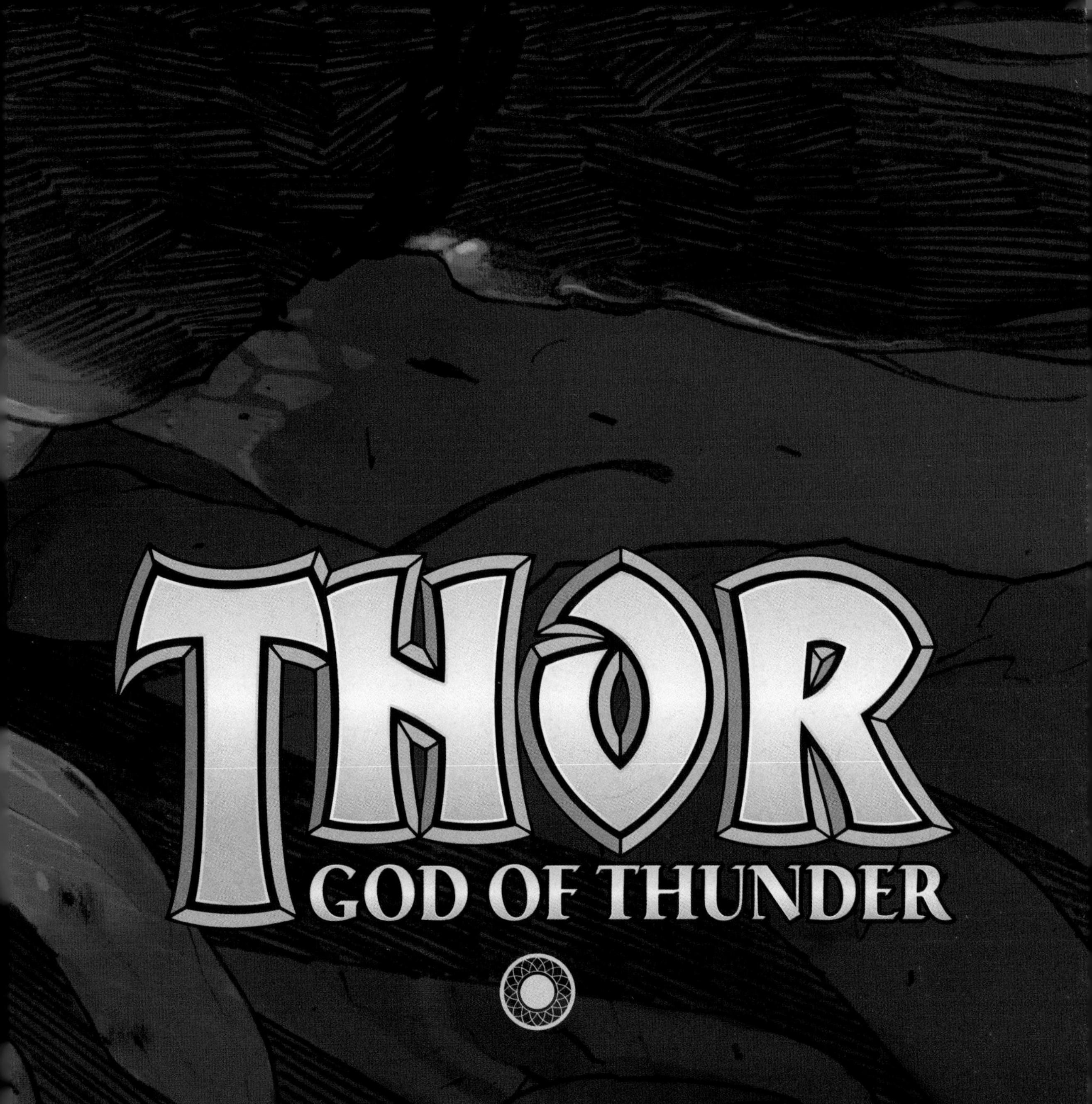

THOR
GOD OF THUNDER

WRITER
JASON AARON

ARTIST, #1-5 & #7-11
ESAD RIBIC

PENCILER, #6
BUTCH GUICE

INKER, #6
TOM PALMER

COLOR ARTIST, #1
DEAN WHITE

COLOR ARTIST, #2-11
IVE SVORCINA

LETTERER
VC'S JOE SABINO

COVER ART
ESAD RIBIC

ASSISTANT EDITOR
JAKE THOMAS

EDITOR
LAUREN SANKOVITCH

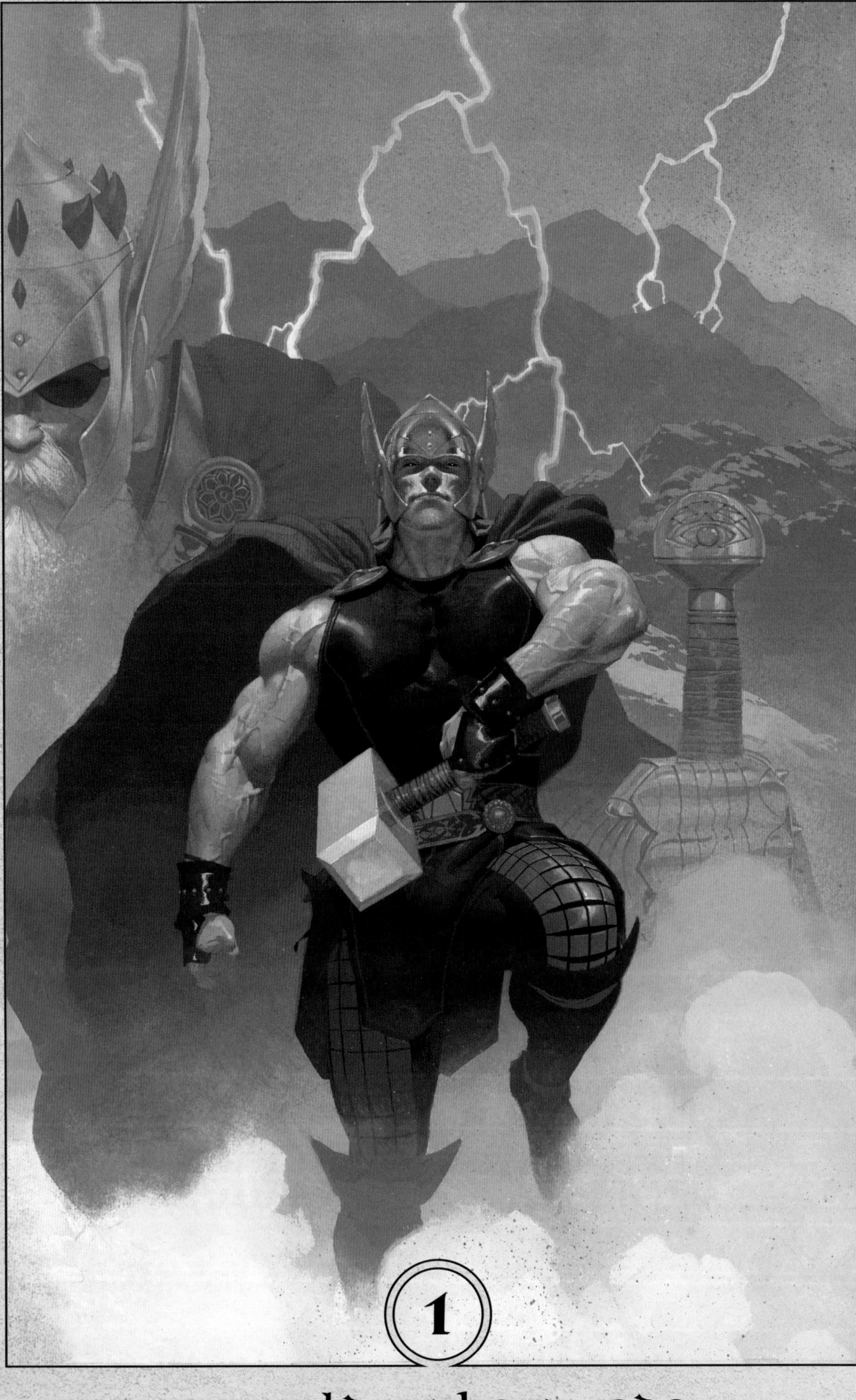
1

A WORLD WITHOUT GODS

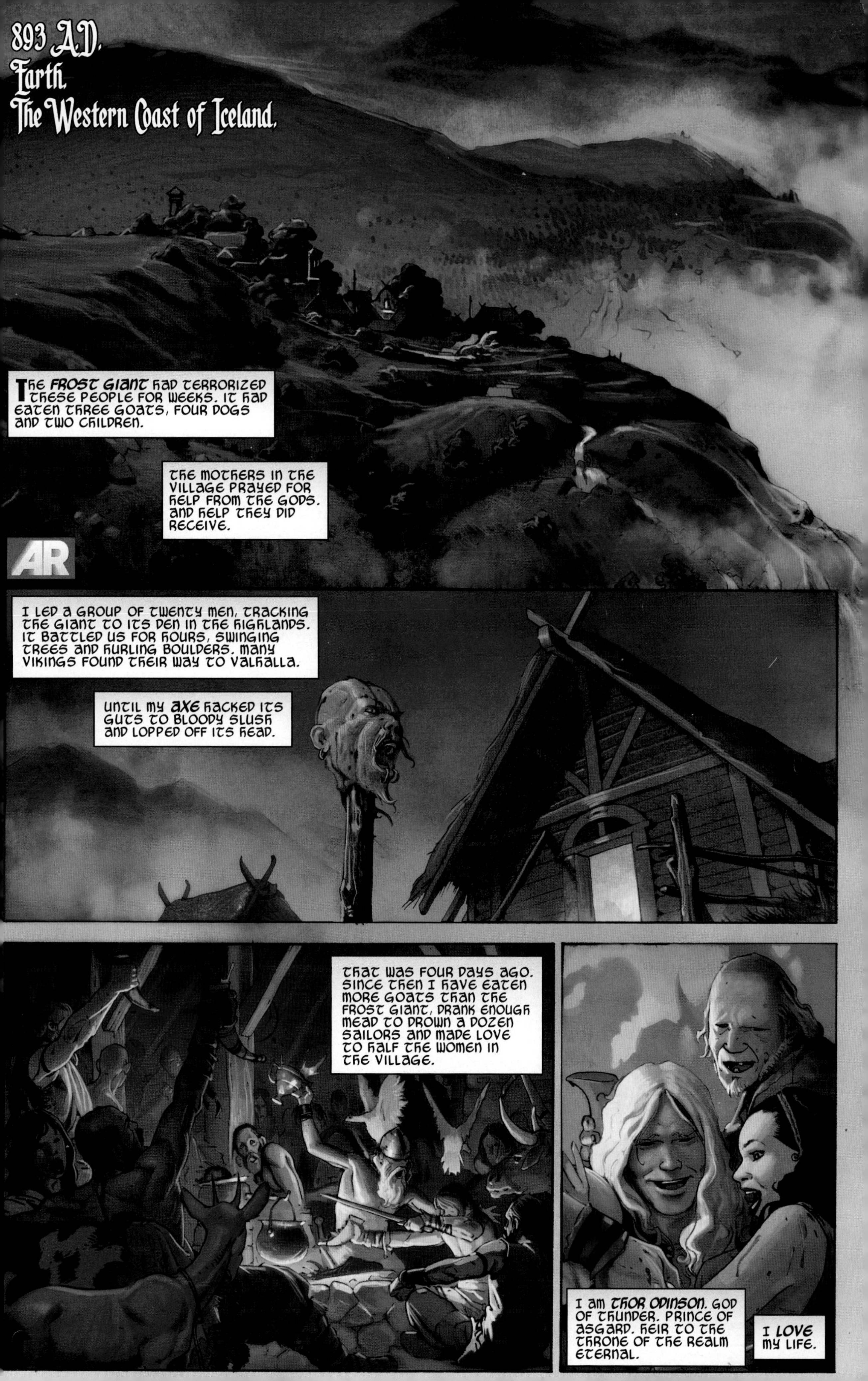
893 A.D.
Earth.
The Western Coast of Iceland.
THE FROST GIANT HAD TERRORIZED THESE PEOPLE FOR WEEKS. IT HAD EATEN THREE GOATS, FOUR DOGS AND TWO CHILDREN.
THE MOTHERS IN THE VILLAGE PRAYED FOR HELP FROM THE GODS. AND HELP THEY DID RECEIVE.
AR
I LED A GROUP OF TWENTY MEN, TRACKING THE GIANT TO ITS DEN IN THE HIGHLANDS. IT BATTLED US FOR HOURS, SWINGING TREES AND HURLING BOULDERS. MANY VIKINGS FOUND THEIR WAY TO VALHALLA.
UNTIL MY AXE HACKED ITS GUTS TO BLOODY SLUSH AND LOPPED OFF ITS HEAD.
THAT WAS FOUR DAYS AGO. SINCE THEN I HAVE EATEN MORE GOATS THAN THE FROST GIANT, DRANK ENOUGH MEAD TO DROWN A DOZEN SAILORS AND MADE LOVE TO HALF THE WOMEN IN THE VILLAGE.
I AM THOR ODINSON. GOD OF THUNDER. PRINCE OF ASGARD. HEIR TO THE THRONE OF THE REALM ETERNAL.
I LOVE MY LIFE.

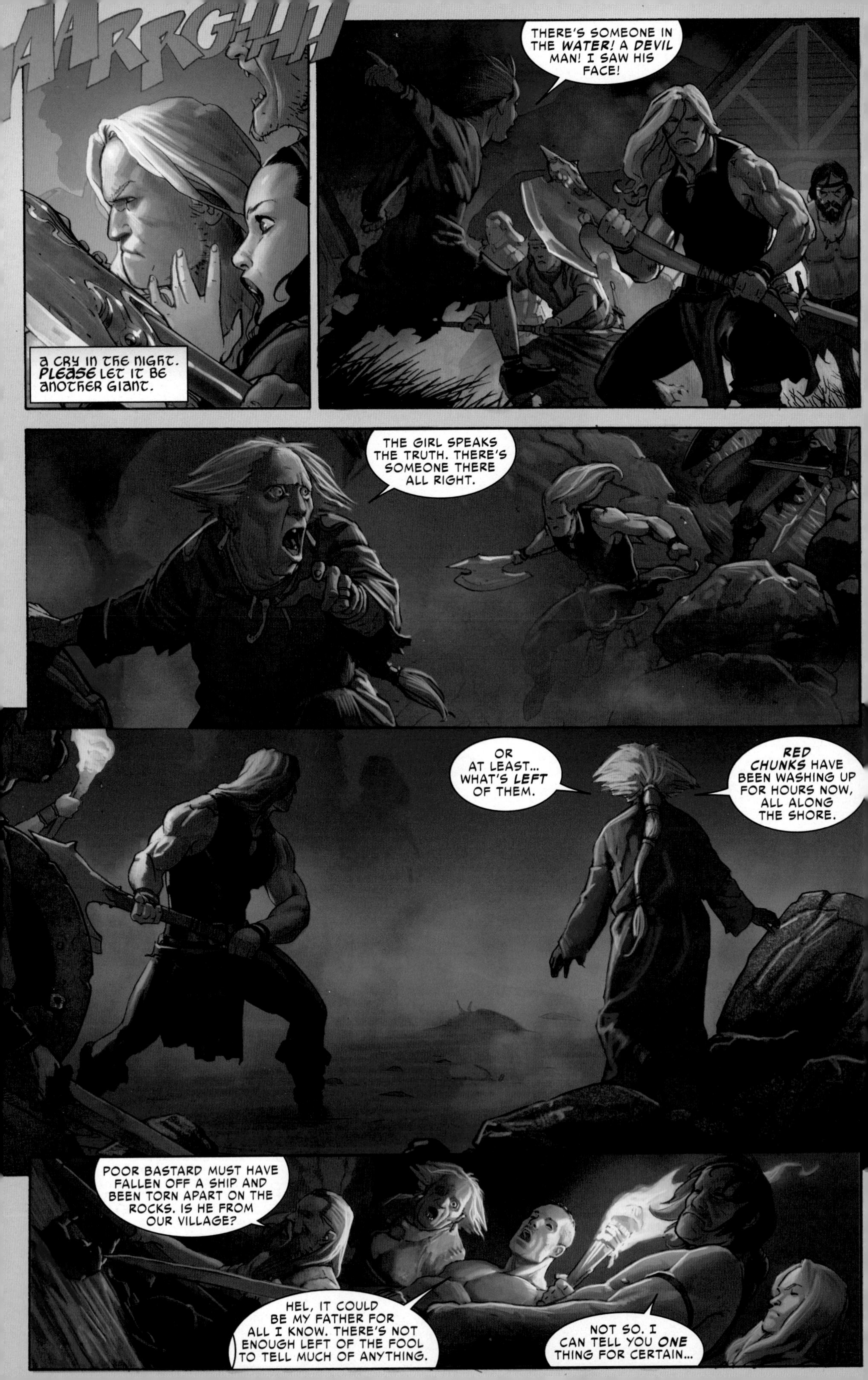
AARRGHHH
A CRY IN THE NIGHT. PLEASE LET IT BE ANOTHER GIANT.
THERE'S SOMEONE IN THE WATER! A DEVIL MAN! I SAW HIS FACE!
THE GIRL SPEAKS THE TRUTH. THERE'S SOMEONE THERE ALL RIGHT.
OR AT LEAST... WHAT'S LEFT OF THEM.
RED CHUNKS HAVE BEEN WASHING UP FOR HOURS NOW, ALL ALONG THE SHORE.
POOR BASTARD MUST HAVE FALLEN OFF A SHIP AND BEEN TORN APART ON THE ROCKS. IS HE FROM OUR VILLAGE?
HEL, IT COULD BE MY FATHER FOR ALL I KNOW. THERE'S NOT ENOUGH LEFT OF THE FOOL TO TELL MUCH OF ANYTHING.
NOT SO. I CAN TELL YOU ONE THING FOR CERTAIN...

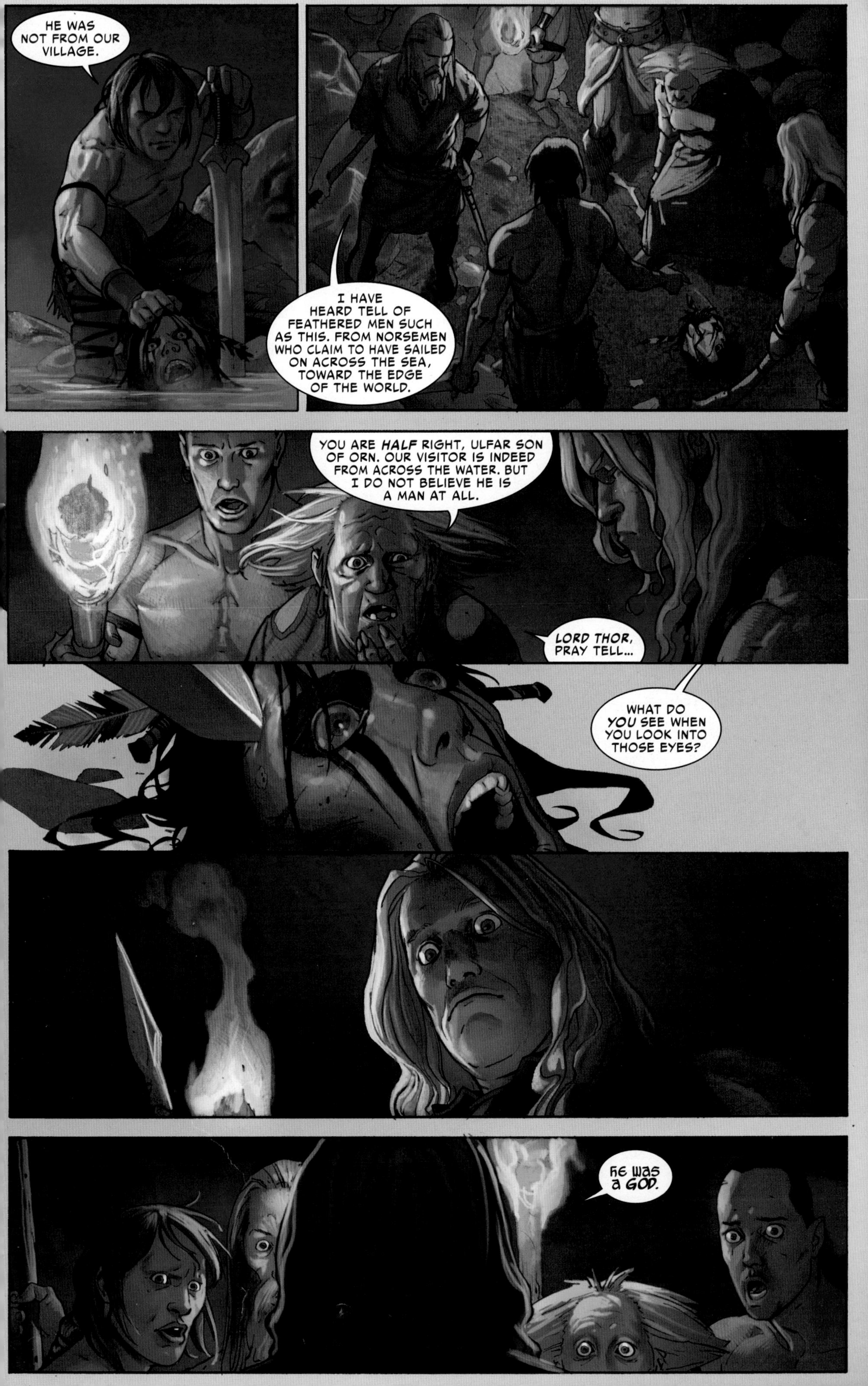
HE WAS NOT FROM OUR VILLAGE.
I HAVE HEARD TELL OF FEATHERED MEN SUCH AS THIS. FROM NORSEMEN WHO CLAIM TO HAVE SAILED ON ACROSS THE SEA, TOWARD THE EDGE OF THE WORLD.
YOU ARE *HALF* RIGHT, ULFAR SON OF ORN. OUR VISITOR IS INDEED FROM ACROSS THE WATER. BUT I DO NOT BELIEVE HE IS A MAN AT ALL.
LORD THOR, PRAY TELL...
WHAT DO *YOU* SEE WHEN YOU LOOK INTO THOSE EYES?
HE WAS A *GOD*.

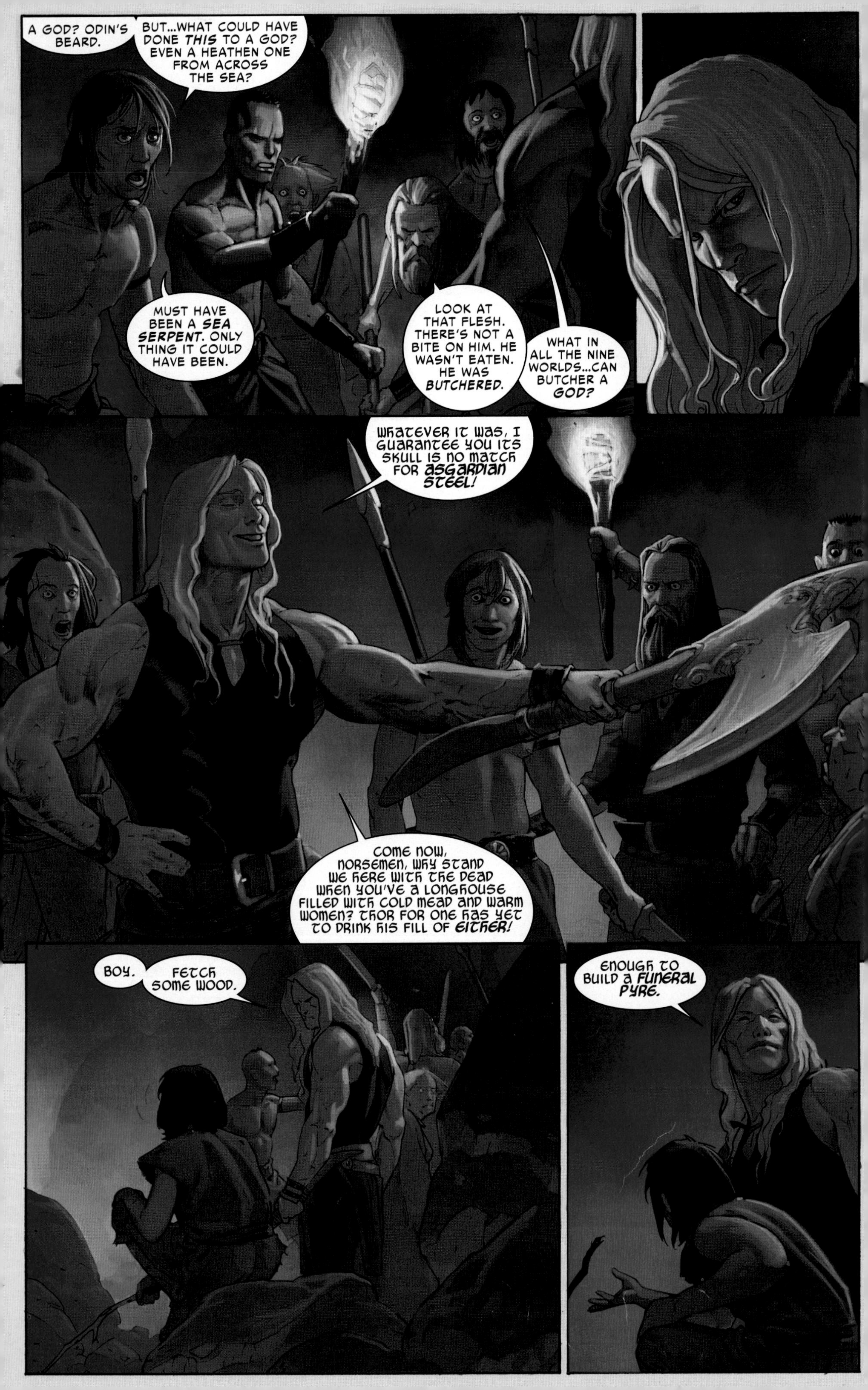

A GOD? ODIN'S BEARD.
BUT...WHAT COULD HAVE DONE *THIS* TO A GOD? EVEN A HEATHEN ONE FROM ACROSS THE SEA?
MUST HAVE BEEN A *SEA SERPENT*. ONLY THING IT COULD HAVE BEEN.
LOOK AT THAT FLESH. THERE'S NOT A BITE ON HIM. HE WASN'T EATEN. HE WAS *BUTCHERED*.
WHAT IN ALL THE NINE WORLDS...CAN BUTCHER A *GOD?*
WHATEVER IT WAS, I GUARANTEE YOU ITS SKULL IS NO MATCH FOR **ASGARDIAN STEEL!**
COME NOW, NORSEMEN, WHY STAND WE HERE WITH THE DEAD WHEN YOU'VE A LONGHOUSE FILLED WITH COLD MEAD AND WARM WOMEN? THOR FOR ONE HAS YET TO DRINK HIS FILL OF *EITHER!*
BOY.
FETCH SOME WOOD.
ENOUGH TO BUILD A *FUNERAL PYRE.*

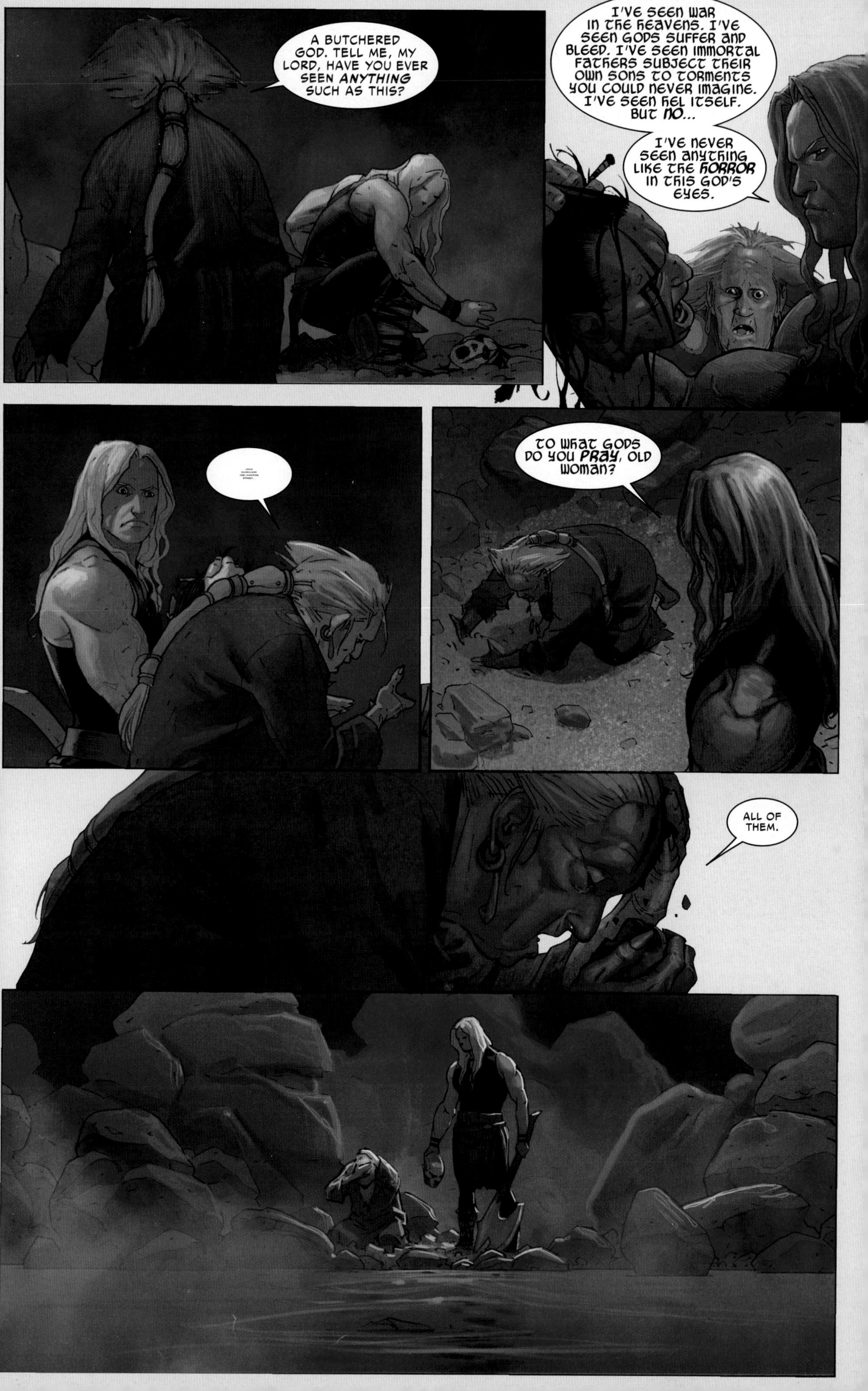
A BUTCHERED GOD. TELL ME, MY LORD, HAVE YOU EVER SEEN ANYTHING SUCH AS THIS?
I'VE SEEN WAR IN THE HEAVENS. I'VE SEEN GODS SUFFER AND BLEED. I'VE SEEN IMMORTAL FATHERS SUBJECT THEIR OWN SONS TO TORMENTS YOU COULD NEVER IMAGINE. I'VE SEEN HEL ITSELF. BUT NO...
I'VE NEVER SEEN ANYTHING LIKE THE HORROR IN THIS GOD'S EYES.
TO WHAT GODS DO YOU PRAY, OLD WOMAN?
ALL OF THEM.

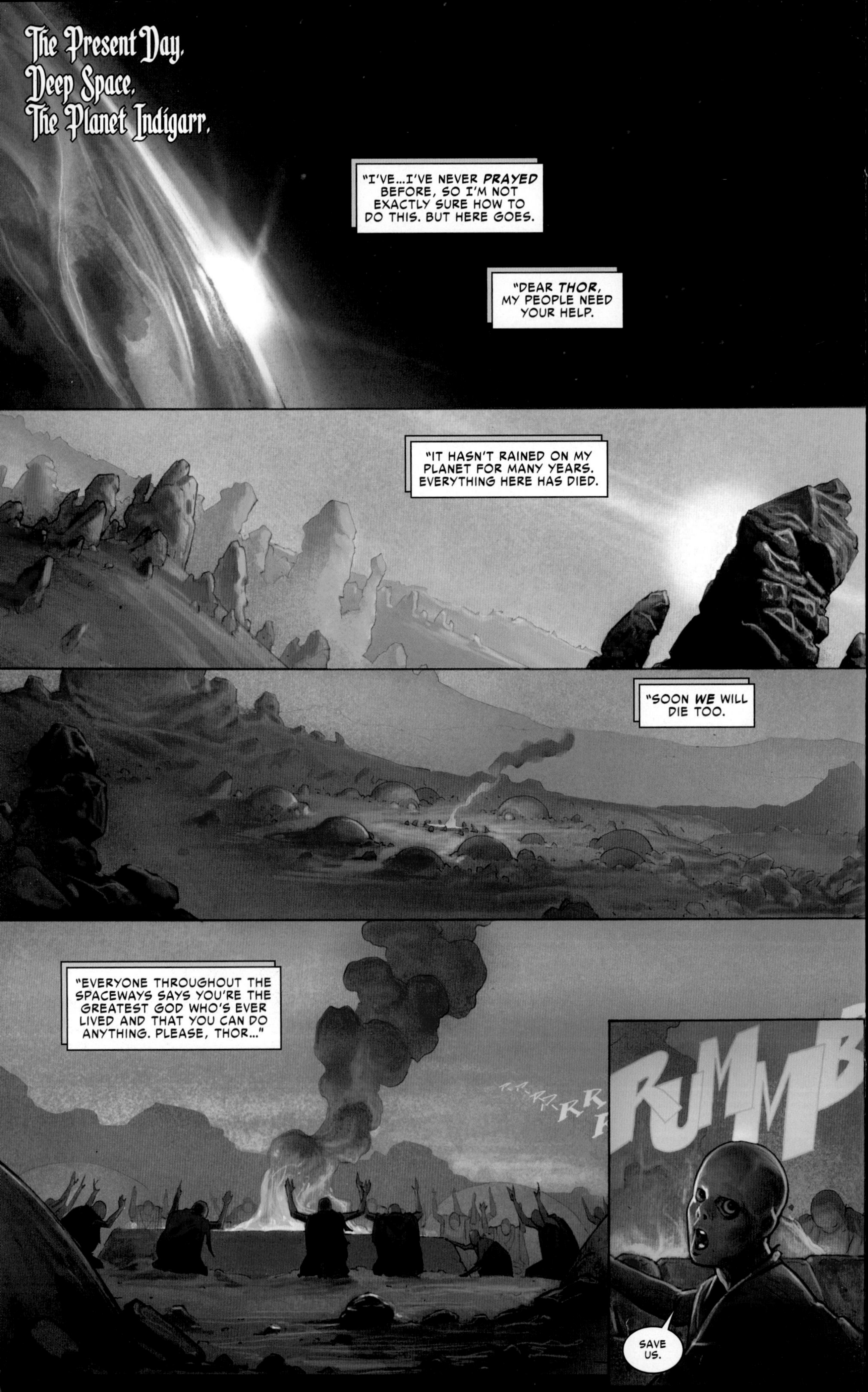
The Present Day.
Deep Space.
The Planet Indigarr.
"I'VE...I'VE NEVER PRAYED BEFORE, SO I'M NOT EXACTLY SURE HOW TO DO THIS. BUT HERE GOES.
"DEAR THOR, MY PEOPLE NEED YOUR HELP.
"IT HASN'T RAINED ON MY PLANET FOR MANY YEARS. EVERYTHING HERE HAS DIED.
"SOON WE WILL DIE TOO.
"EVERYONE THROUGHOUT THE SPACEWAYS SAYS YOU'RE THE GREATEST GOD WHO'S EVER LIVED AND THAT YOU CAN DO ANYTHING. PLEASE, THOR..."
RUMMB
SAVE US.

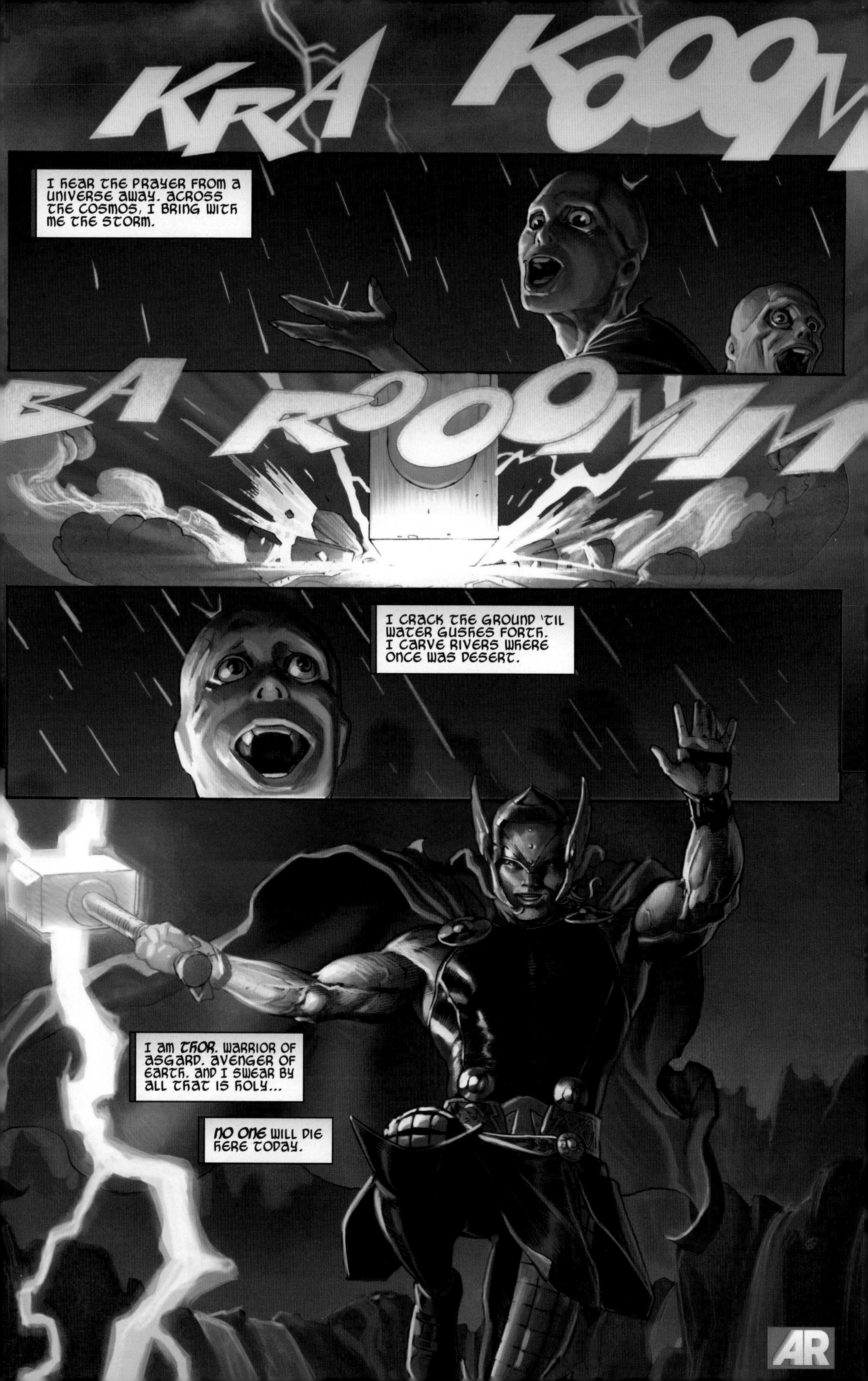
KRA KOOOM
I HEAR THE PRAYER FROM A UNIVERSE AWAY. ACROSS THE COSMOS, I BRING WITH ME THE STORM.
BA ROOOMM
I CRACK THE GROUND 'TIL WATER GUSHES FORTH. I CARVE RIVERS WHERE ONCE WAS DESERT.
I AM THOR. WARRIOR OF ASGARD. AVENGER OF EARTH. AND I SWEAR BY ALL THAT IS HOLY...
NO ONE WILL DIE HERE TODAY.
AR

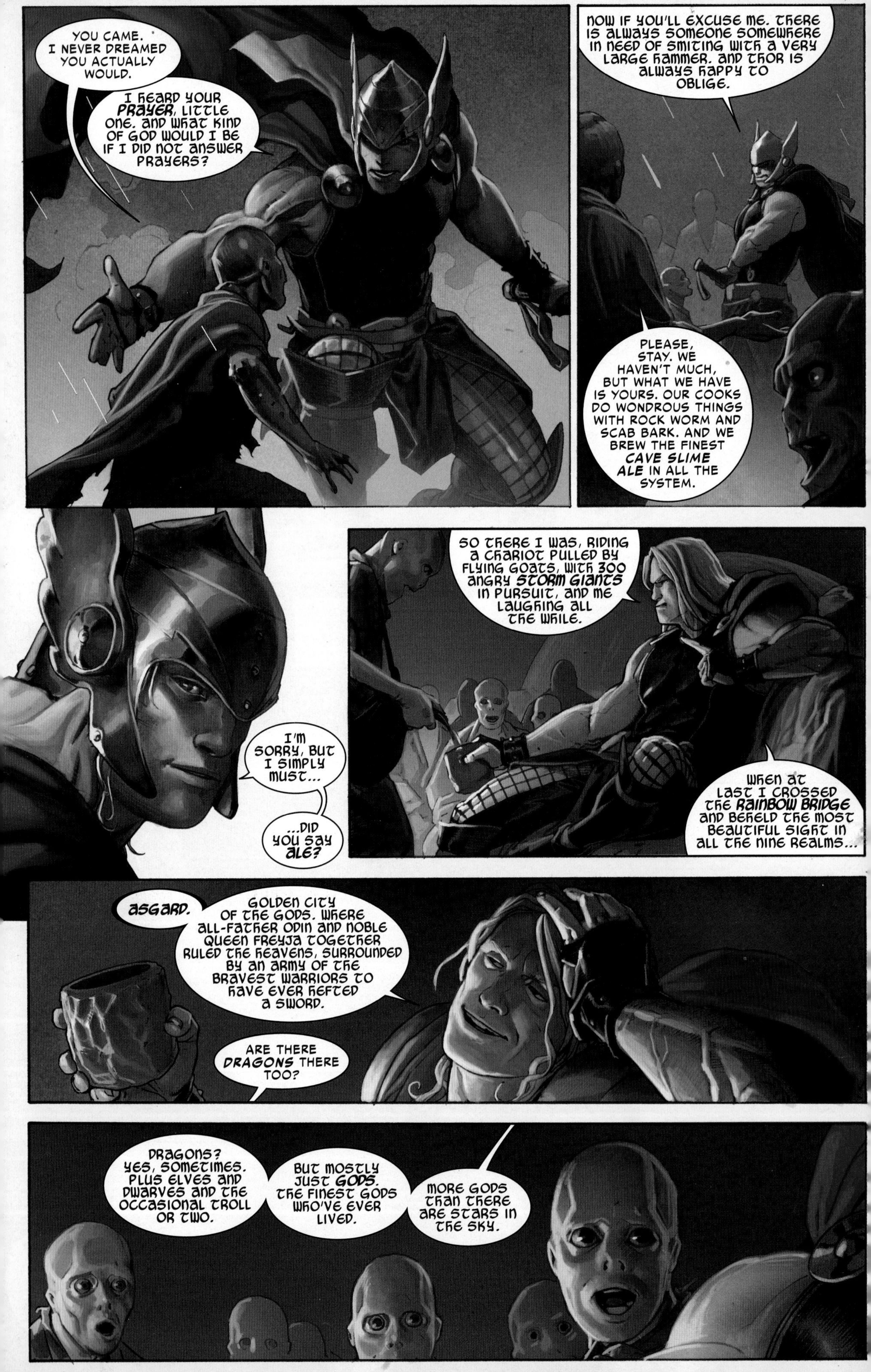
YOU CAME. I NEVER DREAMED YOU ACTUALLY WOULD.
I HEARD YOUR PRAYER, LITTLE ONE. AND WHAT KIND OF GOD WOULD I BE IF I DID NOT ANSWER PRAYERS?
NOW IF YOU'LL EXCUSE ME. THERE IS ALWAYS SOMEONE SOMEWHERE IN NEED OF SMITING WITH A VERY LARGE HAMMER. AND THOR IS ALWAYS HAPPY TO OBLIGE.
PLEASE, STAY. WE HAVEN'T MUCH, BUT WHAT WE HAVE IS YOURS. OUR COOKS DO WONDROUS THINGS WITH ROCK WORM AND SCAB BARK. AND WE BREW THE FINEST CAVE SLIME ALE IN ALL THE SYSTEM.
I'M SORRY, BUT I SIMPLY MUST...
...DID YOU SAY ALE?
SO THERE I WAS, RIDING A CHARIOT PULLED BY FLYING GOATS, WITH 300 ANGRY STORM GIANTS IN PURSUIT, AND ME LAUGHING ALL THE WHILE.
WHEN AT LAST I CROSSED THE RAINBOW BRIDGE AND BEHELD THE MOST BEAUTIFUL SIGHT IN ALL THE NINE REALMS...
ASGARD.
GOLDEN CITY OF THE GODS. WHERE ALL-FATHER ODIN AND NOBLE QUEEN FREYJA TOGETHER RULED THE HEAVENS, SURROUNDED BY AN ARMY OF THE BRAVEST WARRIORS TO HAVE EVER HEFTED A SWORD.
ARE THERE DRAGONS THERE TOO?
DRAGONS? YES, SOMETIMES. PLUS ELVES AND DWARVES AND THE OCCASIONAL TROLL OR TWO.
BUT MOSTLY JUST GODS. THE FINEST GODS WHO'VE EVER LIVED.
MORE GODS THAN THERE ARE STARS IN THE SKY.

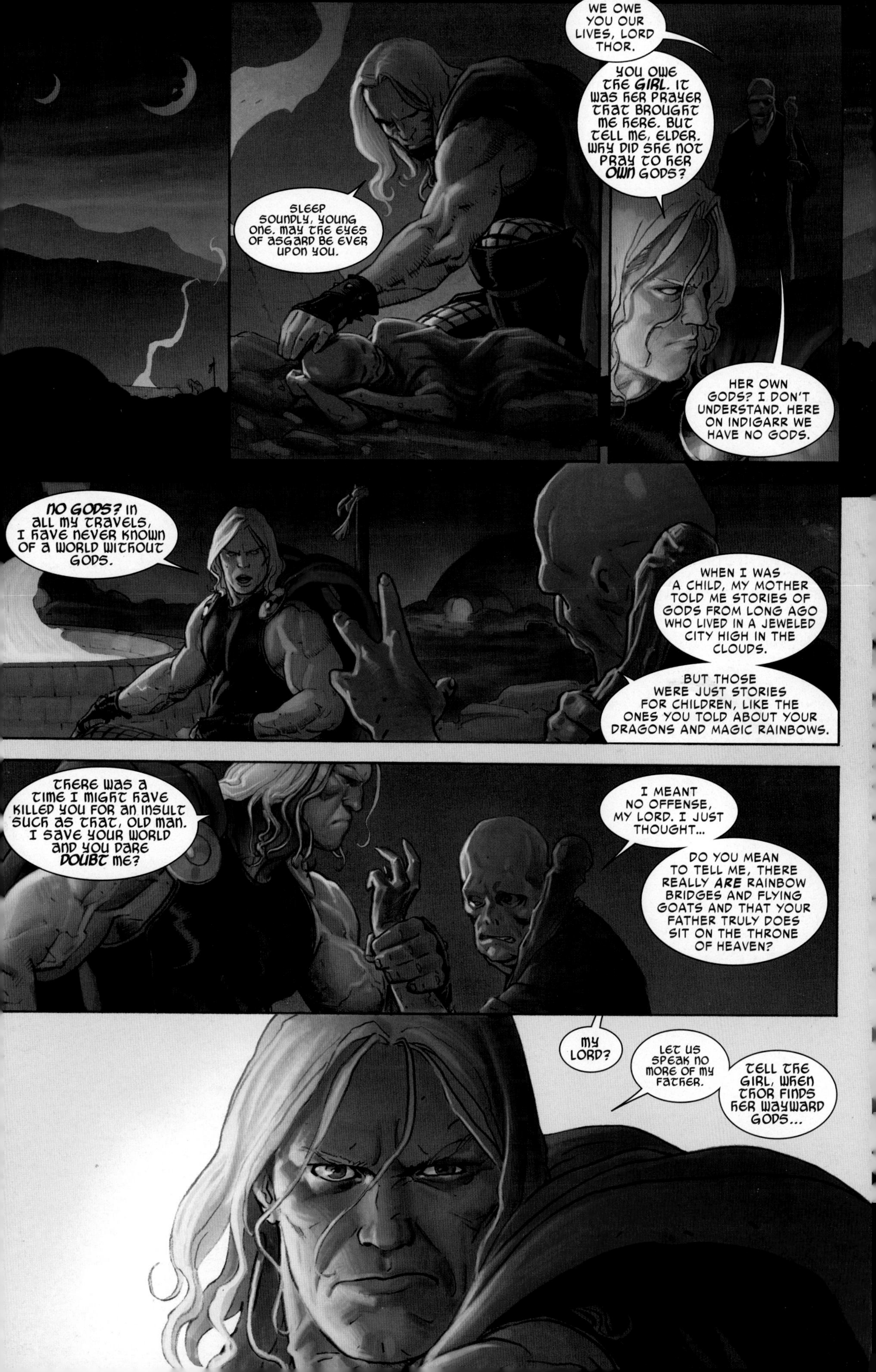
SLEEP SOUNDLY, YOUNG ONE. MAY THE EYES OF ASGARD BE EVER UPON YOU.
WE OWE YOU OUR LIVES, LORD THOR.
YOU OWE THE GIRL. IT WAS HER PRAYER THAT BROUGHT ME HERE. BUT TELL ME, ELDER. WHY DID SHE NOT PRAY TO HER OWN GODS?
HER OWN GODS? I DON'T UNDERSTAND. HERE ON INDIGARR WE HAVE NO GODS.
NO GODS? IN ALL MY TRAVELS, I HAVE NEVER KNOWN OF A WORLD WITHOUT GODS.
WHEN I WAS A CHILD, MY MOTHER TOLD ME STORIES OF GODS FROM LONG AGO WHO LIVED IN A JEWELED CITY HIGH IN THE CLOUDS.
BUT THOSE WERE JUST STORIES FOR CHILDREN, LIKE THE ONES YOU TOLD ABOUT YOUR DRAGONS AND MAGIC RAINBOWS.
THERE WAS A TIME I MIGHT HAVE KILLED YOU FOR AN INSULT SUCH AS THAT, OLD MAN. I SAVE YOUR WORLD AND YOU DARE DOUBT ME?
I MEANT NO OFFENSE, MY LORD. I JUST THOUGHT...
DO YOU MEAN TO TELL ME, THERE REALLY ARE RAINBOW BRIDGES AND FLYING GOATS AND THAT YOUR FATHER TRULY DOES SIT ON THE THRONE OF HEAVEN?
MY LORD?
LET US SPEAK NO MORE OF MY FATHER.
TELL THE GIRL, WHEN THOR FINDS HER WAYWARD GODS...

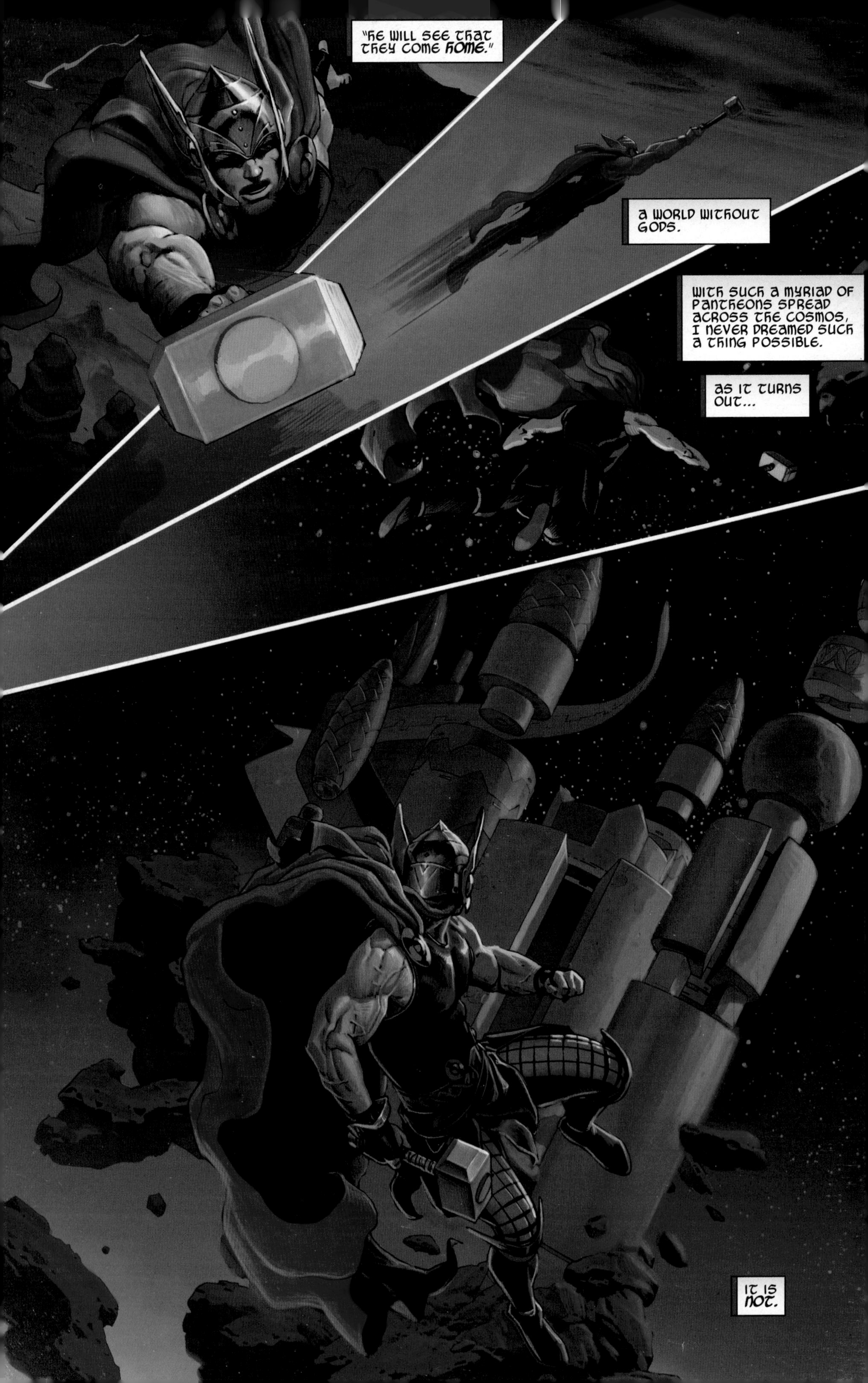
"HE WILL SEE THAT THEY COME *HOME*."
A WORLD WITHOUT GODS.
WITH SUCH A MYRIAD OF PANTHEONS SPREAD ACROSS THE COSMOS, I NEVER DREAMED SUCH A THING POSSIBLE.
AS IT TURNS OUT...
IT IS *NOT*.

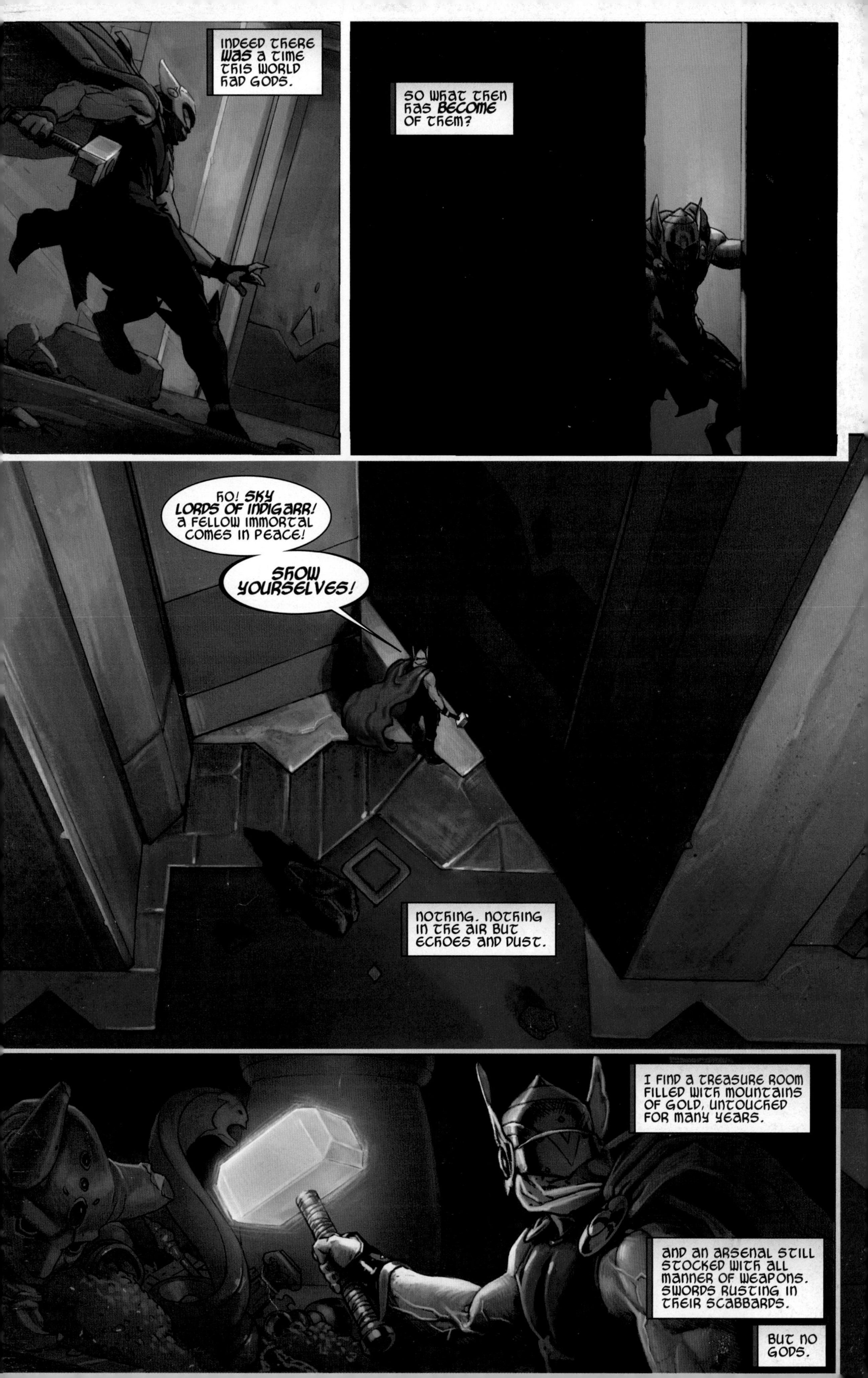
INDEED THERE WAS A TIME THIS WORLD HAD GODS.
SO WHAT THEN HAS BECOME OF THEM?
HO! SKY LORDS OF INDIGARR! A FELLOW IMMORTAL COMES IN PEACE!
SHOW YOURSELVES!
NOTHING. NOTHING IN THE AIR BUT ECHOES AND DUST.
I FIND A TREASURE ROOM FILLED WITH MOUNTAINS OF GOLD, UNTOUCHED FOR MANY YEARS.
AND AN ARSENAL STILL STOCKED WITH ALL MANNER OF WEAPONS. SWORDS RUSTING IN THEIR SCABBARDS.
BUT NO GODS.

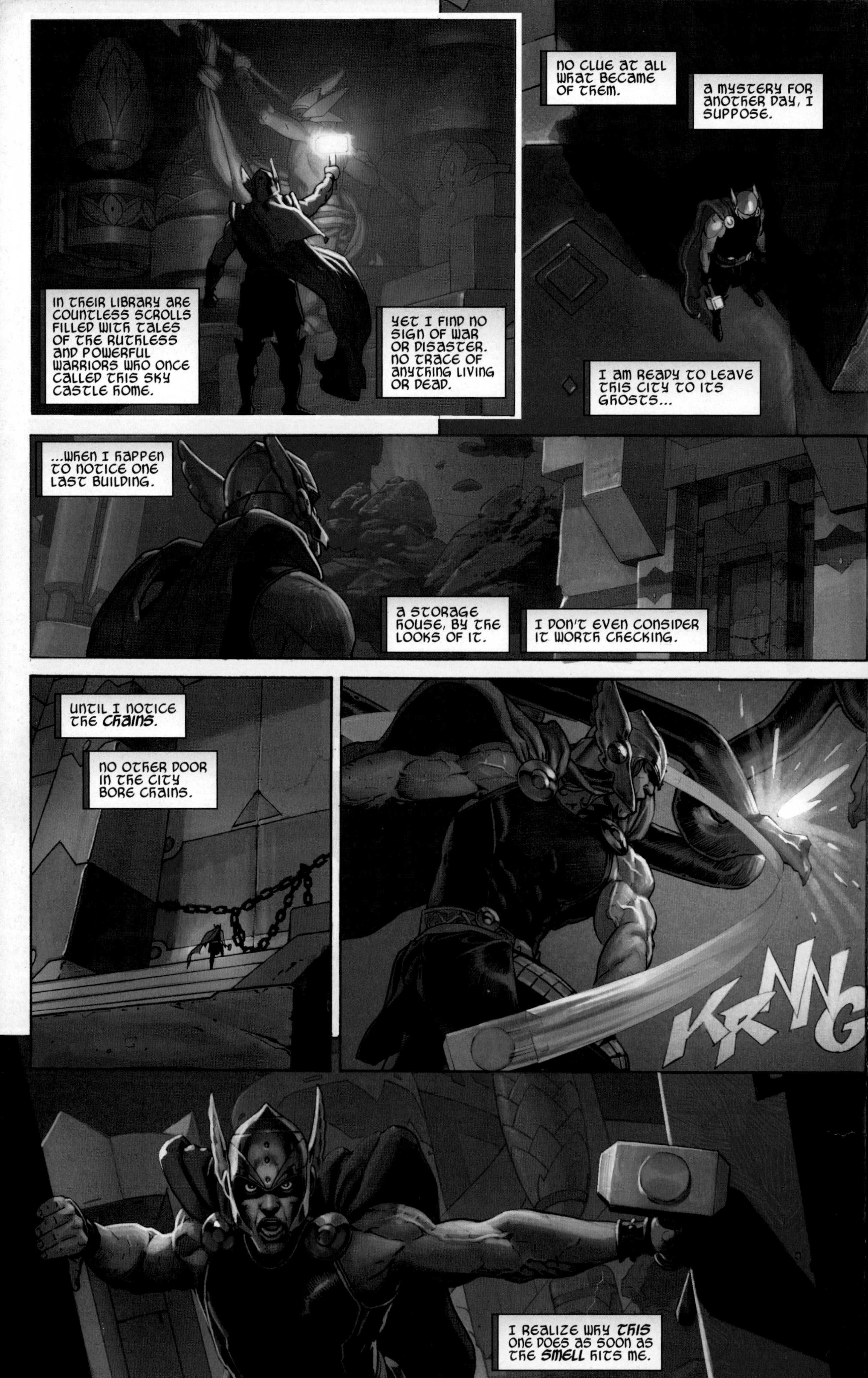
IN THEIR LIBRARY ARE COUNTLESS SCROLLS FILLED WITH TALES OF THE RUTHLESS AND POWERFUL WARRIORS WHO ONCE CALLED THIS SKY CASTLE HOME.
YET I FIND NO SIGN OF WAR OR DISASTER. NO TRACE OF ANYTHING LIVING OR DEAD.
NO CLUE AT ALL WHAT BECAME OF THEM.
A MYSTERY FOR ANOTHER DAY, I SUPPOSE.
I AM READY TO LEAVE THIS CITY TO ITS GHOSTS...
...WHEN I HAPPEN TO NOTICE ONE LAST BUILDING.
A STORAGE HOUSE, BY THE LOOKS OF IT.
I DON'T EVEN CONSIDER IT WORTH CHECKING.
UNTIL I NOTICE THE *CHAINS.*
NO OTHER DOOR IN THE CITY BORE CHAINS.
KRNNG
I REALIZE WHY *THIS* ONE DOES AS SOON AS THE *SMELL* HITS ME.

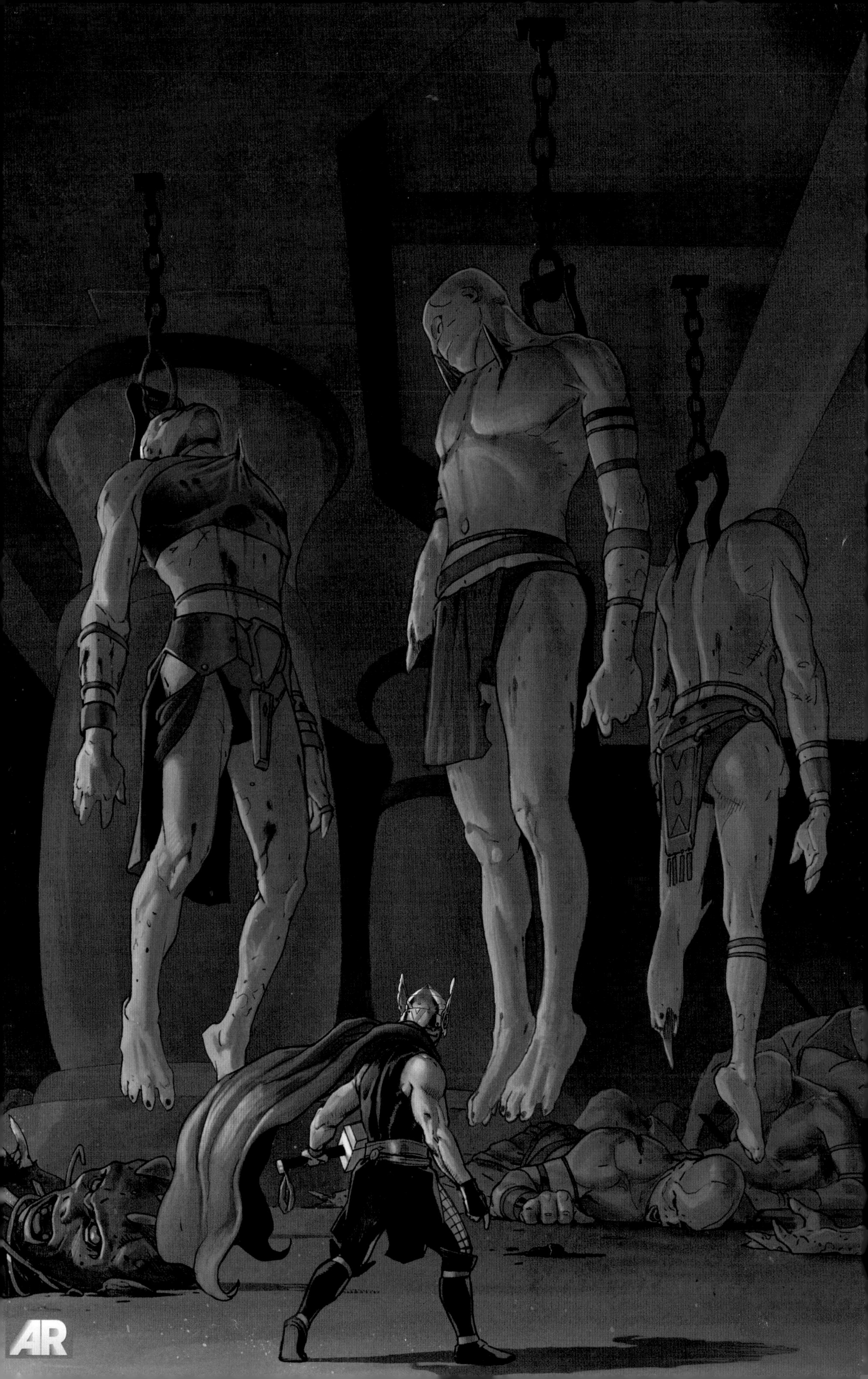

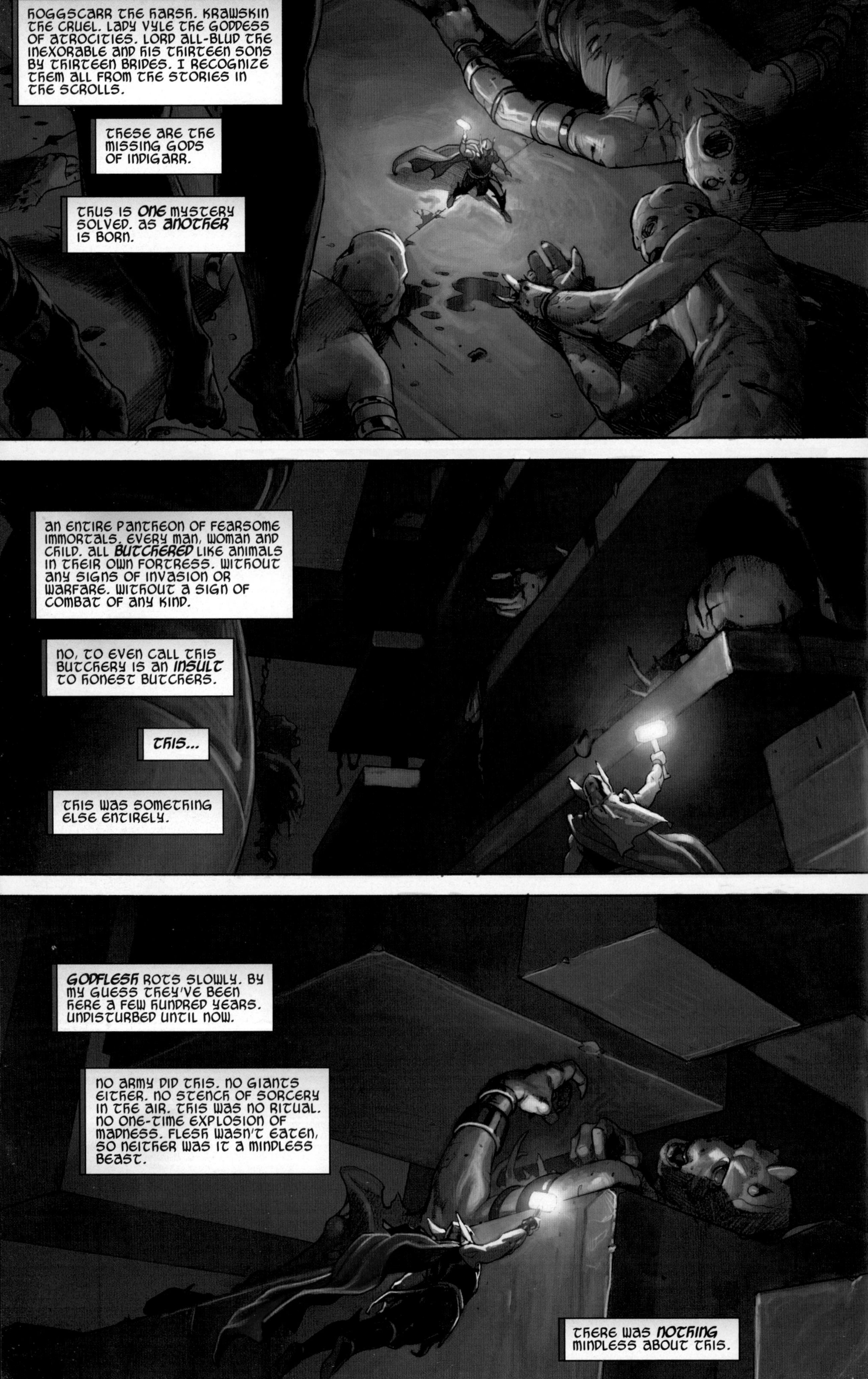
HOGGSCARR THE HARSH. KRAWSKIN THE CRUEL. LADY VYLE THE GODDESS OF ATROCITIES. LORD ALL-BLUD THE INEXORABLE AND HIS THIRTEEN SONS BY THIRTEEN BRIDES. I RECOGNIZE THEM ALL FROM THE STORIES IN THE SCROLLS.
THESE ARE THE MISSING GODS OF INDIGARR.
THUS IS ONE MYSTERY SOLVED. AS ANOTHER IS BORN.
AN ENTIRE PANTHEON OF FEARSOME IMMORTALS. EVERY MAN, WOMAN AND CHILD. ALL BUTCHERED LIKE ANIMALS IN THEIR OWN FORTRESS. WITHOUT ANY SIGNS OF INVASION OR WARFARE. WITHOUT A SIGN OF COMBAT OF ANY KIND.
NO, TO EVEN CALL THIS BUTCHERY IS AN INSULT TO HONEST BUTCHERS.
THIS...
THIS WAS SOMETHING ELSE ENTIRELY.
GODFLESH ROTS SLOWLY. BY MY GUESS THEY'VE BEEN HERE A FEW HUNDRED YEARS. UNDISTURBED UNTIL NOW.
NO ARMY DID THIS. NO GIANTS EITHER. NO STENCH OF SORCERY IN THE AIR. THIS WAS NO RITUAL. NO ONE-TIME EXPLOSION OF MADNESS. FLESH WASN'T EATEN, SO NEITHER WAS IT A MINDLESS BEAST.
THERE WAS NOTHING MINDLESS ABOUT THIS.

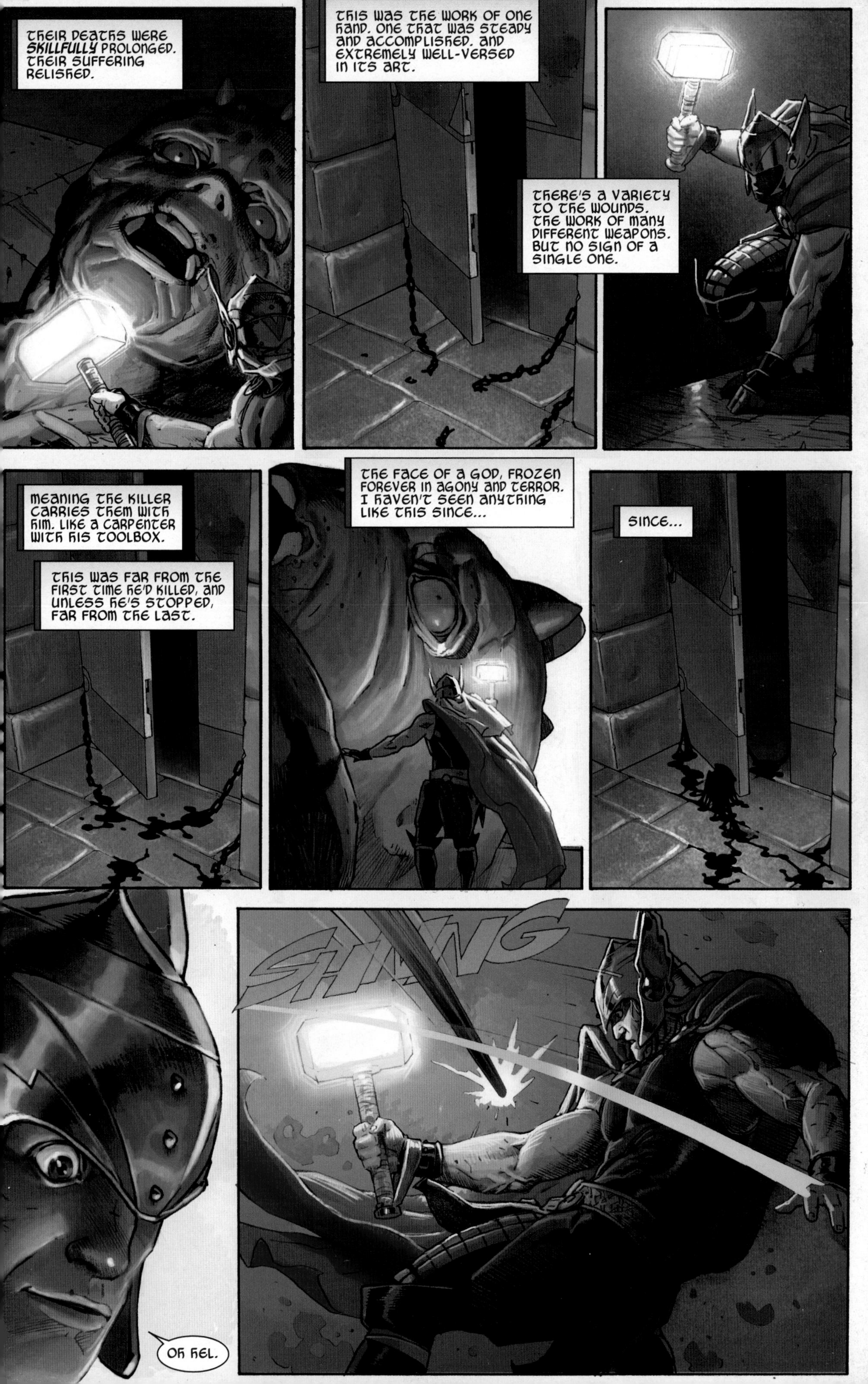
THEIR DEATHS WERE SKILLFULLY PROLONGED. THEIR SUFFERING RELISHED.
THIS WAS THE WORK OF ONE HAND. ONE THAT WAS STEADY AND ACCOMPLISHED. AND EXTREMELY WELL-VERSED IN ITS ART.
THERE'S A VARIETY TO THE WOUNDS. THE WORK OF MANY DIFFERENT WEAPONS. BUT NO SIGN OF A SINGLE ONE.
MEANING THE KILLER CARRIES THEM WITH HIM. LIKE A CARPENTER WITH HIS TOOLBOX.
THIS WAS FAR FROM THE FIRST TIME HE'D KILLED, AND UNLESS HE'S STOPPED, FAR FROM THE LAST.
THE FACE OF A GOD, FROZEN FOREVER IN AGONY AND TERROR. I HAVEN'T SEEN ANYTHING LIKE THIS SINCE...
SINCE...
OH HEL.
SHING

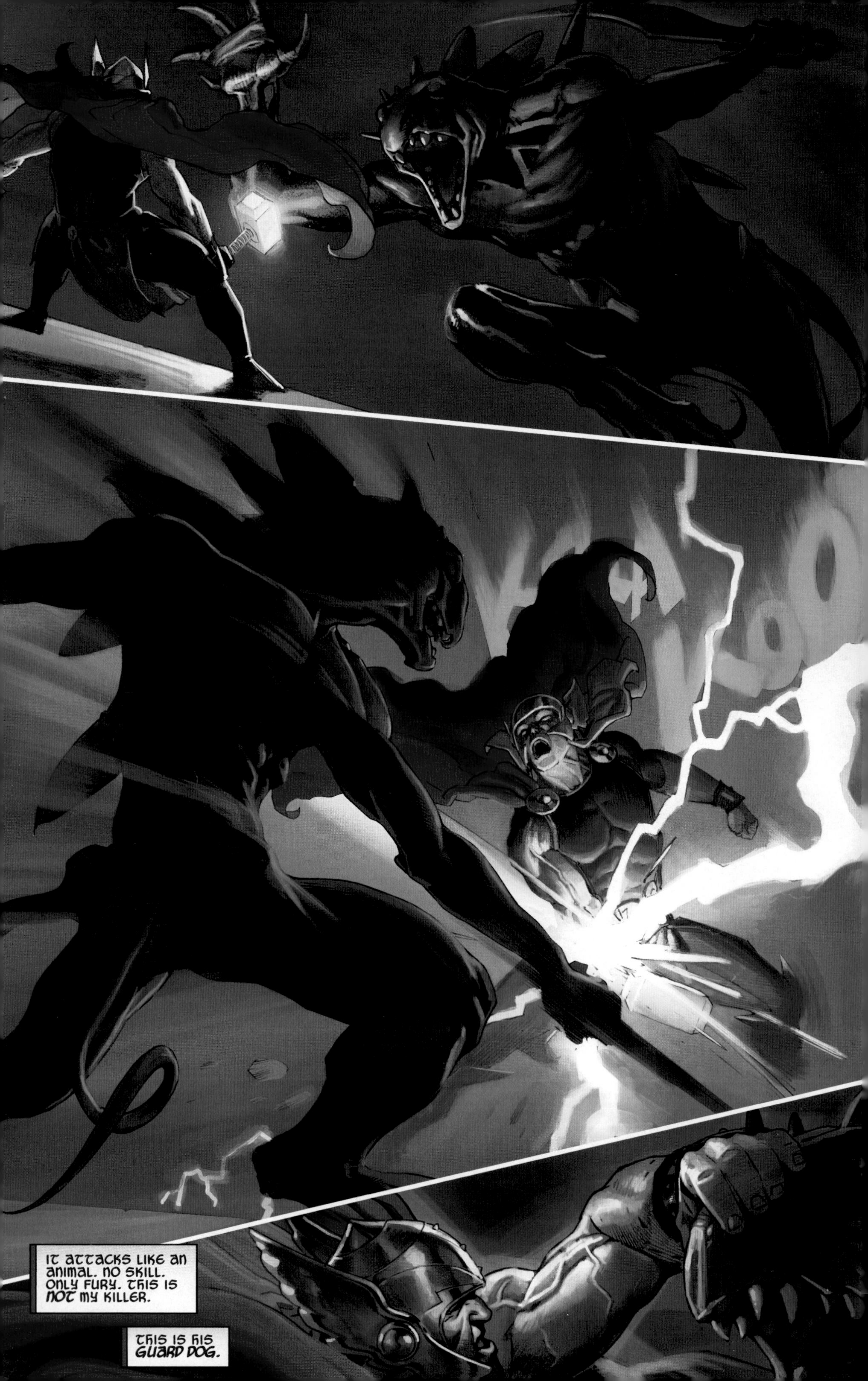
IT ATTACKS LIKE AN ANIMAL. NO SKILL. ONLY FURY. THIS IS *NOT* MY KILLER.
THIS IS HIS **GUARD DOG.**

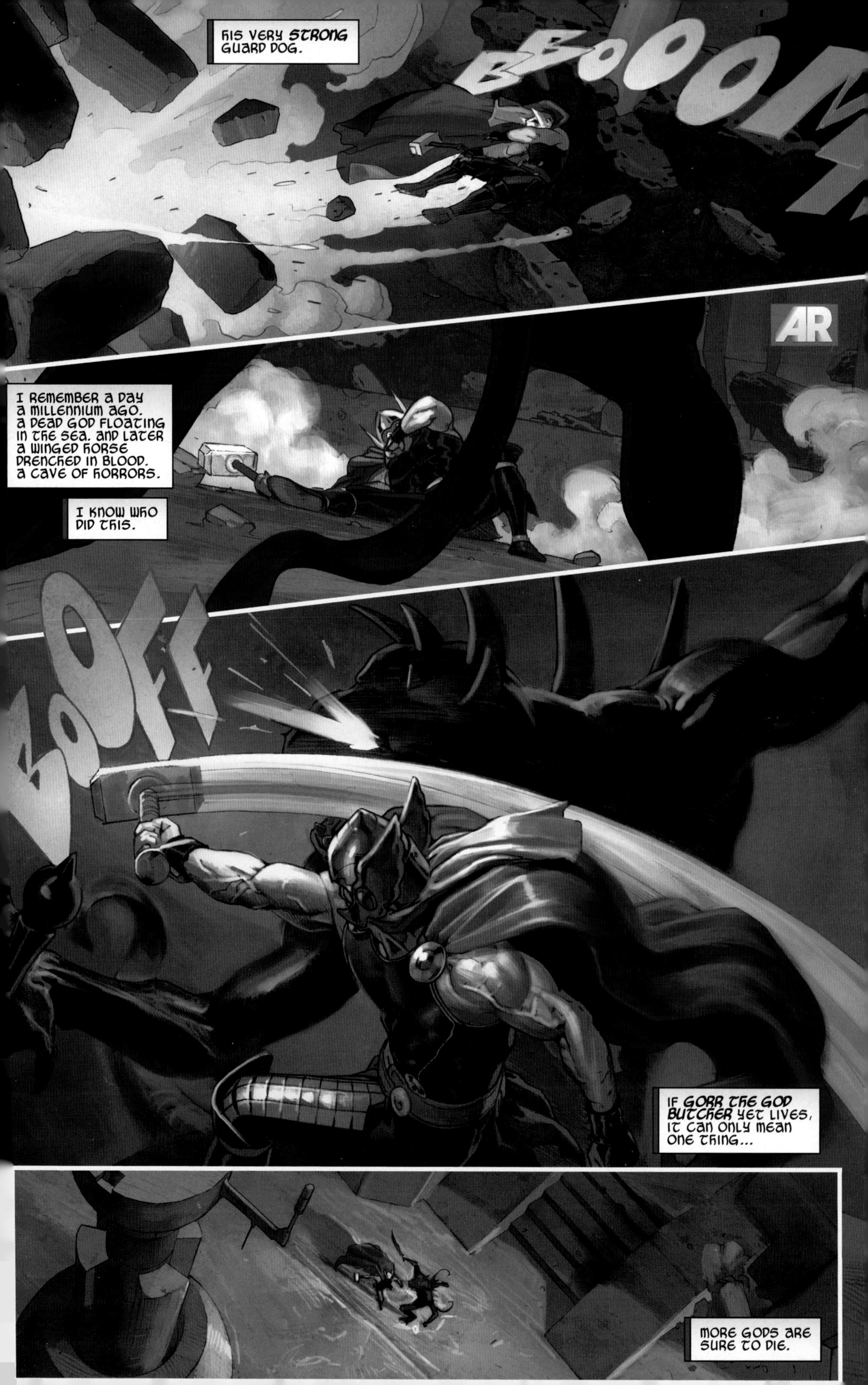

HIS VERY STRONG GUARD DOG.
BBOOOOM
I REMEMBER A DAY A MILLENNIUM AGO. A DEAD GOD FLOATING IN THE SEA. AND LATER A WINGED HORSE DRENCHED IN BLOOD. A CAVE OF HORRORS.
I KNOW WHO DID THIS.
IF GORR THE GOD BUTCHER YET LIVES, IT CAN ONLY MEAN ONE THING...
MORE GODS ARE SURE TO DIE.

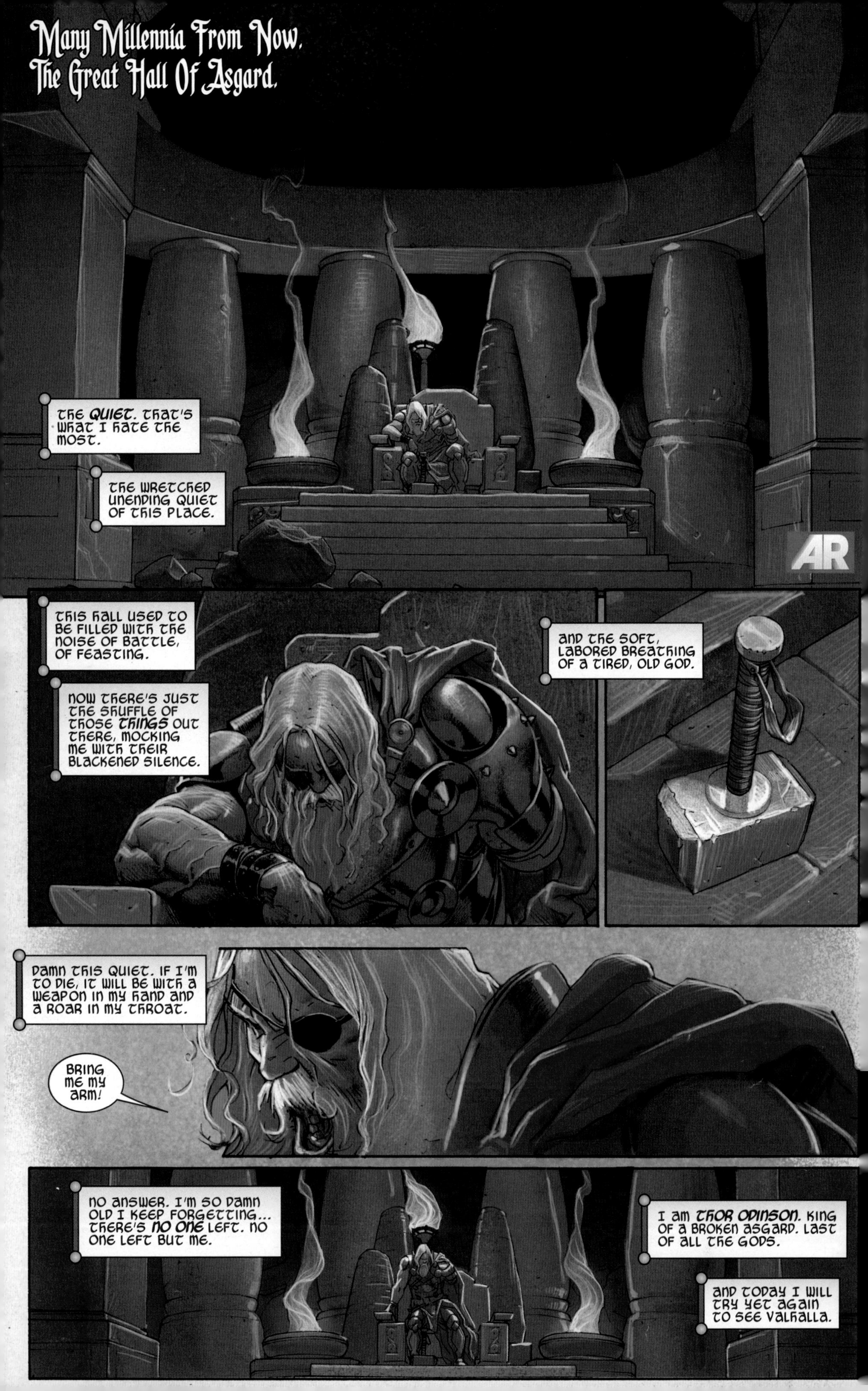

Many Millennia From Now, The Great Hall Of Asgard.
THE QUIET. THAT'S WHAT I HATE THE MOST.
THE WRETCHED UNENDING QUIET OF THIS PLACE.
THIS HALL USED TO BE FILLED WITH THE NOISE OF BATTLE, OF FEASTING.
NOW THERE'S JUST THE SHUFFLE OF THOSE THINGS OUT THERE, MOCKING ME WITH THEIR BLACKENED SILENCE.
AND THE SOFT, LABORED BREATHING OF A TIRED, OLD GOD.
DAMN THIS QUIET. IF I'M TO DIE, IT WILL BE WITH A WEAPON IN MY HAND AND A ROAR IN MY THROAT.
BRING ME MY ARM!
NO ANSWER. I'M SO DAMN OLD I KEEP FORGETTING... THERE'S NO ONE LEFT. NO ONE LEFT BUT ME.
I AM THOR ODINSON. KING OF A BROKEN ASGARD. LAST OF ALL THE GODS.
AND TODAY I WILL TRY YET AGAIN TO SEE VALHALLA.

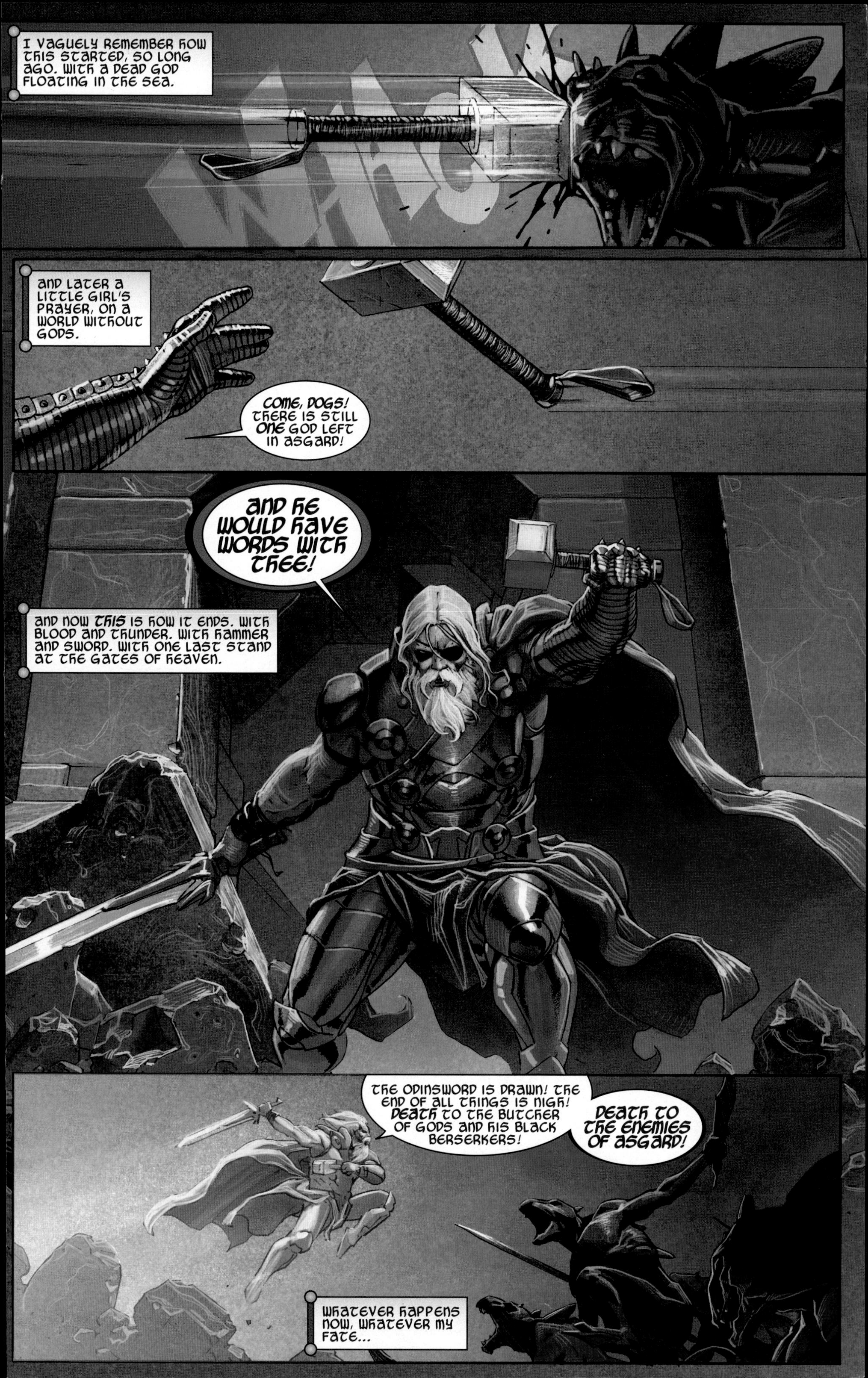
I VAGUELY REMEMBER HOW THIS STARTED, SO LONG AGO. WITH A DEAD GOD FLOATING IN THE SEA.
AND LATER A LITTLE GIRL'S PRAYER, ON A WORLD WITHOUT GODS.
COME, DOGS! THERE IS STILL ONE GOD LEFT IN ASGARD!
AND HE WOULD HAVE WORDS WITH THEE!
AND NOW THIS IS HOW IT ENDS. WITH BLOOD AND THUNDER. WITH HAMMER AND SWORD. WITH ONE LAST STAND AT THE GATES OF HEAVEN.
THE ODINSWORD IS DRAWN! THE END OF ALL THINGS IS NIGH! DEATH TO THE BUTCHER OF GODS AND HIS BLACK BERSERKERS!
DEATH TO THE ENEMIES OF ASGARD!
WHATEVER HAPPENS NOW, WHATEVER MY FATE...

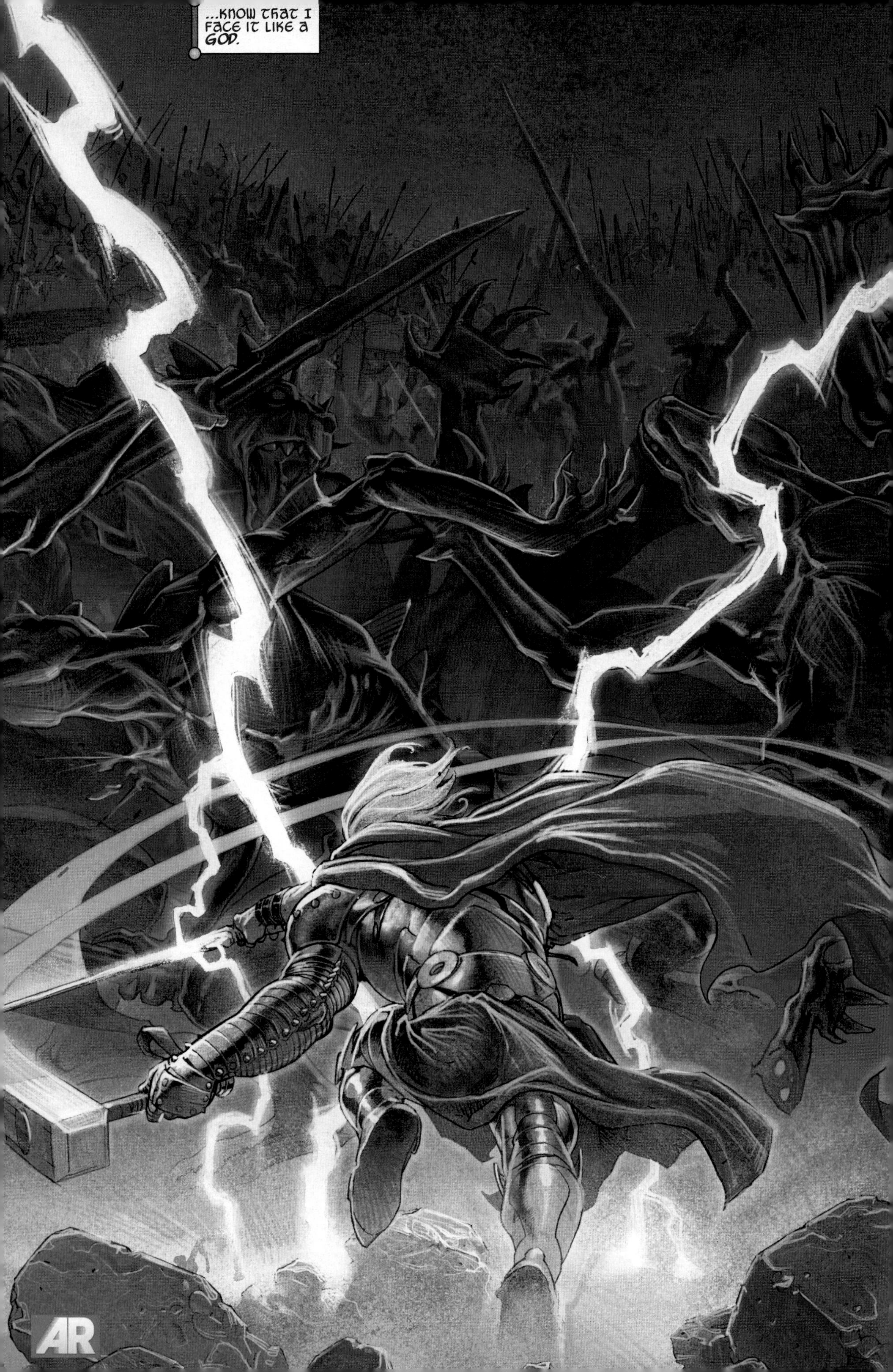
...KNOW THAT I FACE IT LIKE A GOD.
AR

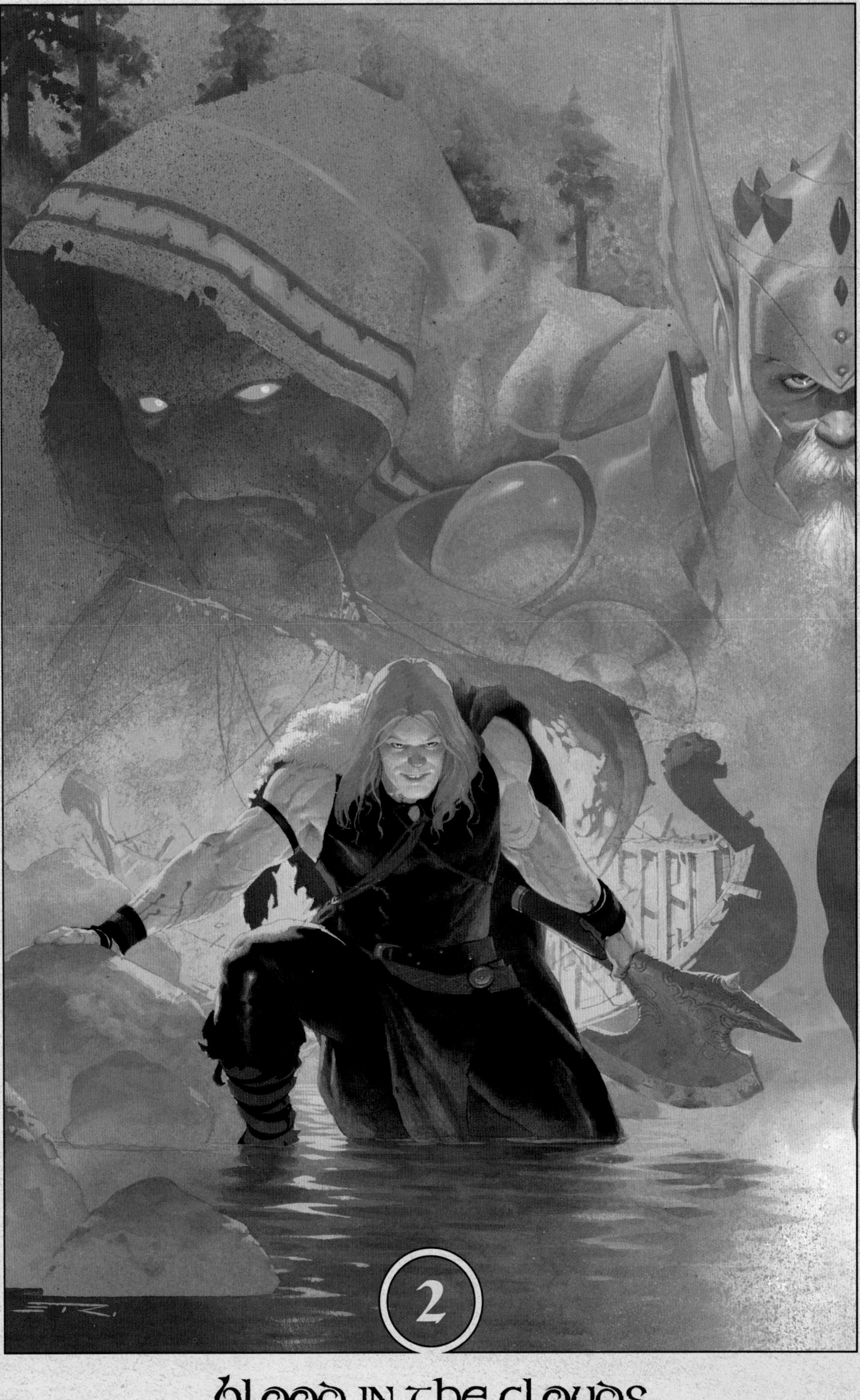
2

BLOOD IN THE CLOUDS

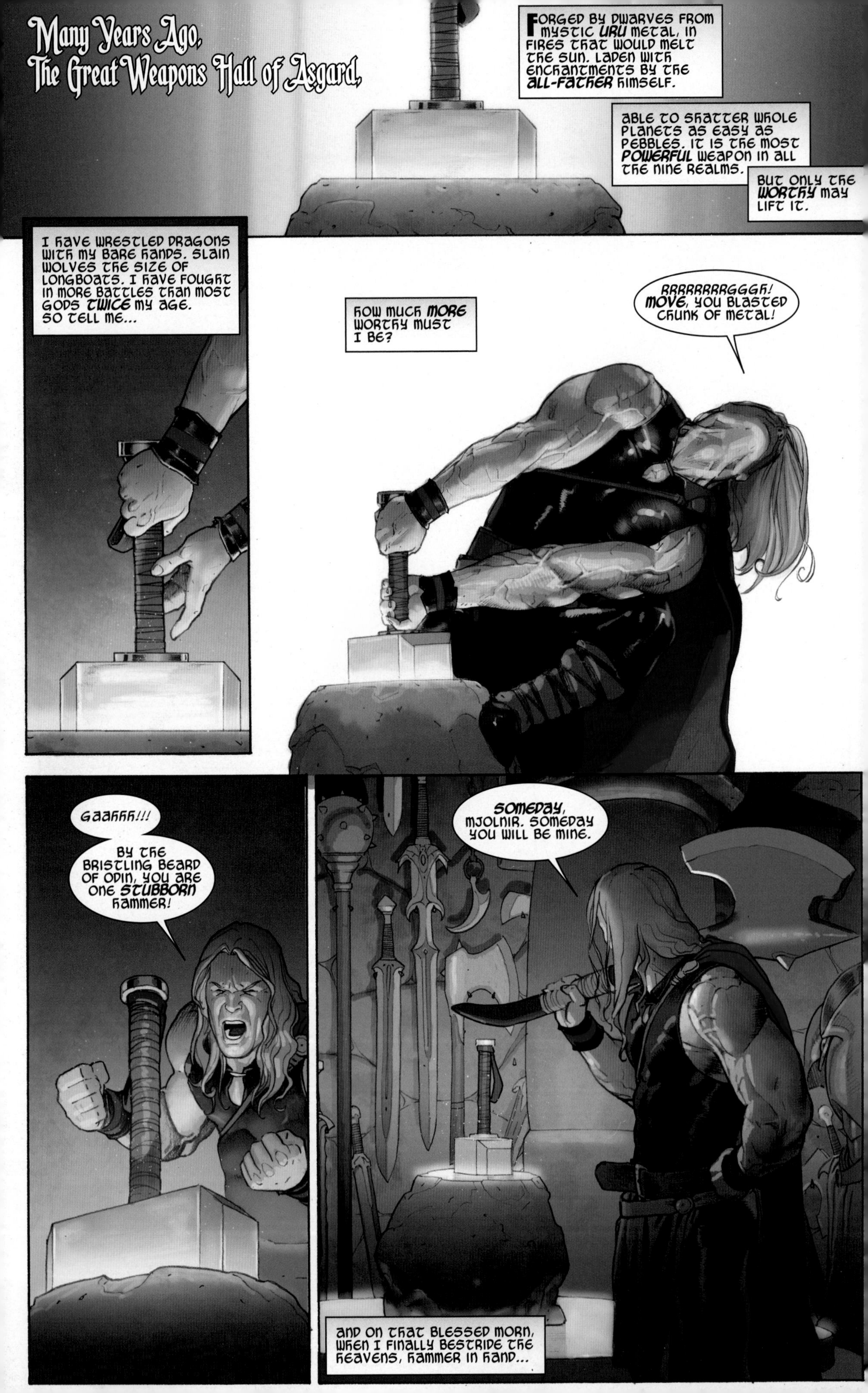

Many Years Ago,
The Great Weapons Hall of Asgard,
FORGED BY DWARVES FROM MYSTIC URU METAL, IN FIRES THAT WOULD MELT THE SUN. LADEN WITH ENCHANTMENTS BY THE ALL-FATHER HIMSELF.
ABLE TO SHATTER WHOLE PLANETS AS EASY AS PEBBLES. IT IS THE MOST POWERFUL WEAPON IN ALL THE NINE REALMS.
BUT ONLY THE WORTHY MAY LIFT IT.
I HAVE WRESTLED DRAGONS WITH MY BARE HANDS. SLAIN WOLVES THE SIZE OF LONGBOATS. I HAVE FOUGHT IN MORE BATTLES THAN MOST GODS TWICE MY AGE. SO TELL ME...
HOW MUCH MORE WORTHY MUST I BE?
RRRRRRRRGGGH! MOVE, YOU BLASTED CHUNK OF METAL!
GAAHHH!!!
BY THE BRISTLING BEARD OF ODIN, YOU ARE ONE STUBBORN HAMMER!
SOMEDAY, MJOLNIR. SOMEDAY YOU WILL BE MINE.
AND ON THAT BLESSED MORN, WHEN I FINALLY BESTRIDE THE HEAVENS, HAMMER IN HAND...

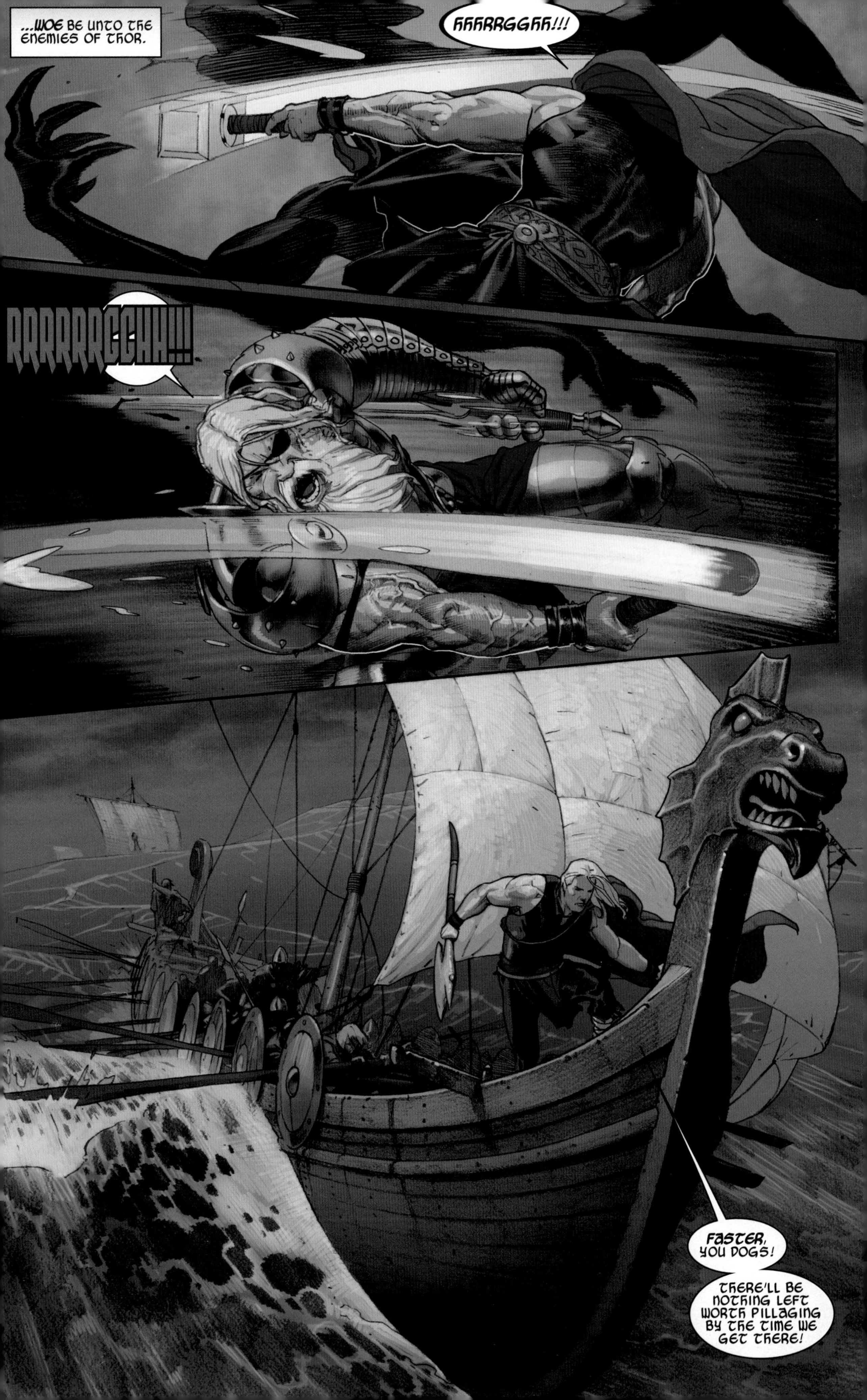
...WOE BE UNTO THE ENEMIES OF THOR.
HHHRRGGHH!!!
RRRRRRGGHH!!!
FASTER, YOU DOGS!
THERE'LL BE NOTHING LEFT WORTH PILLAGING BY THE TIME WE GET THERE!

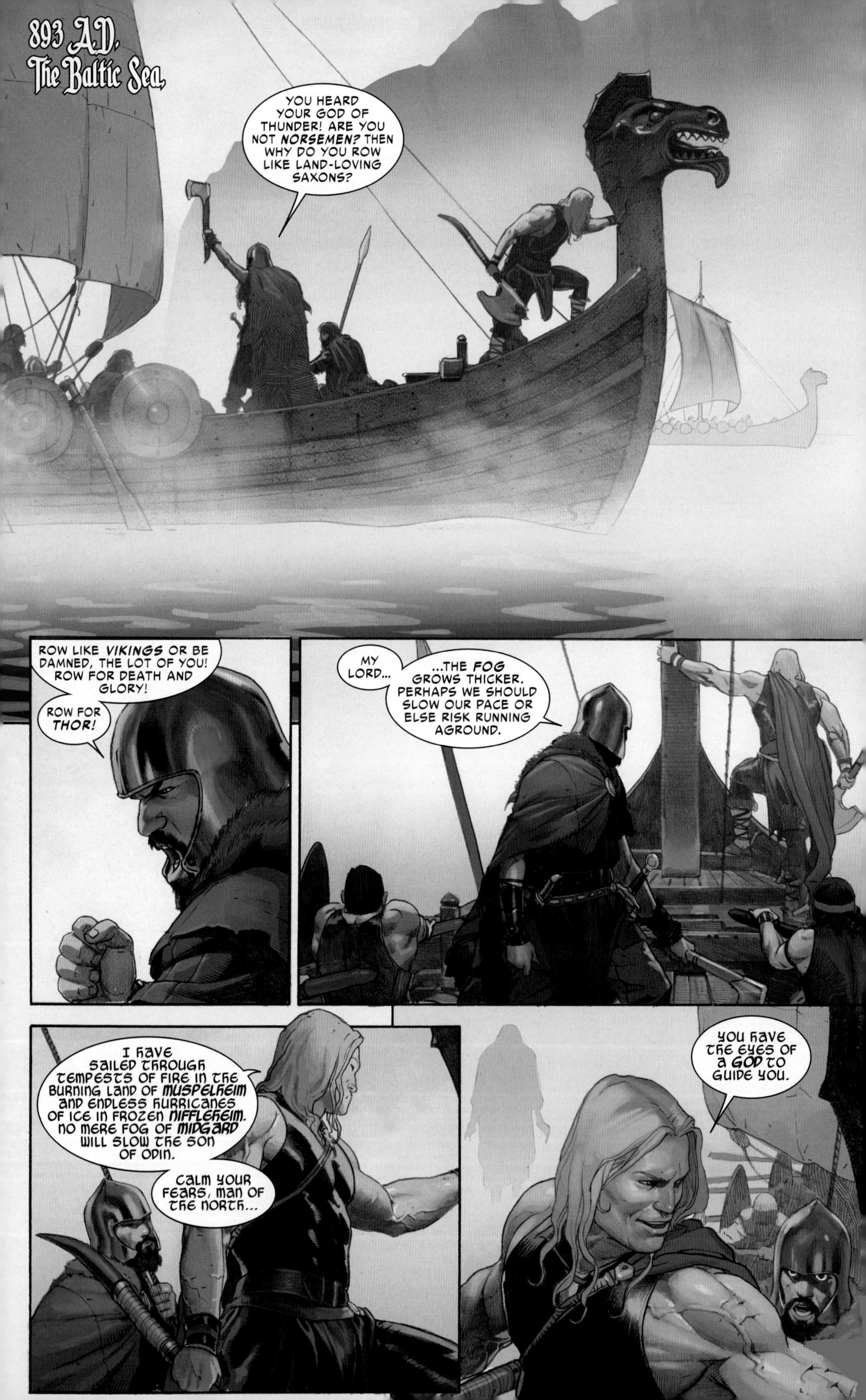
893 A.D.
The Baltic Sea.
YOU HEARD YOUR GOD OF THUNDER! ARE YOU NOT NORSEMEN? THEN WHY DO YOU ROW LIKE LAND-LOVING SAXONS?
ROW LIKE VIKINGS OR BE DAMNED, THE LOT OF YOU! ROW FOR DEATH AND GLORY!
ROW FOR THOR!
MY LORD...
...THE FOG GROWS THICKER. PERHAPS WE SHOULD SLOW OUR PACE OR ELSE RISK RUNNING AGROUND.
I HAVE SAILED THROUGH TEMPESTS OF FIRE IN THE BURNING LAND OF MUSPELHEIM AND ENDLESS HURRICANES OF ICE IN FROZEN NIFFLEHEIM. NO MERE FOG OF MIDGARD WILL SLOW THE SON OF ODIN.
CALM YOUR FEARS, MAN OF THE NORTH...
YOU HAVE THE EYES OF A GOD TO GUIDE YOU.

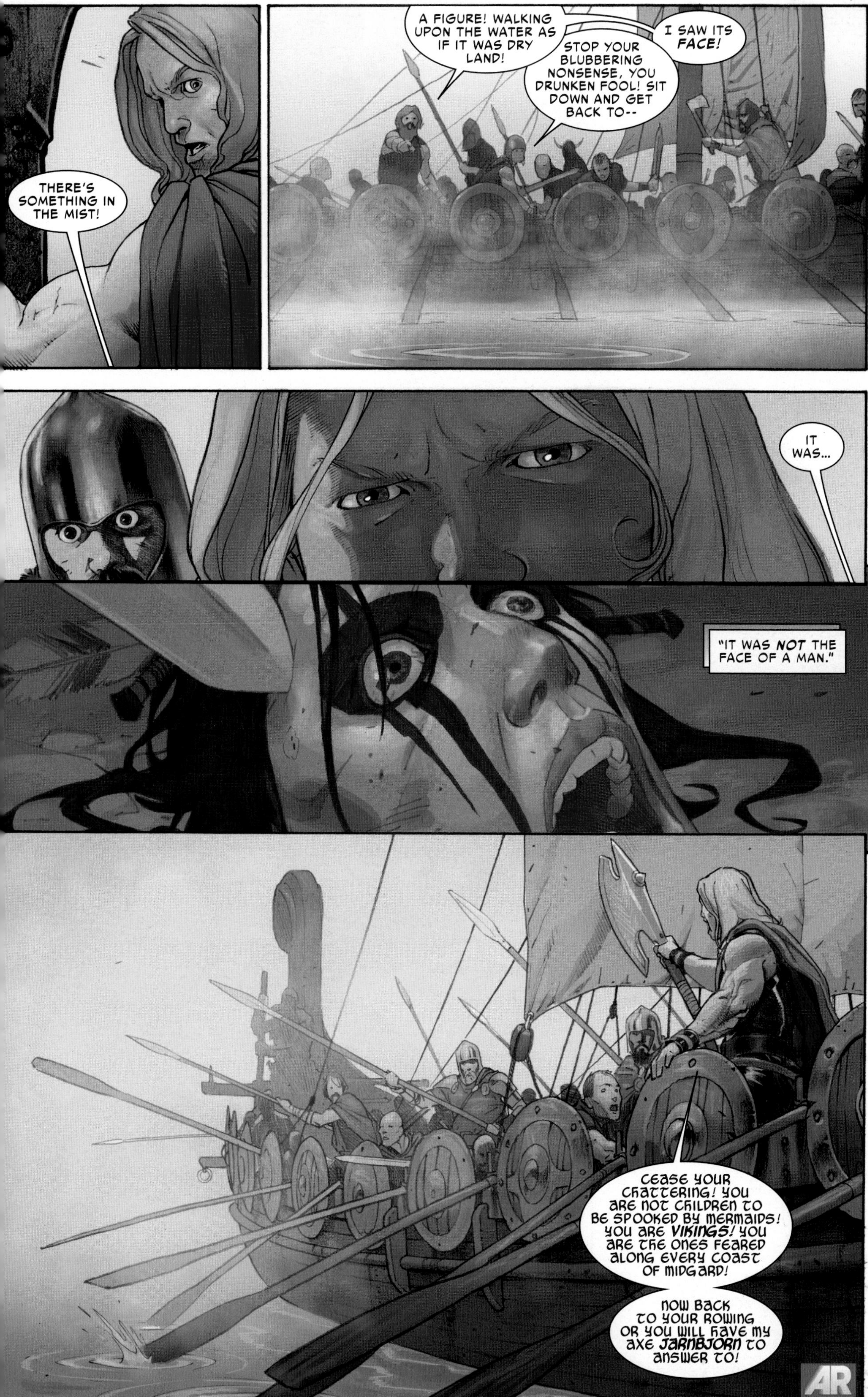
THERE'S SOMETHING IN THE MIST!
A FIGURE! WALKING UPON THE WATER AS IF IT WAS DRY LAND!
I SAW ITS *FACE!*
STOP YOUR BLUBBERING NONSENSE, YOU DRUNKEN FOOL! SIT DOWN AND GET BACK TO--
IT WAS...
"IT WAS *NOT* THE FACE OF A MAN."
CEASE YOUR CHATTERING! YOU ARE NOT CHILDREN TO BE SPOOKED BY MERMAIDS! YOU ARE *VIKINGS!* YOU ARE THE ONES FEARED ALONG EVERY COAST OF MIDGARD!
NOW BACK TO YOUR ROWING OR YOU WILL HAVE MY AXE *JARNBJORN* TO ANSWER TO!

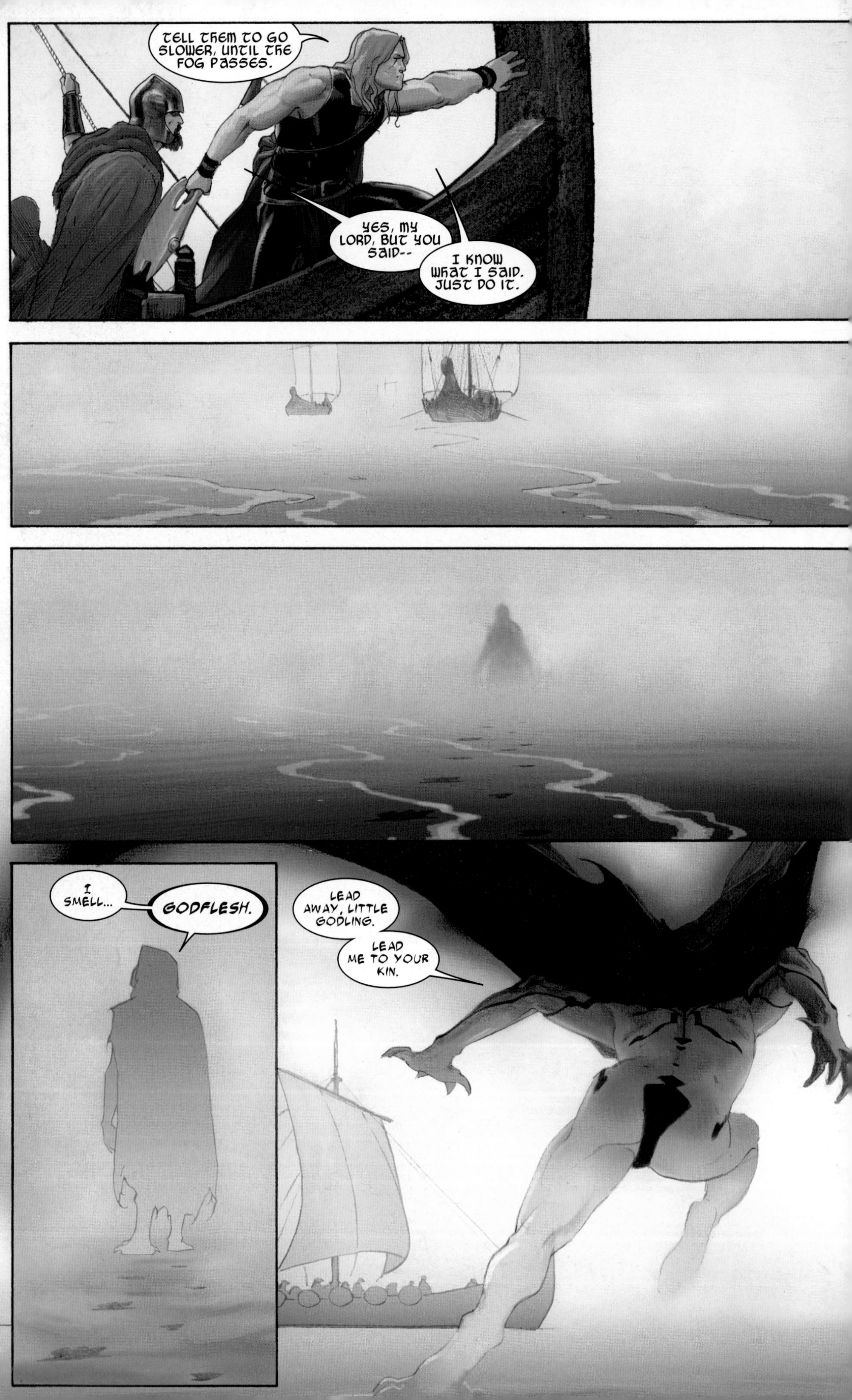
TELL THEM TO GO SLOWER, UNTIL THE FOG PASSES.
YES, MY LORD, BUT YOU SAID--
I KNOW WHAT I SAID. JUST DO IT.
I SMELL...
GODFLESH.
LEAD AWAY, LITTLE GODLING.
LEAD ME TO YOUR KIN.

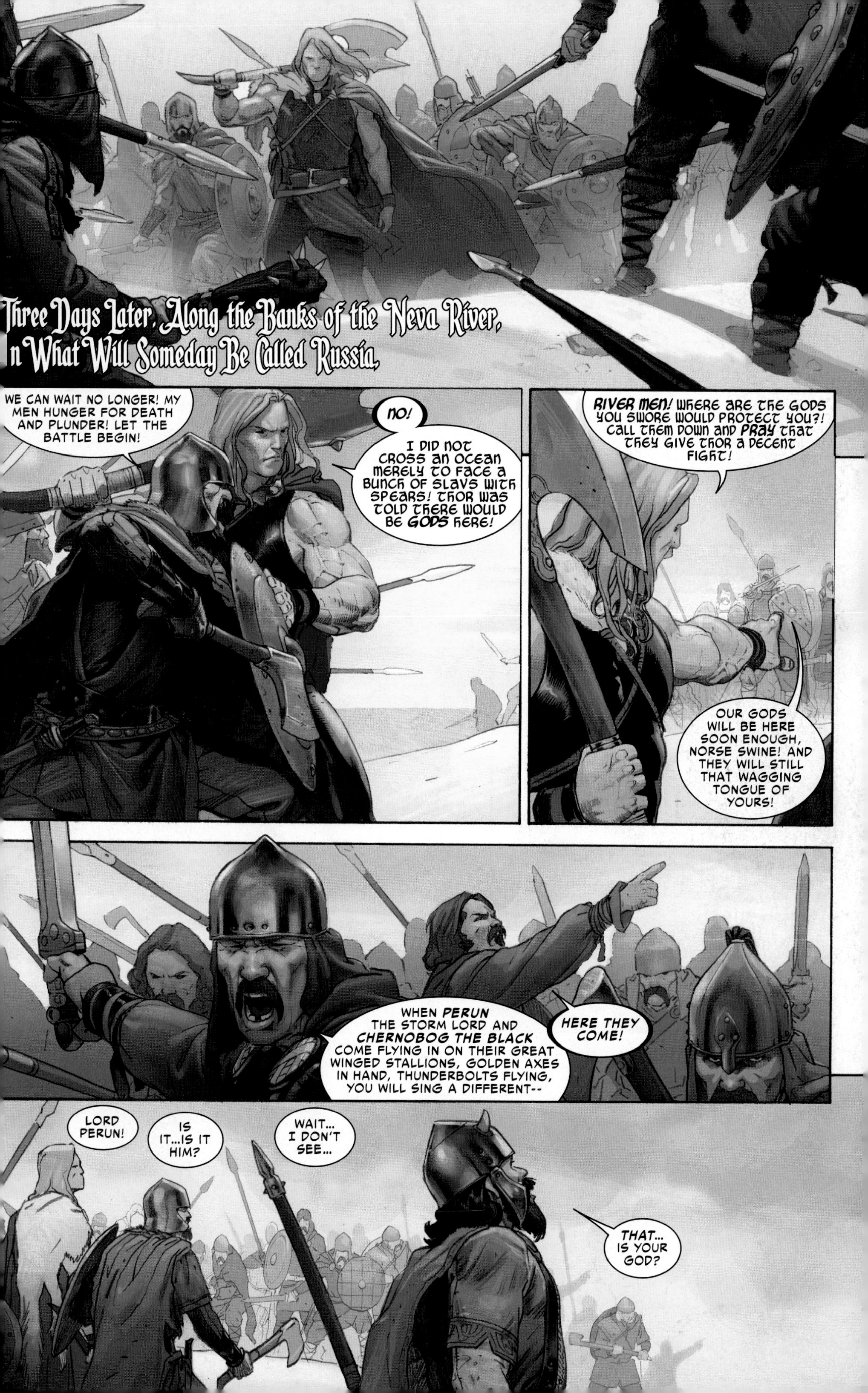
Three Days Later, Along the Banks of the Neva River, n What Will Someday Be Called Russia,
WE CAN WAIT NO LONGER! MY MEN HUNGER FOR DEATH AND PLUNDER! LET THE BATTLE BEGIN!
NO!
I DID NOT CROSS AN OCEAN MERELY TO FACE A BUNCH OF SLAVS WITH SPEARS! THOR WAS TOLD THERE WOULD BE GODS HERE!
RIVER MEN! WHERE ARE THE GODS YOU SWORE WOULD PROTECT YOU?! CALL THEM DOWN AND PRAY THAT THEY GIVE THOR A DECENT FIGHT!
OUR GODS WILL BE HERE SOON ENOUGH, NORSE SWINE! AND THEY WILL STILL THAT WAGGING TONGUE OF YOURS!
WHEN PERUN THE STORM LORD AND CHERNOBOG THE BLACK COME FLYING IN ON THEIR GREAT WINGED STALLIONS, GOLDEN AXES IN HAND, THUNDERBOLTS FLYING, YOU WILL SING A DIFFERENT--
HERE THEY COME!
LORD PERUN!
IS IT...IS IT HIM?
WAIT... I DON'T SEE...
THAT... IS YOUR GOD?

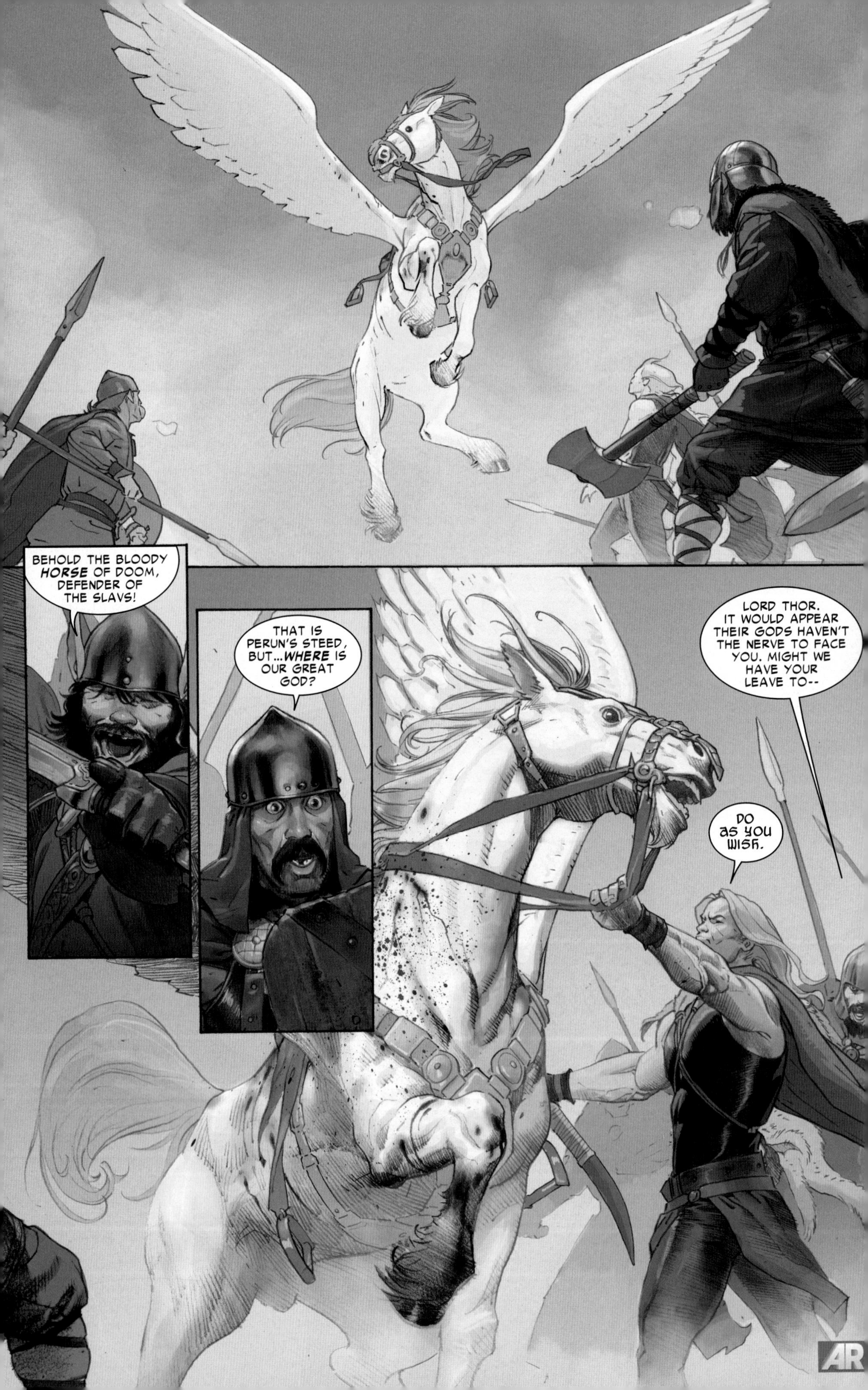
BEHOLD THE BLOODY HORSE OF DOOM, DEFENDER OF THE SLAVS!
THAT IS PERUN'S STEED, BUT...WHERE IS OUR GREAT GOD?
LORD THOR. IT WOULD APPEAR THEIR GODS HAVEN'T THE NERVE TO FACE YOU. MIGHT WE HAVE YOUR LEAVE TO--
DO AS YOU WISH.

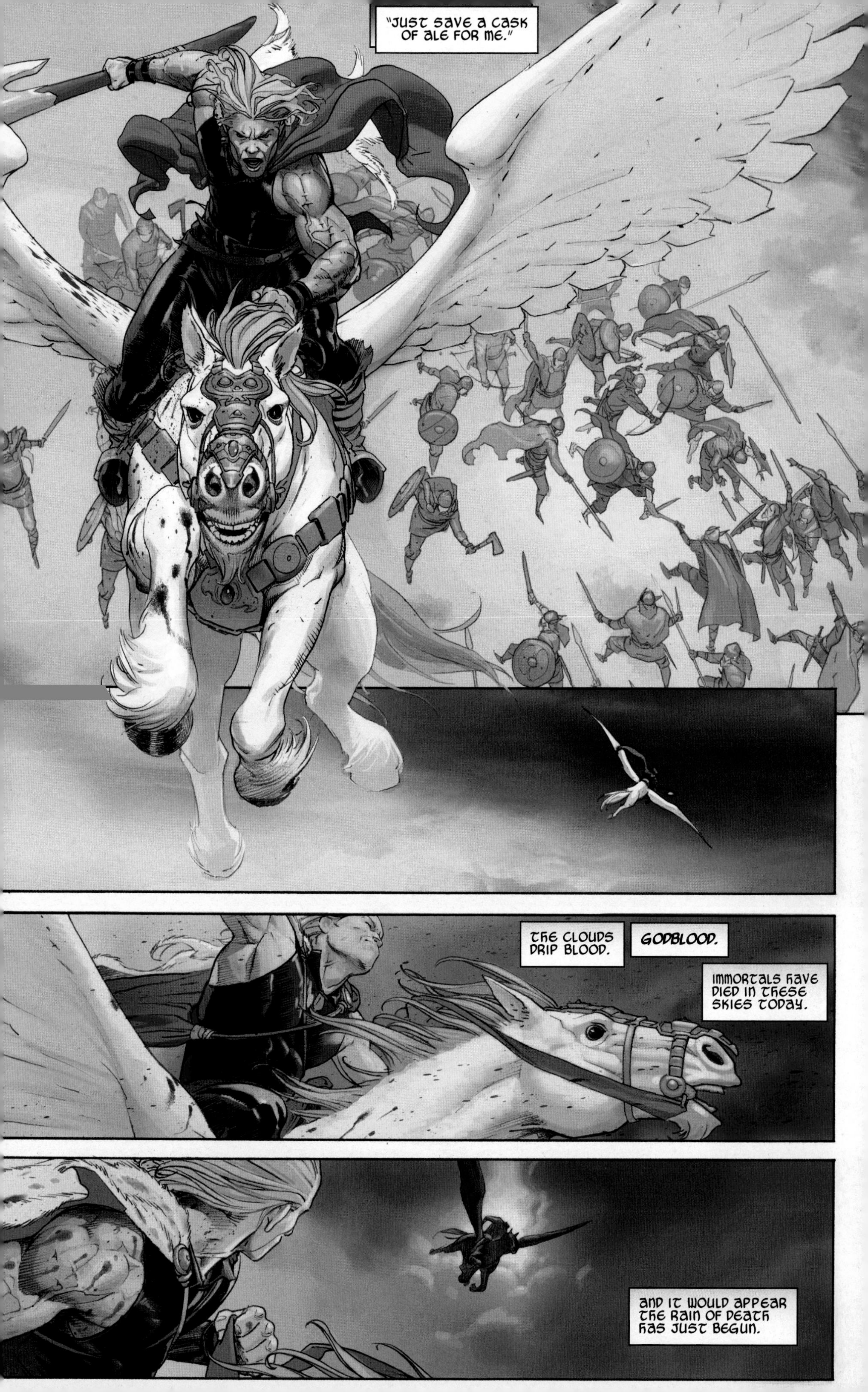
"JUST SAVE A CASK OF ALE FOR ME."
THE CLOUDS DRIP BLOOD.
GODBLOOD.
IMMORTALS HAVE DIED IN THESE SKIES TODAY.
AND IT WOULD APPEAR THE RAIN OF DEATH HAS JUST BEGUN.

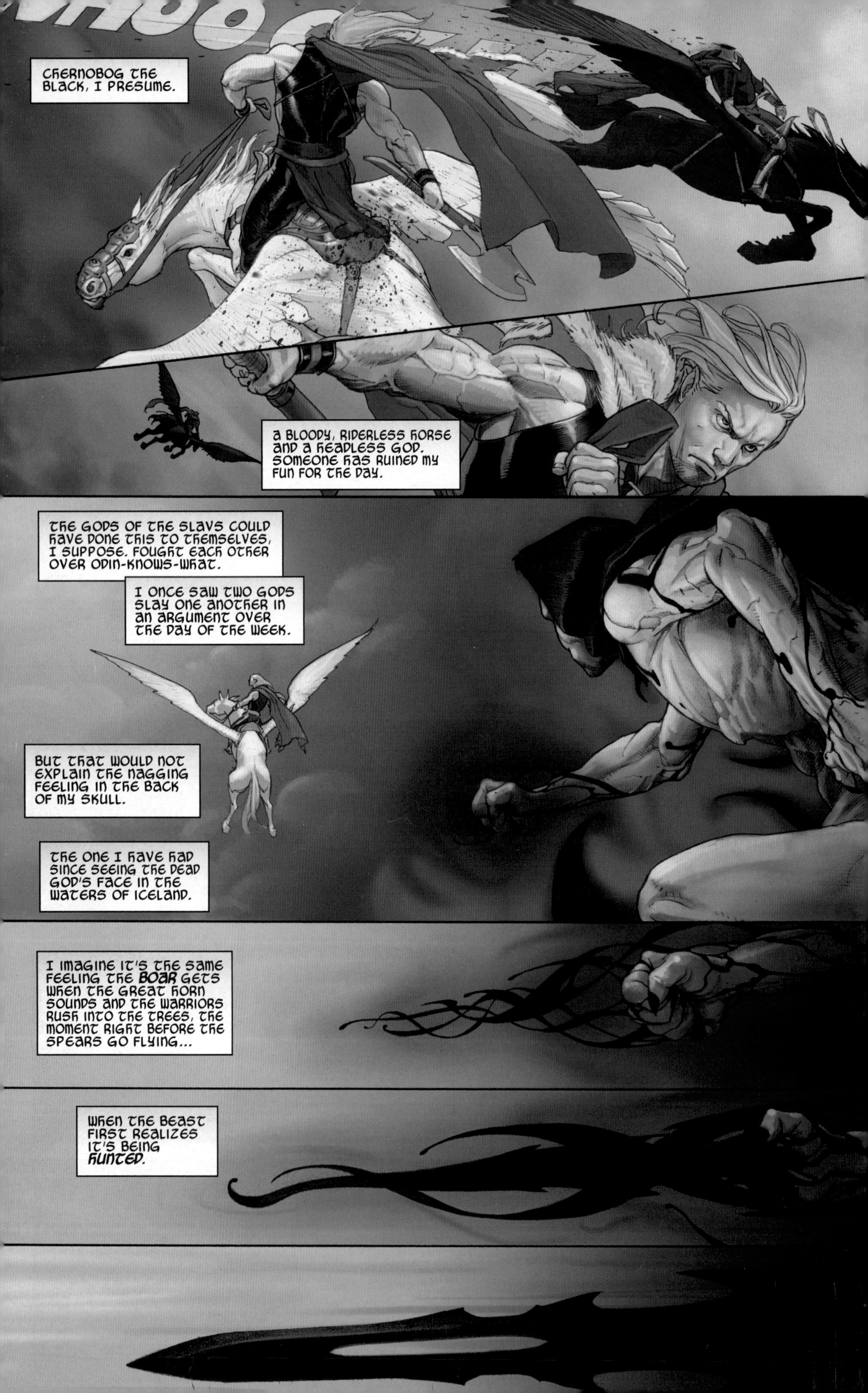
CHERNOBOG THE BLACK, I PRESUME.
A BLOODY, RIDERLESS HORSE AND A HEADLESS GOD. SOMEONE HAS RUINED MY FUN FOR THE DAY.
THE GODS OF THE SLAVS COULD HAVE DONE THIS TO THEMSELVES, I SUPPOSE. FOUGHT EACH OTHER OVER ODIN-KNOWS-WHAT.
I ONCE SAW TWO GODS SLAY ONE ANOTHER IN AN ARGUMENT OVER THE DAY OF THE WEEK.
BUT THAT WOULD NOT EXPLAIN THE NAGGING FEELING IN THE BACK OF MY SKULL.
THE ONE I HAVE HAD SINCE SEEING THE DEAD GOD'S FACE IN THE WATERS OF ICELAND.
I IMAGINE IT'S THE SAME FEELING THE ***BOAR*** GETS WHEN THE GREAT HORN SOUNDS AND THE WARRIORS RUSH INTO THE TREES, THE MOMENT RIGHT BEFORE THE SPEARS GO FLYING...
WHEN THE BEAST FIRST REALIZES IT'S BEING ***HUNTED***.

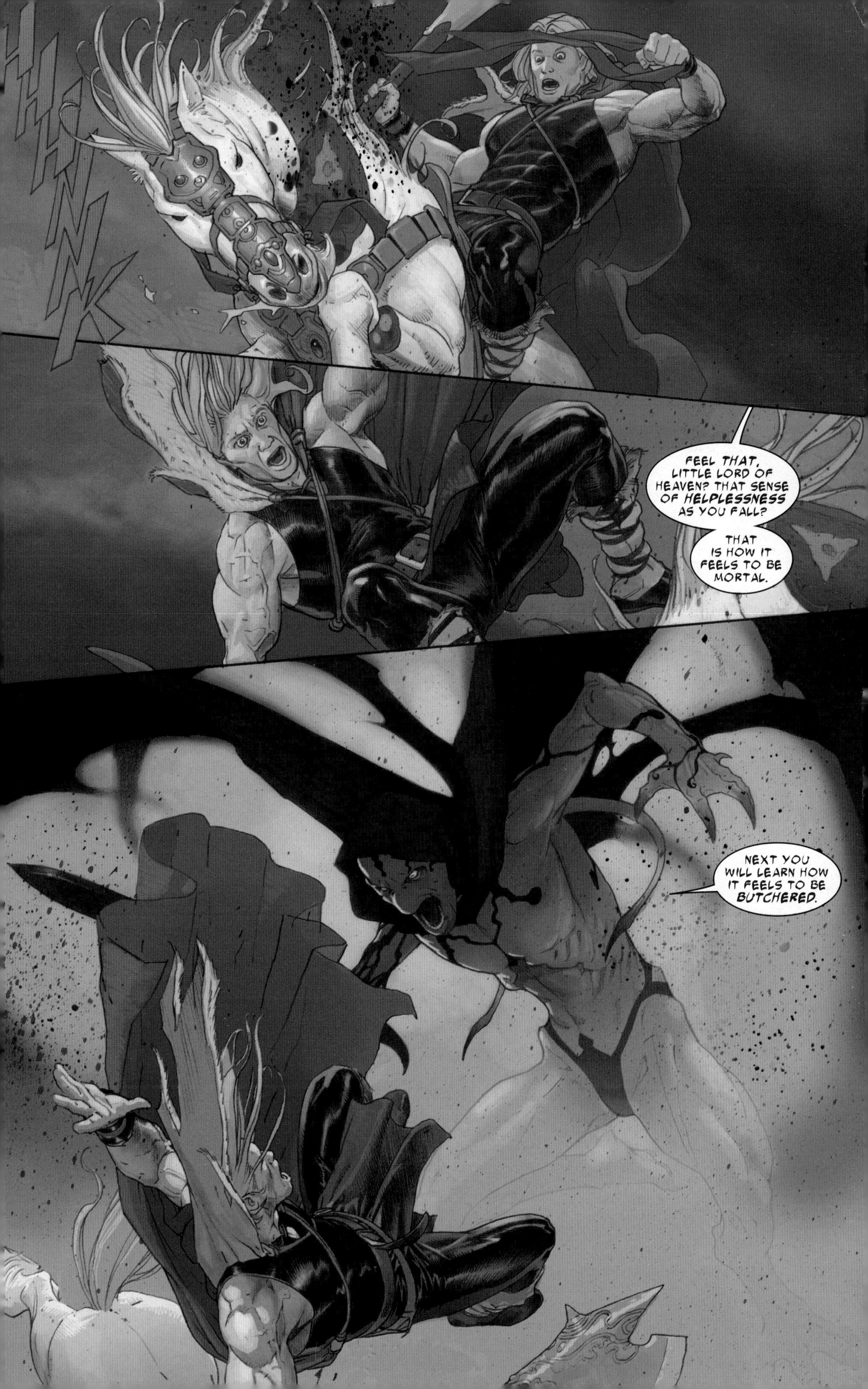

THHHHNNK
FEEL THAT, LITTLE LORD OF HEAVEN? THAT SENSE OF HELPLESSNESS AS YOU FALL?
THAT IS HOW IT FEELS TO BE MORTAL.
NEXT YOU WILL LEARN HOW IT FEELS TO BE BUTCHERED.

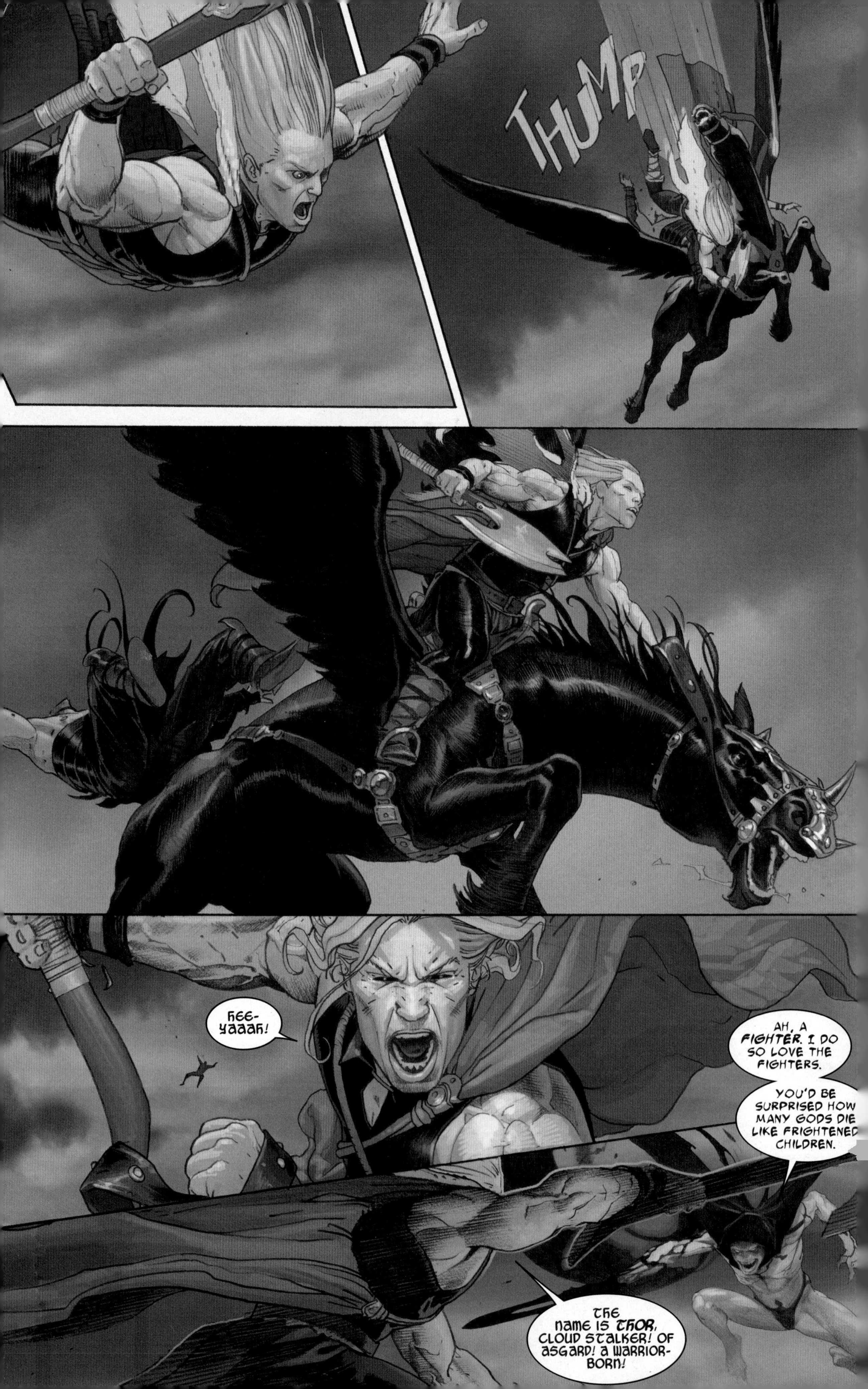
THUMP
HEE-YAAAH!
AH, A FIGHTER. I DO SO LOVE THE FIGHTERS.
YOU'D BE SURPRISED HOW MANY GODS DIE LIKE FRIGHTENED CHILDREN.
THE NAME IS THOR, CLOUD STALKER! OF ASGARD! A WARRIOR-BORN!

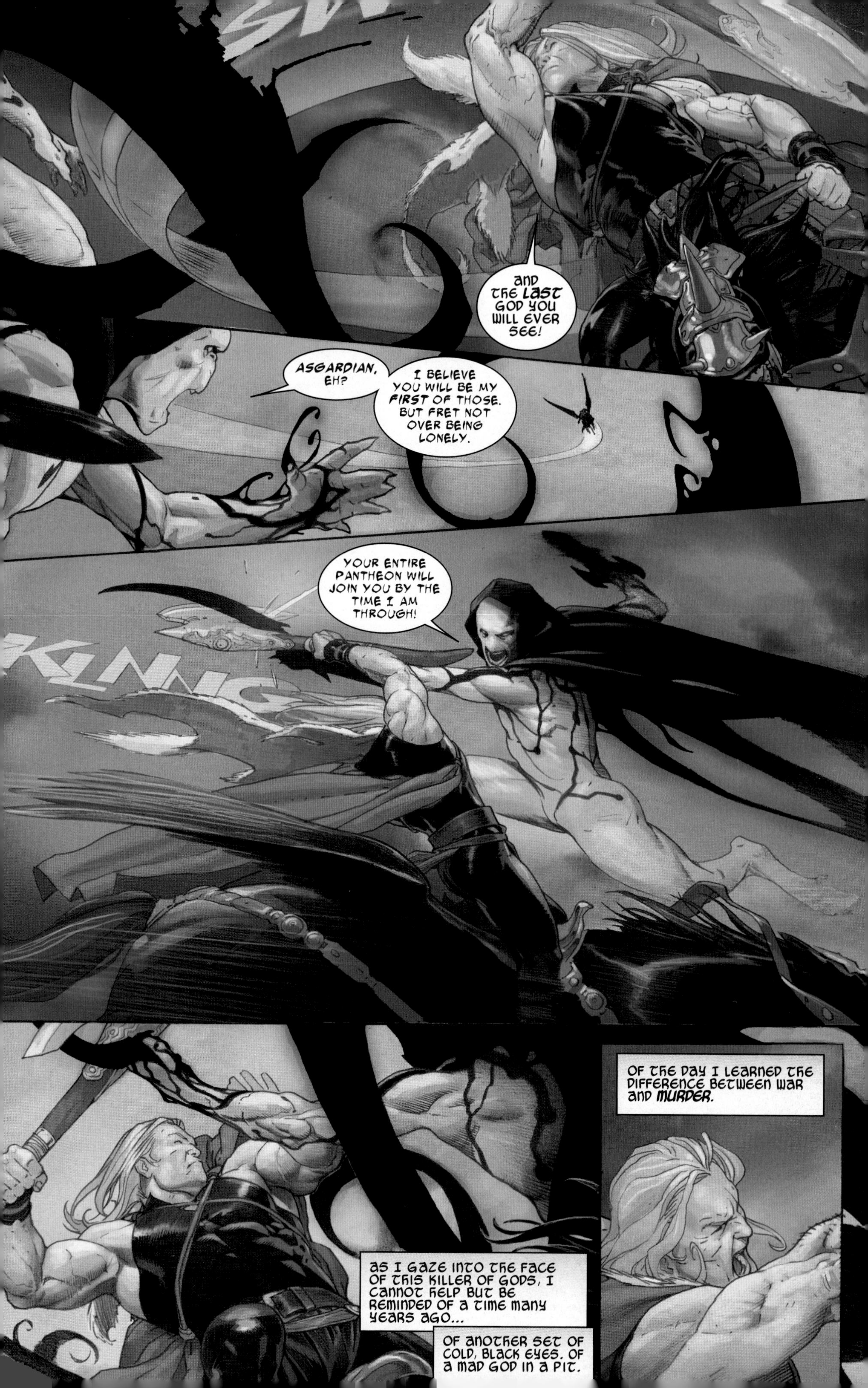
AND THE LAST GOD YOU WILL EVER SEE!
ASGARDIAN, EH?
I BELIEVE YOU WILL BE MY FIRST OF THOSE. BUT FRET NOT OVER BEING LONELY.
YOUR ENTIRE PANTHEON WILL JOIN YOU BY THE TIME I AM THROUGH!
KLNNG
AS I GAZE INTO THE FACE OF THIS KILLER OF GODS, I CANNOT HELP BUT BE REMINDED OF A TIME MANY YEARS AGO...
OF ANOTHER SET OF COLD, BLACK EYES. OF A MAD GOD IN A PIT.
OF THE DAY I LEARNED THE DIFFERENCE BETWEEN WAR AND MURDER.

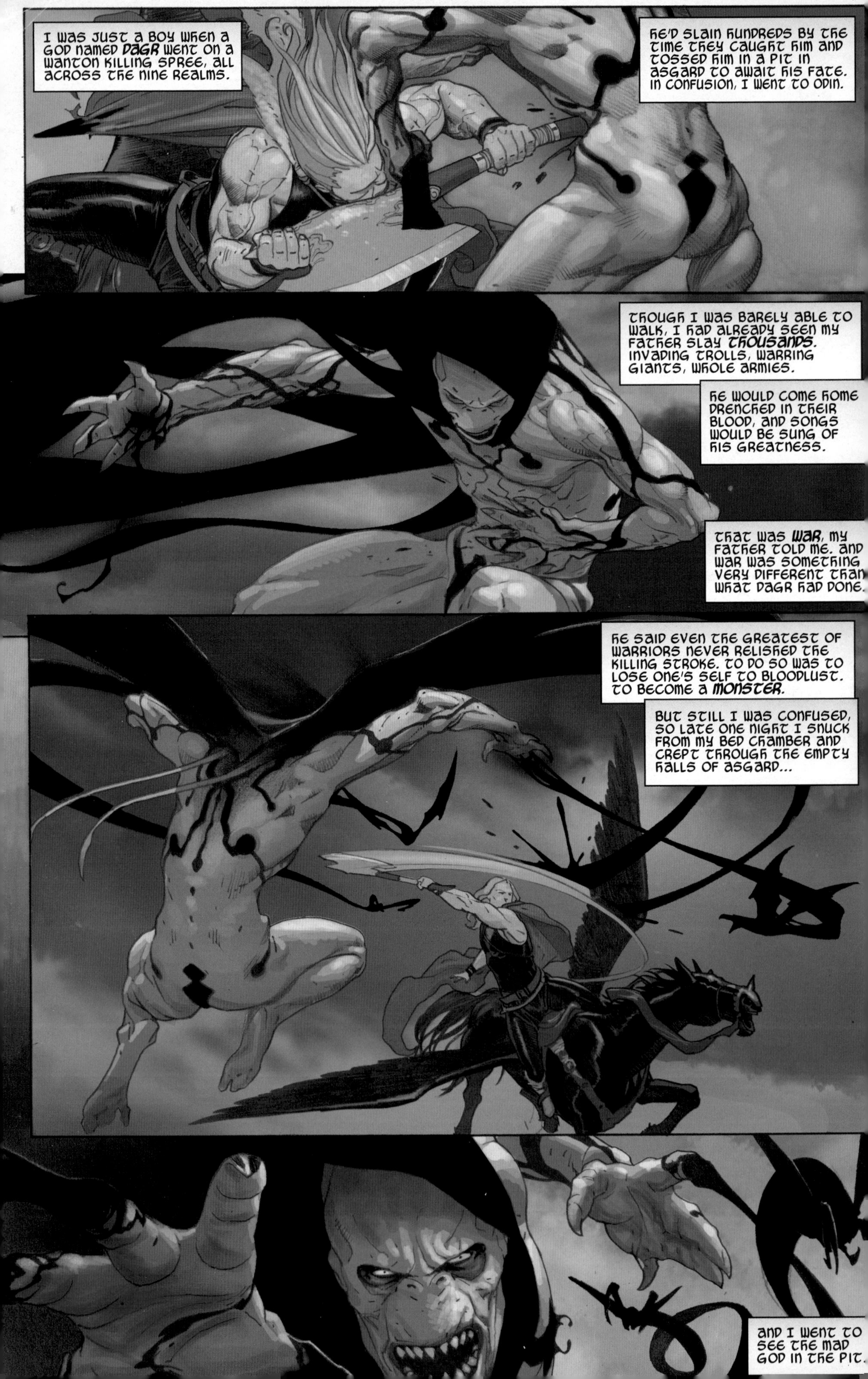
I WAS JUST A BOY WHEN A GOD NAMED DAGR WENT ON A WANTON KILLING SPREE, ALL ACROSS THE NINE REALMS.
HE'D SLAIN HUNDREDS BY THE TIME THEY CAUGHT HIM AND TOSSED HIM IN A PIT IN ASGARD TO AWAIT HIS FATE. IN CONFUSION, I WENT TO ODIN.
THOUGH I WAS BARELY ABLE TO WALK, I HAD ALREADY SEEN MY FATHER SLAY THOUSANDS. INVADING TROLLS, WARRING GIANTS, WHOLE ARMIES.
HE WOULD COME HOME DRENCHED IN THEIR BLOOD, AND SONGS WOULD BE SUNG OF HIS GREATNESS.
THAT WAS WAR, MY FATHER TOLD ME. AND WAR WAS SOMETHING VERY DIFFERENT THAN WHAT DAGR HAD DONE.
HE SAID EVEN THE GREATEST OF WARRIORS NEVER RELISHED THE KILLING STROKE. TO DO SO WAS TO LOSE ONE'S SELF TO BLOODLUST. TO BECOME A MONSTER.
BUT STILL I WAS CONFUSED, SO LATE ONE NIGHT I SNUCK FROM MY BED CHAMBER AND CREPT THROUGH THE EMPTY HALLS OF ASGARD...
AND I WENT TO SEE THE MAD GOD IN THE PIT.

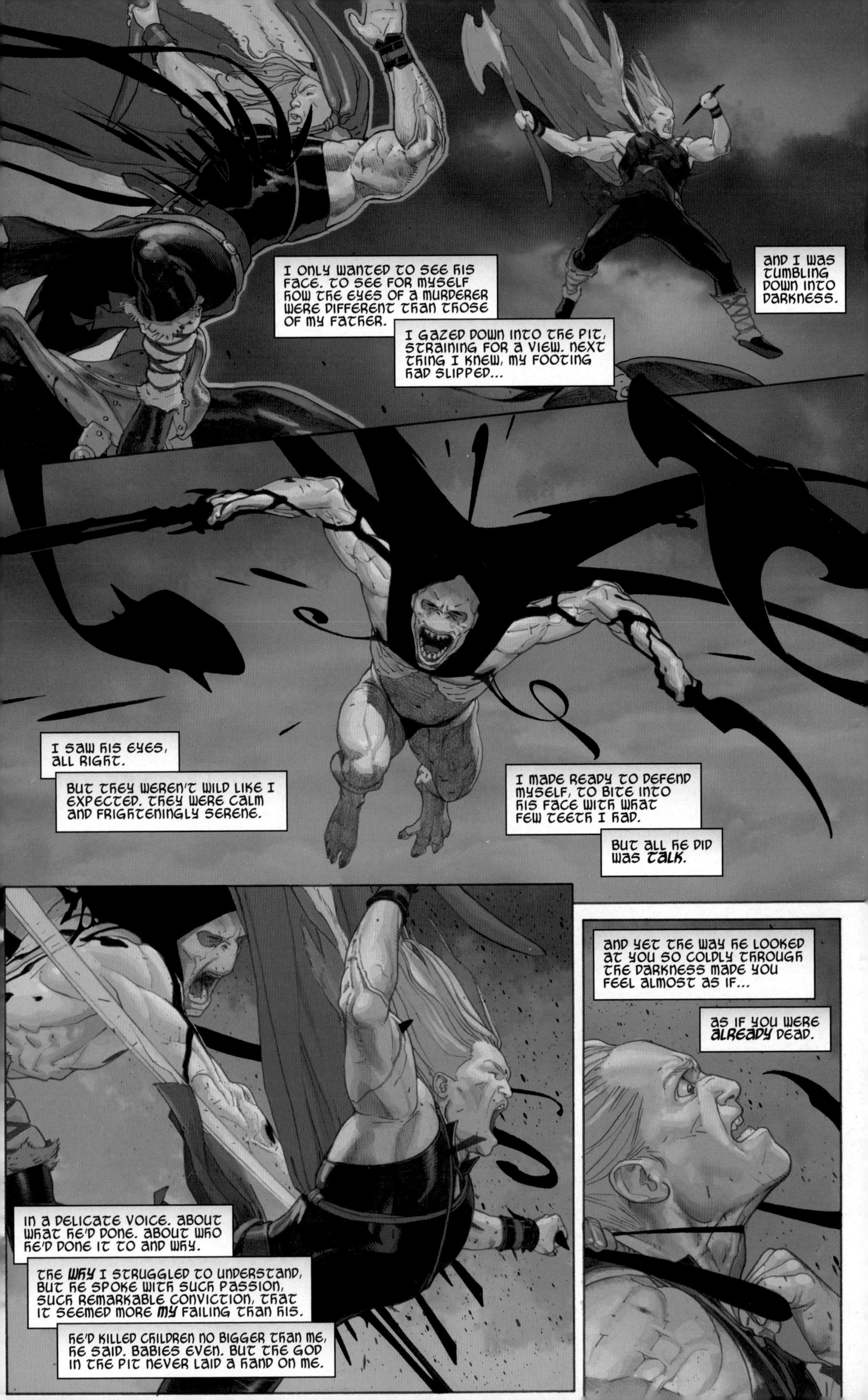
I ONLY WANTED TO SEE HIS FACE. TO SEE FOR MYSELF HOW THE EYES OF A MURDERER WERE DIFFERENT THAN THOSE OF MY FATHER.
I GAZED DOWN INTO THE PIT, STRAINING FOR A VIEW. NEXT THING I KNEW, MY FOOTING HAD SLIPPED...
AND I WAS TUMBLING DOWN INTO DARKNESS.
I SAW HIS EYES, ALL RIGHT.
BUT THEY WEREN'T WILD LIKE I EXPECTED. THEY WERE CALM AND FRIGHTENINGLY SERENE.
I MADE READY TO DEFEND MYSELF, TO BITE INTO HIS FACE WITH WHAT FEW TEETH I HAD.
BUT ALL HE DID WAS TALK.
IN A DELICATE VOICE. ABOUT WHAT HE'D DONE. ABOUT WHO HE'D DONE IT TO AND WHY.
THE WHY I STRUGGLED TO UNDERSTAND, BUT HE SPOKE WITH SUCH PASSION, SUCH REMARKABLE CONVICTION, THAT IT SEEMED MORE MY FAILING THAN HIS.
HE'D KILLED CHILDREN NO BIGGER THAN ME, HE SAID. BABIES EVEN. BUT THE GOD IN THE PIT NEVER LAID A HAND ON ME.
AND YET THE WAY HE LOOKED AT YOU SO COLDLY THROUGH THE DARKNESS MADE YOU FEEL ALMOST AS IF...
AS IF YOU WERE ALREADY DEAD.

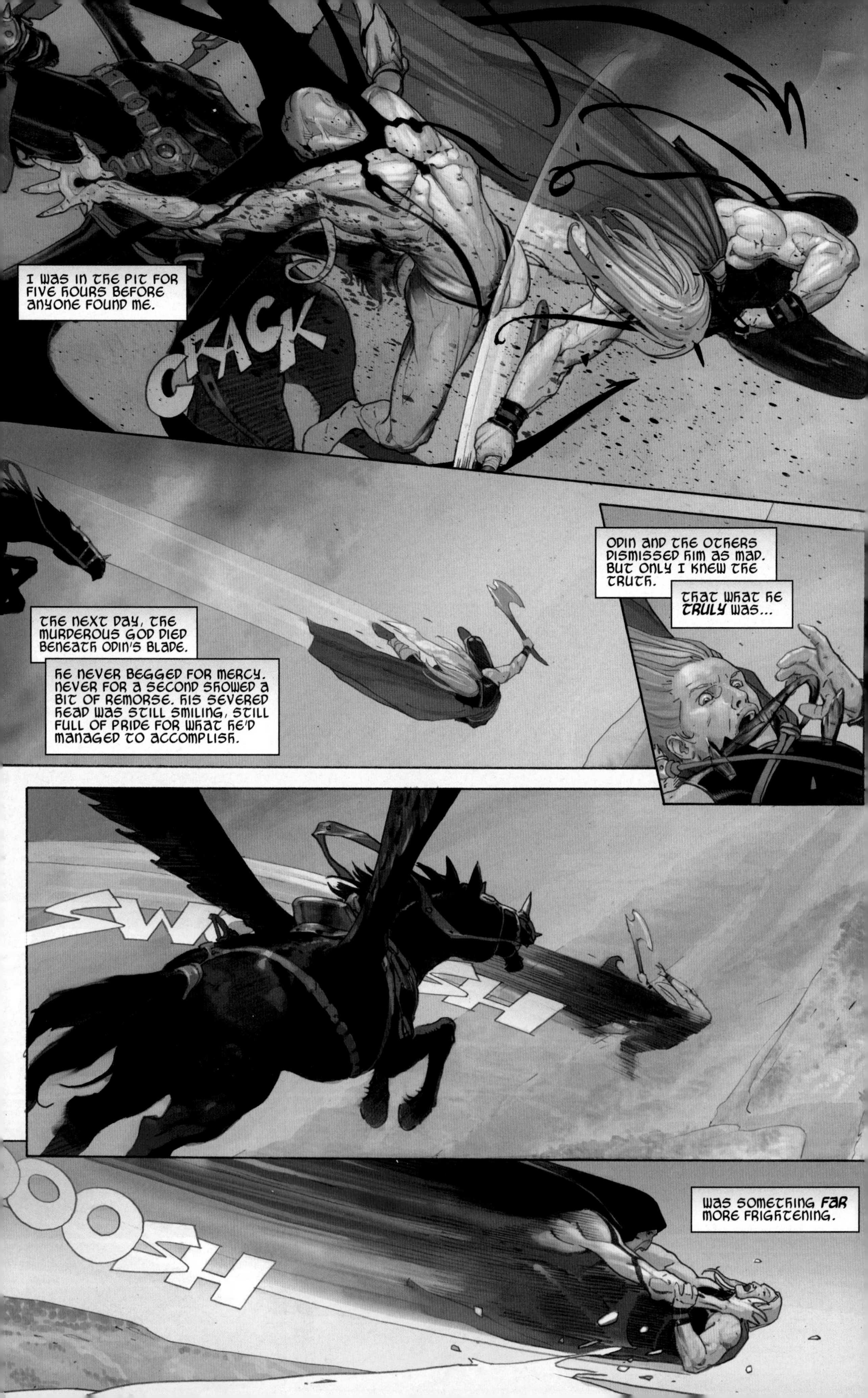
I WAS IN THE PIT FOR FIVE HOURS BEFORE ANYONE FOUND ME.
CRACK
THE NEXT DAY, THE MURDEROUS GOD DIED BENEATH ODIN'S BLADE.
HE NEVER BEGGED FOR MERCY. NEVER FOR A SECOND SHOWED A BIT OF REMORSE. HIS SEVERED HEAD WAS STILL SMILING, STILL FULL OF PRIDE FOR WHAT HE'D MANAGED TO ACCOMPLISH.
ODIN AND THE OTHERS DISMISSED HIM AS MAD. BUT ONLY I KNEW THE TRUTH.
THAT WHAT HE TRULY WAS...
WAS SOMETHING FAR MORE FRIGHTENING.

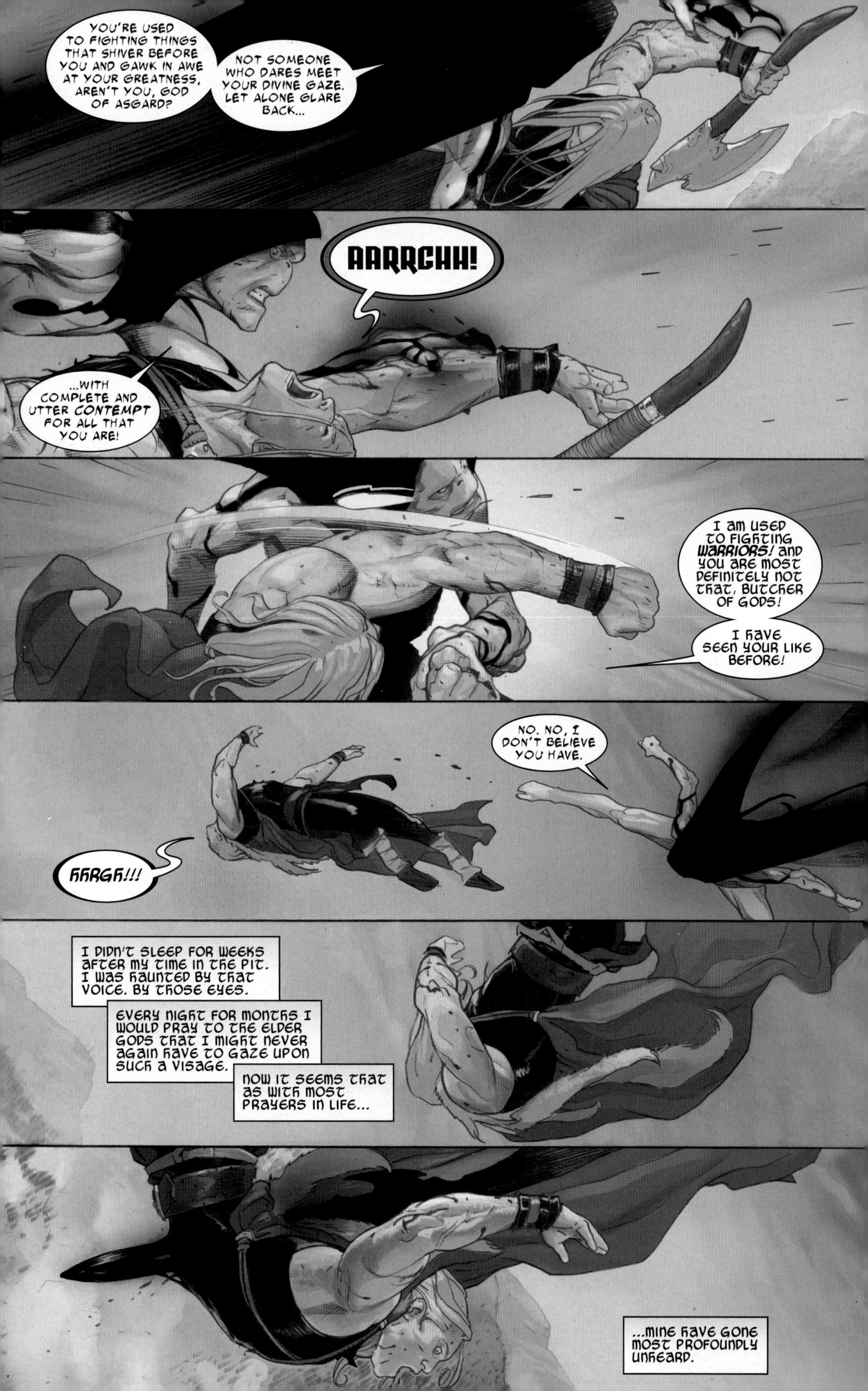
YOU'RE USED TO FIGHTING THINGS THAT SHIVER BEFORE YOU AND GAWK IN AWE AT YOUR GREATNESS, AREN'T YOU, GOD OF ASGARD?
NOT SOMEONE WHO DARES MEET YOUR DIVINE GAZE. LET ALONE GLARE BACK...
AARRGHH!
...WITH COMPLETE AND UTTER CONTEMPT FOR ALL THAT YOU ARE!
I AM USED TO FIGHTING WARRIORS! AND YOU ARE MOST DEFINITELY NOT THAT, BUTCHER OF GODS!
I HAVE SEEN YOUR LIKE BEFORE!
NO. NO, I DON'T BELIEVE YOU HAVE.
HHRGH!!!
I DIDN'T SLEEP FOR WEEKS AFTER MY TIME IN THE PIT. I WAS HAUNTED BY THAT VOICE. BY THOSE EYES.
EVERY NIGHT FOR MONTHS I WOULD PRAY TO THE ELDER GODS THAT I MIGHT NEVER AGAIN HAVE TO GAZE UPON SUCH A VISAGE.
NOW IT SEEMS THAT AS WITH MOST PRAYERS IN LIFE...
...MINE HAVE GONE MOST PROFOUNDLY UNHEARD.

I CANNOT HELP BUT WONDER, LITTLE GOD, TO THE POOR DAMNED FOOLS BELOW US WHO *WORSHIP* YOU...

WHAT ARE YOU THE GOD OF?

AXES? DRUNKENNESS? VANITY?

OR WAR PERHAPS? I HAVE KILLED SO VERY MANY GODS OF WAR.

AND GODS OF FEAR. GODS OF CHAOS. GODS OF BLOOD AND WRATH AND JEALOUSY AND LIES.

OF PLAGUES AND EARTHQUAKES. GENOCIDE AND REVENGE. OF DEGRADATION. OF DEATH.

VERY FEW GODS OF POETRY AND FLOWERS. THOUGH I KILLED THOSE JUST THE SAME.

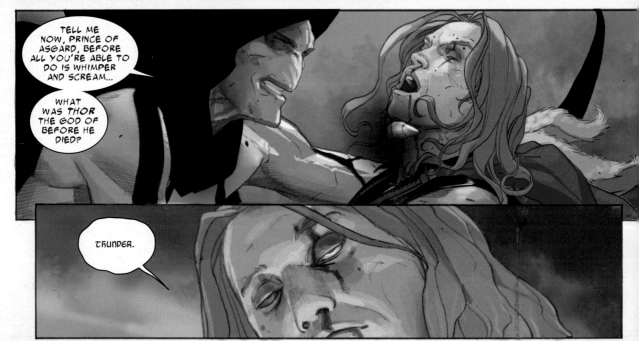

TELL ME NOW, PRINCE OF ASGARD, BEFORE ALL YOU'RE ABLE TO DO IS WHIMPER AND SCREAM...

WHAT WAS *THOR* THE GOD OF BEFORE HE DIED?

THUNDER.

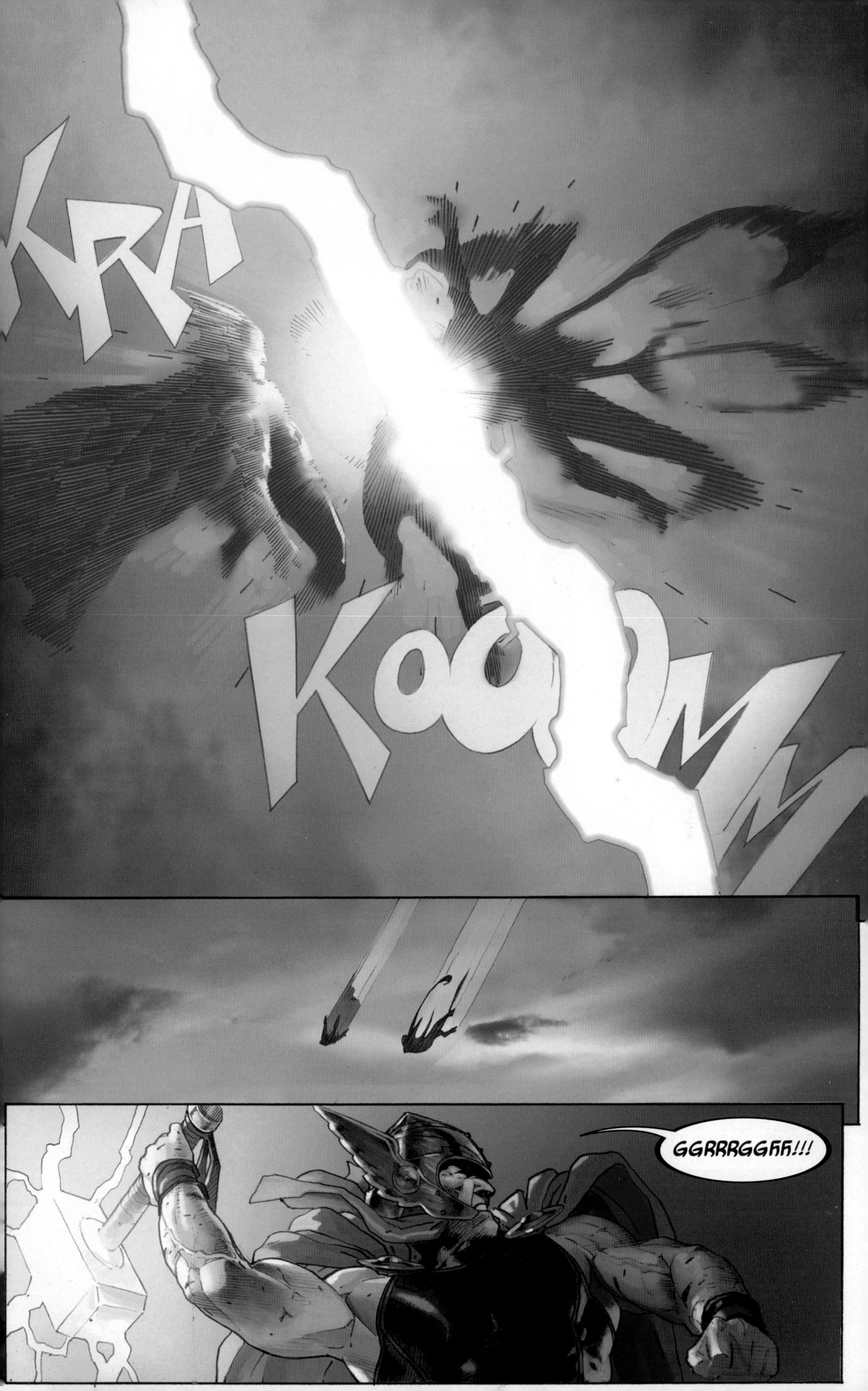
KRA
KOOOM
GGRRRGGHH!!!

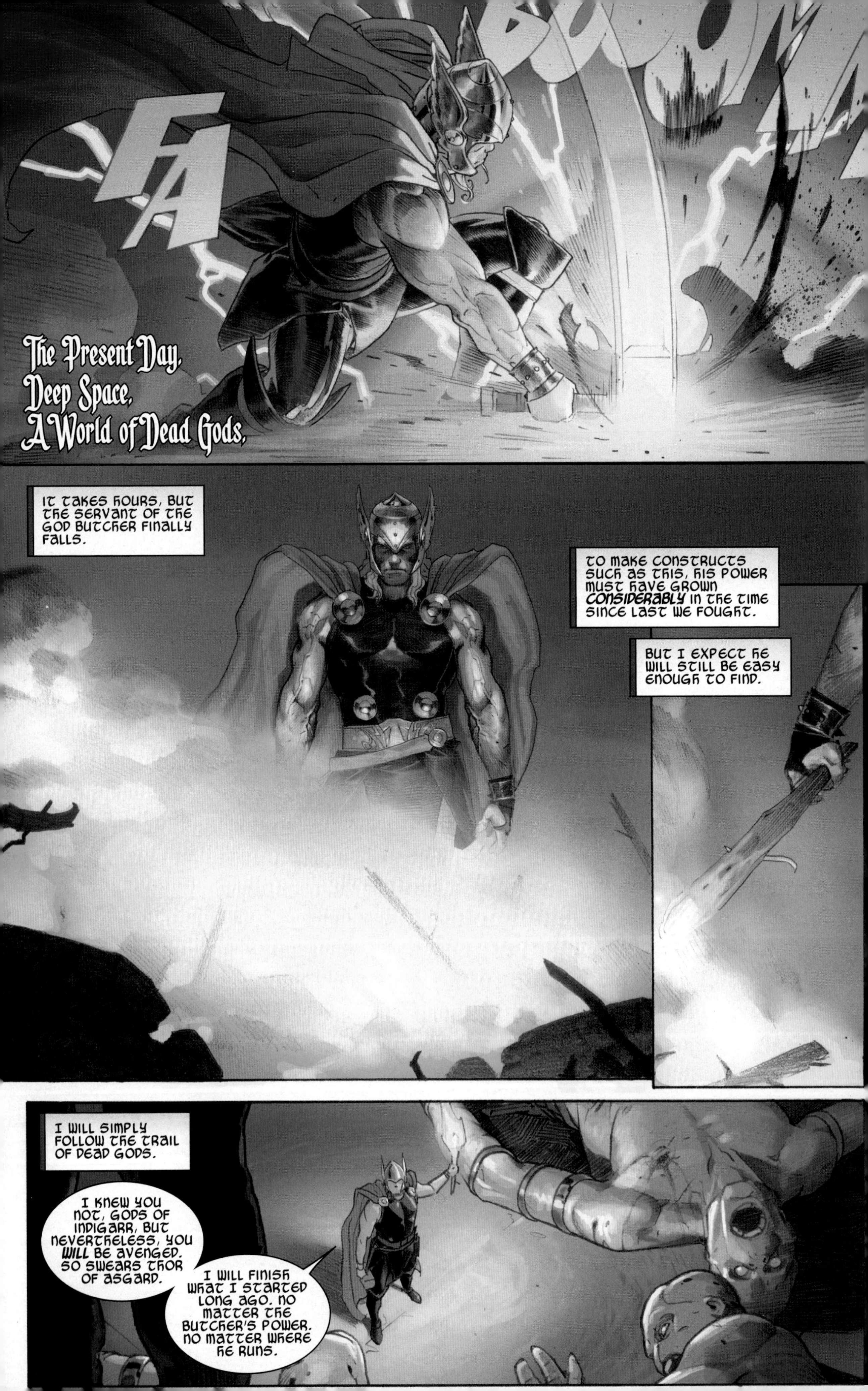
FA
BOOM
The Present Day, Deep Space, A World of Dead Gods.
IT TAKES HOURS, BUT THE SERVANT OF THE GOD BUTCHER FINALLY FALLS.
TO MAKE CONSTRUCTS SUCH AS THIS, HIS POWER MUST HAVE GROWN CONSIDERABLY IN THE TIME SINCE LAST WE FOUGHT.
BUT I EXPECT HE WILL STILL BE EASY ENOUGH TO FIND.
I WILL SIMPLY FOLLOW THE TRAIL OF DEAD GODS.
I KNEW YOU NOT, GODS OF INDIGARR, BUT NEVERTHELESS, YOU WILL BE AVENGED. SO SWEARS THOR OF ASGARD.
I WILL FINISH WHAT I STARTED LONG AGO. NO MATTER THE BUTCHER'S POWER. NO MATTER WHERE HE RUNS.

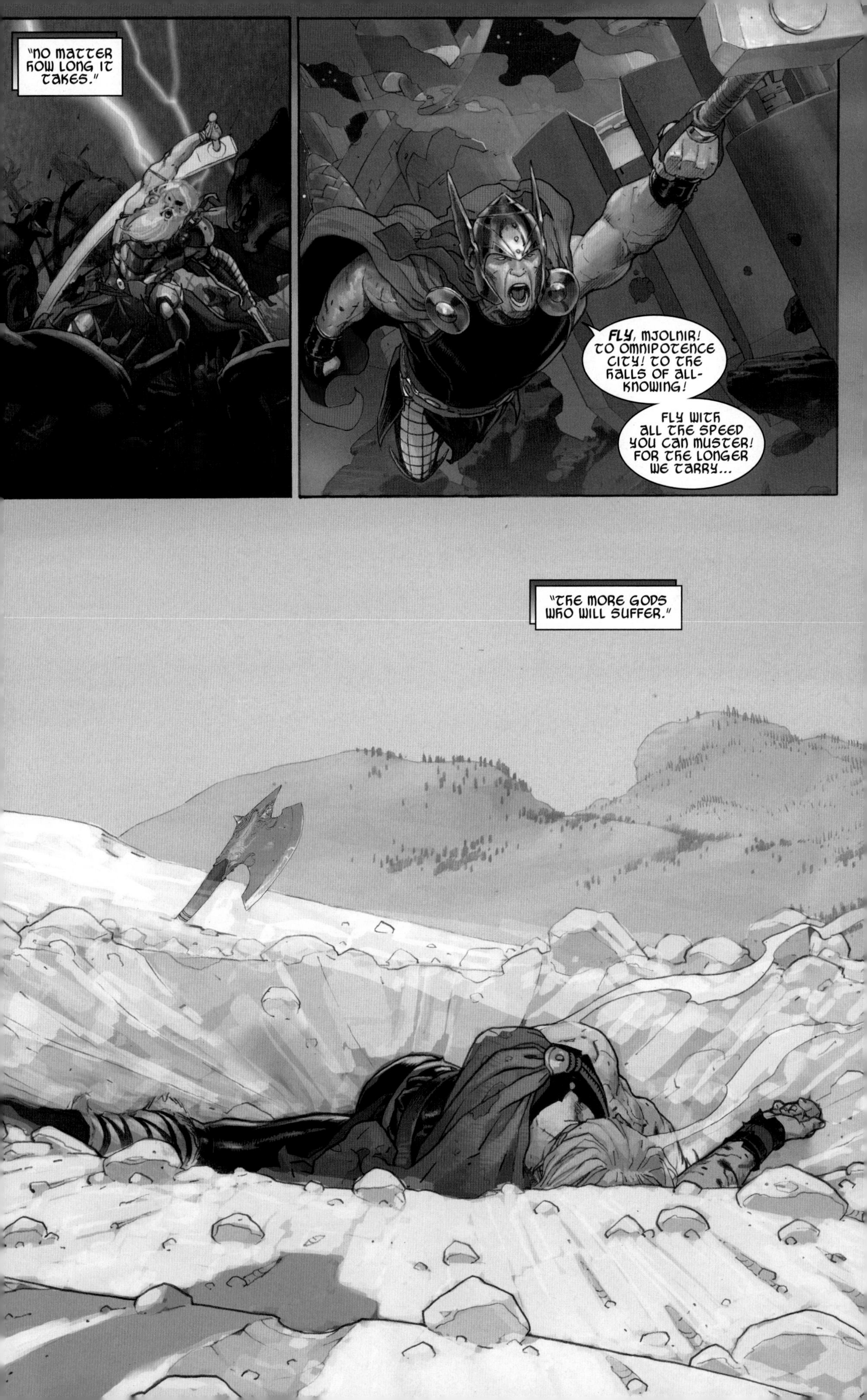
"NO MATTER HOW LONG IT TAKES."
FLY, MJOLNIR! TO OMNIPOTENCE CITY! TO THE HALLS OF ALL-KNOWING!
FLY WITH ALL THE SPEED YOU CAN MUSTER! FOR THE LONGER WE TARRY...
"THE MORE GODS WHO WILL SUFFER."

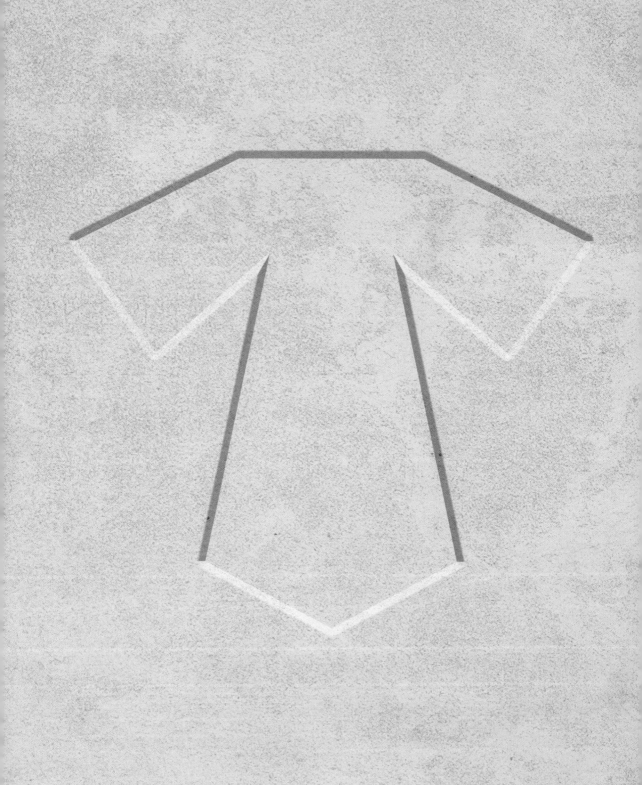

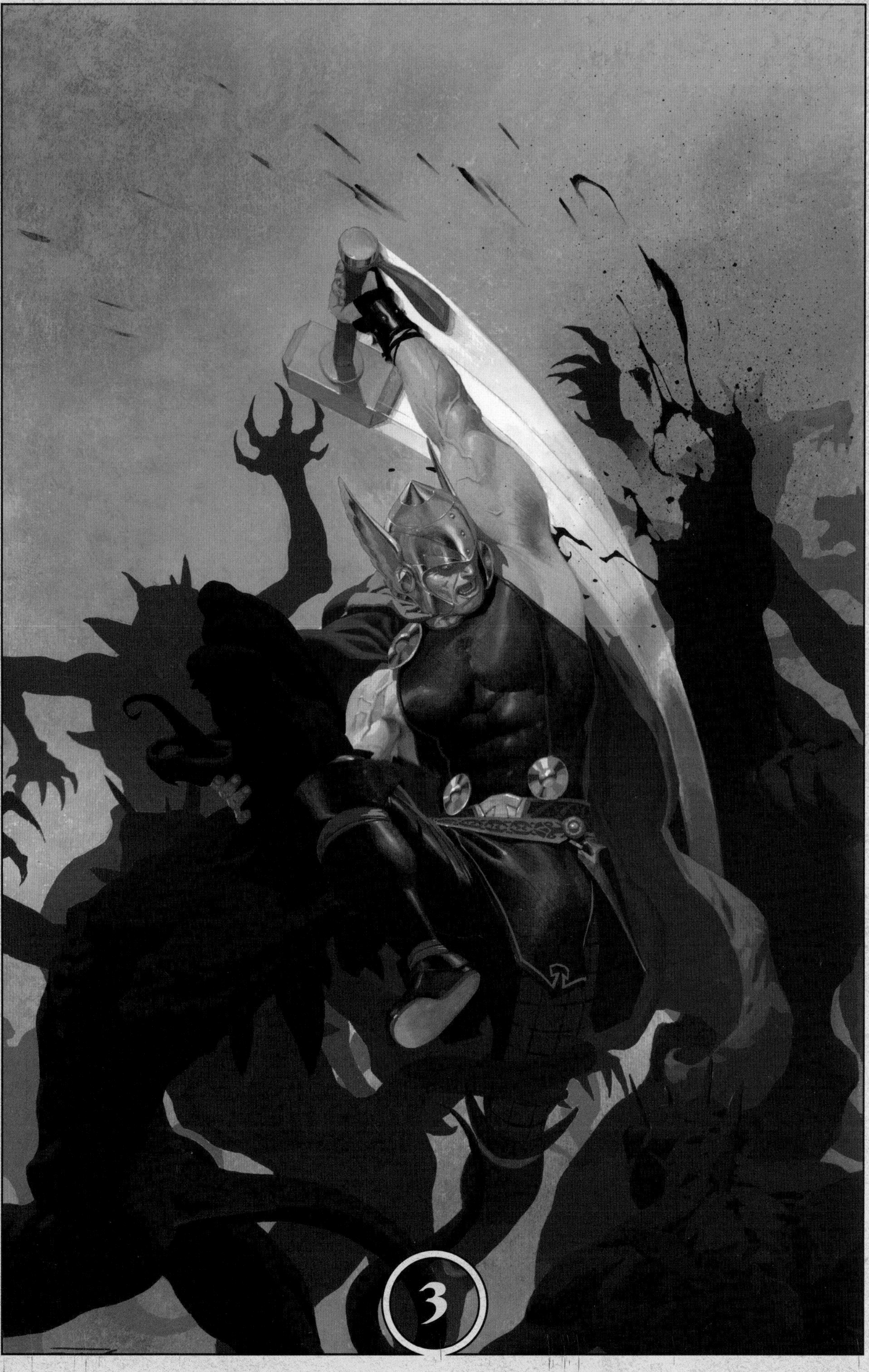
3

THE HALL OF THE LOST

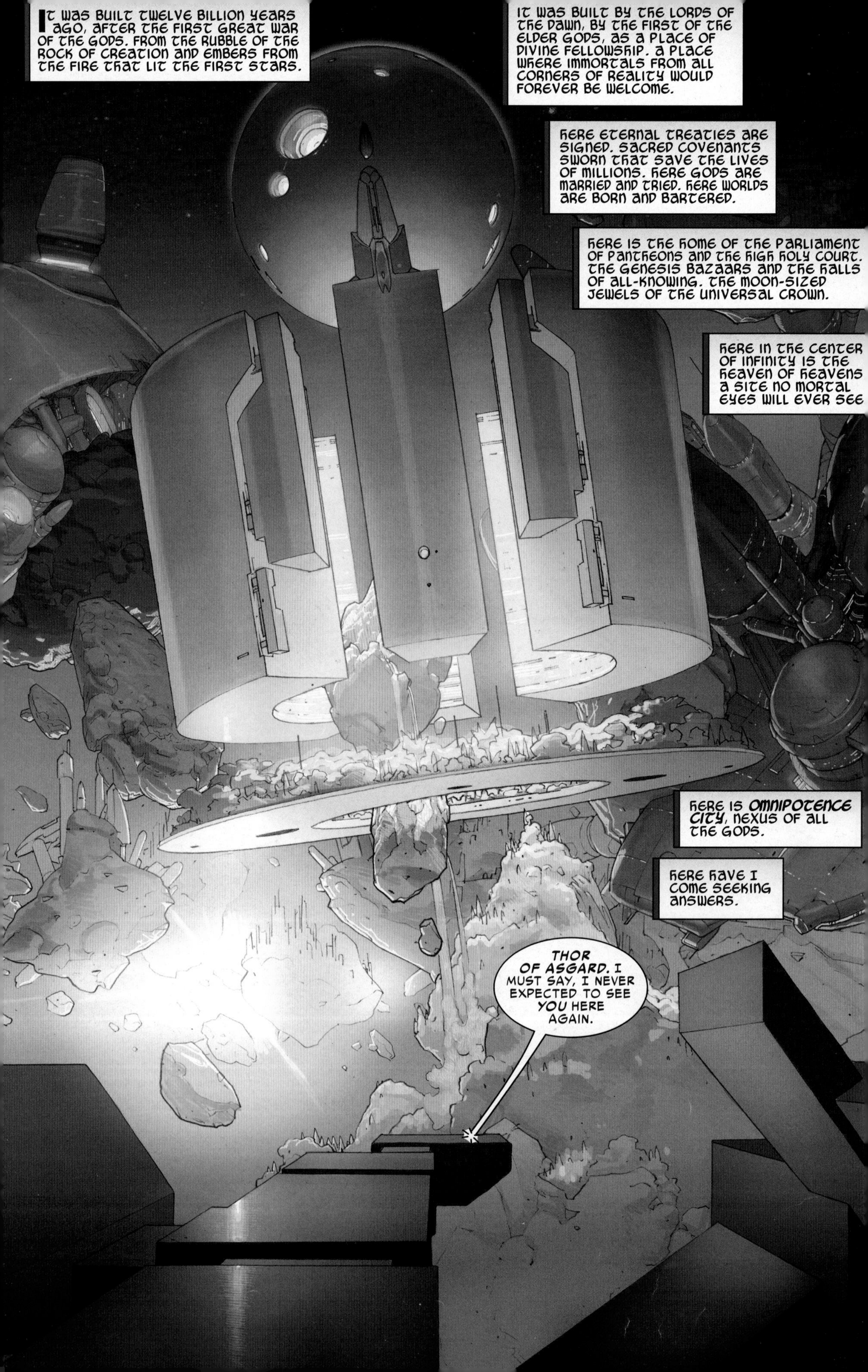
It was built twelve billion years ago, after the first great war of the gods. From the rubble of the Rock of Creation and embers from the fire that lit the first stars.
It was built by the Lords of the Dawn, by the first of the elder gods, as a place of divine fellowship. A place where immortals from all corners of reality would forever be welcome.
Here eternal treaties are signed. Sacred covenants sworn that save the lives of millions. Here gods are married and tried. Here worlds are born and bartered.
Here is the home of the Parliament of Pantheons and the High Holy Court. The Genesis Bazaars and the Halls of All-Knowing. The moon-sized jewels of the Universal Crown.
Here in the center of infinity is the heaven of heavens a site no mortal eyes will ever see
Here is *Omnipotence City*, nexus of all the gods.
Here have I come seeking answers.
THOR OF ASGARD. I MUST SAY, I NEVER EXPECTED TO SEE *YOU* HERE AGAIN.

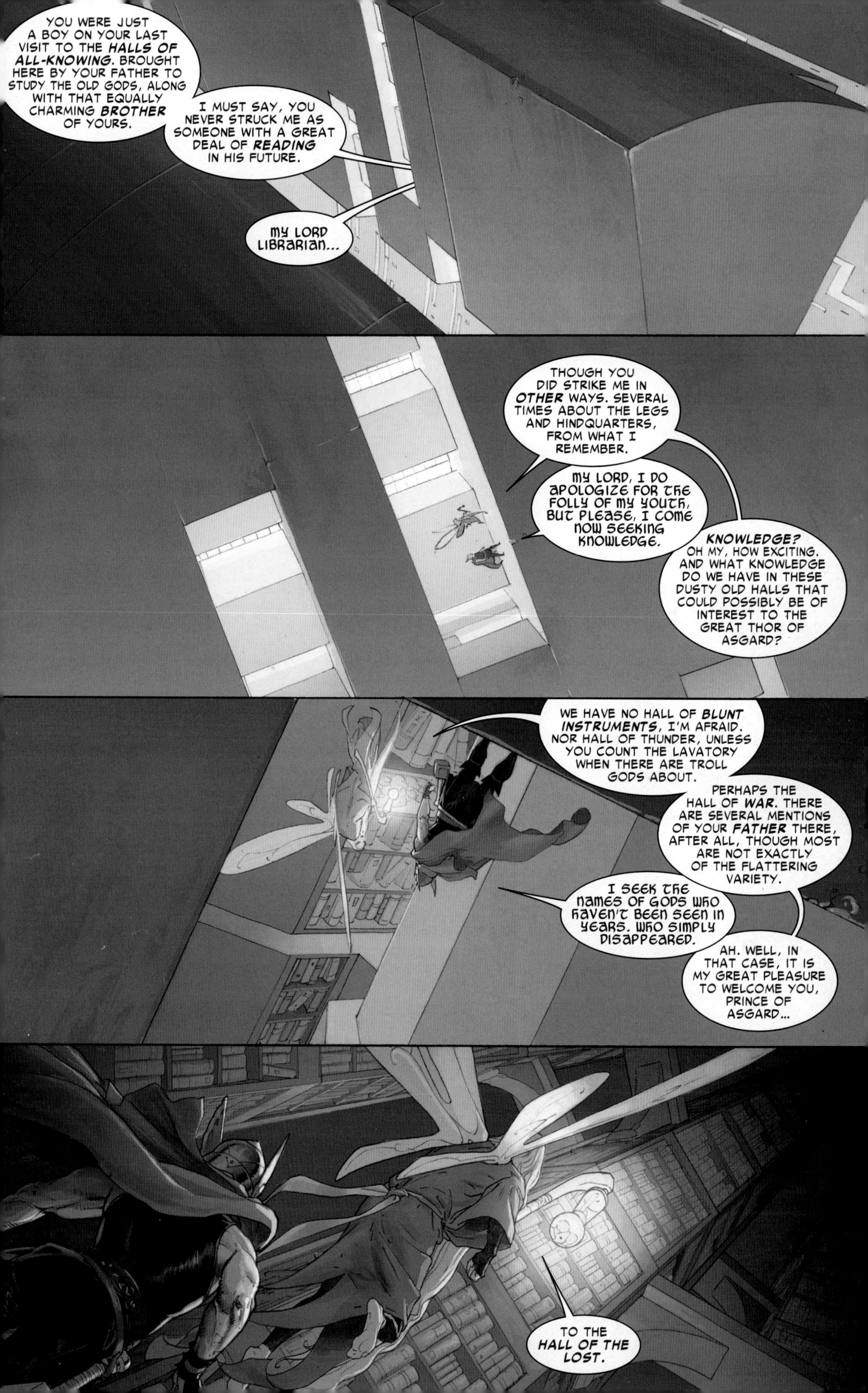
YOU WERE JUST A BOY ON YOUR LAST VISIT TO THE HALLS OF ALL-KNOWING. BROUGHT HERE BY YOUR FATHER TO STUDY THE OLD GODS, ALONG WITH THAT EQUALLY CHARMING BROTHER OF YOURS.
I MUST SAY, YOU NEVER STRUCK ME AS SOMEONE WITH A GREAT DEAL OF READING IN HIS FUTURE.
MY LORD LIBRARIAN...
THOUGH YOU DID STRIKE ME IN OTHER WAYS. SEVERAL TIMES ABOUT THE LEGS AND HINDQUARTERS, FROM WHAT I REMEMBER.
MY LORD, I DO APOLOGIZE FOR THE FOLLY OF MY YOUTH, BUT PLEASE, I COME NOW SEEKING KNOWLEDGE.
KNOWLEDGE? OH MY, HOW EXCITING. AND WHAT KNOWLEDGE DO WE HAVE IN THESE DUSTY OLD HALLS THAT COULD POSSIBLY BE OF INTEREST TO THE GREAT THOR OF ASGARD?
WE HAVE NO HALL OF BLUNT INSTRUMENTS, I'M AFRAID. NOR HALL OF THUNDER, UNLESS YOU COUNT THE LAVATORY WHEN THERE ARE TROLL GODS ABOUT.
PERHAPS THE HALL OF WAR. THERE ARE SEVERAL MENTIONS OF YOUR FATHER THERE, AFTER ALL, THOUGH MOST ARE NOT EXACTLY OF THE FLATTERING VARIETY.
I SEEK THE NAMES OF GODS WHO HAVEN'T BEEN SEEN IN YEARS. WHO SIMPLY DISAPPEARED.
AH. WELL, IN THAT CASE, IT IS MY GREAT PLEASURE TO WELCOME YOU, PRINCE OF ASGARD...
TO THE HALL OF THE LOST.

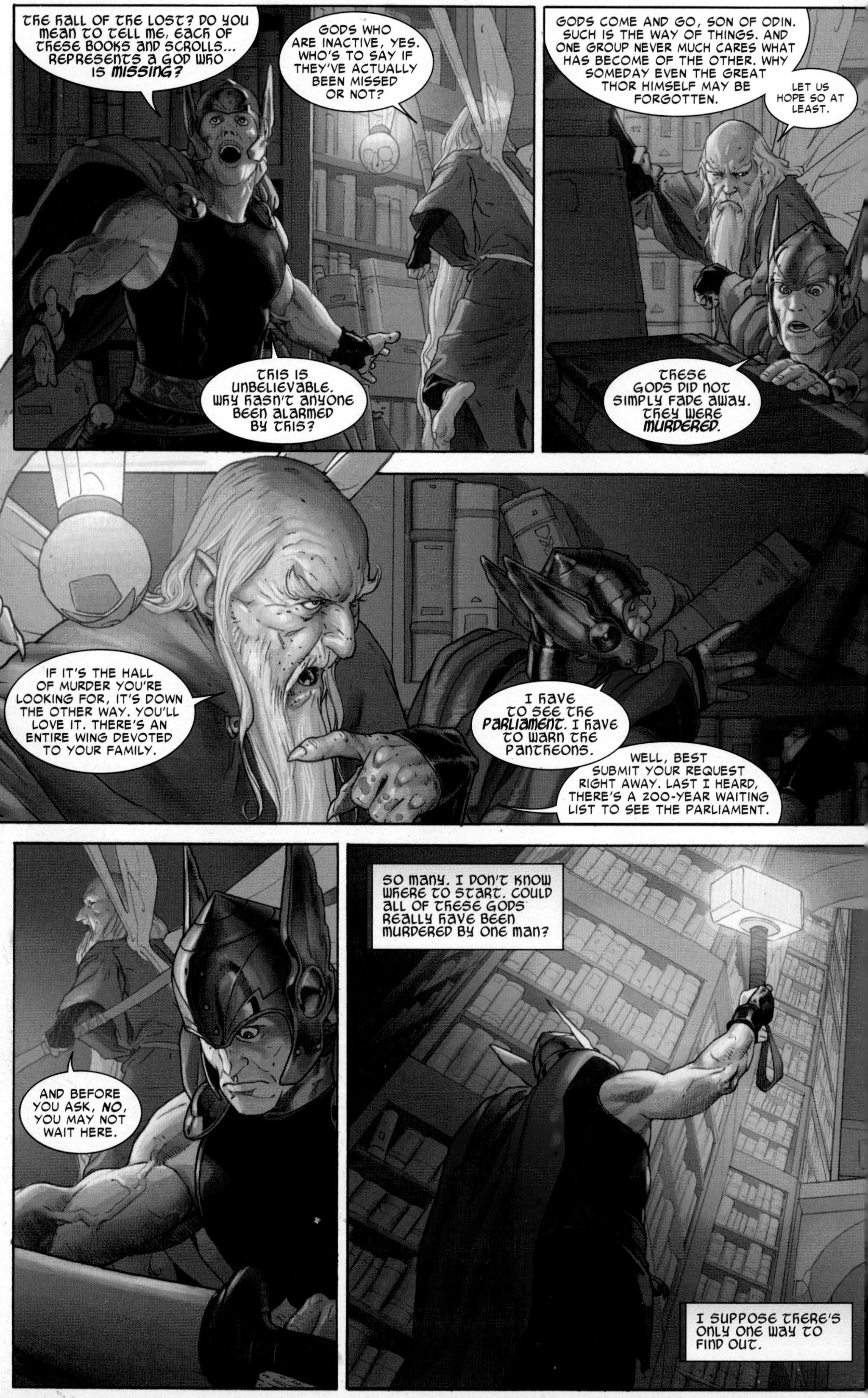
THE HALL OF THE LOST? DO YOU MEAN TO TELL ME, EACH OF THESE BOOKS AND SCROLLS... REPRESENTS A GOD WHO IS MISSING?
GODS WHO ARE INACTIVE, YES. WHO'S TO SAY IF THEY'VE ACTUALLY BEEN MISSED OR NOT?
THIS IS UNBELIEVABLE. WHY HASN'T ANYONE BEEN ALARMED BY THIS?
GODS COME AND GO, SON OF ODIN. SUCH IS THE WAY OF THINGS. AND ONE GROUP NEVER MUCH CARES WHAT HAS BECOME OF THE OTHER. WHY SOMEDAY EVEN THE GREAT THOR HIMSELF MAY BE FORGOTTEN.
LET US HOPE SO AT LEAST.
THESE GODS DID NOT SIMPLY FADE AWAY. THEY WERE MURDERED.
IF IT'S THE HALL OF MURDER YOU'RE LOOKING FOR, IT'S DOWN THE OTHER WAY. YOU'LL LOVE IT. THERE'S AN ENTIRE WING DEVOTED TO YOUR FAMILY.
I HAVE TO SEE THE PARLIAMENT. I HAVE TO WARN THE PANTHEONS.
WELL, BEST SUBMIT YOUR REQUEST RIGHT AWAY. LAST I HEARD, THERE'S A 200-YEAR WAITING LIST TO SEE THE PARLIAMENT.
AND BEFORE YOU ASK, NO, YOU MAY NOT WAIT HERE.
SO MANY. I DON'T KNOW WHERE TO START. COULD ALL OF THESE GODS REALLY HAVE BEEN MURDERED BY ONE MAN?
I SUPPOSE THERE'S ONLY ONE WAY TO FIND OUT.

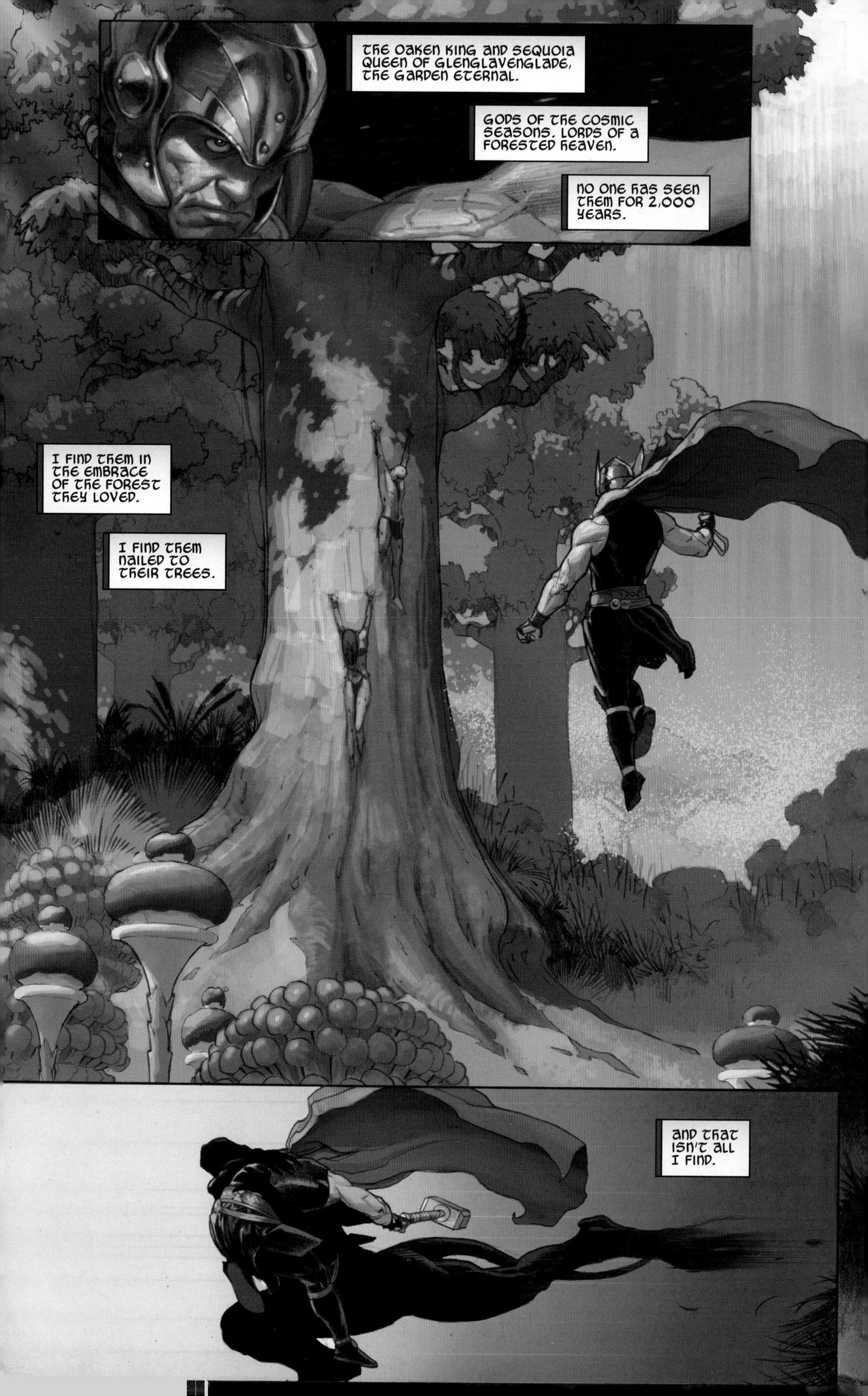
THE OAKEN KING AND SEQUOIA QUEEN OF GLENGLAVENGLADE, THE GARDEN ETERNAL.
GODS OF THE COSMIC SEASONS. LORDS OF A FORESTED HEAVEN.
NO ONE HAS SEEN THEM FOR 2,000 YEARS.
I FIND THEM IN THE EMBRACE OF THE FOREST THEY LOVED.
I FIND THEM NAILED TO THEIR TREES.
AND THAT ISN'T ALL I FIND.

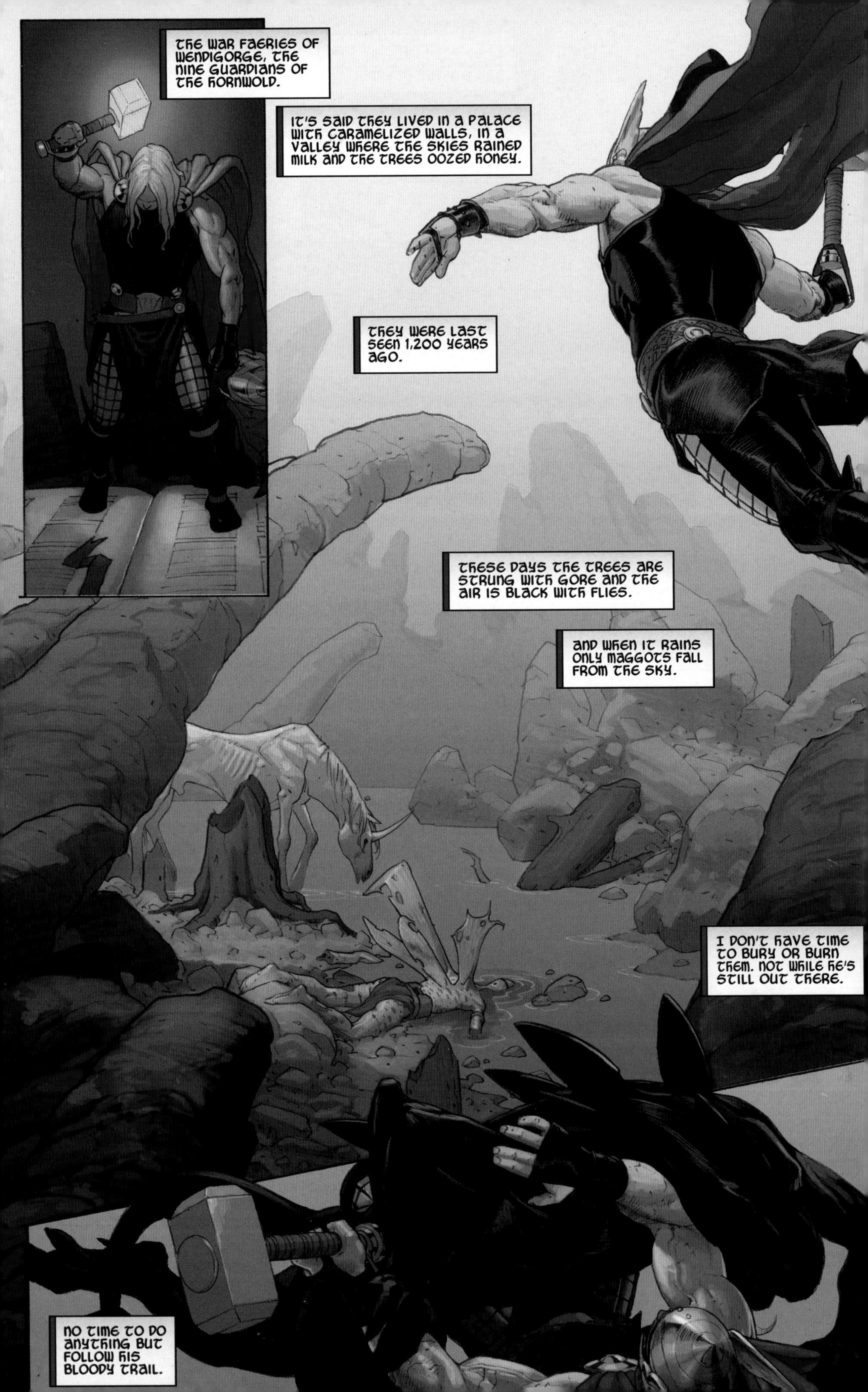
THE WAR FAERIES OF WENDIGORGE, THE NINE GUARDIANS OF THE HORNWOLD.
IT'S SAID THEY LIVED IN A PALACE WITH CARAMELIZED WALLS, IN A VALLEY WHERE THE SKIES RAINED MILK AND THE TREES OOZED HONEY.
THEY WERE LAST SEEN 1,200 YEARS AGO.
THESE DAYS THE TREES ARE STRUNG WITH GORE AND THE AIR IS BLACK WITH FLIES.
AND WHEN IT RAINS ONLY MAGGOTS FALL FROM THE SKY.
I DON'T HAVE TIME TO BURY OR BURN THEM. NOT WHILE HE'S STILL OUT THERE.
NO TIME TO DO ANYTHING BUT FOLLOW HIS BLOODY TRAIL.

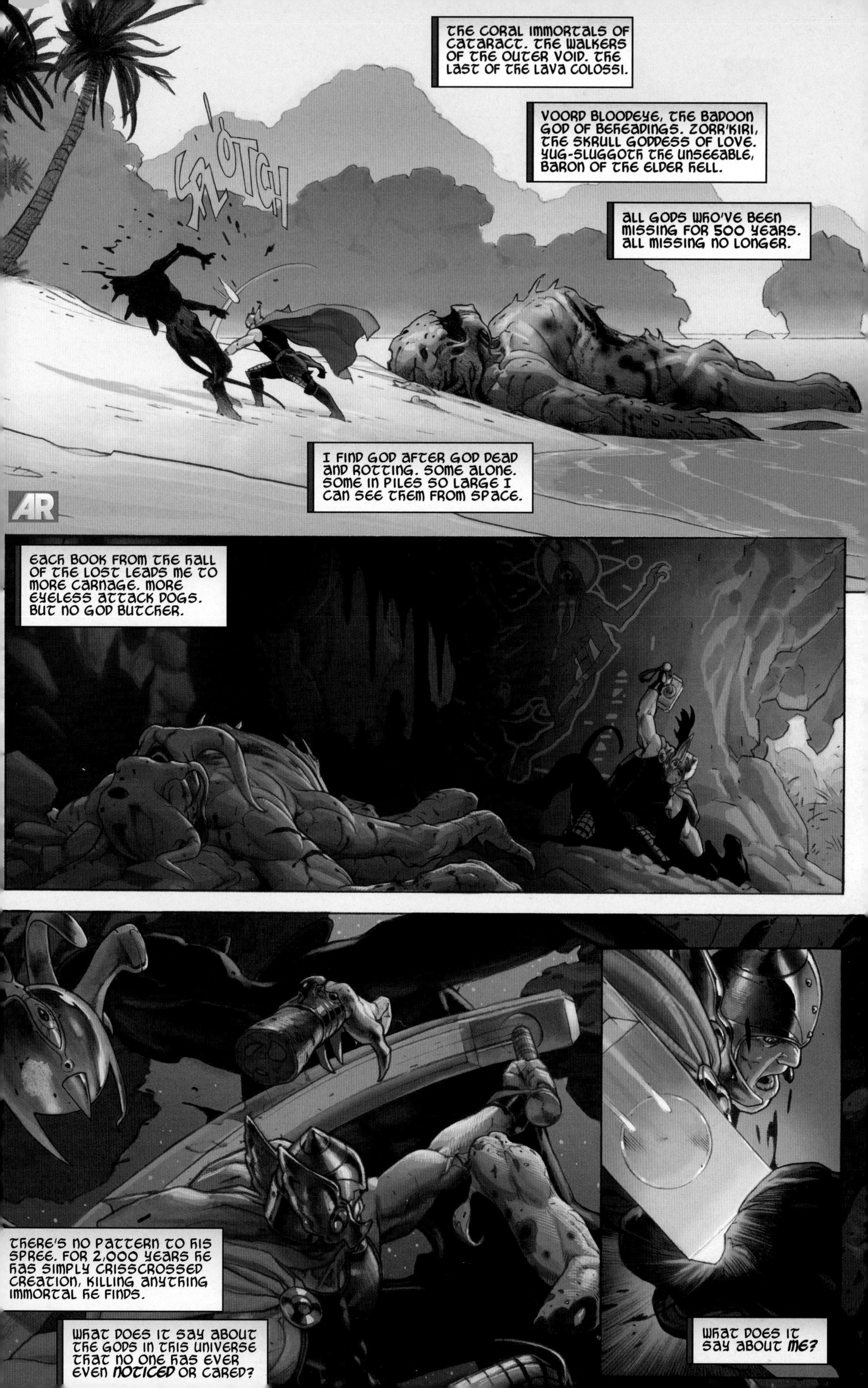
THE CORAL IMMORTALS OF CATARACT. THE WALKERS OF THE OUTER VOID. THE LAST OF THE LAVA COLOSSI.
SKLOTCH
VOORD BLOODEYE, THE BADOON GOD OF BEHEADINGS. ZORR'KIRI, THE SKRULL GODDESS OF LOVE. YUG-SLUGGOTH THE UNSEEABLE, BARON OF THE ELDER HELL.
ALL GODS WHO'VE BEEN MISSING FOR 500 YEARS. ALL MISSING NO LONGER.
I FIND GOD AFTER GOD DEAD AND ROTTING. SOME ALONE. SOME IN PILES SO LARGE I CAN SEE THEM FROM SPACE.
EACH BOOK FROM THE HALL OF THE LOST LEADS ME TO MORE CARNAGE. MORE EYELESS ATTACK DOGS. BUT NO GOD BUTCHER.
THERE'S NO PATTERN TO HIS SPREE. FOR 2,000 YEARS HE HAS SIMPLY CRISSCROSSED CREATION, KILLING ANYTHING IMMORTAL HE FINDS.
WHAT DOES IT SAY ABOUT THE GODS IN THIS UNIVERSE THAT NO ONE HAS EVER EVEN NOTICED OR CARED?
WHAT DOES IT SAY ABOUT ME?

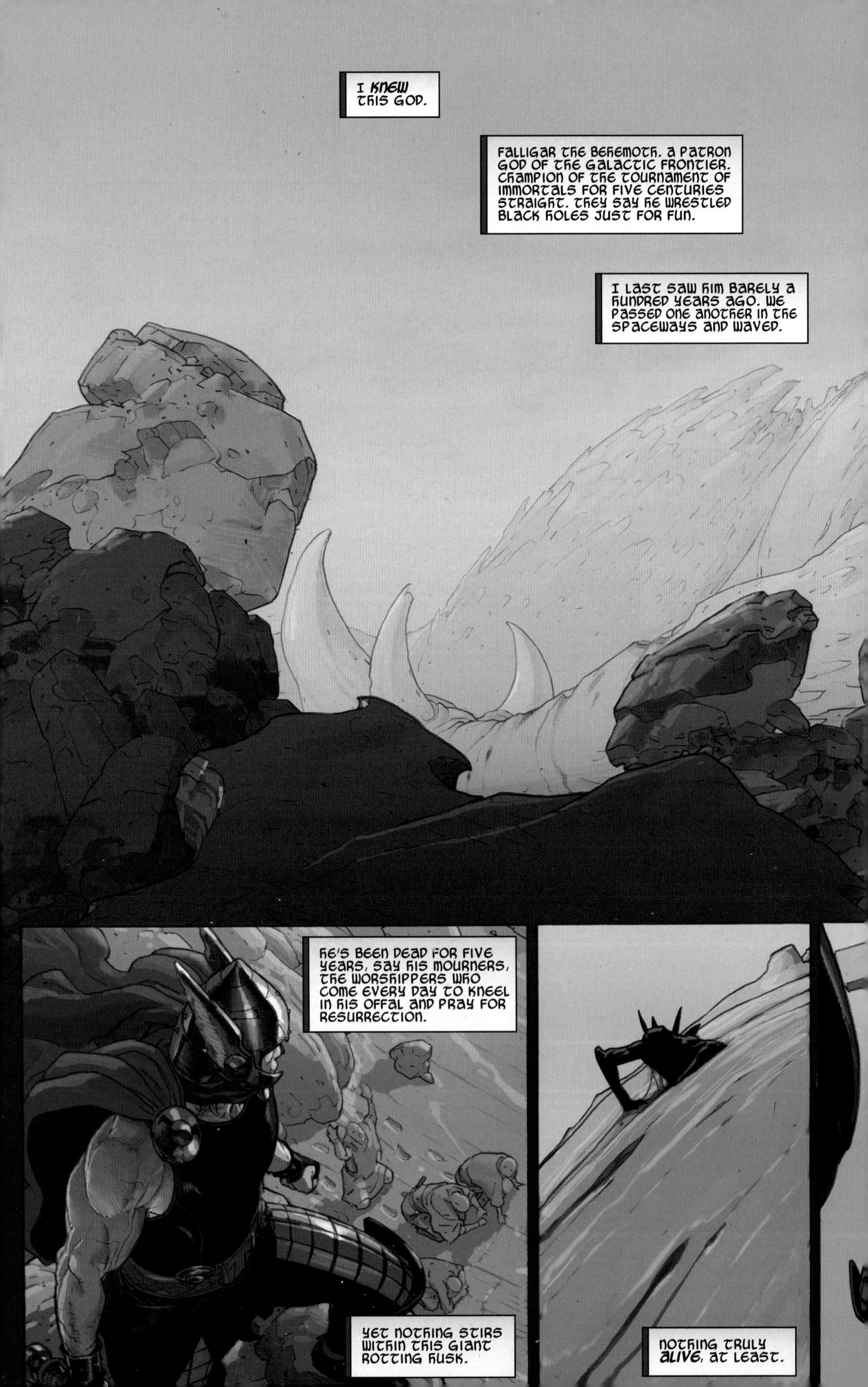
I KNEW THIS GOD.
FALLIGAR THE BEHEMOTH. A PATRON GOD OF THE GALACTIC FRONTIER. CHAMPION OF THE TOURNAMENT OF IMMORTALS FOR FIVE CENTURIES STRAIGHT. THEY SAY HE WRESTLED BLACK HOLES JUST FOR FUN.
I LAST SAW HIM BARELY A HUNDRED YEARS AGO. WE PASSED ONE ANOTHER IN THE SPACEWAYS AND WAVED.
HE'S BEEN DEAD FOR FIVE YEARS, SAY HIS MOURNERS, THE WORSHIPPERS WHO COME EVERY DAY TO KNEEL IN HIS OFFAL AND PRAY FOR RESURRECTION.
YET NOTHING STIRS WITHIN THIS GIANT ROTTING HUSK.
NOTHING TRULY ALIVE, AT LEAST.

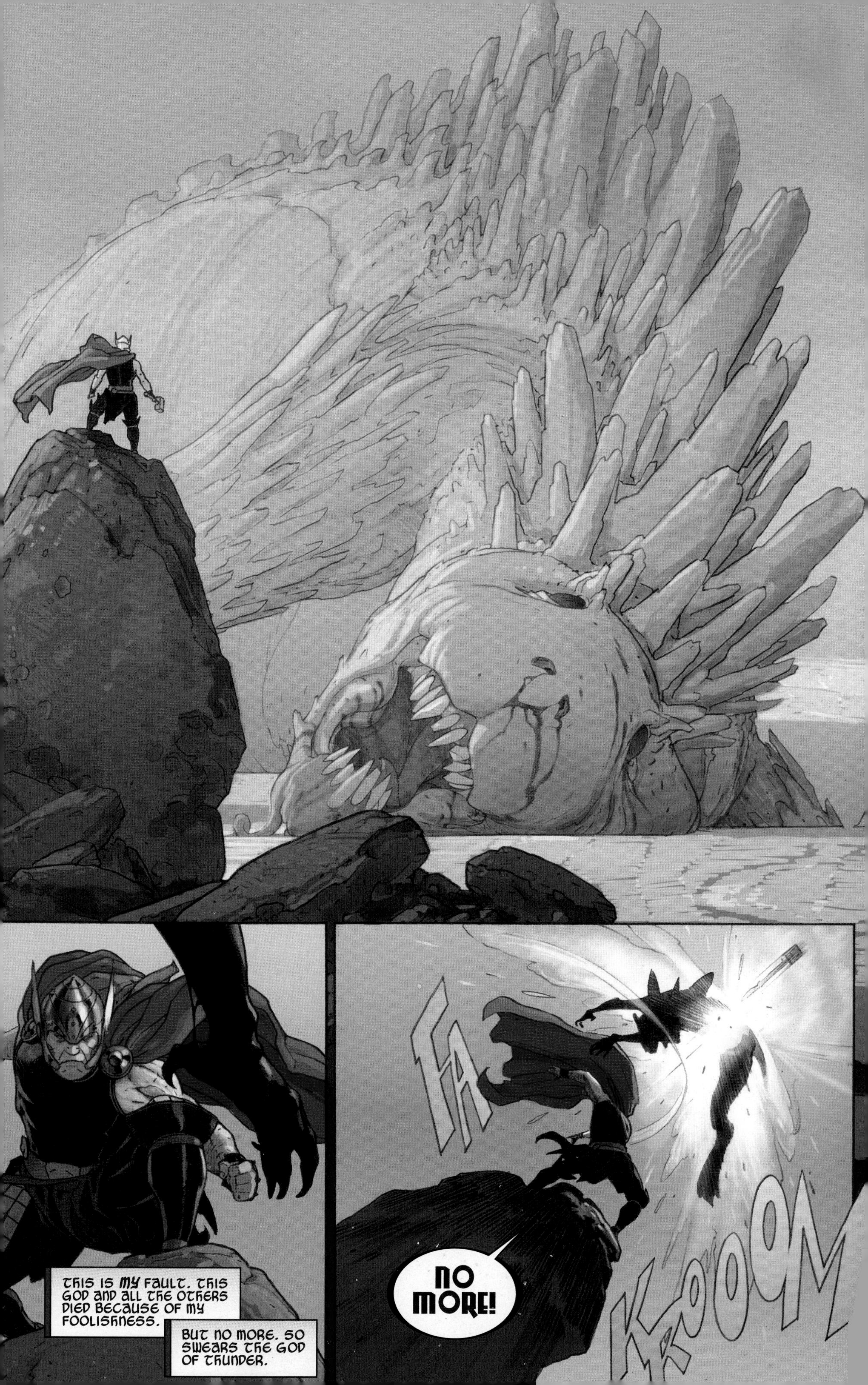
THIS IS MY FAULT. THIS GOD AND ALL THE OTHERS DIED BECAUSE OF MY FOOLISHNESS.
BUT NO MORE. SO SWEARS THE GOD OF THUNDER.
FA
NO MORE!
KROOOM

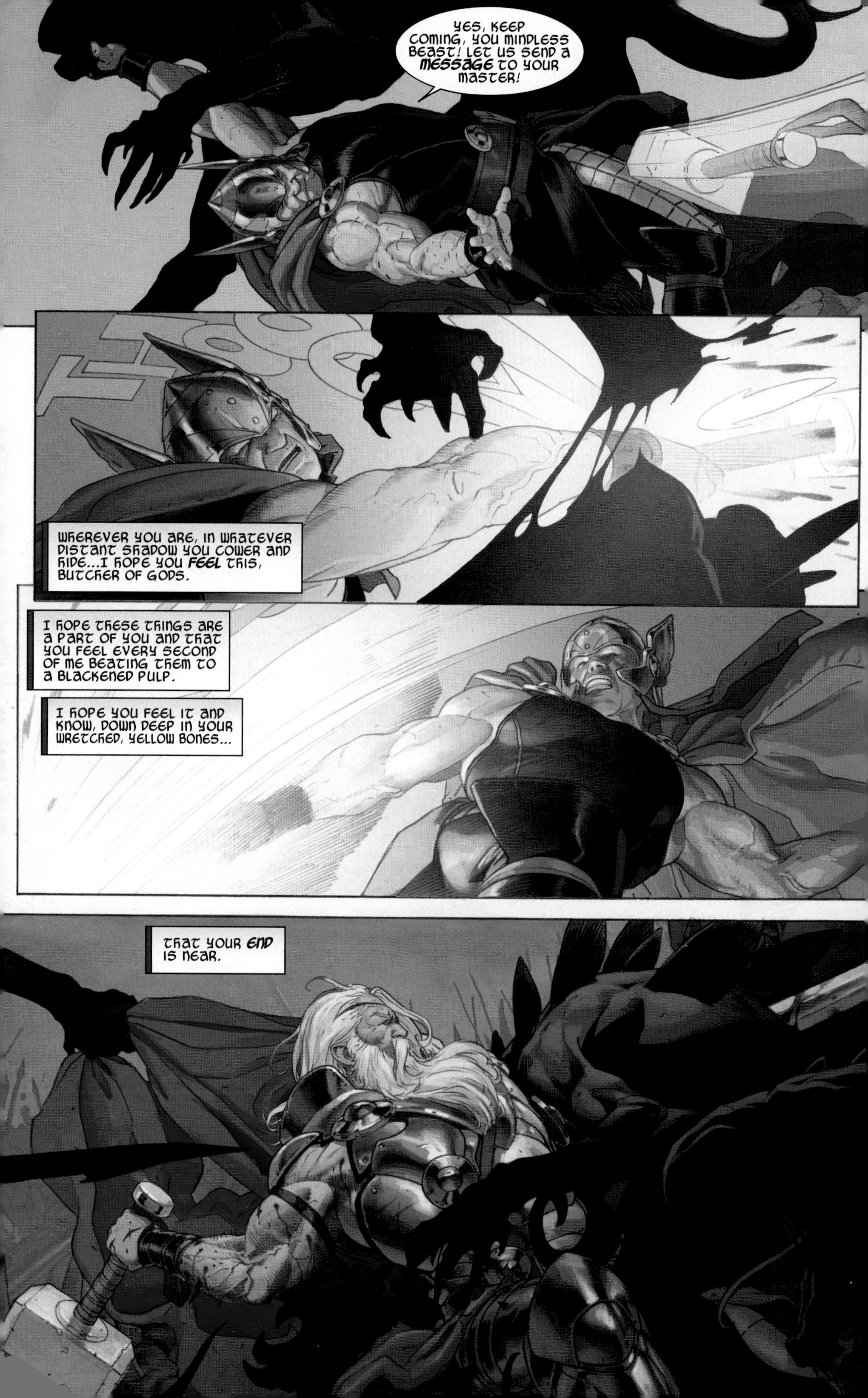

YES, KEEP COMING, YOU MINDLESS BEAST! LET US SEND A MESSAGE TO YOUR MASTER!
WHEREVER YOU ARE, IN WHATEVER DISTANT SHADOW YOU COWER AND HIDE...I HOPE YOU FEEL THIS, BUTCHER OF GODS.
I HOPE THESE THINGS ARE A PART OF YOU AND THAT YOU FEEL EVERY SECOND OF ME BEATING THEM TO A BLACKENED PULP.
I HOPE YOU FEEL IT AND KNOW, DOWN DEEP IN YOUR WRETCHED, YELLOW BONES...
THAT YOUR END IS NEAR.

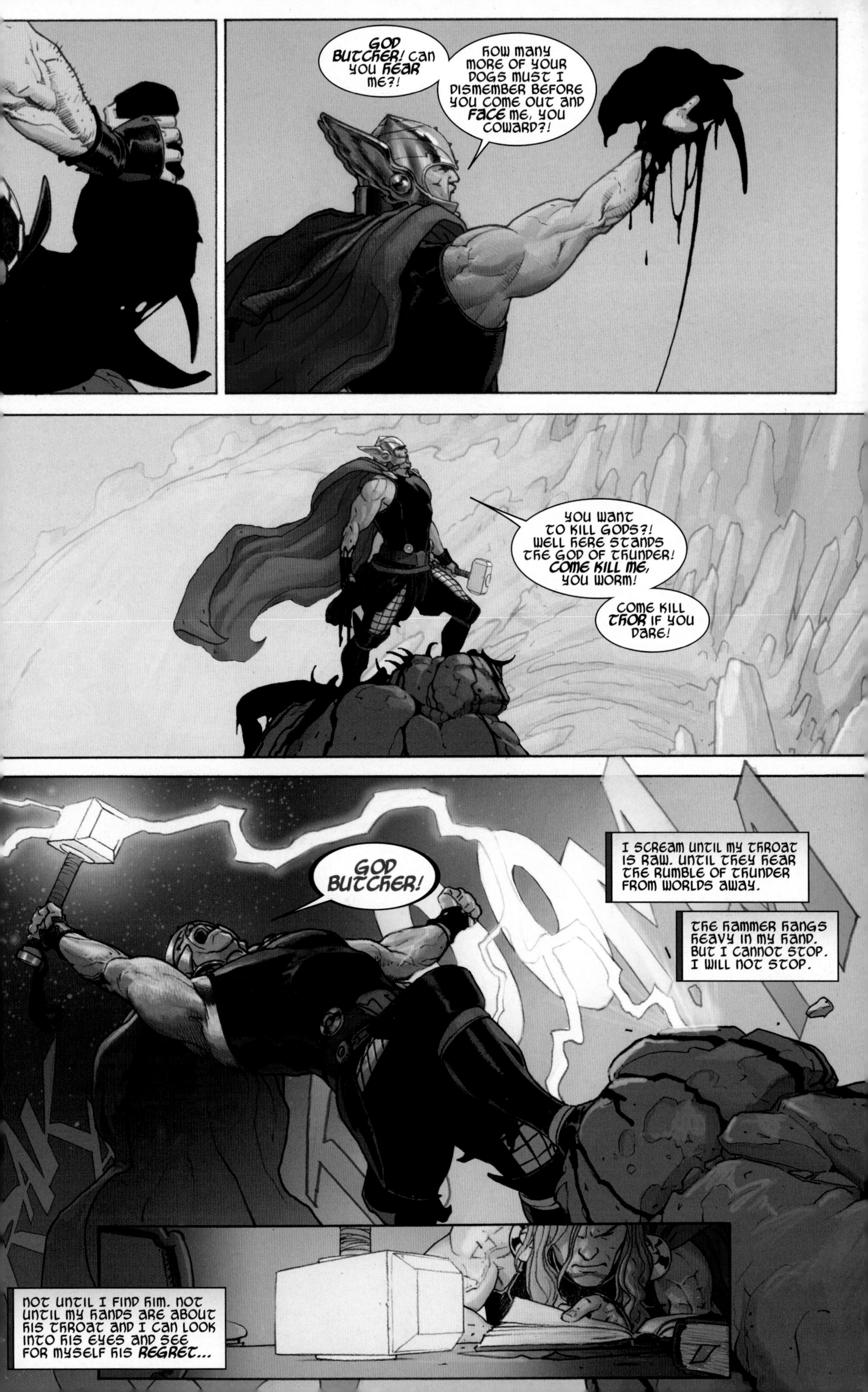
GOD BUTCHER! Can you HEAR me?!
How many more of your dogs must I dismember before you come out and FACE me, you coward?!
You want to kill gods?! Well here stands the God of Thunder! COME KILL ME, you worm!
Come kill THOR if you dare!
GOD BUTCHER!
I scream until my throat is raw. Until they hear the rumble of thunder from worlds away.
The hammer hangs heavy in my hand. But I cannot stop. I will not stop.
Not until I find him. Not until my hands are about his throat and I can look into his eyes and see for myself his REGRET...

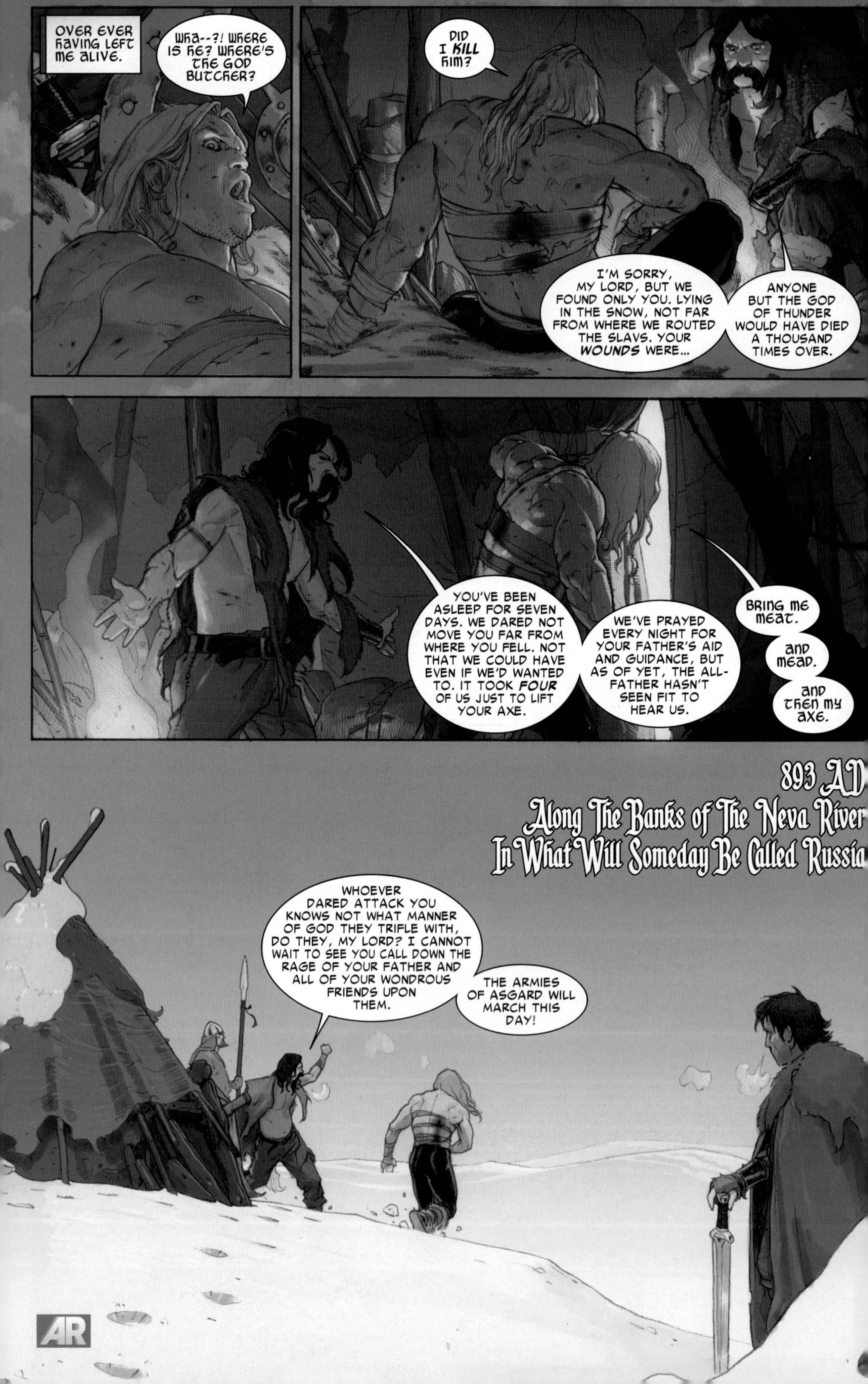
OVER EVER HAVING LEFT ME ALIVE.
WHA--?! WHERE IS HE? WHERE'S THE GOD BUTCHER?
DID I KILL HIM?
I'M SORRY, MY LORD, BUT WE FOUND ONLY YOU. LYING IN THE SNOW, NOT FAR FROM WHERE WE ROUTED THE SLAVS. YOUR WOUNDS WERE...
ANYONE BUT THE GOD OF THUNDER WOULD HAVE DIED A THOUSAND TIMES OVER.
YOU'VE BEEN ASLEEP FOR SEVEN DAYS. WE DARED NOT MOVE YOU FAR FROM WHERE YOU FELL. NOT THAT WE COULD HAVE EVEN IF WE'D WANTED TO. IT TOOK FOUR OF US JUST TO LIFT YOUR AXE.
WE'VE PRAYED EVERY NIGHT FOR YOUR FATHER'S AID AND GUIDANCE, BUT AS OF YET, THE ALL-FATHER HASN'T SEEN FIT TO HEAR US.
BRING ME MEAT.
AND MEAD.
AND THEN MY AXE.
893 AD
Along The Banks of The Neva River
In What Will Someday Be Called Russia
WHOEVER DARED ATTACK YOU KNOWS NOT WHAT MANNER OF GOD THEY TRIFLE WITH, DO THEY, MY LORD? I CANNOT WAIT TO SEE YOU CALL DOWN THE RAGE OF YOUR FATHER AND ALL OF YOUR WONDROUS FRIENDS UPON THEM.
THE ARMIES OF ASGARD WILL MARCH THIS DAY!
AR

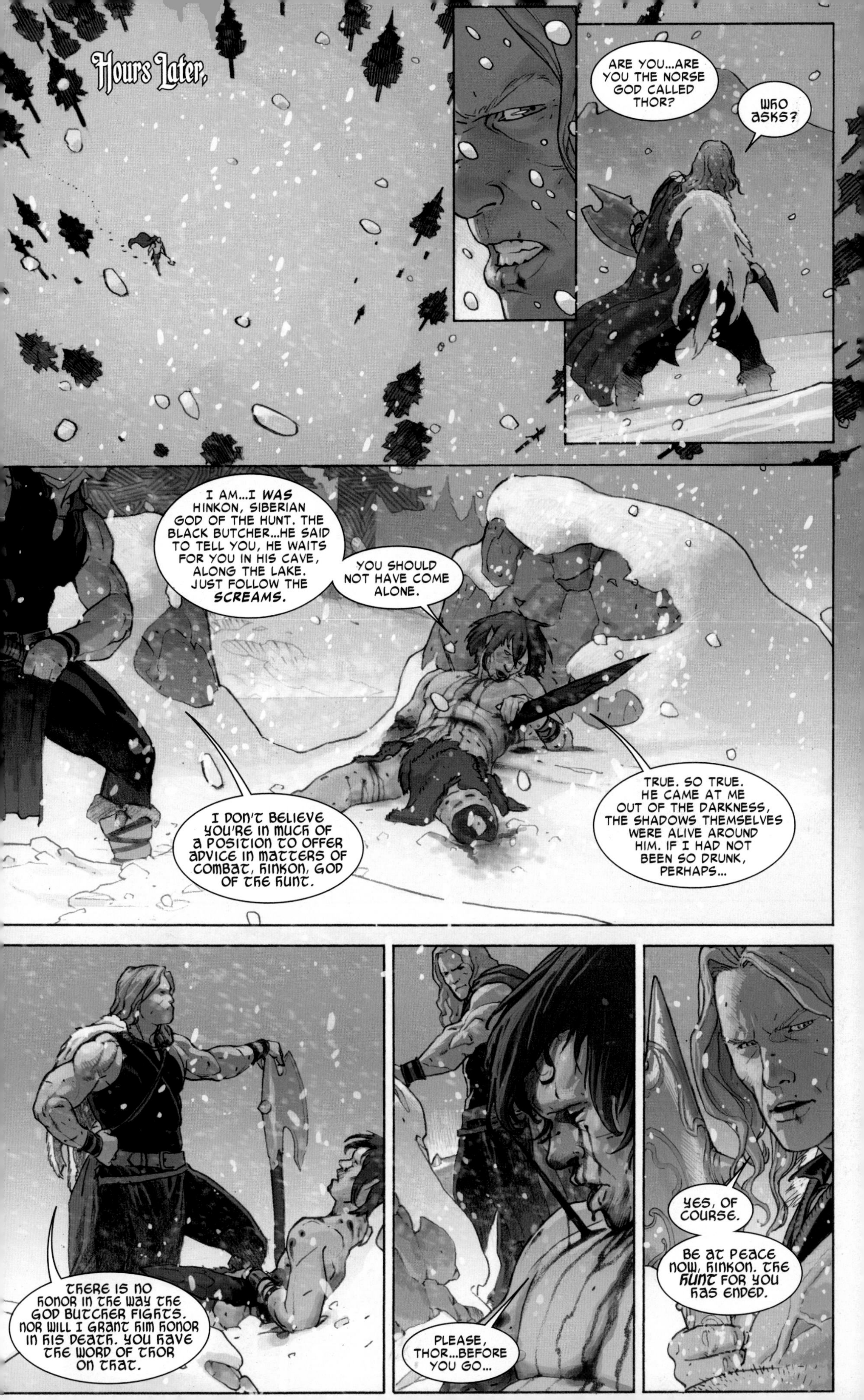
Hours Later,
ARE YOU...ARE YOU THE NORSE GOD CALLED THOR?
WHO ASKS?
I AM...I WAS HINKON, SIBERIAN GOD OF THE HUNT. THE BLACK BUTCHER...HE SAID TO TELL YOU, HE WAITS FOR YOU IN HIS CAVE, ALONG THE LAKE. JUST FOLLOW THE SCREAMS.
YOU SHOULD NOT HAVE COME ALONE.
I DON'T BELIEVE YOU'RE IN MUCH OF A POSITION TO OFFER ADVICE IN MATTERS OF COMBAT, HINKON, GOD OF THE HUNT.
TRUE. SO TRUE. HE CAME AT ME OUT OF THE DARKNESS, THE SHADOWS THEMSELVES WERE ALIVE AROUND HIM. IF I HAD NOT BEEN SO DRUNK, PERHAPS...
THERE IS NO HONOR IN THE WAY THE GOD BUTCHER FIGHTS. NOR WILL I GRANT HIM HONOR IN HIS DEATH. YOU HAVE THE WORD OF THOR ON THAT.
PLEASE, THOR...BEFORE YOU GO...
YES, OF COURSE.
BE AT PEACE NOW, HINKON. THE HUNT FOR YOU HAS ENDED.

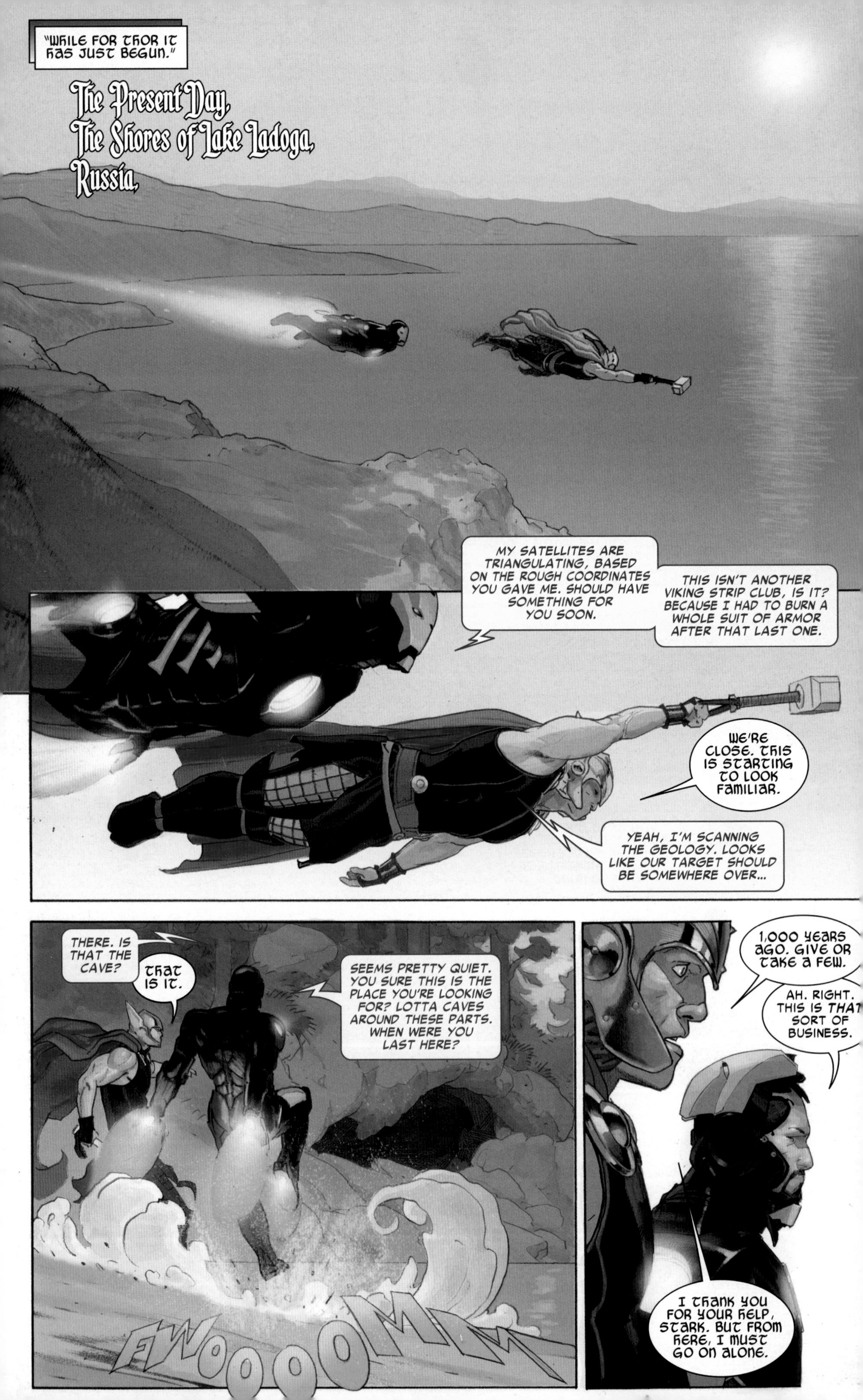
"WHILE FOR THOR IT HAS JUST BEGUN."
The Present Day, The Shores of Lake Ladoga, Russia.
MY SATELLITES ARE TRIANGULATING, BASED ON THE ROUGH COORDINATES YOU GAVE ME. SHOULD HAVE SOMETHING FOR YOU SOON.
THIS ISN'T ANOTHER VIKING STRIP CLUB, IS IT? BECAUSE I HAD TO BURN A WHOLE SUIT OF ARMOR AFTER THAT LAST ONE.
WE'RE CLOSE. THIS IS STARTING TO LOOK FAMILIAR.
YEAH, I'M SCANNING THE GEOLOGY. LOOKS LIKE OUR TARGET SHOULD BE SOMEWHERE OVER...
THERE. IS THAT THE CAVE?
THAT IS IT.
SEEMS PRETTY QUIET. YOU SURE THIS IS THE PLACE YOU'RE LOOKING FOR? LOTTA CAVES AROUND THESE PARTS. WHEN WERE YOU LAST HERE?
FWOOOOMM
1,000 YEARS AGO. GIVE OR TAKE A FEW.
AH. RIGHT. THIS IS THAT SORT OF BUSINESS.
I THANK YOU FOR YOUR HELP, STARK. BUT FROM HERE, I MUST GO ON ALONE.

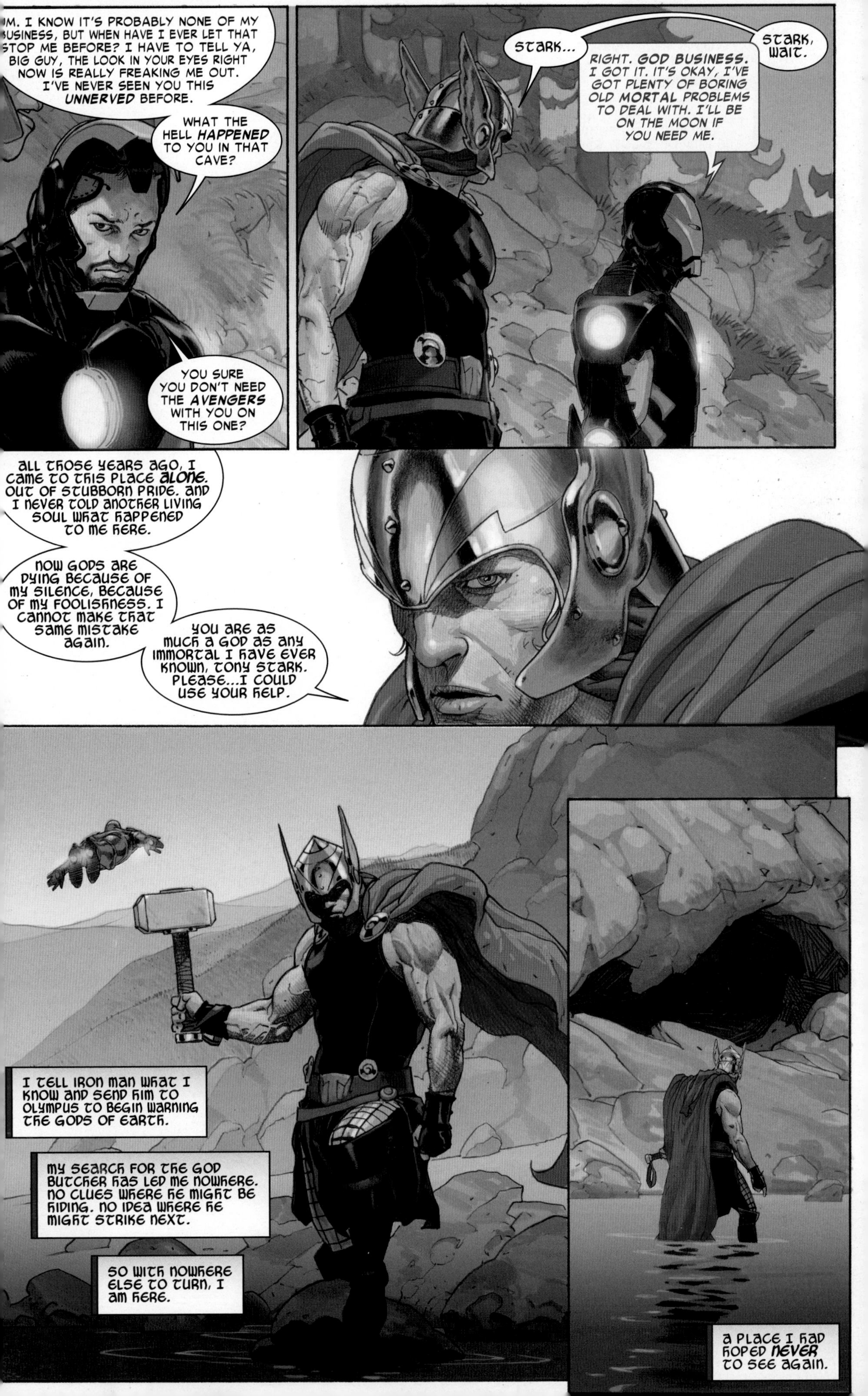

M. I KNOW IT'S PROBABLY NONE OF MY BUSINESS, BUT WHEN HAVE I EVER LET THAT STOP ME BEFORE? I HAVE TO TELL YA, BIG GUY, THE LOOK IN YOUR EYES RIGHT NOW IS REALLY FREAKING ME OUT. I'VE NEVER SEEN YOU THIS UNNERVED BEFORE.
WHAT THE HELL HAPPENED TO YOU IN THAT CAVE?
YOU SURE YOU DON'T NEED THE AVENGERS WITH YOU ON THIS ONE?
STARK...
RIGHT. GOD BUSINESS. I GOT IT. IT'S OKAY, I'VE GOT PLENTY OF BORING OLD MORTAL PROBLEMS TO DEAL WITH. I'LL BE ON THE MOON IF YOU NEED ME.
STARK, WAIT.
ALL THOSE YEARS AGO, I CAME TO THIS PLACE ALONE. OUT OF STUBBORN PRIDE. AND I NEVER TOLD ANOTHER LIVING SOUL WHAT HAPPENED TO ME HERE.
NOW GODS ARE DYING BECAUSE OF MY SILENCE, BECAUSE OF MY FOOLISHNESS. I CANNOT MAKE THAT SAME MISTAKE AGAIN.
YOU ARE AS MUCH A GOD AS ANY IMMORTAL I HAVE EVER KNOWN, TONY STARK. PLEASE...I COULD USE YOUR HELP.
I TELL IRON MAN WHAT I KNOW AND SEND HIM TO OLYMPUS TO BEGIN WARNING THE GODS OF EARTH.
MY SEARCH FOR THE GOD BUTCHER HAS LED ME NOWHERE. NO CLUES WHERE HE MIGHT BE HIDING. NO IDEA WHERE HE MIGHT STRIKE NEXT.
SO WITH NOWHERE ELSE TO TURN, I AM HERE.
A PLACE I HAD HOPED NEVER TO SEE AGAIN.

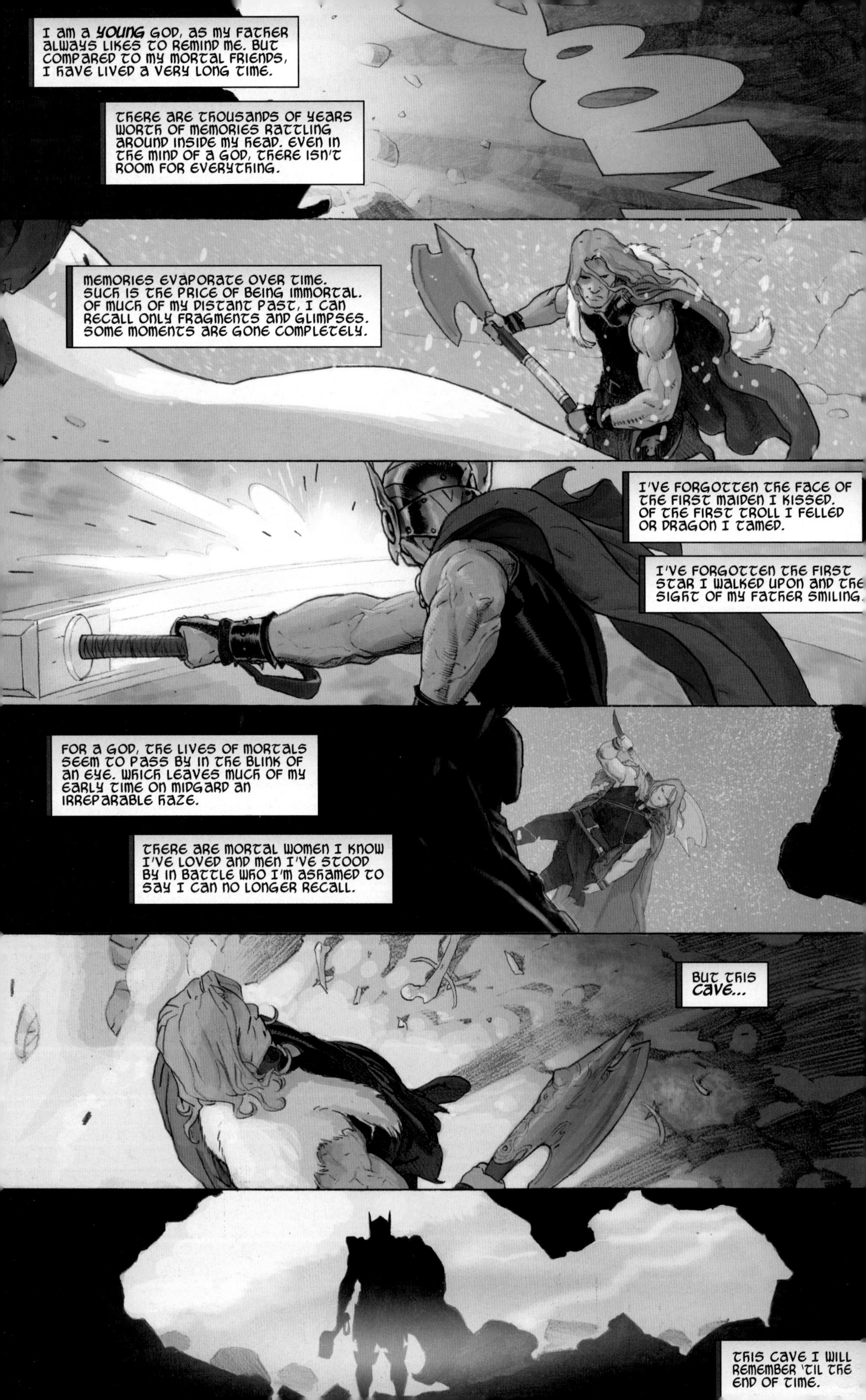
I am a YOUNG GOD, AS MY FATHER ALWAYS LIKES TO REMIND ME. BUT COMPARED TO MY MORTAL FRIENDS, I HAVE LIVED A VERY LONG TIME.
THERE ARE THOUSANDS OF YEARS WORTH OF MEMORIES RATTLING AROUND INSIDE MY HEAD. EVEN IN THE MIND OF A GOD, THERE ISN'T ROOM FOR EVERYTHING.
MEMORIES EVAPORATE OVER TIME. SUCH IS THE PRICE OF BEING IMMORTAL. OF MUCH OF MY DISTANT PAST, I CAN RECALL ONLY FRAGMENTS AND GLIMPSES. SOME MOMENTS ARE GONE COMPLETELY.
I'VE FORGOTTEN THE FACE OF THE FIRST MAIDEN I KISSED. OF THE FIRST TROLL I FELLED OR DRAGON I TAMED.
I'VE FORGOTTEN THE FIRST STAR I WALKED UPON AND THE SIGHT OF MY FATHER SMILING.
FOR A GOD, THE LIVES OF MORTALS SEEM TO PASS BY IN THE BLINK OF AN EYE. WHICH LEAVES MUCH OF MY EARLY TIME ON MIDGARD AN IRREPARABLE HAZE.
THERE ARE MORTAL WOMEN I KNOW I'VE LOVED AND MEN I'VE STOOD BY IN BATTLE WHO I'M ASHAMED TO SAY I CAN NO LONGER RECALL.
BUT THIS CAVE...
THIS CAVE I WILL REMEMBER 'TIL THE END OF TIME.

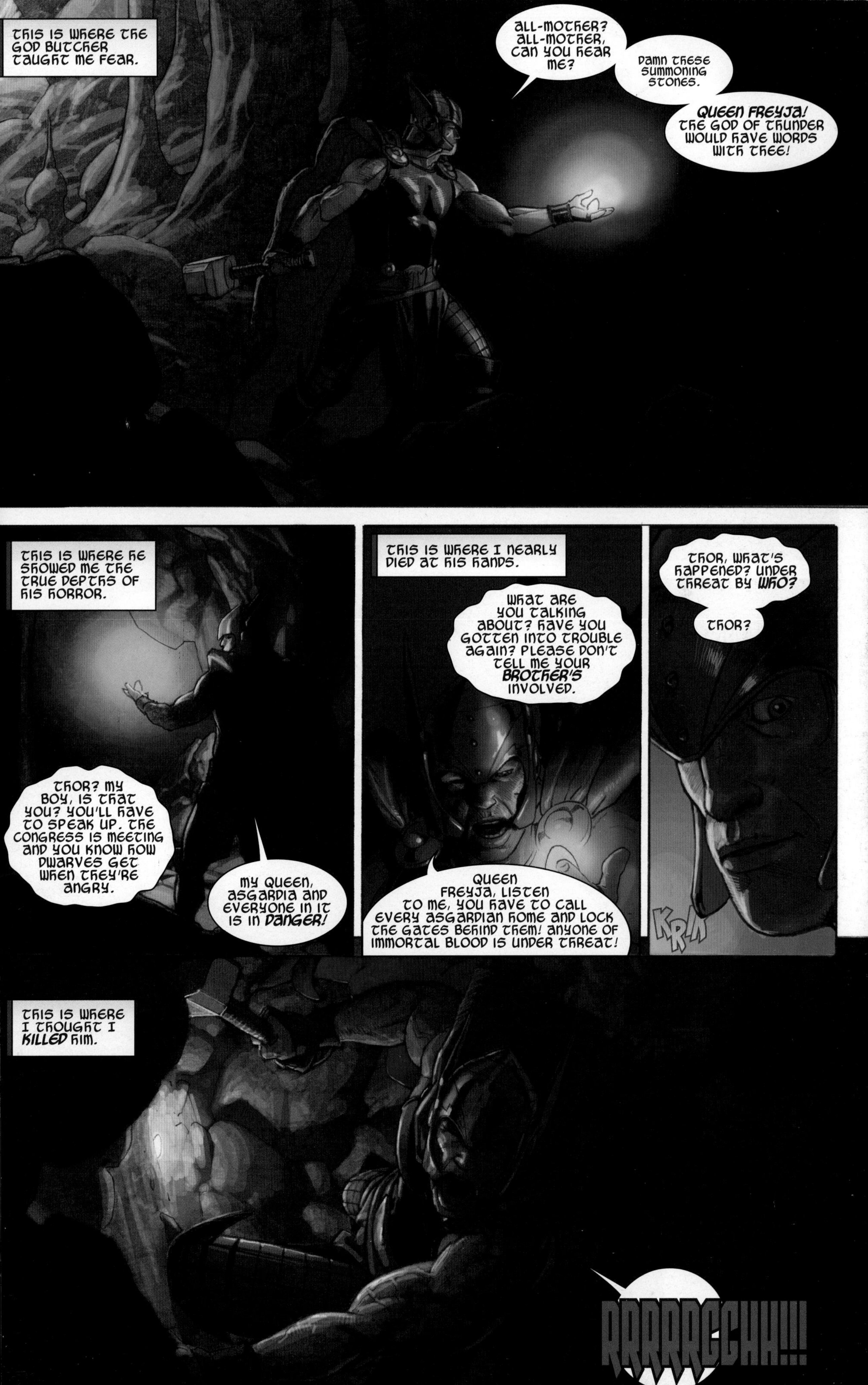
THIS IS WHERE THE GOD BUTCHER TAUGHT ME FEAR.
ALL-MOTHER? ALL-MOTHER, CAN YOU HEAR ME?
DAMN THESE SUMMONING STONES.
QUEEN FREYJA! THE GOD OF THUNDER WOULD HAVE WORDS WITH THEE!
THIS IS WHERE HE SHOWED ME THE TRUE DEPTHS OF HIS HORROR.
THOR? MY BOY, IS THAT YOU? YOU'LL HAVE TO SPEAK UP. THE CONGRESS IS MEETING AND YOU KNOW HOW DWARVES GET WHEN THEY'RE ANGRY.
MY QUEEN, ASGARDIA AND EVERYONE IN IT IS IN DANGER!
THIS IS WHERE I NEARLY DIED AT HIS HANDS.
WHAT ARE YOU TALKING ABOUT? HAVE YOU GOTTEN INTO TROUBLE AGAIN? PLEASE DON'T TELL ME YOUR BROTHER'S INVOLVED.
QUEEN FREYJA, LISTEN TO ME, YOU HAVE TO CALL EVERY ASGARDIAN HOME AND LOCK THE GATES BEHIND THEM! ANYONE OF IMMORTAL BLOOD IS UNDER THREAT!
THOR, WHAT'S HAPPENED? UNDER THREAT BY WHO?
THOR?
KRA
THIS IS WHERE I THOUGHT I KILLED HIM.
RRRRRCCHH!!!

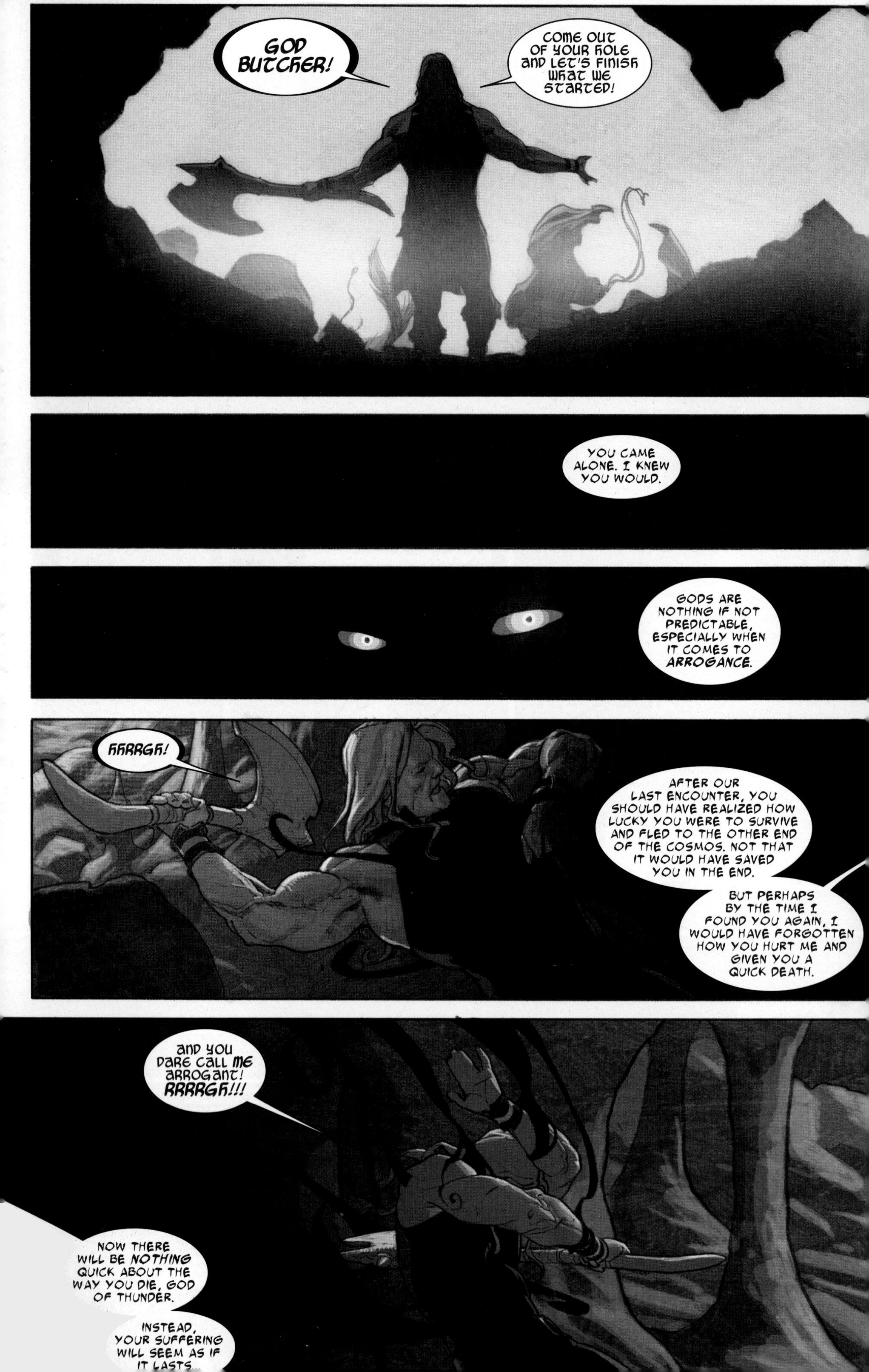
GOD BUTCHER!
COME OUT OF YOUR HOLE AND LET'S FINISH WHAT WE STARTED!
YOU CAME ALONE. I KNEW YOU WOULD.
GODS ARE NOTHING IF NOT PREDICTABLE, ESPECIALLY WHEN IT COMES TO ARROGANCE.
HHRRGH!
AFTER OUR LAST ENCOUNTER, YOU SHOULD HAVE REALIZED HOW LUCKY YOU WERE TO SURVIVE AND FLED TO THE OTHER END OF THE COSMOS. NOT THAT IT WOULD HAVE SAVED YOU IN THE END.
BUT PERHAPS BY THE TIME I FOUND YOU AGAIN, I WOULD HAVE FORGOTTEN HOW YOU HURT ME AND GIVEN YOU A QUICK DEATH.
AND YOU DARE CALL ME ARROGANT! RRRRGH!!!
NOW THERE WILL BE NOTHING QUICK ABOUT THE WAY YOU DIE, GOD OF THUNDER.
INSTEAD, YOUR SUFFERING WILL SEEM AS IF IT LASTS...

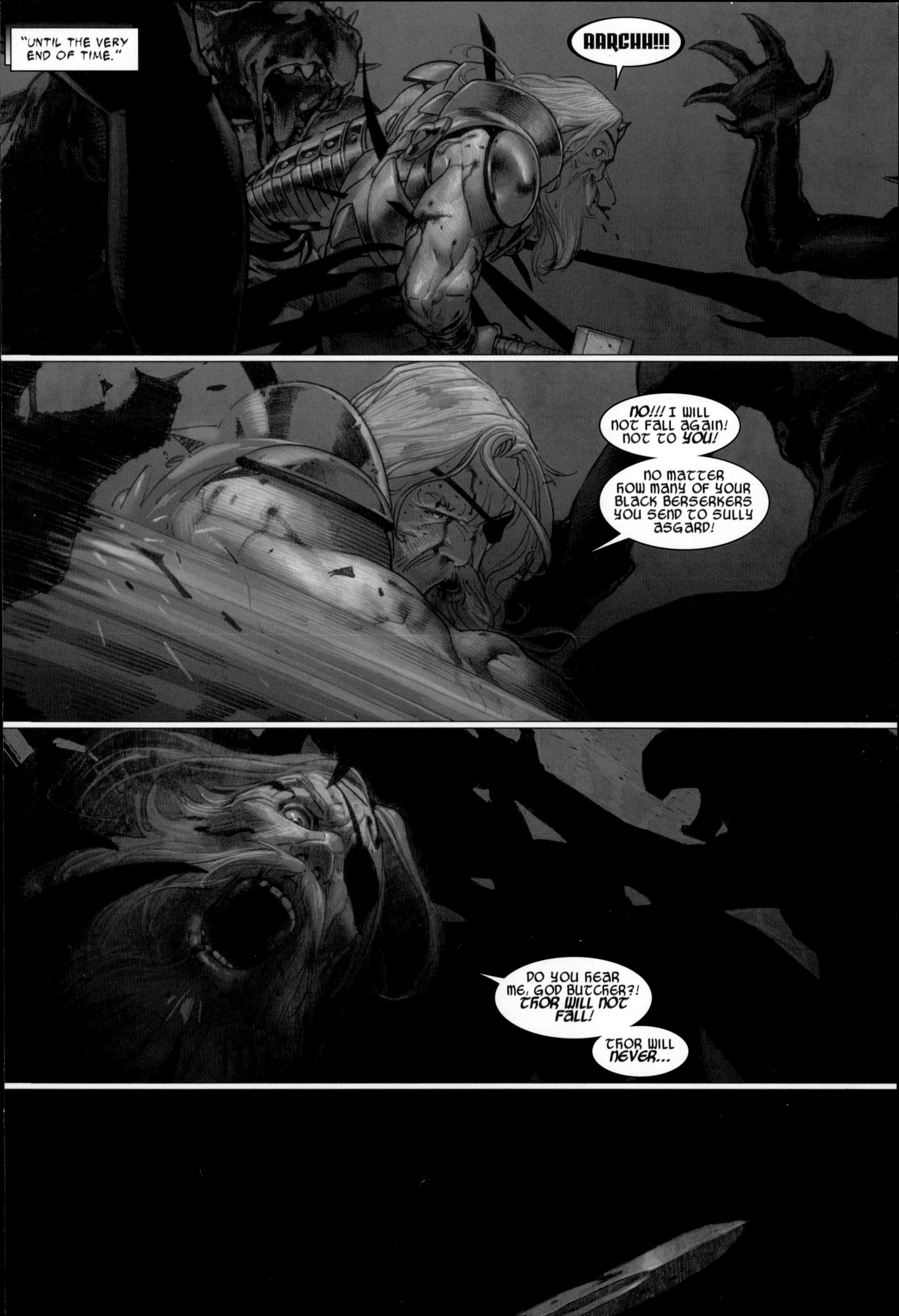

"UNTIL THE VERY END OF TIME."
AARGHH!!!
NO!!! I WILL NOT FALL AGAIN! NOT TO YOU!
NO MATTER HOW MANY OF YOUR BLACK BERSERKERS YOU SEND TO SULLY ASGARD!
DO YOU HEAR ME, GOD BUTCHER?! THOR WILL NOT FALL!
THOR WILL NEVER...

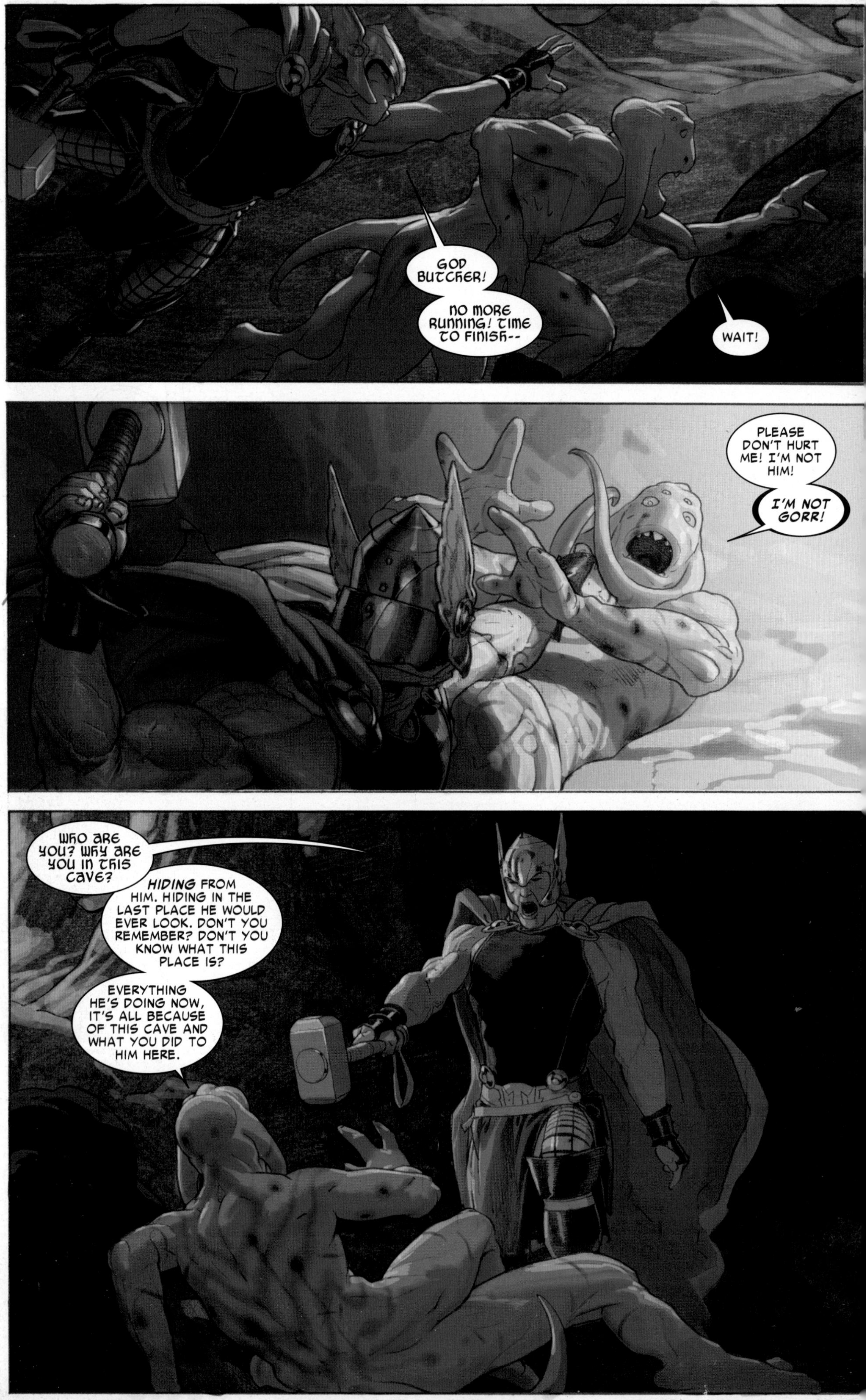
GOD BUTCHER!
NO MORE RUNNING! TIME TO FINISH--
WAIT!
PLEASE DON'T HURT ME! I'M NOT HIM!
I'M NOT GORR!
WHO ARE YOU? WHY ARE YOU IN THIS CAVE?
HIDING FROM HIM. HIDING IN THE LAST PLACE HE WOULD EVER LOOK. DON'T YOU REMEMBER? DON'T YOU KNOW WHAT THIS PLACE IS?
EVERYTHING HE'S DOING NOW, IT'S ALL BECAUSE OF THIS CAVE AND WHAT YOU DID TO HIM HERE.

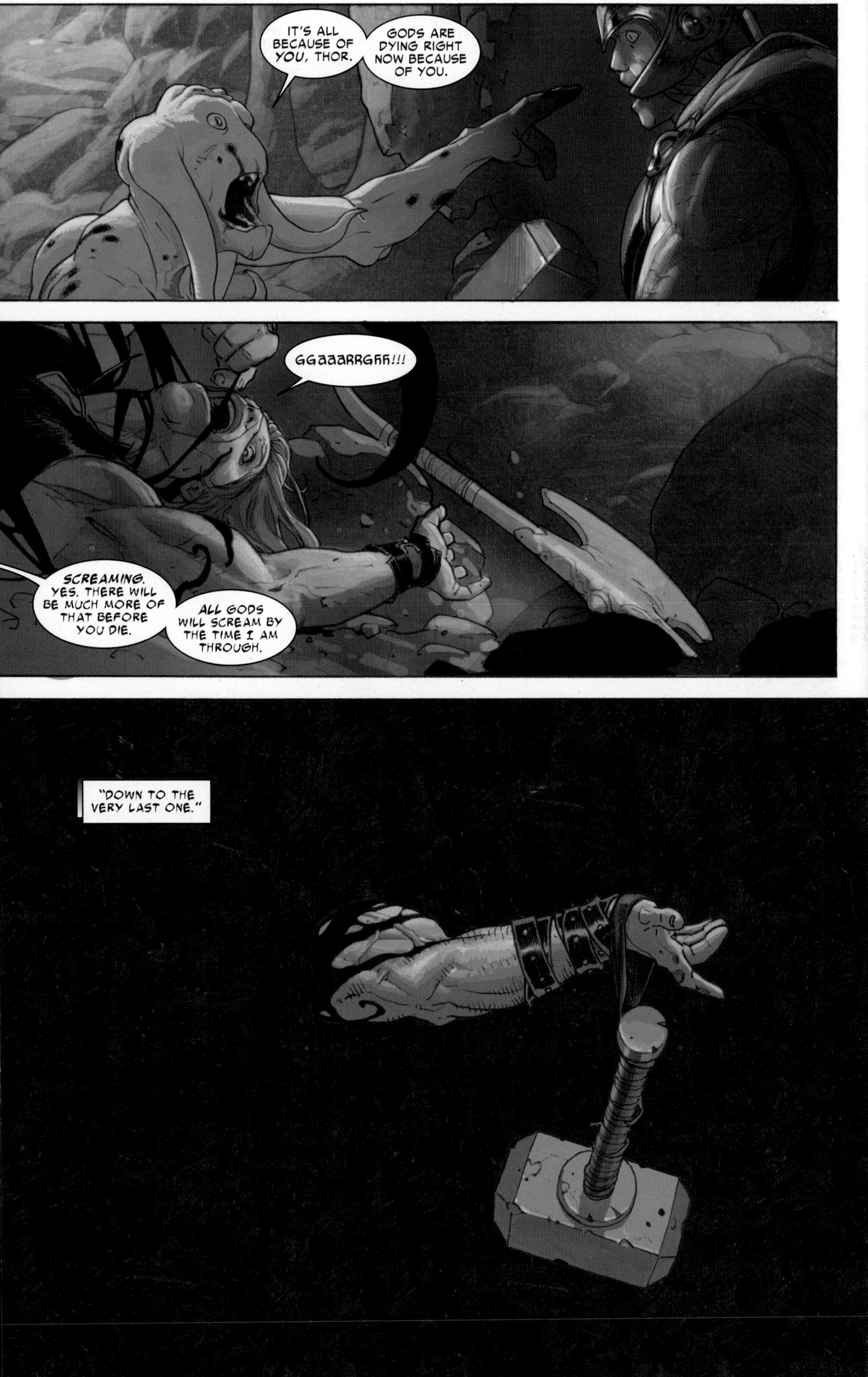
IT'S ALL BECAUSE OF YOU, THOR.
GODS ARE DYING RIGHT NOW BECAUSE OF YOU.
GGAAARRGHH!!!
SCREAMING. YES. THERE WILL BE MUCH MORE OF THAT BEFORE YOU DIE.
ALL GODS WILL SCREAM BY THE TIME I AM THROUGH.
"DOWN TO THE VERY LAST ONE."

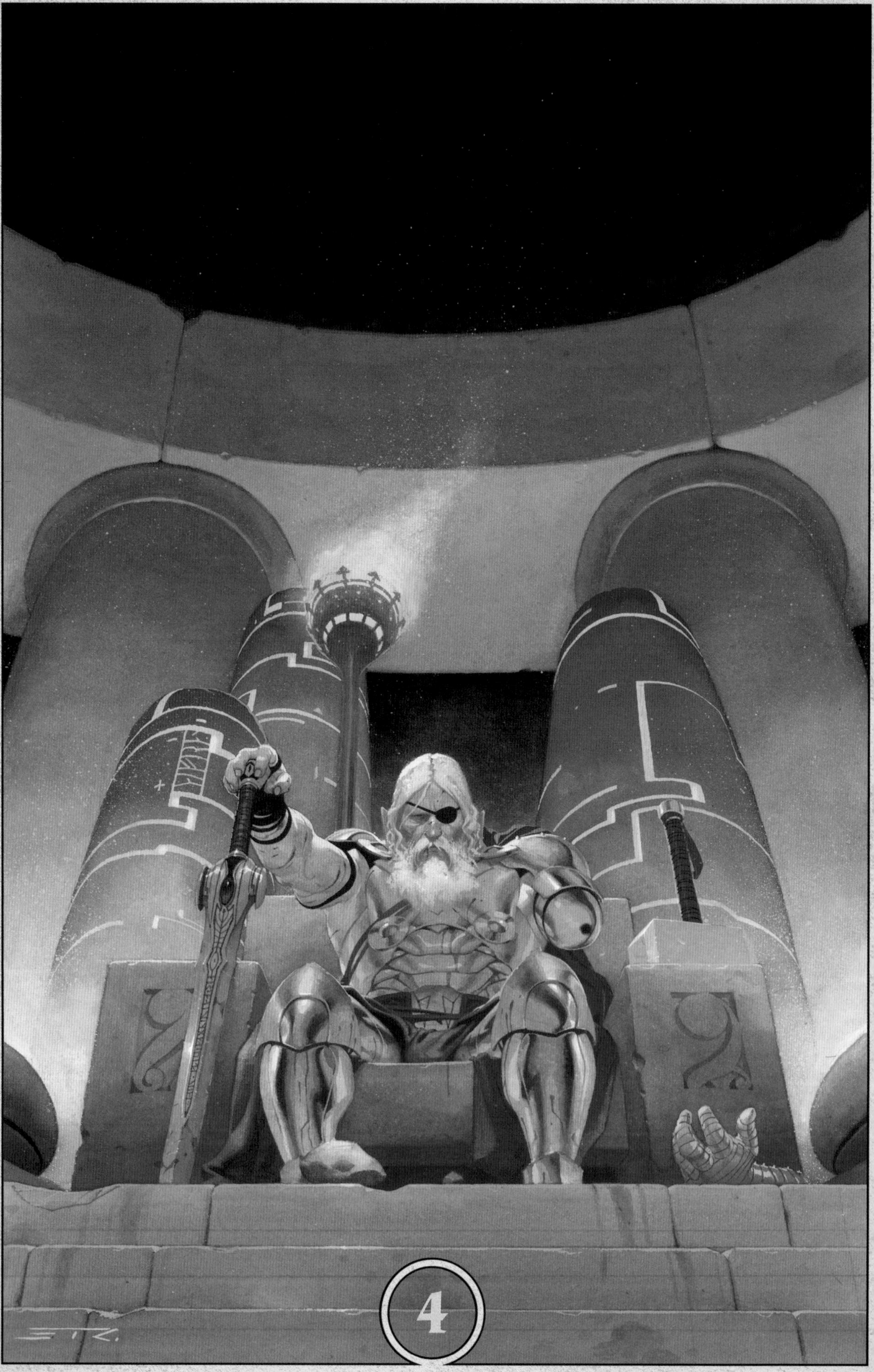
4

THE LAST GOD IN ASGARD

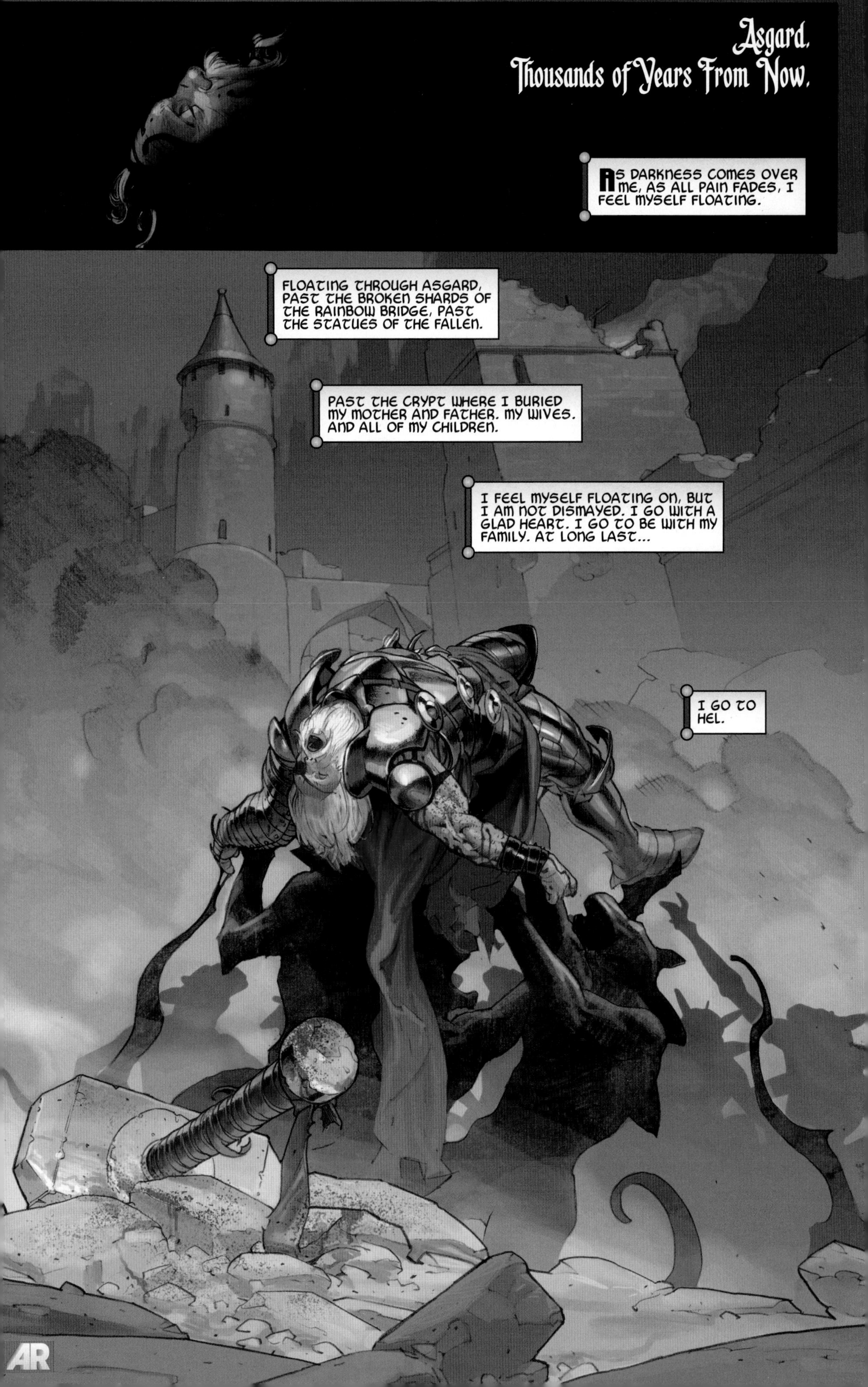
Asgard,
Thousands of Years From Now.
AS DARKNESS COMES OVER ME, AS ALL PAIN FADES, I FEEL MYSELF FLOATING.
FLOATING THROUGH ASGARD, PAST THE BROKEN SHARDS OF THE RAINBOW BRIDGE, PAST THE STATUES OF THE FALLEN.
PAST THE CRYPT WHERE I BURIED MY MOTHER AND FATHER. MY WIVES. AND ALL OF MY CHILDREN.
I FEEL MYSELF FLOATING ON, BUT I AM NOT DISMAYED. I GO WITH A GLAD HEART. I GO TO BE WITH MY FAMILY. AT LONG LAST...
I GO TO HEL.
AR

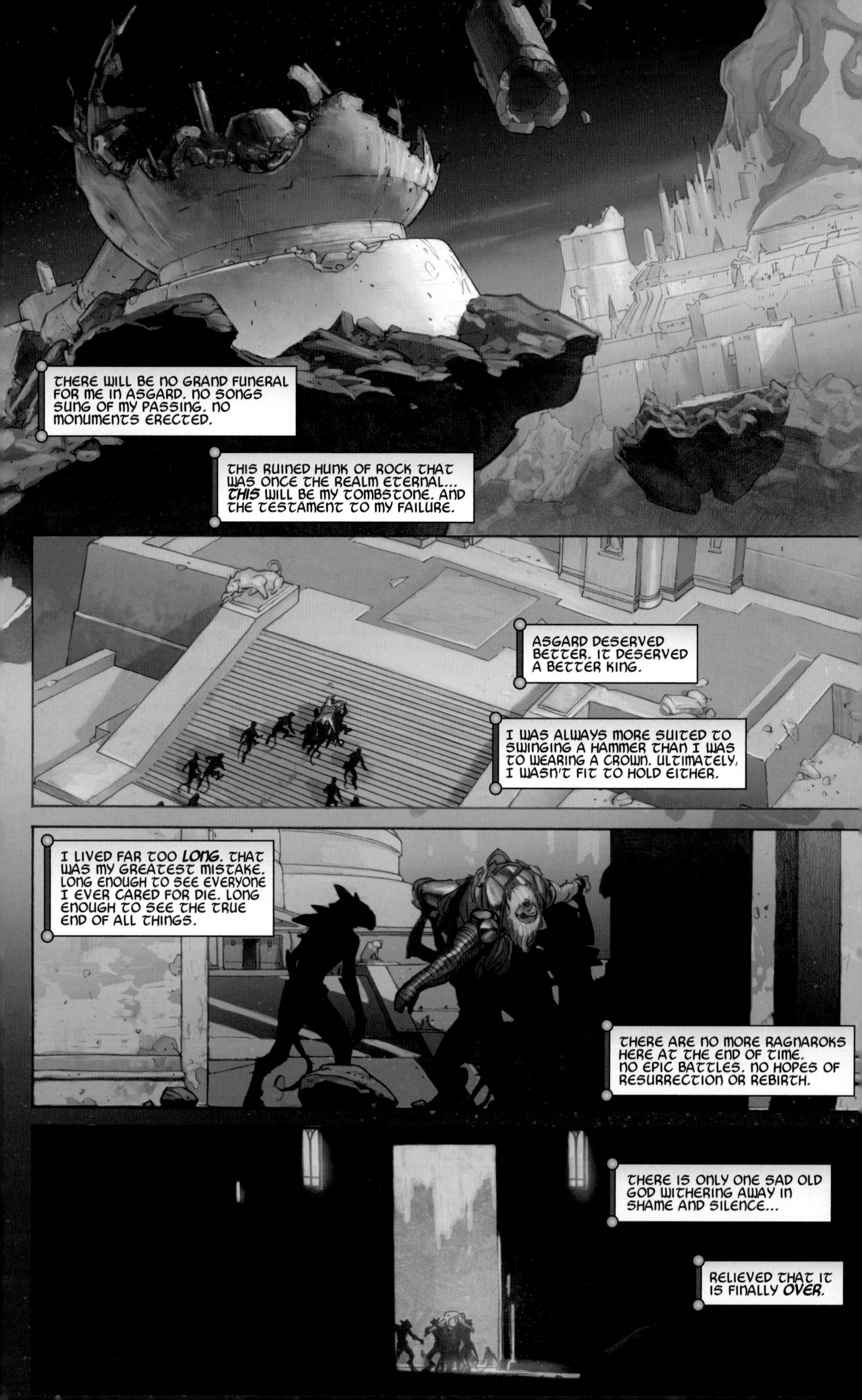
THERE WILL BE NO GRAND FUNERAL FOR ME IN ASGARD. NO SONGS SUNG OF MY PASSING. NO MONUMENTS ERECTED.
THIS RUINED HUNK OF ROCK THAT WAS ONCE THE REALM ETERNAL... *THIS* WILL BE MY TOMBSTONE. AND THE TESTAMENT TO MY FAILURE.
ASGARD DESERVED BETTER. IT DESERVED A BETTER KING.
I WAS ALWAYS MORE SUITED TO SWINGING A HAMMER THAN I WAS TO WEARING A CROWN. ULTIMATELY, I WASN'T FIT TO HOLD EITHER.
I LIVED FAR TOO *LONG*. THAT WAS MY GREATEST MISTAKE. LONG ENOUGH TO SEE EVERYONE I EVER CARED FOR DIE. LONG ENOUGH TO SEE THE TRUE END OF ALL THINGS.
THERE ARE NO MORE RAGNAROKS HERE AT THE END OF TIME. NO EPIC BATTLES. NO HOPES OF RESURRECTION OR REBIRTH.
THERE IS ONLY ONE SAD OLD GOD WITHERING AWAY IN SHAME AND SILENCE...
RELIEVED THAT IT IS FINALLY *OVER*.

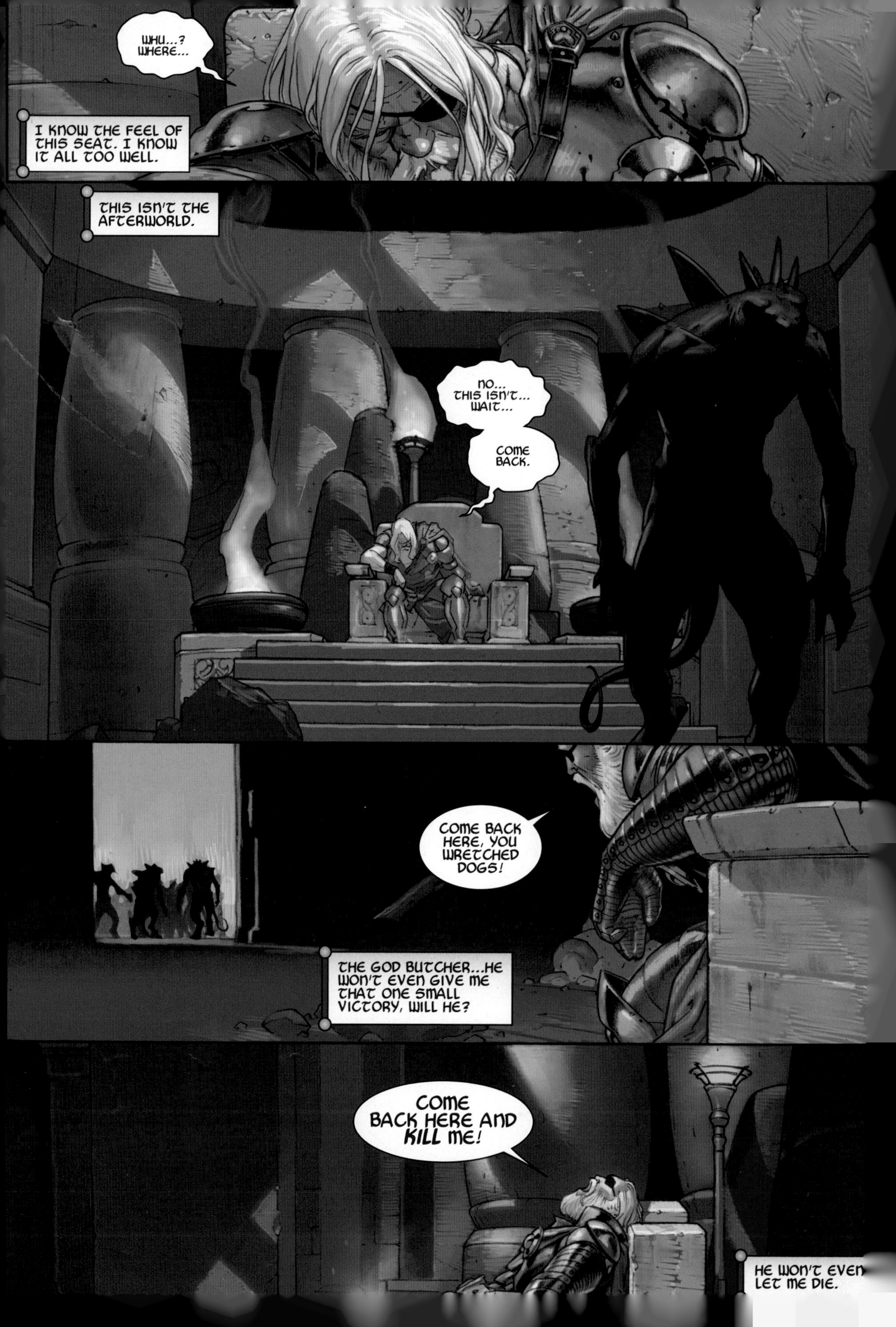
WHU...? WHERE...
I KNOW THE FEEL OF THIS SEAT. I KNOW IT ALL TOO WELL.
THIS ISN'T THE AFTERWORLD.
NO... THIS ISN'T... WAIT...
COME BACK.
COME BACK HERE, YOU WRETCHED DOGS!
THE GOD BUTCHER...HE WON'T EVEN GIVE ME THAT ONE SMALL VICTORY, WILL HE?
COME BACK HERE AND KILL ME!
HE WON'T EVEN LET ME DIE.

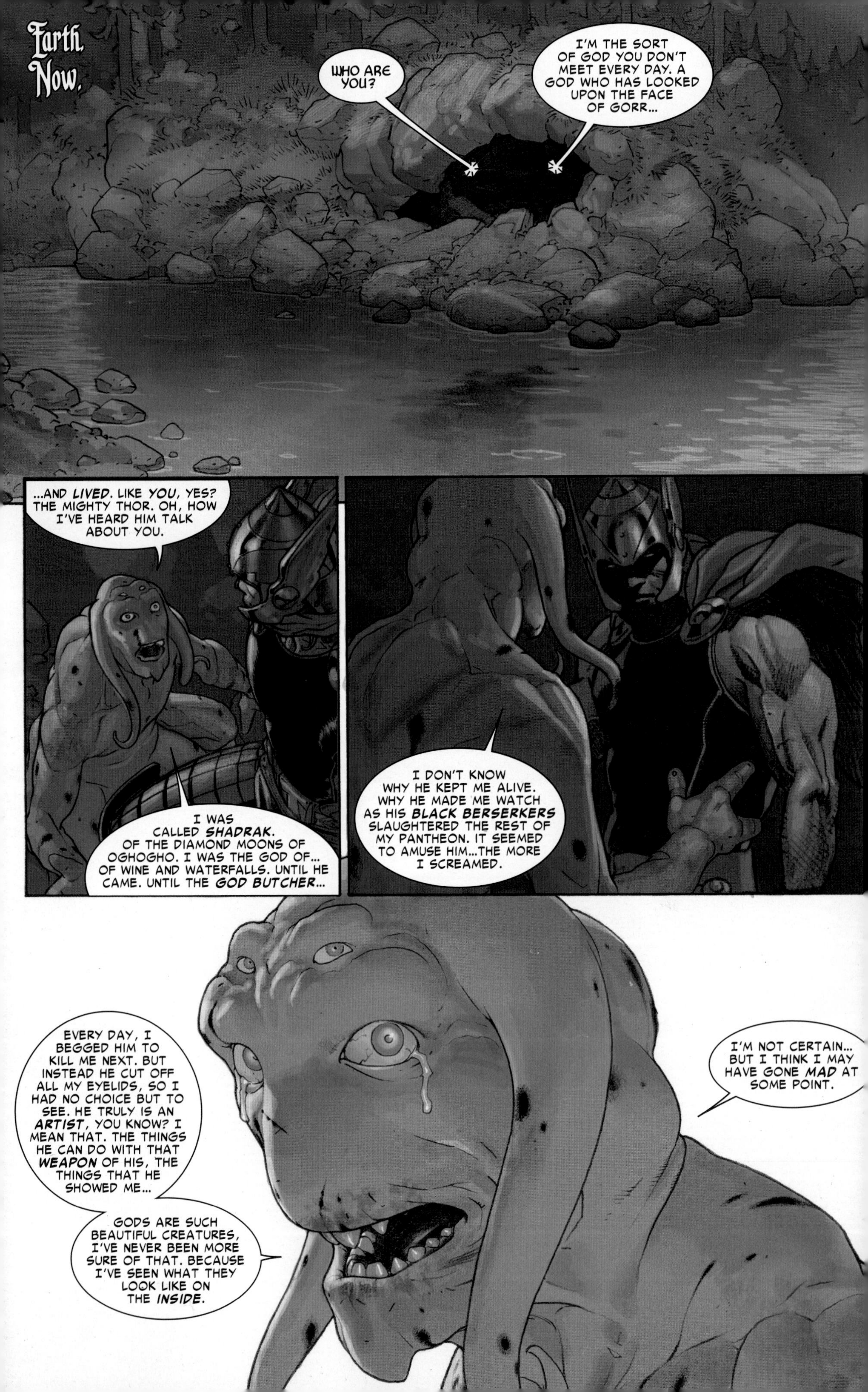
Earth. Now.
WHO ARE YOU?
I'M THE SORT OF GOD YOU DON'T MEET EVERY DAY. A GOD WHO HAS LOOKED UPON THE FACE OF GORR...
...AND LIVED. LIKE YOU, YES? THE MIGHTY THOR. OH, HOW I'VE HEARD HIM TALK ABOUT YOU.
I WAS CALLED SHADRAK. OF THE DIAMOND MOONS OF OGHOGHO. I WAS THE GOD OF... OF WINE AND WATERFALLS. UNTIL HE CAME. UNTIL THE GOD BUTCHER...
I DON'T KNOW WHY HE KEPT ME ALIVE. WHY HE MADE ME WATCH AS HIS BLACK BERSERKERS SLAUGHTERED THE REST OF MY PANTHEON. IT SEEMED TO AMUSE HIM...THE MORE I SCREAMED.
EVERY DAY, I BEGGED HIM TO KILL ME NEXT. BUT INSTEAD HE CUT OFF ALL MY EYELIDS, SO I HAD NO CHOICE BUT TO SEE. HE TRULY IS AN ARTIST, YOU KNOW? I MEAN THAT. THE THINGS HE CAN DO WITH THAT WEAPON OF HIS, THE THINGS THAT HE SHOWED ME...
GODS ARE SUCH BEAUTIFUL CREATURES, I'VE NEVER BEEN MORE SURE OF THAT. BECAUSE I'VE SEEN WHAT THEY LOOK LIKE ON THE INSIDE.
I'M NOT CERTAIN... BUT I THINK I MAY HAVE GONE MAD AT SOME POINT.

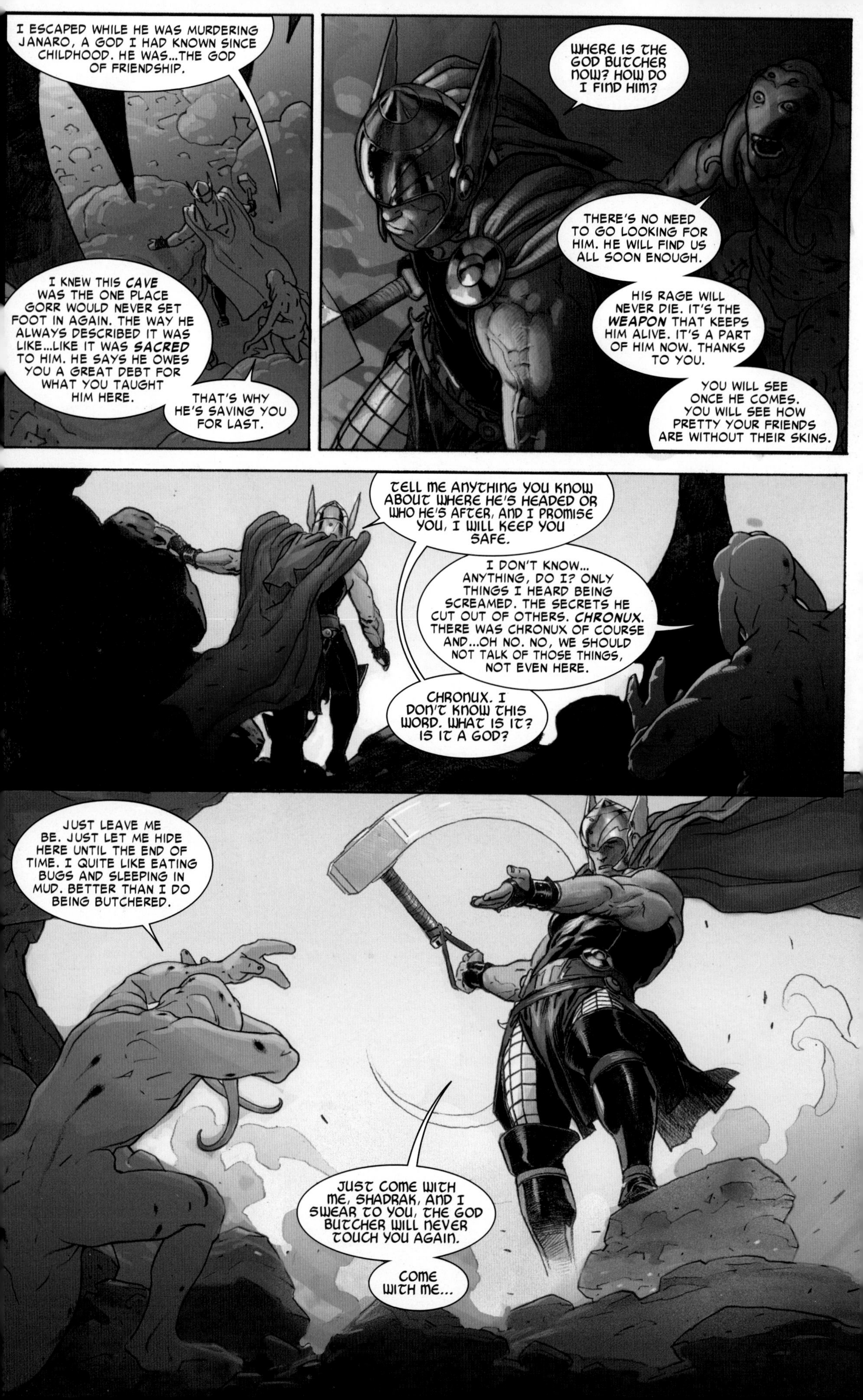
I ESCAPED WHILE HE WAS MURDERING JANARO, A GOD I HAD KNOWN SINCE CHILDHOOD. HE WAS...THE GOD OF FRIENDSHIP.
I KNEW THIS *CAVE* WAS THE ONE PLACE GORR WOULD NEVER SET FOOT IN AGAIN. THE WAY HE ALWAYS DESCRIBED IT WAS LIKE...LIKE IT WAS *SACRED* TO HIM. HE SAYS HE OWES YOU A GREAT DEBT FOR WHAT YOU TAUGHT HIM HERE.
THAT'S WHY HE'S SAVING YOU FOR LAST.
WHERE IS THE GOD BUTCHER NOW? HOW DO I FIND HIM?
THERE'S NO NEED TO GO LOOKING FOR HIM. HE WILL FIND US ALL SOON ENOUGH.
HIS RAGE WILL NEVER DIE. IT'S THE *WEAPON* THAT KEEPS HIM ALIVE. IT'S A PART OF HIM NOW. THANKS TO YOU.
YOU WILL SEE ONCE HE COMES. YOU WILL SEE HOW PRETTY YOUR FRIENDS ARE WITHOUT THEIR SKINS.
TELL ME ANYTHING YOU KNOW ABOUT WHERE HE'S HEADED OR WHO HE'S AFTER, AND I PROMISE YOU, I WILL KEEP YOU SAFE.
I DON'T KNOW... ANYTHING, DO I? ONLY THINGS I HEARD BEING SCREAMED. THE SECRETS HE CUT OUT OF OTHERS. *CHRONUX*. THERE WAS CHRONUX OF COURSE AND...OH NO. NO, WE SHOULD NOT TALK OF THOSE THINGS, NOT EVEN HERE.
CHRONUX. I DON'T KNOW THIS WORD. WHAT IS IT? IS IT A GOD?
JUST LEAVE ME BE. JUST LET ME HIDE HERE UNTIL THE END OF TIME. I QUITE LIKE EATING BUGS AND SLEEPING IN MUD. BETTER THAN I DO BEING BUTCHERED.
JUST COME WITH ME, SHADRAK, AND I SWEAR TO YOU, THE GOD BUTCHER WILL NEVER TOUCH YOU AGAIN.
COME WITH ME...

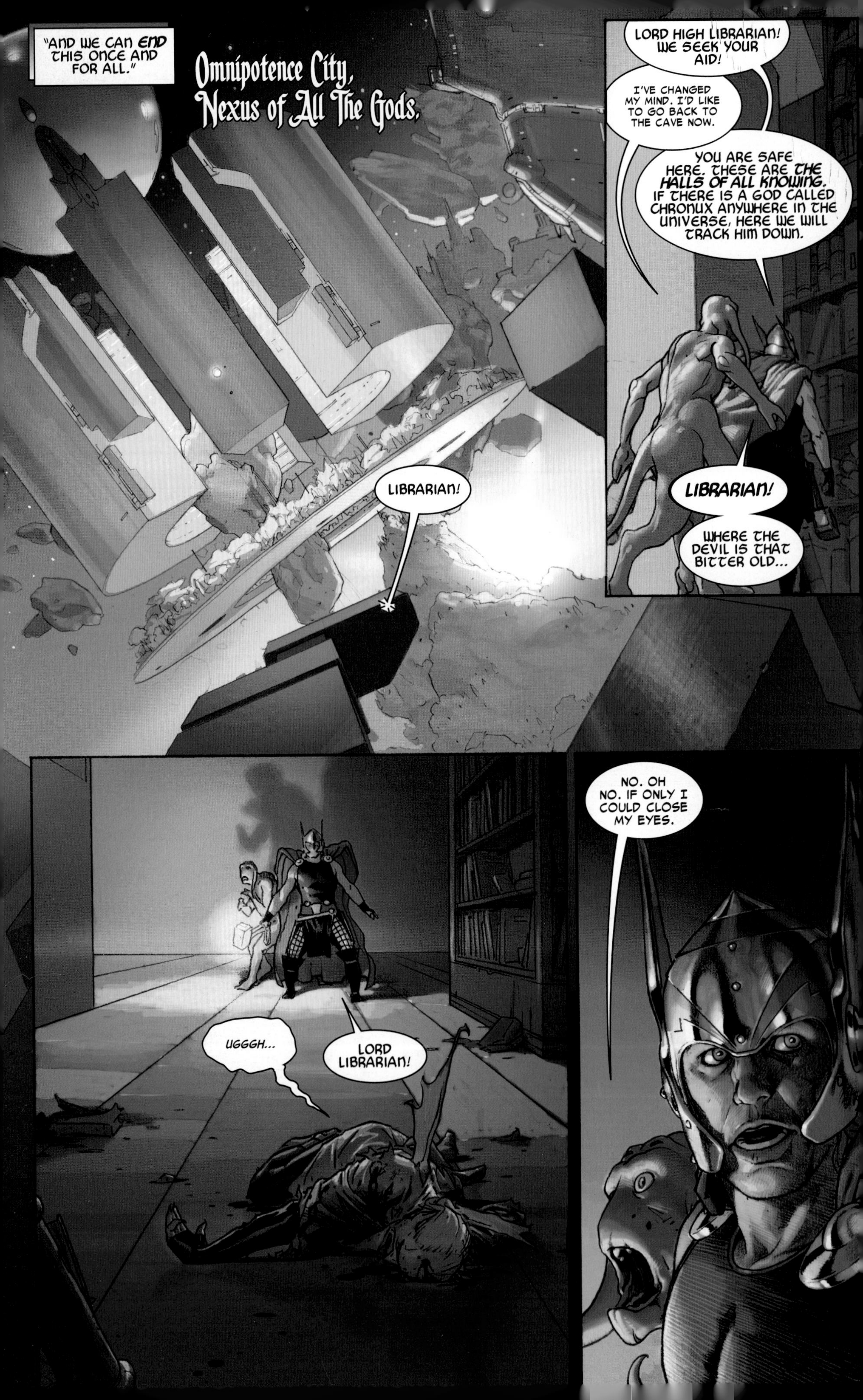
"AND WE CAN END THIS ONCE AND FOR ALL."
Omnipotence City, Nexus of All The Gods,
LIBRARIAN!
LORD HIGH LIBRARIAN! WE SEEK YOUR AID!
I'VE CHANGED MY MIND. I'D LIKE TO GO BACK TO THE CAVE NOW.
YOU ARE SAFE HERE. THESE ARE THE HALLS OF ALL KNOWING. IF THERE IS A GOD CALLED CHRONUX ANYWHERE IN THE UNIVERSE, HERE WE WILL TRACK HIM DOWN.
LIBRARIAN!
WHERE THE DEVIL IS THAT BITTER OLD...
UGGGH...
LORD LIBRARIAN!
NO. OH NO. IF ONLY I COULD CLOSE MY EYES.

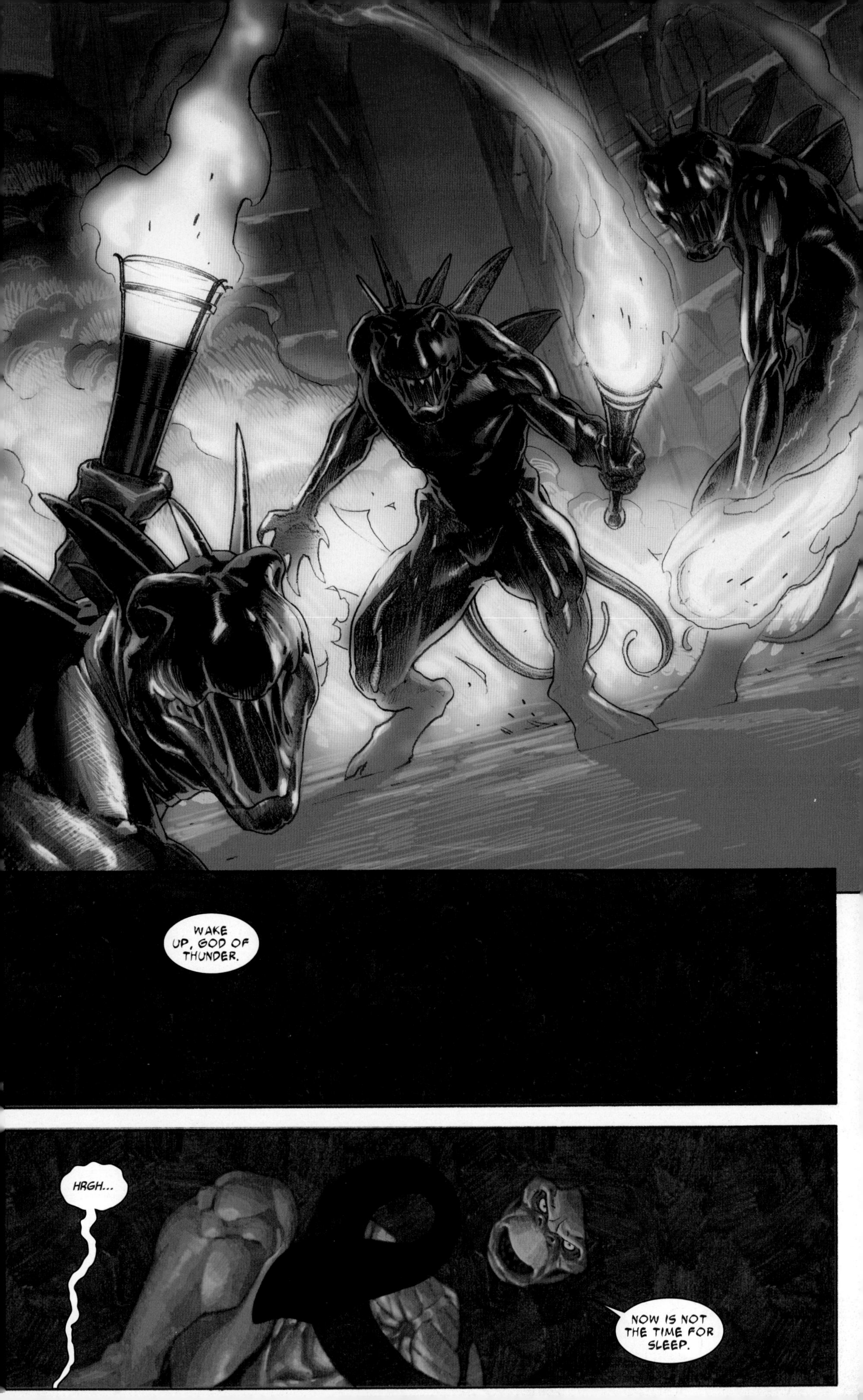
WAKE UP, GOD OF THUNDER.
HRGH...
NOW IS NOT THE TIME FOR SLEEP.

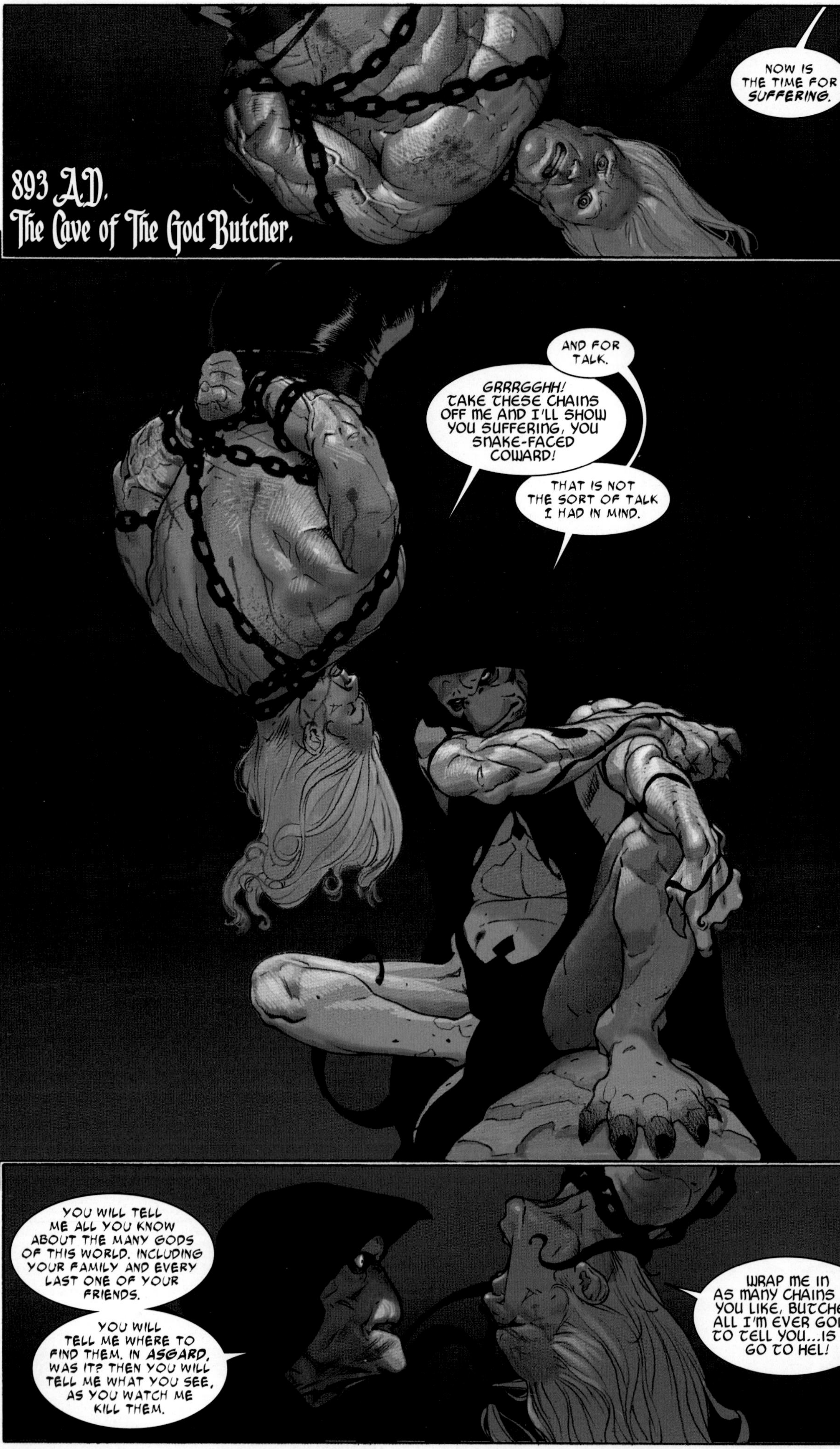
893 A.D.
The Cave of The God Butcher.
NOW IS THE TIME FOR SUFFERING.
AND FOR TALK.
GRRRGGHH! TAKE THESE CHAINS OFF ME AND I'LL SHOW YOU SUFFERING, YOU SNAKE-FACED COWARD!
THAT IS NOT THE SORT OF TALK I HAD IN MIND.
YOU WILL TELL ME ALL YOU KNOW ABOUT THE MANY GODS OF THIS WORLD. INCLUDING YOUR FAMILY AND EVERY LAST ONE OF YOUR FRIENDS.
YOU WILL TELL ME WHERE TO FIND THEM. IN ASGARD, WAS IT? THEN YOU WILL TELL ME WHAT YOU SEE, AS YOU WATCH ME KILL THEM.
WRAP ME IN AS MANY CHAINS AS YOU LIKE, BUTCHER! ALL I'M EVER GOING TO TELL YOU...IS TO GO TO HEL!

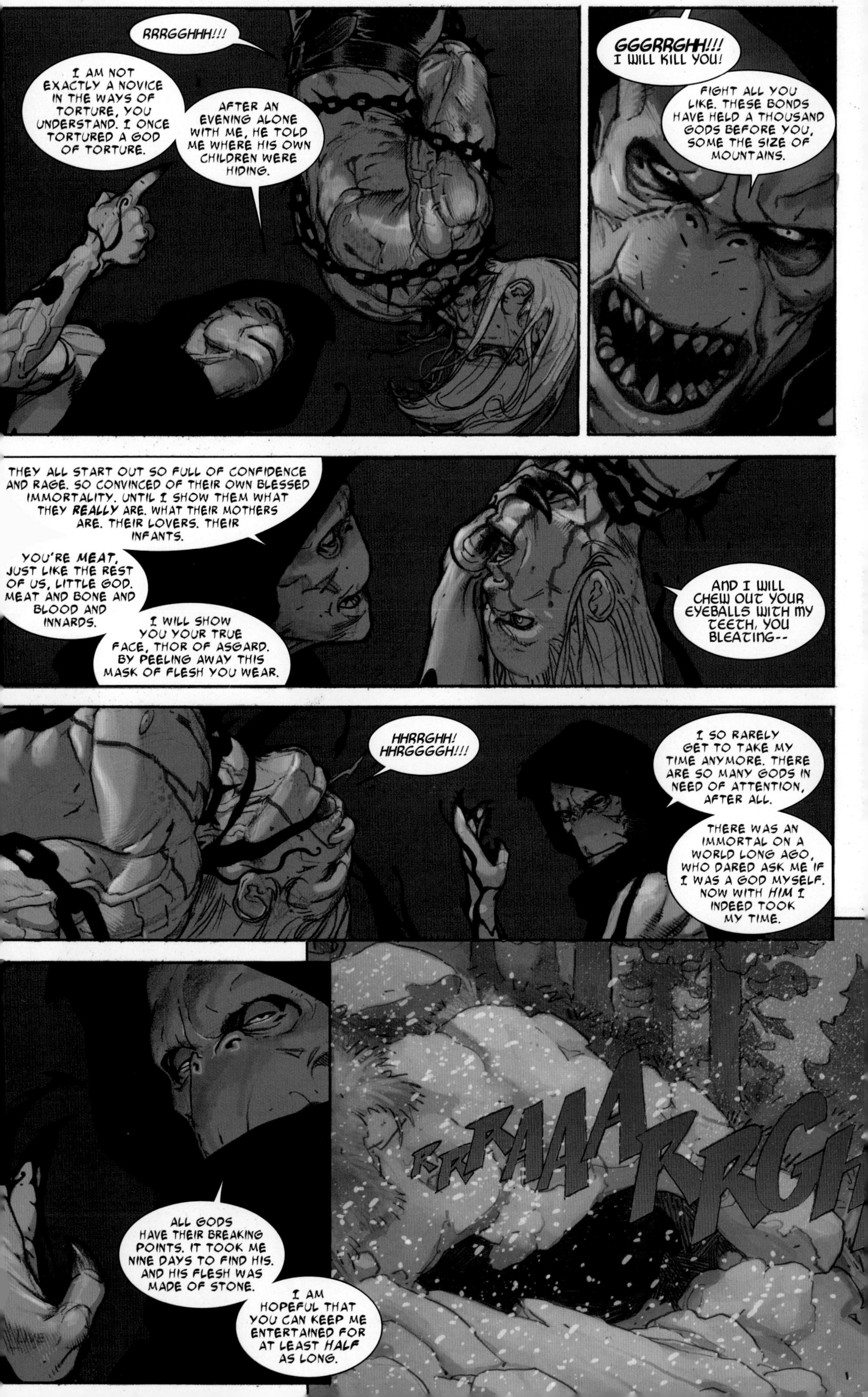
RRRGGHHH!!!
I AM NOT EXACTLY A NOVICE IN THE WAYS OF TORTURE, YOU UNDERSTAND. I ONCE TORTURED A GOD OF TORTURE.
AFTER AN EVENING ALONE WITH ME, HE TOLD ME WHERE HIS OWN CHILDREN WERE HIDING.
GGGRRGHH!!! I WILL KILL YOU!
FIGHT ALL YOU LIKE. THESE BONDS HAVE HELD A THOUSAND GODS BEFORE YOU, SOME THE SIZE OF MOUNTAINS.
THEY ALL START OUT SO FULL OF CONFIDENCE AND RAGE. SO CONVINCED OF THEIR OWN BLESSED IMMORTALITY. UNTIL I SHOW THEM WHAT THEY REALLY ARE. WHAT THEIR MOTHERS ARE. THEIR LOVERS. THEIR INFANTS.
YOU'RE MEAT, JUST LIKE THE REST OF US, LITTLE GOD. MEAT AND BONE AND BLOOD AND INNARDS.
I WILL SHOW YOU YOUR TRUE FACE, THOR OF ASGARD. BY PEELING AWAY THIS MASK OF FLESH YOU WEAR.
AND I WILL CHEW OUT YOUR EYEBALLS WITH MY TEETH, YOU BLEATING--
HHRRGHH! HHRGGGGH!!!
I SO RARELY GET TO TAKE MY TIME ANYMORE. THERE ARE SO MANY GODS IN NEED OF ATTENTION, AFTER ALL.
THERE WAS AN IMMORTAL ON A WORLD LONG AGO, WHO DARED ASK ME IF I WAS A GOD MYSELF. NOW WITH HIM I INDEED TOOK MY TIME.
ALL GODS HAVE THEIR BREAKING POINTS. IT TOOK ME NINE DAYS TO FIND HIS. AND HIS FLESH WAS MADE OF STONE.
I AM HOPEFUL THAT YOU CAN KEEP ME ENTERTAINED FOR AT LEAST HALF AS LONG.
RRRAAARRGH

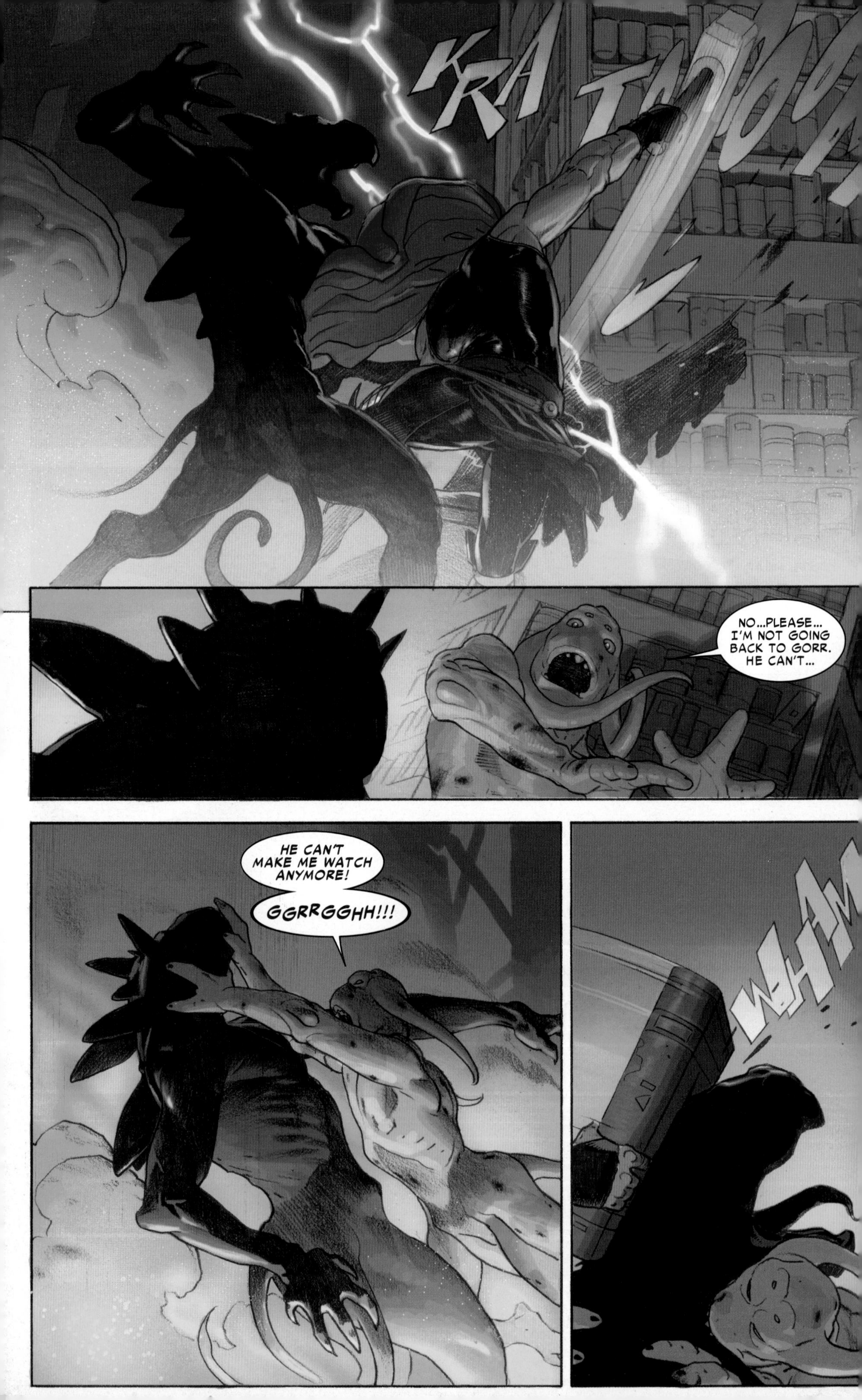
KRA TOOOOM
NO...PLEASE... I'M NOT GOING BACK TO GORR. HE CAN'T...
HE CAN'T MAKE ME WATCH ANYMORE!
GGRRGGHH!!!
WHAM

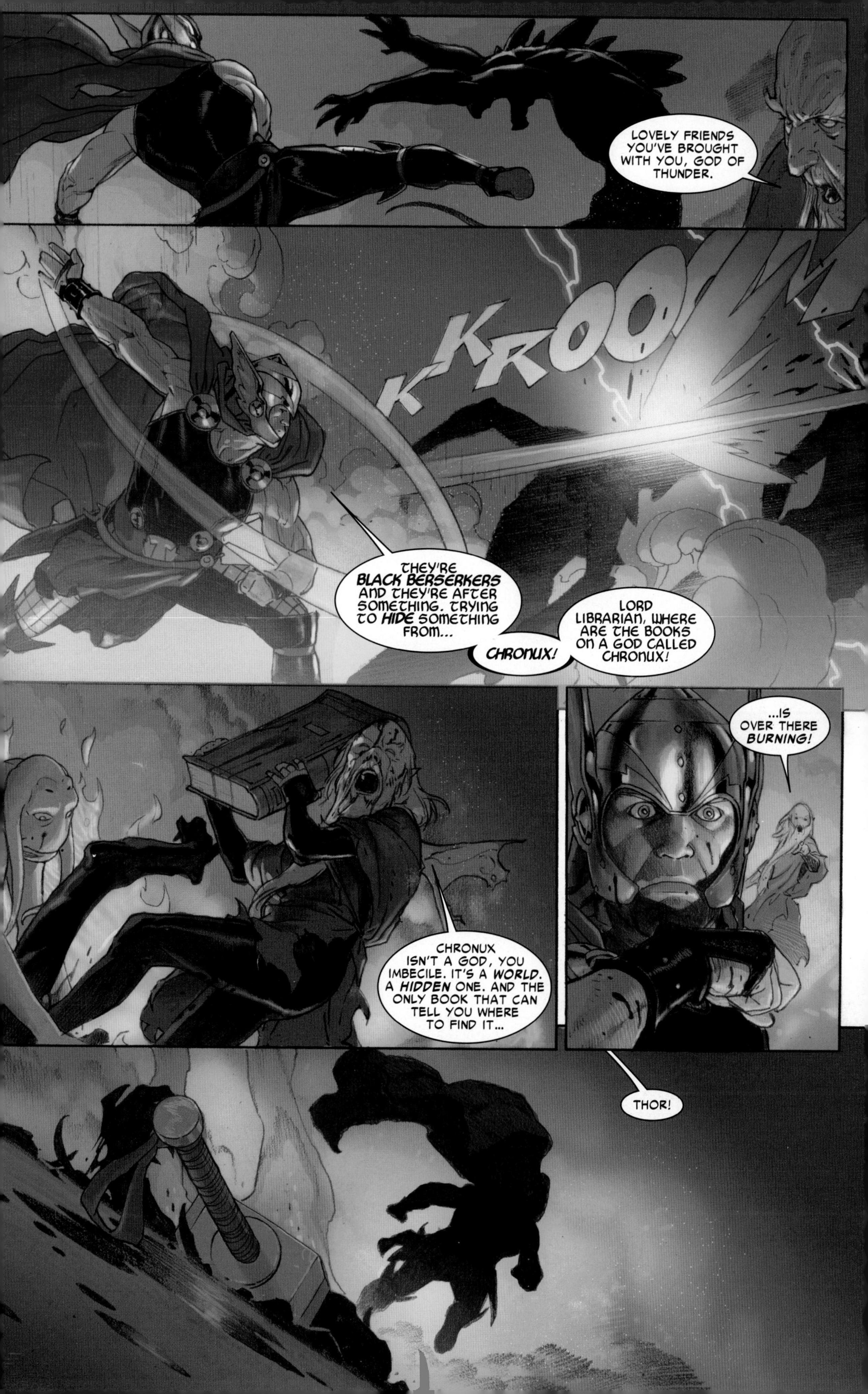
LOVELY FRIENDS YOU'VE BROUGHT WITH YOU, GOD OF THUNDER.
K-K-KROOOOM
THEY'RE BLACK BERSERKERS AND THEY'RE AFTER SOMETHING. TRYING TO HIDE SOMETHING FROM...
CHRONUX!
LORD LIBRARIAN, WHERE ARE THE BOOKS ON A GOD CALLED CHRONUX!
CHRONUX ISN'T A GOD, YOU IMBECILE. IT'S A WORLD. A HIDDEN ONE. AND THE ONLY BOOK THAT CAN TELL YOU WHERE TO FIND IT...
...IS OVER THERE BURNING!
THOR!

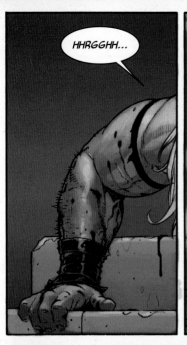

HHRGGHH...

I WILL NOT SIT... ON THAT BLASTED THRONE...A SECOND LONGER.

IF I CANNOT WALK TO MY DEATH LIKE A GOD OF THE VIKINGS...

I WILL *CRAWL* TO IT...LIKE A WOUNDED DOG.

COME, MJOLNIR, OLD FRIEND.

SHOW ME THERE'S STILL SOME MAGIC LEFT IN THESE DEAD HALLS.

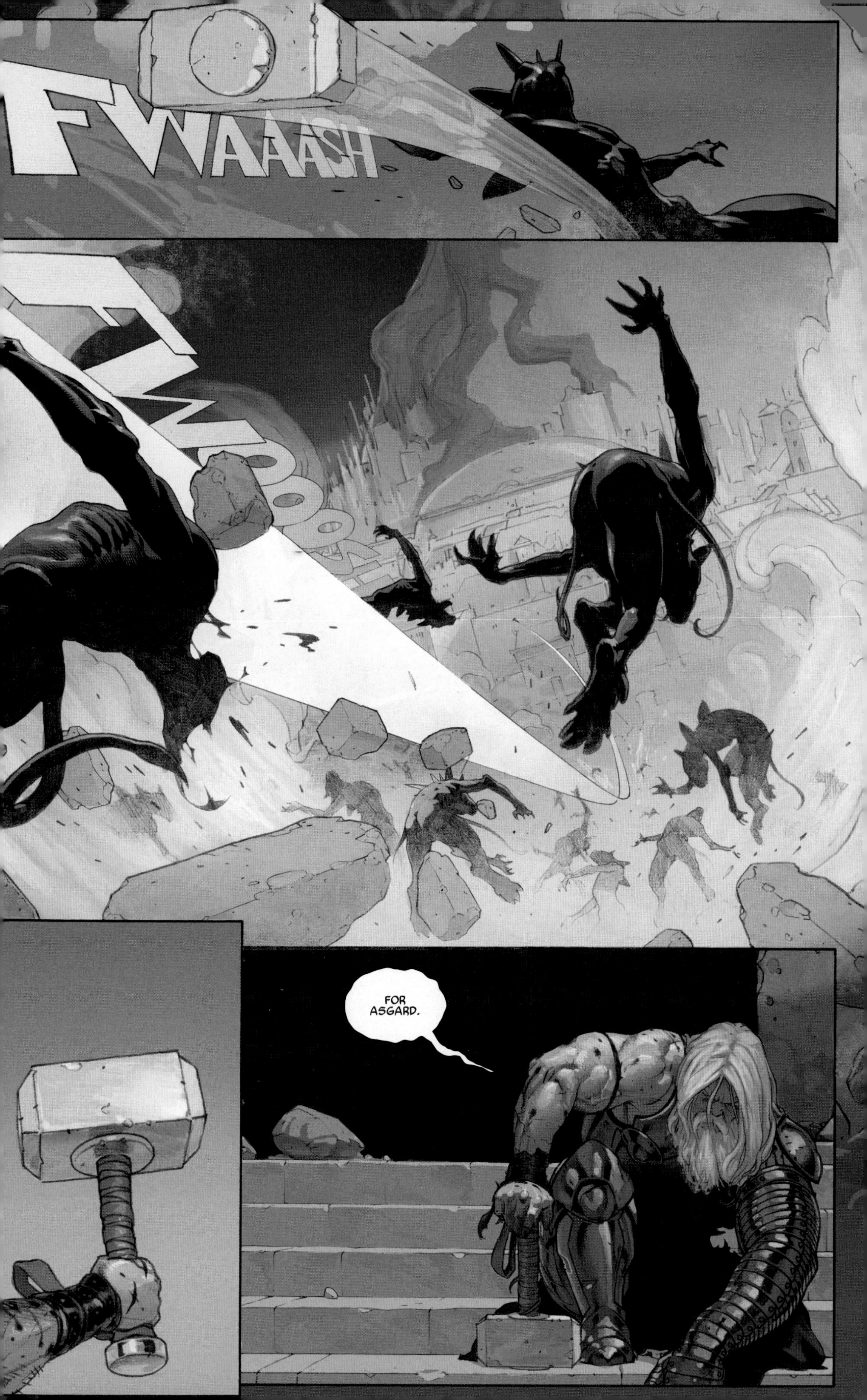
FWAAASH
FWOOOSH
FOR ASGARD.

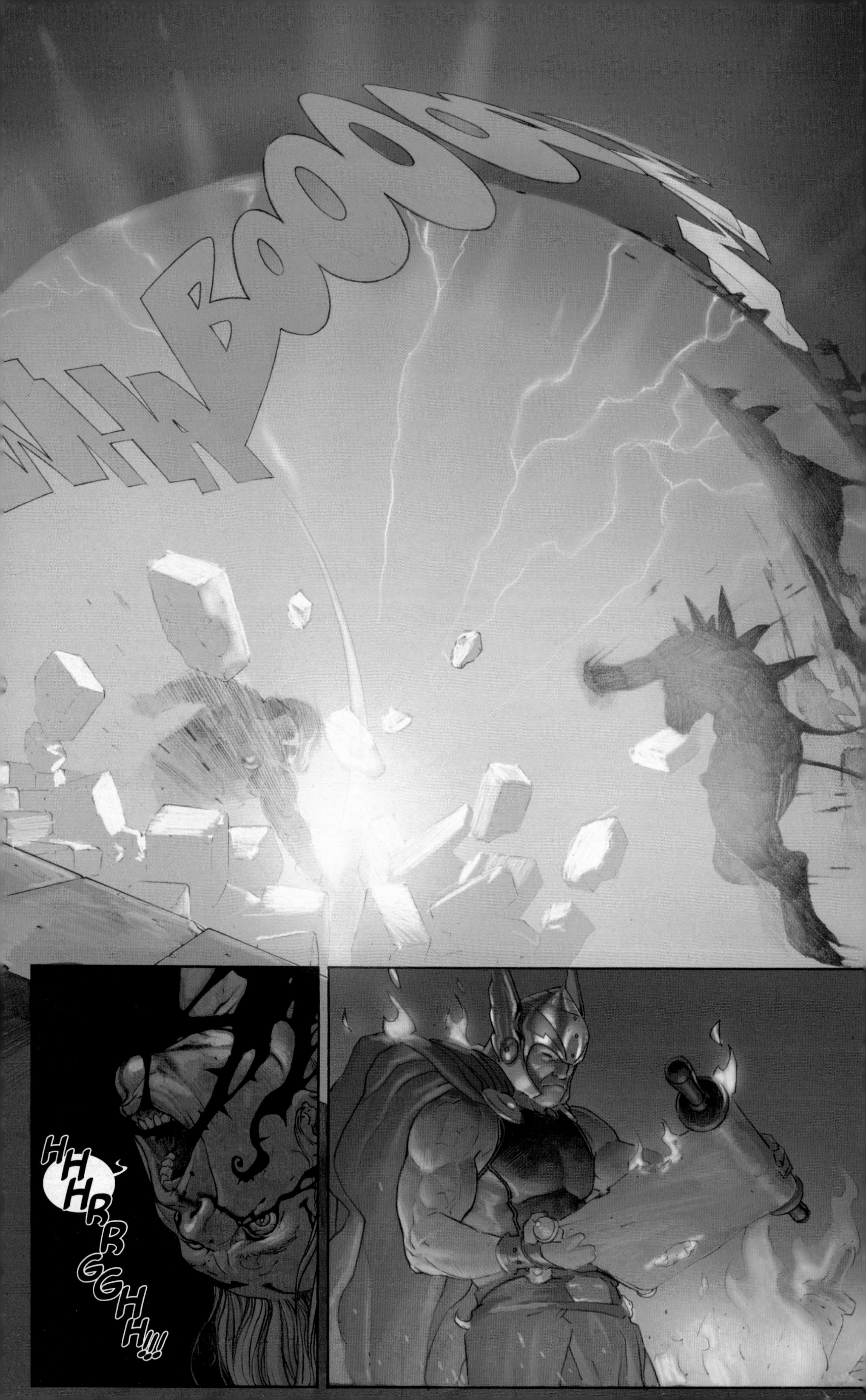
WHABOOOOM
HHHRRGGHH!!!

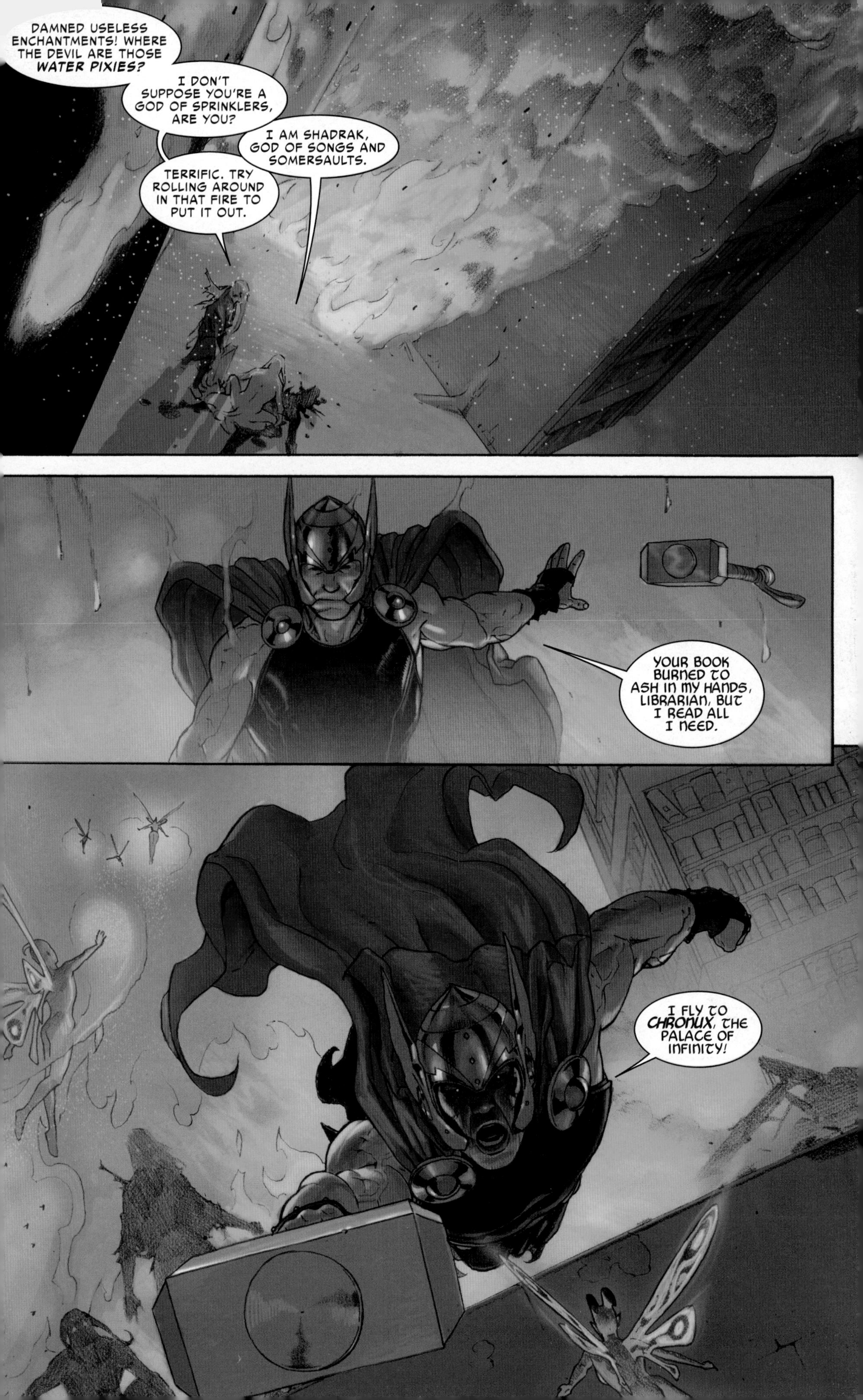
DAMNED USELESS ENCHANTMENTS! WHERE THE DEVIL ARE THOSE WATER PIXIES?
I DON'T SUPPOSE YOU'RE A GOD OF SPRINKLERS, ARE YOU?
I AM SHADRAK, GOD OF SONGS AND SOMERSAULTS.
TERRIFIC. TRY ROLLING AROUND IN THAT FIRE TO PUT IT OUT.
YOUR BOOK BURNED TO ASH IN MY HANDS, LIBRARIAN, BUT I READ ALL I NEED.
I FLY TO CHRONUX, THE PALACE OF INFINITY!

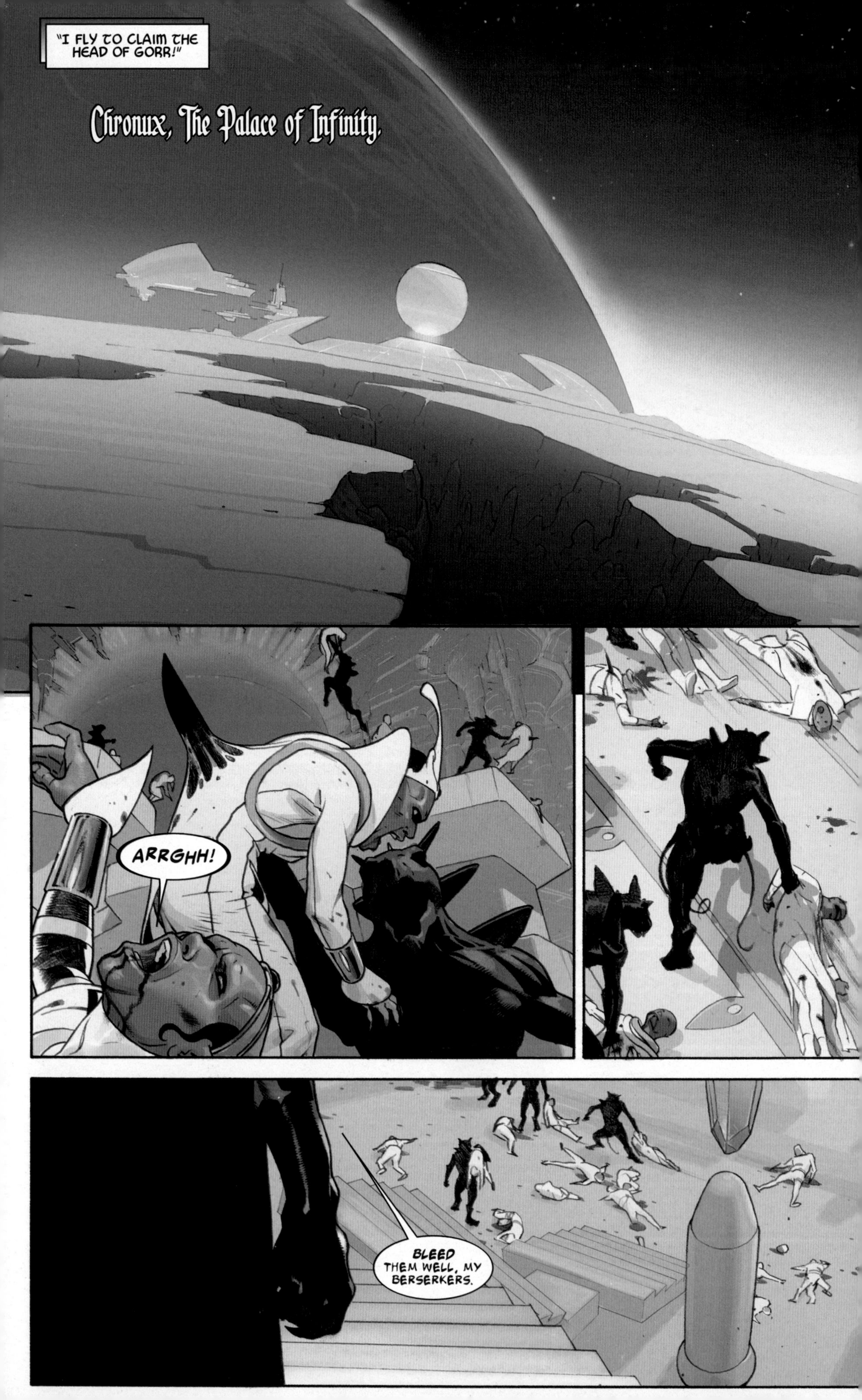
"I FLY TO CLAIM THE HEAD OF GORR!"
Chronux, The Palace of Infinity.
ARRGHH!
BLEED THEM WELL, MY BERSERKERS.

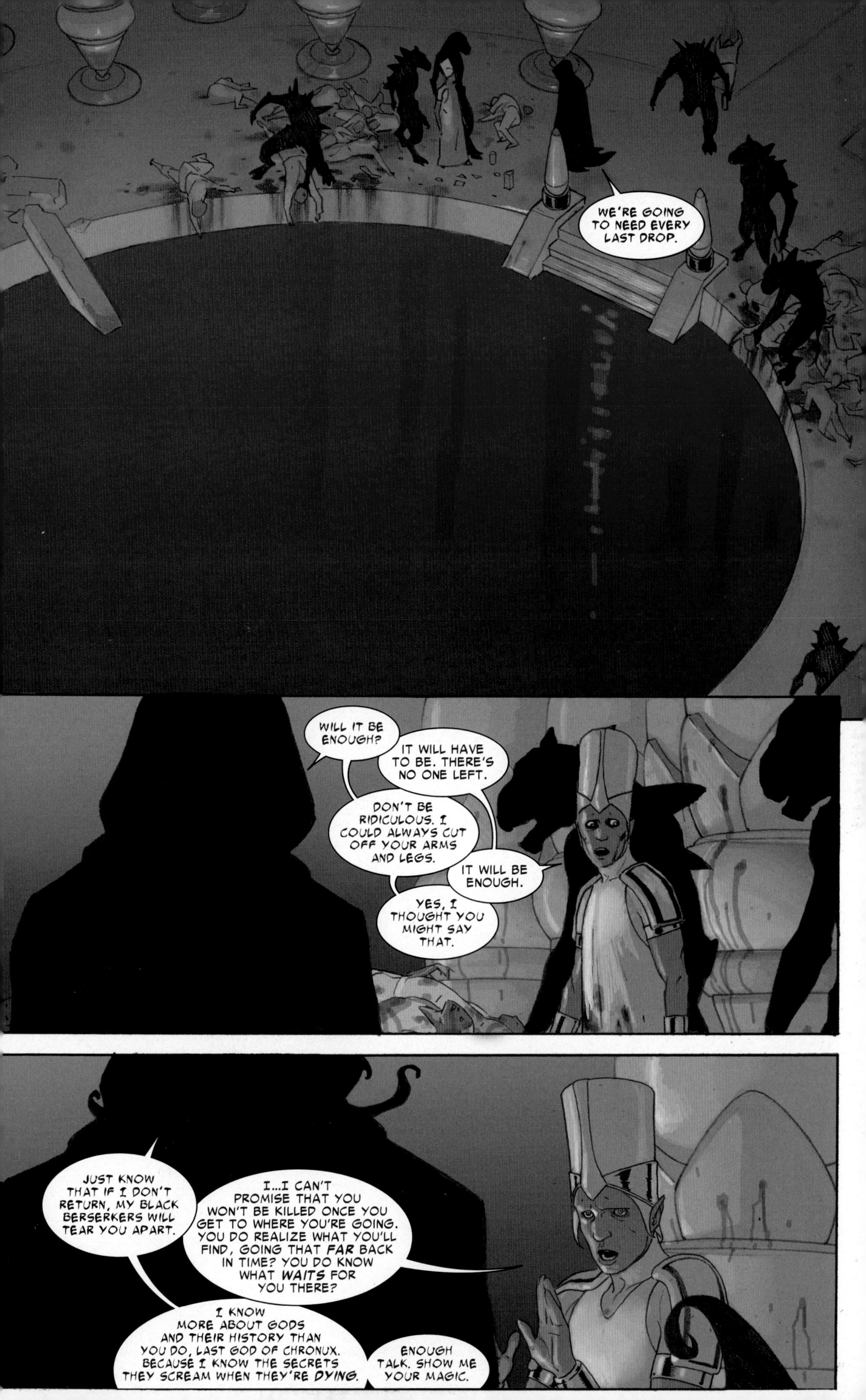
WE'RE GOING TO NEED EVERY LAST DROP.
WILL IT BE ENOUGH?
IT WILL HAVE TO BE. THERE'S NO ONE LEFT.
DON'T BE RIDICULOUS. I COULD ALWAYS CUT OFF YOUR ARMS AND LEGS.
IT WILL BE ENOUGH.
YES, I THOUGHT YOU MIGHT SAY THAT.
JUST KNOW THAT IF I DON'T RETURN, MY BLACK BERSERKERS WILL TEAR YOU APART.
I...I CAN'T PROMISE THAT YOU WON'T BE KILLED ONCE YOU GET TO WHERE YOU'RE GOING. YOU DO REALIZE WHAT YOU'LL FIND, GOING THAT FAR BACK IN TIME? YOU DO KNOW WHAT WAITS FOR YOU THERE?
I KNOW MORE ABOUT GODS AND THEIR HISTORY THAN YOU DO, LAST GOD OF CHRONUX. BECAUSE I KNOW THE SECRETS THEY SCREAM WHEN THEY'RE DYING.
ENOUGH TALK. SHOW ME YOUR MAGIC.

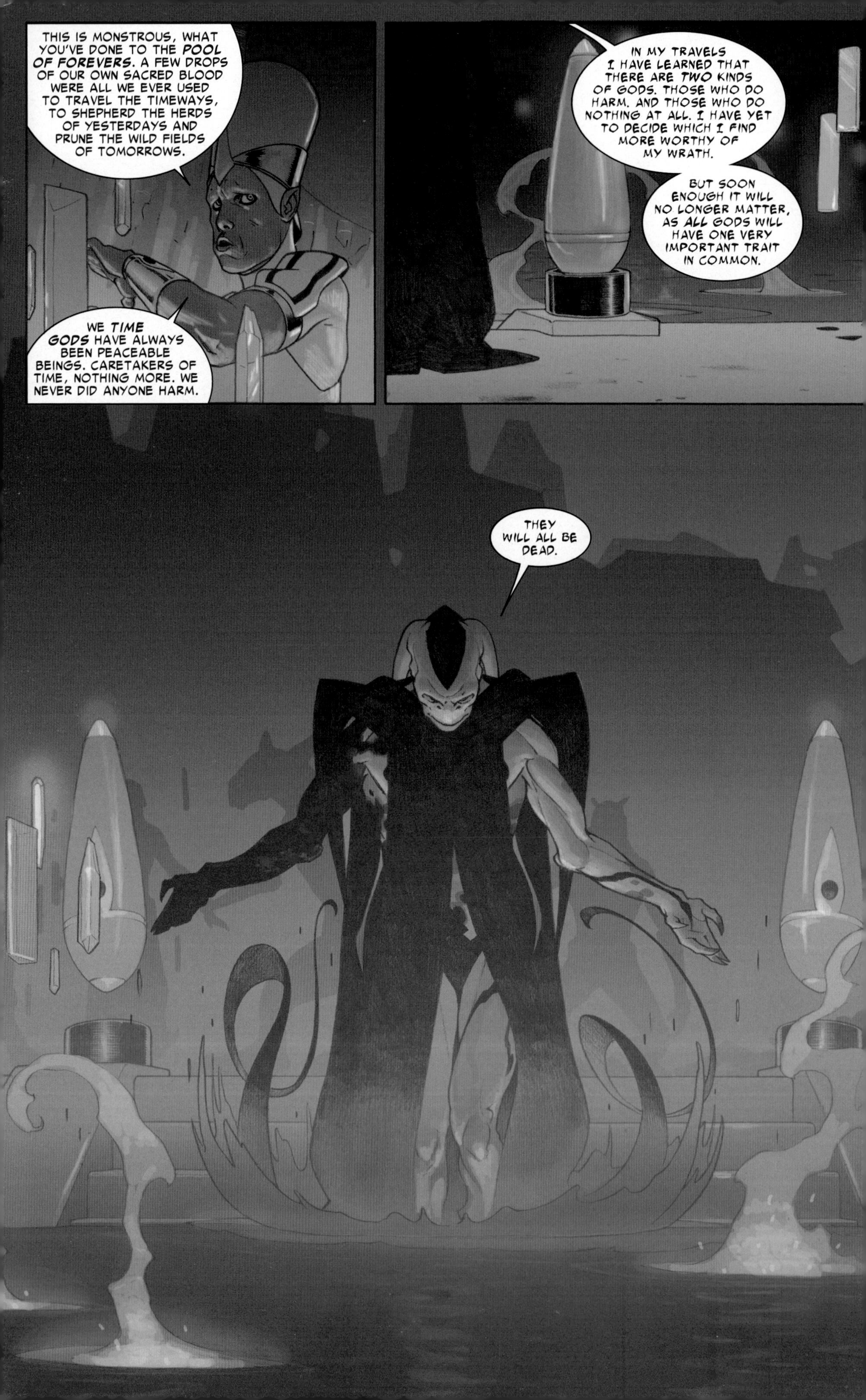
THIS IS MONSTROUS, WHAT YOU'VE DONE TO THE POOL OF FOREVERS. A FEW DROPS OF OUR OWN SACRED BLOOD WERE ALL WE EVER USED TO TRAVEL THE TIMEWAYS, TO SHEPHERD THE HERDS OF YESTERDAYS AND PRUNE THE WILD FIELDS OF TOMORROWS.
WE TIME GODS HAVE ALWAYS BEEN PEACEABLE BEINGS. CARETAKERS OF TIME, NOTHING MORE. WE NEVER DID ANYONE HARM.
IN MY TRAVELS I HAVE LEARNED THAT THERE ARE TWO KINDS OF GODS. THOSE WHO DO HARM. AND THOSE WHO DO NOTHING AT ALL. I HAVE YET TO DECIDE WHICH I FIND MORE WORTHY OF MY WRATH.
BUT SOON ENOUGH IT WILL NO LONGER MATTER, AS ALL GODS WILL HAVE ONE VERY IMPORTANT TRAIT IN COMMON.
THEY WILL ALL BE DEAD.

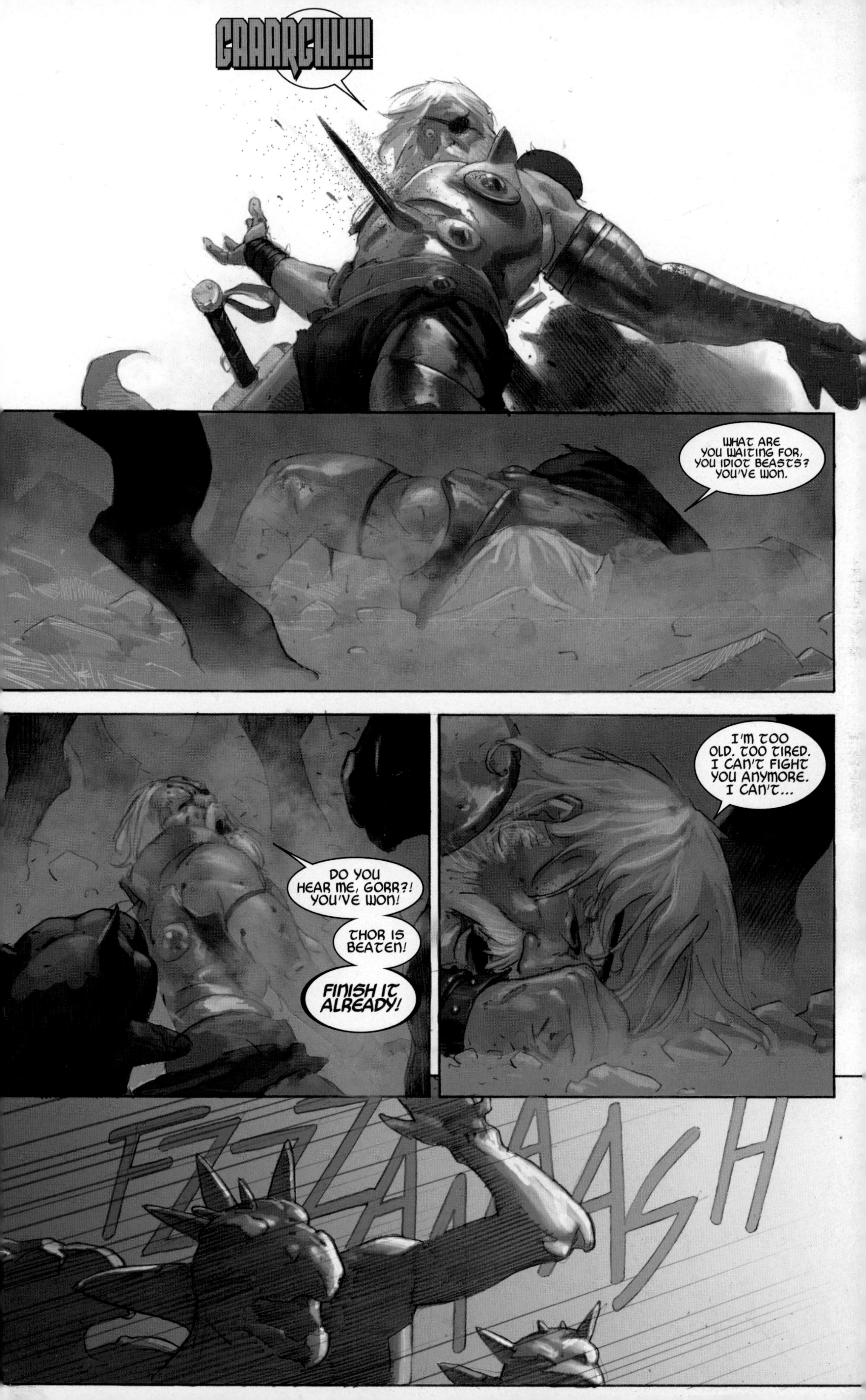

CAAARCHH!!!
WHAT ARE YOU WAITING FOR, YOU IDIOT BEASTS? YOU'VE WON.
DO YOU HEAR ME, GORR?! YOU'VE WON!
THOR IS BEATEN!
FINISH IT ALREADY!
I'M TOO OLD. TOO TIRED. I CAN'T FIGHT YOU ANYMORE. I CAN'T...
FZZZAAAASH

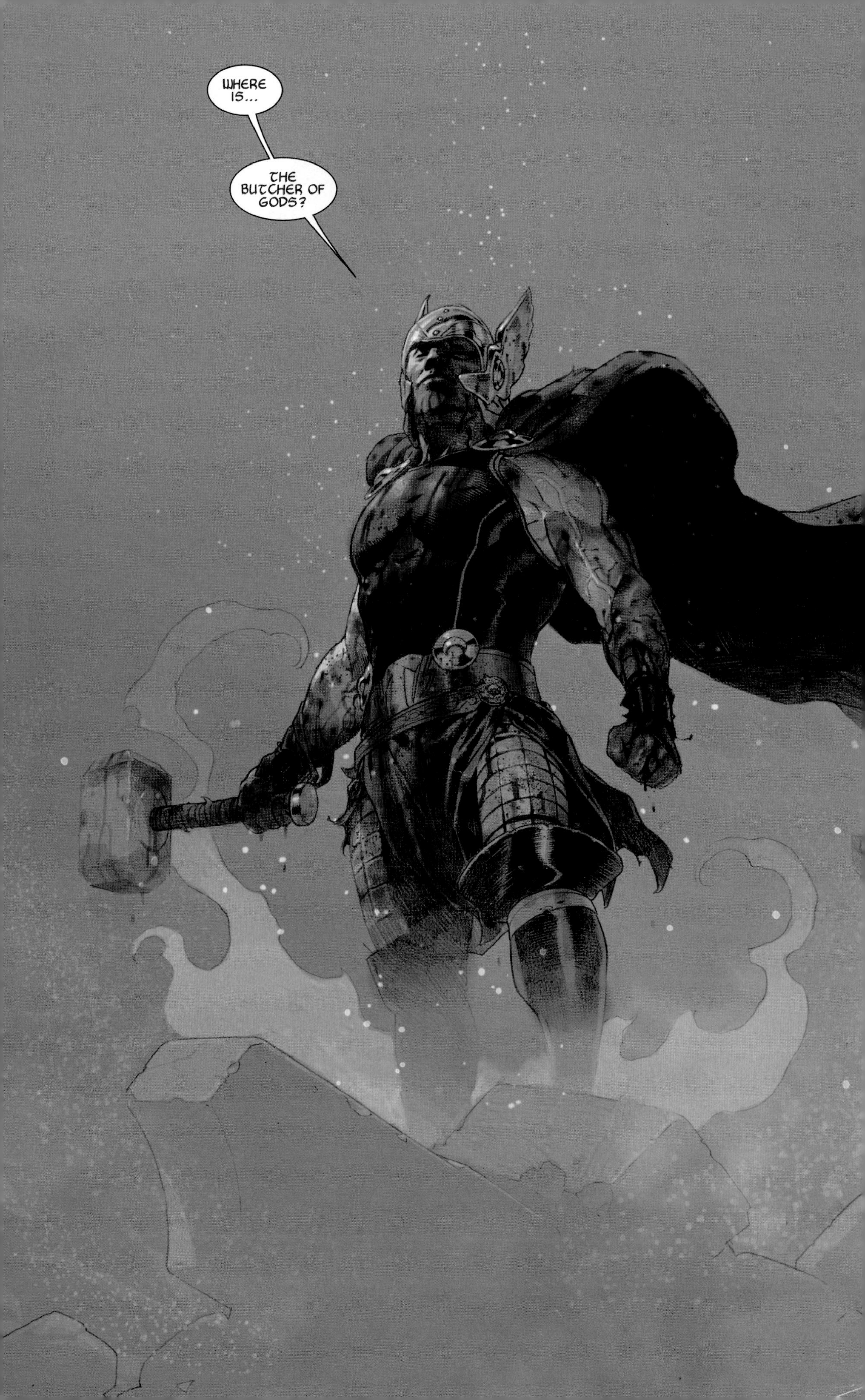
WHERE IS...
THE BUTCHER OF GODS?

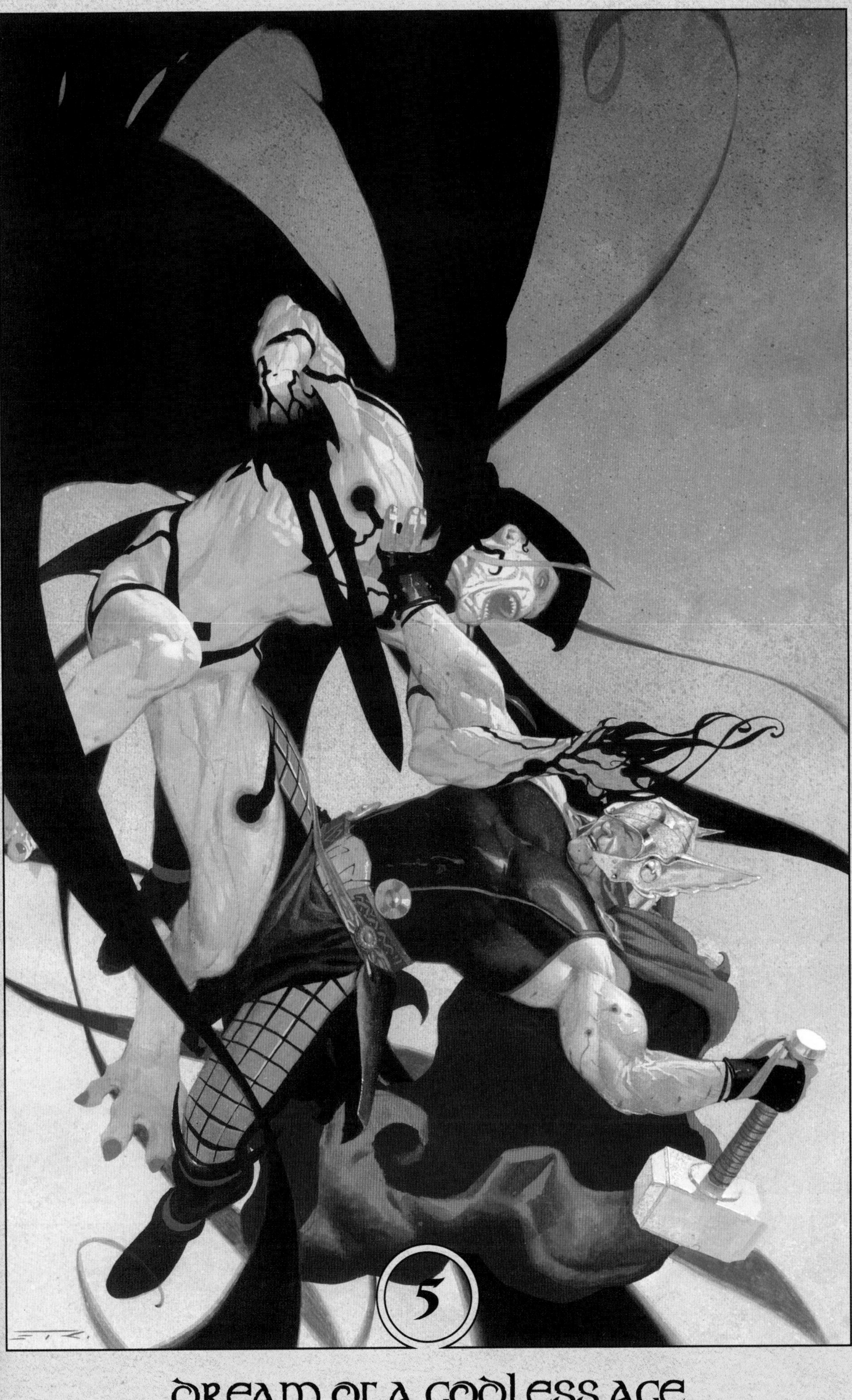
5

DREAM OF A GODLESS AGE

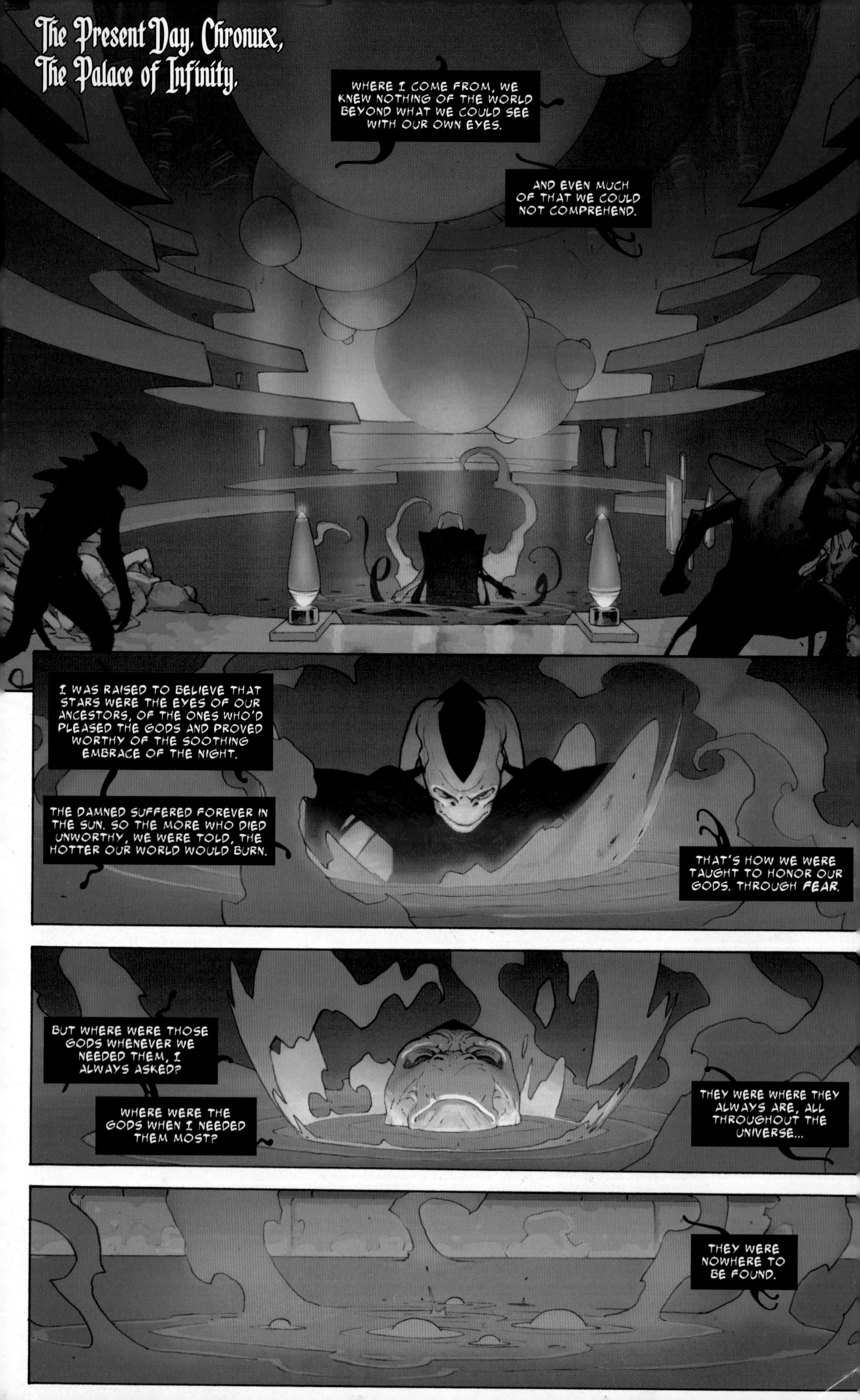
The Present Day, Chronux, The Palace of Infinity.
WHERE I COME FROM, WE KNEW NOTHING OF THE WORLD BEYOND WHAT WE COULD SEE WITH OUR OWN EYES.
AND EVEN MUCH OF THAT WE COULD NOT COMPREHEND.
I WAS RAISED TO BELIEVE THAT STARS WERE THE EYES OF OUR ANCESTORS, OF THE ONES WHO'D PLEASED THE GODS AND PROVED WORTHY OF THE SOOTHING EMBRACE OF THE NIGHT.
THE DAMNED SUFFERED FOREVER IN THE SUN. SO THE MORE WHO DIED UNWORTHY, WE WERE TOLD, THE HOTTER OUR WORLD WOULD BURN.
THAT'S HOW WE WERE TAUGHT TO HONOR OUR GODS. THROUGH FEAR.
BUT WHERE WERE THOSE GODS WHENEVER WE NEEDED THEM, I ALWAYS ASKED?
WHERE WERE THE GODS WHEN I NEEDED THEM MOST?
THEY WERE WHERE THEY ALWAYS ARE, ALL THROUGHOUT THE UNIVERSE...
THEY WERE NOWHERE TO BE FOUND.

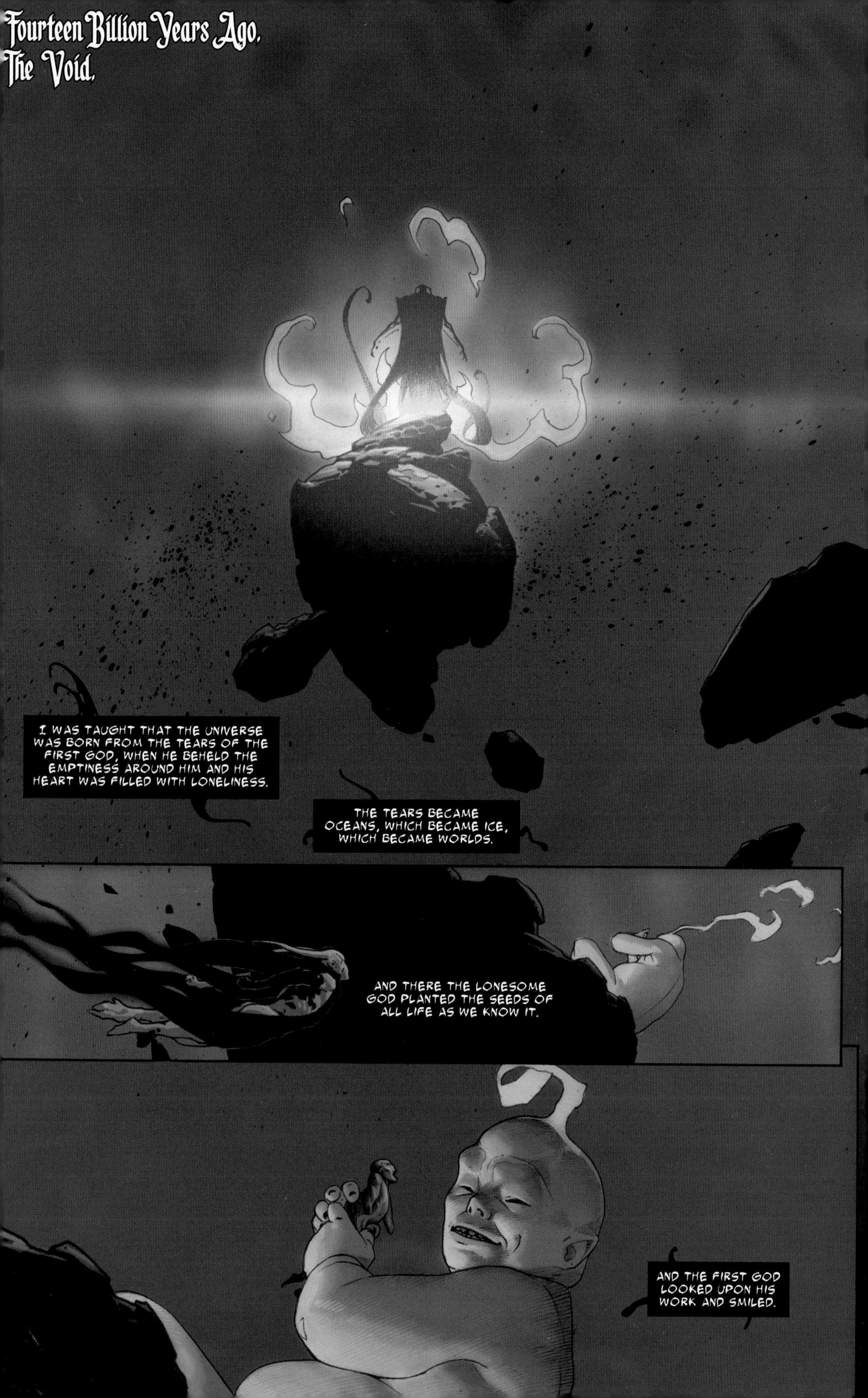
Fourteen Billion Years Ago,
The Void,
I WAS TAUGHT THAT THE UNIVERSE WAS BORN FROM THE TEARS OF THE FIRST GOD, WHEN HE BEHELD THE EMPTINESS AROUND HIM AND HIS HEART WAS FILLED WITH LONELINESS.
THE TEARS BECAME OCEANS, WHICH BECAME ICE, WHICH BECAME WORLDS.
AND THERE THE LONESOME GOD PLANTED THE SEEDS OF ALL LIFE AS WE KNOW IT.
AND THE FIRST GOD LOOKED UPON HIS WORK AND SMILED.

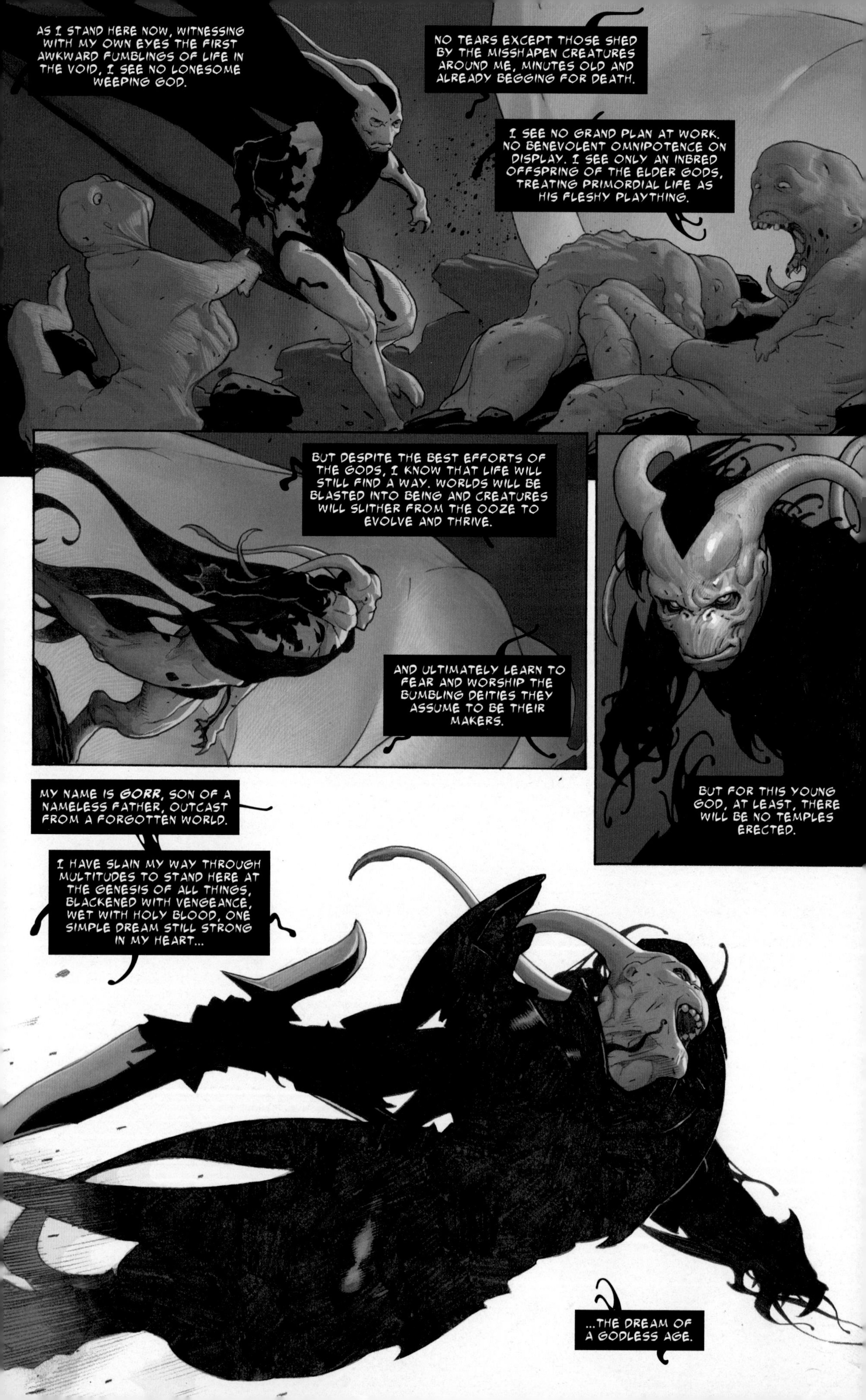
AS I STAND HERE NOW, WITNESSING WITH MY OWN EYES THE FIRST AWKWARD FUMBLINGS OF LIFE IN THE VOID, I SEE NO LONESOME WEEPING GOD.
NO TEARS EXCEPT THOSE SHED BY THE MISSHAPEN CREATURES AROUND ME, MINUTES OLD AND ALREADY BEGGING FOR DEATH.
I SEE NO GRAND PLAN AT WORK. NO BENEVOLENT OMNIPOTENCE ON DISPLAY. I SEE ONLY AN INBRED OFFSPRING OF THE ELDER GODS, TREATING PRIMORDIAL LIFE AS HIS FLESHY PLAYTHING.
BUT DESPITE THE BEST EFFORTS OF THE GODS, I KNOW THAT LIFE WILL STILL FIND A WAY. WORLDS WILL BE BLASTED INTO BEING AND CREATURES WILL SLITHER FROM THE OOZE TO EVOLVE AND THRIVE.
AND ULTIMATELY LEARN TO FEAR AND WORSHIP THE BUMBLING DEITIES THEY ASSUME TO BE THEIR MAKERS.
BUT FOR THIS YOUNG GOD, AT LEAST, THERE WILL BE NO TEMPLES ERECTED.
MY NAME IS GORR, SON OF A NAMELESS FATHER, OUTCAST FROM A FORGOTTEN WORLD.
I HAVE SLAIN MY WAY THROUGH MULTITUDES TO STAND HERE AT THE GENESIS OF ALL THINGS, BLACKENED WITH VENGEANCE, WET WITH HOLY BLOOD, ONE SIMPLE DREAM STILL STRONG IN MY HEART...
...THE DREAM OF A GODLESS AGE.

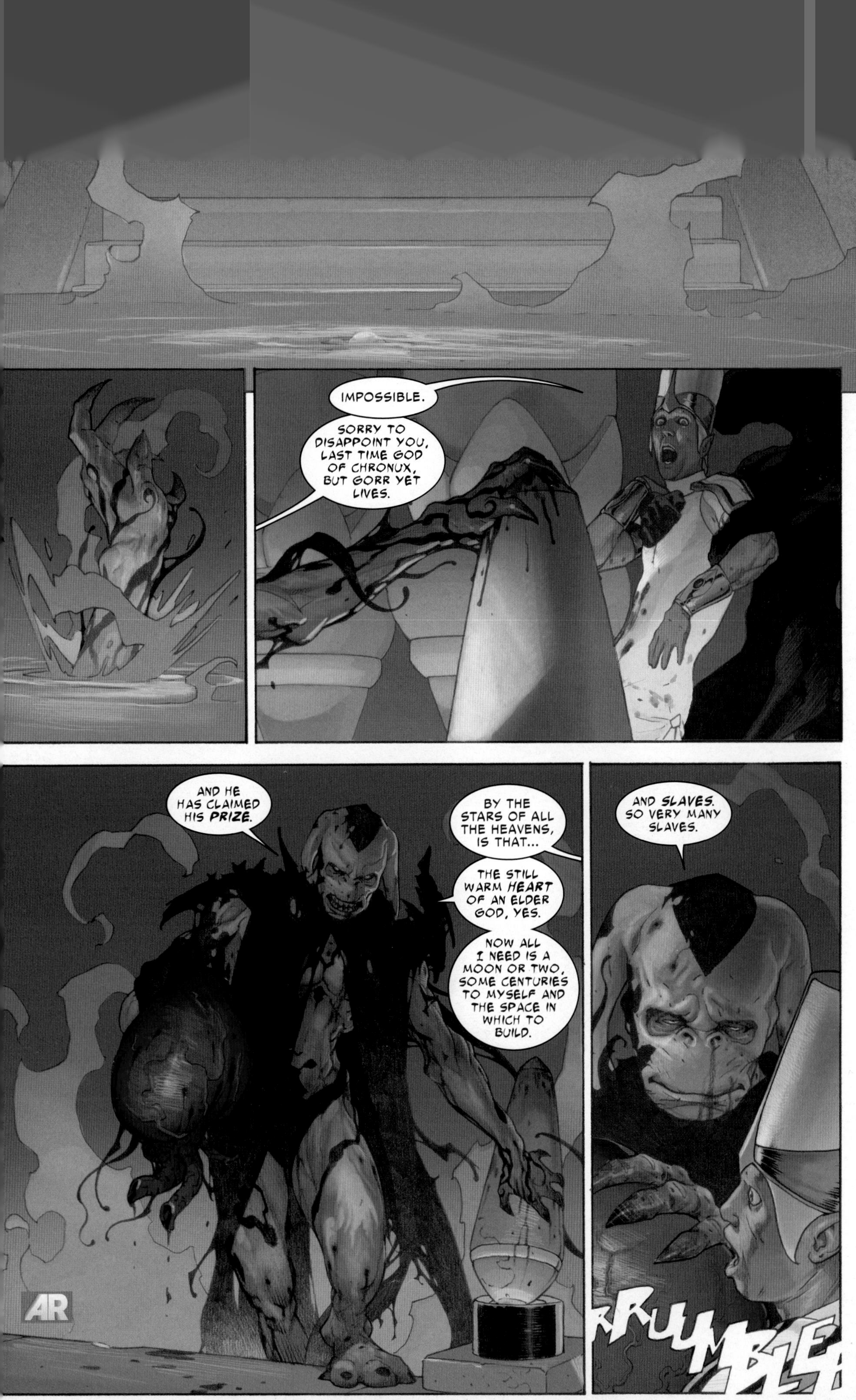
IMPOSSIBLE.
SORRY TO DISAPPOINT YOU, LAST TIME GOD OF CHRONUX, BUT GORR YET LIVES.
AND HE HAS CLAIMED HIS **PRIZE**.
BY THE STARS OF ALL THE HEAVENS, IS THAT...
THE STILL WARM *HEART* OF AN ELDER GOD, YES.
NOW ALL I NEED IS A MOON OR TWO, SOME CENTURIES TO MYSELF AND THE SPACE IN WHICH TO BUILD.
AND *SLAVES*. SO VERY MANY SLAVES.
RRUUMBLE

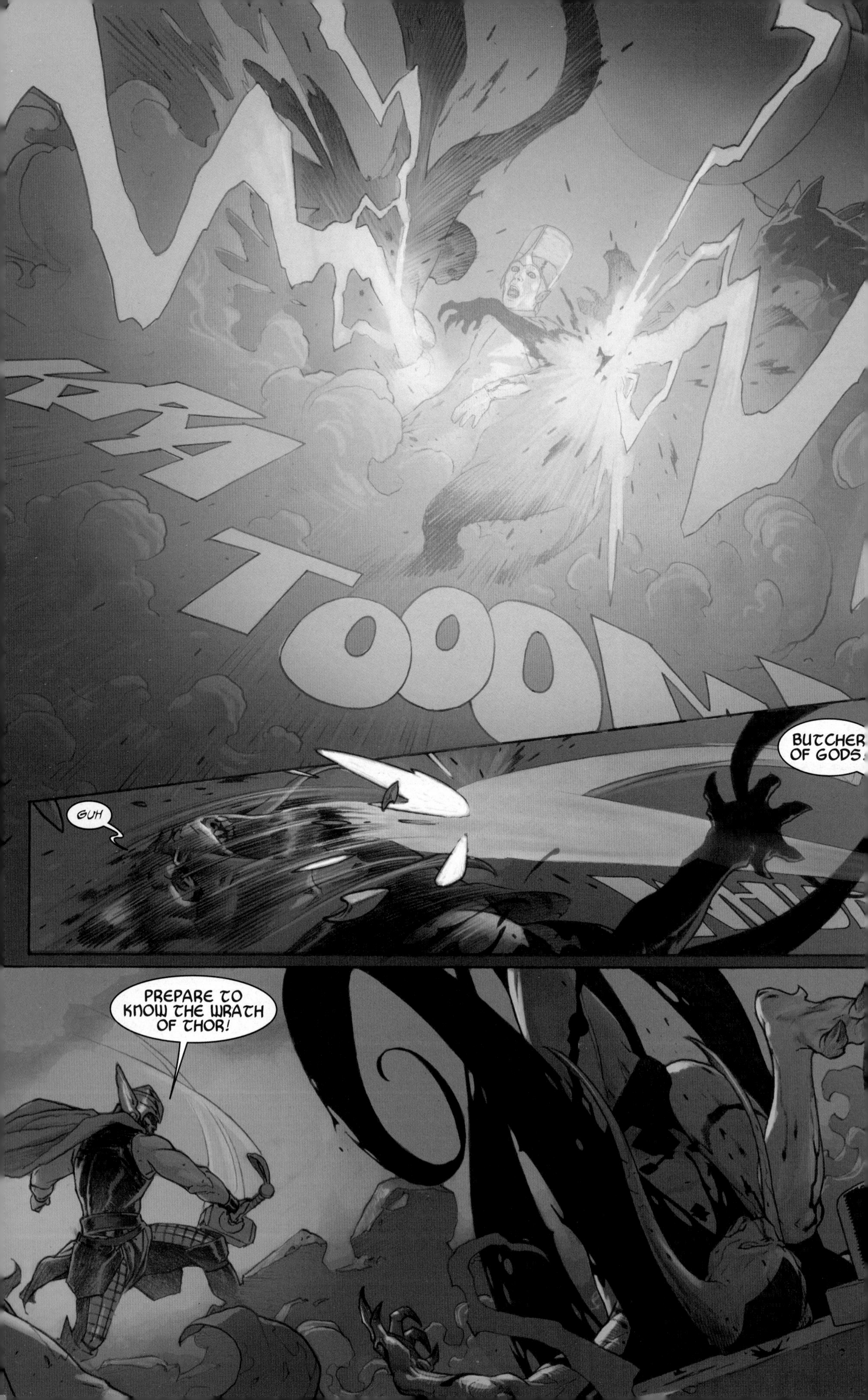
BUTCHER OF GODS!
GUH
PREPARE TO KNOW THE WRATH OF THOR!

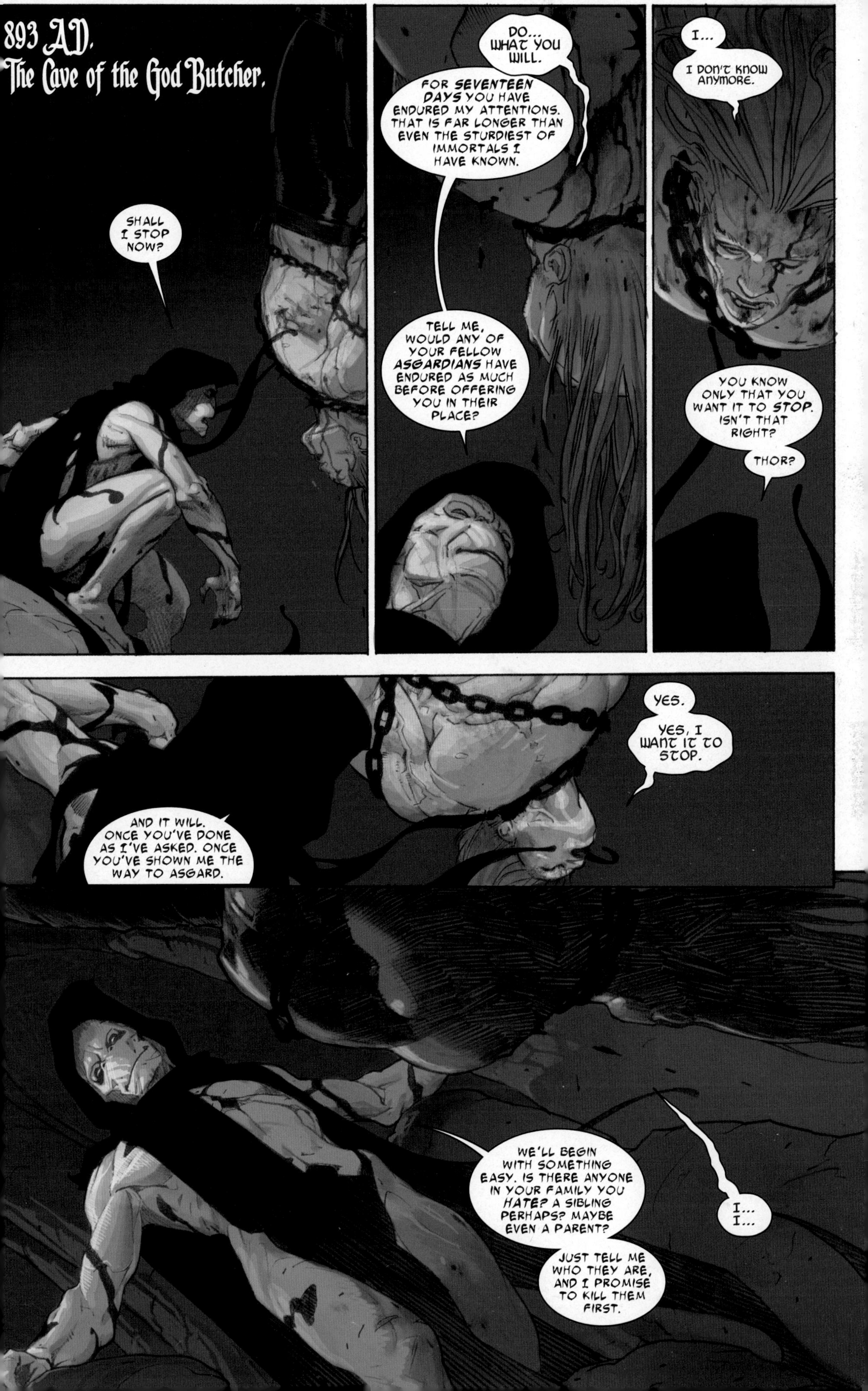
893 A.D.
The Cave of the God Butcher.
SHALL I STOP NOW?
DO... WHAT YOU WILL.
FOR SEVENTEEN DAYS YOU HAVE ENDURED MY ATTENTIONS. THAT IS FAR LONGER THAN EVEN THE STURDIEST OF IMMORTALS I HAVE KNOWN.
TELL ME, WOULD ANY OF YOUR FELLOW ASGARDIANS HAVE ENDURED AS MUCH BEFORE OFFERING YOU IN THEIR PLACE?
I...
I DON'T KNOW ANYMORE.
YOU KNOW ONLY THAT YOU WANT IT TO STOP. ISN'T THAT RIGHT?
THOR?
YES.
YES, I WANT IT TO STOP.
AND IT WILL. ONCE YOU'VE DONE AS I'VE ASKED. ONCE YOU'VE SHOWN ME THE WAY TO ASGARD.
WE'LL BEGIN WITH SOMETHING EASY. IS THERE ANYONE IN YOUR FAMILY YOU HATE? A SIBLING PERHAPS? MAYBE EVEN A PARENT?
JUST TELL ME WHO THEY ARE, AND I PROMISE TO KILL THEM FIRST.
I... I...

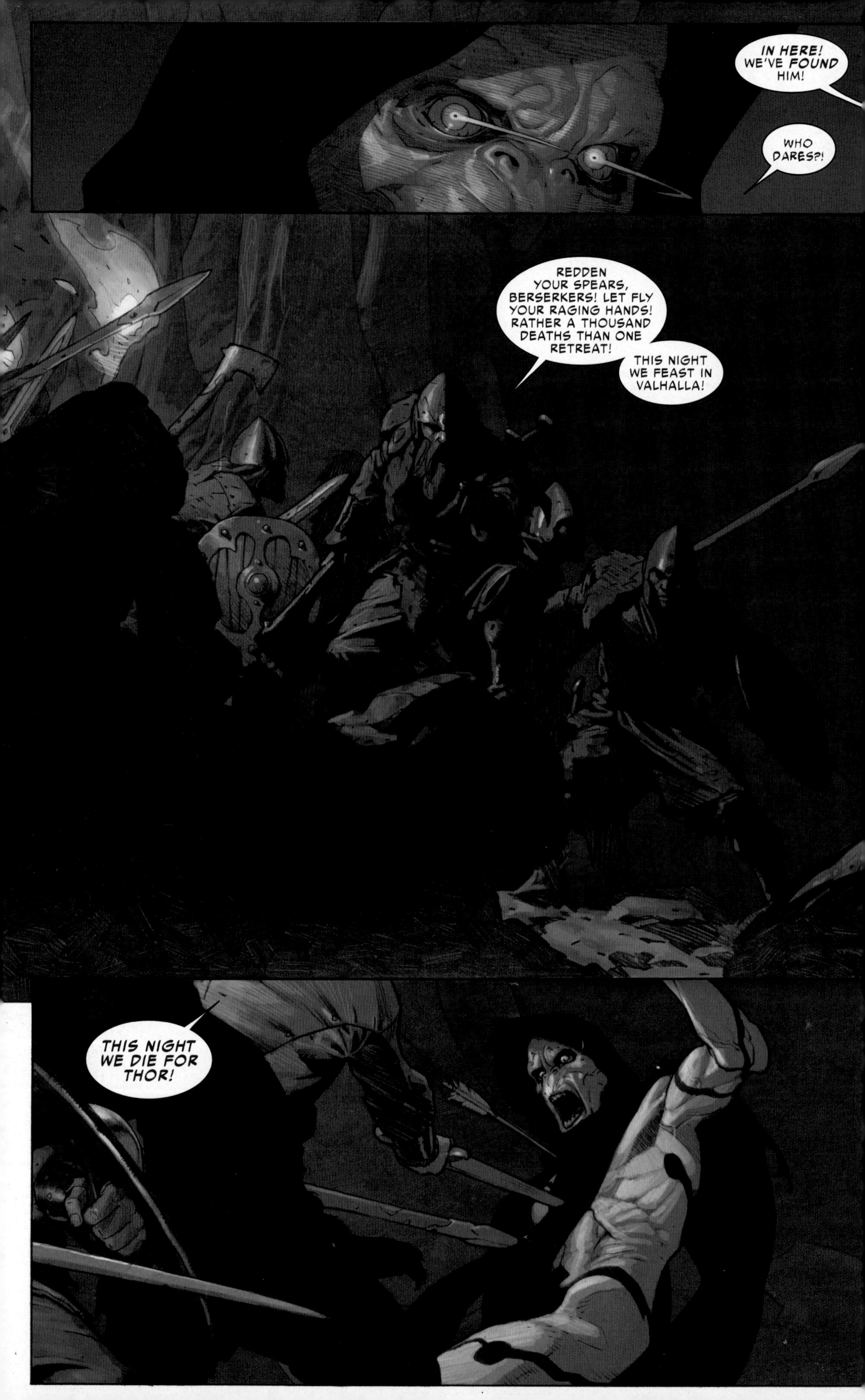
IN HERE! WE'VE FOUND HIM!
WHO DARES?!
REDDEN YOUR SPEARS, BERSERKERS! LET FLY YOUR RAGING HANDS! RATHER A THOUSAND DEATHS THAN ONE RETREAT!
THIS NIGHT WE FEAST IN VALHALLA!
THIS NIGHT WE DIE FOR THOR!

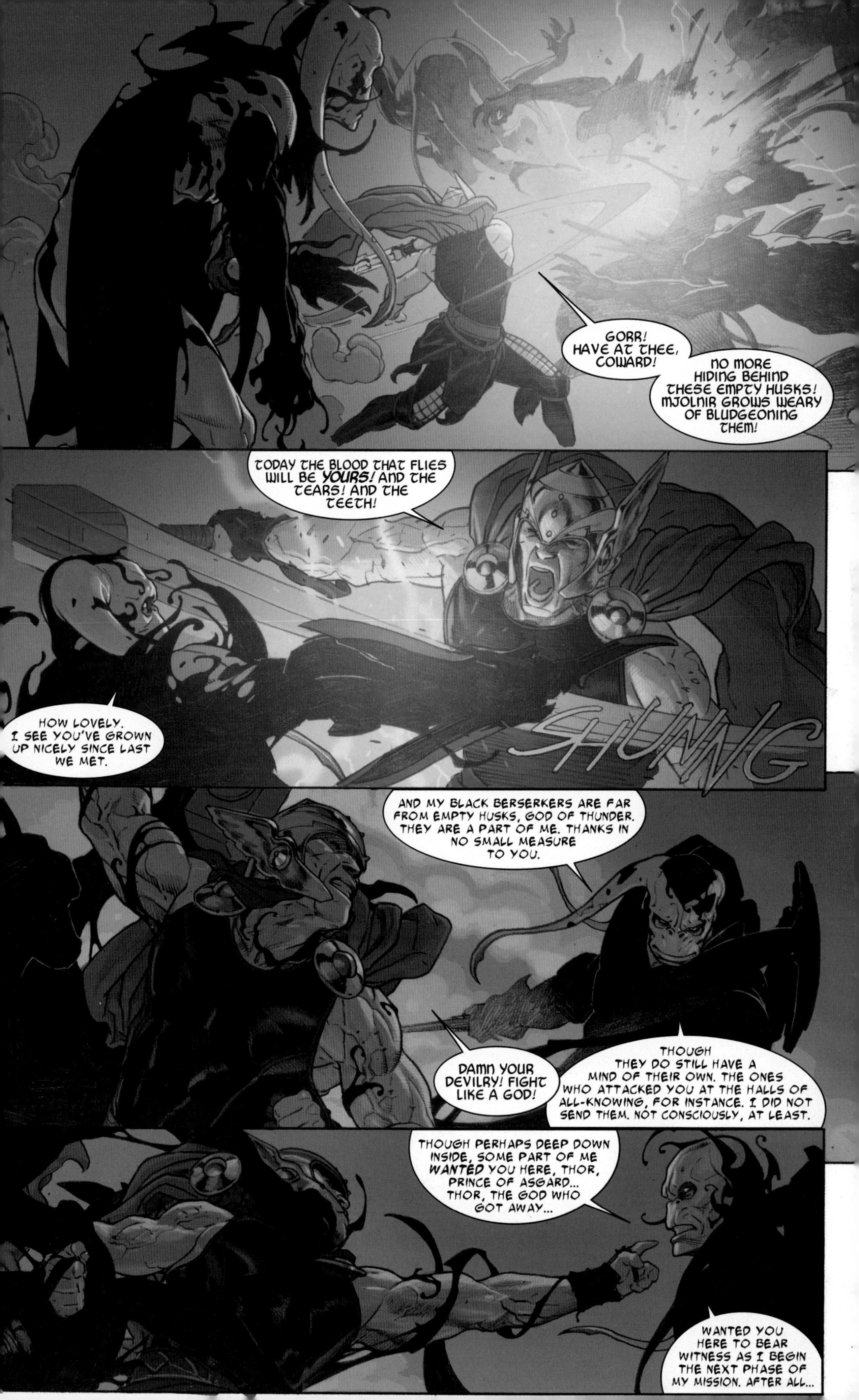
GORR! HAVE AT THEE, COWARD!
NO MORE HIDING BEHIND THESE EMPTY HUSKS! MJOLNIR GROWS WEARY OF BLUDGEONING THEM!
TODAY THE BLOOD THAT FLIES WILL BE YOURS! AND THE TEARS! AND THE TEETH!
HOW LOVELY. I SEE YOU'VE GROWN UP NICELY SINCE LAST WE MET.
SHUNNG
AND MY BLACK BERSERKERS ARE FAR FROM EMPTY HUSKS, GOD OF THUNDER. THEY ARE A PART OF ME. THANKS IN NO SMALL MEASURE TO YOU.
DAMN YOUR DEVILRY! FIGHT LIKE A GOD!
THOUGH THEY DO STILL HAVE A MIND OF THEIR OWN. THE ONES WHO ATTACKED YOU AT THE HALLS OF ALL-KNOWING, FOR INSTANCE. I DID NOT SEND THEM. NOT CONSCIOUSLY, AT LEAST.
THOUGH PERHAPS DEEP DOWN INSIDE, SOME PART OF ME WANTED YOU HERE, THOR, PRINCE OF ASGARD... THOR, THE GOD WHO GOT AWAY...
WANTED YOU HERE TO BEAR WITNESS AS I BEGIN THE NEXT PHASE OF MY MISSION. AFTER ALL...

"NONE OF THIS WOULD HAVE BEEN POSSIBLE WITHOUT YOU."

STOP THIS! I AM NOT HERE TO HURT YOU, MEN OF EARTH! I COME INSTEAD TO LIBERATE YOU AND YOUR KIND FROM THE YOKE OF DIVINE SERVITUDE!

DON'T WORRY, LORD THOR, WE'LL HAVE YOU FREE OF THESE CHAINS OR DIE TRY--

AND WE COME TO LIBERATE THAT HIDEOUS HEAD OF YOURS FROM ITS SHOULDERS! CUT HIM DOWN!

LISTEN TO ME, YOU FOOLS! DO NOT THROW YOUR LIVES AWAY ON SOMETHING AS USELESS AS A GOD!

GAAHHHK!!!

HE ISN'T WORTH YOUR DEVOTION! NONE OF THEM ARE! JUST LISTEN TO ME! LISTEN AND LET ME TELL YOU OF MY DREAM! A DREAM OF A--

FOR THE LOVE OF ODIN, SOMEONE GET A SPEAR IN THAT THROAT AND STOP THIS WRETCH'S MEWLING!

VERY WELL. DIE FOR YOUR GOD IF YOU WISH. SEE IF HE EVEN TAKES NOTICE.

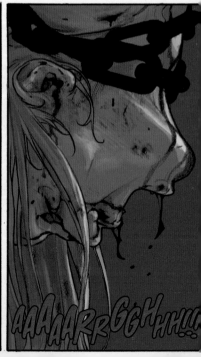

AAAAARRGGHHH!!!

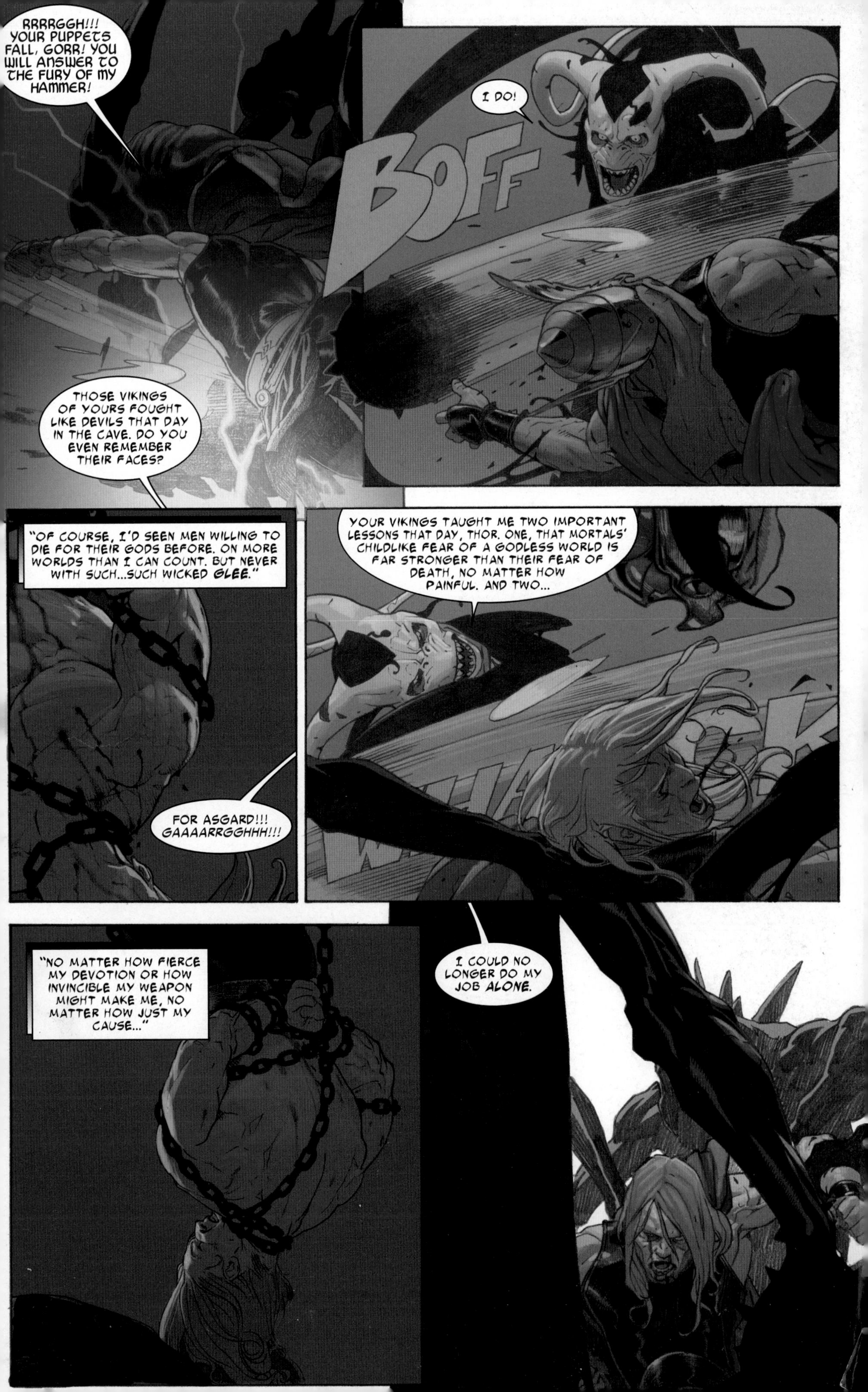

RRRRGGH!!! YOUR PUPPETS FALL, GORR! YOU WILL ANSWER TO THE FURY OF MY HAMMER!
I DO!
BOFF
THOSE VIKINGS OF YOURS FOUGHT LIKE DEVILS THAT DAY IN THE CAVE. DO YOU EVEN REMEMBER THEIR FACES?
"OF COURSE, I'D SEEN MEN WILLING TO DIE FOR THEIR GODS BEFORE. ON MORE WORLDS THAN I CAN COUNT. BUT NEVER WITH SUCH...SUCH WICKED GLEE."
FOR ASGARD!!! GAAAARRGGHHH!!!
YOUR VIKINGS TAUGHT ME TWO IMPORTANT LESSONS THAT DAY, THOR. ONE, THAT MORTALS' CHILDLIKE FEAR OF A GODLESS WORLD IS FAR STRONGER THAN THEIR FEAR OF DEATH, NO MATTER HOW PAINFUL. AND TWO...
"NO MATTER HOW FIERCE MY DEVOTION OR HOW INVINCIBLE MY WEAPON MIGHT MAKE ME, NO MATTER HOW JUST MY CAUSE..."
I COULD NO LONGER DO MY JOB ALONE.

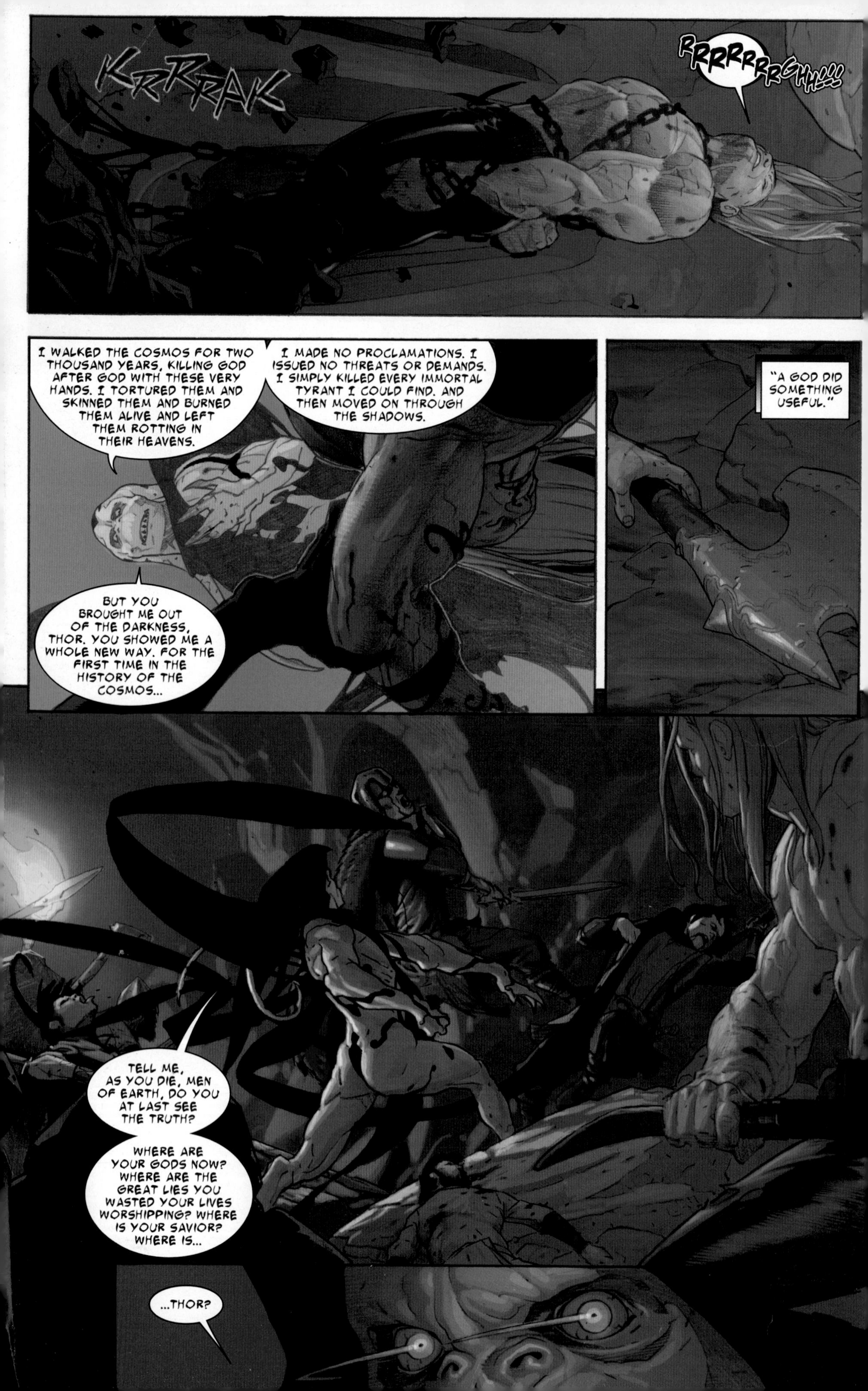
KRRRAK
RRRRRRRGHH!!!
I WALKED THE COSMOS FOR TWO THOUSAND YEARS, KILLING GOD AFTER GOD WITH THESE VERY HANDS. I TORTURED THEM AND SKINNED THEM AND BURNED THEM ALIVE AND LEFT THEM ROTTING IN THEIR HEAVENS.
I MADE NO PROCLAMATIONS. I ISSUED NO THREATS OR DEMANDS. I SIMPLY KILLED EVERY IMMORTAL TYRANT I COULD FIND, AND THEN MOVED ON THROUGH THE SHADOWS.
BUT YOU BROUGHT ME OUT OF THE DARKNESS, THOR. YOU SHOWED ME A WHOLE NEW WAY. FOR THE FIRST TIME IN THE HISTORY OF THE COSMOS...
"A GOD DID SOMETHING USEFUL."
TELL ME, AS YOU DIE, MEN OF EARTH, DO YOU AT LAST SEE THE TRUTH?
WHERE ARE YOUR GODS NOW? WHERE ARE THE GREAT LIES YOU WASTED YOUR LIVES WORSHIPPING? WHERE IS YOUR SAVIOR? WHERE IS...
...THOR?

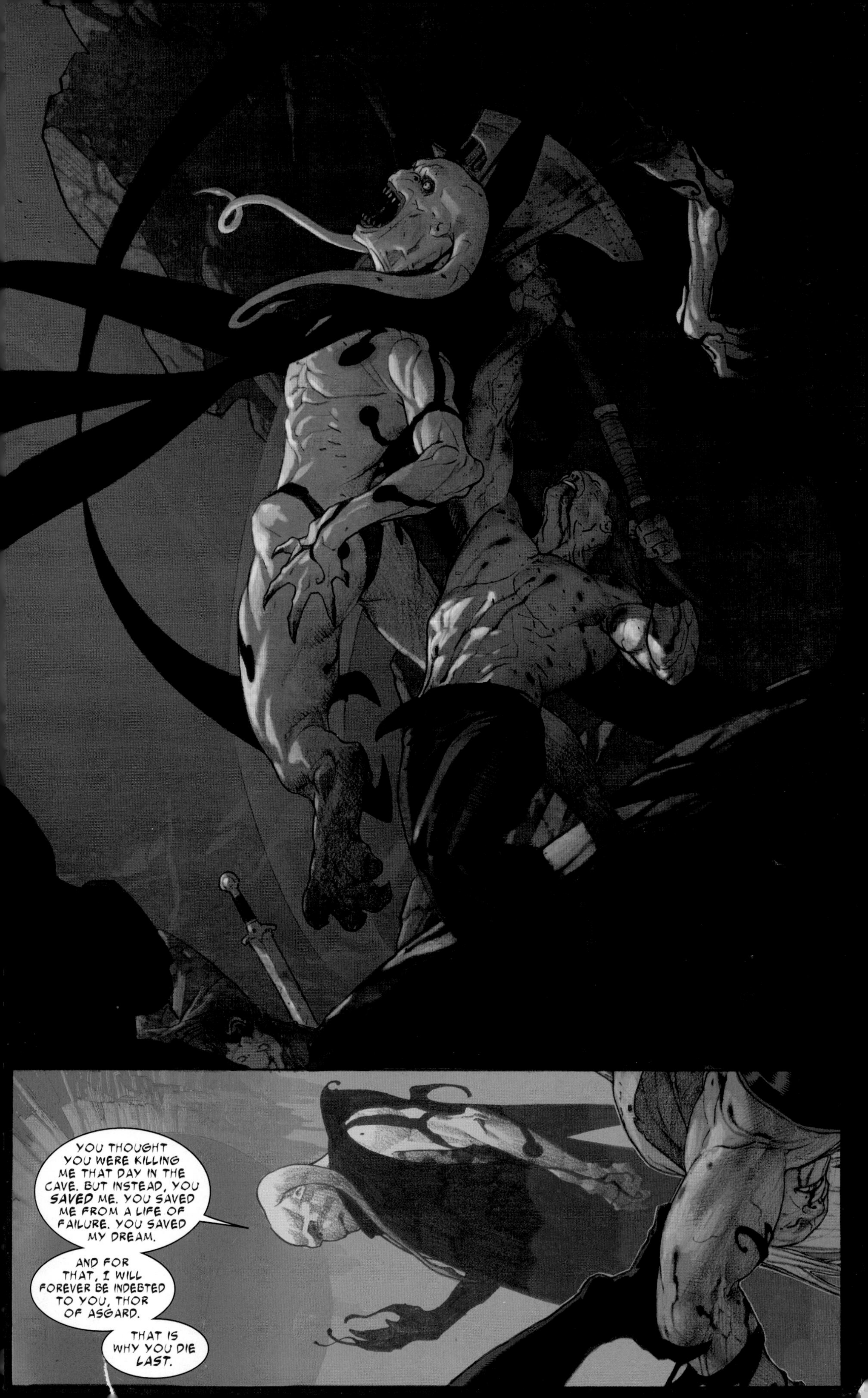
YOU THOUGHT YOU WERE KILLING ME THAT DAY IN THE CAVE. BUT INSTEAD, YOU SAVED ME. YOU SAVED ME FROM A LIFE OF FAILURE. YOU SAVED MY DREAM.
AND FOR THAT, I WILL FOREVER BE INDEBTED TO YOU, THOR OF ASGARD.
THAT IS WHY YOU DIE LAST.

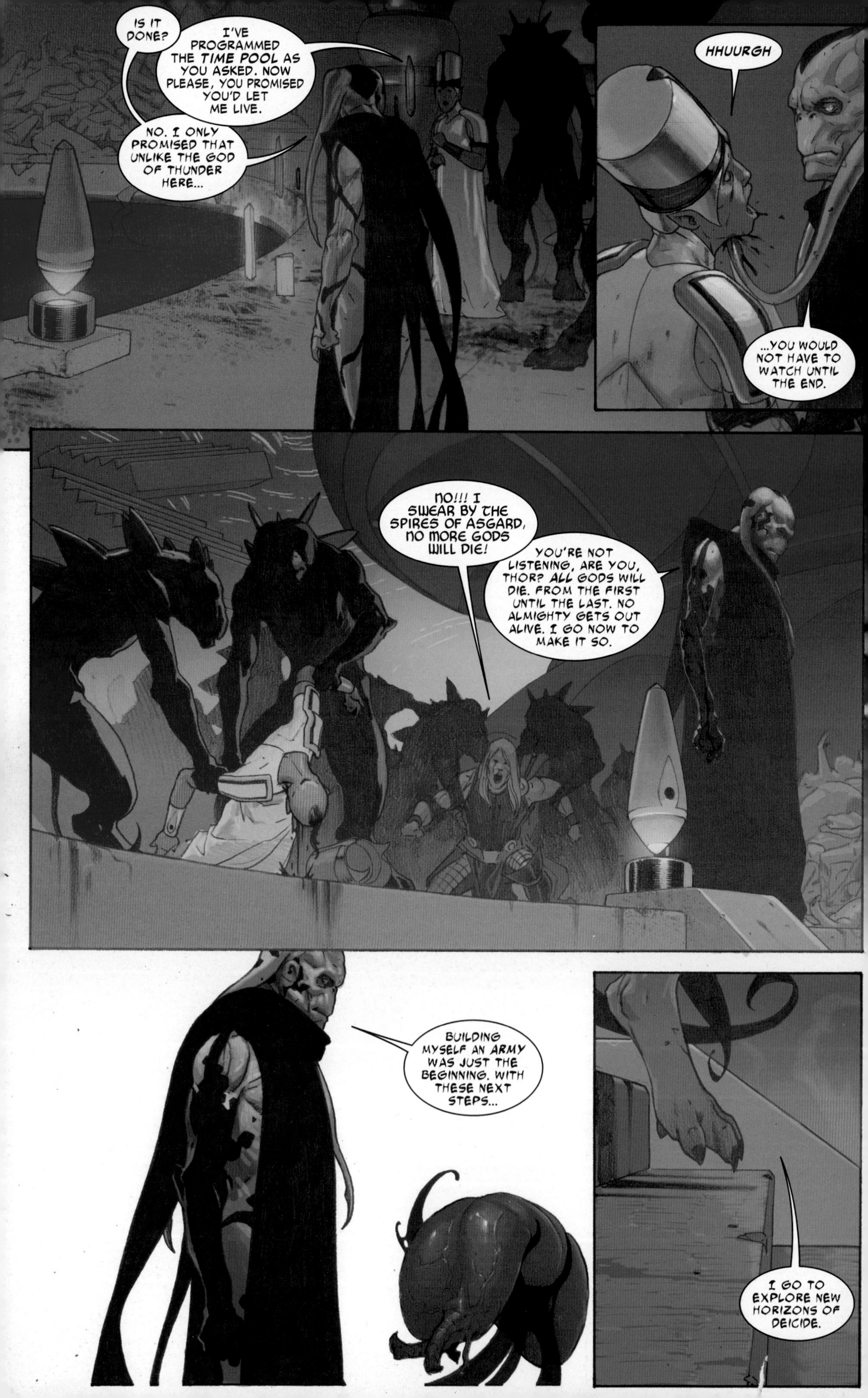
IS IT DONE?
I'VE PROGRAMMED THE TIME POOL AS YOU ASKED. NOW PLEASE, YOU PROMISED YOU'D LET ME LIVE.
NO. I ONLY PROMISED THAT UNLIKE THE GOD OF THUNDER HERE...
HHUURGH
...YOU WOULD NOT HAVE TO WATCH UNTIL THE END.
NO!!! I SWEAR BY THE SPIRES OF ASGARD, NO MORE GODS WILL DIE!
YOU'RE NOT LISTENING, ARE YOU, THOR? ALL GODS WILL DIE. FROM THE FIRST UNTIL THE LAST. NO ALMIGHTY GETS OUT ALIVE. I GO NOW TO MAKE IT SO.
BUILDING MYSELF AN ARMY WAS JUST THE BEGINNING. WITH THESE NEXT STEPS...
I GO TO EXPLORE NEW HORIZONS OF DEICIDE.

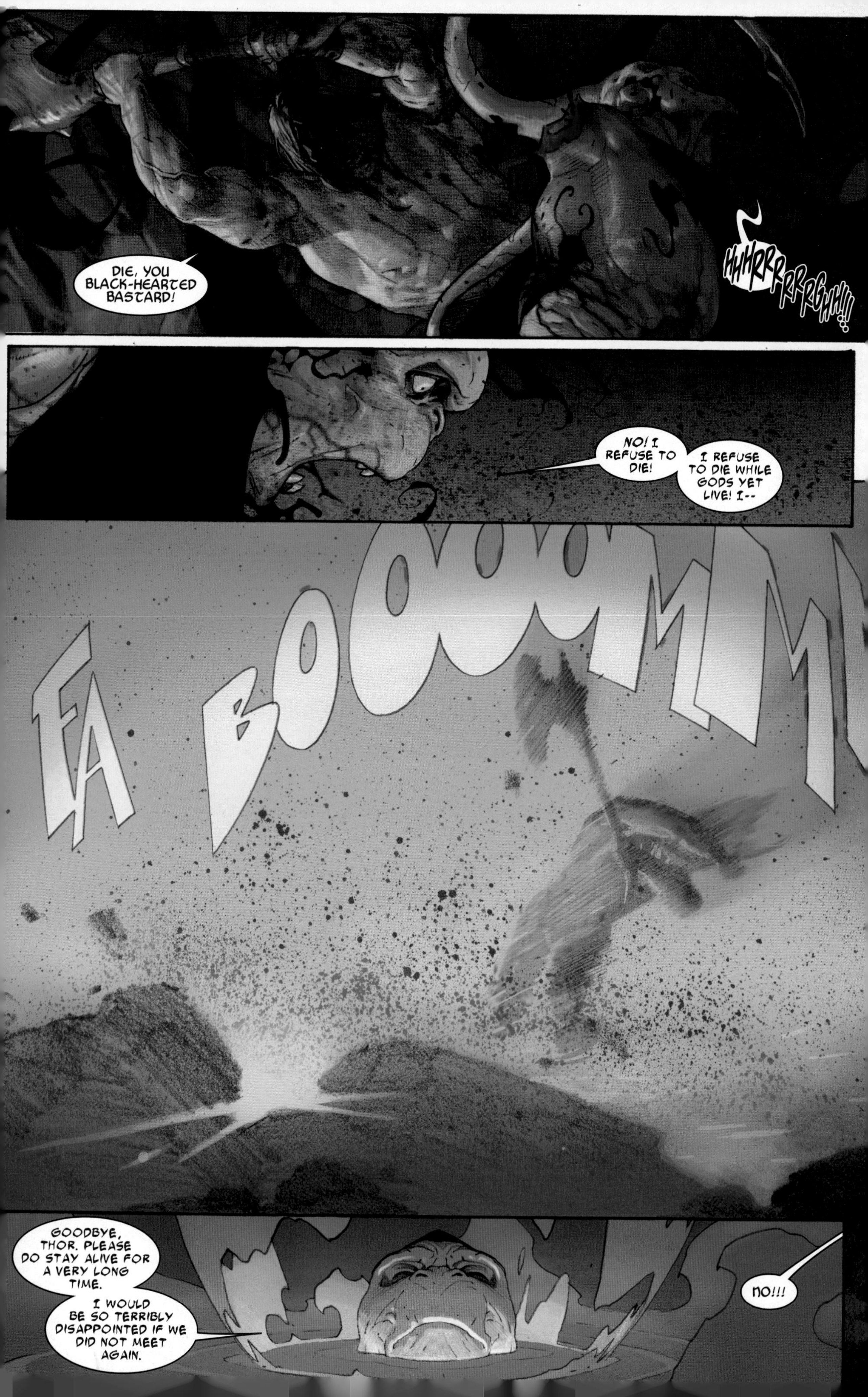

DIE, YOU BLACK-HEARTED BASTARD!
HHHRRRRRRGHH!!!
NO! I REFUSE TO DIE!
I REFUSE TO DIE WHILE GODS YET LIVE! I--
FA BOOOOMMM
GOODBYE, THOR. PLEASE DO STAY ALIVE FOR A VERY LONG TIME.
I WOULD BE SO TERRIBLY DISAPPOINTED IF WE DID NOT MEET AGAIN.
no!!!

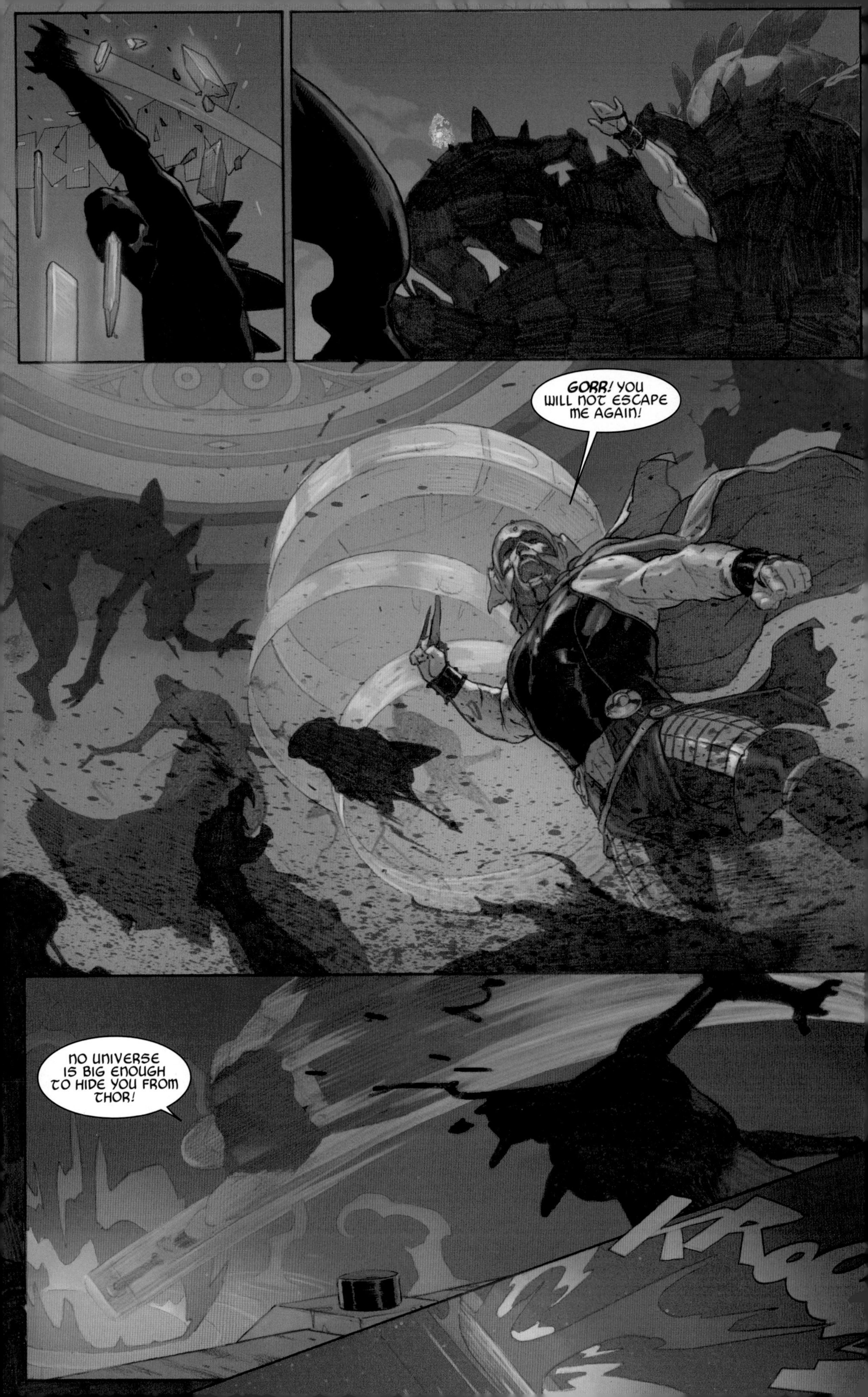
GORR! YOU WILL NOT ESCAPE ME AGAIN!
NO UNIVERSE IS BIG ENOUGH TO HIDE YOU FROM THOR!

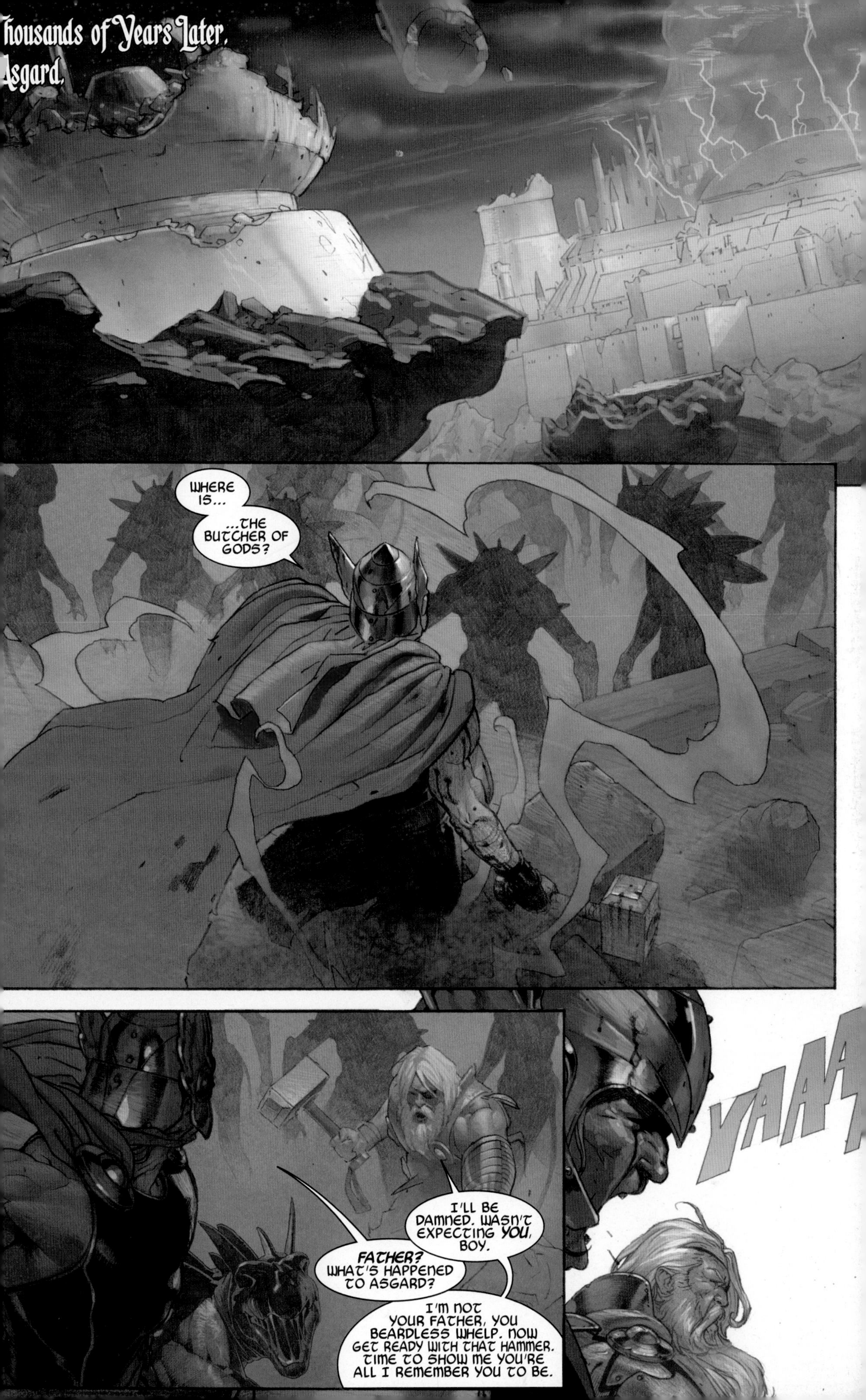

Thousands of Years Later,
Asgard.
WHERE IS... ...THE BUTCHER OF GODS?
FATHER? WHAT'S HAPPENED TO ASGARD?
I'LL BE DAMNED. WASN'T EXPECTING YOU, BOY.
I'M NOT YOUR FATHER, YOU BEARDLESS WHELP. NOW GET READY WITH THAT HAMMER. TIME TO SHOW ME YOU'RE ALL I REMEMBER YOU TO BE.
YAAA

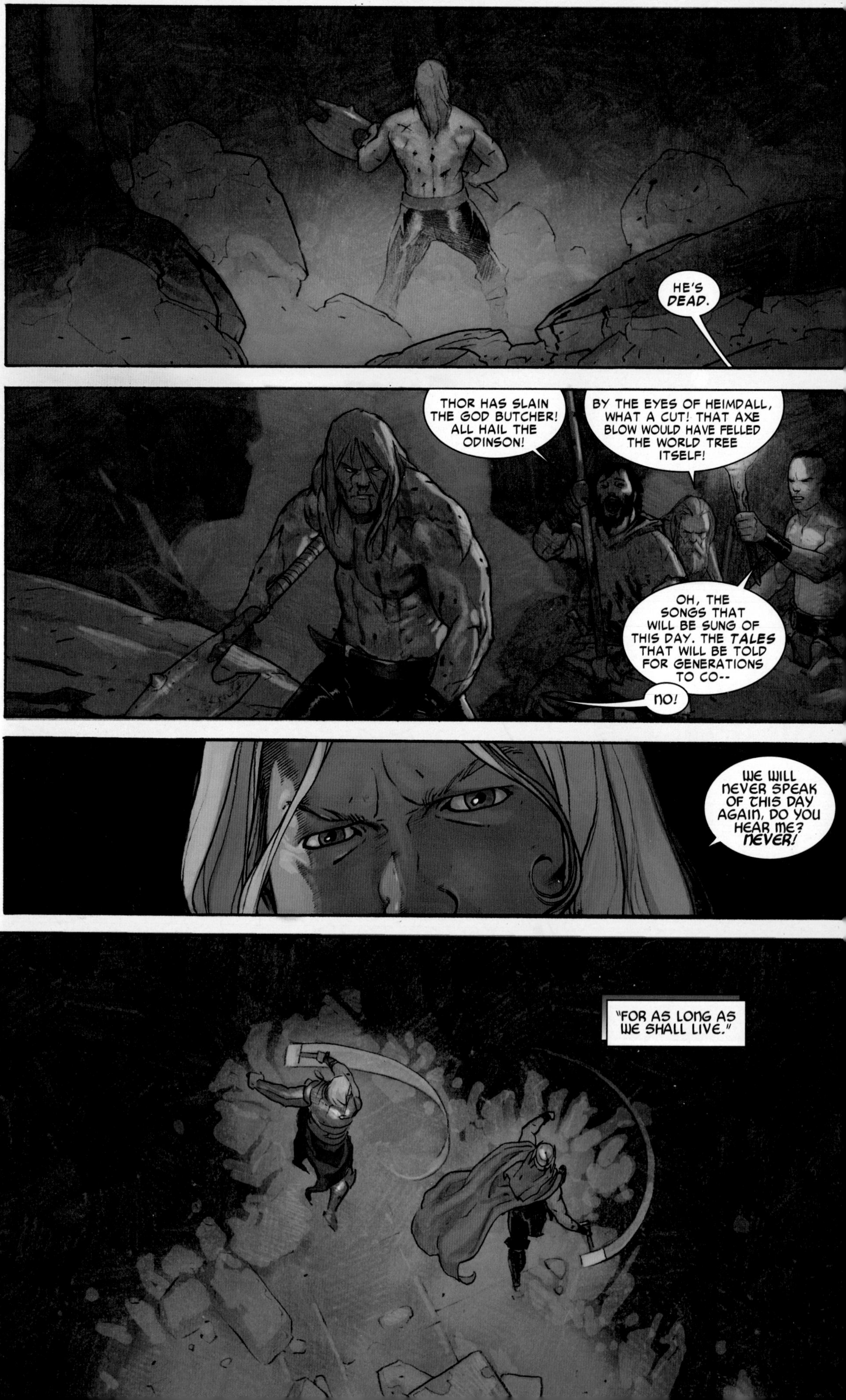
HE'S *DEAD*.
THOR HAS SLAIN THE GOD BUTCHER! ALL HAIL THE ODINSON!
BY THE EYES OF HEIMDALL, WHAT A CUT! THAT AXE BLOW WOULD HAVE FELLED THE WORLD TREE ITSELF!
OH, THE SONGS THAT WILL BE SUNG OF THIS DAY. THE *TALES* THAT WILL BE TOLD FOR GENERATIONS TO CO--
NO!
WE WILL NEVER SPEAK OF THIS DAY AGAIN, DO YOU HEAR ME? *NEVER!*
"FOR AS LONG AS WE SHALL LIVE."

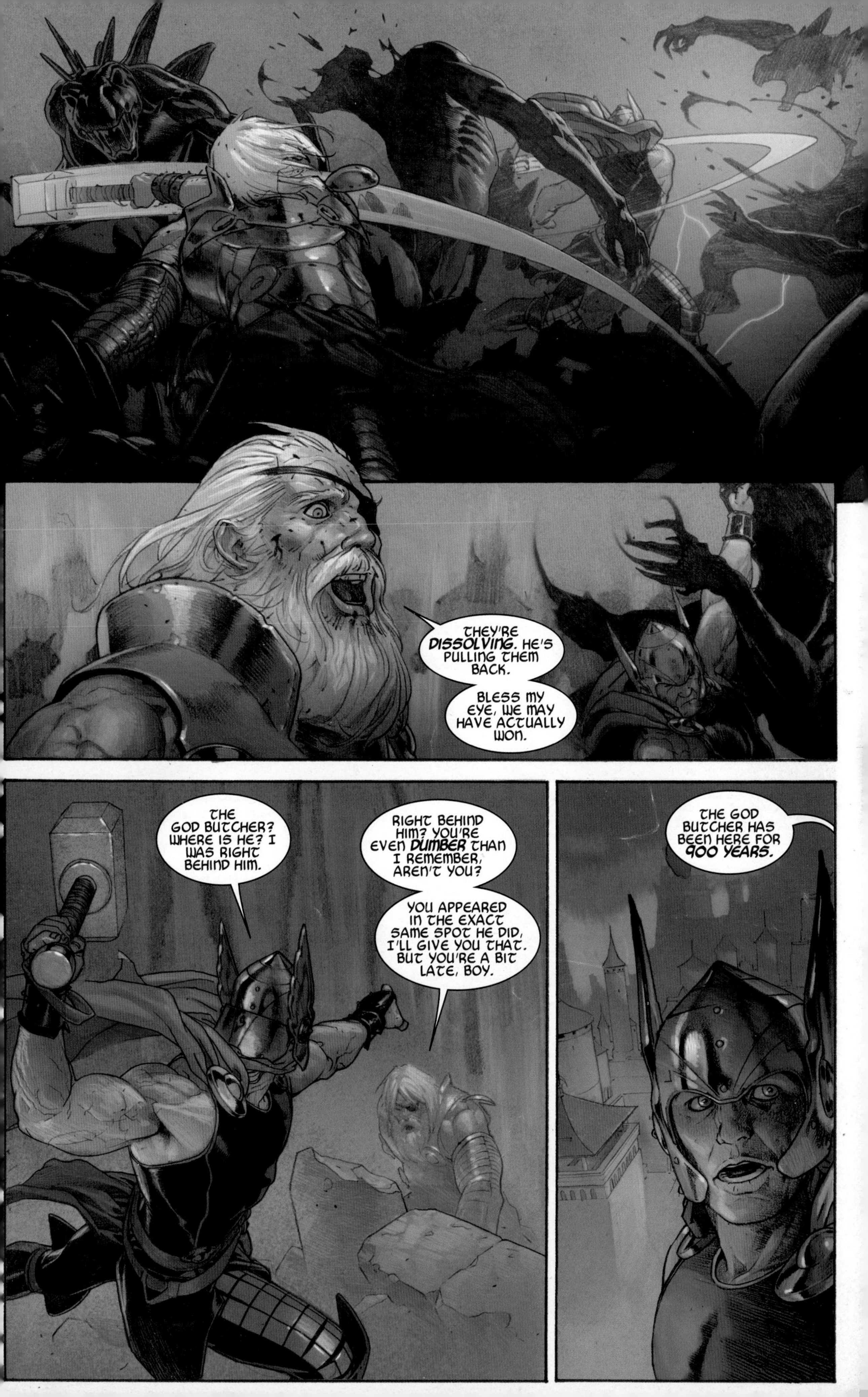
THEY'RE DISSOLVING. HE'S PULLING THEM BACK.
BLESS MY EYE, WE MAY HAVE ACTUALLY WON.
THE GOD BUTCHER? WHERE IS HE? I WAS RIGHT BEHIND HIM.
RIGHT BEHIND HIM? YOU'RE EVEN DUMBER THAN I REMEMBER, AREN'T YOU?
YOU APPEARED IN THE EXACT SAME SPOT HE DID, I'LL GIVE YOU THAT. BUT YOU'RE A BIT LATE, BOY.
THE GOD BUTCHER HAS BEEN HERE FOR 900 YEARS.

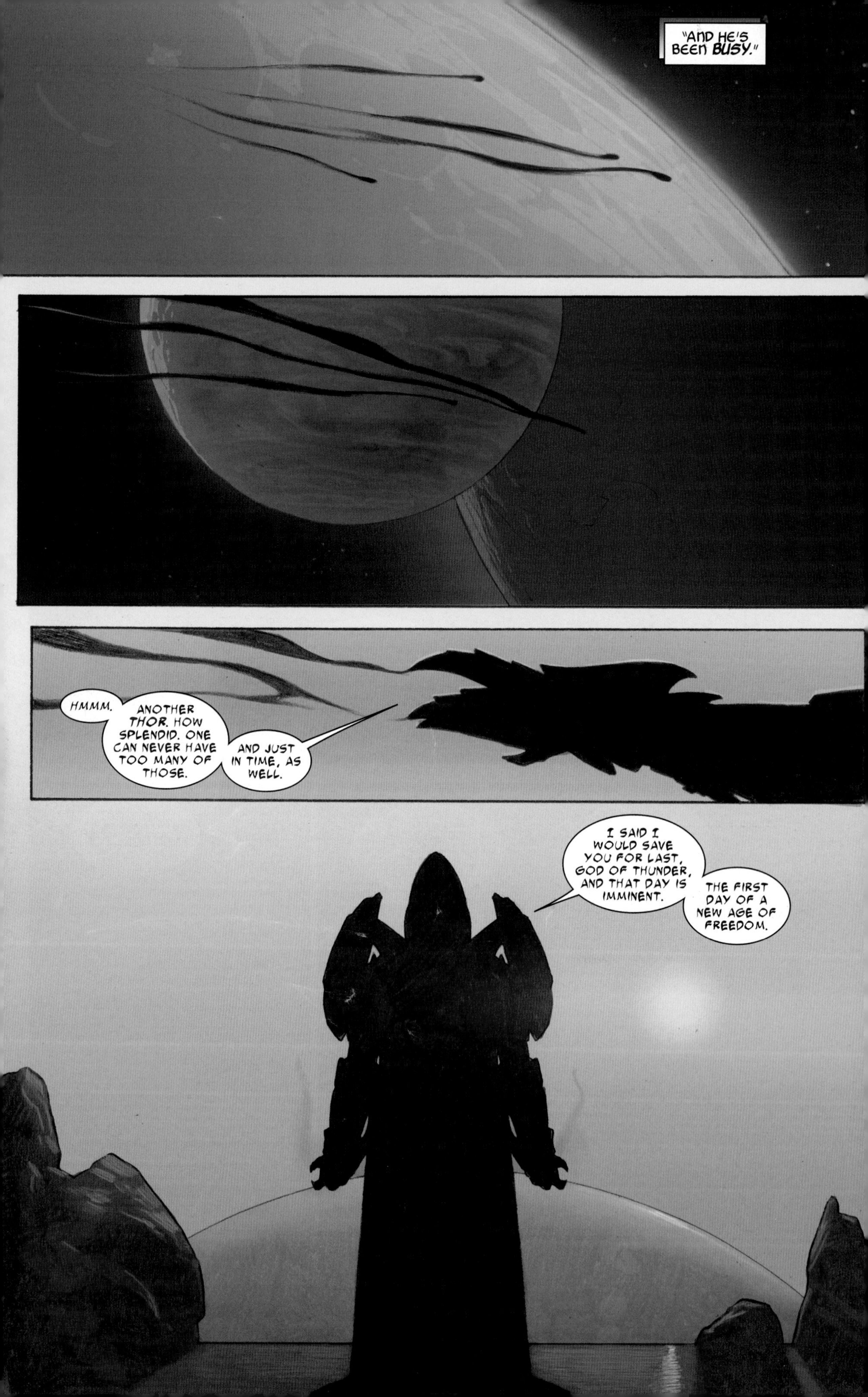
"AND HE'S BEEN BUSY."
HMMM.
ANOTHER THOR. HOW SPLENDID. ONE CAN NEVER HAVE TOO MANY OF THOSE.
AND JUST IN TIME, AS WELL.
I SAID I WOULD SAVE YOU FOR LAST, GOD OF THUNDER, AND THAT DAY IS IMMINENT.
THE FIRST DAY OF A NEW AGE OF FREEDOM.

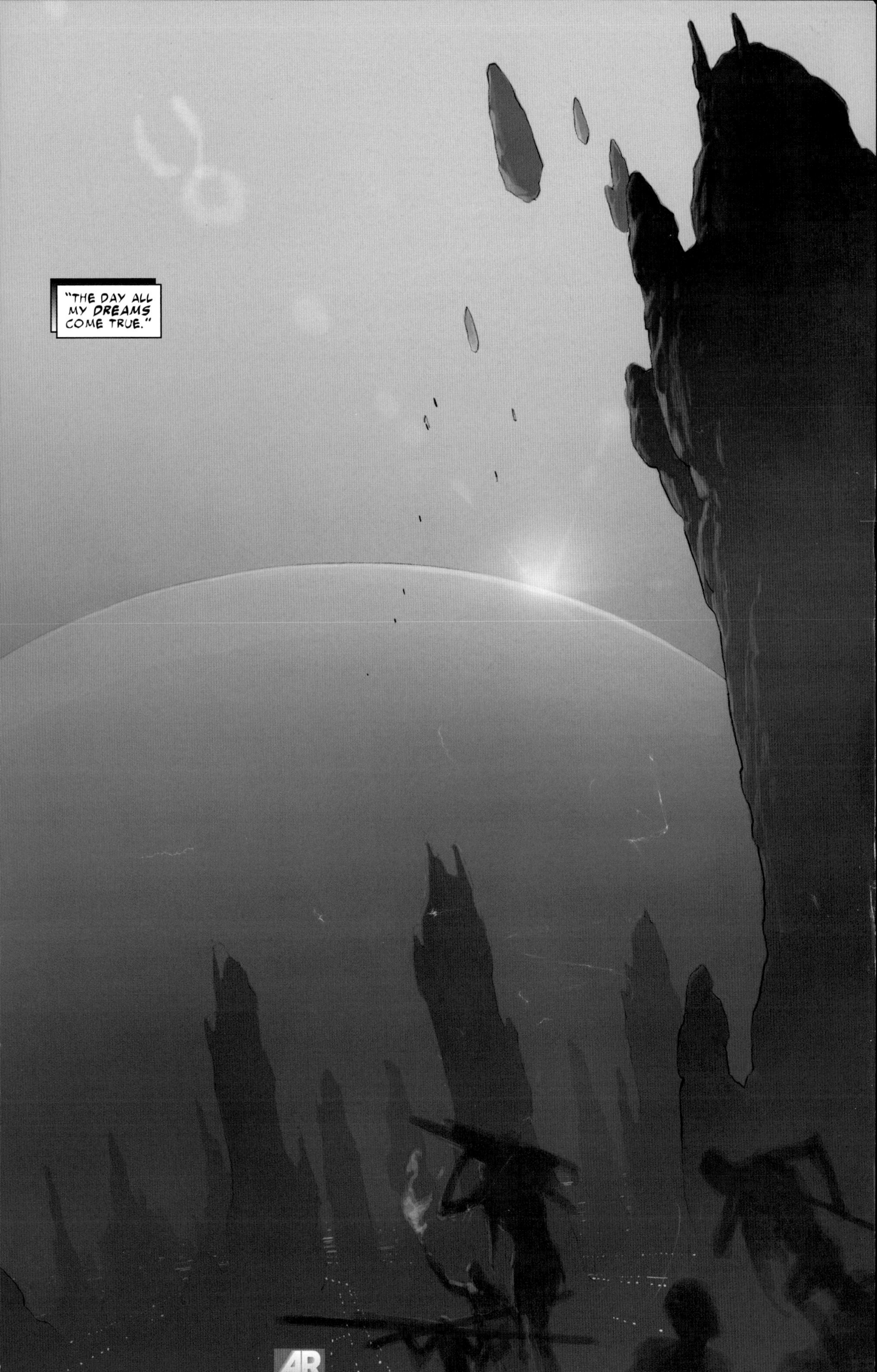
"THE DAY ALL MY DREAMS COME TRUE."

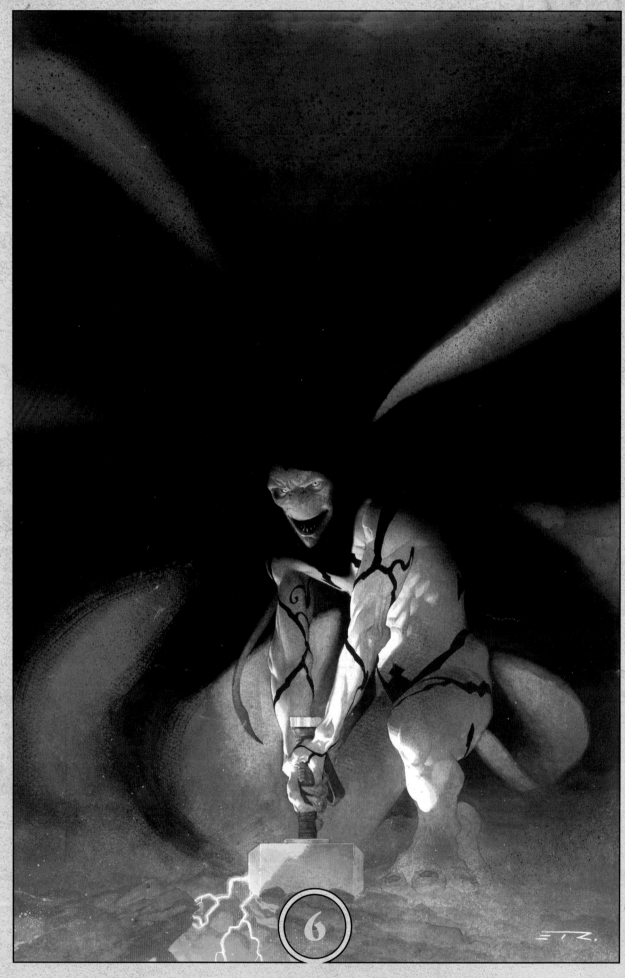

WHAT THE GODS HAVE WROUGHT

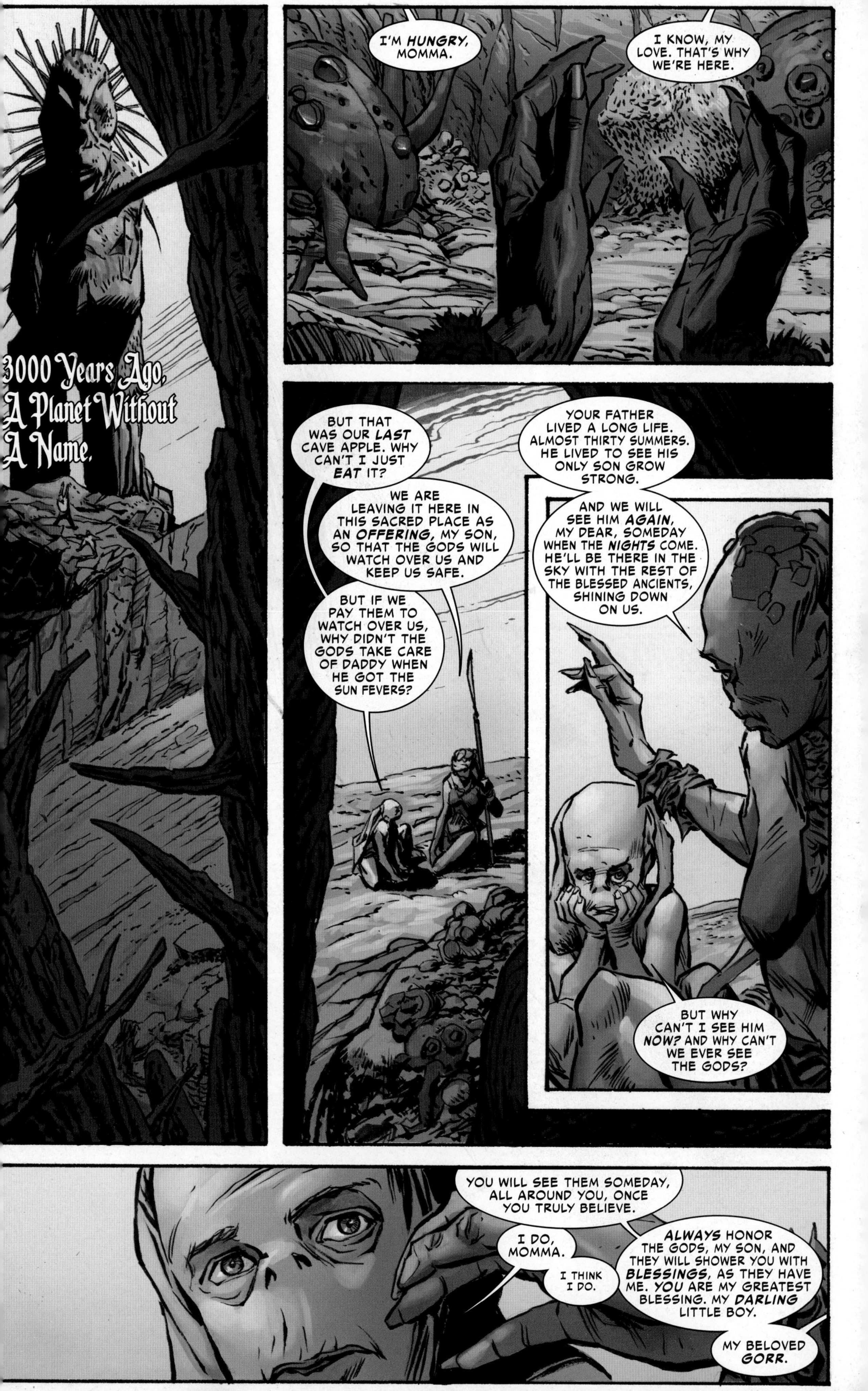
3000 Years Ago, A Planet Without A Name.
I'M HUNGRY, MOMMA.
I KNOW, MY LOVE. THAT'S WHY WE'RE HERE.
BUT THAT WAS OUR LAST CAVE APPLE. WHY CAN'T I JUST EAT IT?
WE ARE LEAVING IT HERE IN THIS SACRED PLACE AS AN OFFERING, MY SON, SO THAT THE GODS WILL WATCH OVER US AND KEEP US SAFE.
BUT IF WE PAY THEM TO WATCH OVER US, WHY DIDN'T THE GODS TAKE CARE OF DADDY WHEN HE GOT THE SUN FEVERS?
YOUR FATHER LIVED A LONG LIFE. ALMOST THIRTY SUMMERS. HE LIVED TO SEE HIS ONLY SON GROW STRONG.
AND WE WILL SEE HIM AGAIN, MY DEAR, SOMEDAY WHEN THE NIGHTS COME. HE'LL BE THERE IN THE SKY WITH THE REST OF THE BLESSED ANCIENTS, SHINING DOWN ON US.
BUT WHY CAN'T I SEE HIM NOW? AND WHY CAN'T WE EVER SEE THE GODS?
YOU WILL SEE THEM SOMEDAY, ALL AROUND YOU, ONCE YOU TRULY BELIEVE.
I DO, MOMMA.
I THINK I DO.
ALWAYS HONOR THE GODS, MY SON, AND THEY WILL SHOWER YOU WITH BLESSINGS, AS THEY HAVE ME. YOU ARE MY GREATEST BLESSING. MY DARLING LITTLE BOY.
MY BELOVED GORR.

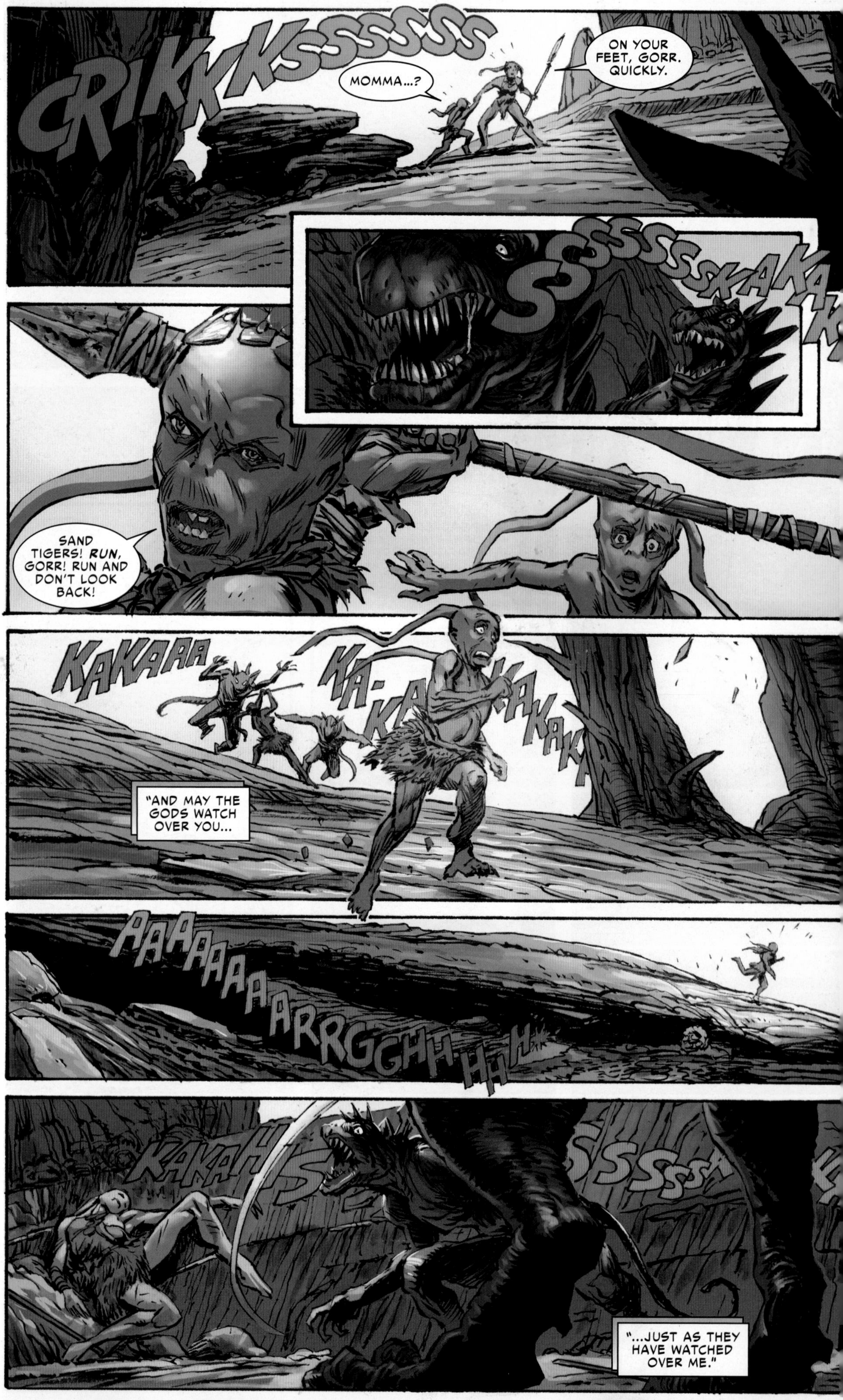
CRIKKKSSSSSSS
MOMMA...?
ON YOUR FEET, GORR. QUICKLY.
SSSSSSSSKAKAKAK
SAND TIGERS! RUN, GORR! RUN AND DON'T LOOK BACK!
KAKAAA
KA-KA-KAKAKAKA
"AND MAY THE GODS WATCH OVER YOU...
AAAAAAAAARRRGGHHHHH
KAKAKAH
SSSSSS
"...JUST AS THEY HAVE WATCHED OVER ME."

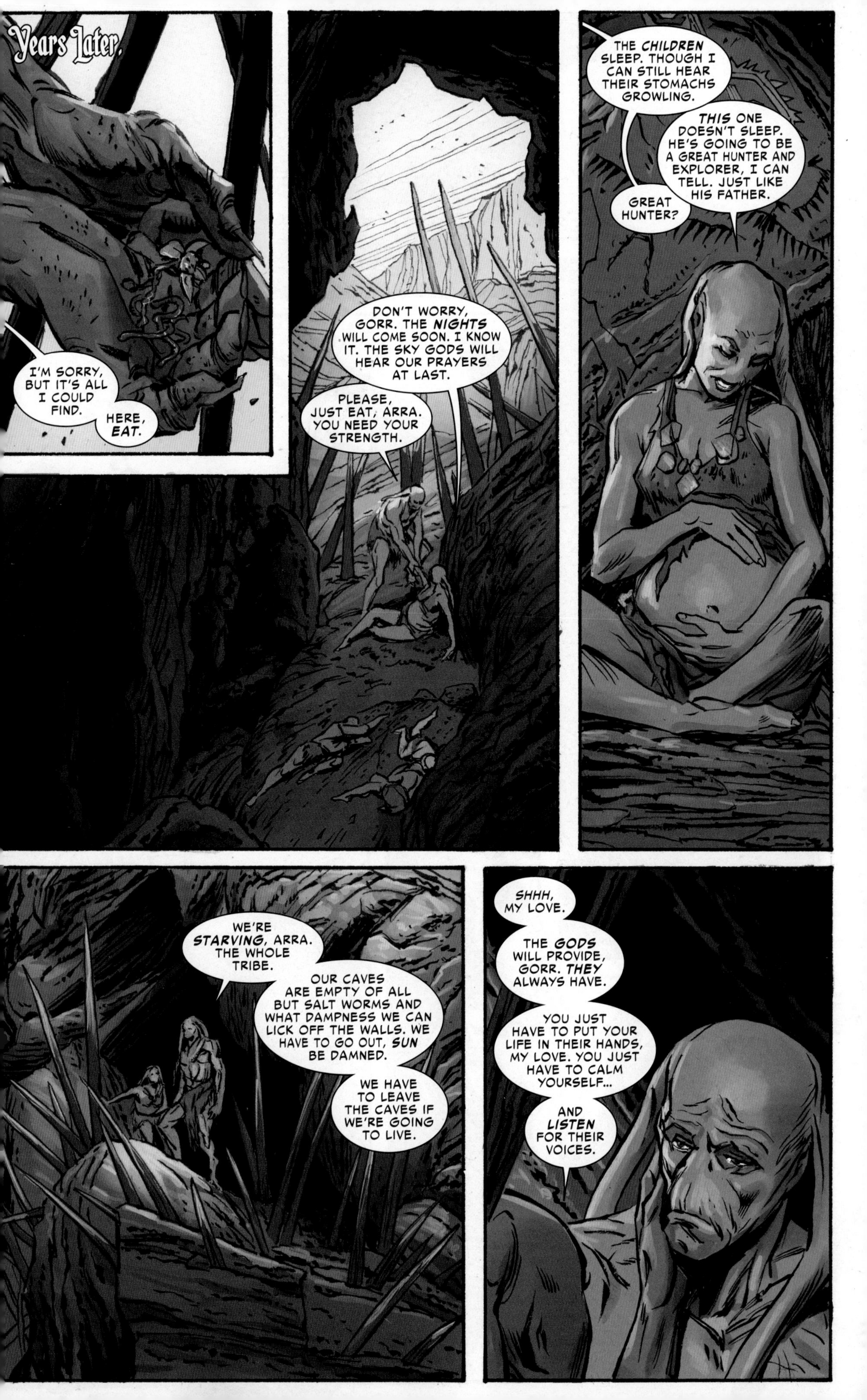
Years Later.
I'M SORRY, BUT IT'S ALL I COULD FIND.
HERE, EAT.
DON'T WORRY, GORR. THE NIGHTS WILL COME SOON. I KNOW IT. THE SKY GODS WILL HEAR OUR PRAYERS AT LAST.
PLEASE, JUST EAT, ARRA. YOU NEED YOUR STRENGTH.
THE CHILDREN SLEEP. THOUGH I CAN STILL HEAR THEIR STOMACHS GROWLING.
THIS ONE DOESN'T SLEEP. HE'S GOING TO BE A GREAT HUNTER AND EXPLORER, I CAN TELL. JUST LIKE HIS FATHER.
GREAT HUNTER?
WE'RE STARVING, ARRA. THE WHOLE TRIBE.
OUR CAVES ARE EMPTY OF ALL BUT SALT WORMS AND WHAT DAMPNESS WE CAN LICK OFF THE WALLS. WE HAVE TO GO OUT, SUN BE DAMNED.
WE HAVE TO LEAVE THE CAVES IF WE'RE GOING TO LIVE.
SHHH, MY LOVE.
THE GODS WILL PROVIDE, GORR. THEY ALWAYS HAVE.
YOU JUST HAVE TO PUT YOUR LIFE IN THEIR HANDS, MY LOVE. YOU JUST HAVE TO CALM YOURSELF...
AND LISTEN FOR THEIR VOICES.

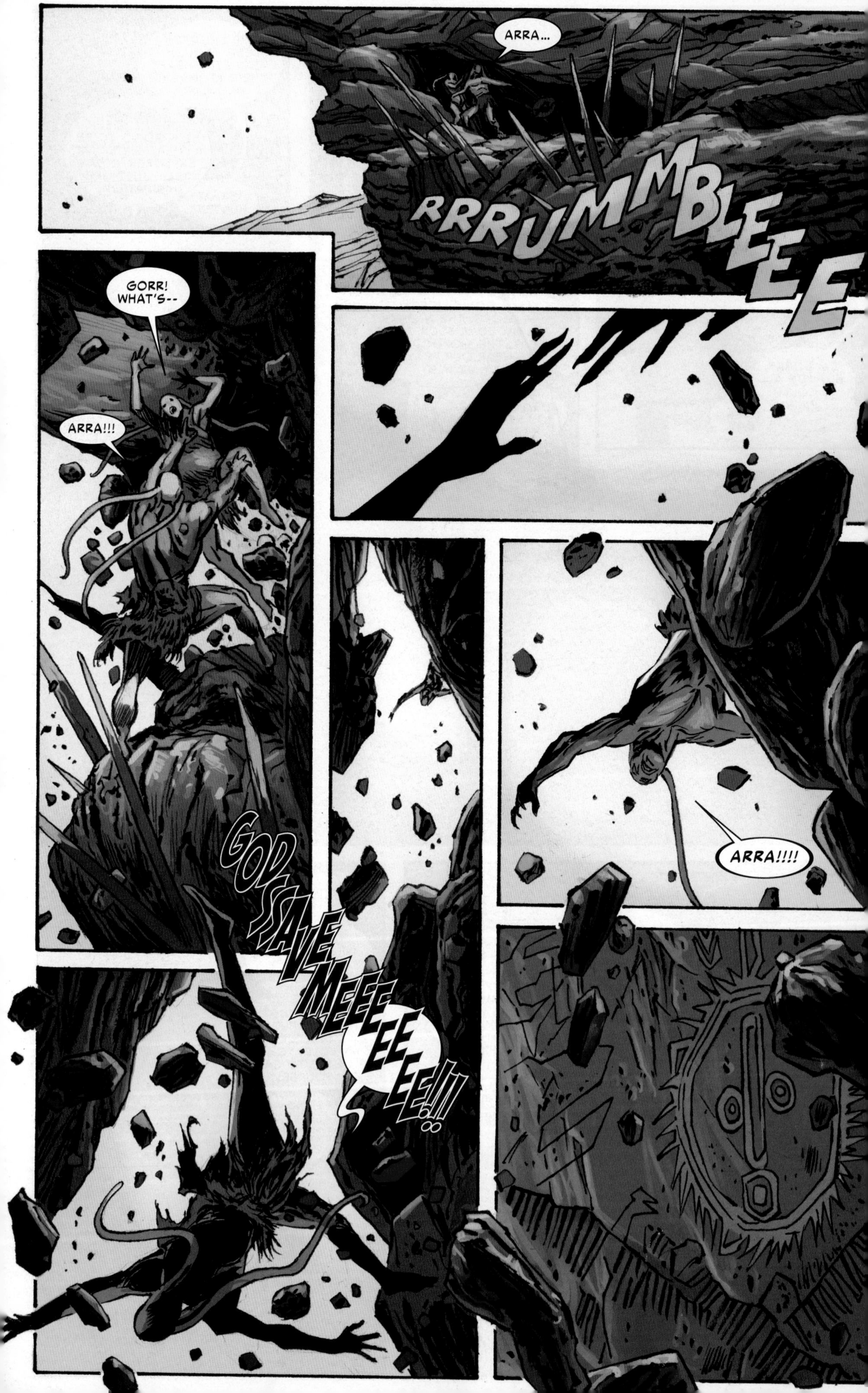

ARRA...
RRRUMMBLEEEE
GORR! WHAT'S--
ARRA!!!
ARRA!!!!
GODS SAVE MEEEEEEE!!!

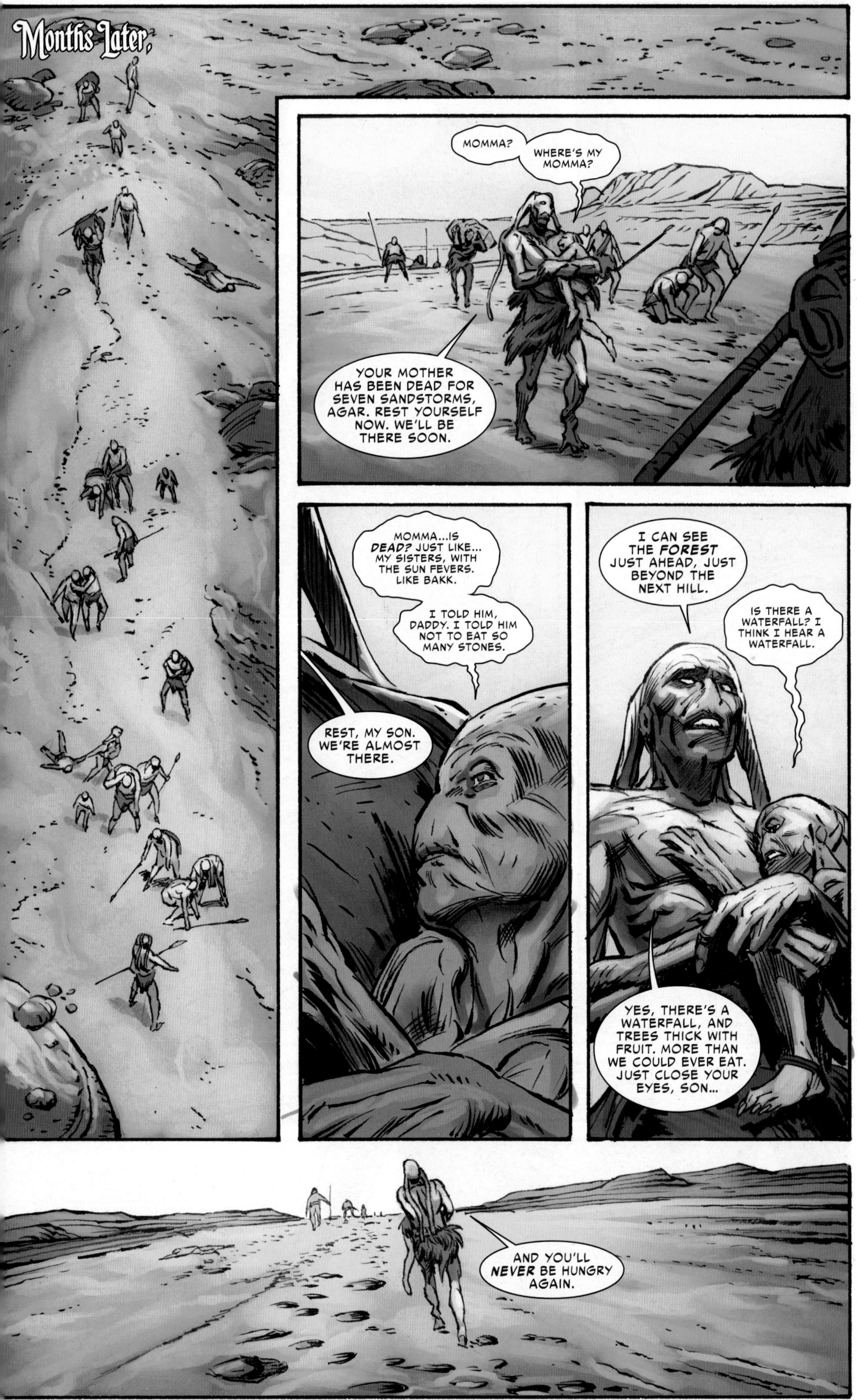
Months Later,
MOMMA?
WHERE'S MY MOMMA?
YOUR MOTHER HAS BEEN DEAD FOR SEVEN SANDSTORMS, AGAR. REST YOURSELF NOW. WE'LL BE THERE SOON.
MOMMA...IS DEAD? JUST LIKE... MY SISTERS, WITH THE SUN FEVERS. LIKE BAKK.
I TOLD HIM, DADDY. I TOLD HIM NOT TO EAT SO MANY STONES.
REST, MY SON. WE'RE ALMOST THERE.
I CAN SEE THE FOREST JUST AHEAD, JUST BEYOND THE NEXT HILL.
IS THERE A WATERFALL? I THINK I HEAR A WATERFALL.
YES, THERE'S A WATERFALL, AND TREES THICK WITH FRUIT. MORE THAN WE COULD EVER EAT. JUST CLOSE YOUR EYES, SON...
AND YOU'LL NEVER BE HUNGRY AGAIN.

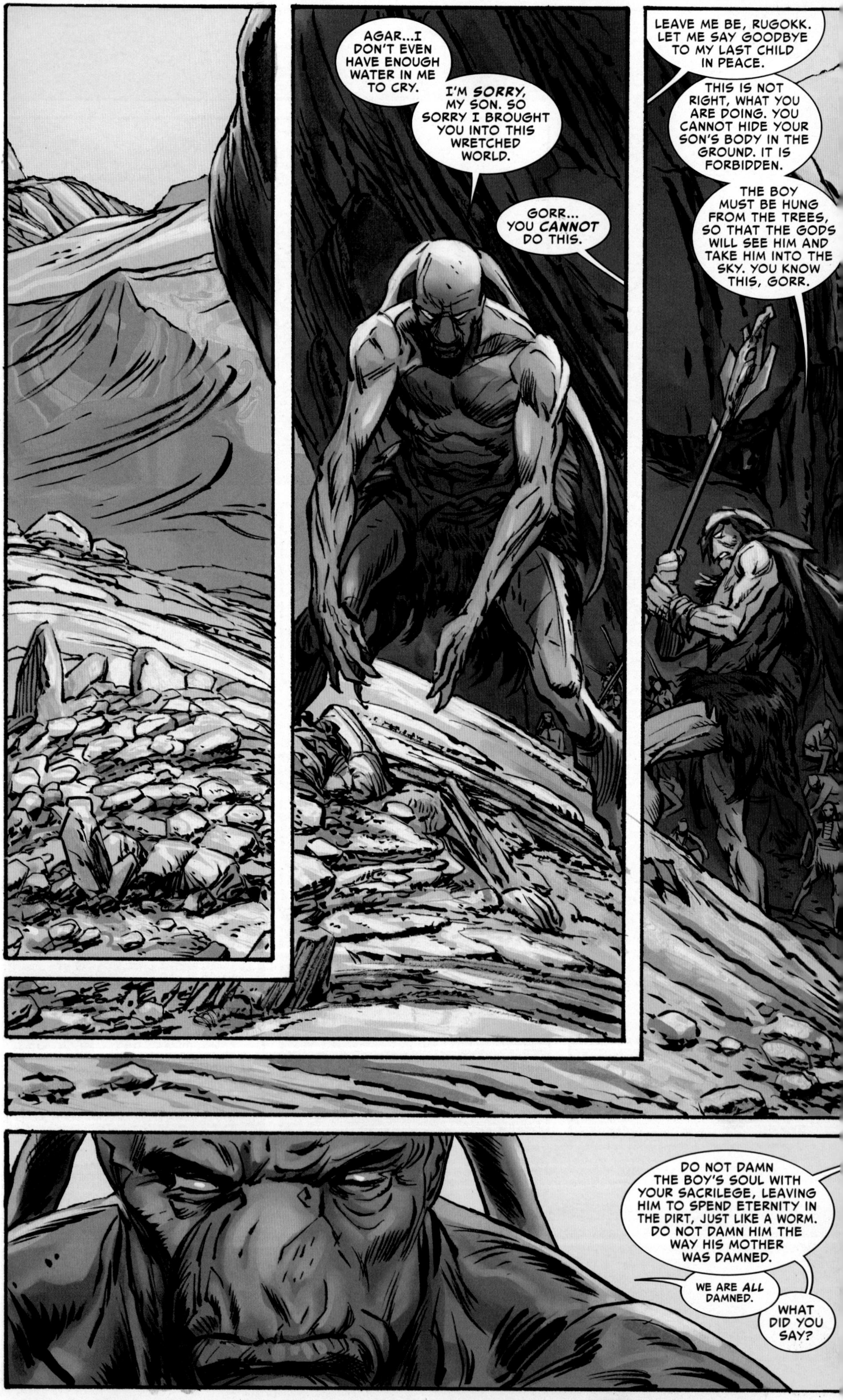

AGAR...I DON'T EVEN HAVE ENOUGH WATER IN ME TO CRY.
I'M SORRY, MY SON. SO SORRY I BROUGHT YOU INTO THIS WRETCHED WORLD.
GORR... YOU CANNOT DO THIS.
LEAVE ME BE, RUGOKK. LET ME SAY GOODBYE TO MY LAST CHILD IN PEACE.
THIS IS NOT RIGHT, WHAT YOU ARE DOING. YOU CANNOT HIDE YOUR SON'S BODY IN THE GROUND. IT IS FORBIDDEN.
THE BOY MUST BE HUNG FROM THE TREES, SO THAT THE GODS WILL SEE HIM AND TAKE HIM INTO THE SKY. YOU KNOW THIS, GORR.
DO NOT DAMN THE BOY'S SOUL WITH YOUR SACRILEGE, LEAVING HIM TO SPEND ETERNITY IN THE DIRT, JUST LIKE A WORM. DO NOT DAMN HIM THE WAY HIS MOTHER WAS DAMNED.
WE ARE ALL DAMNED.
WHAT DID YOU SAY?

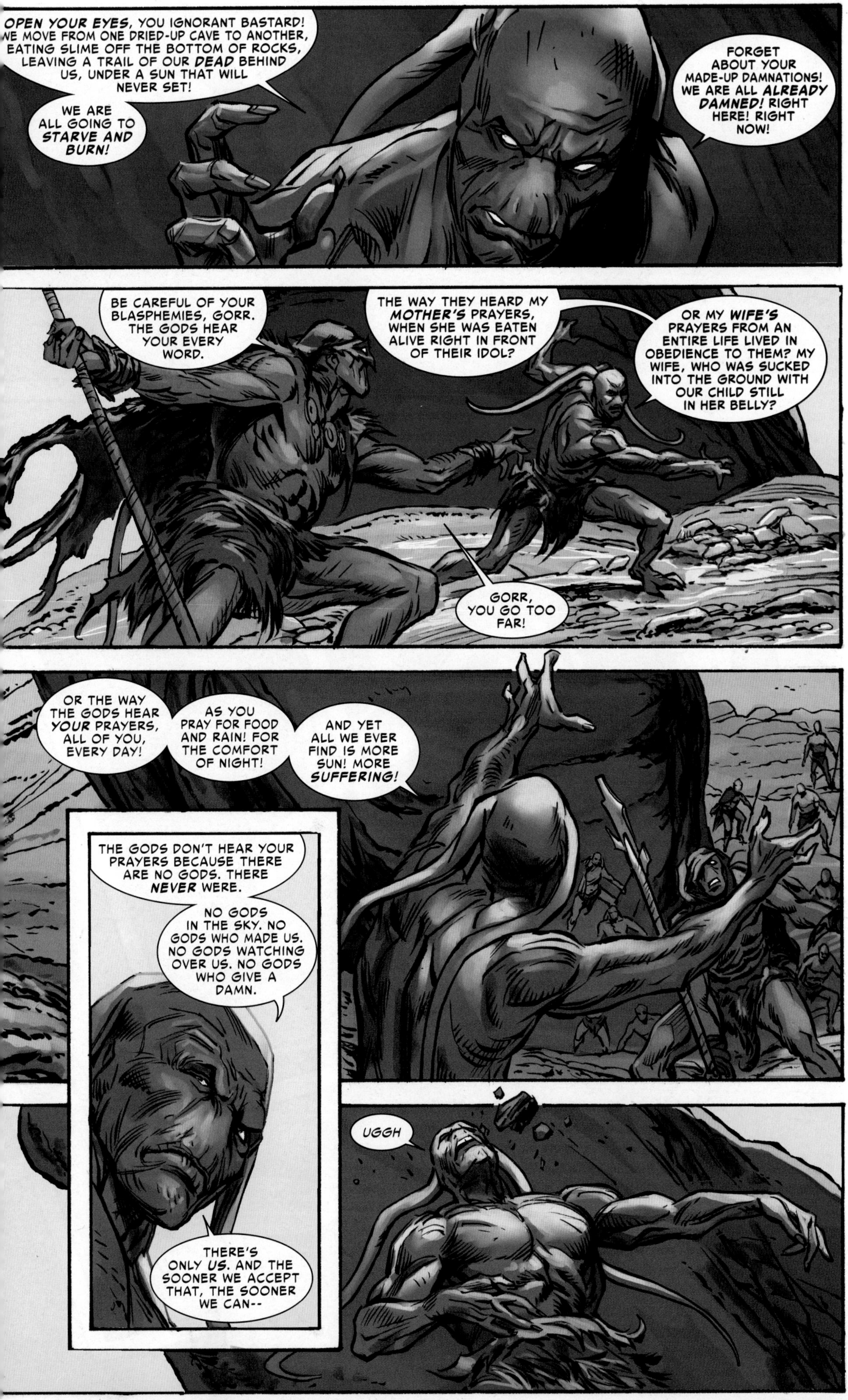
OPEN YOUR EYES, YOU IGNORANT BASTARD! WE MOVE FROM ONE DRIED-UP CAVE TO ANOTHER, EATING SLIME OFF THE BOTTOM OF ROCKS, LEAVING A TRAIL OF OUR DEAD BEHIND US, UNDER A SUN THAT WILL NEVER SET!
WE ARE ALL GOING TO STARVE AND BURN!
FORGET ABOUT YOUR MADE-UP DAMNATIONS! WE ARE ALL ALREADY DAMNED! RIGHT HERE! RIGHT NOW!
BE CAREFUL OF YOUR BLASPHEMIES, GORR. THE GODS HEAR YOUR EVERY WORD.
THE WAY THEY HEARD MY MOTHER'S PRAYERS, WHEN SHE WAS EATEN ALIVE RIGHT IN FRONT OF THEIR IDOL?
OR MY WIFE'S PRAYERS FROM AN ENTIRE LIFE LIVED IN OBEDIENCE TO THEM? MY WIFE, WHO WAS SUCKED INTO THE GROUND WITH OUR CHILD STILL IN HER BELLY?
GORR, YOU GO TOO FAR!
OR THE WAY THE GODS HEAR YOUR PRAYERS, ALL OF YOU, EVERY DAY!
AS YOU PRAY FOR FOOD AND RAIN! FOR THE COMFORT OF NIGHT!
AND YET ALL WE EVER FIND IS MORE SUN! MORE SUFFERING!
THE GODS DON'T HEAR YOUR PRAYERS BECAUSE THERE ARE NO GODS. THERE NEVER WERE.
NO GODS IN THE SKY. NO GODS WHO MADE US. NO GODS WATCHING OVER US. NO GODS WHO GIVE A DAMN.
THERE'S ONLY US. AND THE SOONER WE ACCEPT THAT, THE SOONER WE CAN--
UGGH

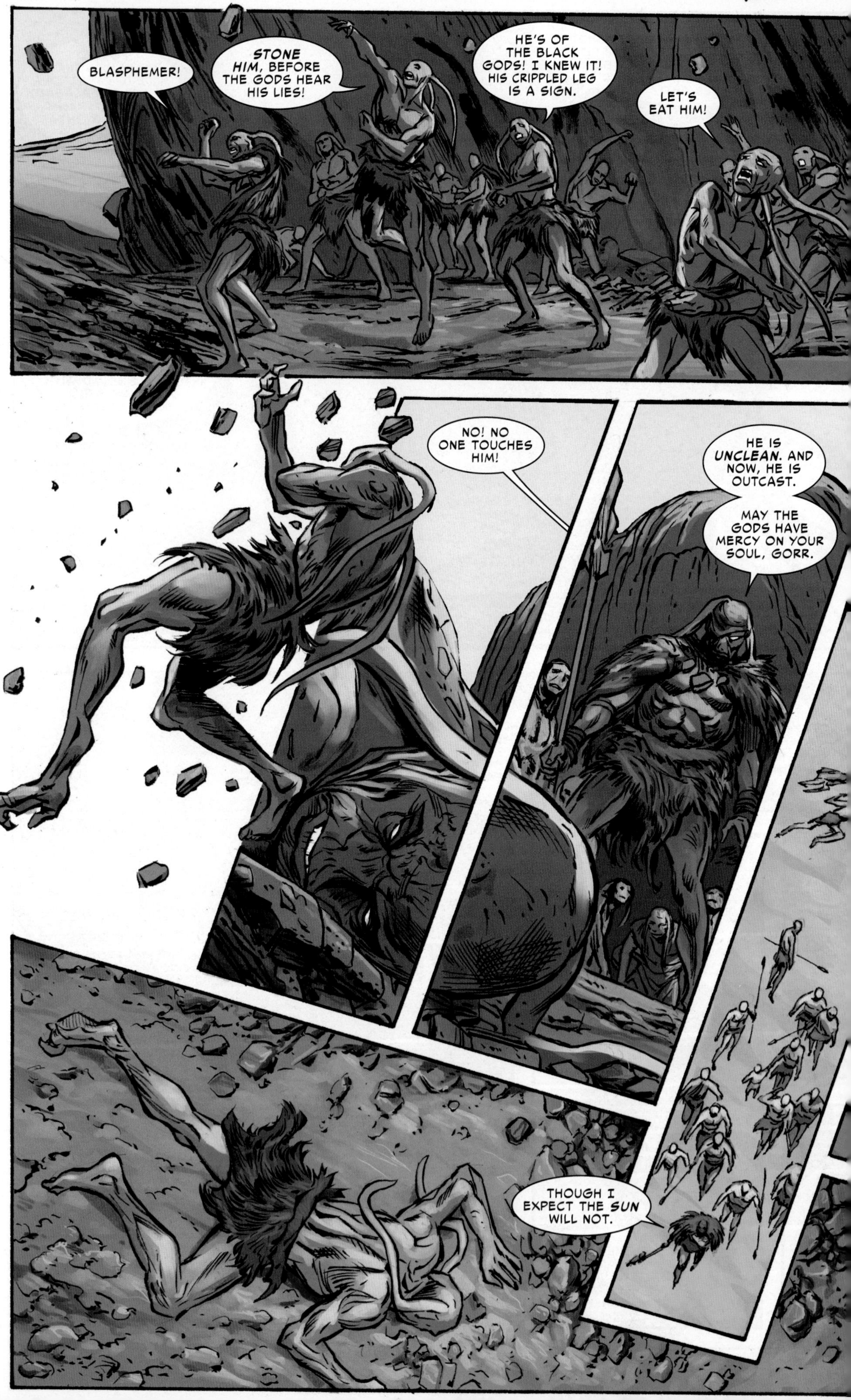
BLASPHEMER!
STONE HIM, BEFORE THE GODS HEAR HIS LIES!
HE'S OF THE BLACK GODS! I KNEW IT! HIS CRIPPLED LEG IS A SIGN.
LET'S EAT HIM!
NO! NO ONE TOUCHES HIM!
HE IS UNCLEAN. AND NOW, HE IS OUTCAST.
MAY THE GODS HAVE MERCY ON YOUR SOUL, GORR.
THOUGH I EXPECT THE SUN WILL NOT.

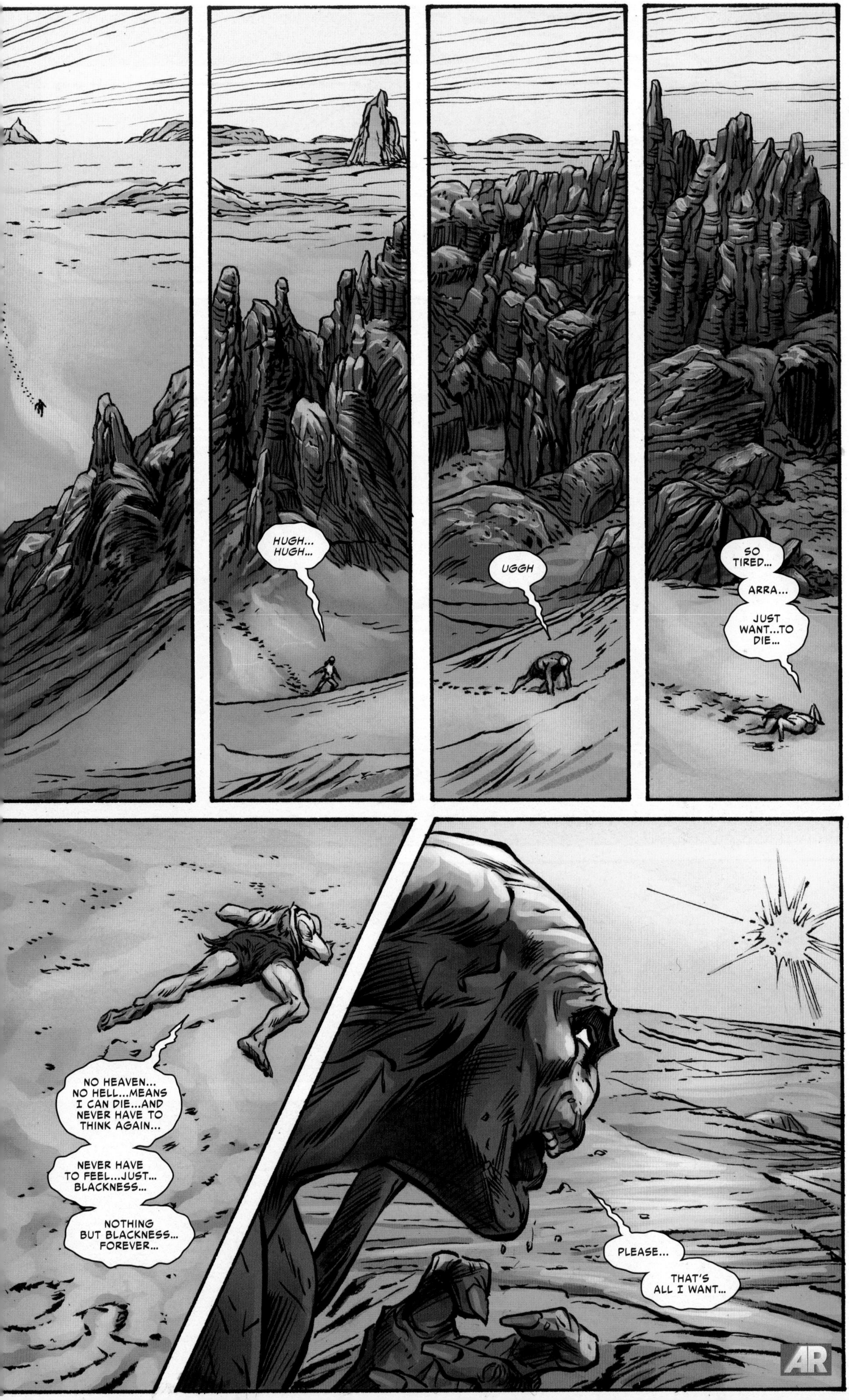
HUGH... HUGH...
UGGH
SO TIRED...
ARRA...
JUST WANT...TO DIE...
NO HEAVEN... NO HELL...MEANS I CAN DIE...AND NEVER HAVE TO THINK AGAIN...
NEVER HAVE TO FEEL...JUST... BLACKNESS...
NOTHING BUT BLACKNESS... FOREVER...
PLEASE...
THAT'S ALL I WANT...

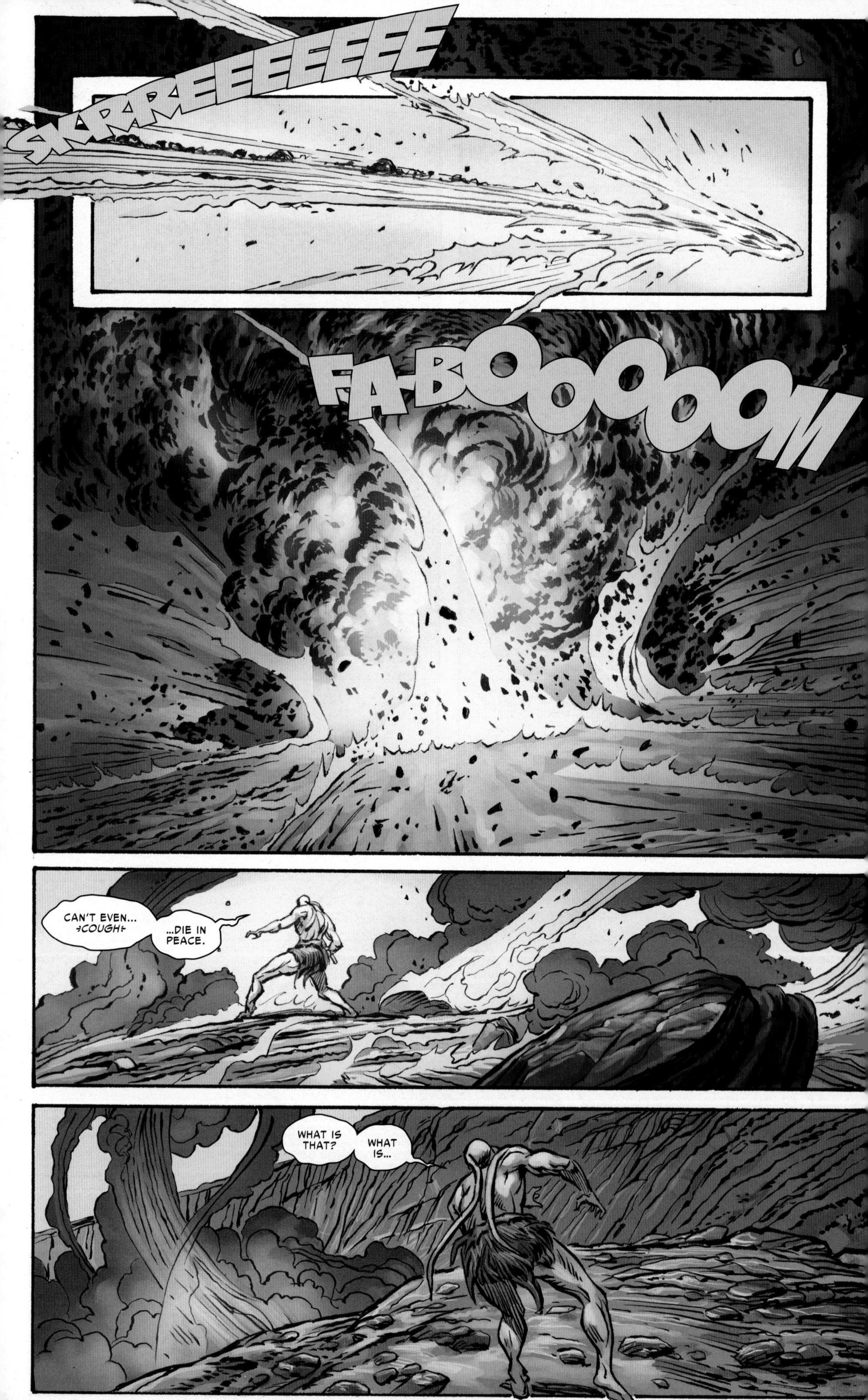
SKRREEEEEEEE
FA-BOOOOOOM
CAN'T EVEN... ~COUGH~
...DIE IN PEACE.
WHAT IS THAT?
WHAT IS...

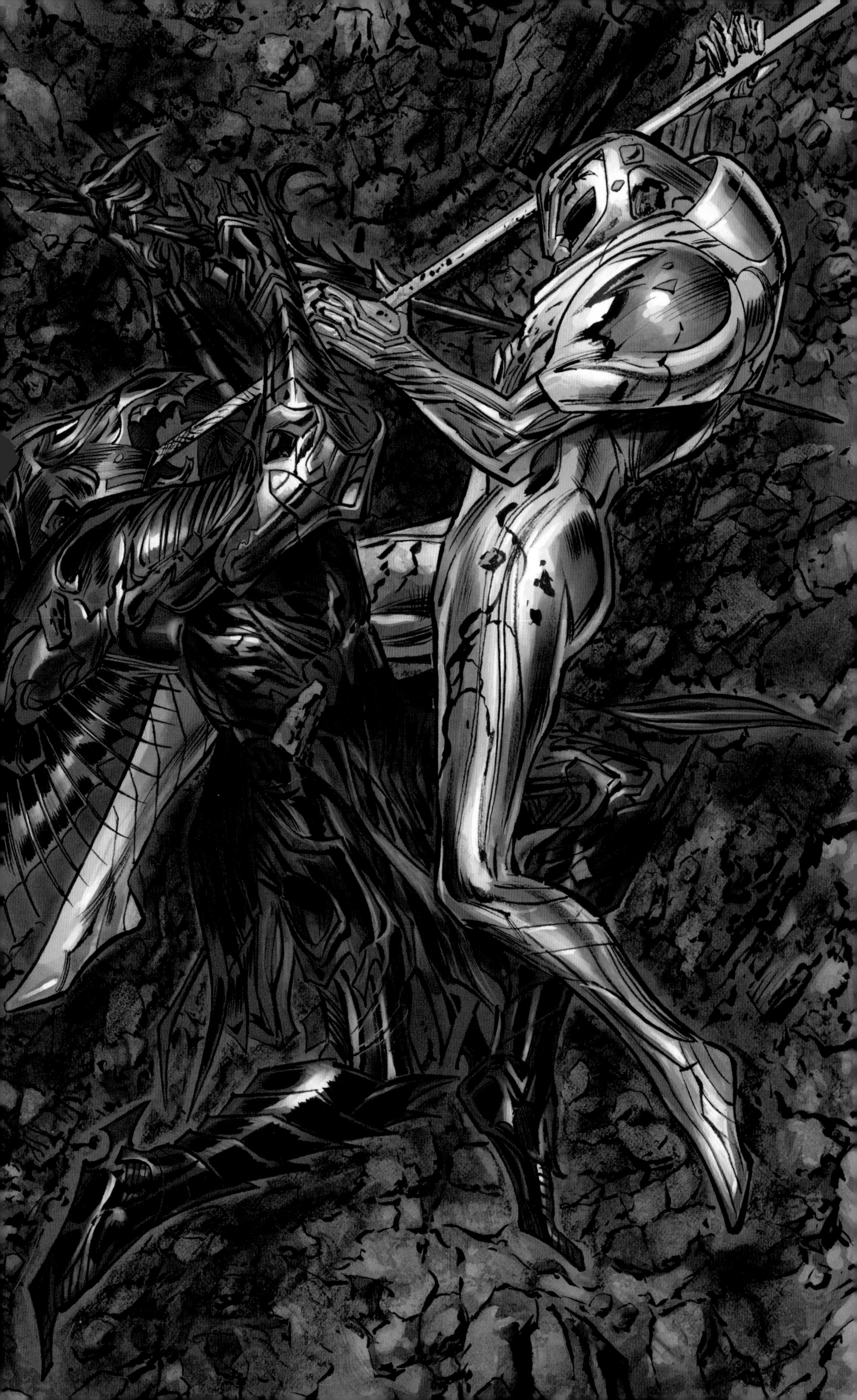

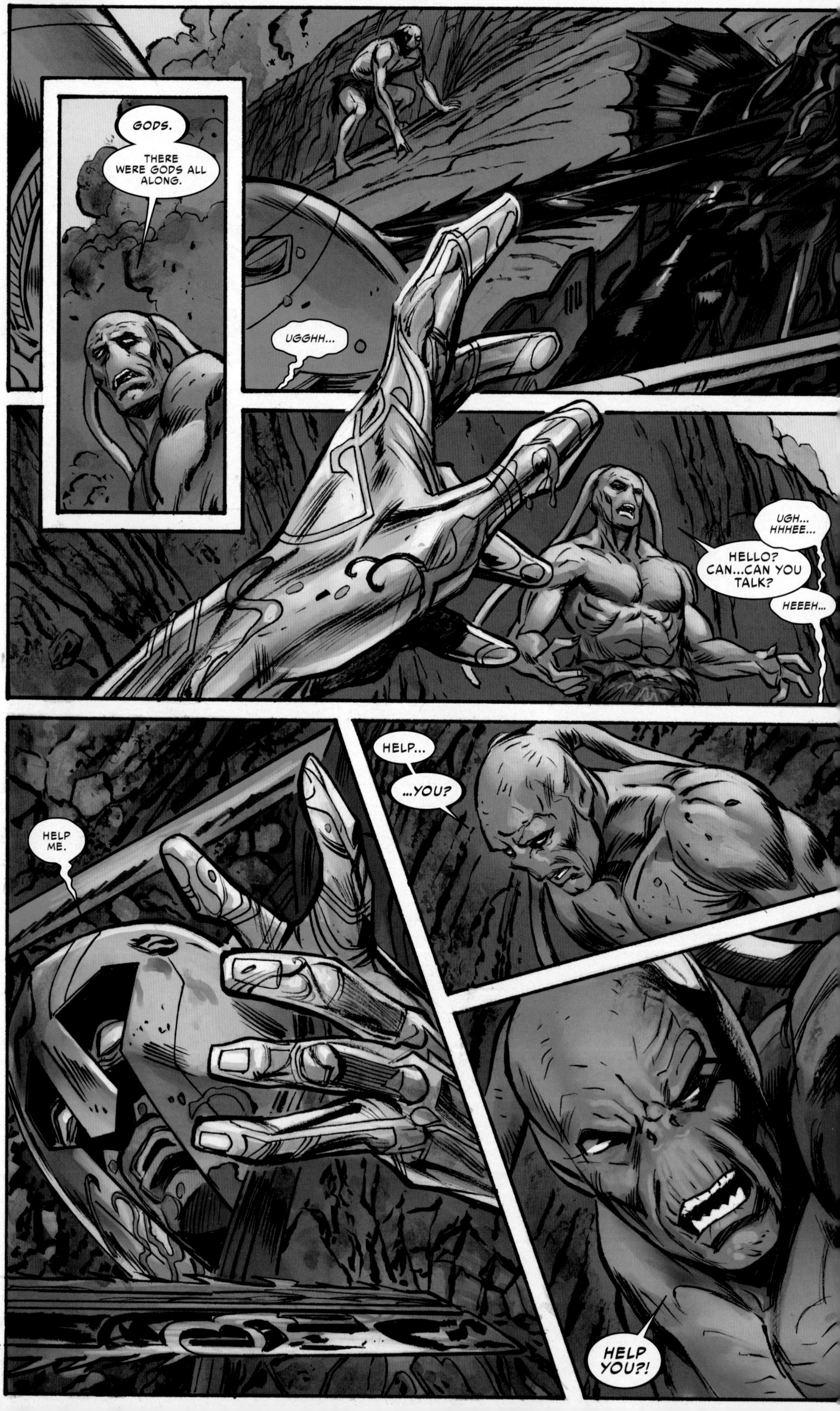
GODS.
THERE WERE GODS ALL ALONG.
UGGHH...
UGH... HHHEE...
HELLO? CAN...CAN YOU TALK?
HEEEH...
HELP ME.
HELP...
...YOU?
HELP YOU?!

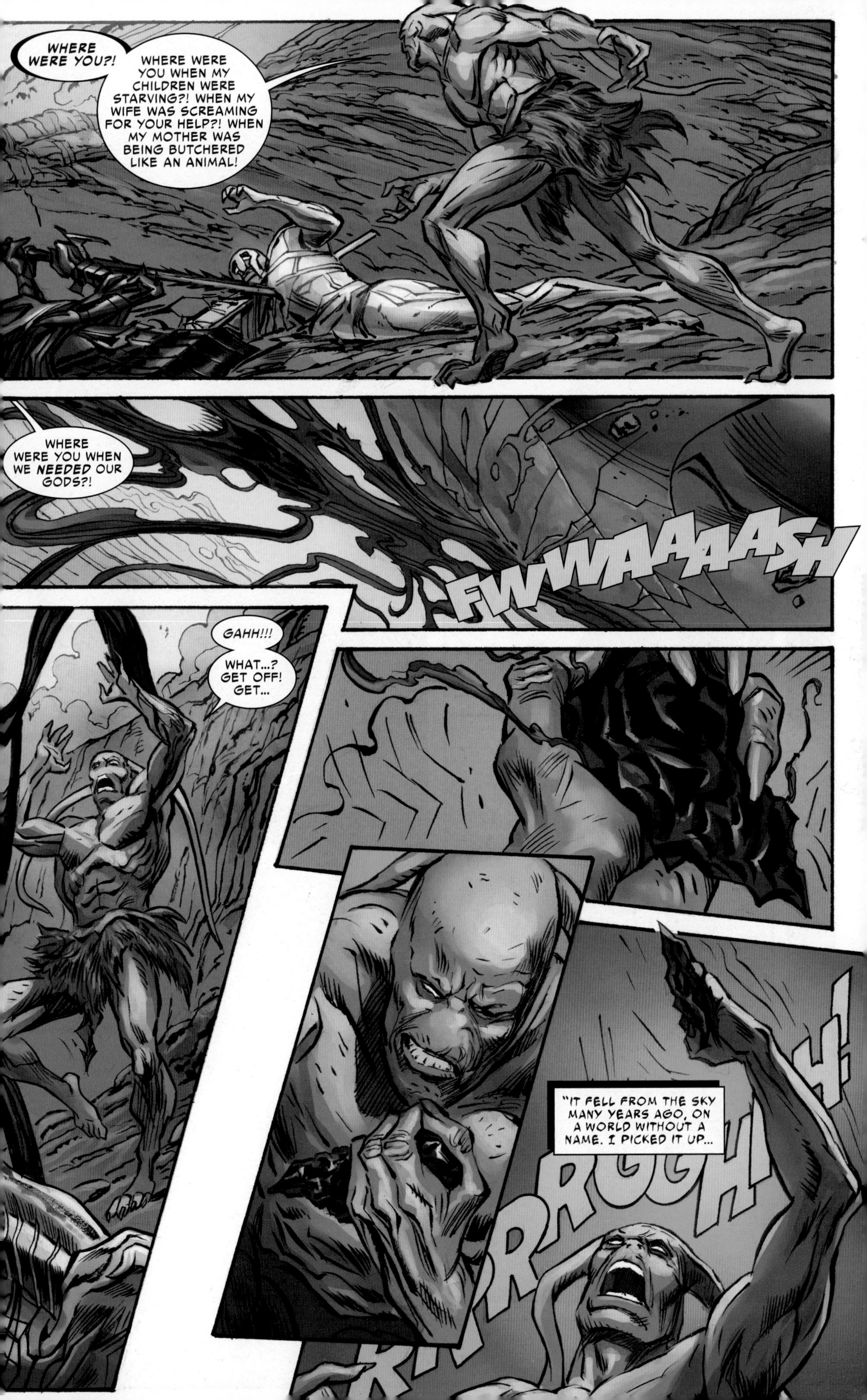
WHERE WERE YOU?!
WHERE WERE YOU WHEN MY CHILDREN WERE STARVING?! WHEN MY WIFE WAS SCREAMING FOR YOUR HELP?! WHEN MY MOTHER WAS BEING BUTCHERED LIKE AN ANIMAL!
WHERE WERE YOU WHEN WE NEEDED OUR GODS?!
FWWAAAASH
GAHH!!!
WHAT...? GET OFF! GET...
"IT FELL FROM THE SKY MANY YEARS AGO, ON A WORLD WITHOUT A NAME. I PICKED IT UP...
RRRAGGHH!

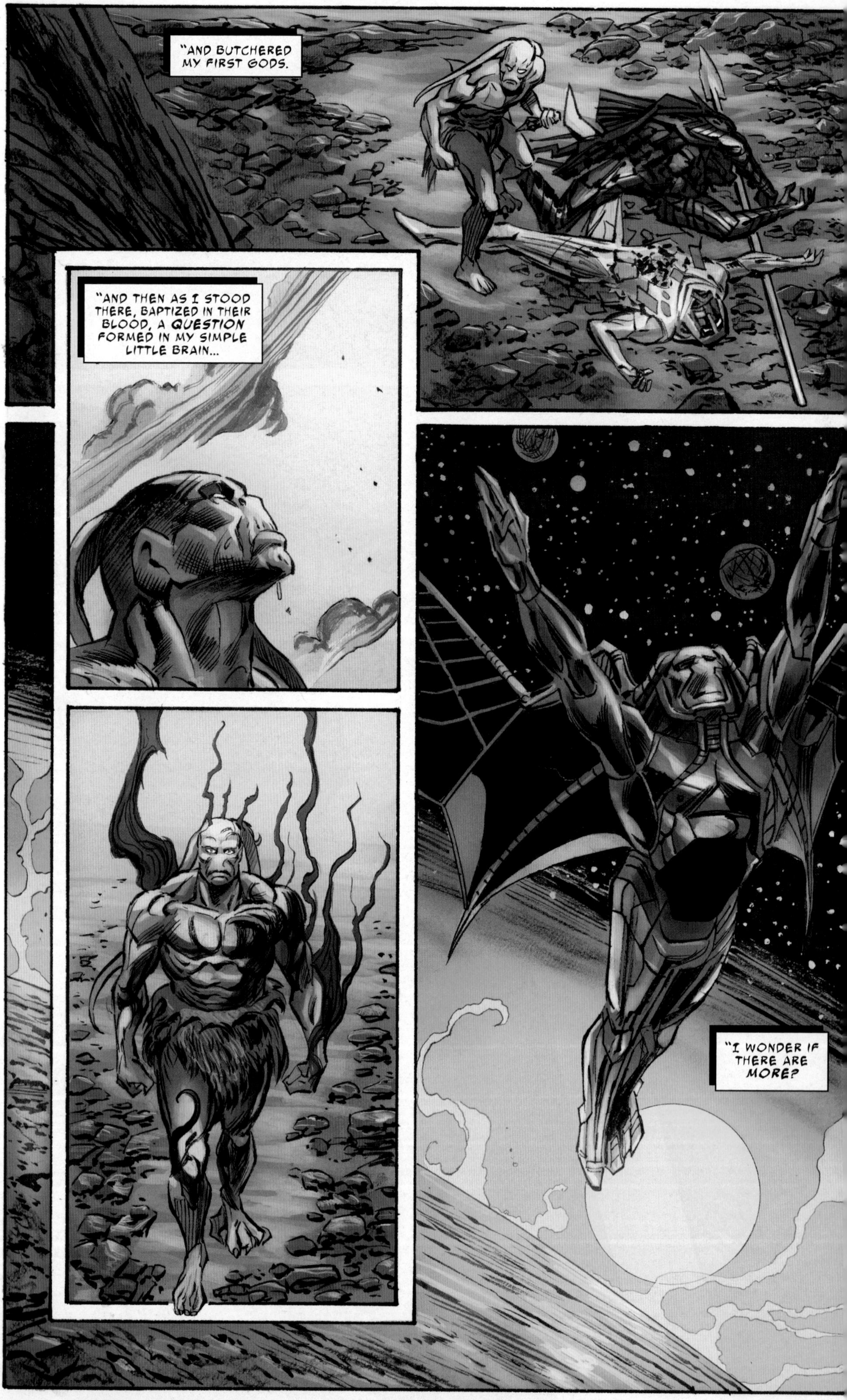
"AND BUTCHERED MY FIRST GODS.
"AND THEN AS I STOOD THERE, BAPTIZED IN THEIR BLOOD, A QUESTION FORMED IN MY SIMPLE LITTLE BRAIN...
"I WONDER IF THERE ARE MORE?

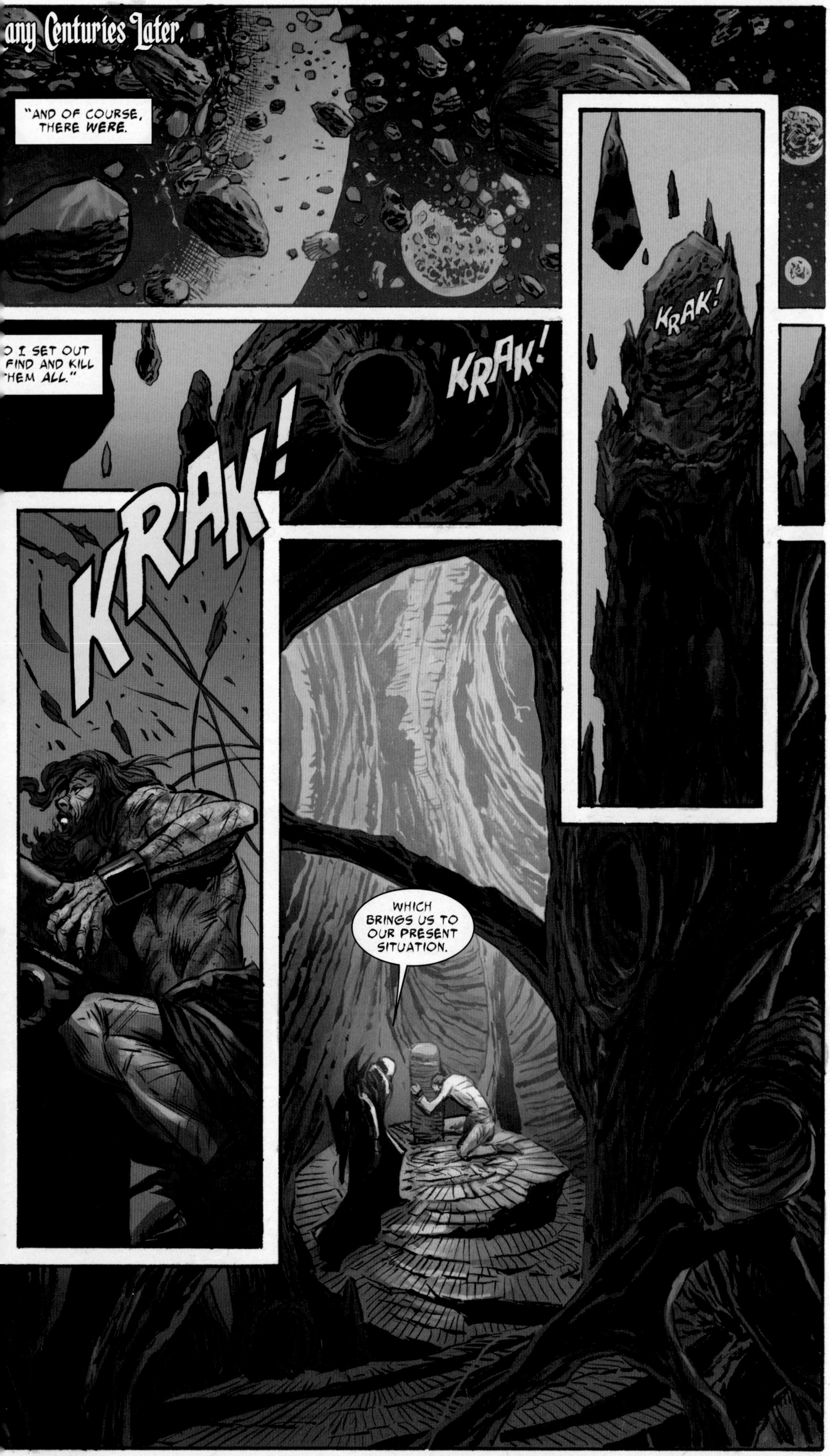
any Centuries Later.
"AND OF COURSE, THERE WERE.
KRAK!
O I SET OUT FIND AND KILL THEM ALL."
KRAK!
KRAK!
KRAK!
WHICH BRINGS US TO OUR PRESENT SITUATION.

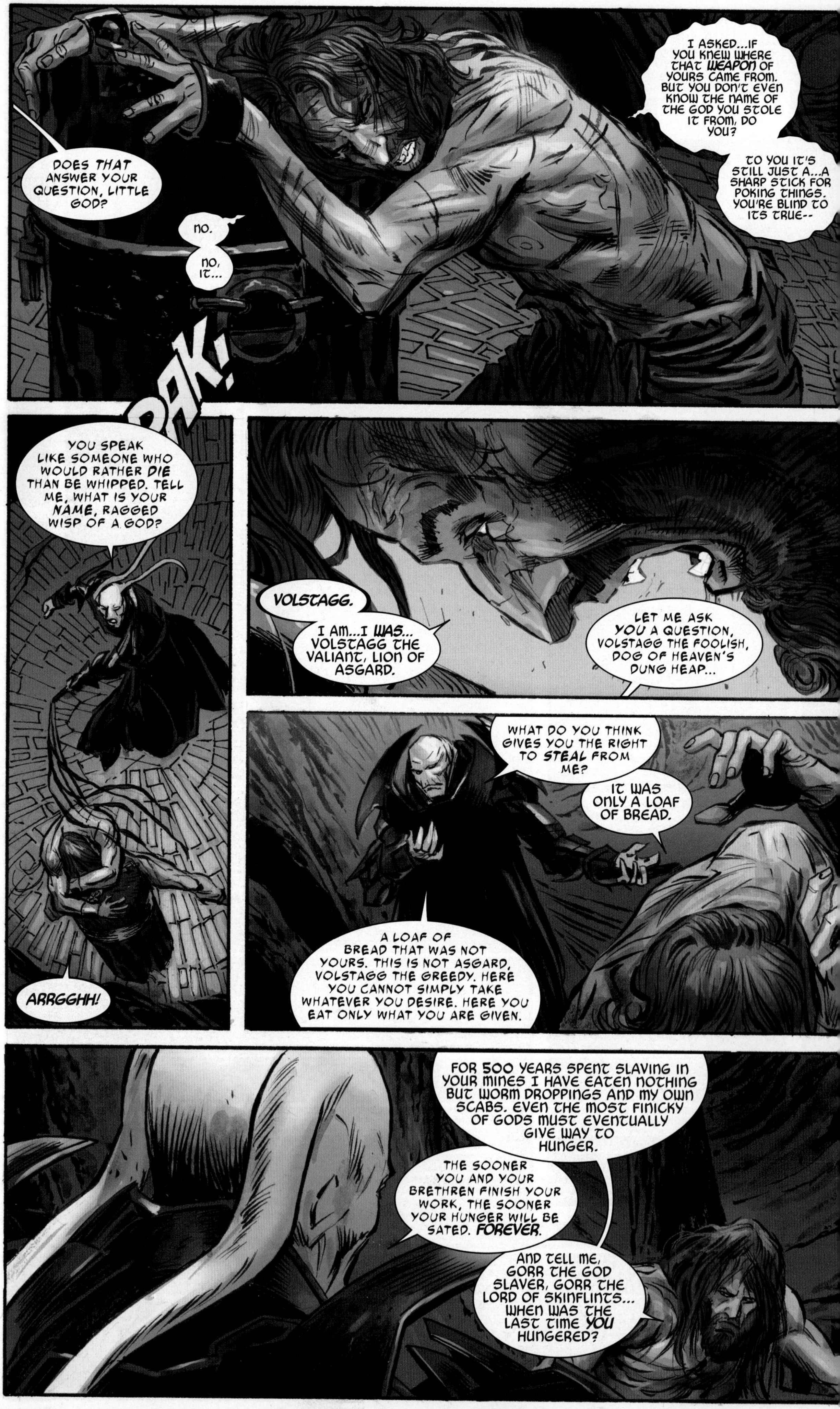
I ASKED...IF YOU KNEW WHERE THAT WEAPON OF YOURS CAME FROM. BUT YOU DON'T EVEN KNOW THE NAME OF THE GOD YOU STOLE IT FROM, DO YOU?
TO YOU IT'S STILL JUST A...A SHARP STICK FOR POKING THINGS. YOU'RE BLIND TO ITS TRUE--
DOES THAT ANSWER YOUR QUESTION, LITTLE GOD?
no.
no, it...
YOU SPEAK LIKE SOMEONE WHO WOULD RATHER DIE THAN BE WHIPPED. TELL ME, WHAT IS YOUR NAME, RAGGED WISP OF A GOD?
ARRGGHH!
VOLSTAGG.
I AM...I WAS... VOLSTAGG THE VALIANT, LION OF ASGARD.
LET ME ASK YOU A QUESTION, VOLSTAGG THE FOOLISH, DOG OF HEAVEN'S DUNG HEAP...
WHAT DO YOU THINK GIVES YOU THE RIGHT TO STEAL FROM ME?
IT WAS ONLY A LOAF OF BREAD.
A LOAF OF BREAD THAT WAS NOT YOURS. THIS IS NOT ASGARD, VOLSTAGG THE GREEDY. HERE YOU CANNOT SIMPLY TAKE WHATEVER YOU DESIRE. HERE YOU EAT ONLY WHAT YOU ARE GIVEN.
FOR 500 YEARS SPENT SLAVING IN YOUR MINES I HAVE EATEN NOTHING BUT WORM DROPPINGS AND MY OWN SCABS. EVEN THE MOST FINICKY OF GODS MUST EVENTUALLY GIVE WAY TO HUNGER.
THE SOONER YOU AND YOUR BRETHREN FINISH YOUR WORK, THE SOONER YOUR HUNGER WILL BE SATED. FOREVER.
AND TELL ME, GORR THE GOD SLAVER, GORR THE LORD OF SKINFLINTS... WHEN WAS THE LAST TIME YOU HUNGERED?

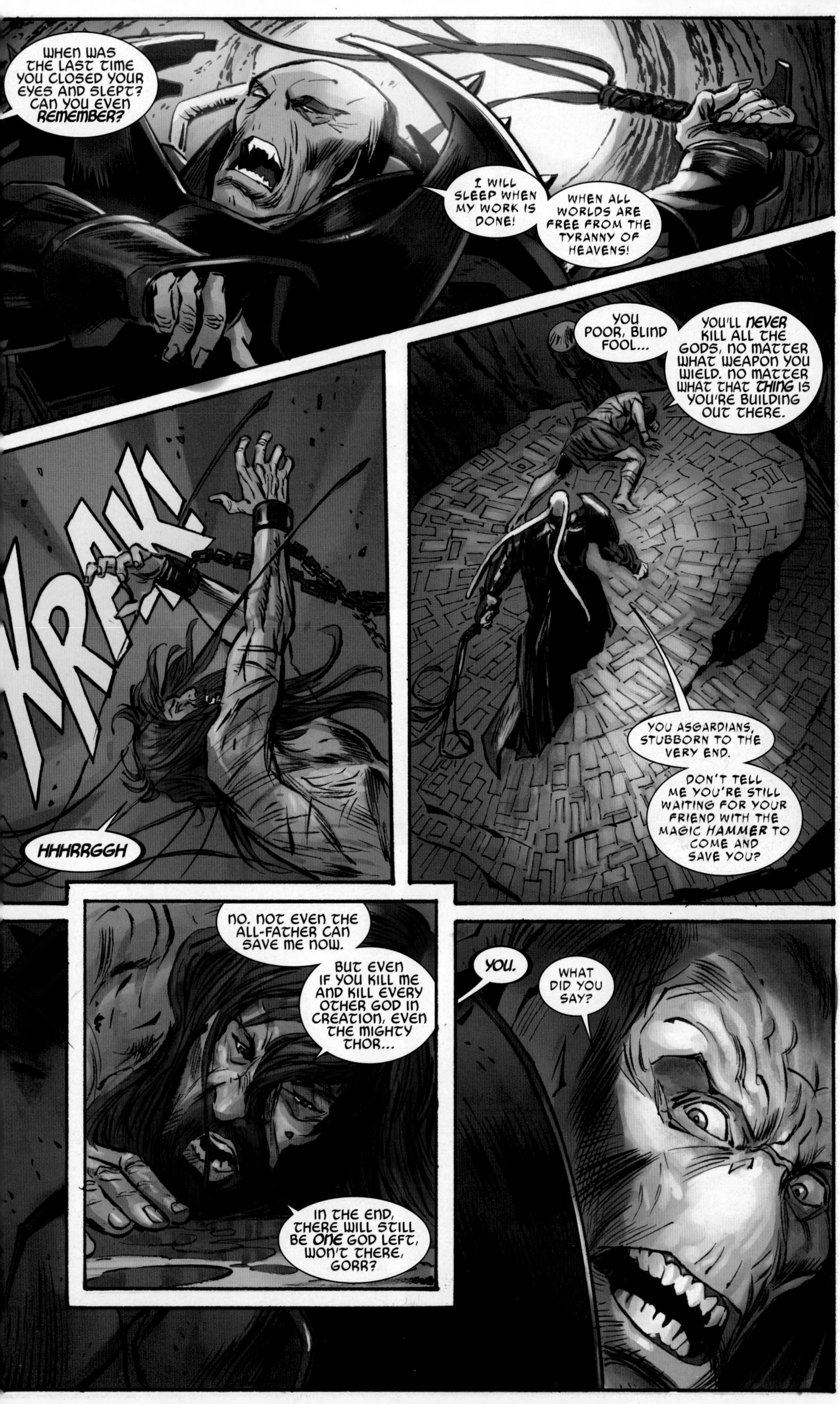
WHEN WAS THE LAST TIME YOU CLOSED YOUR EYES AND SLEPT? CAN YOU EVEN REMEMBER?
I WILL SLEEP WHEN MY WORK IS DONE!
WHEN ALL WORLDS ARE FREE FROM THE TYRANNY OF HEAVENS!
KRAK
HHHRRGGH
YOU POOR, BLIND FOOL...
YOU'LL NEVER KILL ALL THE GODS, NO MATTER WHAT WEAPON YOU WIELD. NO MATTER WHAT THAT THING IS YOU'RE BUILDING OUT THERE.
YOU ASGARDIANS, STUBBORN TO THE VERY END.
DON'T TELL ME YOU'RE STILL WAITING FOR YOUR FRIEND WITH THE MAGIC HAMMER TO COME AND SAVE YOU?
NO. NOT EVEN THE ALL-FATHER CAN SAVE ME NOW.
BUT EVEN IF YOU KILL ME AND KILL EVERY OTHER GOD IN CREATION, EVEN THE MIGHTY THOR...
IN THE END, THERE WILL STILL BE ONE GOD LEFT, WON'T THERE, GORR?
YOU.
WHAT DID YOU SAY?

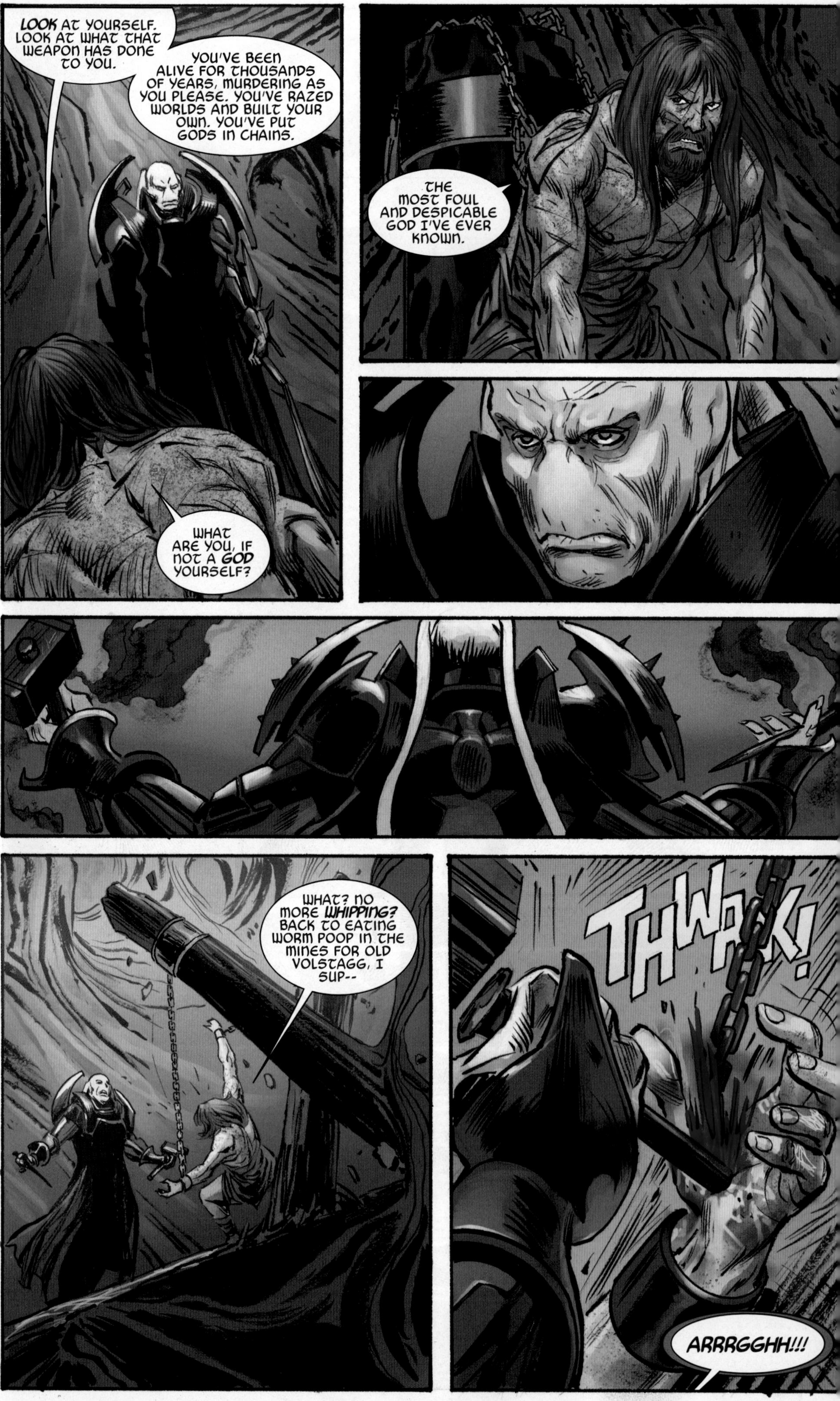
LOOK AT YOURSELF. LOOK AT WHAT THAT WEAPON HAS DONE TO YOU.
YOU'VE BEEN ALIVE FOR THOUSANDS OF YEARS, MURDERING AS YOU PLEASE. YOU'VE RAZED WORLDS AND BUILT YOUR OWN. YOU'VE PUT GODS IN CHAINS.
WHAT ARE YOU, IF NOT A GOD YOURSELF?
THE MOST FOUL AND DESPICABLE GOD I'VE EVER KNOWN.
WHAT? NO MORE WHIPPING? BACK TO EATING WORM POOP IN THE MINES FOR OLD VOLSTAGG, I SUP--
THWACK!
ARRRGGHH!!!

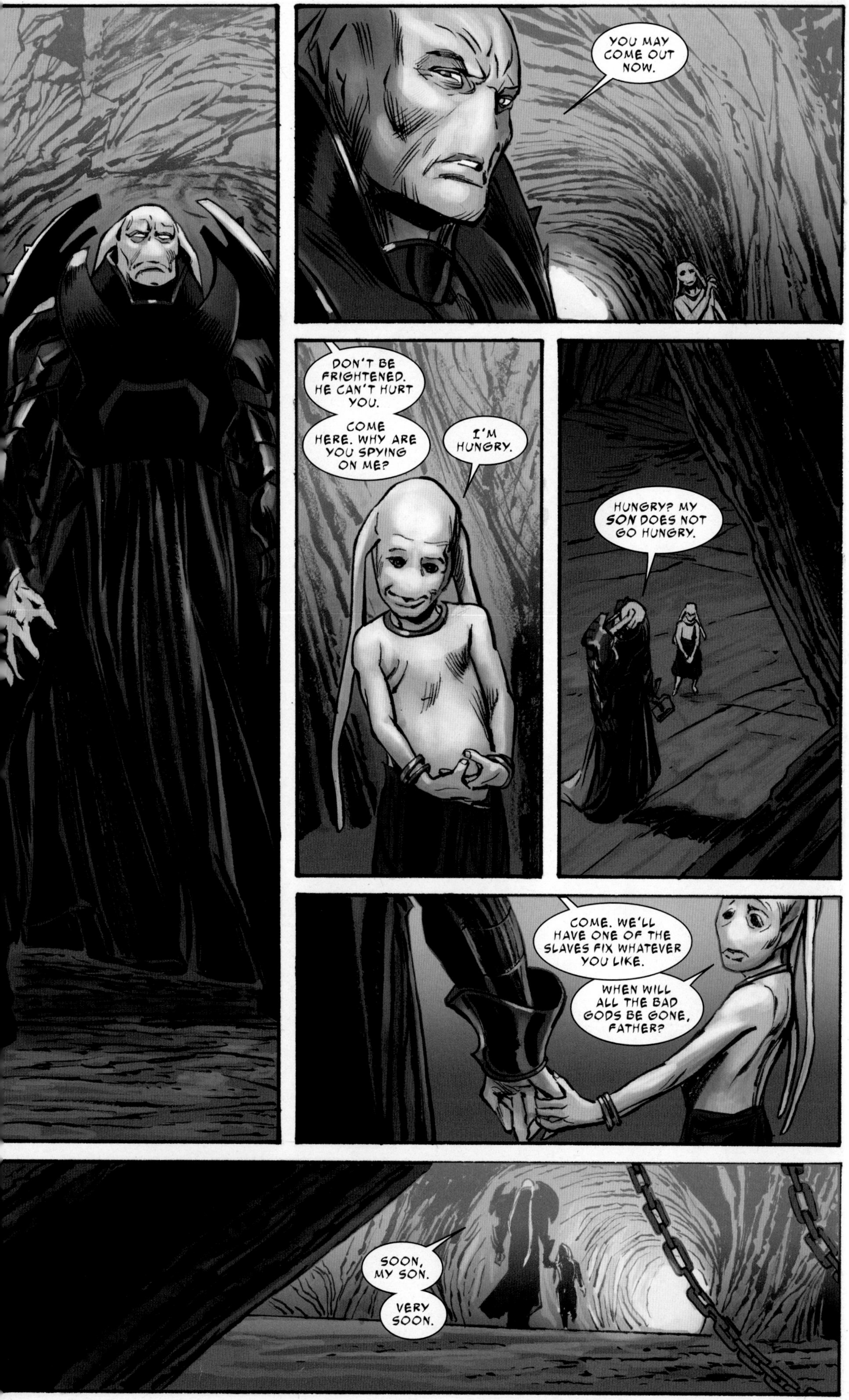
YOU MAY COME OUT NOW.
DON'T BE FRIGHTENED. HE CAN'T HURT YOU.
COME HERE. WHY ARE YOU SPYING ON ME?
I'M HUNGRY.
HUNGRY? MY SON DOES NOT GO HUNGRY.
COME. WE'LL HAVE ONE OF THE SLAVES FIX WHATEVER YOU LIKE.
WHEN WILL ALL THE BAD GODS BE GONE, FATHER?
SOON, MY SON.
VERY SOON.

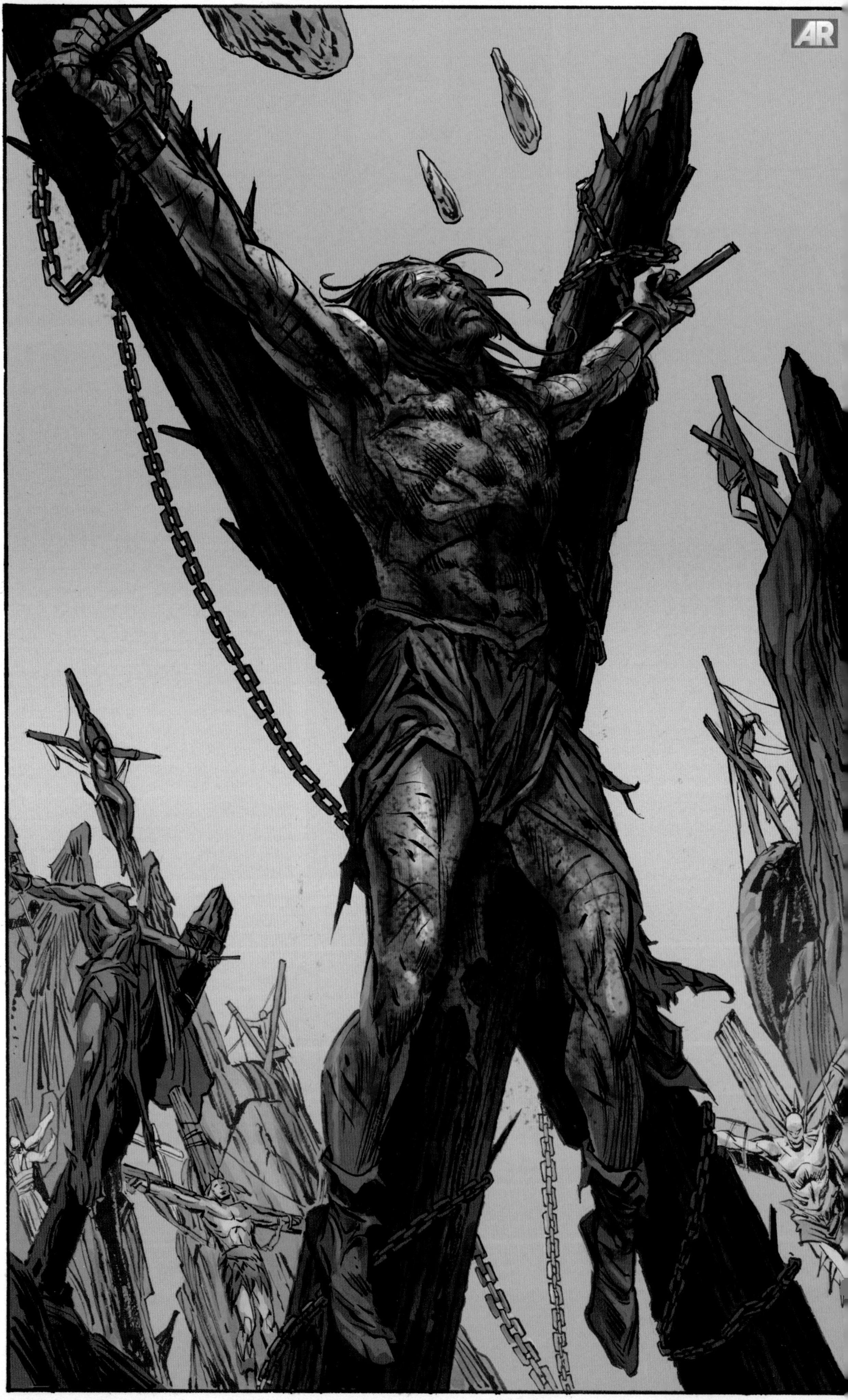

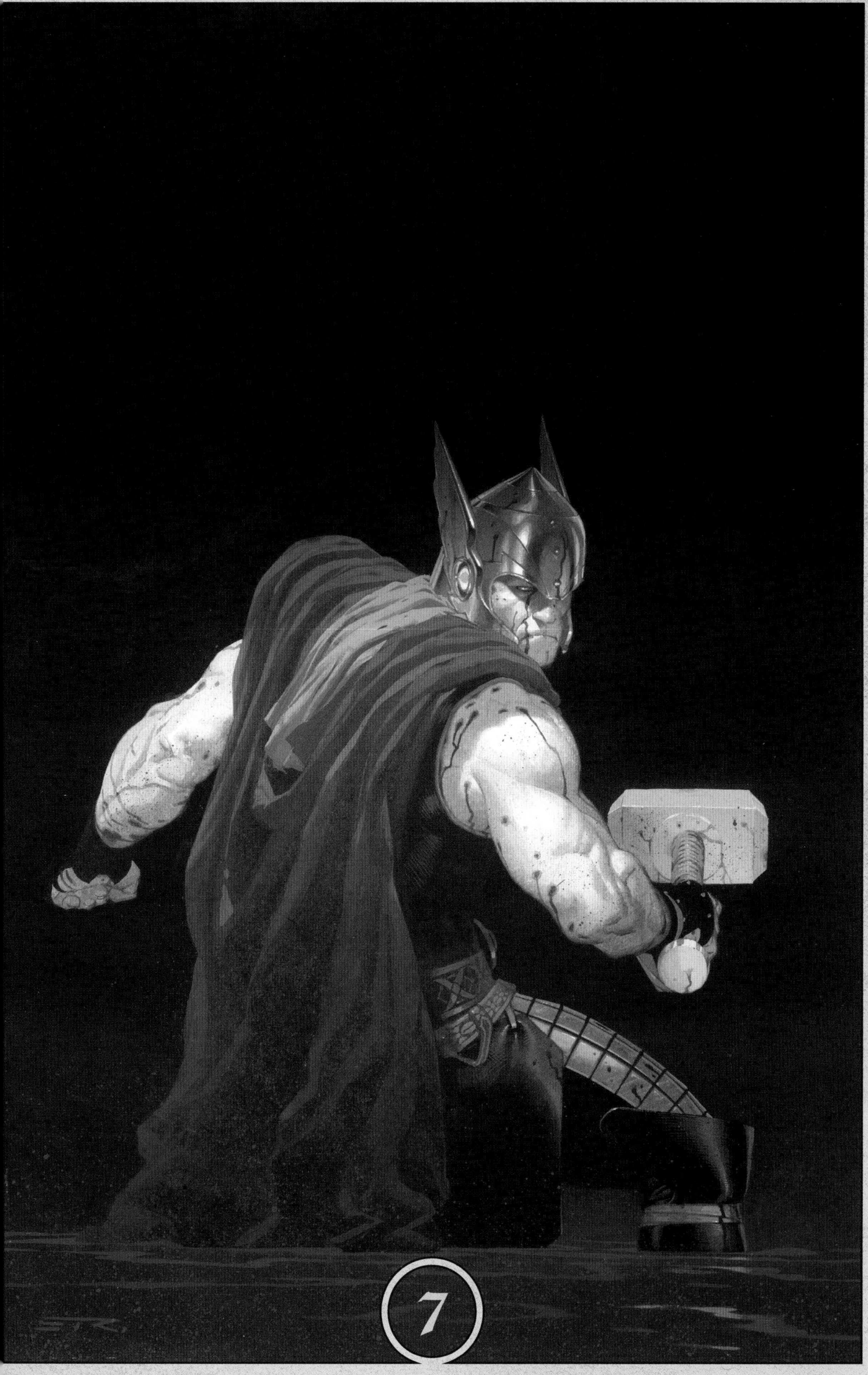
7

GODBOMB PART 1: WHERE GODS GO TO DIE

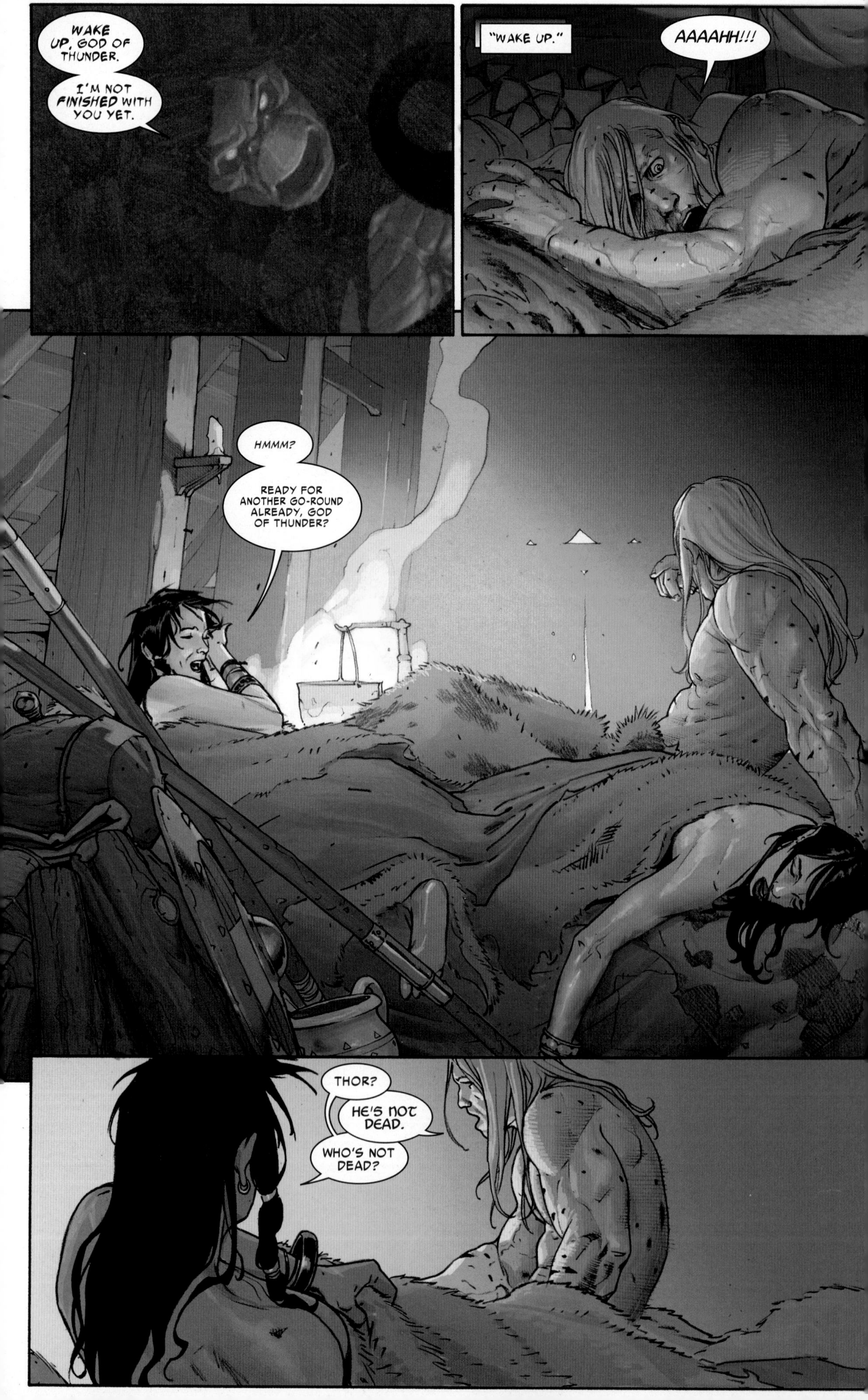
WAKE UP, GOD OF THUNDER.
I'M NOT FINISHED WITH YOU YET.
"WAKE UP."
AAAAHH!!!
HMMM?
READY FOR ANOTHER GO-ROUND ALREADY, GOD OF THUNDER?
THOR?
HE'S NOT DEAD.
WHO'S NOT DEAD?

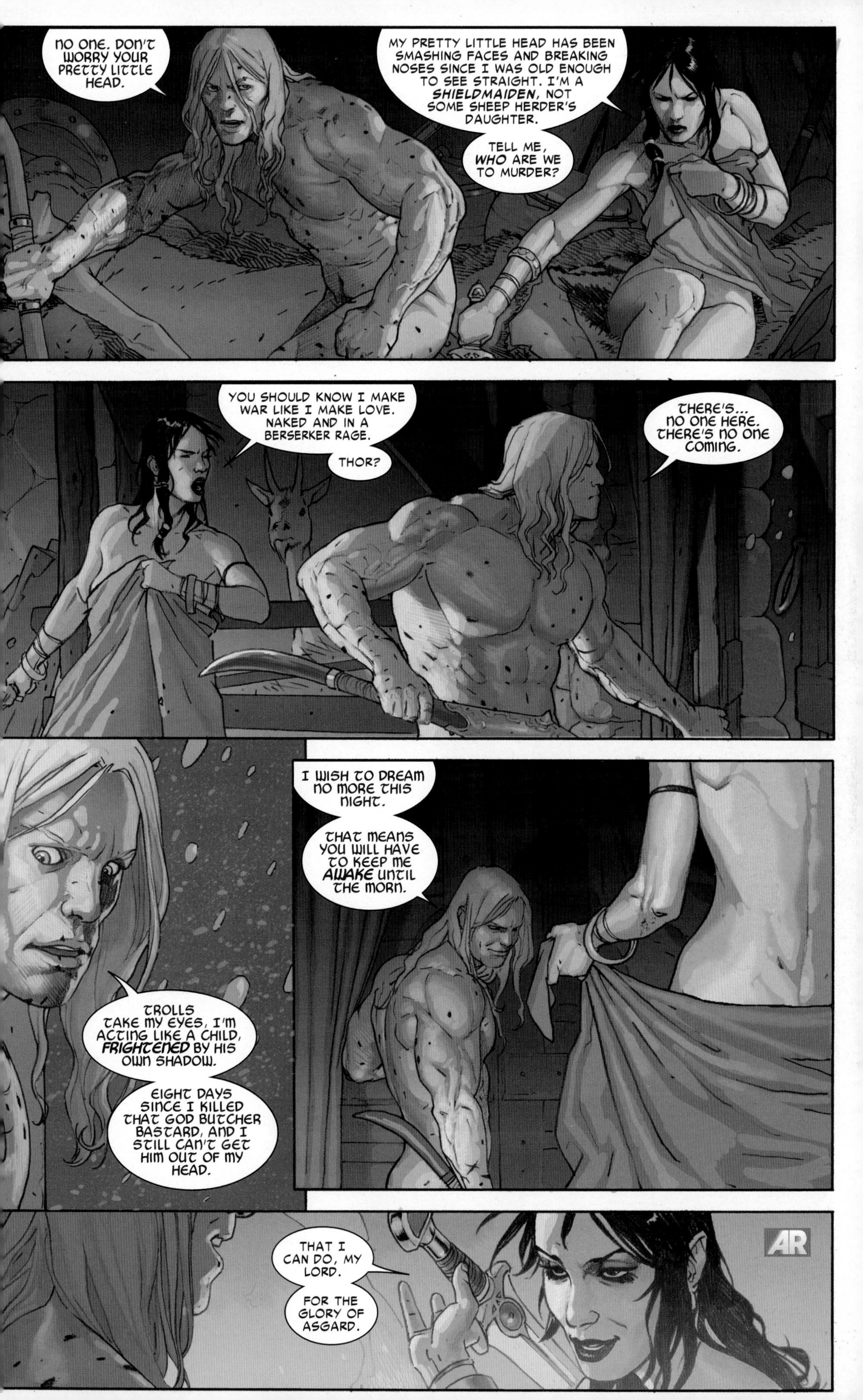
NO ONE. DON'T WORRY YOUR PRETTY LITTLE HEAD.
MY PRETTY LITTLE HEAD HAS BEEN SMASHING FACES AND BREAKING NOSES SINCE I WAS OLD ENOUGH TO SEE STRAIGHT. I'M A SHIELDMAIDEN, NOT SOME SHEEP HERDER'S DAUGHTER.
TELL ME, WHO ARE WE TO MURDER?
YOU SHOULD KNOW I MAKE WAR LIKE I MAKE LOVE. NAKED AND IN A BERSERKER RAGE.
THOR?
THERE'S... NO ONE HERE. THERE'S NO ONE COMING.
TROLLS TAKE MY EYES, I'M ACTING LIKE A CHILD, FRIGHTENED BY HIS OWN SHADOW.
EIGHT DAYS SINCE I KILLED THAT GOD BUTCHER BASTARD, AND I STILL CAN'T GET HIM OUT OF MY HEAD.
I WISH TO DREAM NO MORE THIS NIGHT.
THAT MEANS YOU WILL HAVE TO KEEP ME AWAKE UNTIL THE MORN.
THAT I CAN DO, MY LORD.
FOR THE GLORY OF ASGARD.
AR

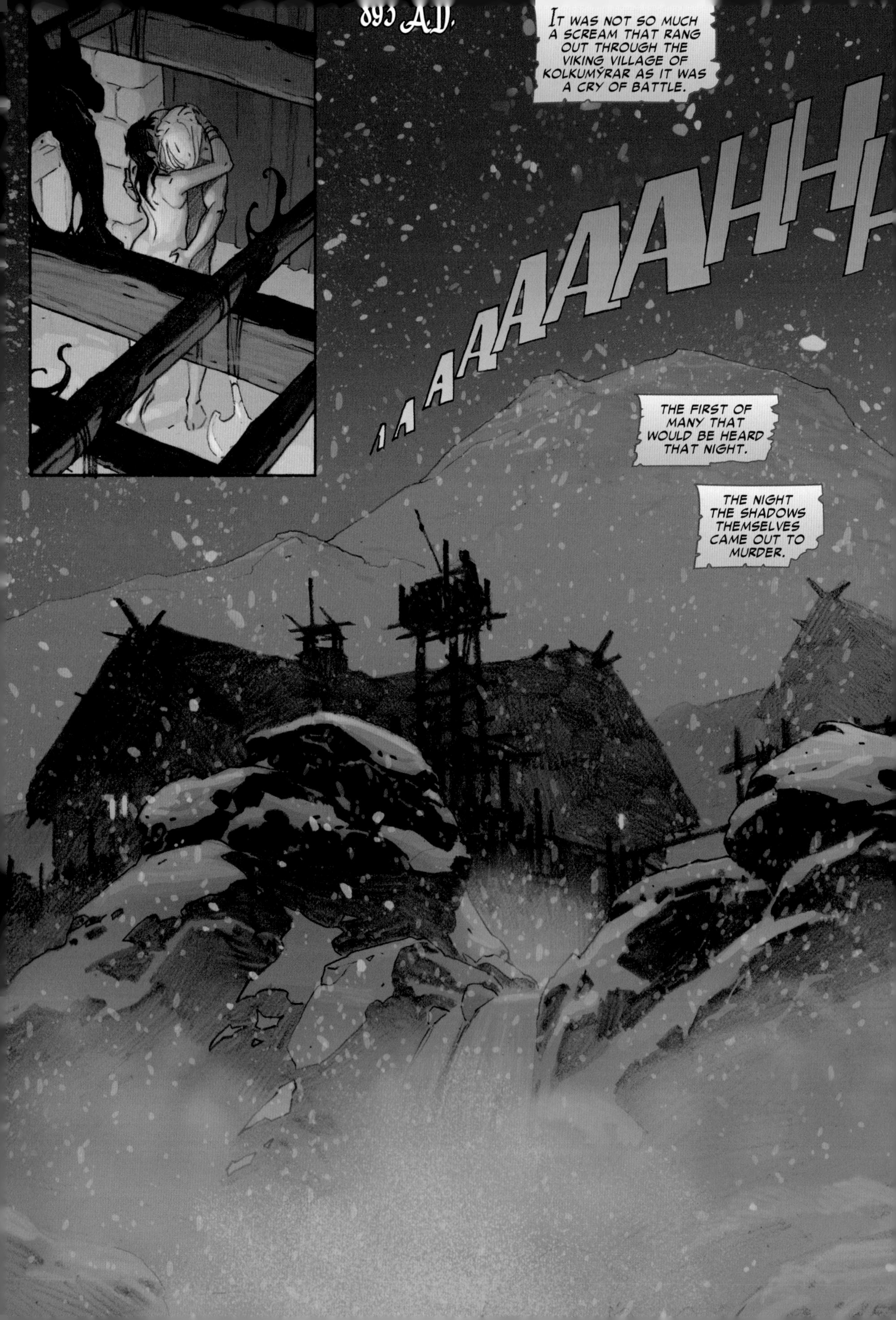
893 A.D.
It was not so much a scream that rang out through the Viking village of Kolkumýrar as it was a cry of battle.
AAAAAAAAAHHH
The first of many that would be heard that night.
The night the shadows themselves came out to murder.

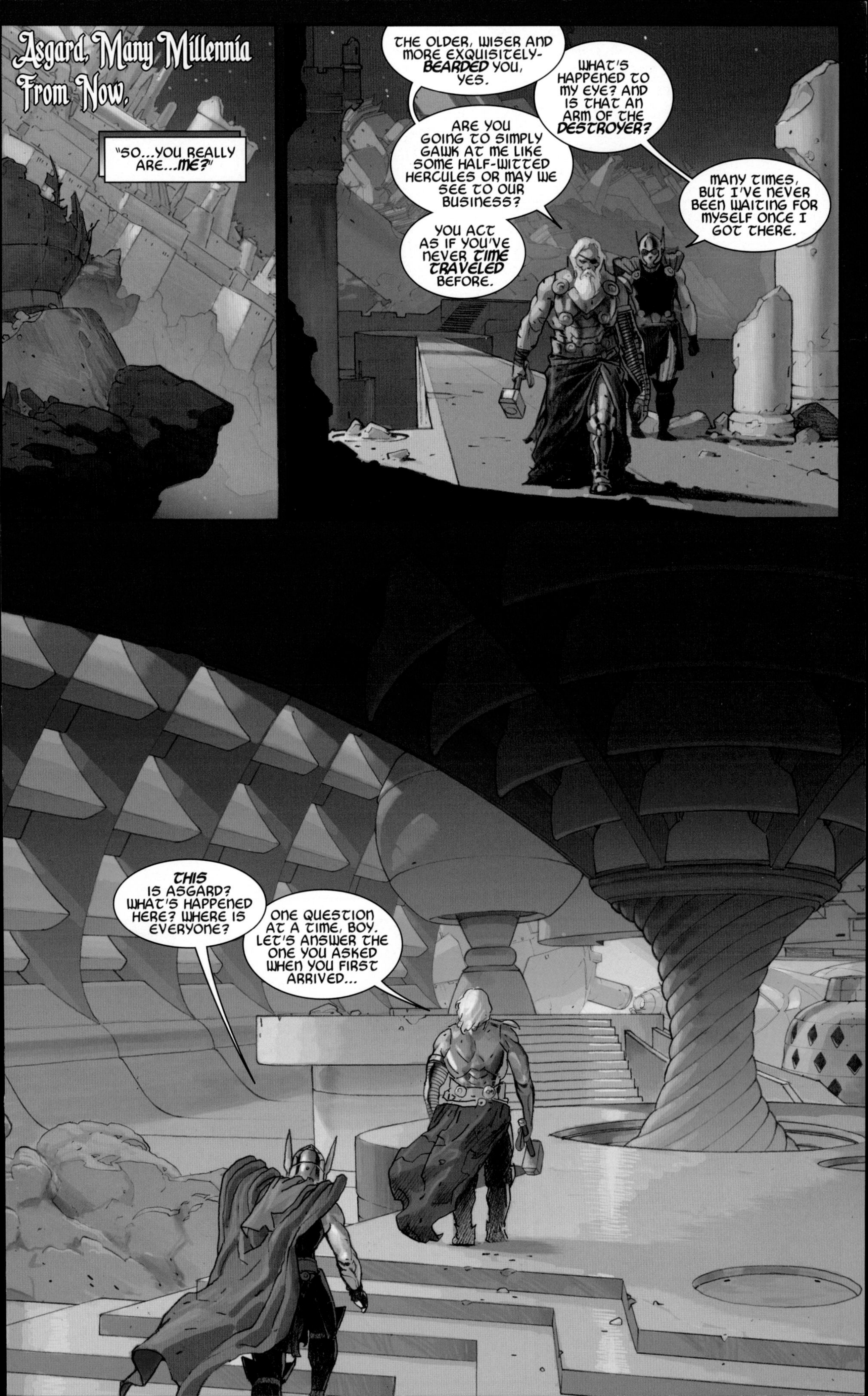
Asgard, Many Millennia From Now.
"SO...YOU REALLY ARE...ME?"
THE OLDER, WISER AND MORE EXQUISITELY-BEARDED YOU, YES.
ARE YOU GOING TO SIMPLY GAWK AT ME LIKE SOME HALF-WITTED HERCULES OR MAY WE SEE TO OUR BUSINESS?
YOU ACT AS IF YOU'VE NEVER TIME TRAVELED BEFORE.
WHAT'S HAPPENED TO MY EYE? AND IS THAT AN ARM OF THE DESTROYER?
MANY TIMES, BUT I'VE NEVER BEEN WAITING FOR MYSELF ONCE I GOT THERE.
THIS IS ASGARD? WHAT'S HAPPENED HERE? WHERE IS EVERYONE?
ONE QUESTION AT A TIME, BOY. LET'S ANSWER THE ONE YOU ASKED WHEN YOU FIRST ARRIVED...

"WHERE IS THE *GOD BUTCHER?*"

THIS... THIS IS... *HLIDSKJALF.* THE HIGH SEAT OF ODIN.

NO ONE BUT THE *ALL-FATHER* HIMSELF IS ALLOWED IN HERE.

YOU ARE *RIGHT* ABOUT THAT.

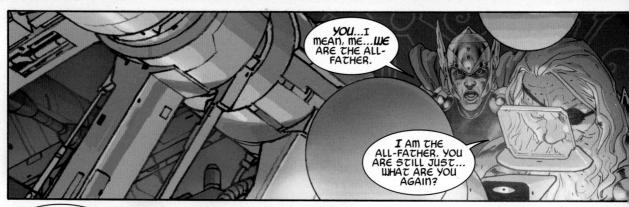

YOU...I MEAN, ME...*WE* ARE THE ALL-FATHER.

I AM THE ALL-FATHER. YOU ARE STILL JUST... WHAT ARE YOU AGAIN?

AN AVENGER? GUARDIAN OF THE GALAXY? THE HEAD OF THAT RIDICULOUS LITTLE *ORDER* OF YOURS?

HAVE YOU MOVED TO THE SUN AND BECOME A COSMIC GOD COP YET?

WHAT? NO.

OH. THEN FORGET I SAID ANYTHING.

WAIT, IF YOU TRULY ARE ME...THEN SHOULDN'T YOU REMEMBER THIS HAPPENING? REMEMBER COMING HERE AND *MEETING* YOURSELF?

I CAN HARDLY REMEMBER HOW TO BUCKLE MY OWN TROUSERS, CAN I? AND THIS IS *TIME TRAVEL* WE'RE TALKING ABOUT. THERE ARE ALL MANNER OF ANNOYING *RULES* GOVERNING THIS SORT OF THING.

I'VE ALWAYS *HATED* TIME TRAVEL.

AND YOU ALWAYS WILL.

WHAT ARE WE LOOKING FOR?

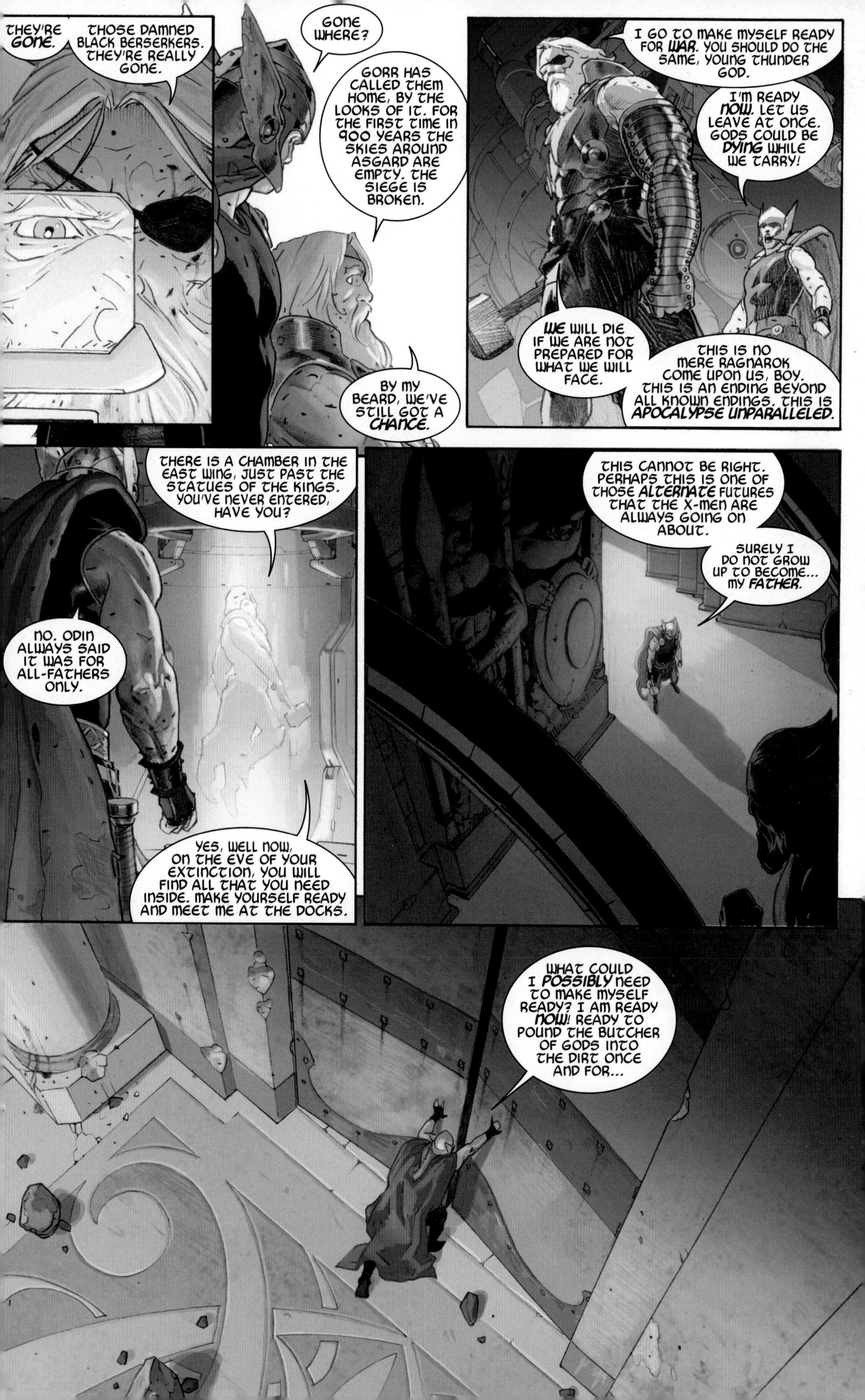
THEY'RE GONE.
THOSE DAMNED BLACK BERSERKERS. THEY'RE REALLY GONE.
GONE WHERE?
GORR HAS CALLED THEM HOME, BY THE LOOKS OF IT. FOR THE FIRST TIME IN 900 YEARS THE SKIES AROUND ASGARD ARE EMPTY. THE SIEGE IS BROKEN.
BY MY BEARD, WE'VE STILL GOT A CHANCE.
I GO TO MAKE MYSELF READY FOR WAR. YOU SHOULD DO THE SAME, YOUNG THUNDER GOD.
I'M READY NOW. LET US LEAVE AT ONCE. GODS COULD BE DYING WHILE WE TARRY!
WE WILL DIE IF WE ARE NOT PREPARED FOR WHAT WE WILL FACE.
THIS IS NO MERE RAGNAROK COME UPON US, BOY. THIS IS AN ENDING BEYOND ALL KNOWN ENDINGS. THIS IS APOCALYPSE UNPARALLELED.
THERE IS A CHAMBER IN THE EAST WING, JUST PAST THE STATUES OF THE KINGS. YOU'VE NEVER ENTERED, HAVE YOU?
NO. ODIN ALWAYS SAID IT WAS FOR ALL-FATHERS ONLY.
YES, WELL NOW, ON THE EVE OF YOUR EXTINCTION, YOU WILL FIND ALL THAT YOU NEED INSIDE. MAKE YOURSELF READY AND MEET ME AT THE DOCKS.
THIS CANNOT BE RIGHT. PERHAPS THIS IS ONE OF THOSE ALTERNATE FUTURES THAT THE X-MEN ARE ALWAYS GOING ON ABOUT.
SURELY I DO NOT GROW UP TO BECOME... MY FATHER.
WHAT COULD I POSSIBLY NEED TO MAKE MYSELF READY? I AM READY NOW! READY TO POUND THE BUTCHER OF GODS INTO THE DIRT ONCE AND FOR...

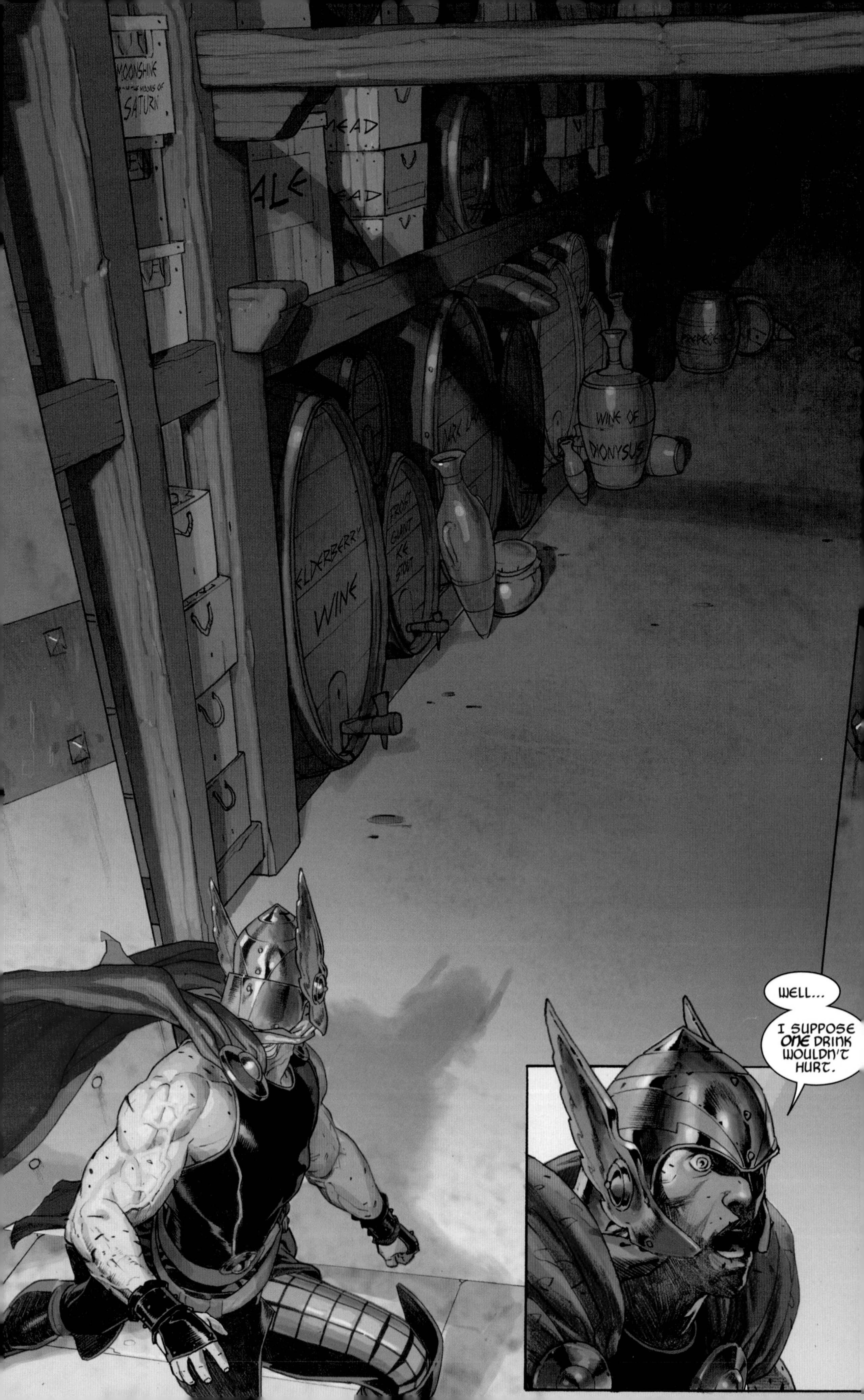

MEAD
ALE
MEAD
ELDERBERRY WINE
WINE OF DIONYSUS
WELL...
I SUPPOSE ONE DRINK WOULDN'T HURT.

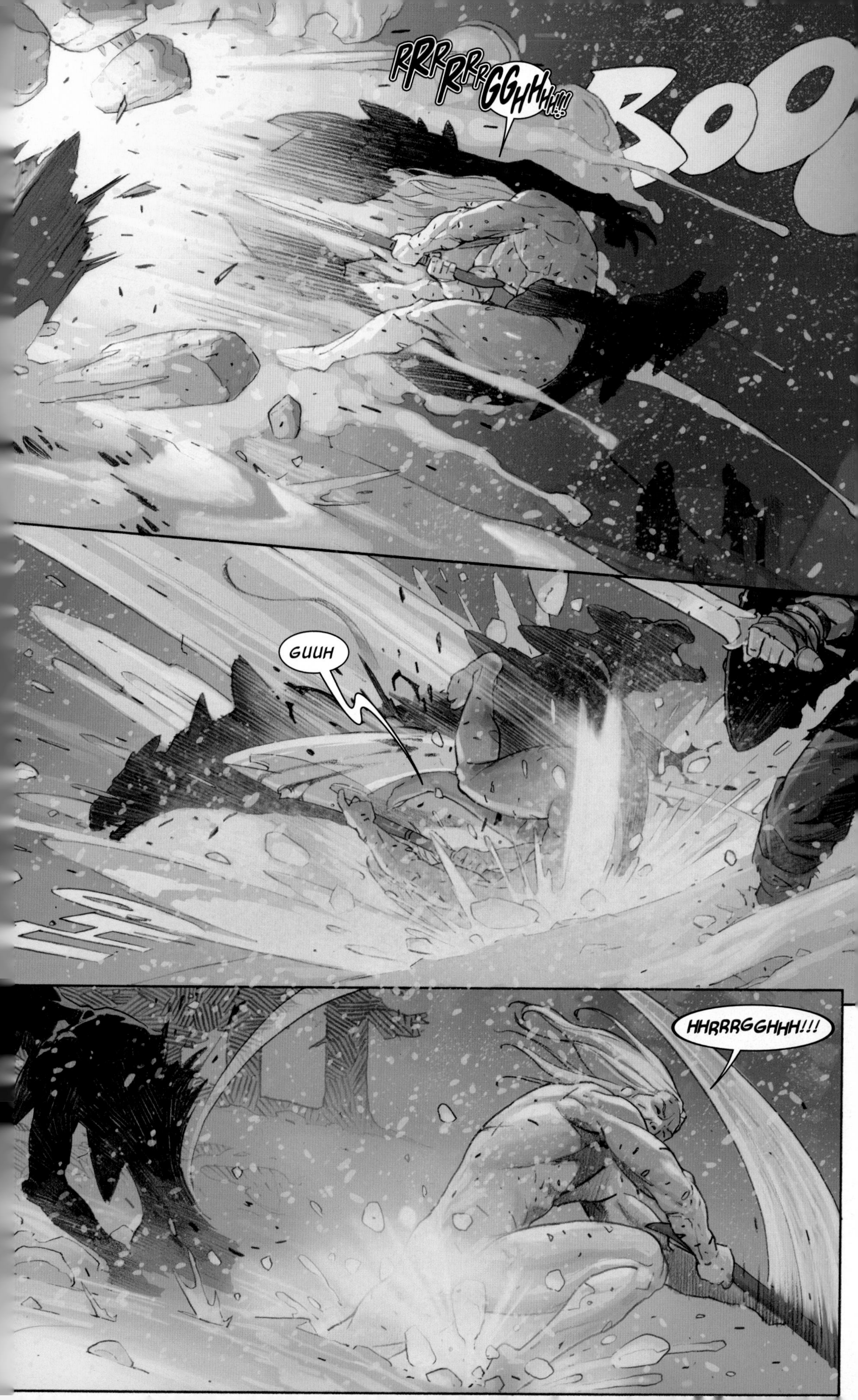
RRRRRRGGHHHH!!!
BOO
GUUH
HHRRRGGHHH!!!

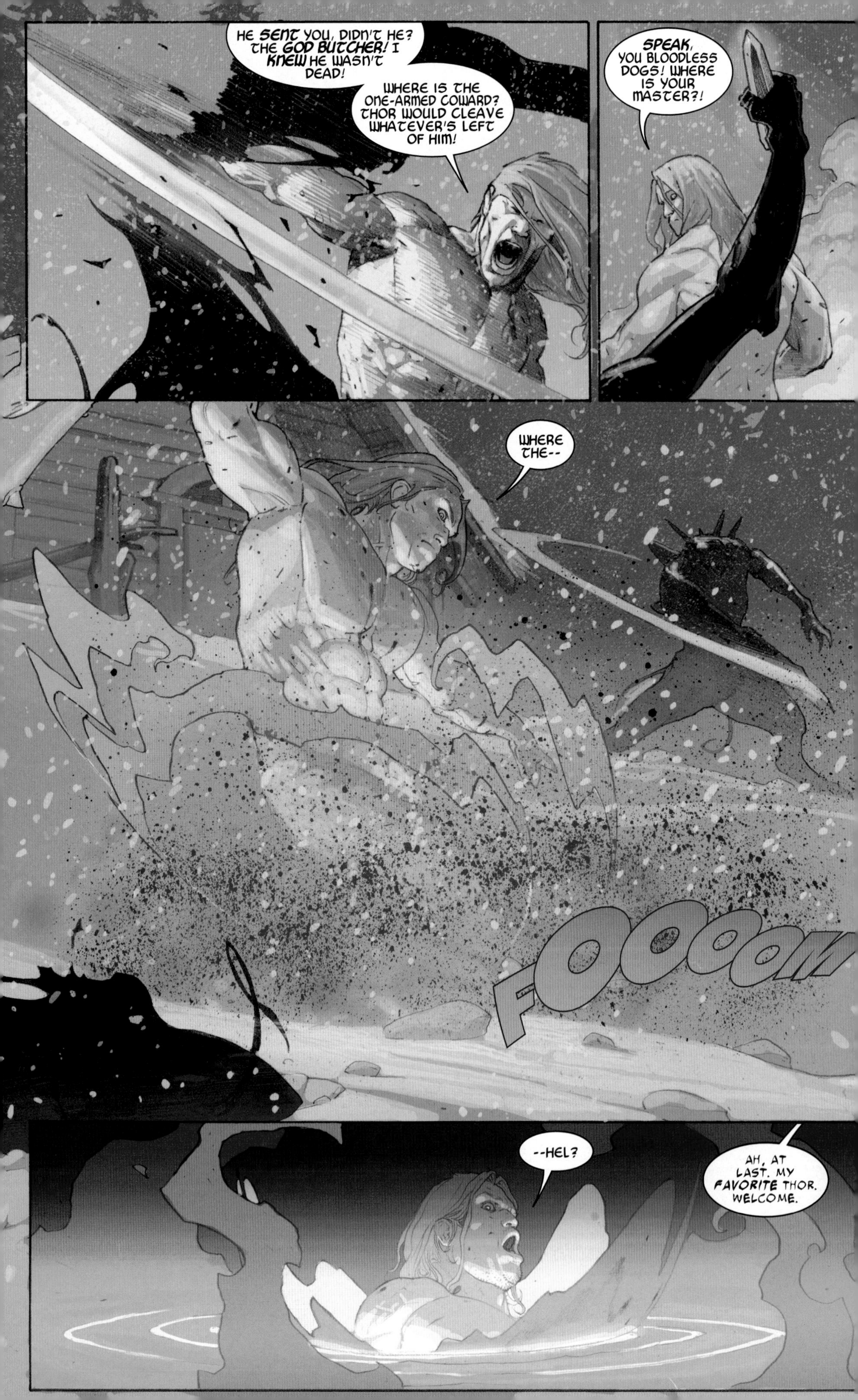
HE SENT YOU, DIDN'T HE? THE GOD BUTCHER! I KNEW HE WASN'T DEAD!
WHERE IS THE ONE-ARMED COWARD? THOR WOULD CLEAVE WHATEVER'S LEFT OF HIM!
SPEAK, YOU BLOODLESS DOGS! WHERE IS YOUR MASTER?!
WHERE THE--
FOOOOM
--HEL?
AH, AT LAST. MY FAVORITE THOR. WELCOME.

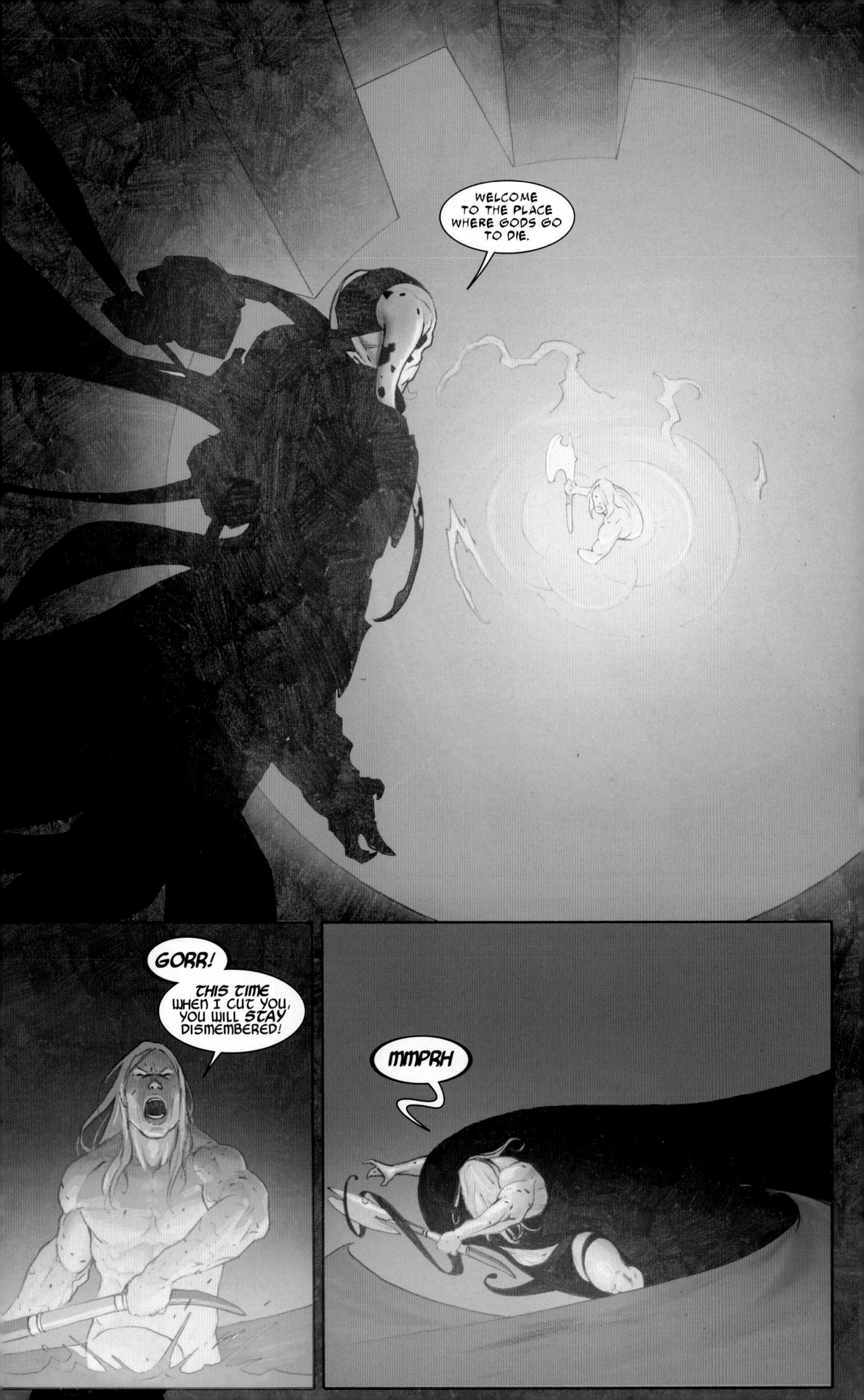
WELCOME TO THE PLACE WHERE GODS GO TO DIE.
GORR!
THIS TIME WHEN I CUT YOU, YOU WILL STAY DISMEMBERED!
MMPRH

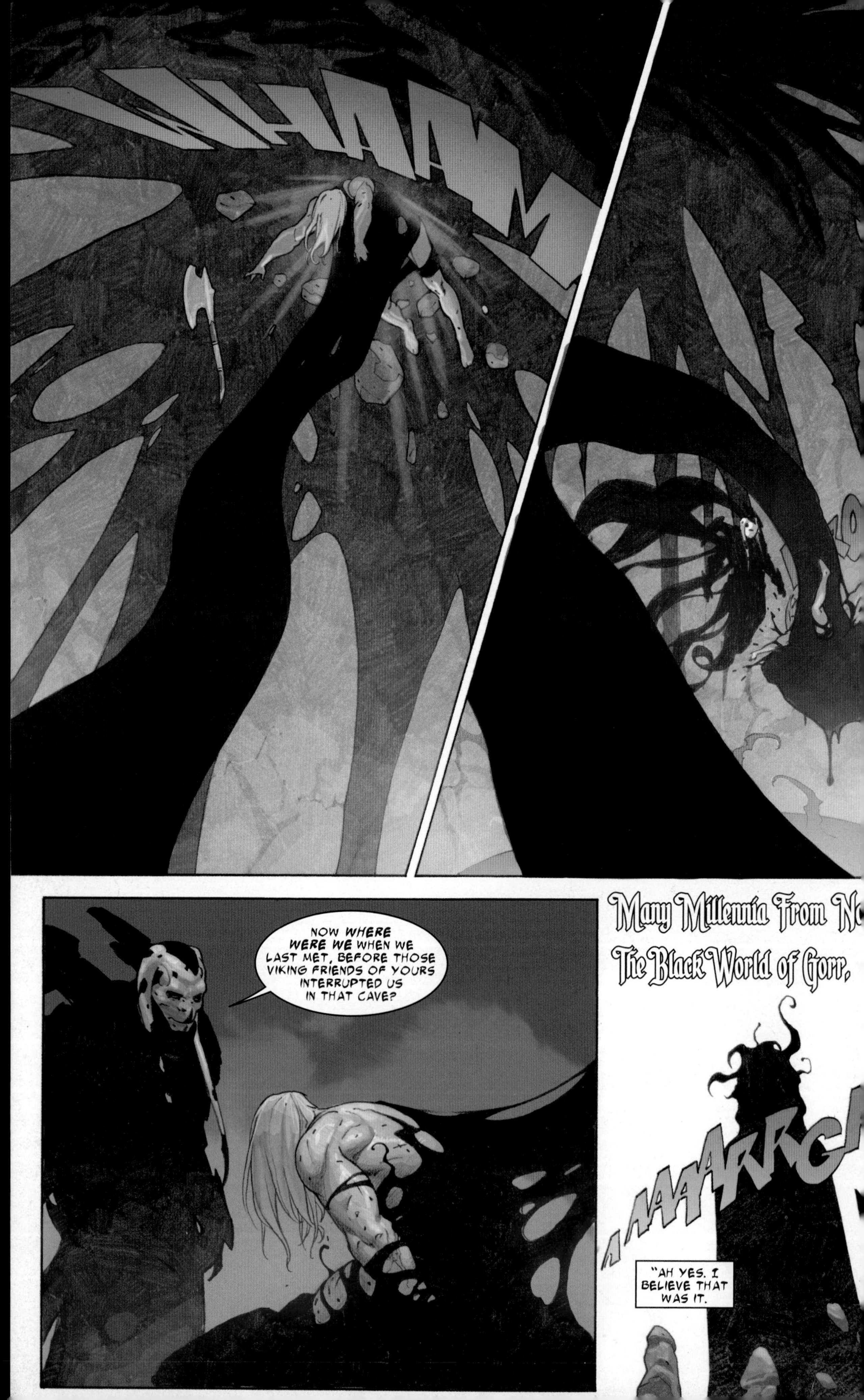
NOW WHERE WERE WE WHEN WE LAST MET, BEFORE THOSE VIKING FRIENDS OF YOURS INTERRUPTED US IN THAT CAVE?
Many Millennia From
The Black World of Gorr,
"AH YES. I BELIEVE THAT WAS IT.

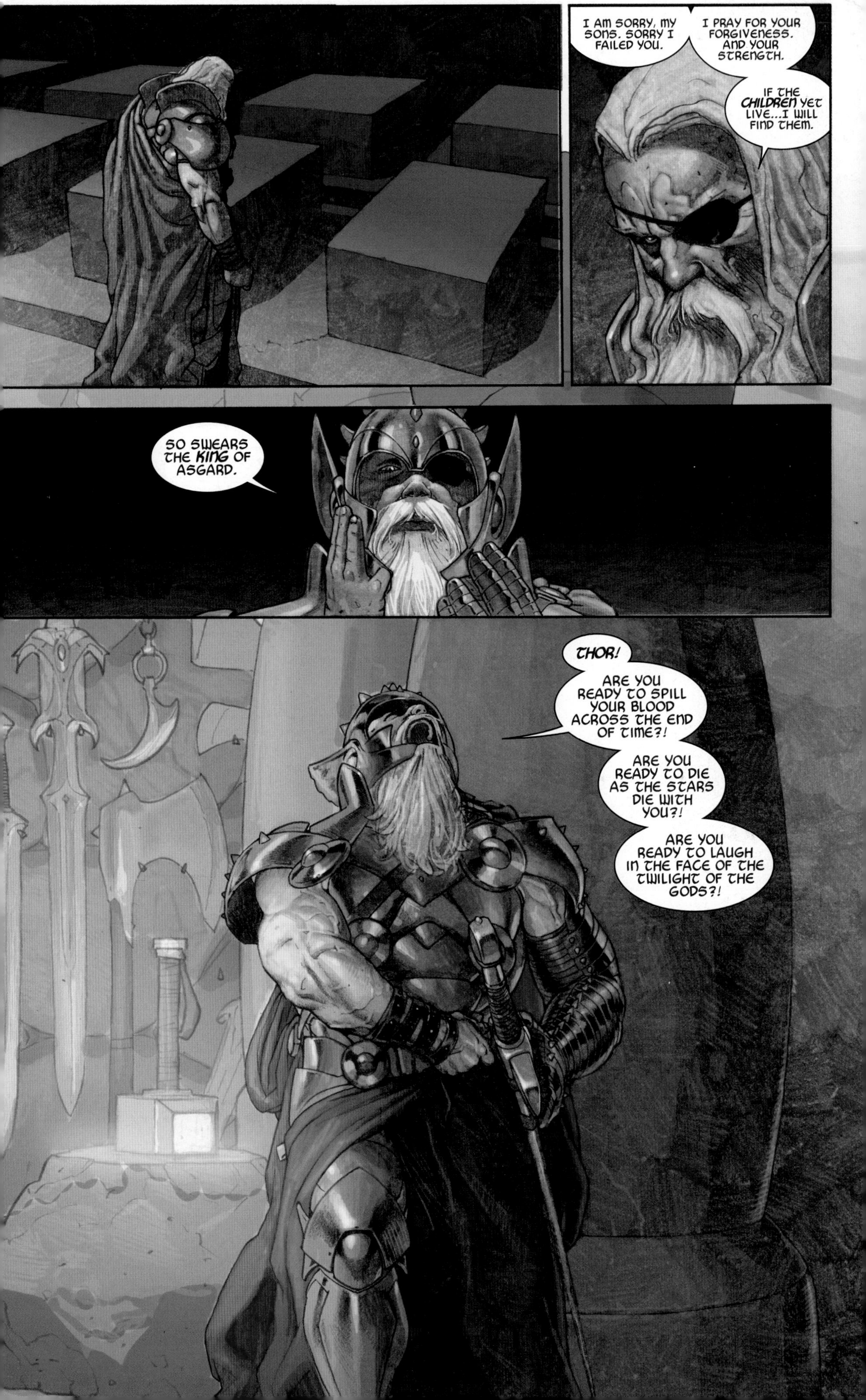
I AM SORRY, MY SONS. SORRY I FAILED YOU.
I PRAY FOR YOUR FORGIVENESS. AND YOUR STRENGTH.
IF THE CHILDREN YET LIVE...I WILL FIND THEM.
SO SWEARS THE KING OF ASGARD.
THOR!
ARE YOU READY TO SPILL YOUR BLOOD ACROSS THE END OF TIME?!
ARE YOU READY TO DIE AS THE STARS DIE WITH YOU?!
ARE YOU READY TO LAUGH IN THE FACE OF THE TWILIGHT OF THE GODS?!

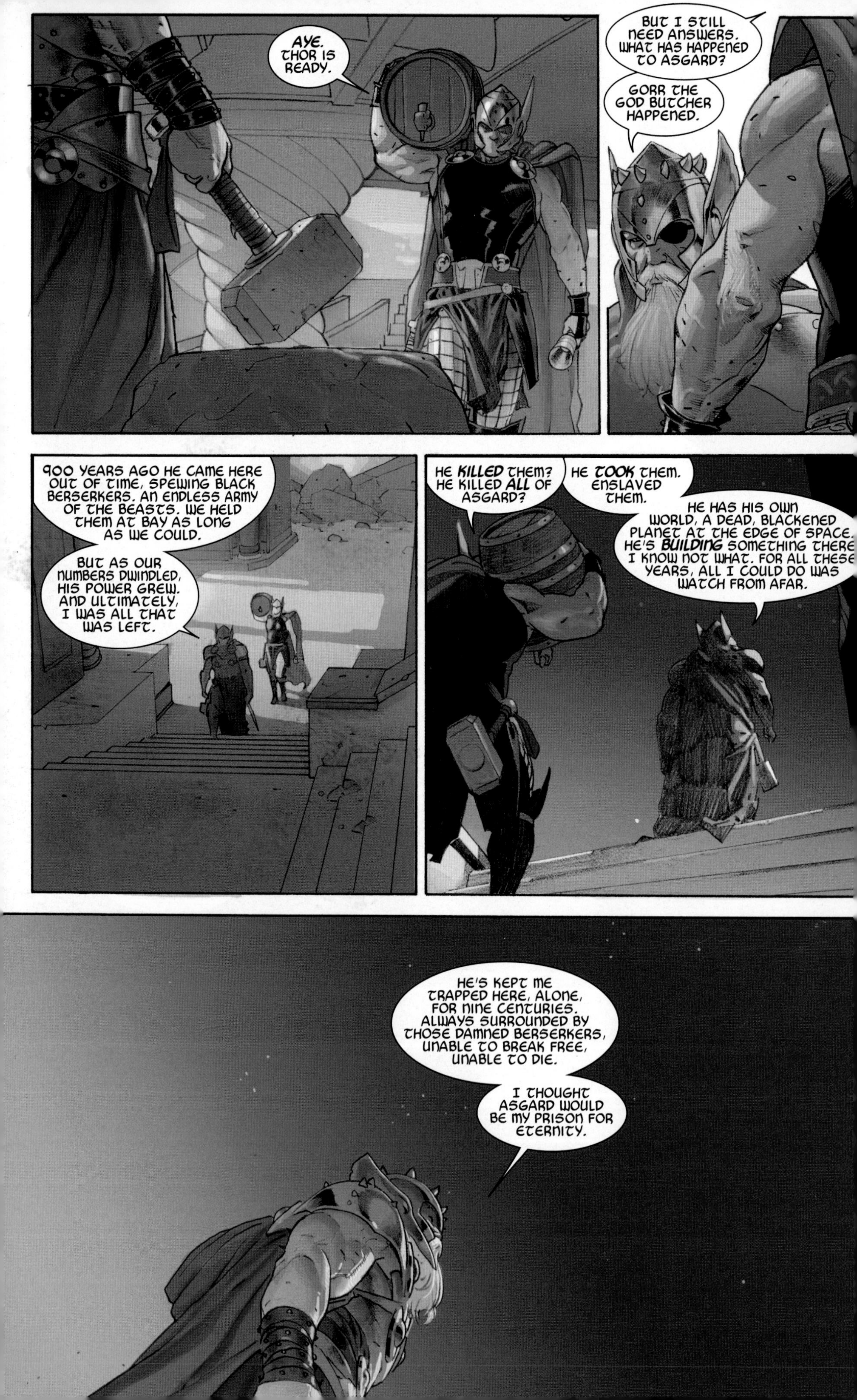
AYE. THOR IS READY.
BUT I STILL NEED ANSWERS. WHAT HAS HAPPENED TO ASGARD?
GORR THE GOD BUTCHER HAPPENED.
900 YEARS AGO HE CAME HERE OUT OF TIME, SPEWING BLACK BERSERKERS. AN ENDLESS ARMY OF THE BEASTS. WE HELD THEM AT BAY AS LONG AS WE COULD.
BUT AS OUR NUMBERS DWINDLED, HIS POWER GREW. AND ULTIMATELY, I WAS ALL THAT WAS LEFT.
HE KILLED THEM? HE KILLED ALL OF ASGARD?
HE TOOK THEM. ENSLAVED THEM.
HE HAS HIS OWN WORLD, A DEAD, BLACKENED PLANET AT THE EDGE OF SPACE. HE'S BUILDING SOMETHING THERE. I KNOW NOT WHAT. FOR ALL THESE YEARS, ALL I COULD DO WAS WATCH FROM AFAR.
HE'S KEPT ME TRAPPED HERE, ALONE, FOR NINE CENTURIES. ALWAYS SURROUNDED BY THOSE DAMNED BERSERKERS, UNABLE TO BREAK FREE, UNABLE TO DIE.
I THOUGHT ASGARD WOULD BE MY PRISON FOR ETERNITY.

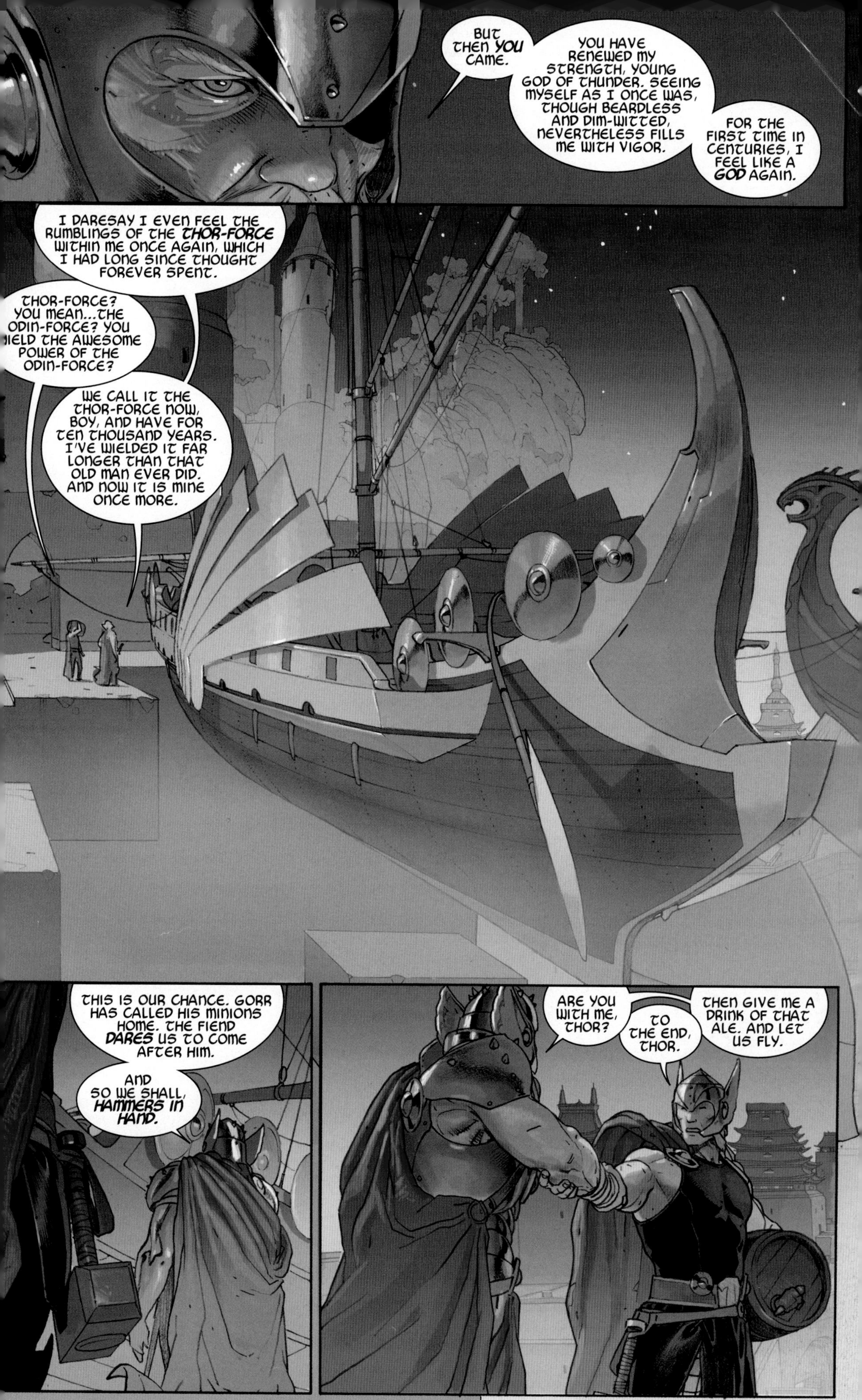
BUT THEN **YOU** CAME.
YOU HAVE RENEWED MY STRENGTH, YOUNG GOD OF THUNDER. SEEING MYSELF AS I ONCE WAS, THOUGH BEARDLESS AND DIM-WITTED, NEVERTHELESS FILLS ME WITH VIGOR.
FOR THE FIRST TIME IN CENTURIES, I FEEL LIKE A **GOD** AGAIN.
I DARESAY I EVEN FEEL THE RUMBLINGS OF THE ***THOR-FORCE*** WITHIN ME ONCE AGAIN, WHICH I HAD LONG SINCE THOUGHT FOREVER SPENT.
THOR-FORCE? YOU MEAN...THE ODIN-FORCE? YOU WIELD THE AWESOME POWER OF THE ODIN-FORCE?
WE CALL IT THE THOR-FORCE NOW, BOY, AND HAVE FOR TEN THOUSAND YEARS. I'VE WIELDED IT FAR LONGER THAN THAT OLD MAN EVER DID. AND NOW IT IS MINE ONCE MORE.
THIS IS OUR CHANCE. GORR HAS CALLED HIS MINIONS HOME. THE FIEND ***DARES*** US TO COME AFTER HIM.
AND SO WE SHALL, ***HAMMERS IN HAND.***
ARE YOU WITH ME, THOR?
TO THE END, THOR.
THEN GIVE ME A DRINK OF THAT ALE. AND LET US FLY.

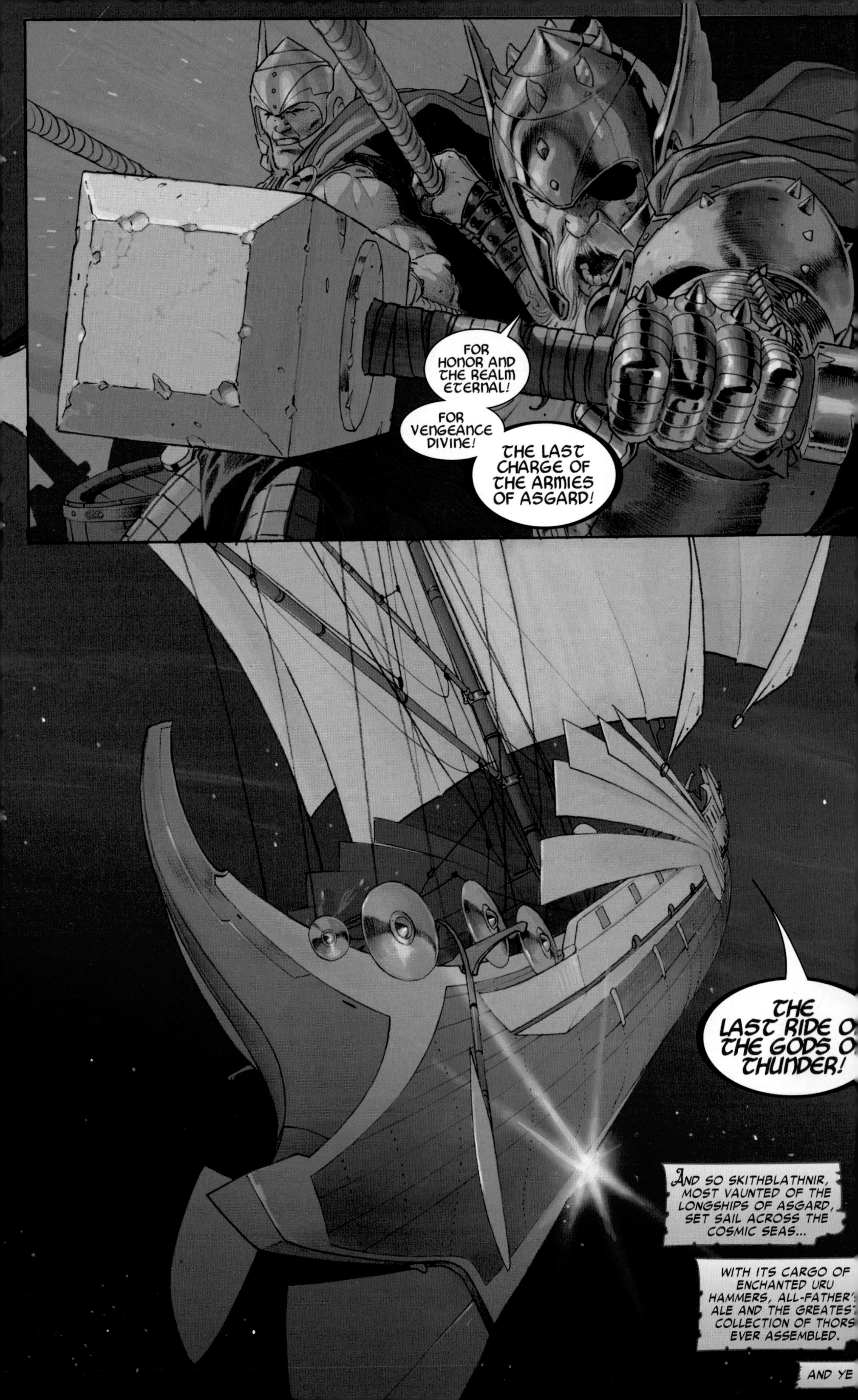

FOR HONOR AND THE REALM ETERNAL!
FOR VENGEANCE DIVINE!
THE LAST CHARGE OF THE ARMIES OF ASGARD!
THE LAST RIDE O THE GODS O THUNDER!
AND SO SKITHBLATHNIR, MOST VAUNTED OF THE LONGSHIPS OF ASGARD, SET SAIL ACROSS THE COSMIC SEAS...
WITH ITS CARGO OF ENCHANTED URU HAMMERS, ALL-FATHER' ALE AND THE GREATES COLLECTION OF THORS EVER ASSEMBLED.
AND YE

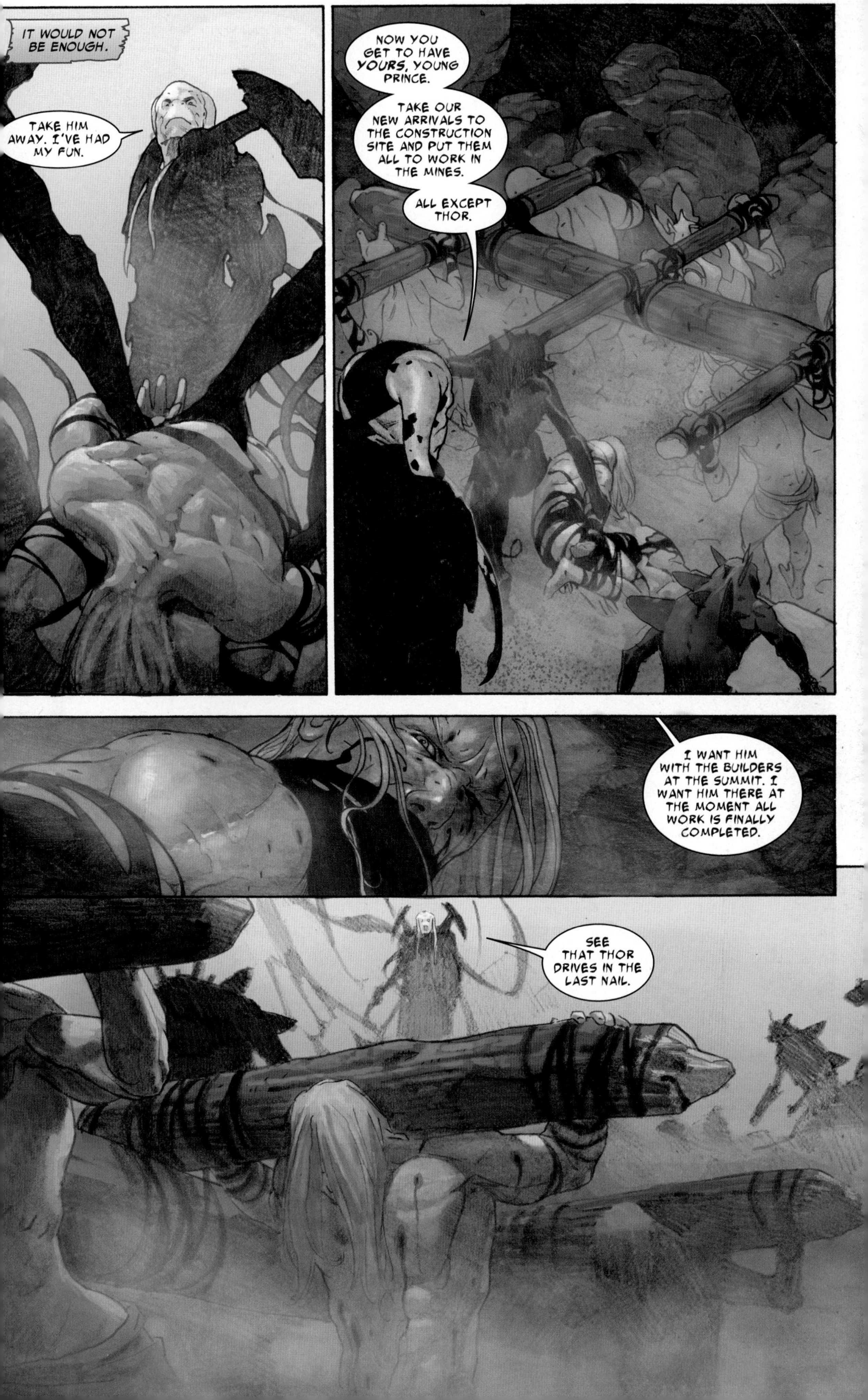
IT WOULD NOT BE ENOUGH.
TAKE HIM AWAY. I'VE HAD MY FUN.
NOW YOU GET TO HAVE YOURS, YOUNG PRINCE.
TAKE OUR NEW ARRIVALS TO THE CONSTRUCTION SITE AND PUT THEM ALL TO WORK IN THE MINES.
ALL EXCEPT THOR.
I WANT HIM WITH THE BUILDERS AT THE SUMMIT. I WANT HIM THERE AT THE MOMENT ALL WORK IS FINALLY COMPLETED.
SEE THAT THOR DRIVES IN THE LAST NAIL.

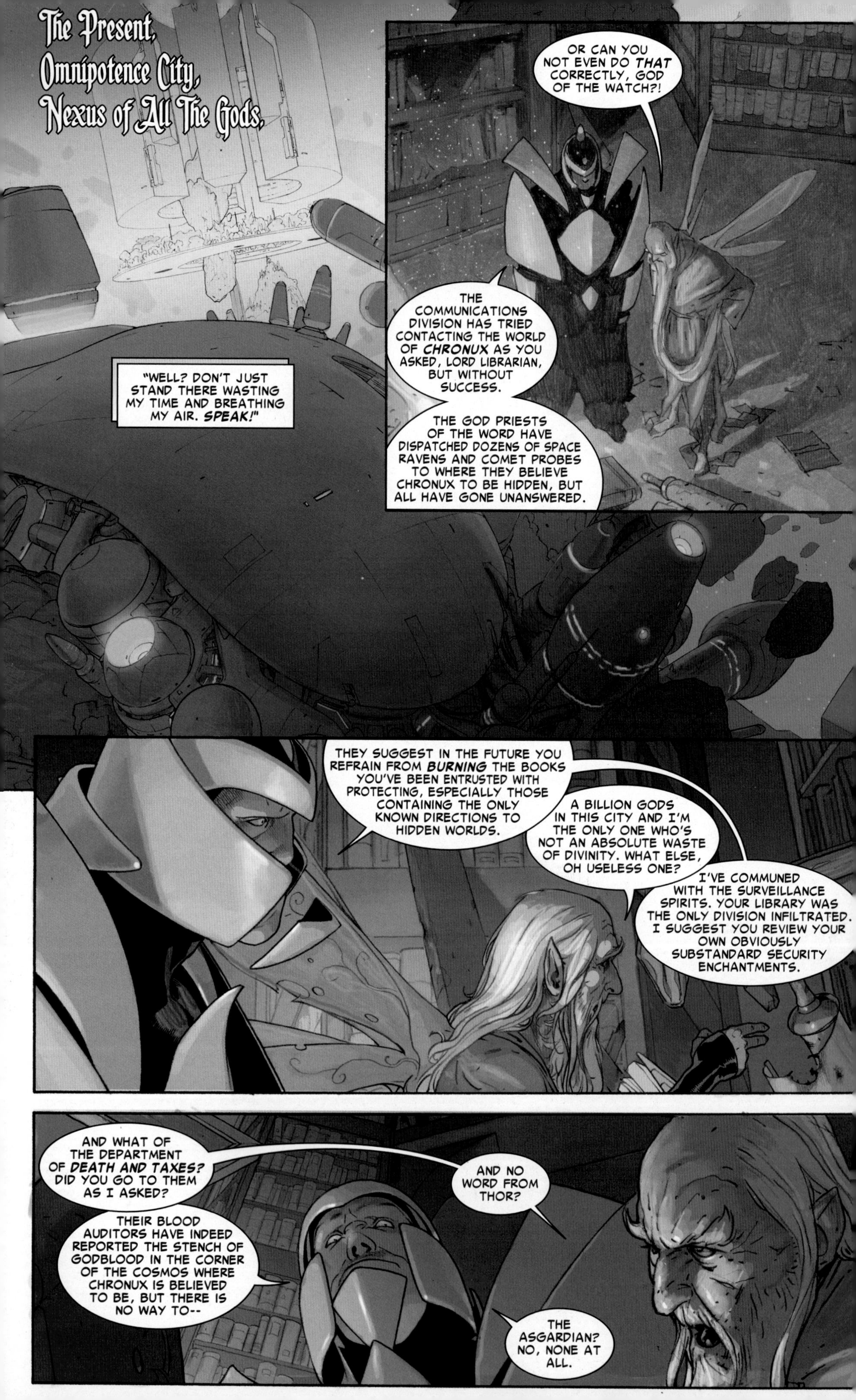
The Present,
Omnipotence City,
Nexus of All The Gods,
"WELL? DON'T JUST STAND THERE WASTING MY TIME AND BREATHING MY AIR. SPEAK!"
OR CAN YOU NOT EVEN DO THAT CORRECTLY, GOD OF THE WATCH?!
THE COMMUNICATIONS DIVISION HAS TRIED CONTACTING THE WORLD OF CHRONUX AS YOU ASKED, LORD LIBRARIAN, BUT WITHOUT SUCCESS.
THE GOD PRIESTS OF THE WORD HAVE DISPATCHED DOZENS OF SPACE RAVENS AND COMET PROBES TO WHERE THEY BELIEVE CHRONUX TO BE HIDDEN, BUT ALL HAVE GONE UNANSWERED.
THEY SUGGEST IN THE FUTURE YOU REFRAIN FROM BURNING THE BOOKS YOU'VE BEEN ENTRUSTED WITH PROTECTING, ESPECIALLY THOSE CONTAINING THE ONLY KNOWN DIRECTIONS TO HIDDEN WORLDS.
A BILLION GODS IN THIS CITY AND I'M THE ONLY ONE WHO'S NOT AN ABSOLUTE WASTE OF DIVINITY. WHAT ELSE, OH USELESS ONE?
I'VE COMMUNED WITH THE SURVEILLANCE SPIRITS. YOUR LIBRARY WAS THE ONLY DIVISION INFILTRATED. I SUGGEST YOU REVIEW YOUR OWN OBVIOUSLY SUBSTANDARD SECURITY ENCHANTMENTS.
AND WHAT OF THE DEPARTMENT OF DEATH AND TAXES? DID YOU GO TO THEM AS I ASKED?
THEIR BLOOD AUDITORS HAVE INDEED REPORTED THE STENCH OF GODBLOOD IN THE CORNER OF THE COSMOS WHERE CHRONUX IS BELIEVED TO BE, BUT THERE IS NO WAY TO--
AND NO WORD FROM THOR?
THE ASGARDIAN? NO, NONE AT ALL.

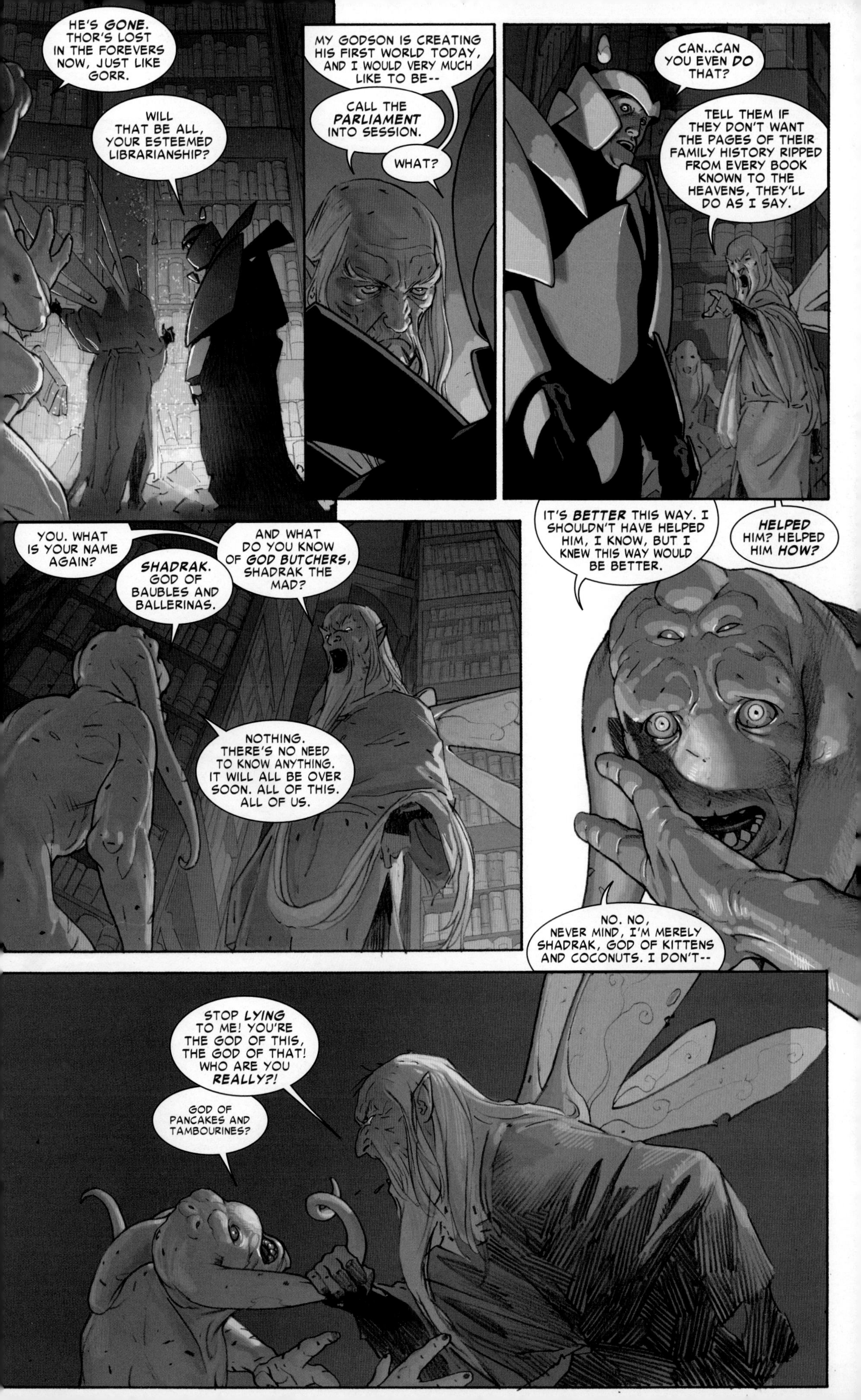
HE'S GONE. THOR'S LOST IN THE FOREVERS NOW, JUST LIKE GORR.
WILL THAT BE ALL, YOUR ESTEEMED LIBRARIANSHIP?
MY GODSON IS CREATING HIS FIRST WORLD TODAY, AND I WOULD VERY MUCH LIKE TO BE--
CALL THE PARLIAMENT INTO SESSION.
WHAT?
CAN...CAN YOU EVEN DO THAT?
TELL THEM IF THEY DON'T WANT THE PAGES OF THEIR FAMILY HISTORY RIPPED FROM EVERY BOOK KNOWN TO THE HEAVENS, THEY'LL DO AS I SAY.
YOU. WHAT IS YOUR NAME AGAIN?
SHADRAK. GOD OF BAUBLES AND BALLERINAS.
AND WHAT DO YOU KNOW OF GOD BUTCHERS, SHADRAK THE MAD?
NOTHING. THERE'S NO NEED TO KNOW ANYTHING. IT WILL ALL BE OVER SOON. ALL OF THIS. ALL OF US.
IT'S BETTER THIS WAY. I SHOULDN'T HAVE HELPED HIM, I KNOW, BUT I KNEW THIS WAY WOULD BE BETTER.
HELPED HIM? HELPED HIM HOW?
NO. NO, NEVER MIND, I'M MERELY SHADRAK, GOD OF KITTENS AND COCONUTS. I DON'T--
STOP LYING TO ME! YOU'RE THE GOD OF THIS, THE GOD OF THAT! WHO ARE YOU REALLY?!
GOD OF PANCAKES AND TAMBOURINES?

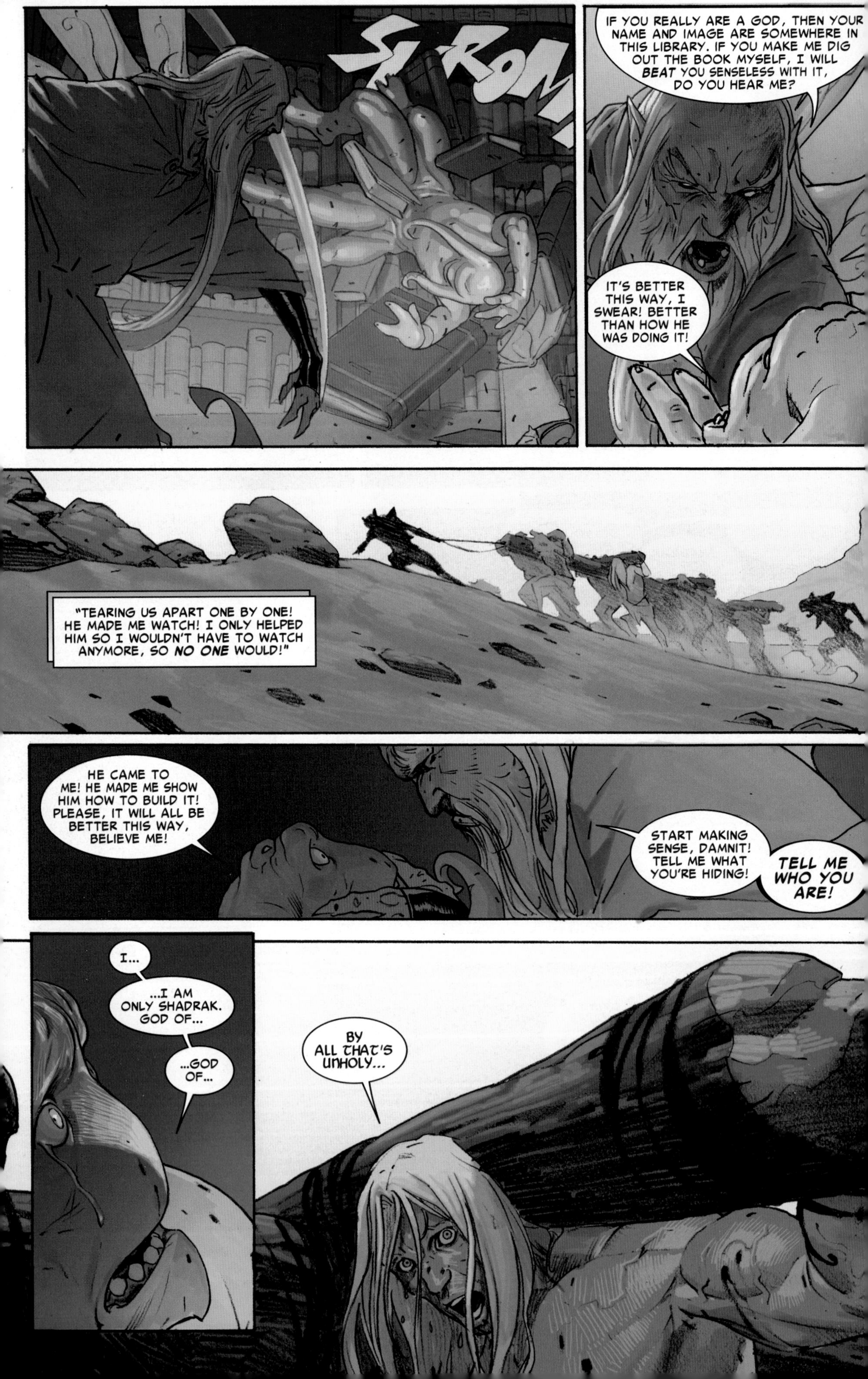

SKROM
IF YOU REALLY ARE A GOD, THEN YOUR NAME AND IMAGE ARE SOMEWHERE IN THIS LIBRARY. IF YOU MAKE ME DIG OUT THE BOOK MYSELF, I WILL BEAT YOU SENSELESS WITH IT, DO YOU HEAR ME?
IT'S BETTER THIS WAY, I SWEAR! BETTER THAN HOW HE WAS DOING IT!
"TEARING US APART ONE BY ONE! HE MADE ME WATCH! I ONLY HELPED HIM SO I WOULDN'T HAVE TO WATCH ANYMORE, SO NO ONE WOULD!"
HE CAME TO ME! HE MADE ME SHOW HIM HOW TO BUILD IT! PLEASE, IT WILL ALL BE BETTER THIS WAY, BELIEVE ME!
START MAKING SENSE, DAMNIT! TELL ME WHAT YOU'RE HIDING!
TELL ME WHO YOU ARE!
I...
...I AM ONLY SHADRAK. GOD OF...
...GOD OF...
BY ALL THAT'S UNHOLY...

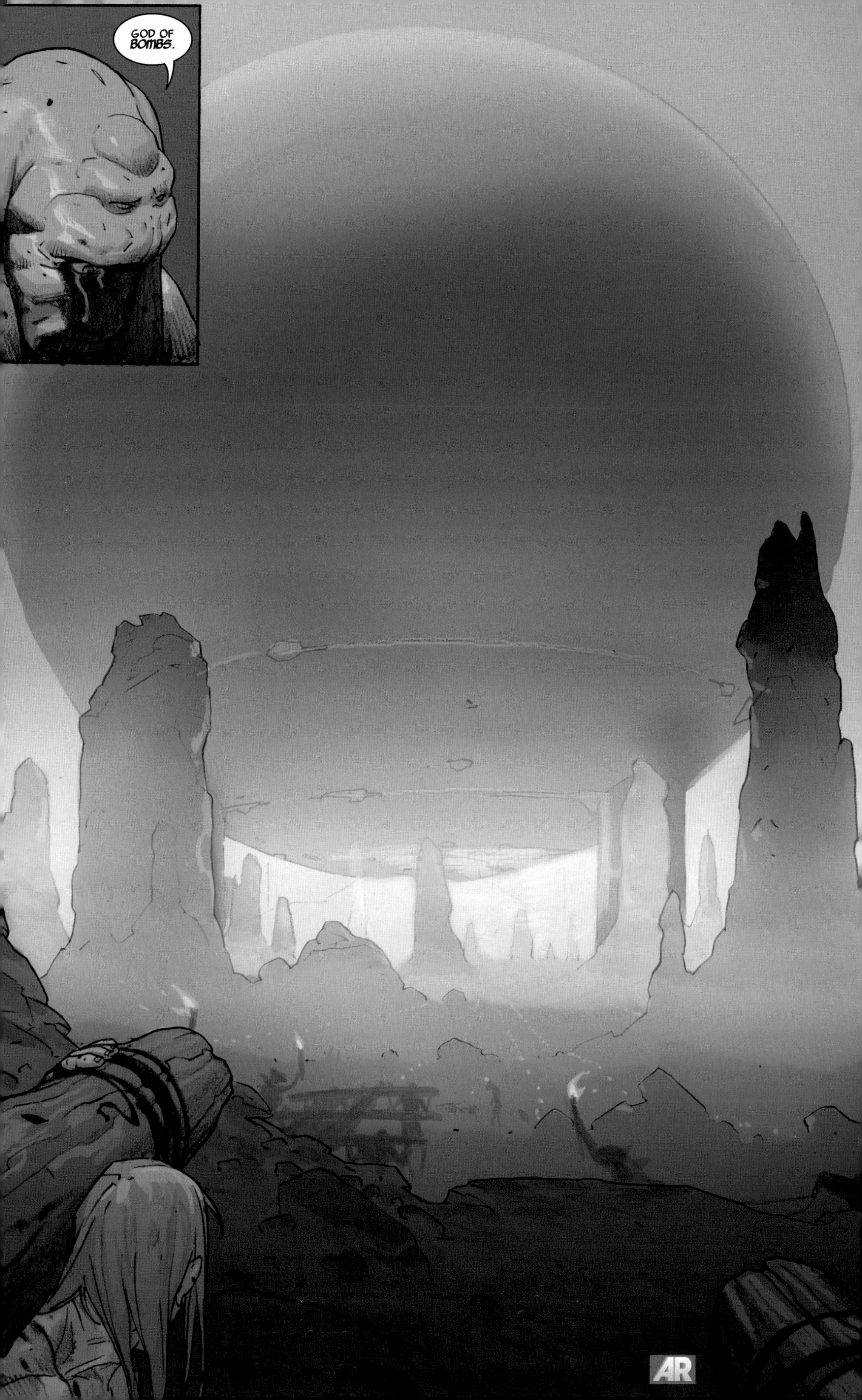
GOD OF BOMBS.

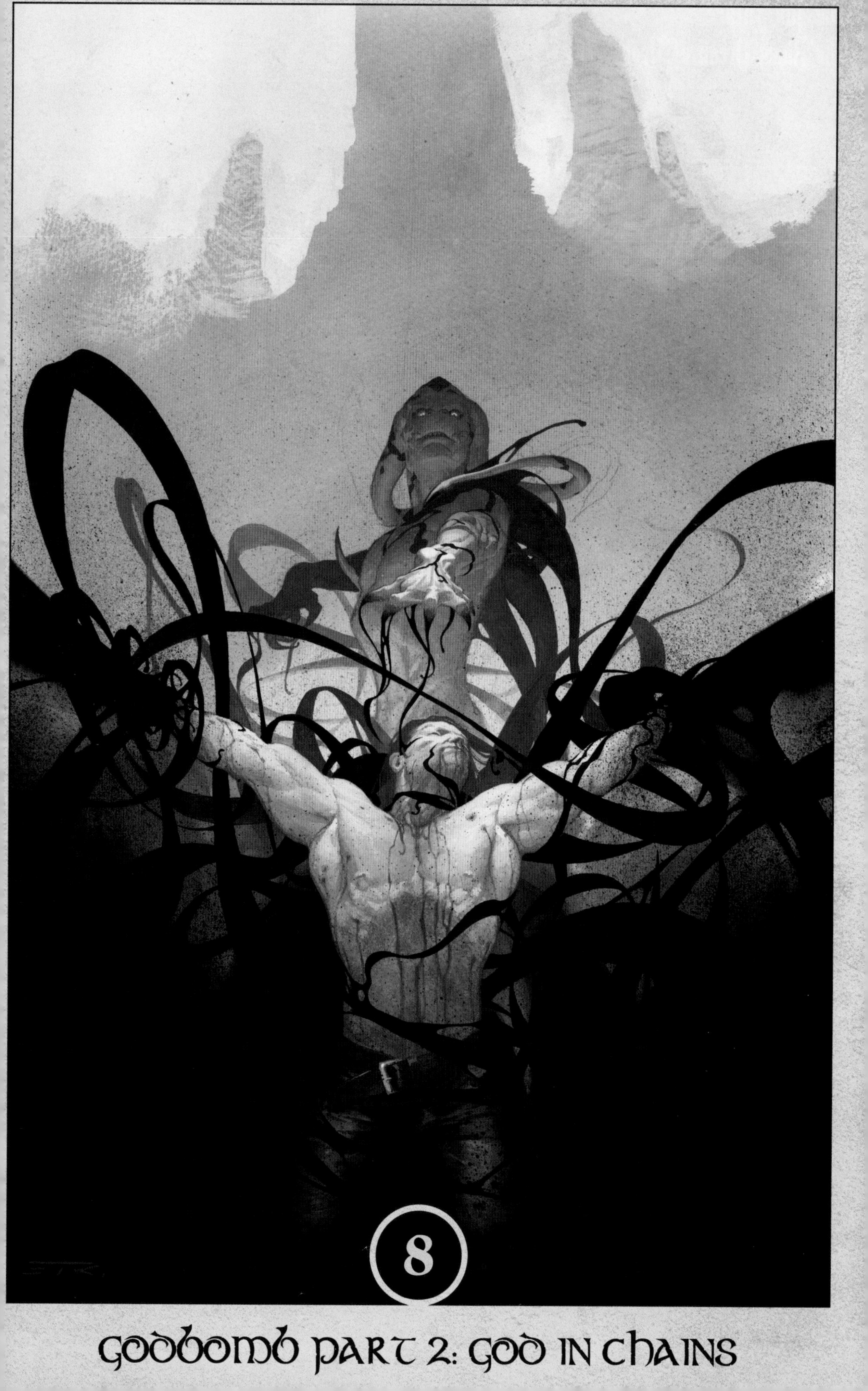
8

GODBOMB PART 2: GOD IN CHAINS

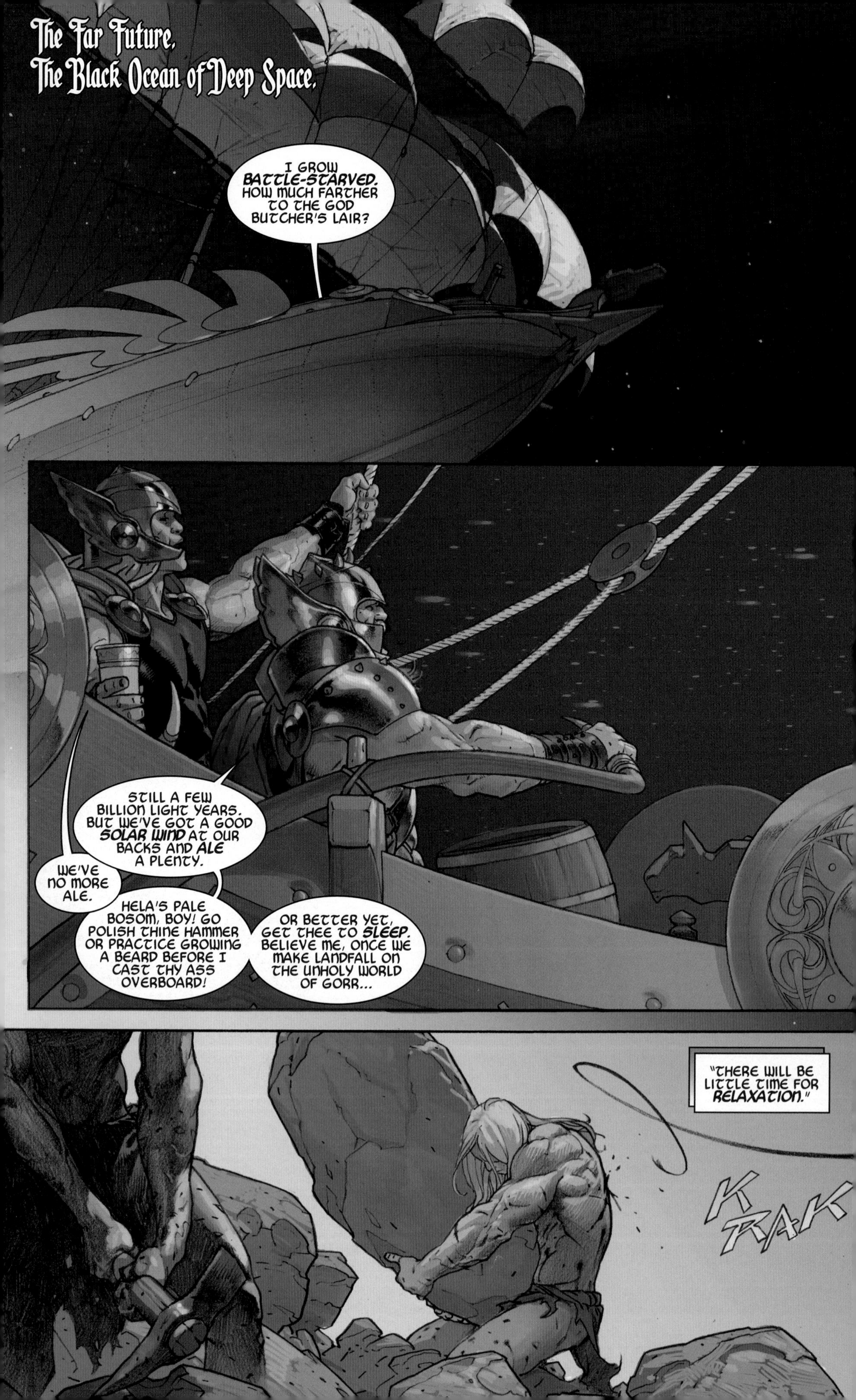
The Far Future,
The Black Ocean of Deep Space,
I GROW BATTLE-STARVED. HOW MUCH FARTHER TO THE GOD BUTCHER'S LAIR?
STILL A FEW BILLION LIGHT YEARS. BUT WE'VE GOT A GOOD SOLAR WIND AT OUR BACKS AND ALE A PLENTY.
WE'VE NO MORE ALE.
HELA'S PALE BOSOM, BOY! GO POLISH THINE HAMMER OR PRACTICE GROWING A BEARD BEFORE I CAST THY ASS OVERBOARD!
OR BETTER YET, GET THEE TO SLEEP. BELIEVE ME, ONCE WE MAKE LANDFALL ON THE UNHOLY WORLD OF GORR...
"THERE WILL BE LITTLE TIME FOR RELAXATION."
KRAK

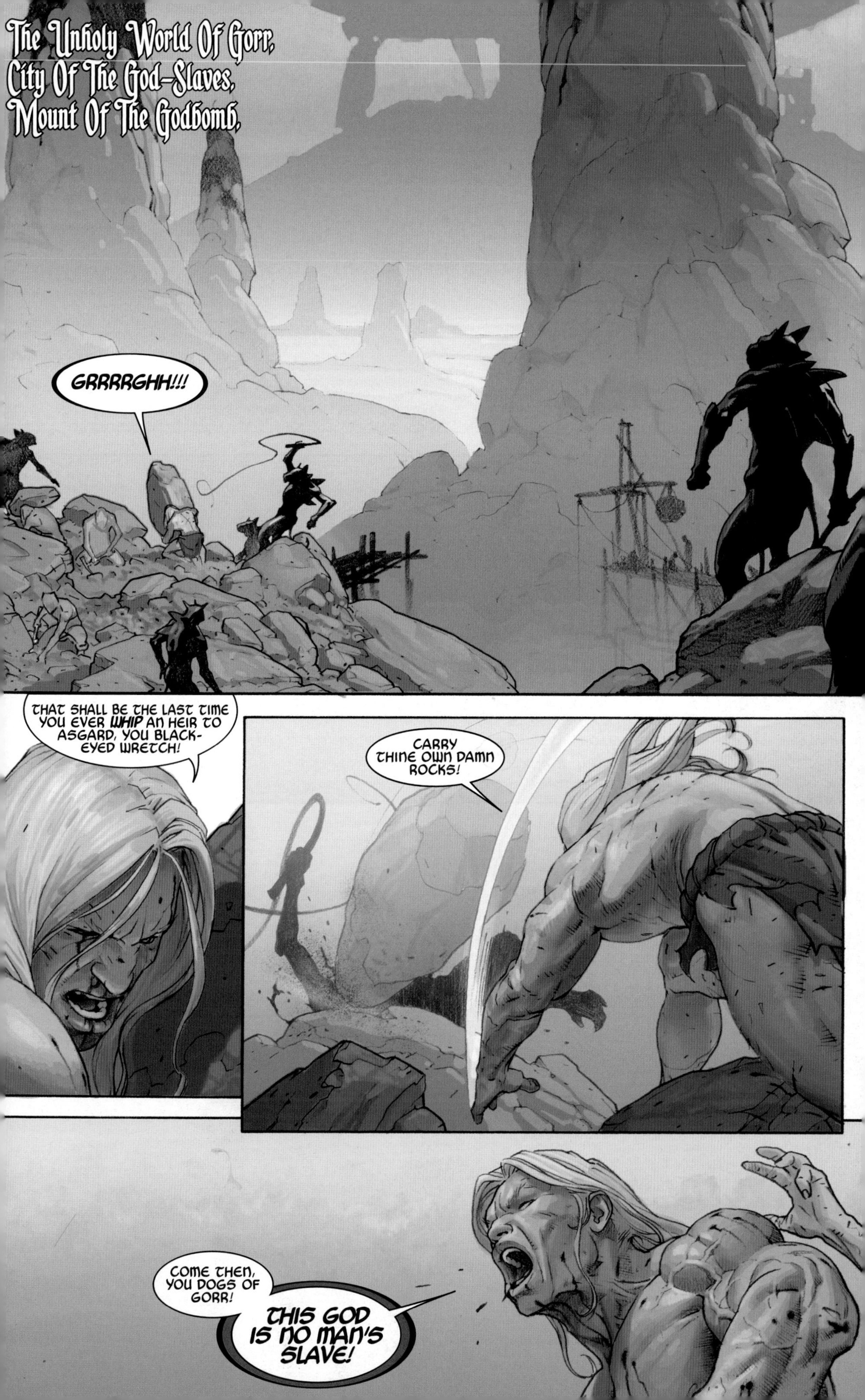
The Unholy World Of Gorr,
City Of The God-Slaves,
Mount Of The Godbomb.
GRRRRGHH!!!
THAT SHALL BE THE LAST TIME YOU EVER WHIP AN HEIR TO ASGARD, YOU BLACK-EYED WRETCH!
CARRY THINE OWN DAMN ROCKS!
COME THEN, YOU DOGS OF GORR!
THIS GOD IS NO MAN'S SLAVE!

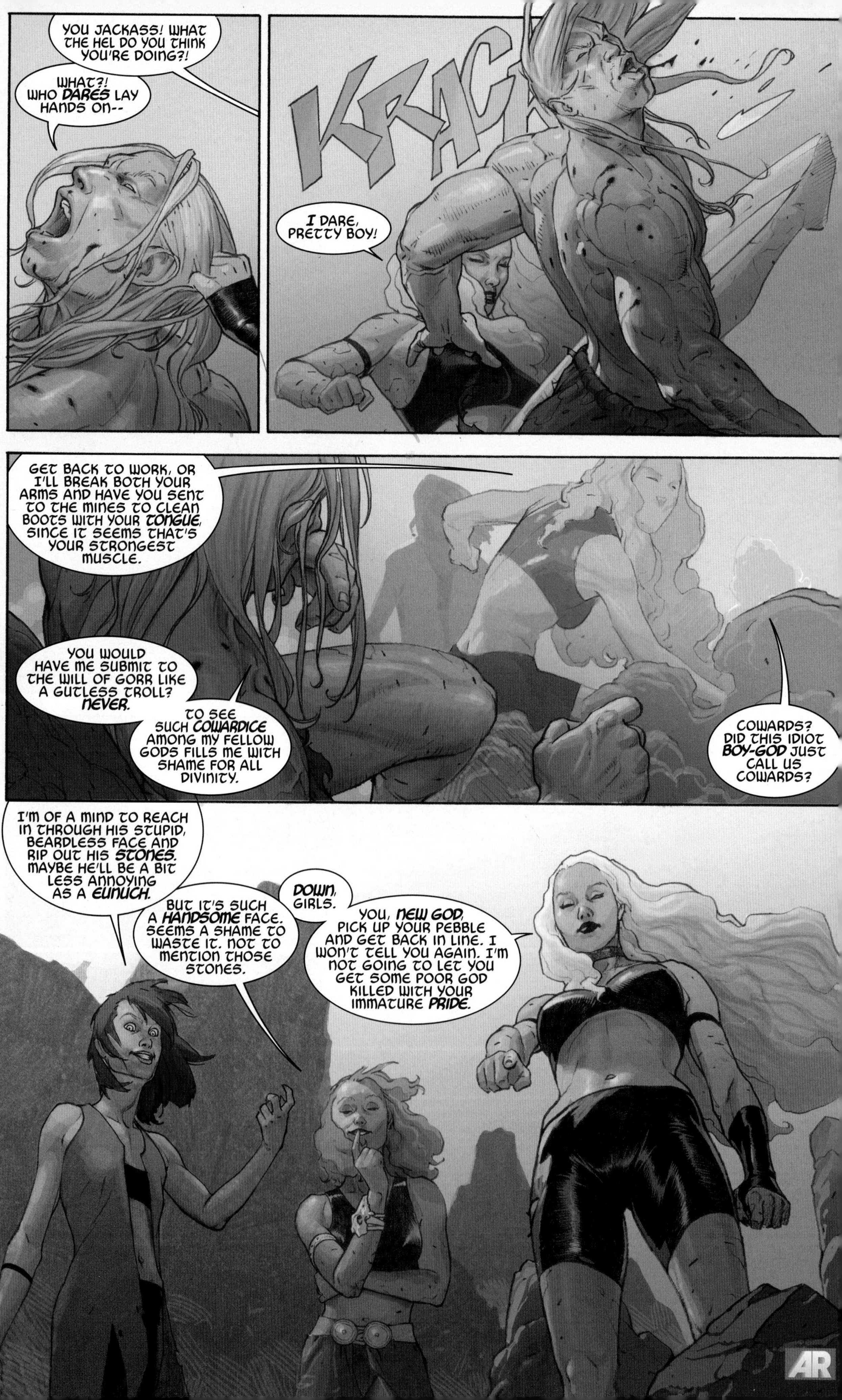
YOU JACKASS! WHAT THE HEL DO YOU THINK YOU'RE DOING?!
WHAT?! WHO DARES LAY HANDS ON--
KRAC
I DARE, PRETTY BOY!
GET BACK TO WORK, OR I'LL BREAK BOTH YOUR ARMS AND HAVE YOU SENT TO THE MINES TO CLEAN BOOTS WITH YOUR TONGUE, SINCE IT SEEMS THAT'S YOUR STRONGEST MUSCLE.
YOU WOULD HAVE ME SUBMIT TO THE WILL OF GORR LIKE A GUTLESS TROLL? NEVER.
TO SEE SUCH COWARDICE AMONG MY FELLOW GODS FILLS ME WITH SHAME FOR ALL DIVINITY.
COWARDS? DID THIS IDIOT BOY-GOD JUST CALL US COWARDS?
I'M OF A MIND TO REACH IN THROUGH HIS STUPID, BEARDLESS FACE AND RIP OUT HIS STONES. MAYBE HE'LL BE A BIT LESS ANNOYING AS A EUNUCH.
BUT IT'S SUCH A HANDSOME FACE. SEEMS A SHAME TO WASTE IT. NOT TO MENTION THOSE STONES.
DOWN, GIRLS.
YOU, NEW GOD, PICK UP YOUR PEBBLE AND GET BACK IN LINE. I WON'T TELL YOU AGAIN. I'M NOT GOING TO LET YOU GET SOME POOR GOD KILLED WITH YOUR IMMATURE PRIDE.
AR

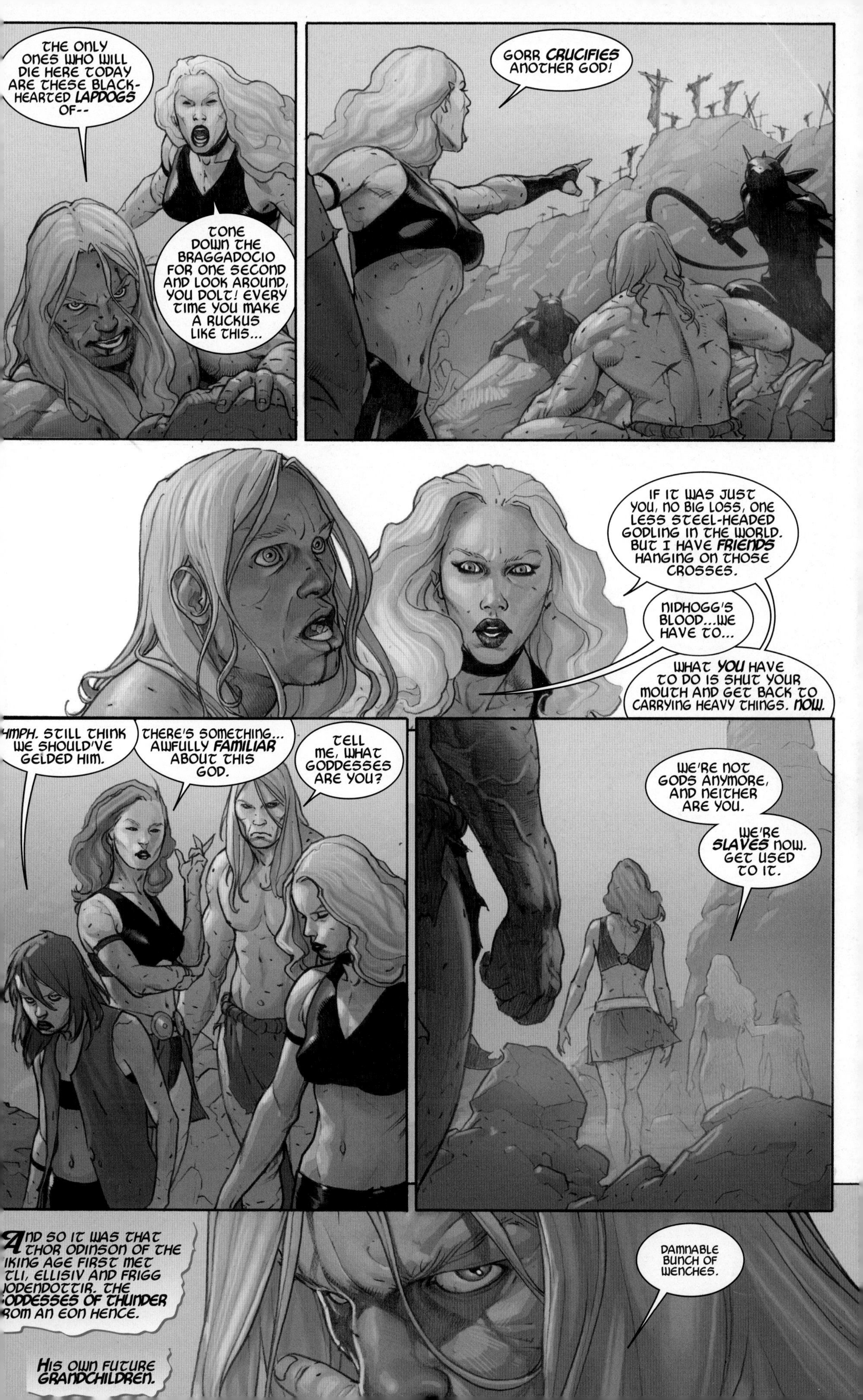
THE ONLY ONES WHO WILL DIE HERE TODAY ARE THESE BLACK-HEARTED LAPDOGS OF--
TONE DOWN THE BRAGGADOCIO FOR ONE SECOND AND LOOK AROUND, YOU DOLT! EVERY TIME YOU MAKE A RUCKUS LIKE THIS...
GORR CRUCIFIES ANOTHER GOD!
IF IT WAS JUST YOU, NO BIG LOSS, ONE LESS STEEL-HEADED GODLING IN THE WORLD. BUT I HAVE FRIENDS HANGING ON THOSE CROSSES.
NIDHOGG'S BLOOD...WE HAVE TO...
WHAT YOU HAVE TO DO IS SHUT YOUR MOUTH AND GET BACK TO CARRYING HEAVY THINGS. NOW.
HMPH. STILL THINK WE SHOULD'VE GELDED HIM.
THERE'S SOMETHING... AWFULLY FAMILIAR ABOUT THIS GOD.
TELL ME, WHAT GODDESSES ARE YOU?
WE'RE NOT GODS ANYMORE, AND NEITHER ARE YOU.
WE'RE SLAVES NOW. GET USED TO IT.
AND SO IT WAS THAT THOR ODINSON OF THE VIKING AGE FIRST MET ATLI, ELLISIV AND FRIGG THORDENDOTTIR. THE GODDESSES OF THUNDER FROM AN EON HENCE.
DAMNABLE BUNCH OF WENCHES.
HIS OWN FUTURE GRANDCHILDREN.

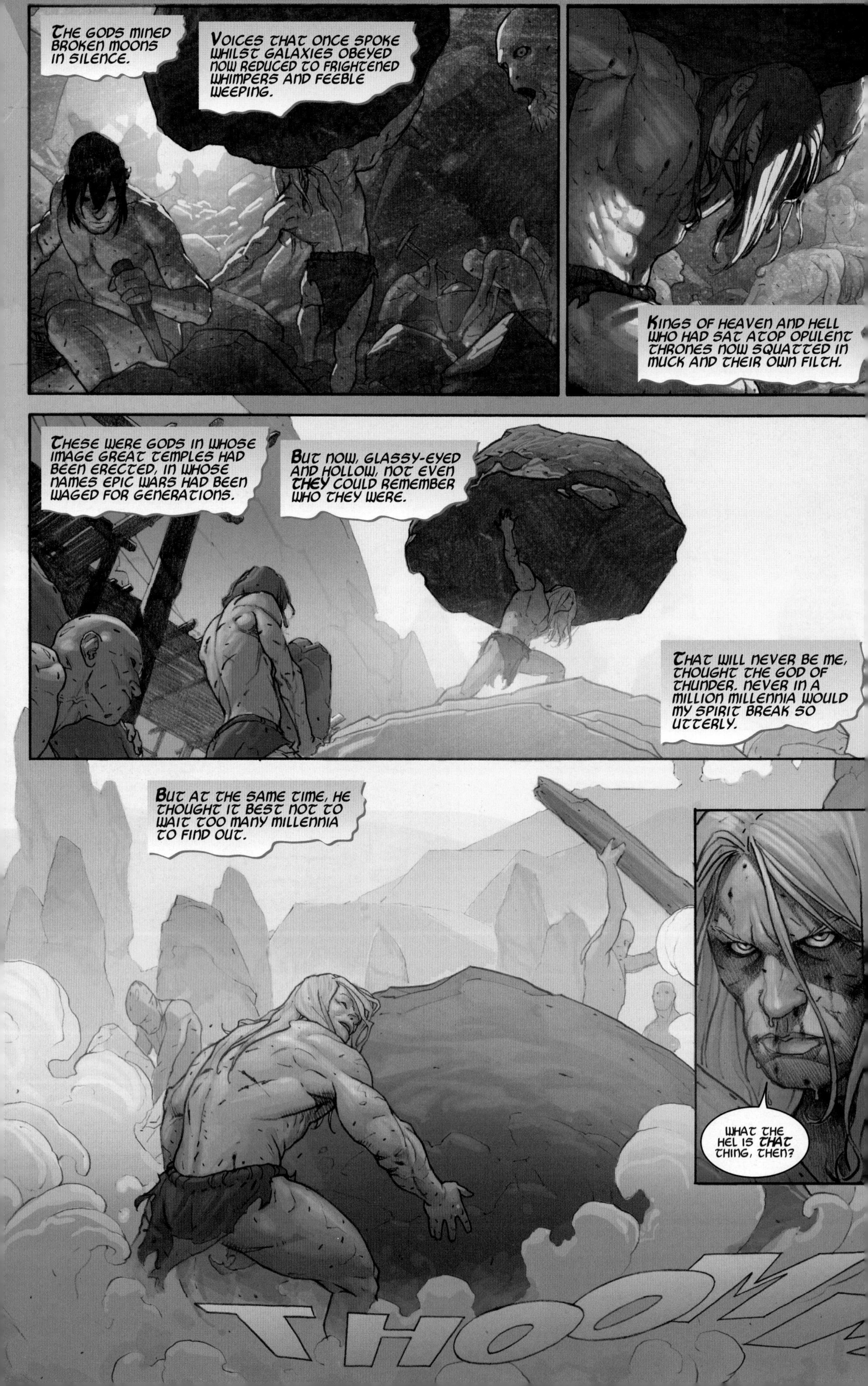
The gods mined broken moons in silence.
Voices that once spoke whilst galaxies obeyed now reduced to frightened whimpers and feeble weeping.
Kings of heaven and hell who had sat atop opulent thrones now squatted in muck and their own filth.
These were gods in whose image great temples had been erected, in whose names epic wars had been waged for generations.
But now, glassy-eyed and hollow, not even THEY could remember who they were.
That will never be me, thought the god of thunder. Never in a million millennia would my spirit break so utterly.
But at the same time, he thought it best not to wait too many millennia to find out.
What the Hel is THAT thing, then?

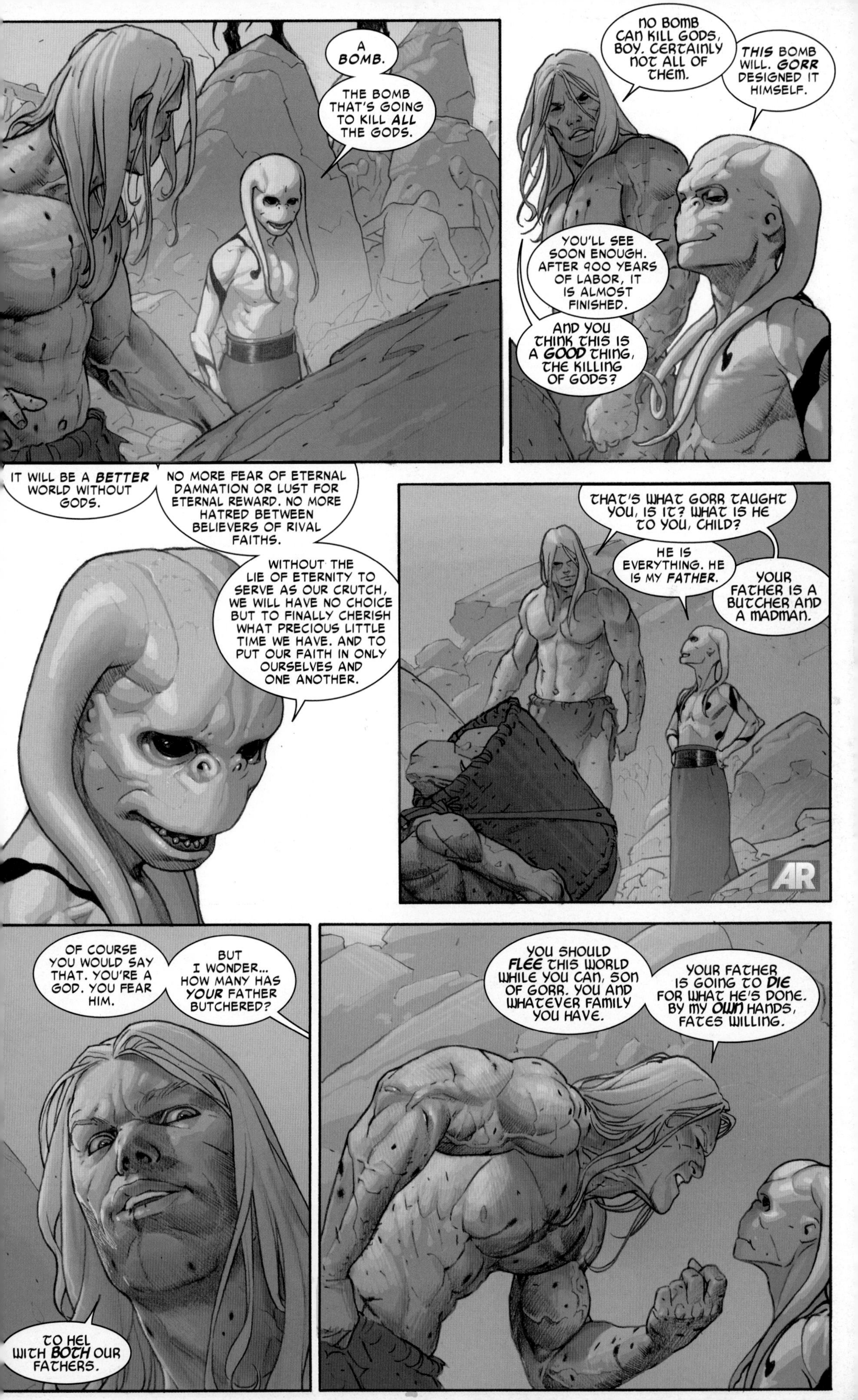
A BOMB.
THE BOMB THAT'S GOING TO KILL ALL THE GODS.
NO BOMB CAN KILL GODS, BOY. CERTAINLY NOT ALL OF THEM.
THIS BOMB WILL. GORR DESIGNED IT HIMSELF.
YOU'LL SEE SOON ENOUGH. AFTER 900 YEARS OF LABOR, IT IS ALMOST FINISHED.
AND YOU THINK THIS IS A GOOD THING, THE KILLING OF GODS?
IT WILL BE A BETTER WORLD WITHOUT GODS.
NO MORE FEAR OF ETERNAL DAMNATION OR LUST FOR ETERNAL REWARD. NO MORE HATRED BETWEEN BELIEVERS OF RIVAL FAITHS.
WITHOUT THE LIE OF ETERNITY TO SERVE AS OUR CRUTCH, WE WILL HAVE NO CHOICE BUT TO FINALLY CHERISH WHAT PRECIOUS LITTLE TIME WE HAVE. AND TO PUT OUR FAITH IN ONLY OURSELVES AND ONE ANOTHER.
THAT'S WHAT GORR TAUGHT YOU, IS IT? WHAT IS HE TO YOU, CHILD?
HE IS EVERYTHING. HE IS MY FATHER.
YOUR FATHER IS A BUTCHER AND A MADMAN.
AR
OF COURSE YOU WOULD SAY THAT. YOU'RE A GOD. YOU FEAR HIM.
BUT I WONDER... HOW MANY HAS YOUR FATHER BUTCHERED?
TO HEL WITH BOTH OUR FATHERS.
YOU SHOULD FLEE THIS WORLD WHILE YOU CAN, SON OF GORR. YOU AND WHATEVER FAMILY YOU HAVE.
YOUR FATHER IS GOING TO DIE FOR WHAT HE'S DONE. BY MY OWN HANDS, FATES WILLING.

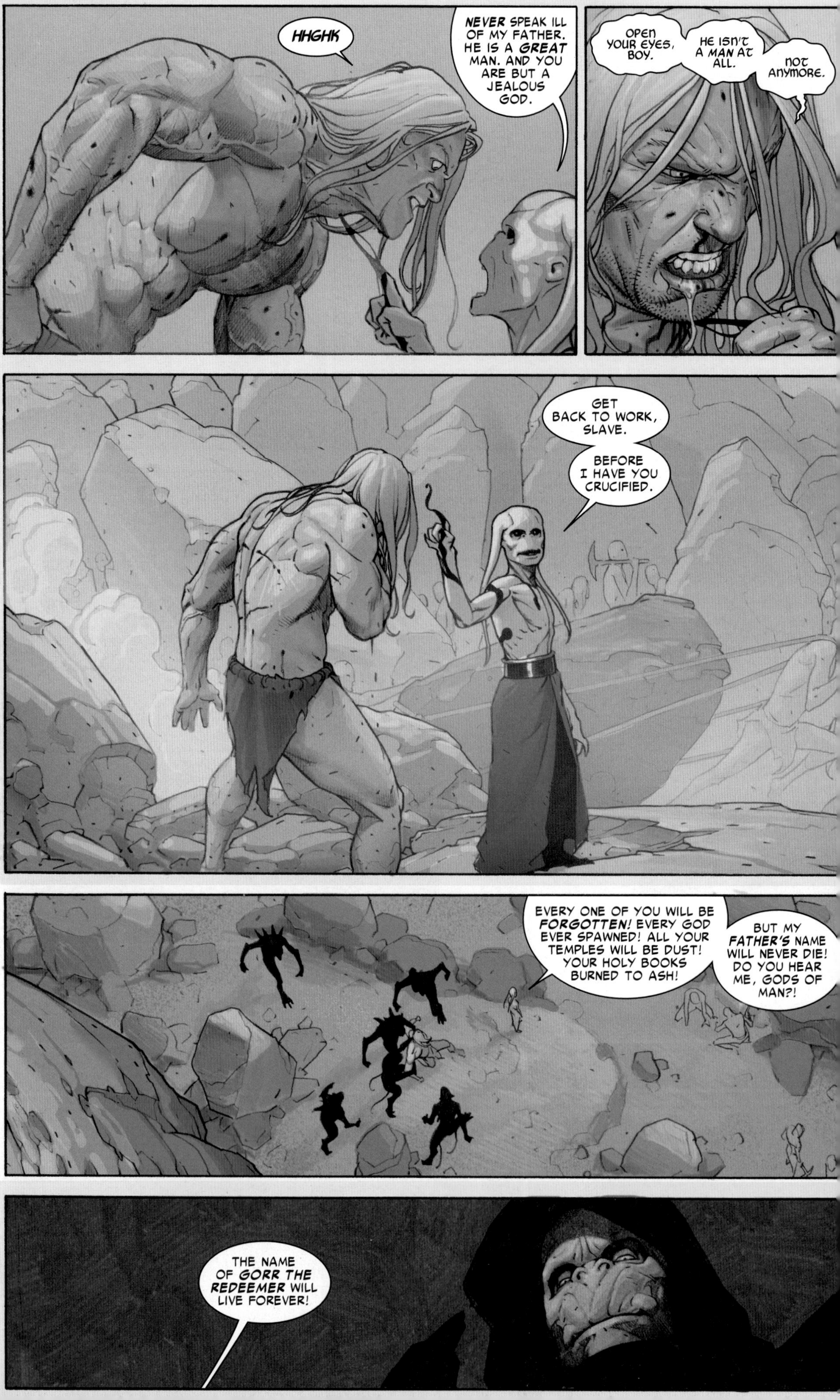
HHGHK
NEVER SPEAK ILL OF MY FATHER. HE IS A GREAT MAN. AND YOU ARE BUT A JEALOUS GOD.
OPEN YOUR EYES, BOY.
HE ISN'T A MAN AT ALL.
NOT ANYMORE.
GET BACK TO WORK, SLAVE.
BEFORE I HAVE YOU CRUCIFIED.
EVERY ONE OF YOU WILL BE FORGOTTEN! EVERY GOD EVER SPAWNED! ALL YOUR TEMPLES WILL BE DUST! YOUR HOLY BOOKS BURNED TO ASH!
BUT MY FATHER'S NAME WILL NEVER DIE! DO YOU HEAR ME, GODS OF MAN?!
THE NAME OF GORR THE REDEEMER WILL LIVE FOREVER!

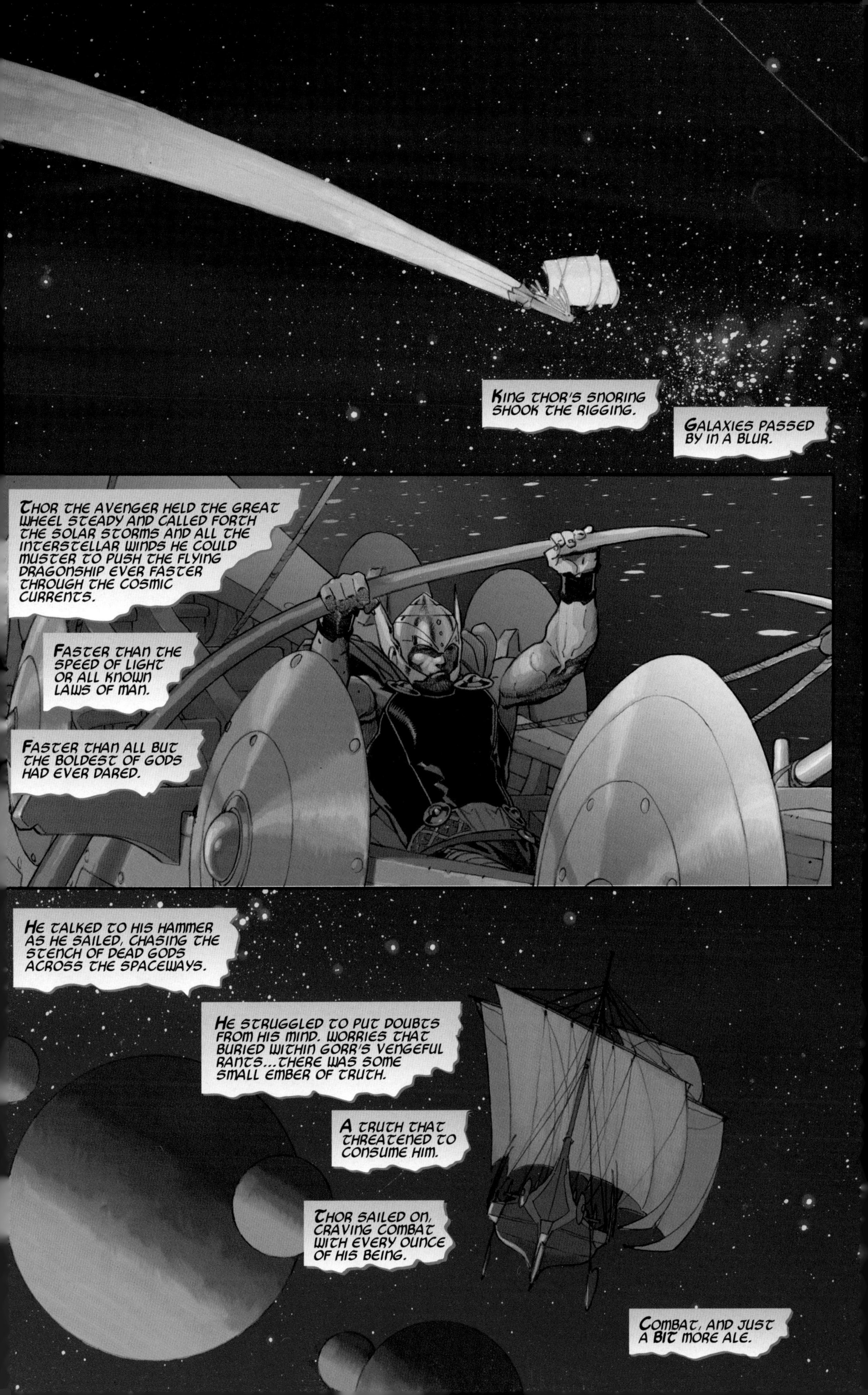

King Thor's snoring shook the rigging.
Galaxies passed by in a blur.
Thor the Avenger held the great wheel steady and called forth the solar storms and all the interstellar winds he could muster to push the flying dragonship ever faster through the cosmic currents.
Faster than the speed of light or all known laws of man.
Faster than all but the boldest of gods had ever dared.
He talked to his hammer as he sailed, chasing the stench of dead gods across the spaceways.
He struggled to put doubts from his mind. Worries that buried within Gorr's vengeful rants...there was some small ember of truth.
A truth that threatened to consume him.
Thor sailed on, craving combat with every ounce of his being.
Combat, and just a BIT more ale.

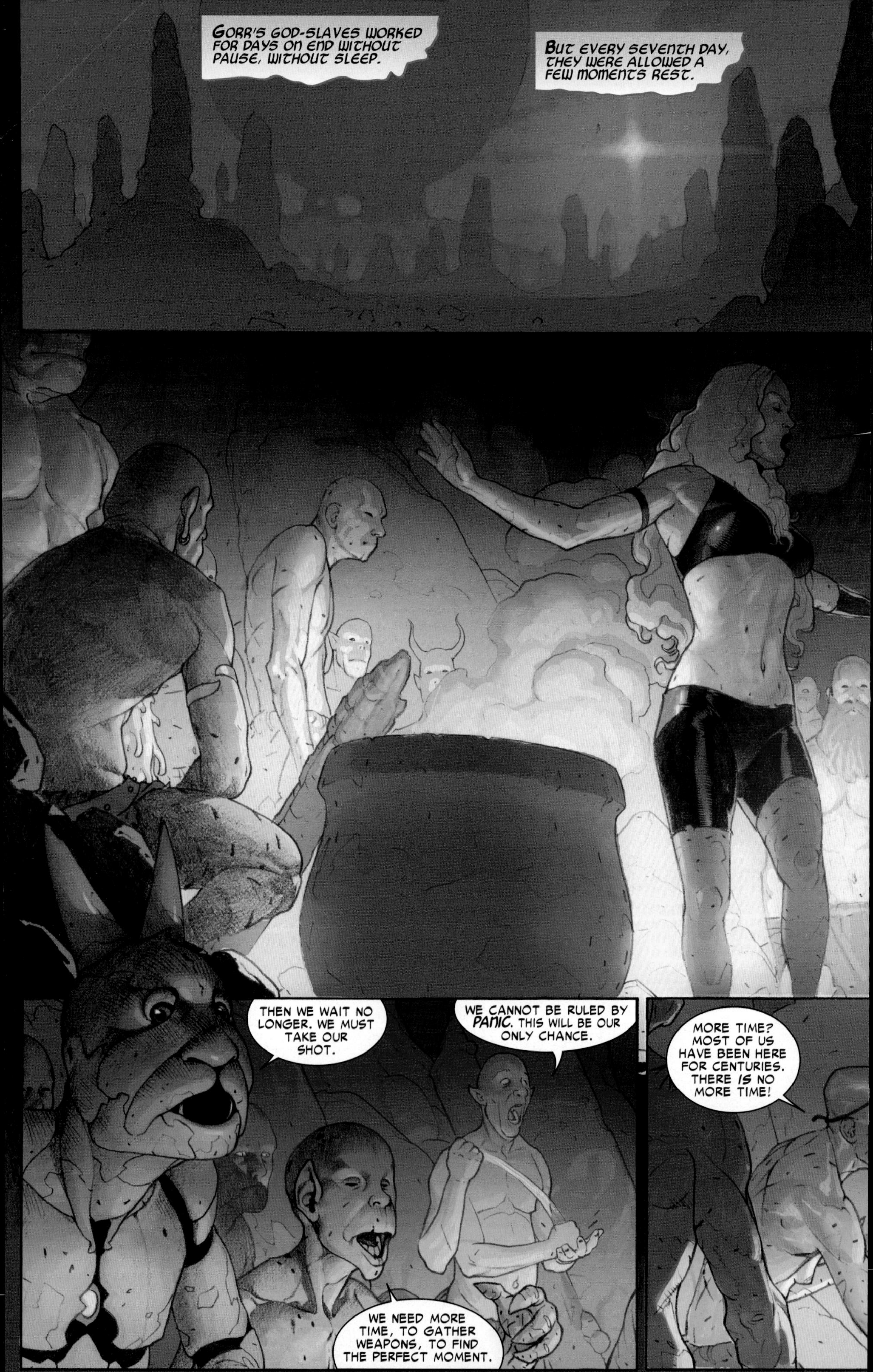
GORR'S GOD-SLAVES WORKED FOR DAYS ON END WITHOUT PAUSE, WITHOUT SLEEP.
BUT EVERY SEVENTH DAY, THEY WERE ALLOWED A FEW MOMENTS REST.
THEN WE WAIT NO LONGER. WE MUST TAKE OUR SHOT.
WE CANNOT BE RULED BY PANIC. THIS WILL BE OUR ONLY CHANCE.
WE NEED MORE TIME, TO GATHER WEAPONS, TO FIND THE PERFECT MOMENT.
MORE TIME? MOST OF US HAVE BEEN HERE FOR CENTURIES. THERE IS NO MORE TIME!

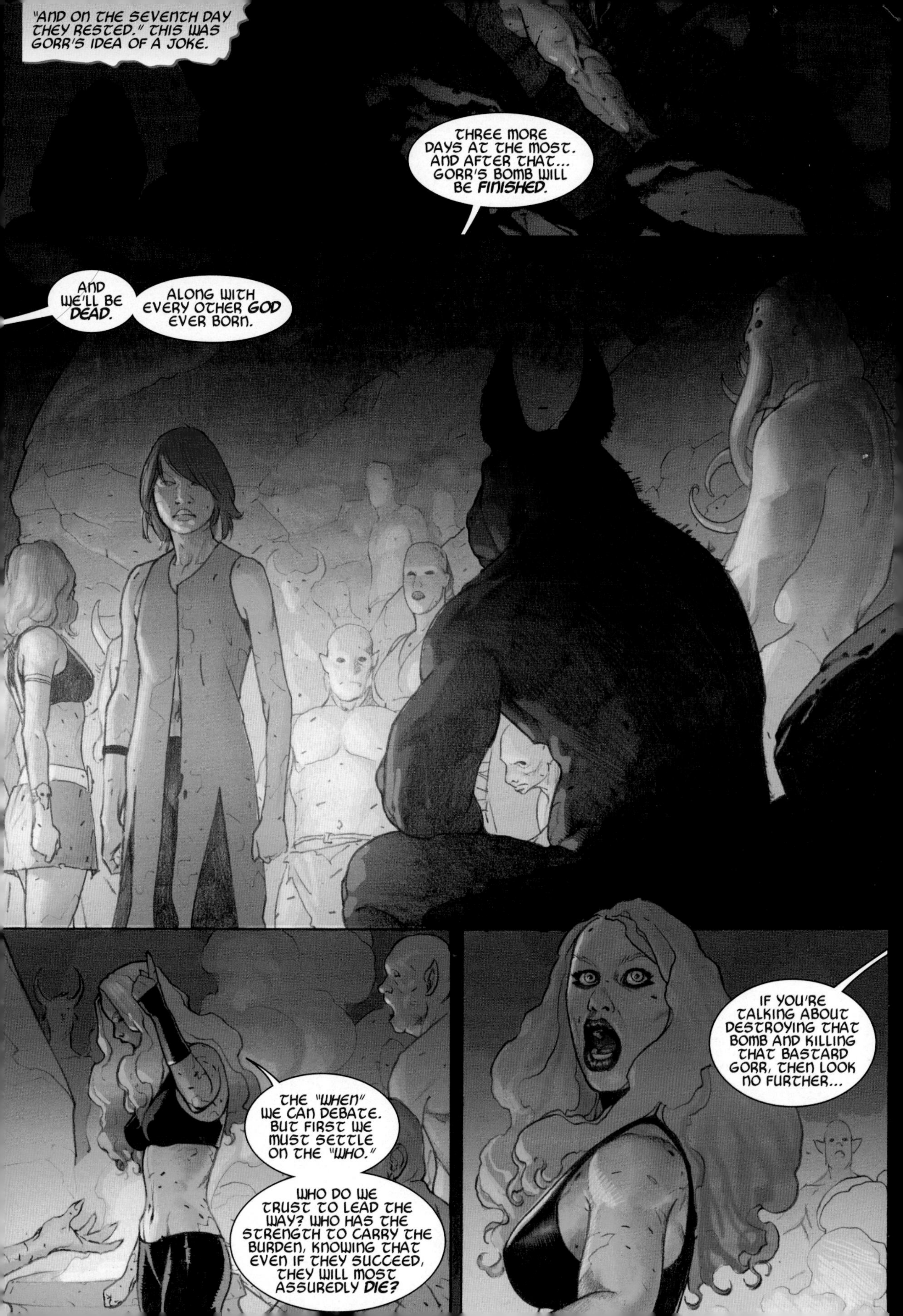
"AND ON THE SEVENTH DAY THEY RESTED." THIS WAS GORR'S IDEA OF A JOKE.
THREE MORE DAYS AT THE MOST. AND AFTER THAT... GORR'S BOMB WILL BE FINISHED.
AND WE'LL BE DEAD.
ALONG WITH EVERY OTHER GOD EVER BORN.
THE "WHEN" WE CAN DEBATE. BUT FIRST WE MUST SETTLE ON THE "WHO."
WHO DO WE TRUST TO LEAD THE WAY? WHO HAS THE STRENGTH TO CARRY THE BURDEN, KNOWING THAT EVEN IF THEY SUCCEED, THEY WILL MOST ASSUREDLY DIE?
IF YOU'RE TALKING ABOUT DESTROYING THAT BOMB AND KILLING THAT BASTARD GORR, THEN LOOK NO FURTHER...

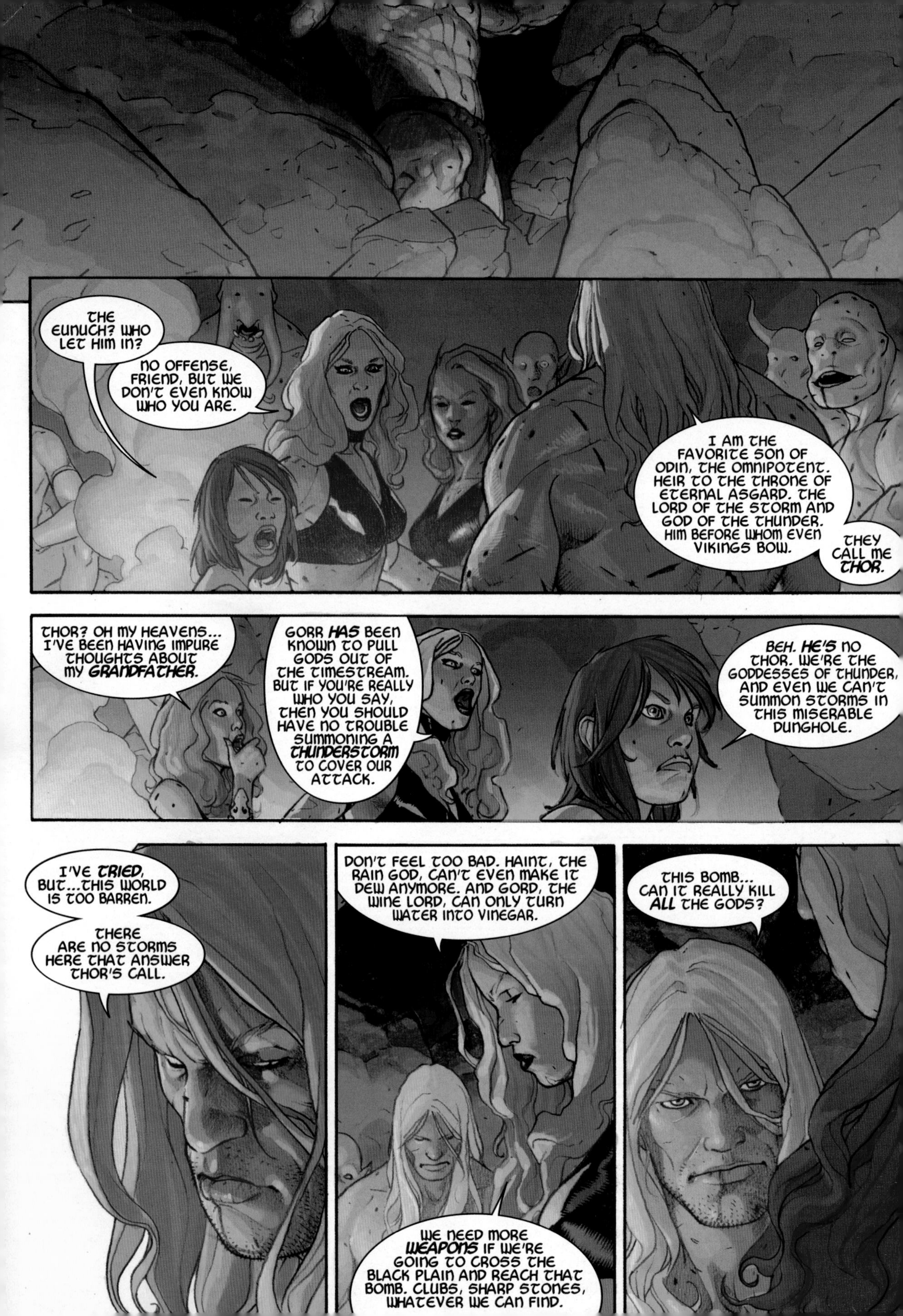
THE EUNUCH? WHO LET HIM IN?
NO OFFENSE, FRIEND, BUT WE DON'T EVEN KNOW WHO YOU ARE.
I AM THE FAVORITE SON OF ODIN, THE OMNIPOTENT. HEIR TO THE THRONE OF ETERNAL ASGARD. THE LORD OF THE STORM AND GOD OF THE THUNDER. HIM BEFORE WHOM EVEN VIKINGS BOW.
THEY CALL ME THOR.
THOR? OH MY HEAVENS... I'VE BEEN HAVING IMPURE THOUGHTS ABOUT MY GRANDFATHER.
GORR HAS BEEN KNOWN TO PULL GODS OUT OF THE TIMESTREAM. BUT IF YOU'RE REALLY WHO YOU SAY, THEN YOU SHOULD HAVE NO TROUBLE SUMMONING A THUNDERSTORM TO COVER OUR ATTACK.
BEH. HE'S NO THOR. WE'RE THE GODDESSES OF THUNDER, AND EVEN WE CAN'T SUMMON STORMS IN THIS MISERABLE DUNGHOLE.
I'VE TRIED, BUT...THIS WORLD IS TOO BARREN.
THERE ARE NO STORMS HERE THAT ANSWER THOR'S CALL.
DON'T FEEL TOO BAD. HAINT, THE RAIN GOD, CAN'T EVEN MAKE IT DEW ANYMORE. AND GORD, THE WINE LORD, CAN ONLY TURN WATER INTO VINEGAR.
WE NEED MORE WEAPONS IF WE'RE GOING TO CROSS THE BLACK PLAIN AND REACH THAT BOMB. CLUBS, SHARP STONES, WHATEVER WE CAN FIND.
THIS BOMB... CAN IT REALLY KILL ALL THE GODS?

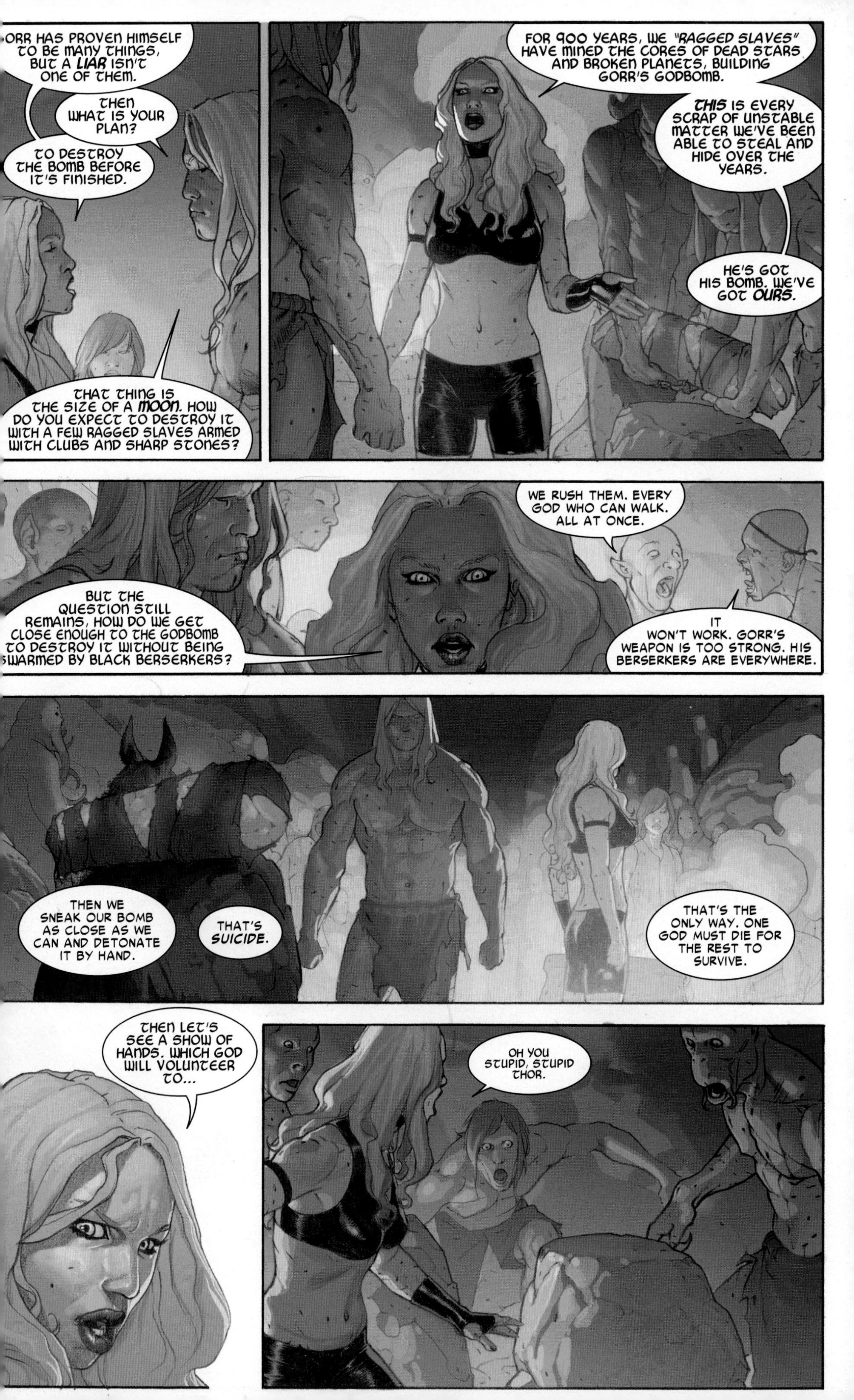
ORR HAS PROVEN HIMSELF TO BE MANY THINGS, BUT A LIAR ISN'T ONE OF THEM.
THEN WHAT IS YOUR PLAN?
TO DESTROY THE BOMB BEFORE IT'S FINISHED.
THAT THING IS THE SIZE OF A MOON. HOW DO YOU EXPECT TO DESTROY IT WITH A FEW RAGGED SLAVES ARMED WITH CLUBS AND SHARP STONES?
FOR 900 YEARS, WE "RAGGED SLAVES" HAVE MINED THE CORES OF DEAD STARS AND BROKEN PLANETS, BUILDING GORR'S GODBOMB.
THIS IS EVERY SCRAP OF UNSTABLE MATTER WE'VE BEEN ABLE TO STEAL AND HIDE OVER THE YEARS.
HE'S GOT HIS BOMB. WE'VE GOT OURS.
BUT THE QUESTION STILL REMAINS, HOW DO WE GET CLOSE ENOUGH TO THE GODBOMB TO DESTROY IT WITHOUT BEING SWARMED BY BLACK BERSERKERS?
WE RUSH THEM. EVERY GOD WHO CAN WALK. ALL AT ONCE.
IT WON'T WORK. GORR'S WEAPON IS TOO STRONG. HIS BERSERKERS ARE EVERYWHERE.
THEN WE SNEAK OUR BOMB AS CLOSE AS WE CAN AND DETONATE IT BY HAND.
THAT'S SUICIDE.
THAT'S THE ONLY WAY. ONE GOD MUST DIE FOR THE REST TO SURVIVE.
THEN LET'S SEE A SHOW OF HANDS. WHICH GOD WILL VOLUNTEER TO...
OH YOU STUPID, STUPID THOR.

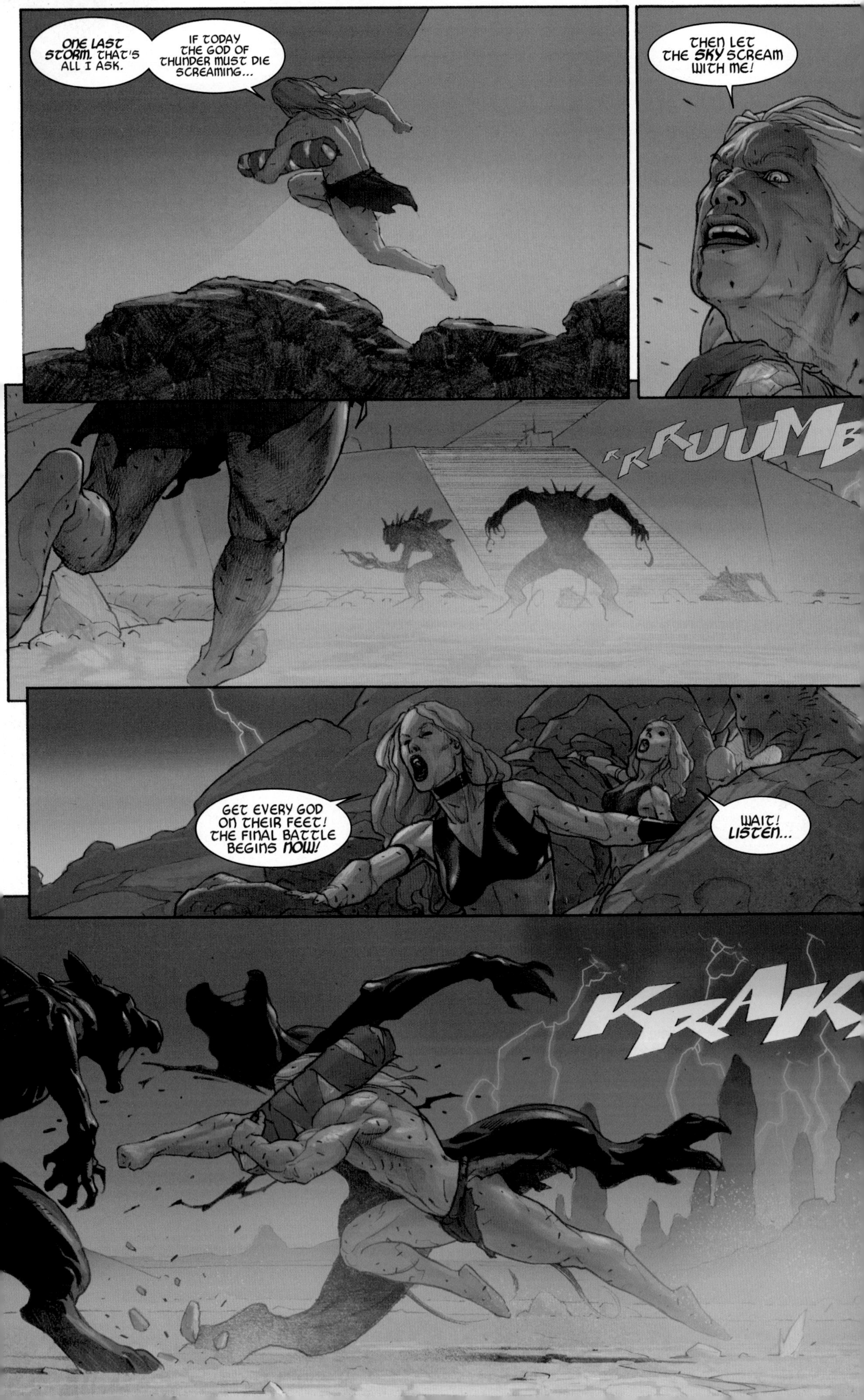
ONE LAST STORM. THAT'S ALL I ASK.
IF TODAY THE GOD OF THUNDER MUST DIE SCREAMING...
THEN LET THE SKY SCREAM WITH ME!
KRRUUMB
GET EVERY GOD ON THEIR FEET! THE FINAL BATTLE BEGINS NOW!
WAIT! LISTEN...
KRAK

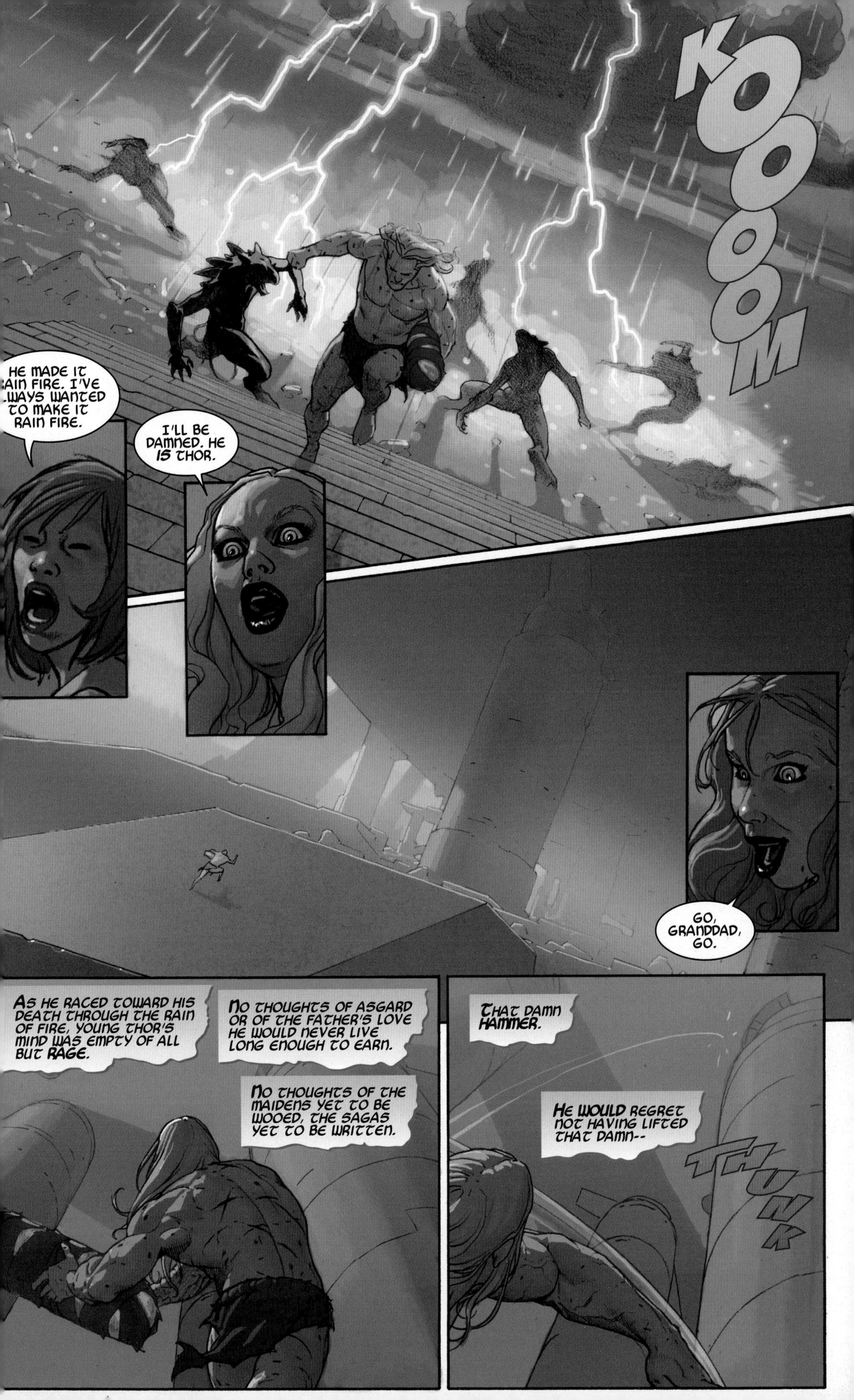
KOOOOOM
HE MADE IT RAIN FIRE. I'VE ALWAYS WANTED TO MAKE IT RAIN FIRE.
I'LL BE DAMNED. HE IS THOR.
GO, GRANDDAD, GO.
AS HE RACED TOWARD HIS DEATH THROUGH THE RAIN OF FIRE, YOUNG THOR'S MIND WAS EMPTY OF ALL BUT RAGE.
NO THOUGHTS OF ASGARD OR OF THE FATHER'S LOVE HE WOULD NEVER LIVE LONG ENOUGH TO EARN.
NO THOUGHTS OF THE MAIDENS YET TO BE WOOED, THE SAGAS YET TO BE WRITTEN.
THAT DAMN HAMMER.
HE WOULD REGRET NOT HAVING LIFTED THAT DAMN--
THUNK

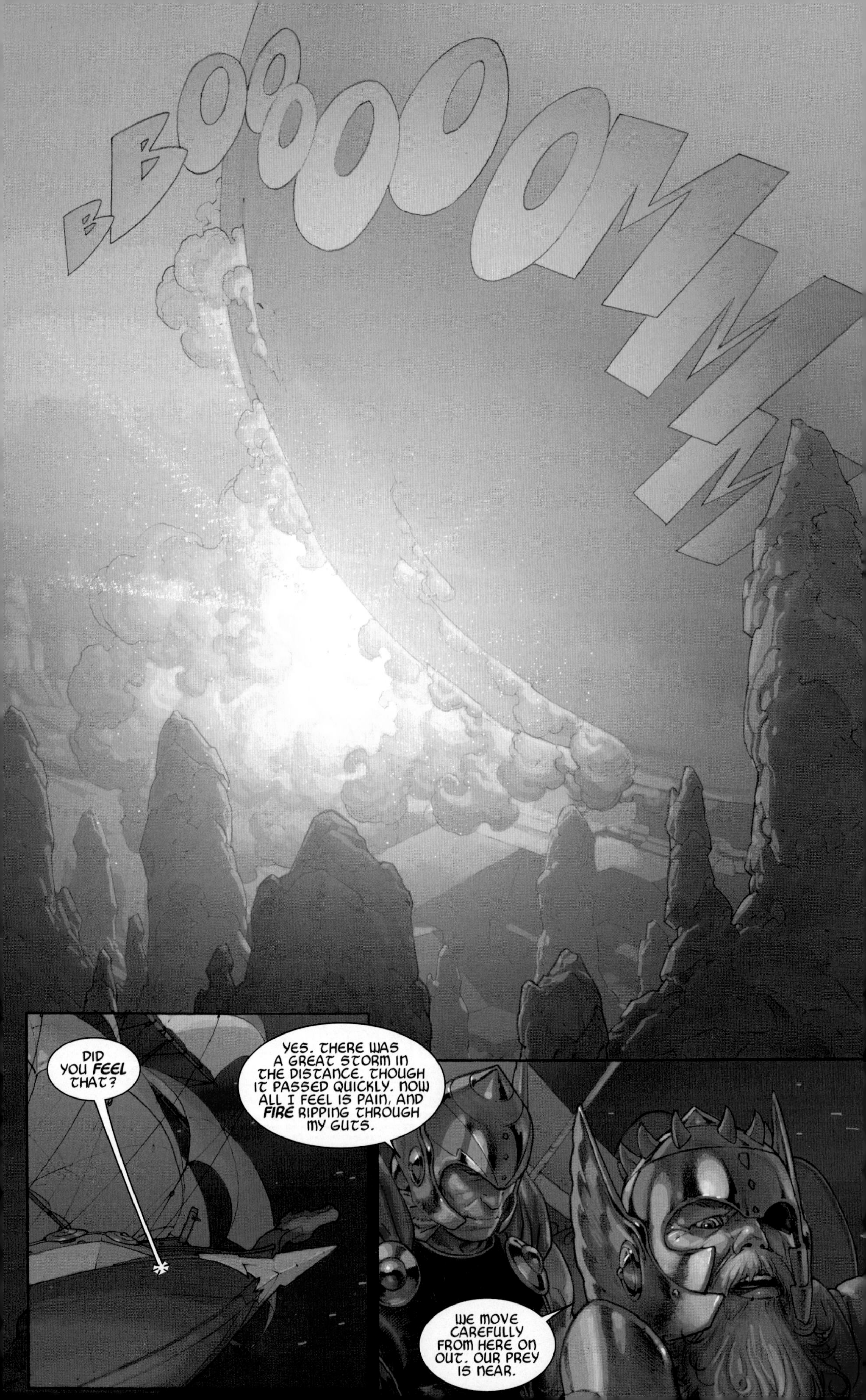
BBOOOOOMMMM
DID YOU FEEL THAT?
YES. THERE WAS A GREAT STORM IN THE DISTANCE. THOUGH IT PASSED QUICKLY. NOW ALL I FEEL IS PAIN, AND FIRE RIPPING THROUGH MY GUTS.
WE MOVE CAREFULLY FROM HERE ON OUT. OUR PREY IS NEAR.

In orbit around Gorr's world, *starsharks* feed on the flesh of dead gods, cast into the void over the centuries.

Best fetch your *hammer*, boy. I sense something stirring. Something close. Something...

...strangely *familiar*.

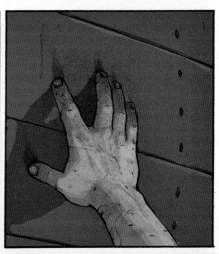

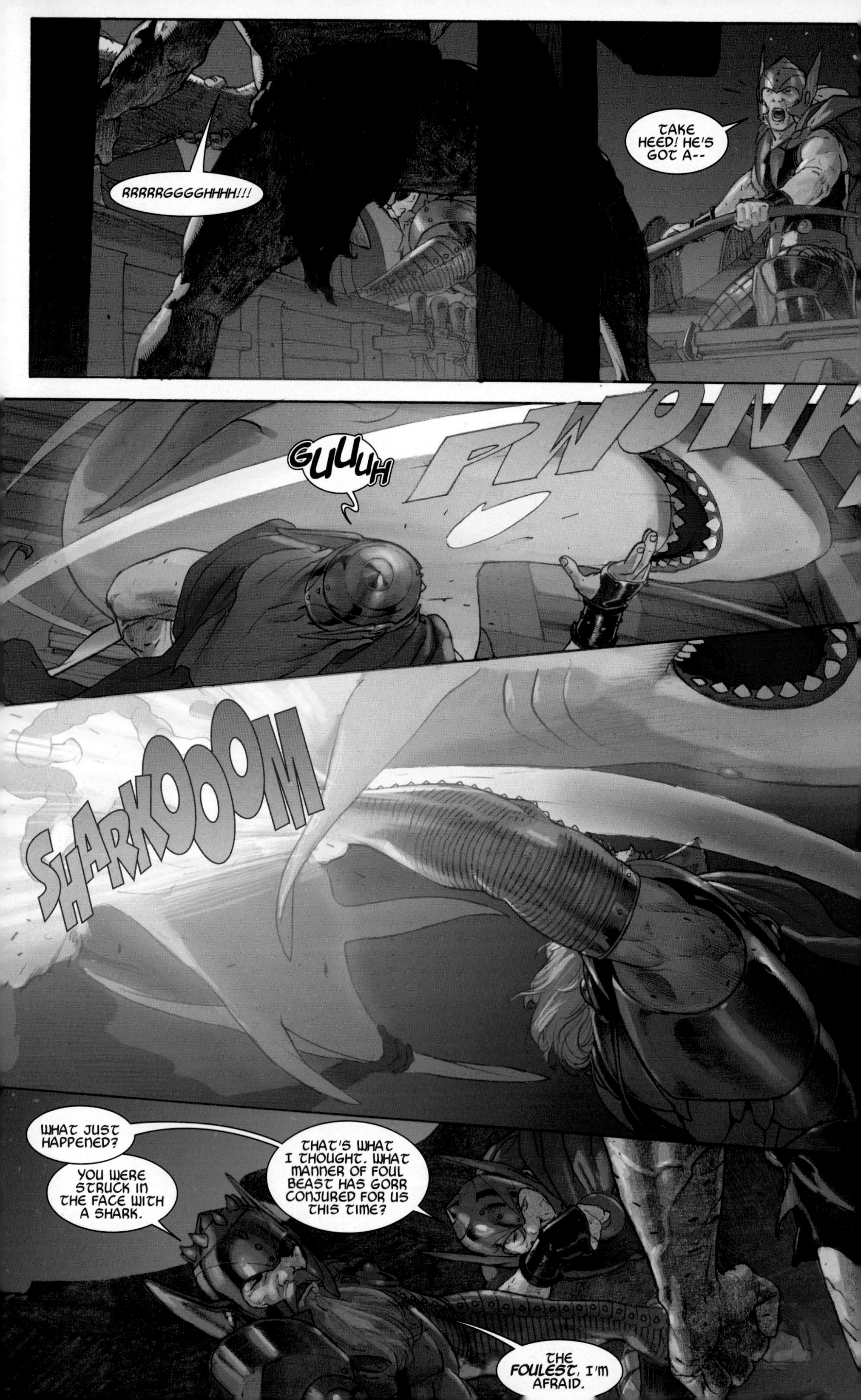
RRRRRGGGGHHHH!!!
TAKE HEED! HE'S GOT A--
GUUUH
FWONK
SHARKOOOM
WHAT JUST HAPPENED?
YOU WERE STRUCK IN THE FACE WITH A SHARK.
THAT'S WHAT I THOUGHT. WHAT MANNER OF FOUL BEAST HAS GORR CONJURED FOR US THIS TIME?
THE FOULEST, I'M AFRAID.

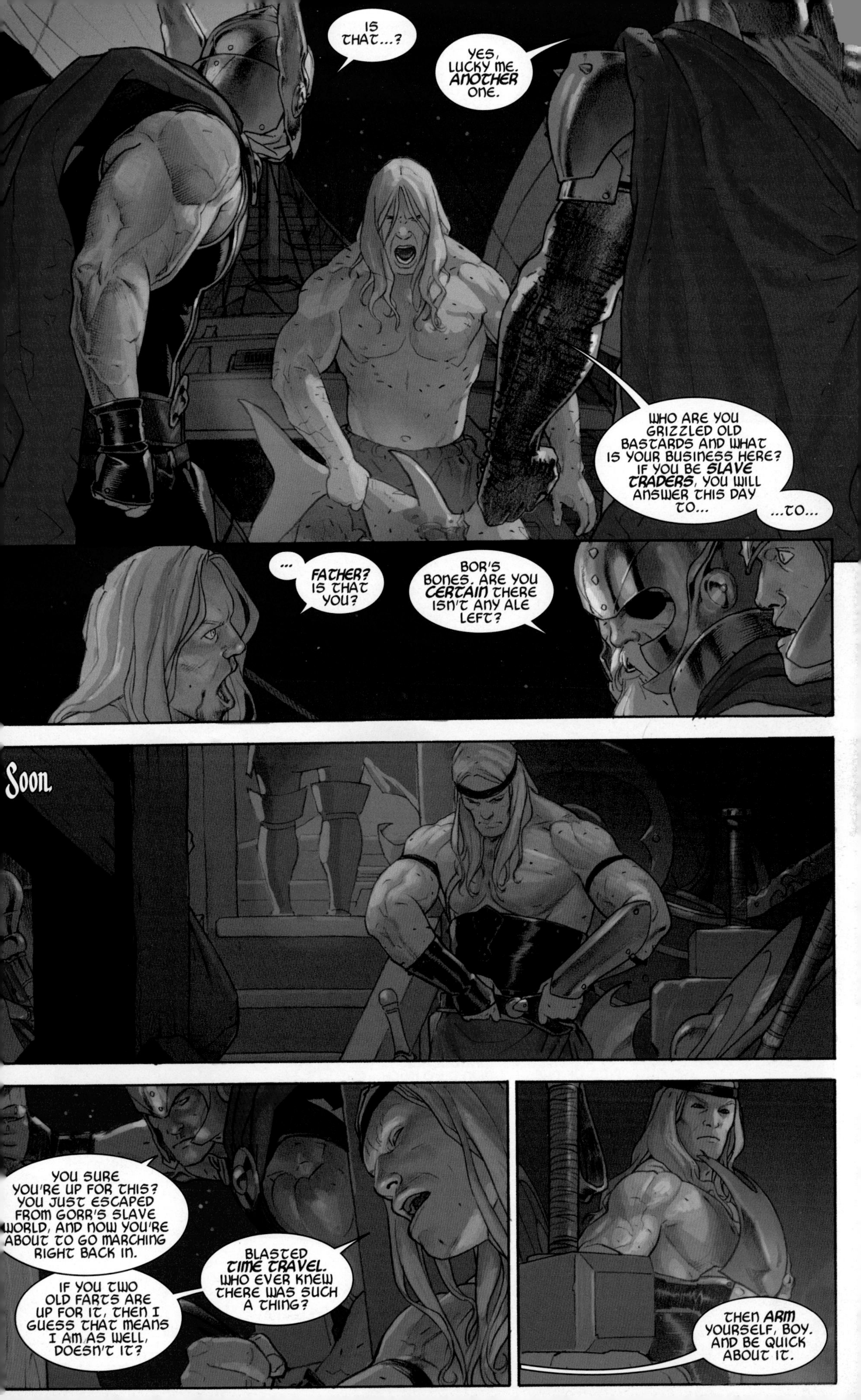
IS THAT...?
YES, LUCKY ME. ANOTHER ONE.
WHO ARE YOU GRIZZLED OLD BASTARDS AND WHAT IS YOUR BUSINESS HERE? IF YOU BE SLAVE TRADERS, YOU WILL ANSWER THIS DAY TO...
...TO...
...FATHER? IS THAT YOU?
BOR'S BONES. ARE YOU CERTAIN THERE ISN'T ANY ALE LEFT?
Soon.
YOU SURE YOU'RE UP FOR THIS? YOU JUST ESCAPED FROM GORR'S SLAVE WORLD, AND NOW YOU'RE ABOUT TO GO MARCHING RIGHT BACK IN.
BLASTED TIME TRAVEL. WHO EVER KNEW THERE WAS SUCH A THING?
IF YOU TWO OLD FARTS ARE UP FOR IT, THEN I GUESS THAT MEANS I AM AS WELL, DOESN'T IT?
THEN ARM YOURSELF, BOY. AND BE QUICK ABOUT IT.

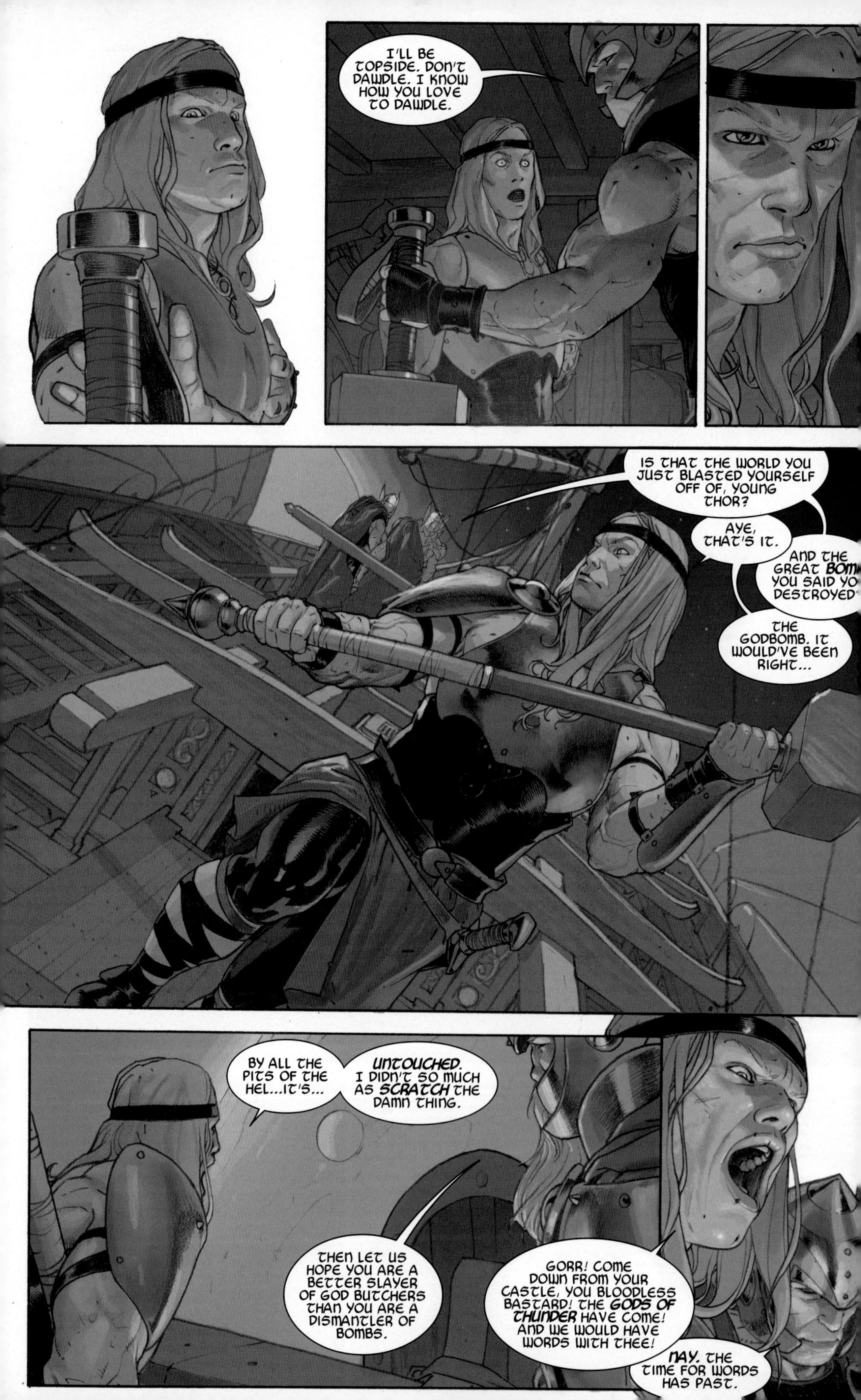
I'LL BE TOPSIDE. DON'T DAWDLE. I KNOW HOW YOU LOVE TO DAWDLE.
IS THAT THE WORLD YOU JUST BLASTED YOURSELF OFF OF, YOUNG THOR?
AYE, THAT'S IT.
AND THE GREAT BOM YOU SAID YO DESTROYED
THE GODBOMB. IT WOULD'VE BEEN RIGHT...
BY ALL THE PITS OF THE HEL...IT'S...
UNTOUCHED. I DIDN'T SO MUCH AS SCRATCH THE DAMN THING.
THEN LET US HOPE YOU ARE A BETTER SLAYER OF GOD BUTCHERS THAN YOU ARE A DISMANTLER OF BOMBS.
GORR! COME DOWN FROM YOUR CASTLE, YOU BLOODLESS BASTARD! THE GODS OF THUNDER HAVE COME! AND WE WOULD HAVE WORDS WITH THEE!
NAY. THE TIME FOR WORDS HAS PAST.

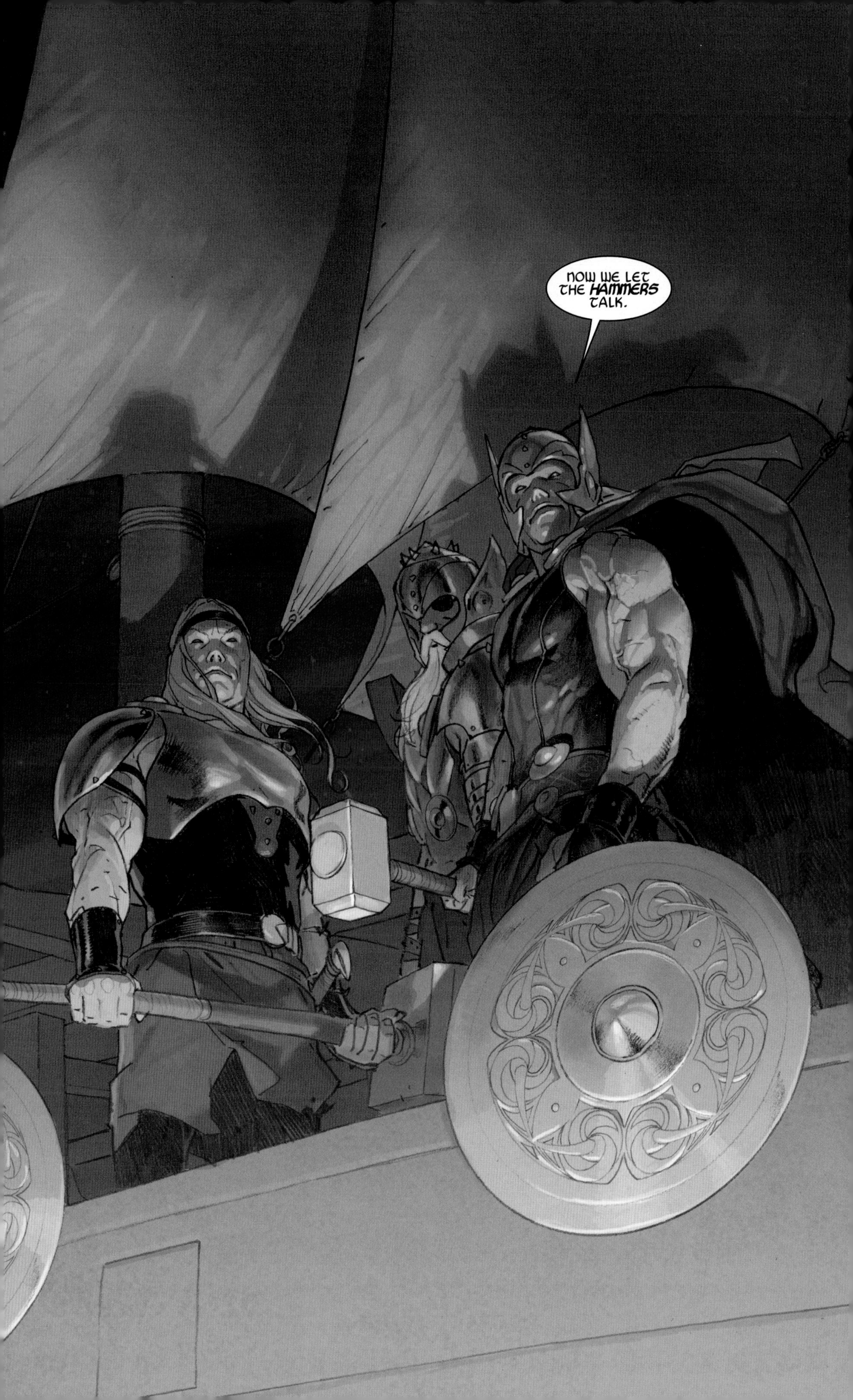
NOW WE LET THE HAMMERS TALK.

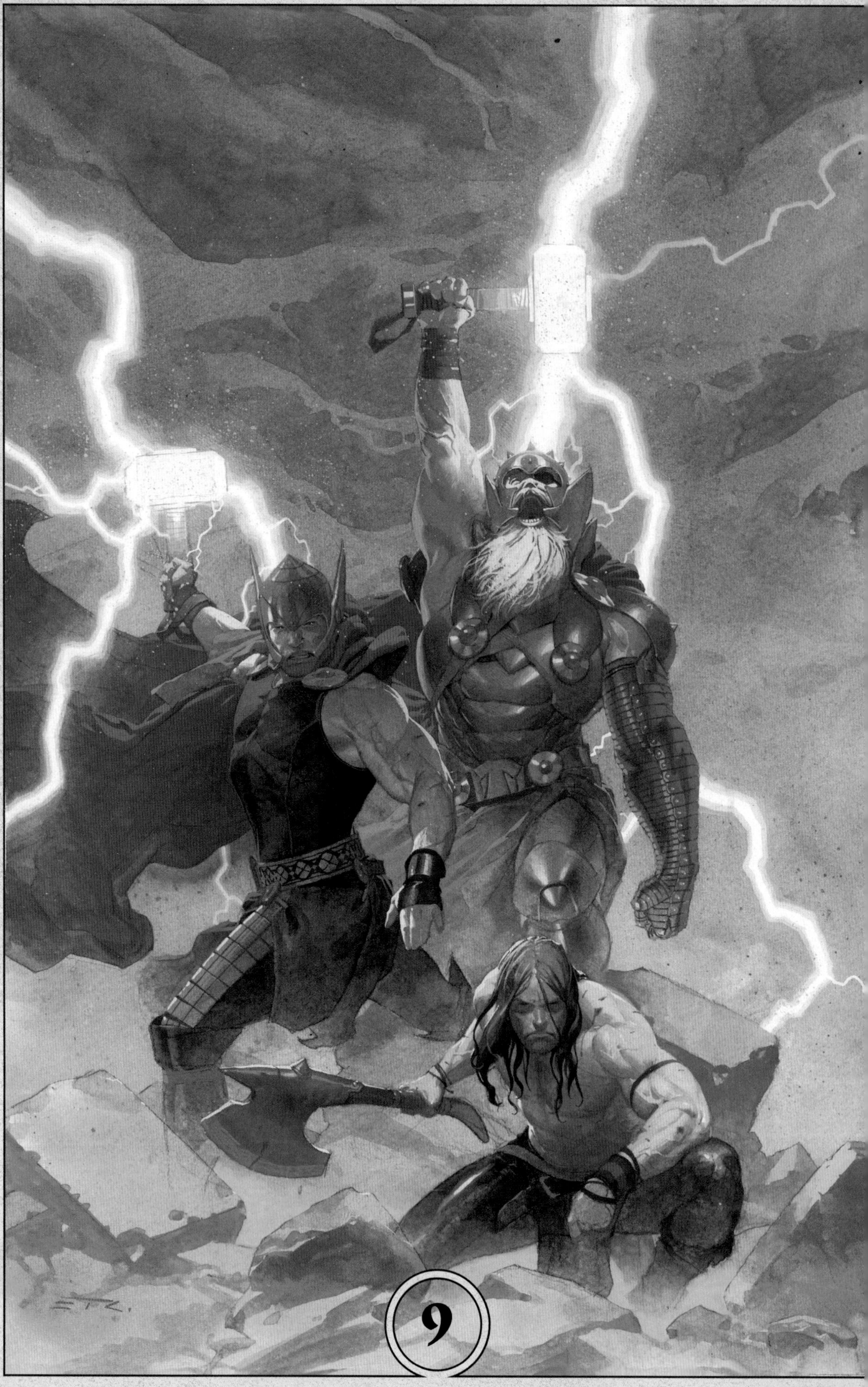
9

GODBOMB PART 3: THUNDER IN THE BLOOD

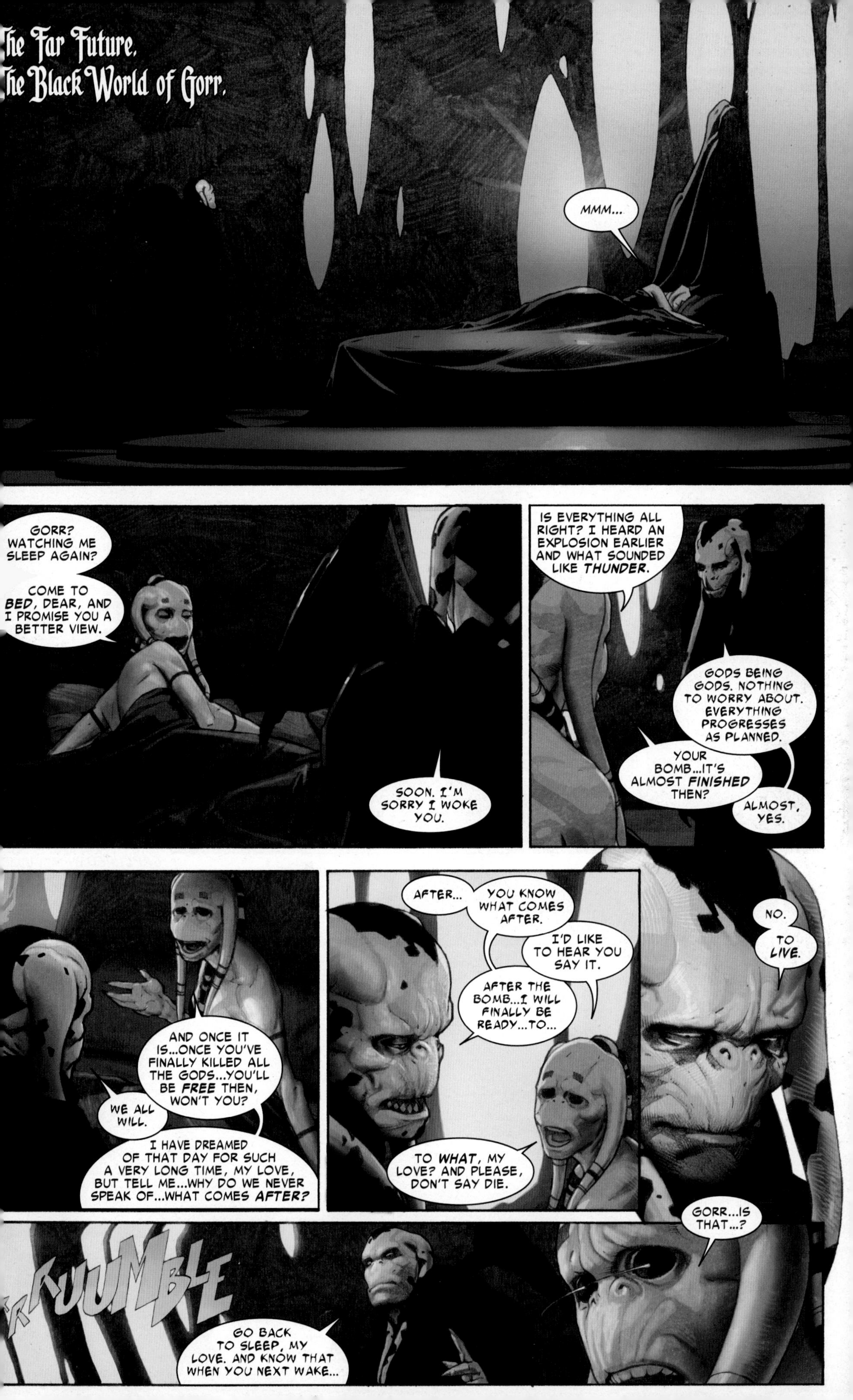
The Far Future.
The Black World of Gorr.
MMM...
GORR? WATCHING ME SLEEP AGAIN?
COME TO BED, DEAR, AND I PROMISE YOU A BETTER VIEW.
SOON. I'M SORRY I WOKE YOU.
IS EVERYTHING ALL RIGHT? I HEARD AN EXPLOSION EARLIER AND WHAT SOUNDED LIKE THUNDER.
GODS BEING GODS. NOTHING TO WORRY ABOUT. EVERYTHING PROGRESSES AS PLANNED.
YOUR BOMB...IT'S ALMOST FINISHED THEN?
ALMOST, YES.
AND ONCE IT IS...ONCE YOU'VE FINALLY KILLED ALL THE GODS...YOU'LL BE FREE THEN, WON'T YOU?
WE ALL WILL.
I HAVE DREAMED OF THAT DAY FOR SUCH A VERY LONG TIME, MY LOVE, BUT TELL ME...WHY DO WE NEVER SPEAK OF...WHAT COMES AFTER?
AFTER...
YOU KNOW WHAT COMES AFTER.
I'D LIKE TO HEAR YOU SAY IT.
AFTER THE BOMB...I WILL FINALLY BE READY...TO...
TO WHAT, MY LOVE? AND PLEASE, DON'T SAY DIE.
NO.
TO LIVE.
KRRUUMBLE
GORR...IS THAT...?
GO BACK TO SLEEP, MY LOVE. AND KNOW THAT WHEN YOU NEXT WAKE...

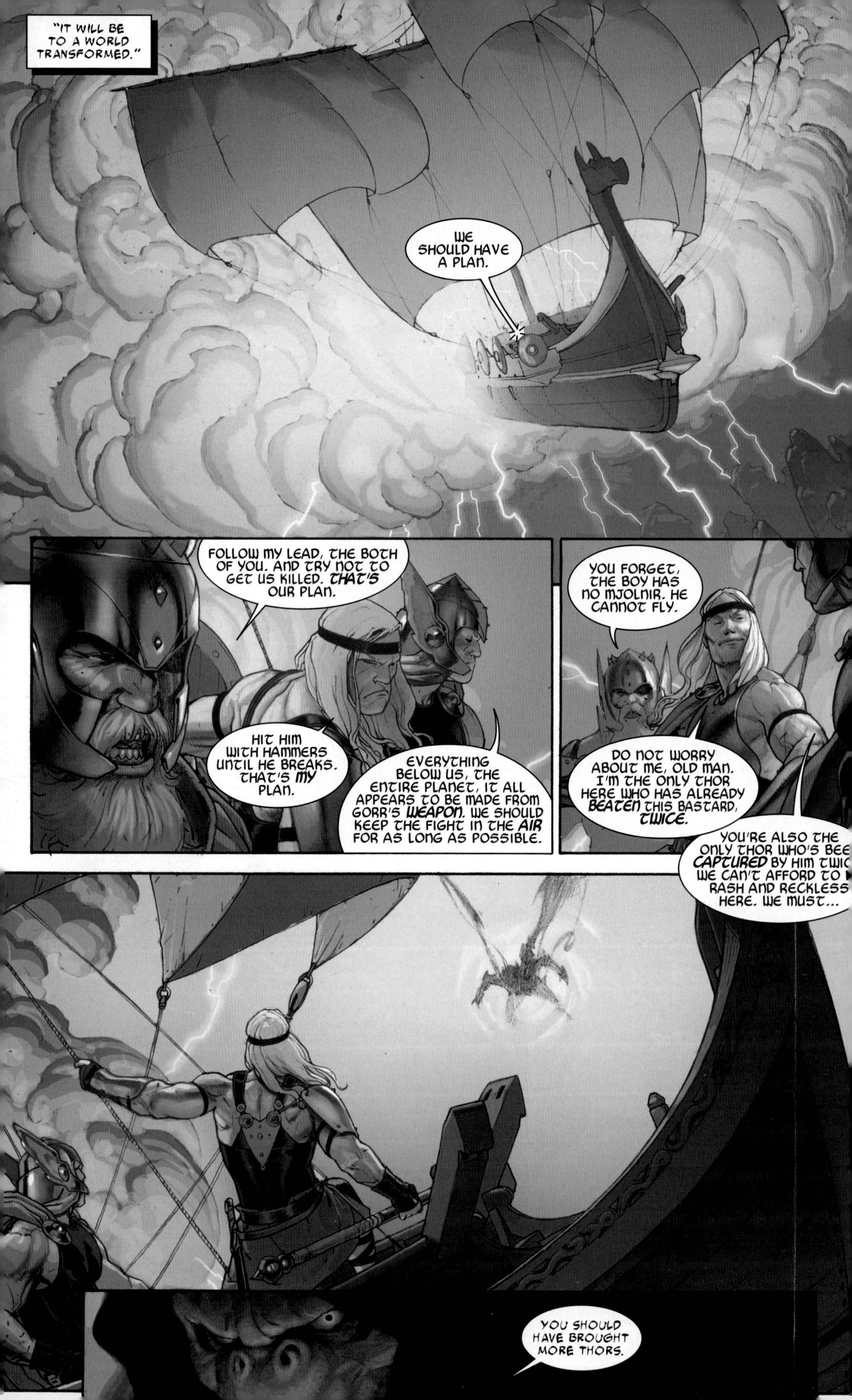
"IT WILL BE TO A WORLD TRANSFORMED."
WE SHOULD HAVE A PLAN.
FOLLOW MY LEAD, THE BOTH OF YOU. AND TRY NOT TO GET US KILLED. THAT'S OUR PLAN.
HIT HIM WITH HAMMERS UNTIL HE BREAKS. THAT'S MY PLAN.
EVERYTHING BELOW US, THE ENTIRE PLANET, IT ALL APPEARS TO BE MADE FROM GORR'S WEAPON. WE SHOULD KEEP THE FIGHT IN THE AIR FOR AS LONG AS POSSIBLE.
YOU FORGET, THE BOY HAS NO MJOLNIR. HE CANNOT FLY.
DO NOT WORRY ABOUT ME, OLD MAN. I'M THE ONLY THOR HERE WHO HAS ALREADY BEATEN THIS BASTARD, TWICE.
YOU'RE ALSO THE ONLY THOR WHO'S BEE CAPTURED BY HIM TWIC WE CAN'T AFFORD TO RASH AND RECKLESS HERE. WE MUST...
YOU SHOULD HAVE BROUGHT MORE THORS.

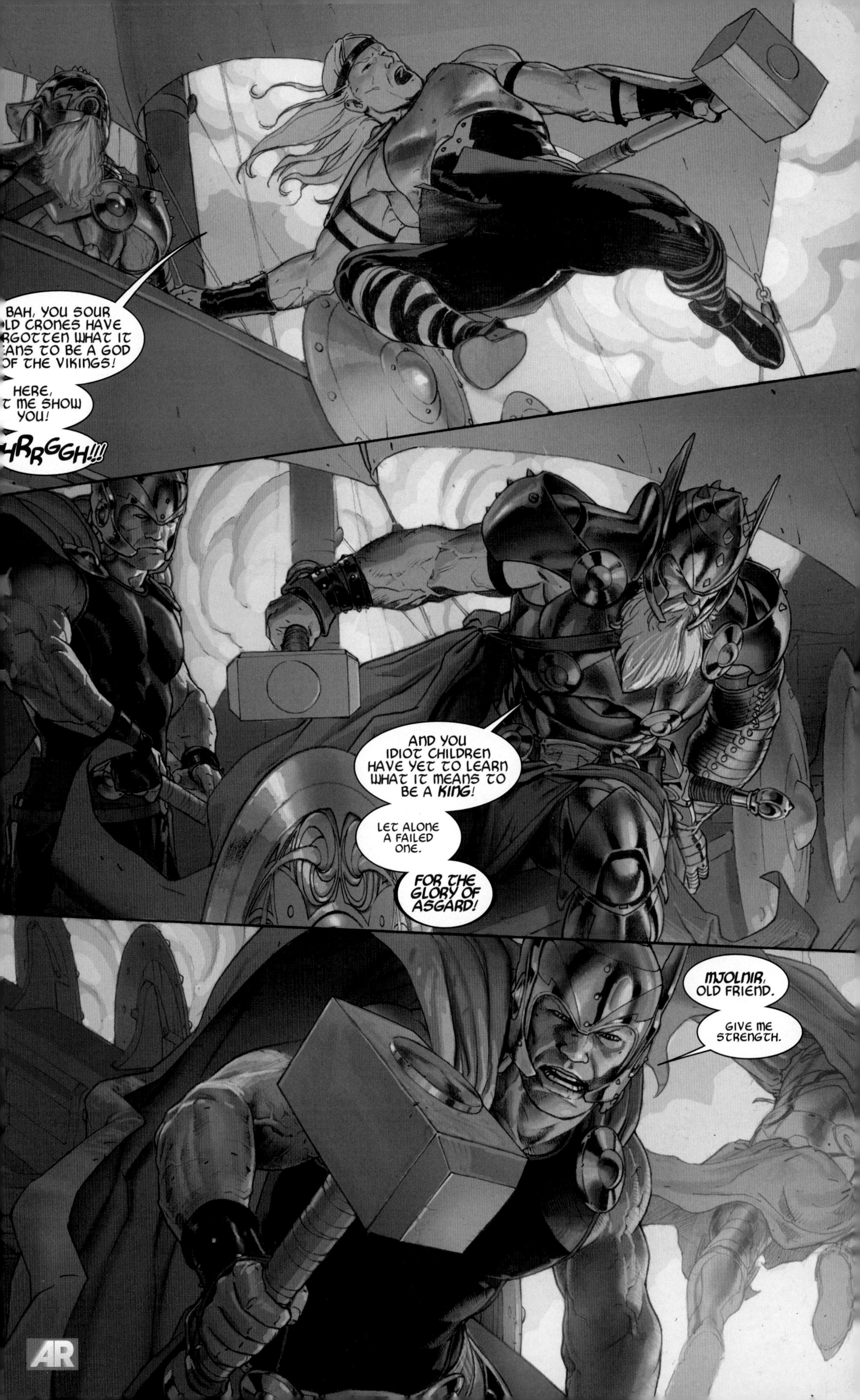

BAH, YOU SOUR LD CRONES HAVE RGOTTEN WHAT IT EANS TO BE A GOD OF THE VIKINGS!
HERE, T ME SHOW YOU!
HRRGGH!!!
AND YOU IDIOT CHILDREN HAVE YET TO LEARN WHAT IT MEANS TO BE A KING!
LET ALONE A FAILED ONE.
FOR THE GLORY OF ASGARD!
MJOLNIR, OLD FRIEND.
GIVE ME STRENGTH.

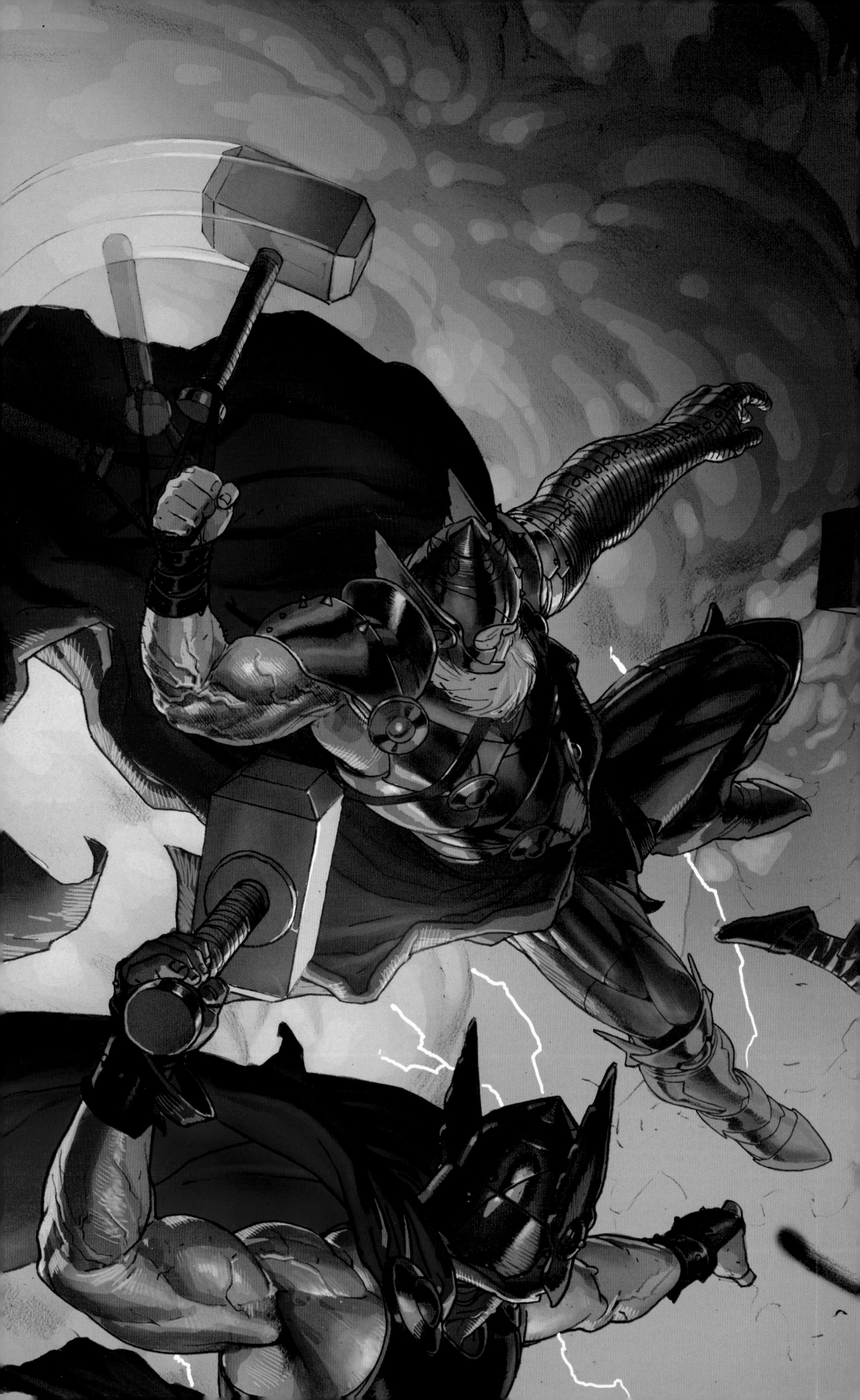

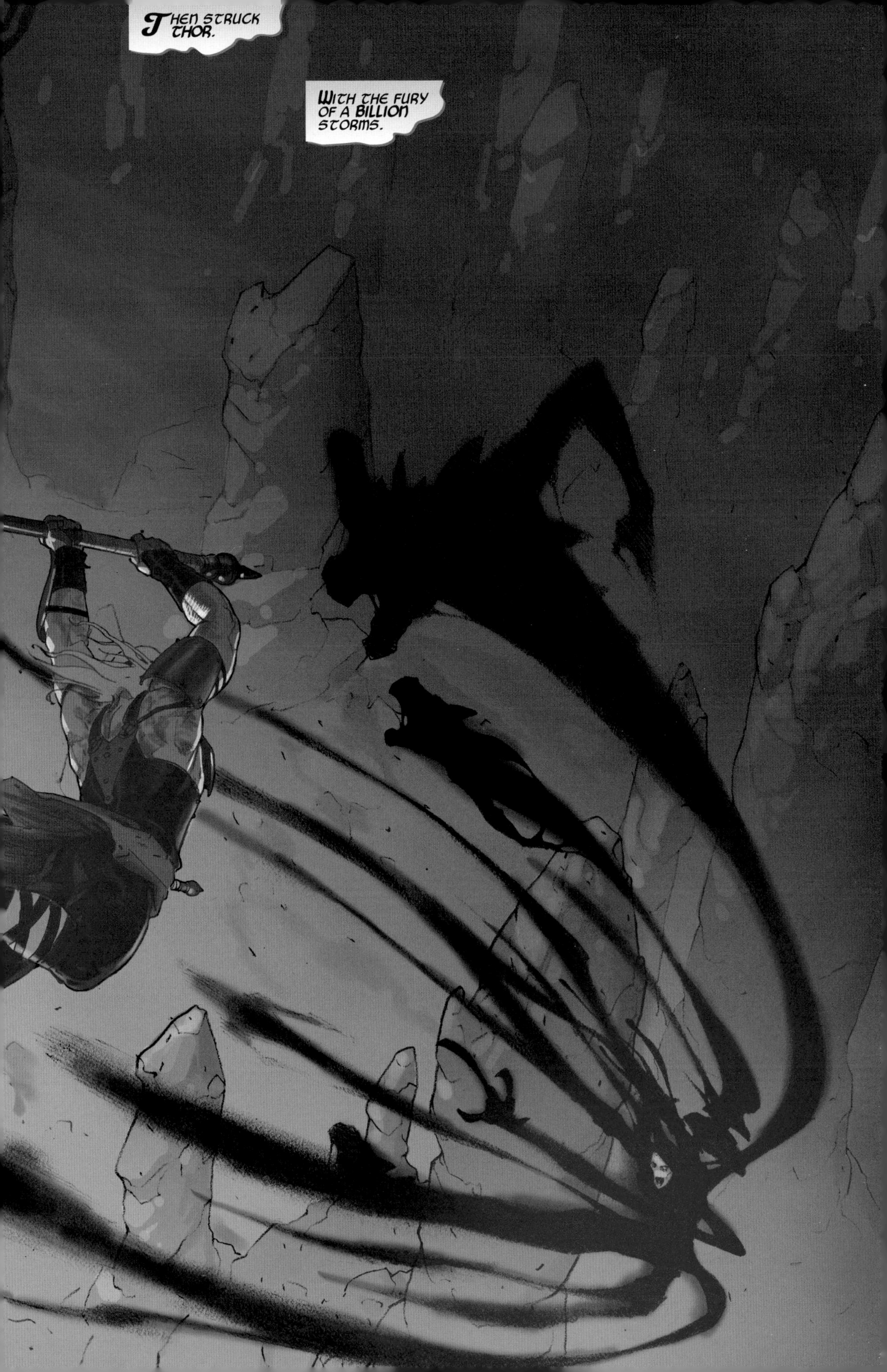
THEN STRUCK THOR.
WITH THE FURY OF A BILLION STORMS.

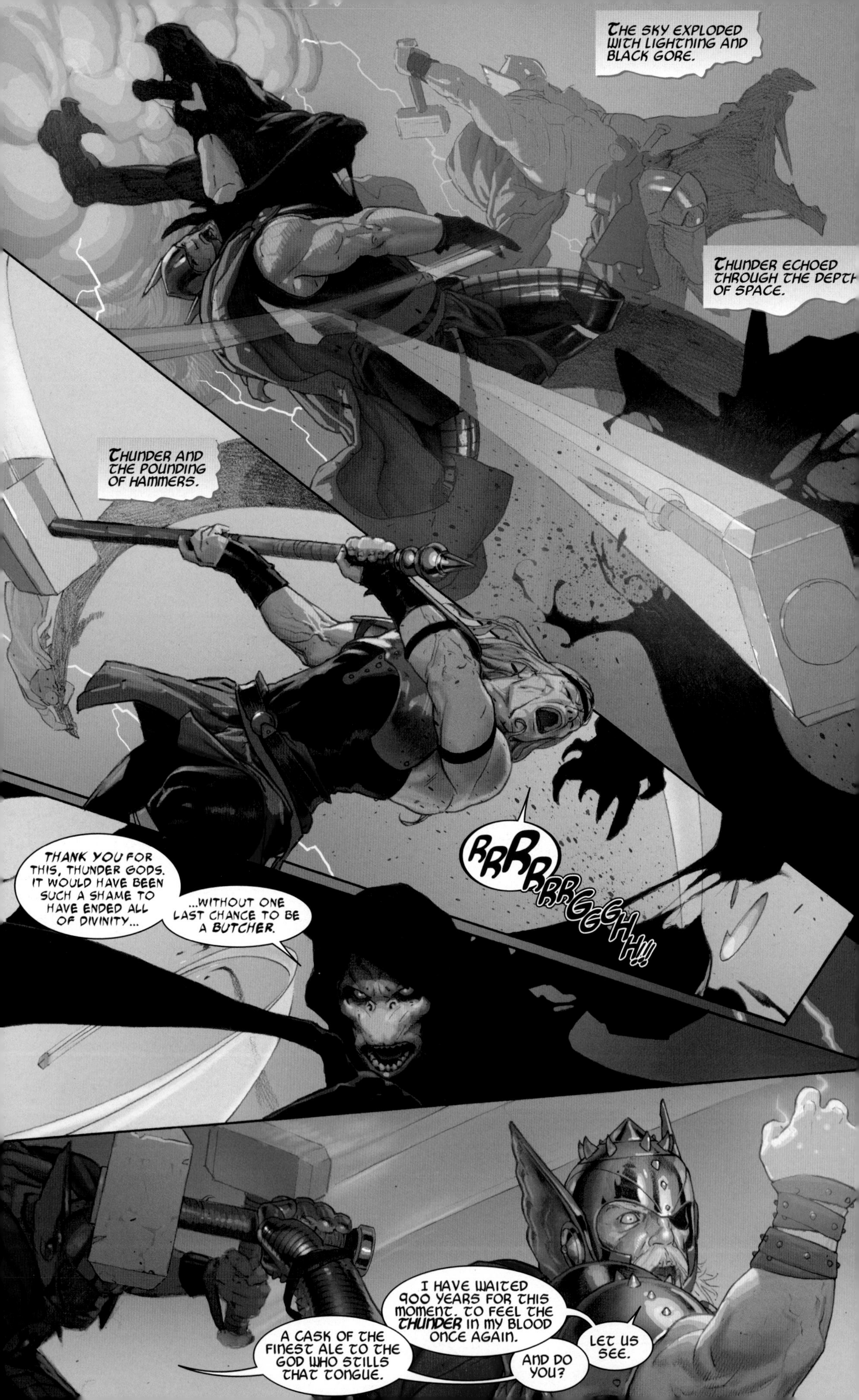
THE SKY EXPLODED WITH LIGHTNING AND BLACK GORE.
THUNDER ECHOED THROUGH THE DEPTH OF SPACE.
THUNDER AND THE POUNDING OF HAMMERS.
RRRRRRGGGHH!!
THANK YOU FOR THIS, THUNDER GODS. IT WOULD HAVE BEEN SUCH A SHAME TO HAVE ENDED ALL OF DIVINITY...
...WITHOUT ONE LAST CHANCE TO BE A BUTCHER.
A CASK OF THE FINEST ALE TO THE GOD WHO STILLS THAT TONGUE.
I HAVE WAITED 900 YEARS FOR THIS MOMENT. TO FEEL THE THUNDER IN MY BLOOD ONCE AGAIN.
AND DO YOU?
LET US SEE.

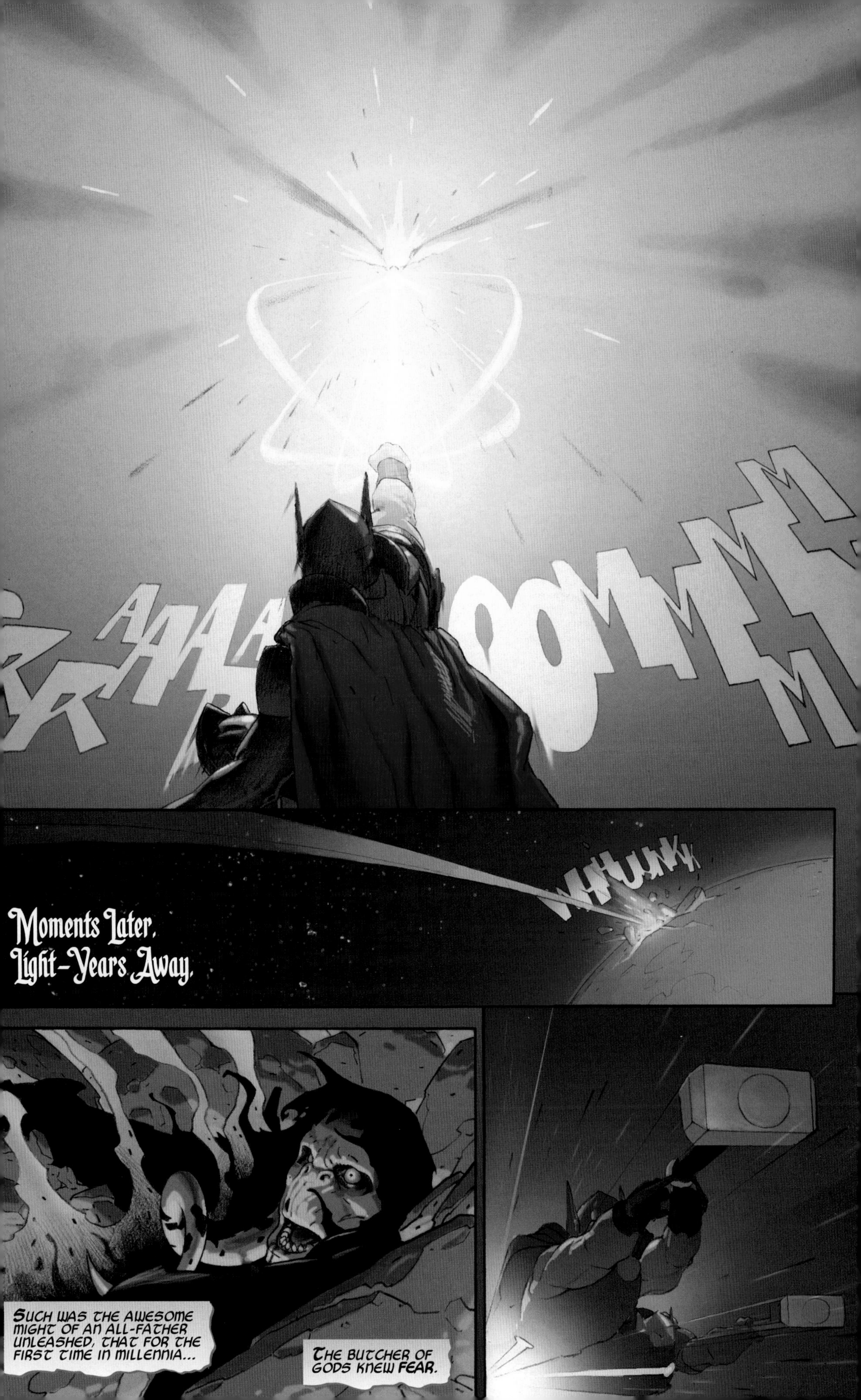
WHUNK
Moments Later,
Light-Years Away.
Such was the awesome might of an All-Father unleashed, that for the first time in millennia...
The Butcher of Gods knew fear.

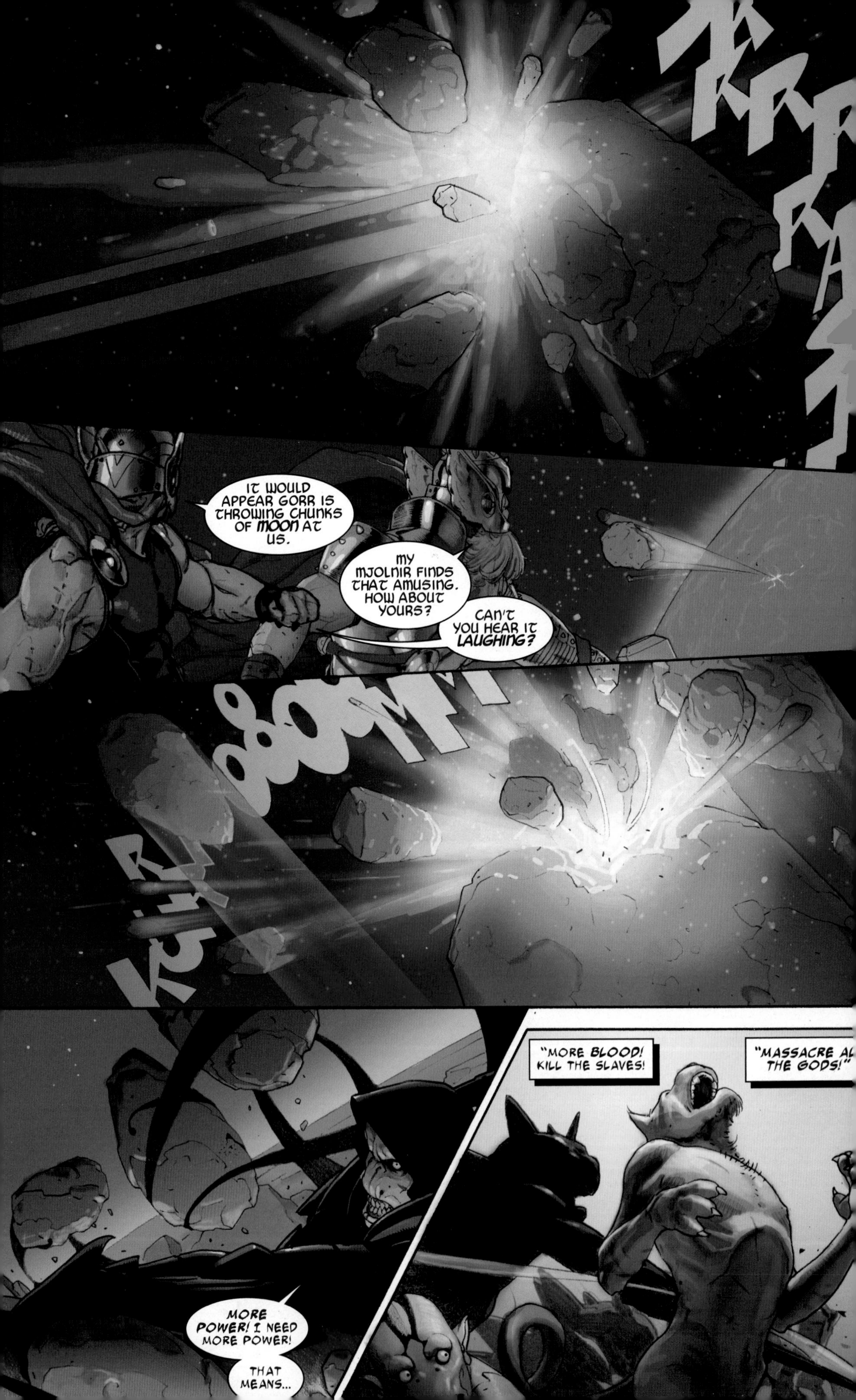
IT WOULD APPEAR GORR IS THROWING CHUNKS OF MOON AT US.
MY MJOLNIR FINDS THAT AMUSING. HOW ABOUT YOURS?
CAN'T YOU HEAR IT LAUGHING?
MORE POWER! I NEED MORE POWER!
THAT MEANS...
"MORE BLOOD! KILL THE SLAVES!
"MASSACRE AL THE GODS!"

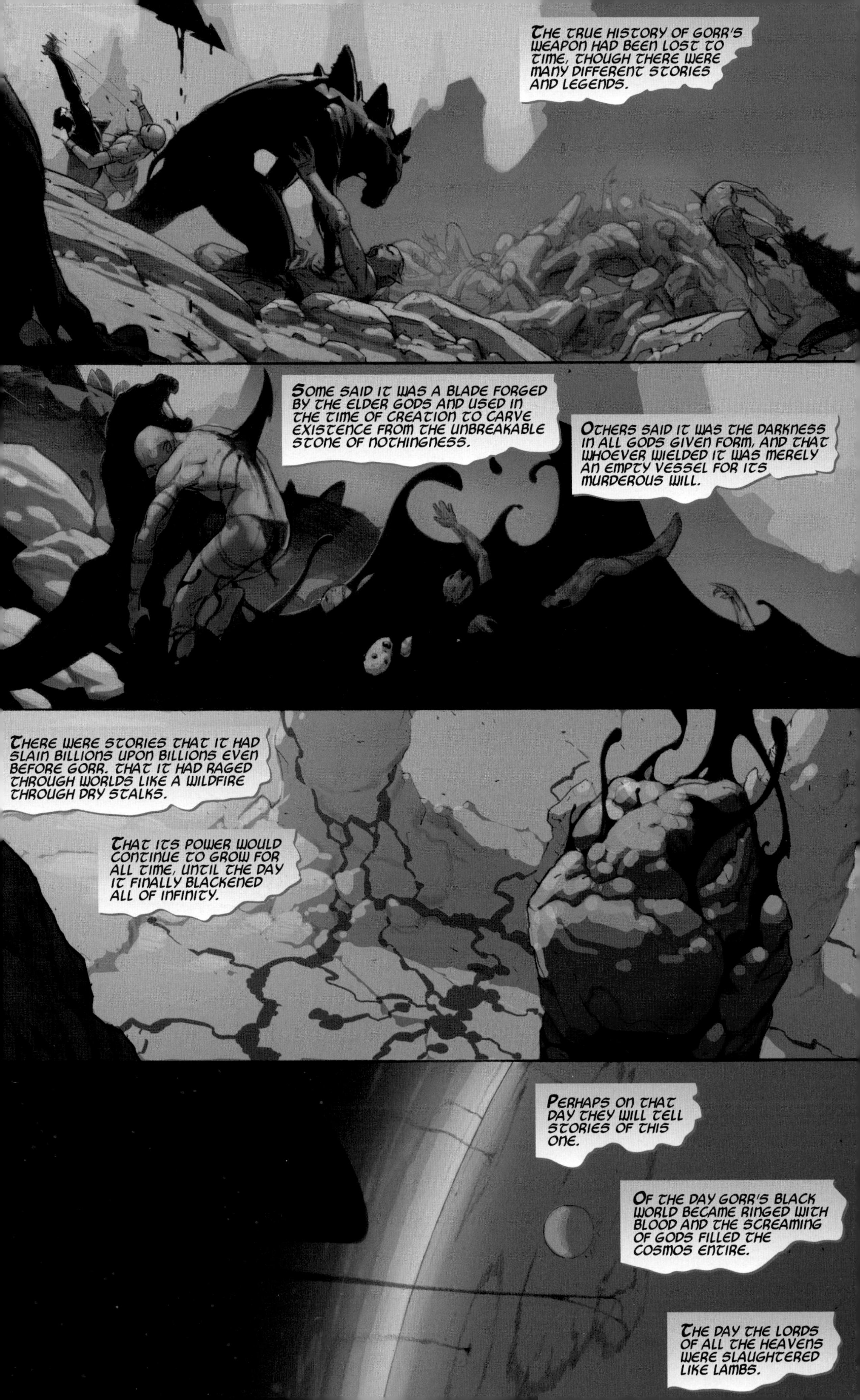
THE TRUE HISTORY OF GORR'S WEAPON HAD BEEN LOST TO TIME, THOUGH THERE WERE MANY DIFFERENT STORIES AND LEGENDS.
SOME SAID IT WAS A BLADE FORGED BY THE ELDER GODS AND USED IN THE TIME OF CREATION TO CARVE EXISTENCE FROM THE UNBREAKABLE STONE OF NOTHINGNESS.
OTHERS SAID IT WAS THE DARKNESS IN ALL GODS GIVEN FORM, AND THAT WHOEVER WIELDED IT WAS MERELY AN EMPTY VESSEL FOR ITS MURDEROUS WILL.
THERE WERE STORIES THAT IT HAD SLAIN BILLIONS UPON BILLIONS EVEN BEFORE GORR. THAT IT HAD RAGED THROUGH WORLDS LIKE A WILDFIRE THROUGH DRY STALKS.
THAT ITS POWER WOULD CONTINUE TO GROW FOR ALL TIME, UNTIL THE DAY IT FINALLY BLACKENED ALL OF INFINITY.
PERHAPS ON THAT DAY THEY WILL TELL STORIES OF THIS ONE.
OF THE DAY GORR'S BLACK WORLD BECAME RINGED WITH BLOOD AND THE SCREAMING OF GODS FILLED THE COSMOS ENTIRE.
THE DAY THE LORDS OF ALL THE HEAVENS WERE SLAUGHTERED LIKE LAMBS.

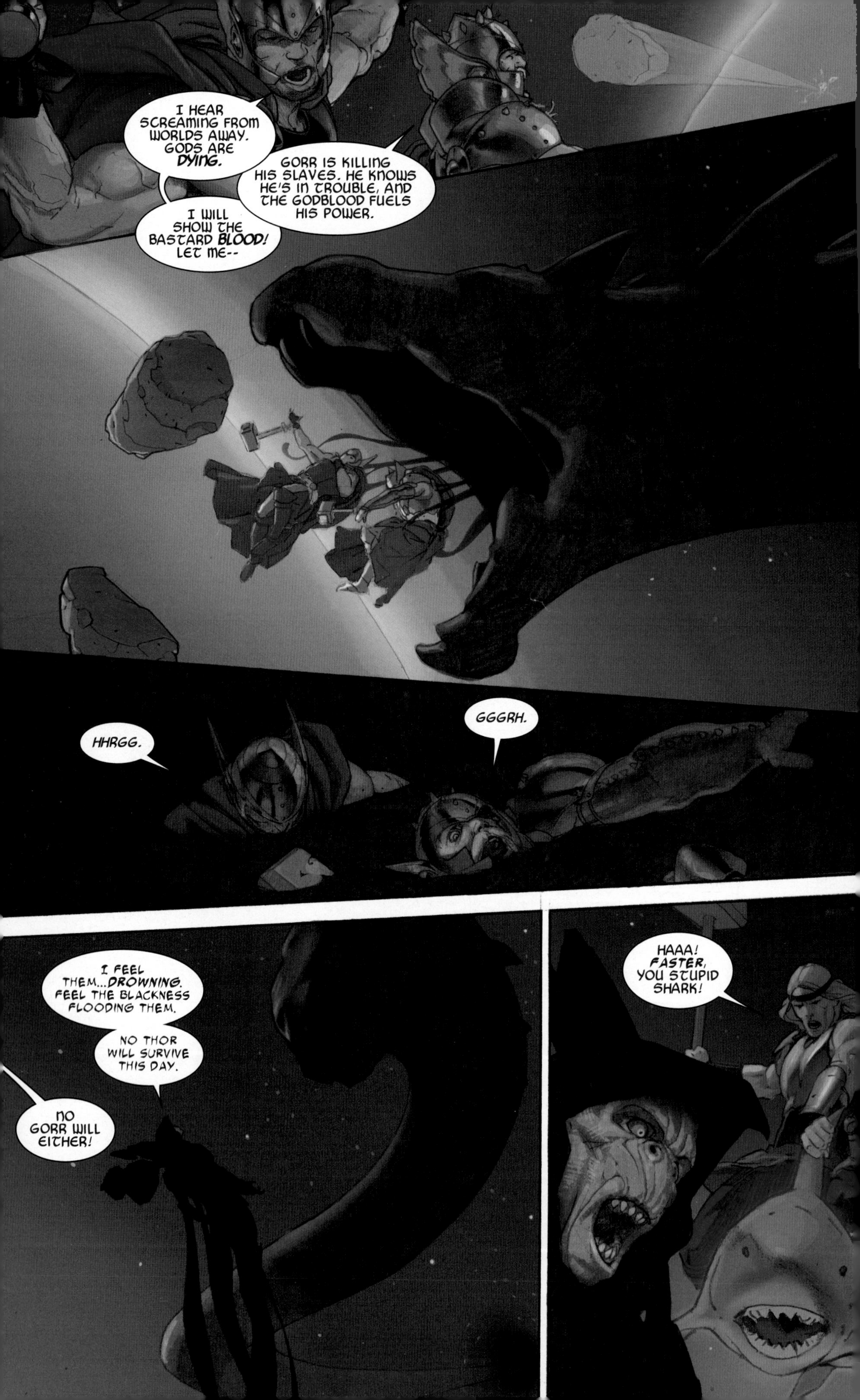
I HEAR SCREAMING FROM WORLDS AWAY. GODS ARE DYING.
GORR IS KILLING HIS SLAVES. HE KNOWS HE'S IN TROUBLE, AND THE GODBLOOD FUELS HIS POWER.
I WILL SHOW THE BASTARD BLOOD! LET ME--
HHRGG.
GGGRH.
I FEEL THEM...DROWNING. FEEL THE BLACKNESS FLOODING THEM.
NO THOR WILL SURVIVE THIS DAY.
NO GORR WILL EITHER!
HAAA! FASTER, YOU STUPID SHARK!

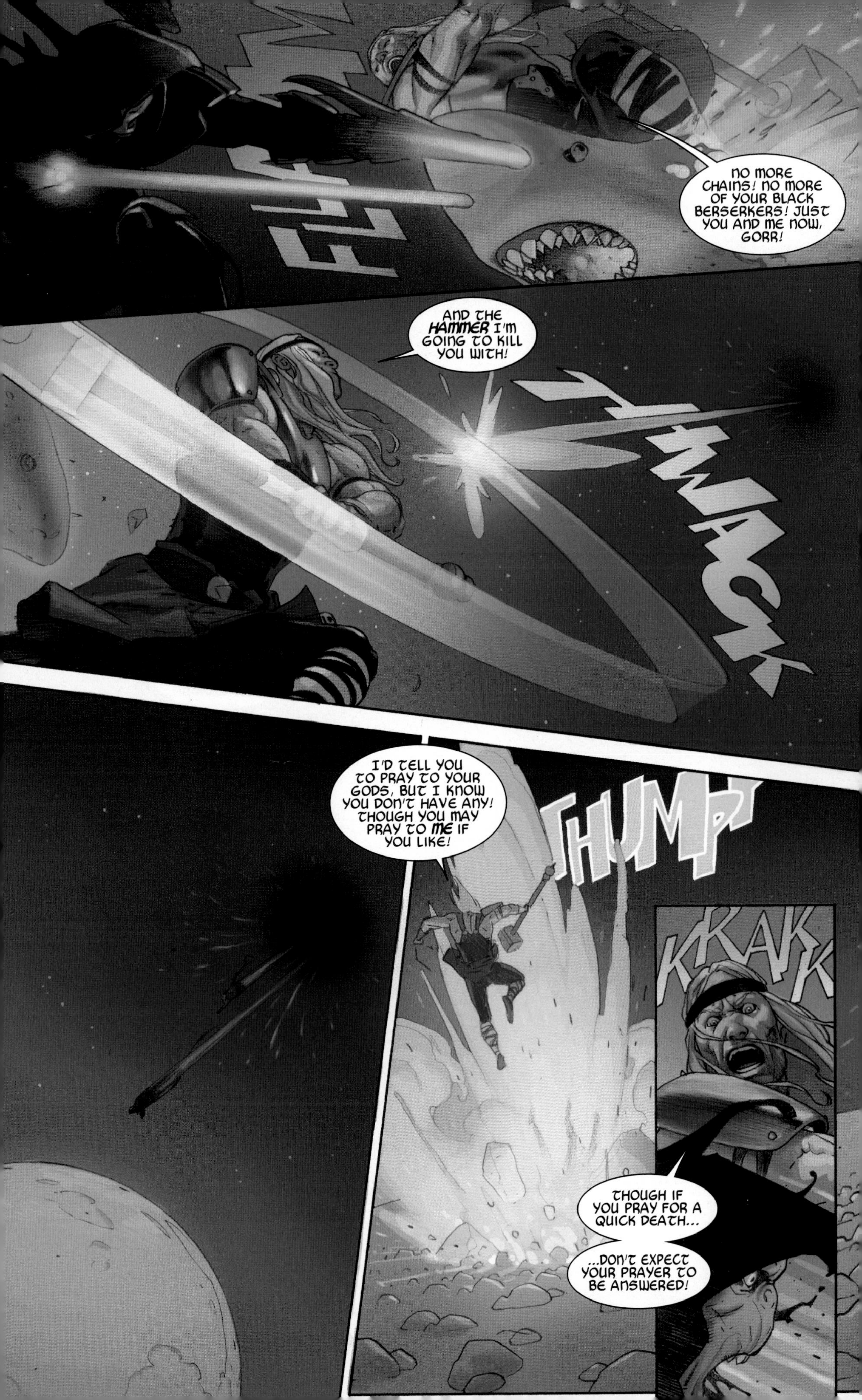

NO MORE CHAINS! NO MORE OF YOUR BLACK BERSERKERS! JUST YOU AND ME NOW, GORR!
AND THE HAMMER I'M GOING TO KILL YOU WITH!
THWACK
I'D TELL YOU TO PRAY TO YOUR GODS, BUT I KNOW YOU DON'T HAVE ANY! THOUGH YOU MAY PRAY TO ME IF YOU LIKE!
THUMP
KRAK
THOUGH IF YOU PRAY FOR A QUICK DEATH...
...DON'T EXPECT YOUR PRAYER TO BE ANSWERED!

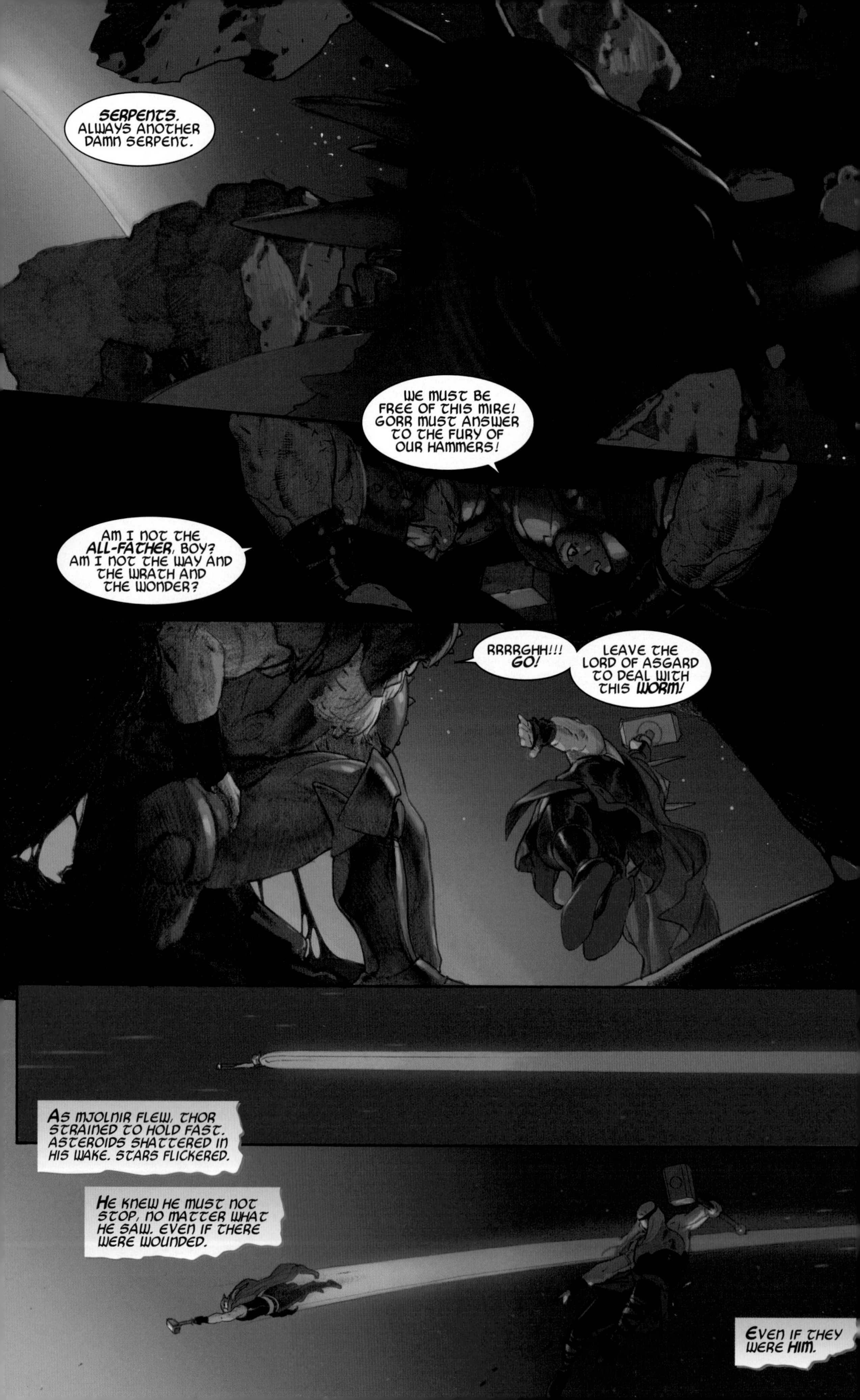
SERPENTS. ALWAYS ANOTHER DAMN SERPENT.
WE MUST BE FREE OF THIS MIRE! GORR MUST ANSWER TO THE FURY OF OUR HAMMERS!
AM I NOT THE ALL-FATHER, BOY? AM I NOT THE WAY AND THE WRATH AND THE WONDER?
RRRRGHH!!! GO!
LEAVE THE LORD OF ASGARD TO DEAL WITH THIS WORM!
AS MJOLNIR FLEW, THOR STRAINED TO HOLD FAST. ASTEROIDS SHATTERED IN HIS WAKE. STARS FLICKERED.
HE KNEW HE MUST NOT STOP, NO MATTER WHAT HE SAW. EVEN IF THERE WERE WOUNDED.
EVEN IF THEY WERE HIM.

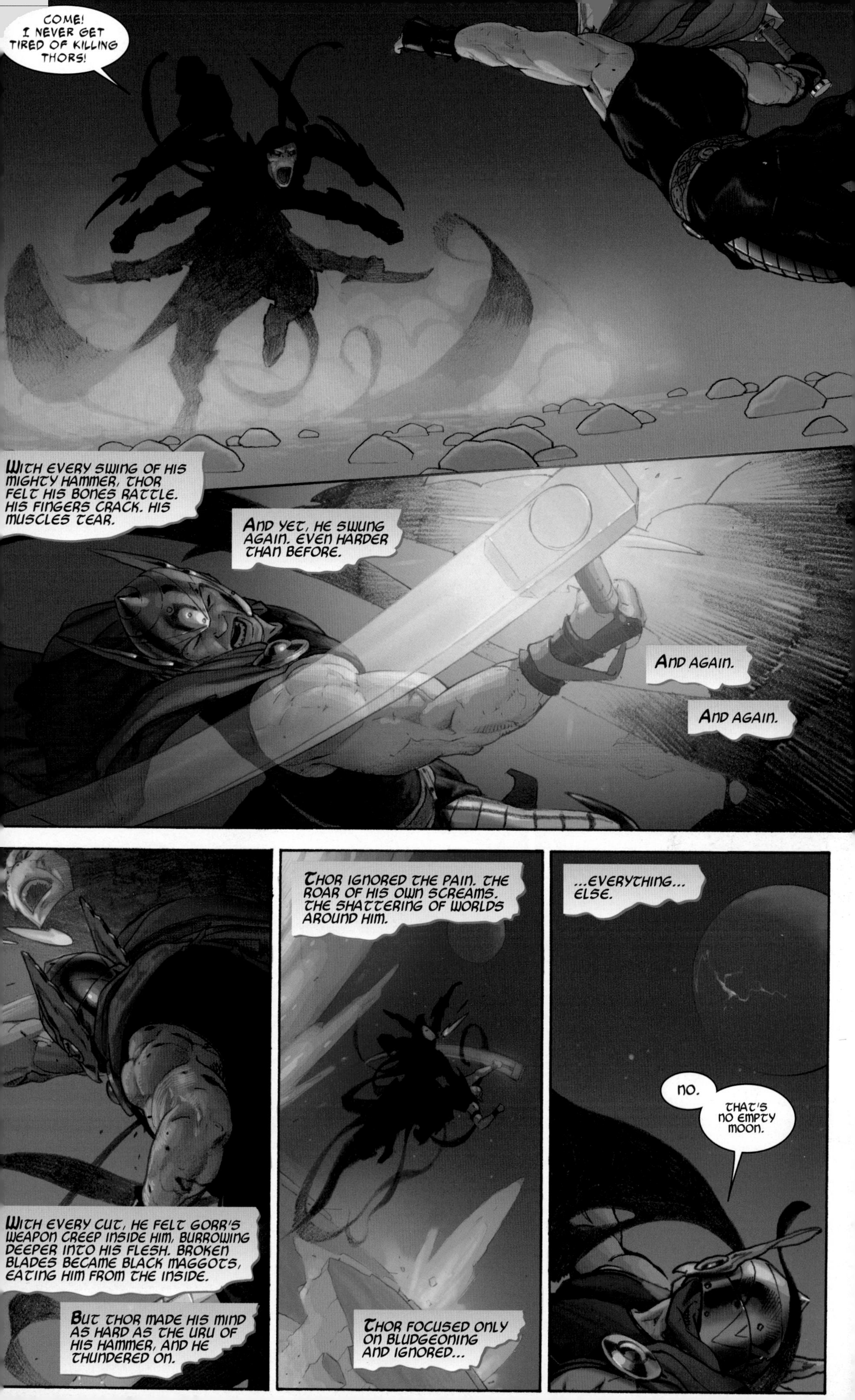
COME! I NEVER GET TIRED OF KILLING THORS!
WITH EVERY SWING OF HIS MIGHTY HAMMER, THOR FELT HIS BONES RATTLE. HIS FINGERS CRACK. HIS MUSCLES TEAR.
AND YET, HE SWUNG AGAIN. EVEN HARDER THAN BEFORE.
AND AGAIN.
AND AGAIN.
WITH EVERY CUT, HE FELT GORR'S WEAPON CREEP INSIDE HIM, BURROWING DEEPER INTO HIS FLESH. BROKEN BLADES BECAME BLACK MAGGOTS, EATING HIM FROM THE INSIDE.
BUT THOR MADE HIS MIND AS HARD AS THE URU OF HIS HAMMER, AND HE THUNDERED ON.
THOR IGNORED THE PAIN. THE ROAR OF HIS OWN SCREAMS. THE SHATTERING OF WORLDS AROUND HIM.
THOR FOCUSED ONLY ON BLUDGEONING AND IGNORED...
...EVERYTHING... ELSE.
NO.
THAT'S NO EMPTY MOON.

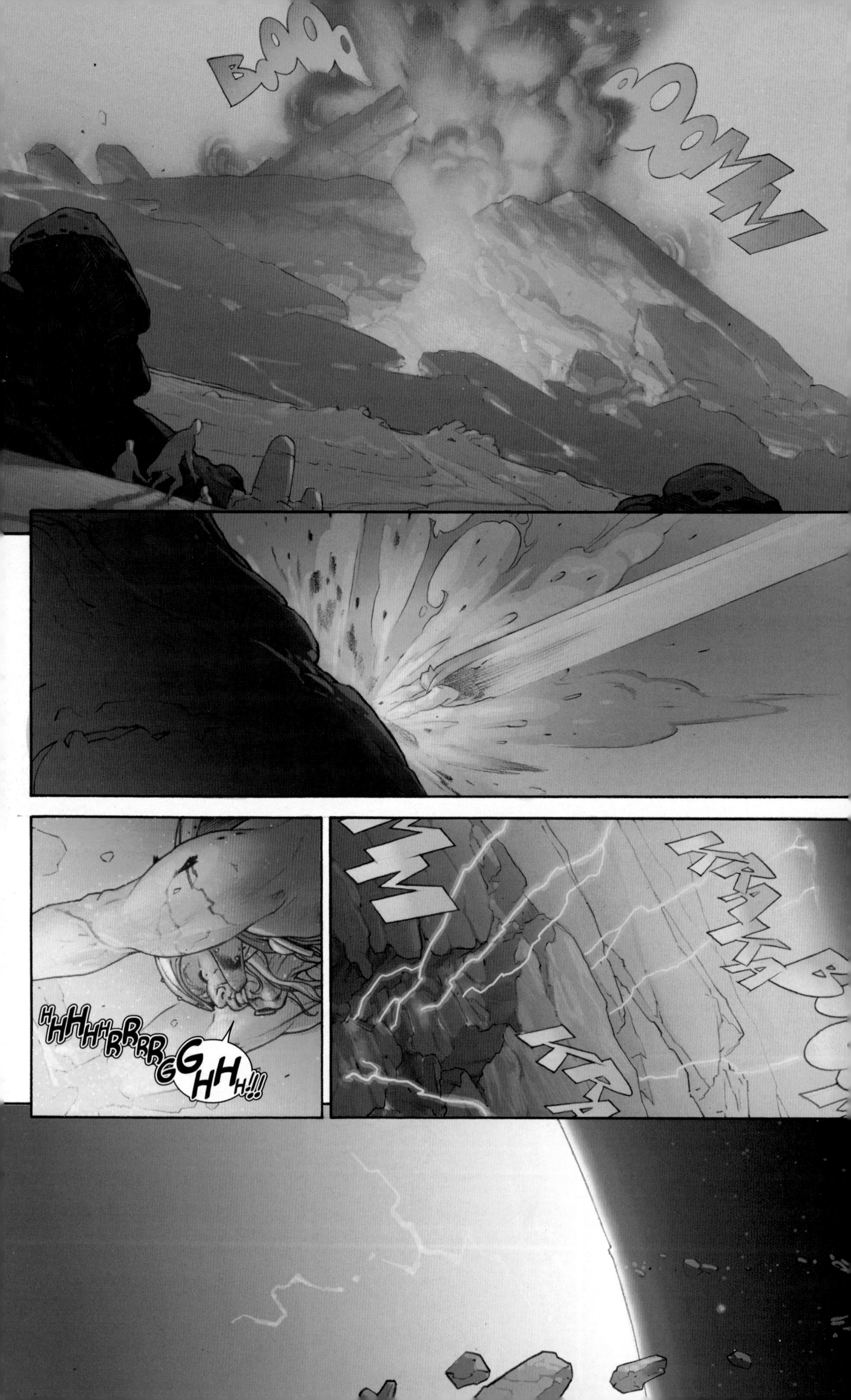
BOOOO
OOOMM
HHHHHRRRRRGGHHH!!!
KRAKA
KRA

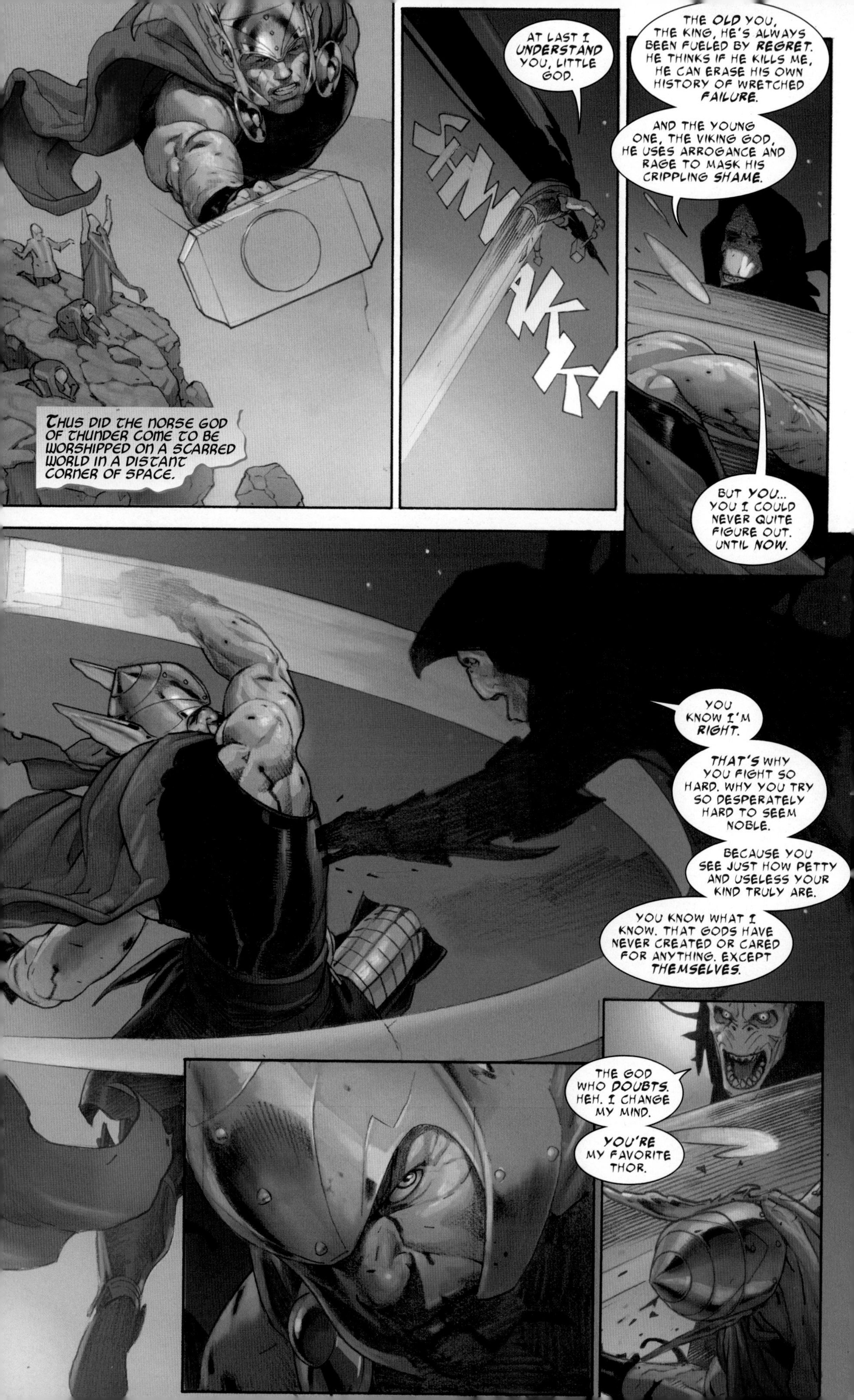
THUS DID THE NORSE GOD OF THUNDER COME TO BE WORSHIPPED ON A SCARRED WORLD IN A DISTANT CORNER OF SPACE.
AT LAST I UNDERSTAND YOU, LITTLE GOD.
SHNAKK
THE OLD YOU, THE KING, HE'S ALWAYS BEEN FUELED BY REGRET. HE THINKS IF HE KILLS ME, HE CAN ERASE HIS OWN HISTORY OF WRETCHED FAILURE.
AND THE YOUNG ONE, THE VIKING GOD, HE USES ARROGANCE AND RAGE TO MASK HIS CRIPPLING SHAME.
BUT YOU... YOU I COULD NEVER QUITE FIGURE OUT. UNTIL NOW.
YOU KNOW I'M RIGHT.
THAT'S WHY YOU FIGHT SO HARD. WHY YOU TRY SO DESPERATELY HARD TO SEEM NOBLE.
BECAUSE YOU SEE JUST HOW PETTY AND USELESS YOUR KIND TRULY ARE.
YOU KNOW WHAT I KNOW. THAT GODS HAVE NEVER CREATED OR CARED FOR ANYTHING. EXCEPT THEMSELVES.
THE GOD WHO DOUBTS. HEH. I CHANGE MY MIND.
YOU'RE MY FAVORITE THOR.

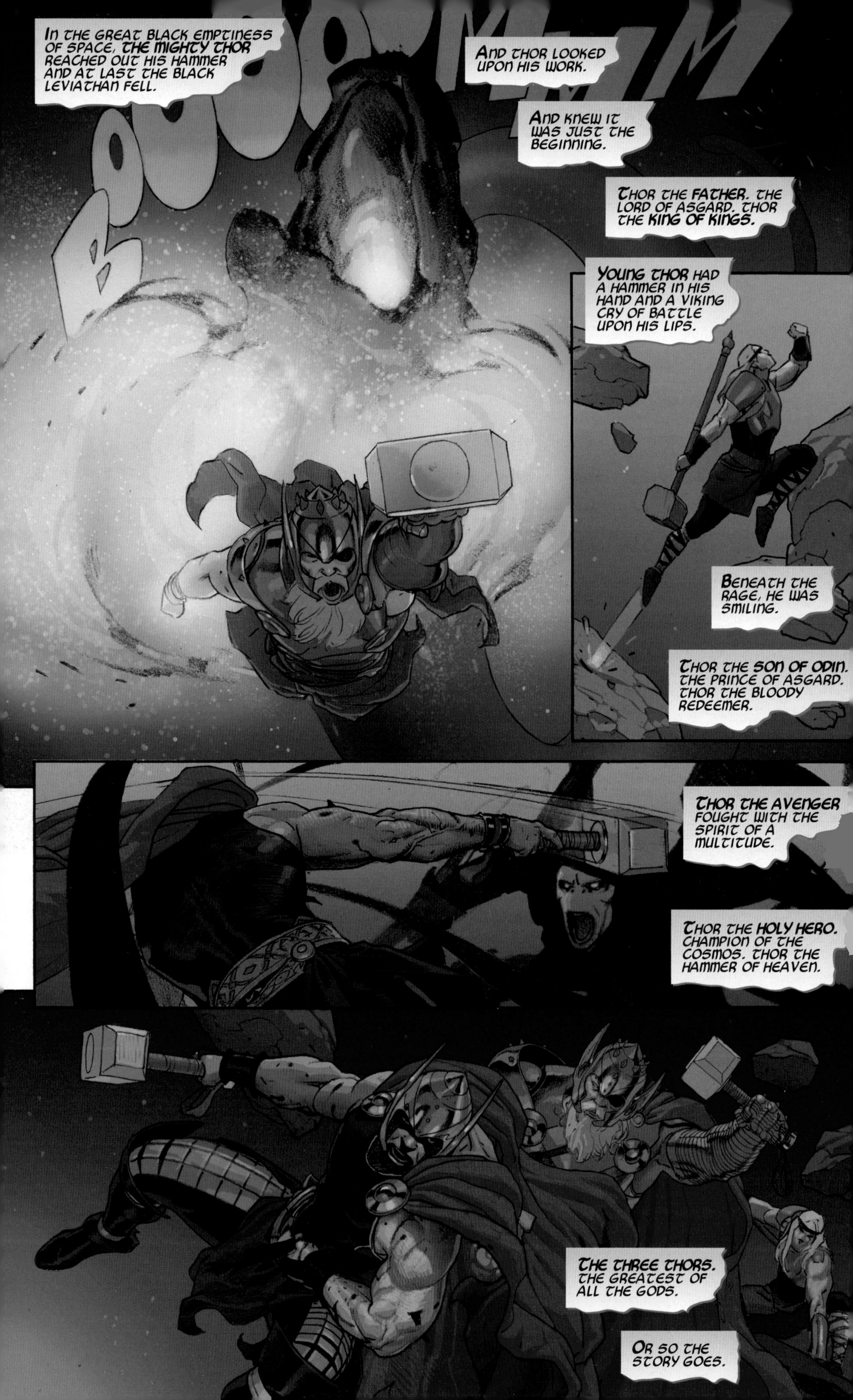
In the great black emptiness of space, THE MIGHTY THOR reached out his hammer and at last the black leviathan fell.
And Thor looked upon his work.
And knew it was just the beginning.
Thor the FATHER. The Lord of Asgard. Thor the KING OF KINGS.
YOUNG THOR had a hammer in his hand and a Viking cry of battle upon his lips.
Beneath the rage, he was smiling.
Thor the SON OF ODIN. The Prince of Asgard. Thor the Bloody Redeemer.
THOR THE AVENGER fought with the spirit of a multitude.
Thor the HOLY HERO. Champion of the Cosmos. Thor the Hammer of Heaven.
THE THREE THORS. The greatest of all the gods.
Or so the story goes.

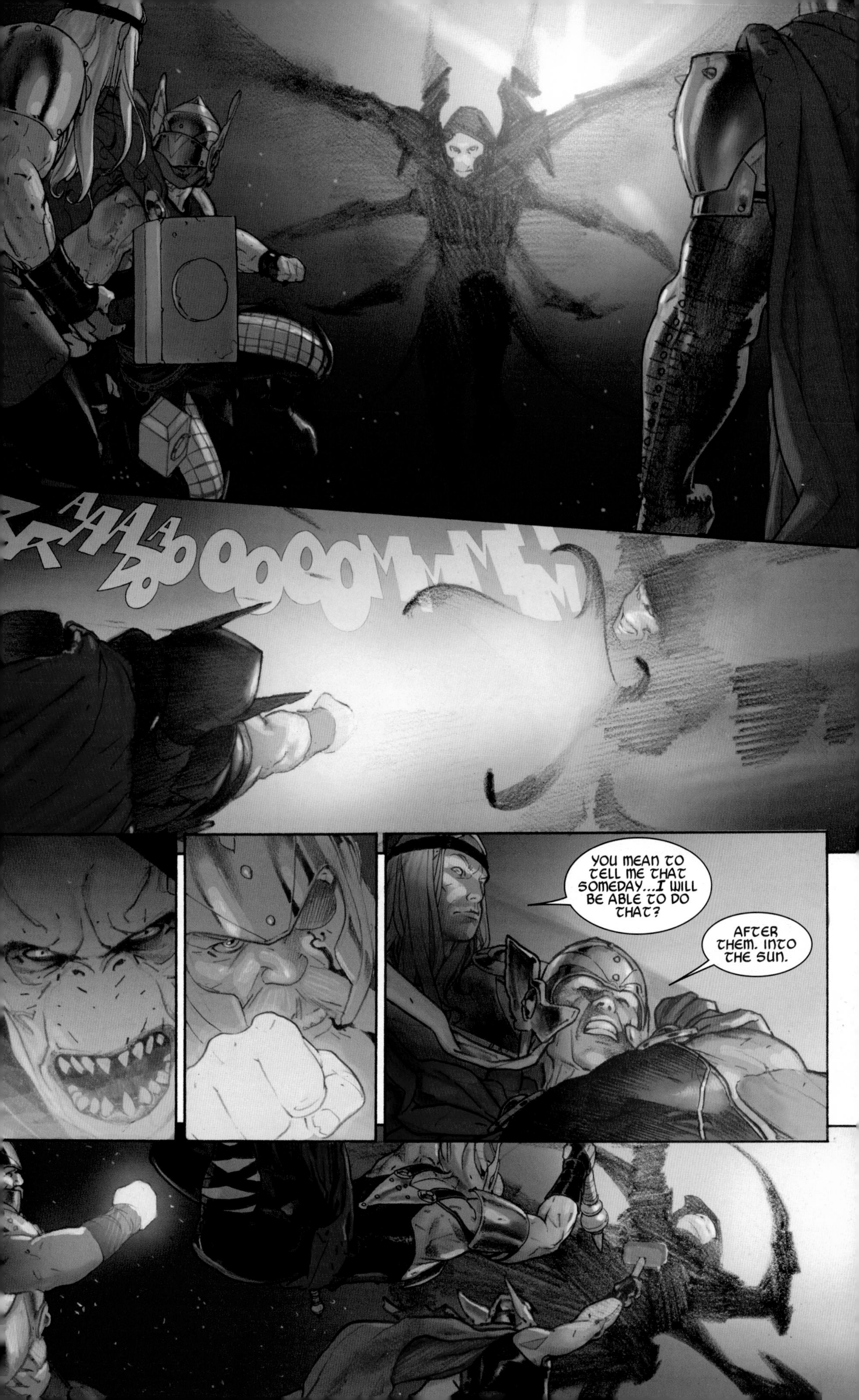

RRAAAAABOOOOOMMM!
YOU MEAN TO TELL ME THAT SOMEDAY...I WILL BE ABLE TO DO THAT?
AFTER THEM. INTO THE SUN.

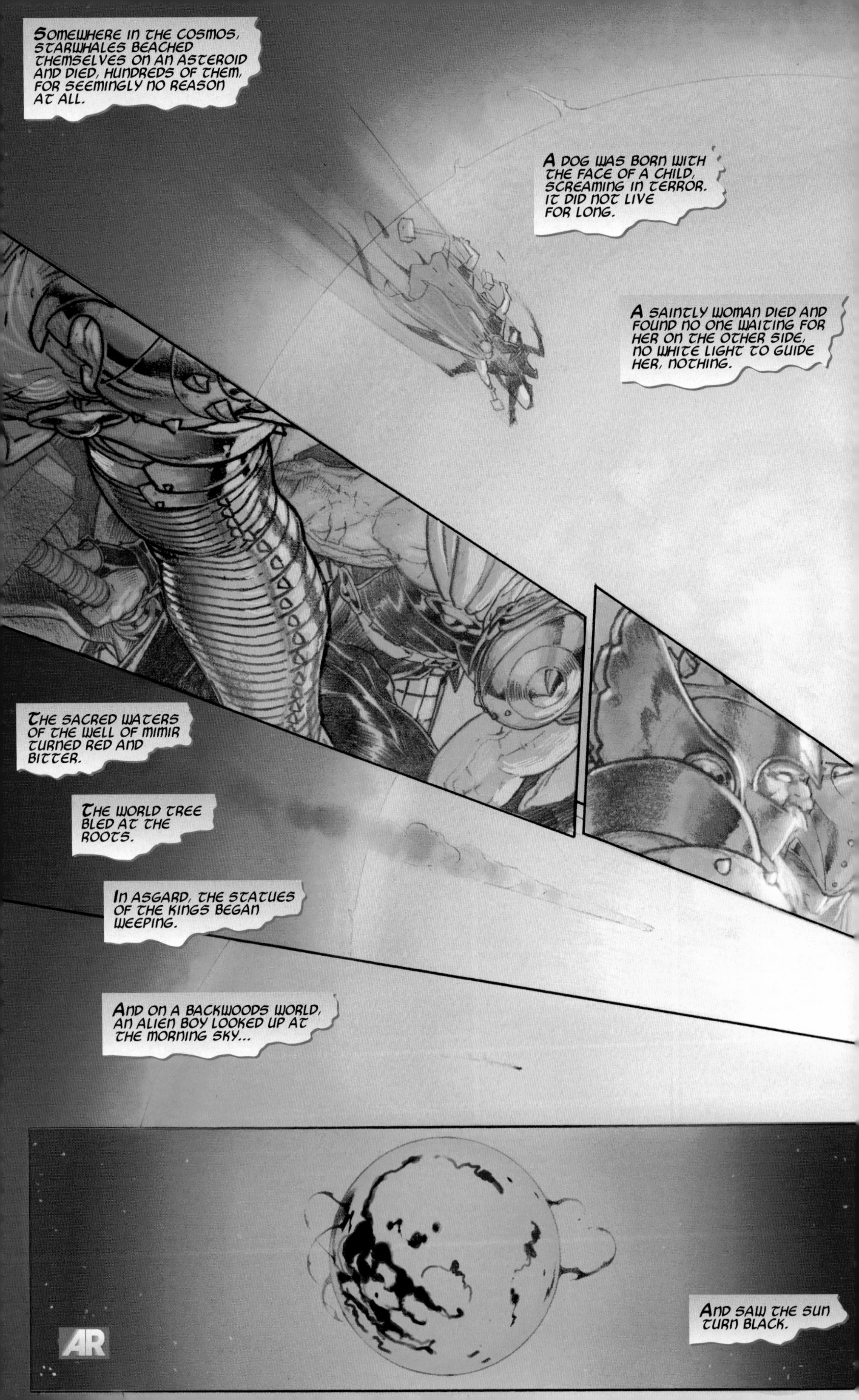

SOMEWHERE IN THE COSMOS, STARWHALES BEACHED THEMSELVES ON AN ASTEROID AND DIED, HUNDREDS OF THEM, FOR SEEMINGLY NO REASON AT ALL.
A DOG WAS BORN WITH THE FACE OF A CHILD, SCREAMING IN TERROR. IT DID NOT LIVE FOR LONG.
A SAINTLY WOMAN DIED AND FOUND NO ONE WAITING FOR HER ON THE OTHER SIDE, NO WHITE LIGHT TO GUIDE HER, NOTHING.
THE SACRED WATERS OF THE WELL OF MIMIR TURNED RED AND BITTER.
THE WORLD TREE BLED AT THE ROOTS.
IN ASGARD, THE STATUES OF THE KINGS BEGAN WEEPING.
AND ON A BACKWOODS WORLD, AN ALIEN BOY LOOKED UP AT THE MORNING SKY...
AND SAW THE SUN TURN BLACK.

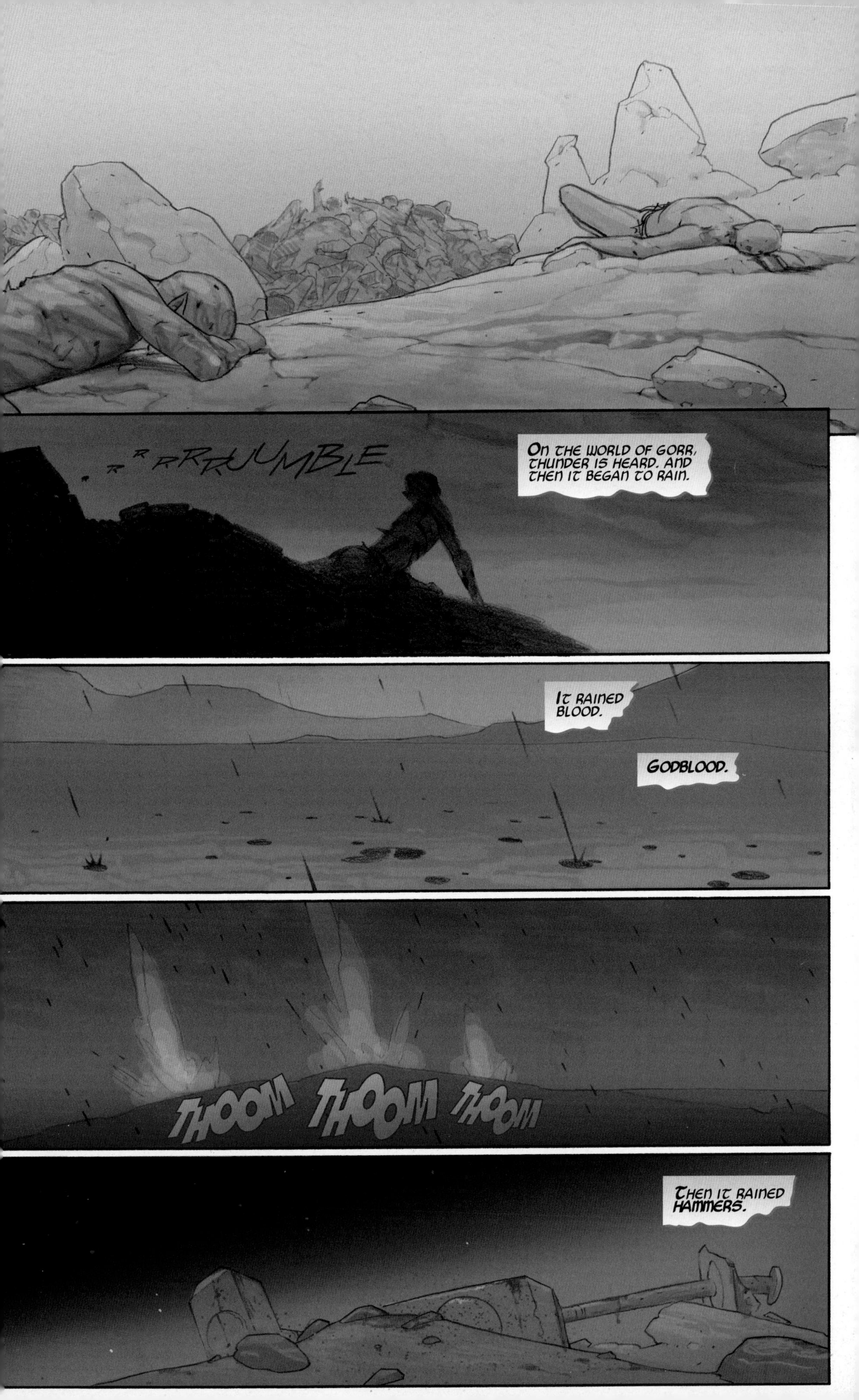
RRRRRUUMBLE
On the world of Gorr, thunder is heard. And then it began to rain.
It rained blood.
Godblood.
THOOM THOOM THOOM
Then it rained hammers.

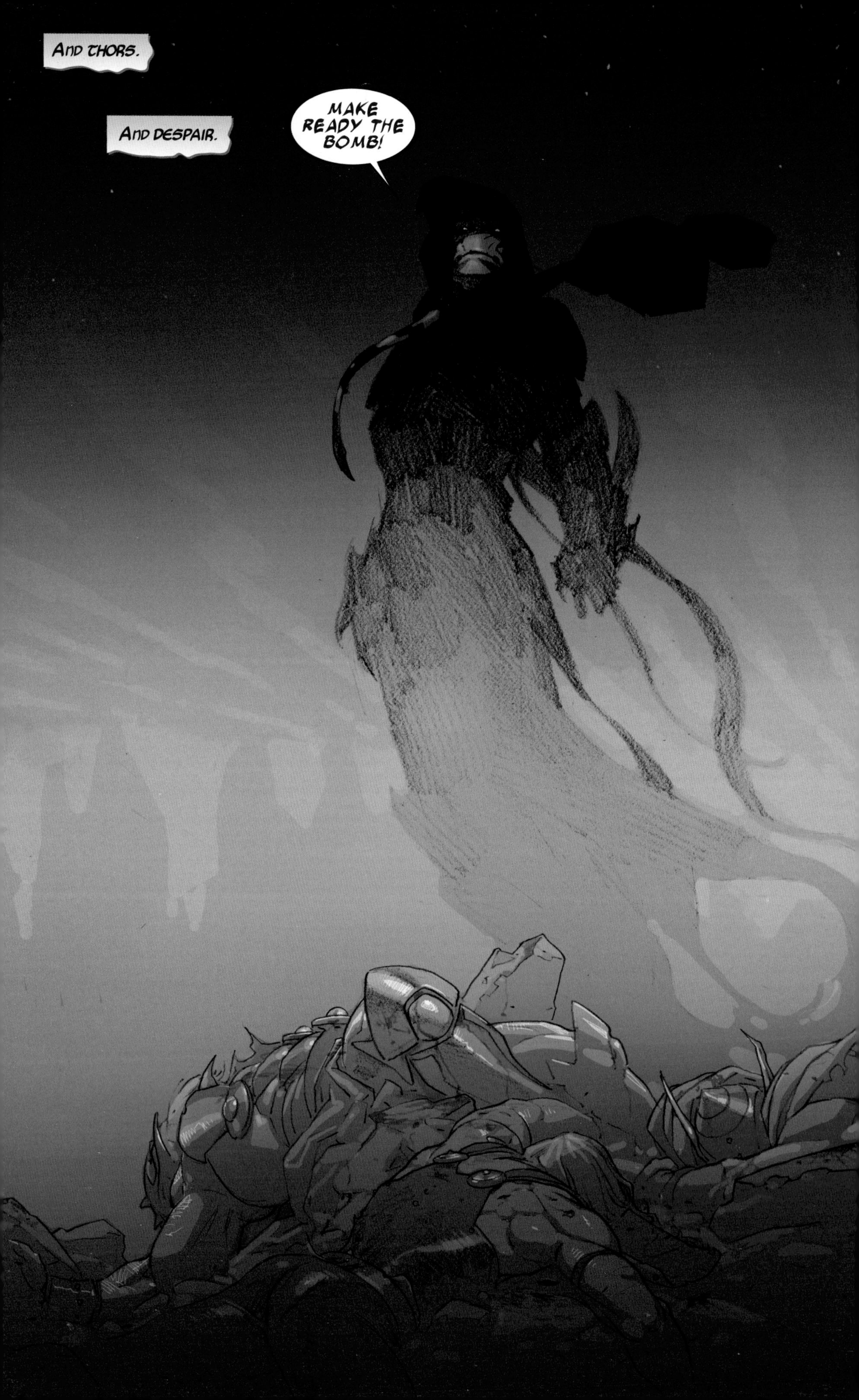
And THORS.
And DESPAIR.
MAKE READY THE BOMB!

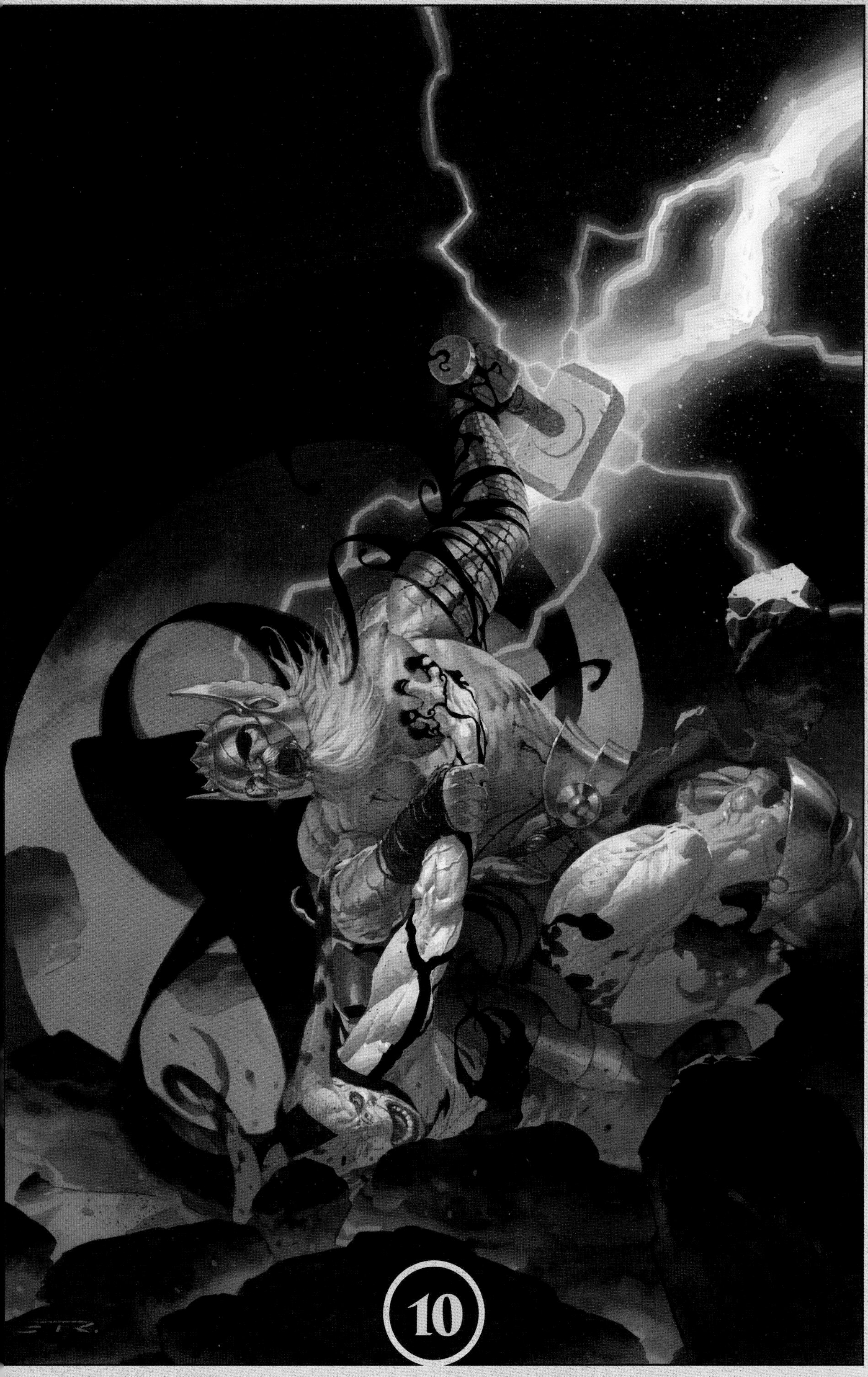
10

GODBOMB PART 4: TO THE LAST GOD

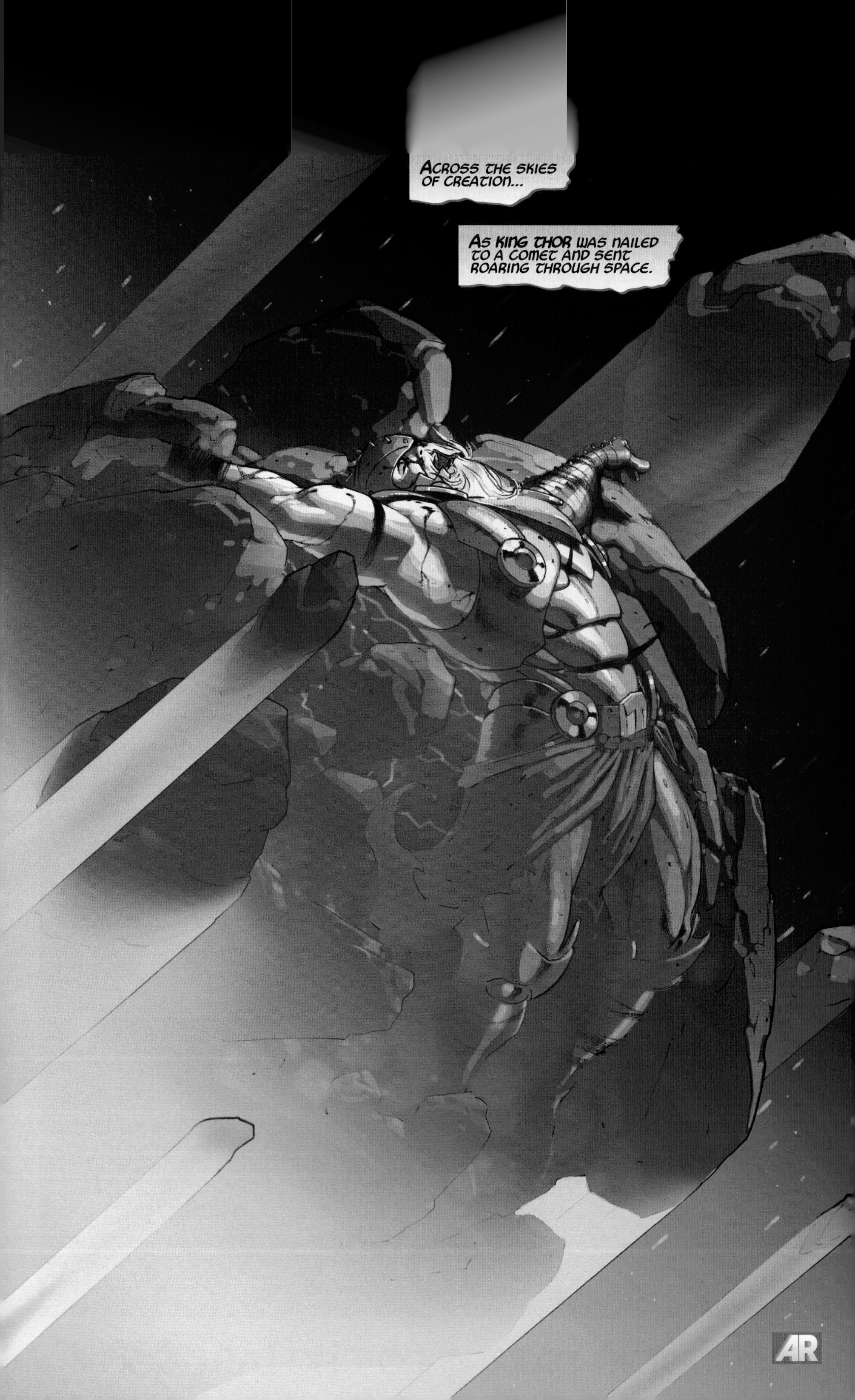
ACROSS THE SKIES OF CREATION...
AS KING THOR WAS NAILED TO A COMET AND SENT ROARING THROUGH SPACE.

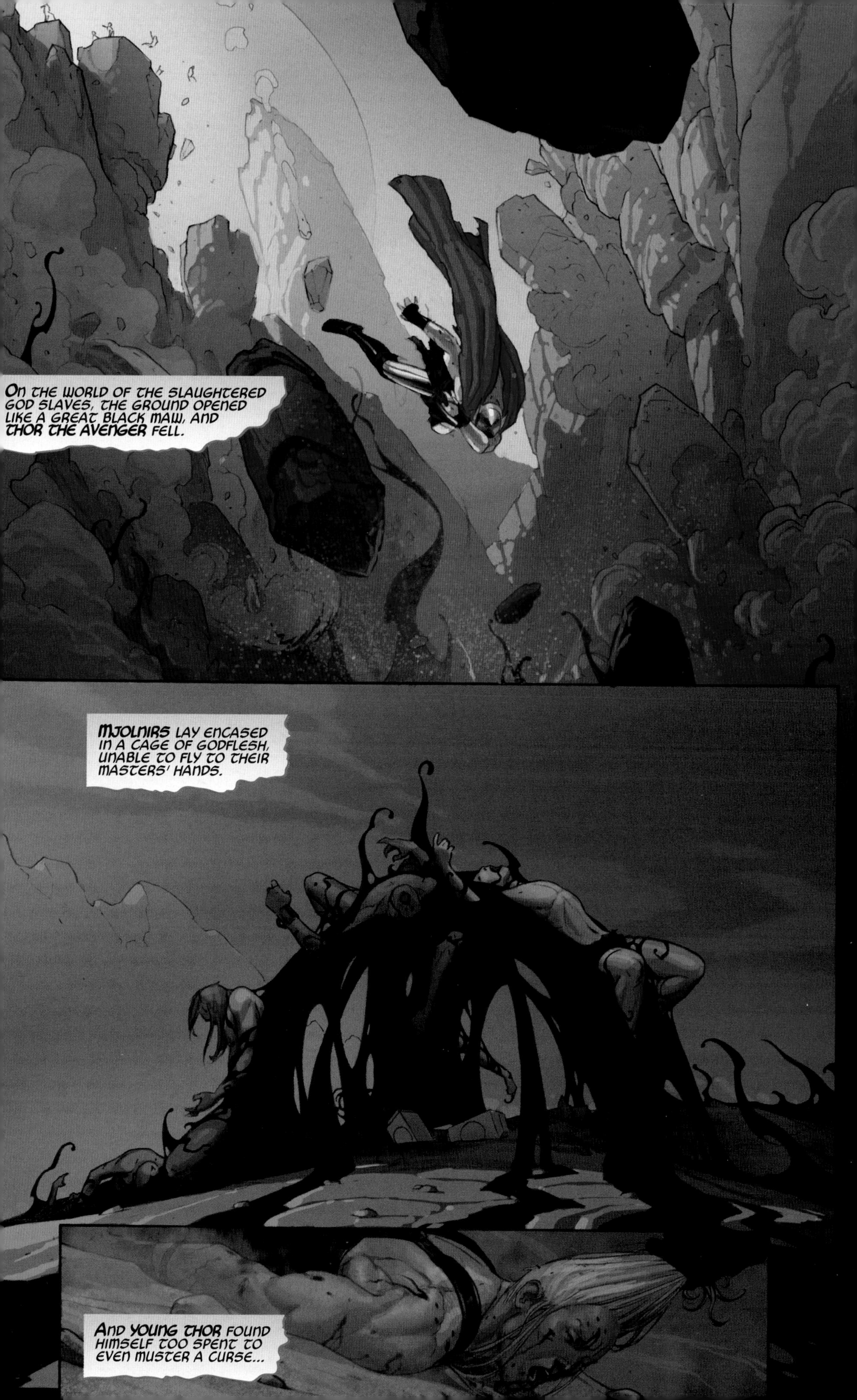
On the world of the slaughtered god slaves, the ground opened like a great black maw, and Thor the Avenger fell.
Mjolnirs lay encased in a cage of godflesh, unable to fly to their masters' hands.
And young Thor found himself too spent to even muster a curse...

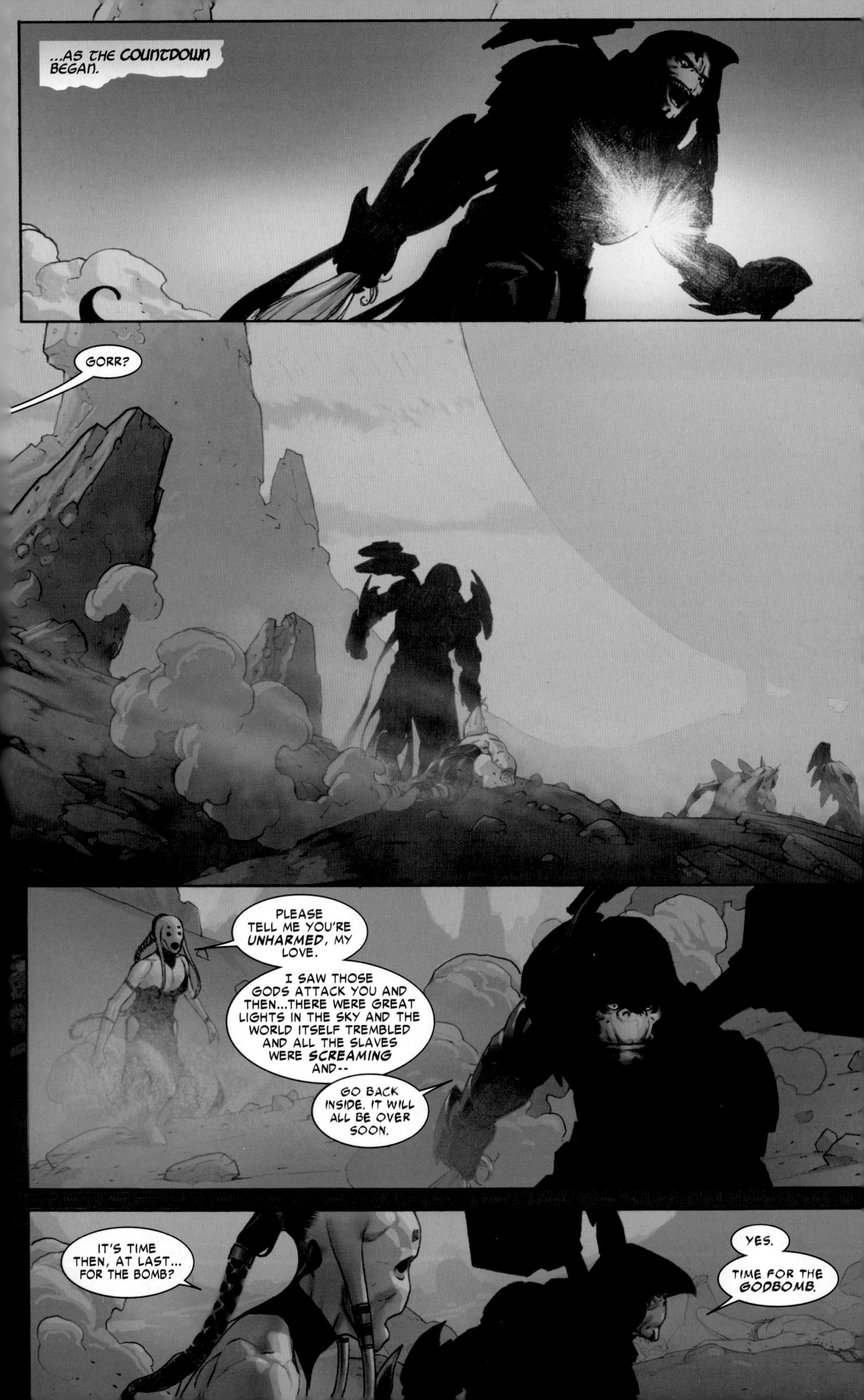
...AS THE COUNTDOWN BEGAN.
GORR?
PLEASE TELL ME YOU'RE UNHARMED, MY LOVE.
I SAW THOSE GODS ATTACK YOU AND THEN...THERE WERE GREAT LIGHTS IN THE SKY AND THE WORLD ITSELF TREMBLED AND ALL THE SLAVES WERE SCREAMING AND--
GO BACK INSIDE. IT WILL ALL BE OVER SOON.
IT'S TIME THEN, AT LAST... FOR THE BOMB?
YES.
TIME FOR THE GODBOMB.

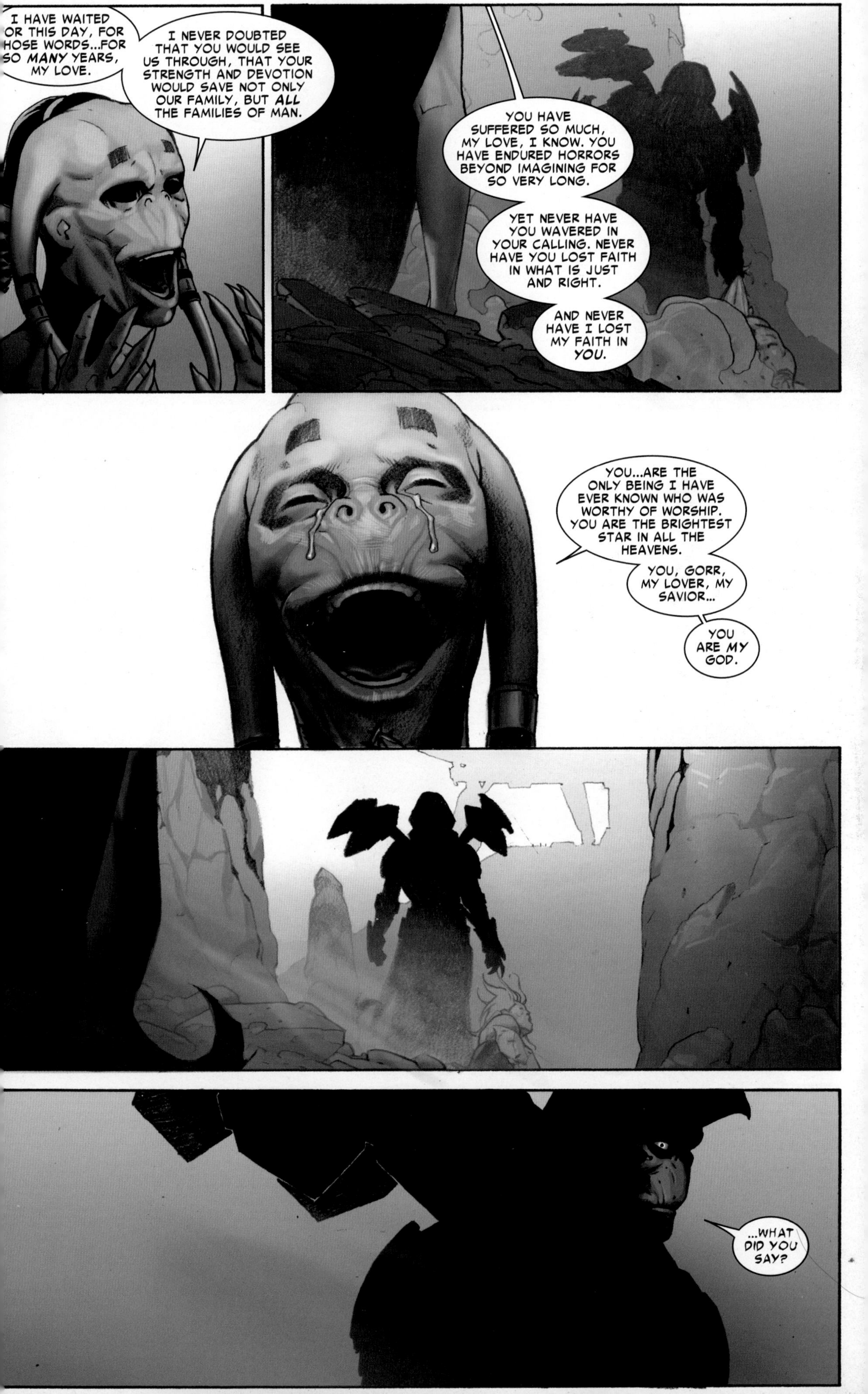
I HAVE WAITED
OR THIS DAY, FOR
HOSE WORDS...FOR
SO MANY YEARS,
MY LOVE.
I NEVER DOUBTED THAT YOU WOULD SEE US THROUGH, THAT YOUR STRENGTH AND DEVOTION WOULD SAVE NOT ONLY OUR FAMILY, BUT ALL THE FAMILIES OF MAN.
YOU HAVE SUFFERED SO MUCH, MY LOVE, I KNOW. YOU HAVE ENDURED HORRORS BEYOND IMAGINING FOR SO VERY LONG.
YET NEVER HAVE YOU WAVERED IN YOUR CALLING. NEVER HAVE YOU LOST FAITH IN WHAT IS JUST AND RIGHT.
AND NEVER HAVE I LOST MY FAITH IN YOU.
YOU...ARE THE ONLY BEING I HAVE EVER KNOWN WHO WAS WORTHY OF WORSHIP. YOU ARE THE BRIGHTEST STAR IN ALL THE HEAVENS.
YOU, GORR, MY LOVER, MY SAVIOR...
YOU ARE MY GOD.
...WHAT DID YOU SAY?

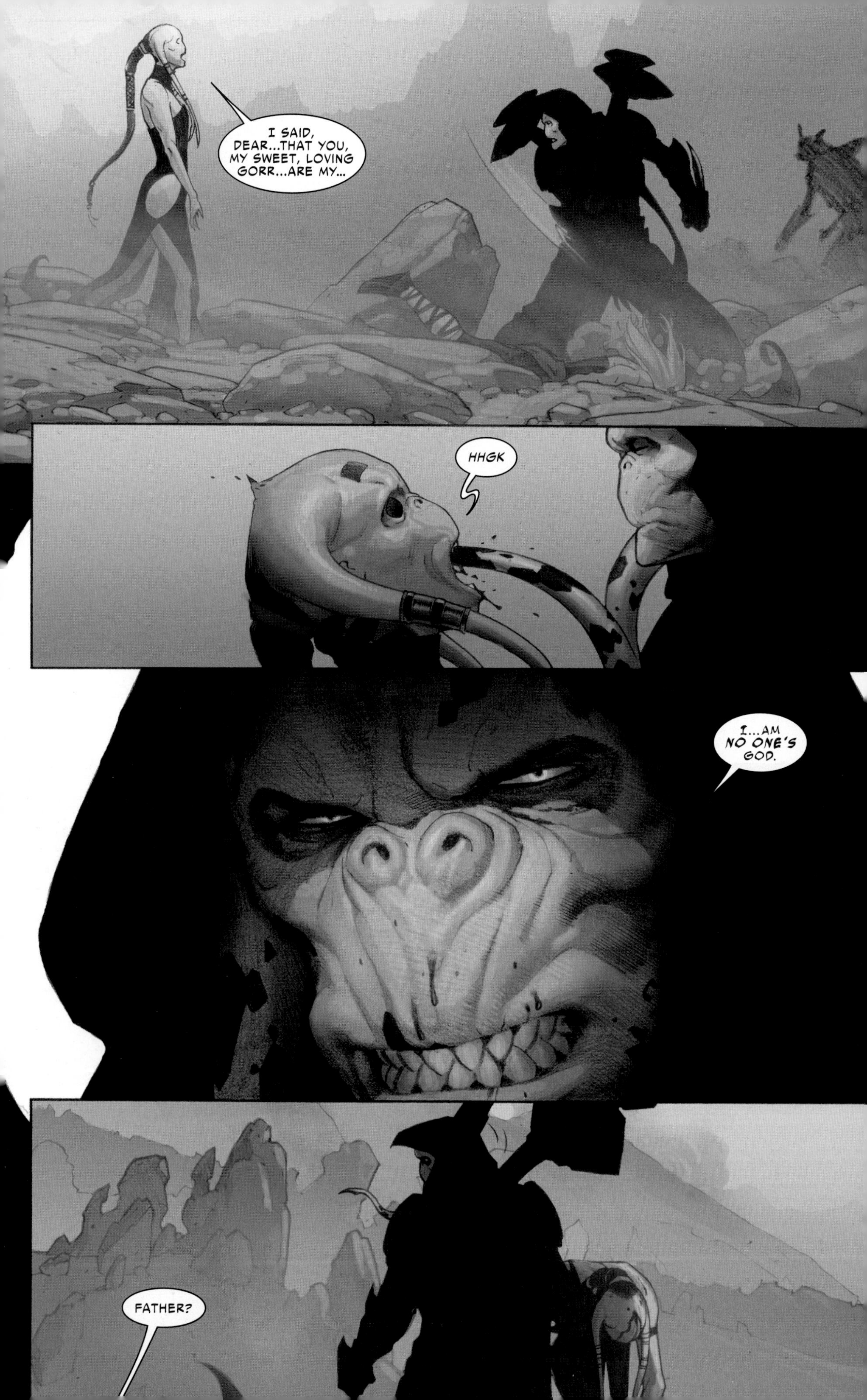
I SAID, DEAR...THAT YOU, MY SWEET, LOVING GORR...ARE MY...
HHGK
I...AM NO ONE'S GOD.
FATHER?

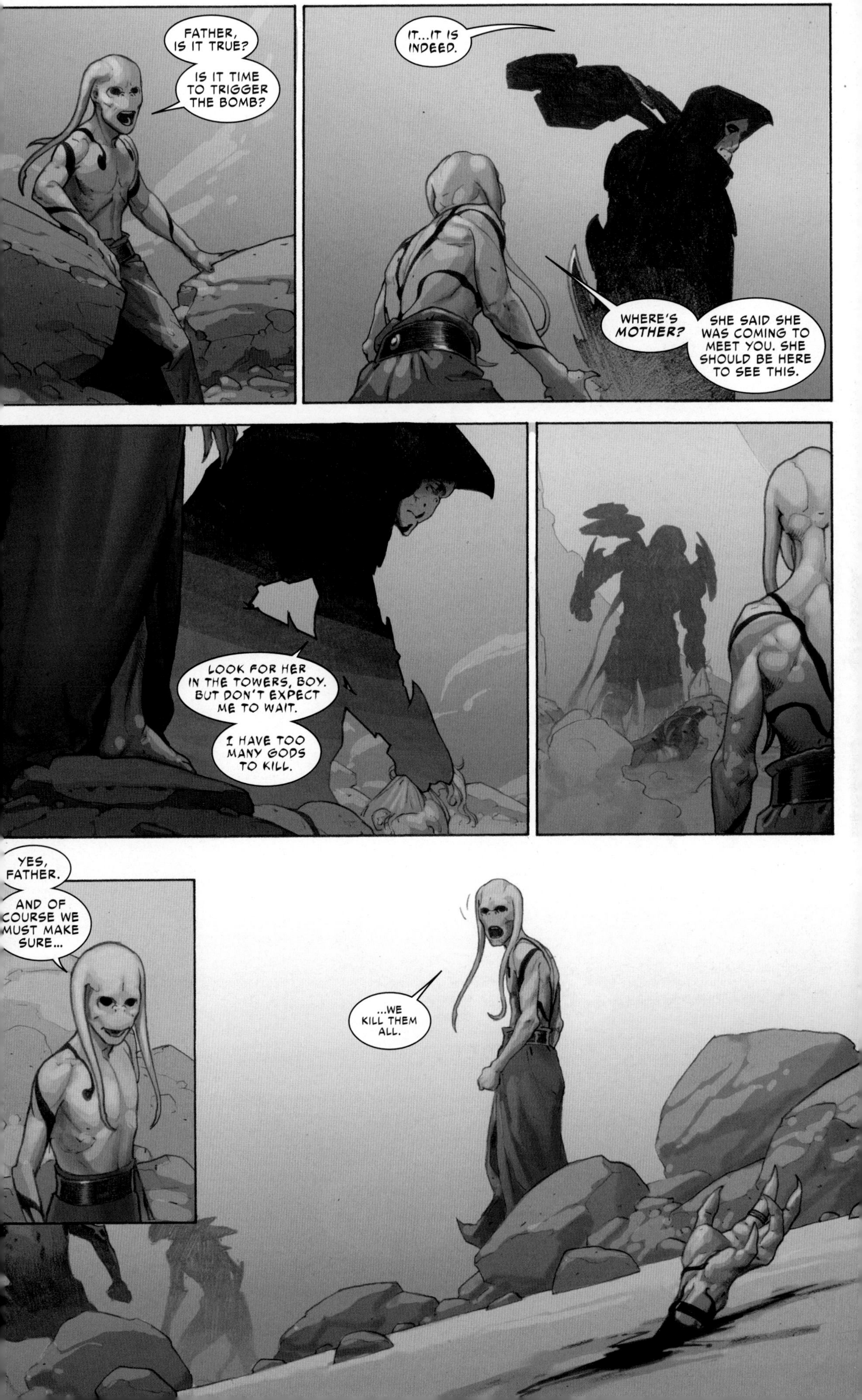
FATHER, IS IT TRUE?
IS IT TIME TO TRIGGER THE BOMB?
IT...IT IS INDEED.
WHERE'S *MOTHER?*
SHE SAID SHE WAS COMING TO MEET YOU. SHE SHOULD BE HERE TO SEE THIS.
LOOK FOR HER IN THE TOWERS, BOY. BUT DON'T EXPECT ME TO WAIT.
I HAVE TOO MANY GODS TO KILL.
YES, FATHER.
AND OF COURSE WE MUST MAKE SURE...
...WE KILL THEM ALL.

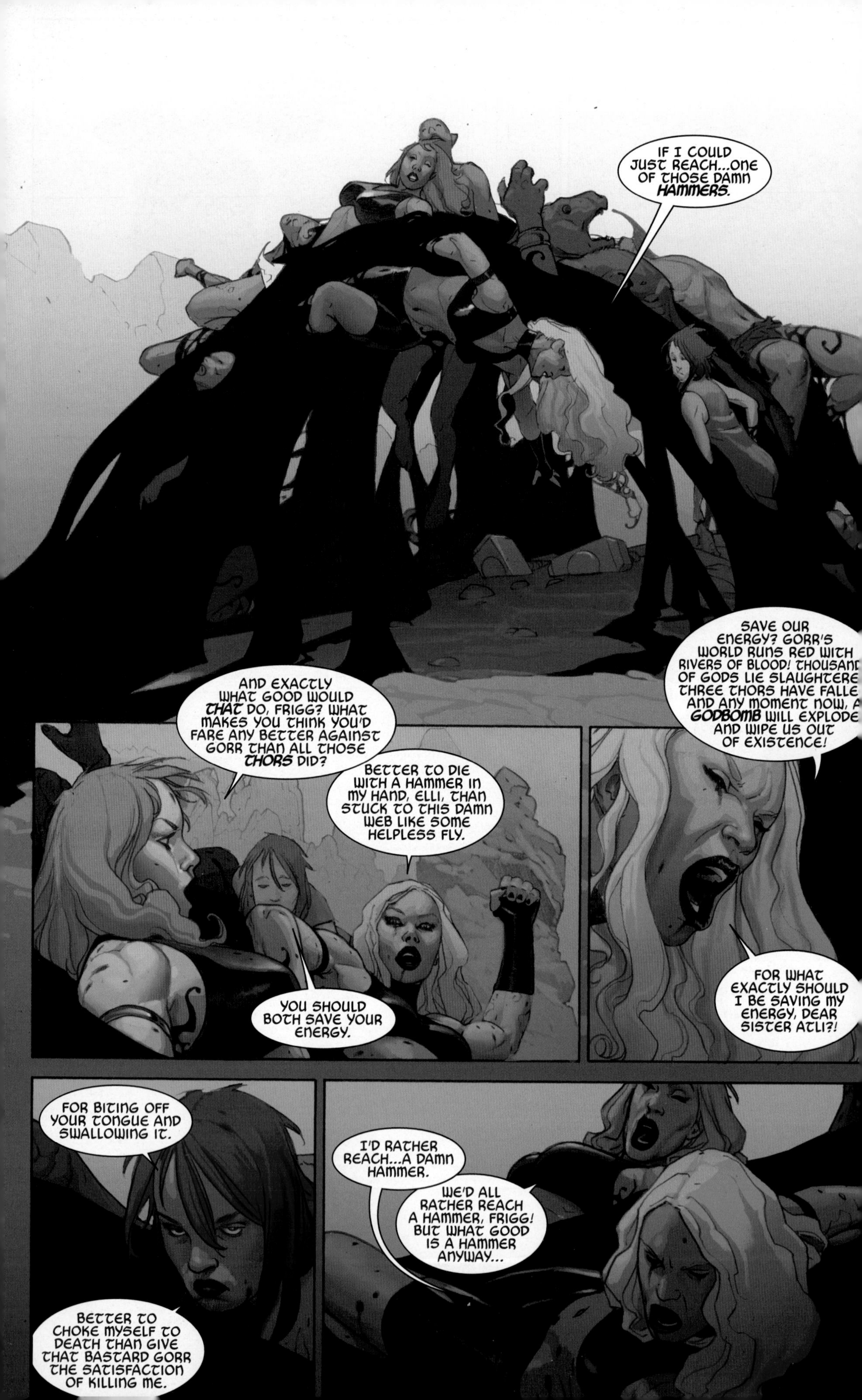
IF I COULD JUST REACH...ONE OF THOSE DAMN HAMMERS.
AND EXACTLY WHAT GOOD WOULD THAT DO, FRIGG? WHAT MAKES YOU THINK YOU'D FARE ANY BETTER AGAINST GORR THAN ALL THOSE THORS DID?
BETTER TO DIE WITH A HAMMER IN MY HAND, ELLI, THAN STUCK TO THIS DAMN WEB LIKE SOME HELPLESS FLY.
YOU SHOULD BOTH SAVE YOUR ENERGY.
SAVE OUR ENERGY? GORR'S WORLD RUNS RED WITH RIVERS OF BLOOD! THOUSAND OF GODS LIE SLAUGHTERE THREE THORS HAVE FALLE AND ANY MOMENT NOW, A GODBOMB WILL EXPLODE AND WIPE US OUT OF EXISTENCE!
FOR WHAT EXACTLY SHOULD I BE SAVING MY ENERGY, DEAR SISTER ATLI?!
FOR BITING OFF YOUR TONGUE AND SWALLOWING IT.
BETTER TO CHOKE MYSELF TO DEATH THAN GIVE THAT BASTARD GORR THE SATISFACTION OF KILLING ME.
I'D RATHER REACH...A DAMN HAMMER.
WE'D ALL RATHER REACH A HAMMER, FRIGG! BUT WHAT GOOD IS A HAMMER ANYWAY...

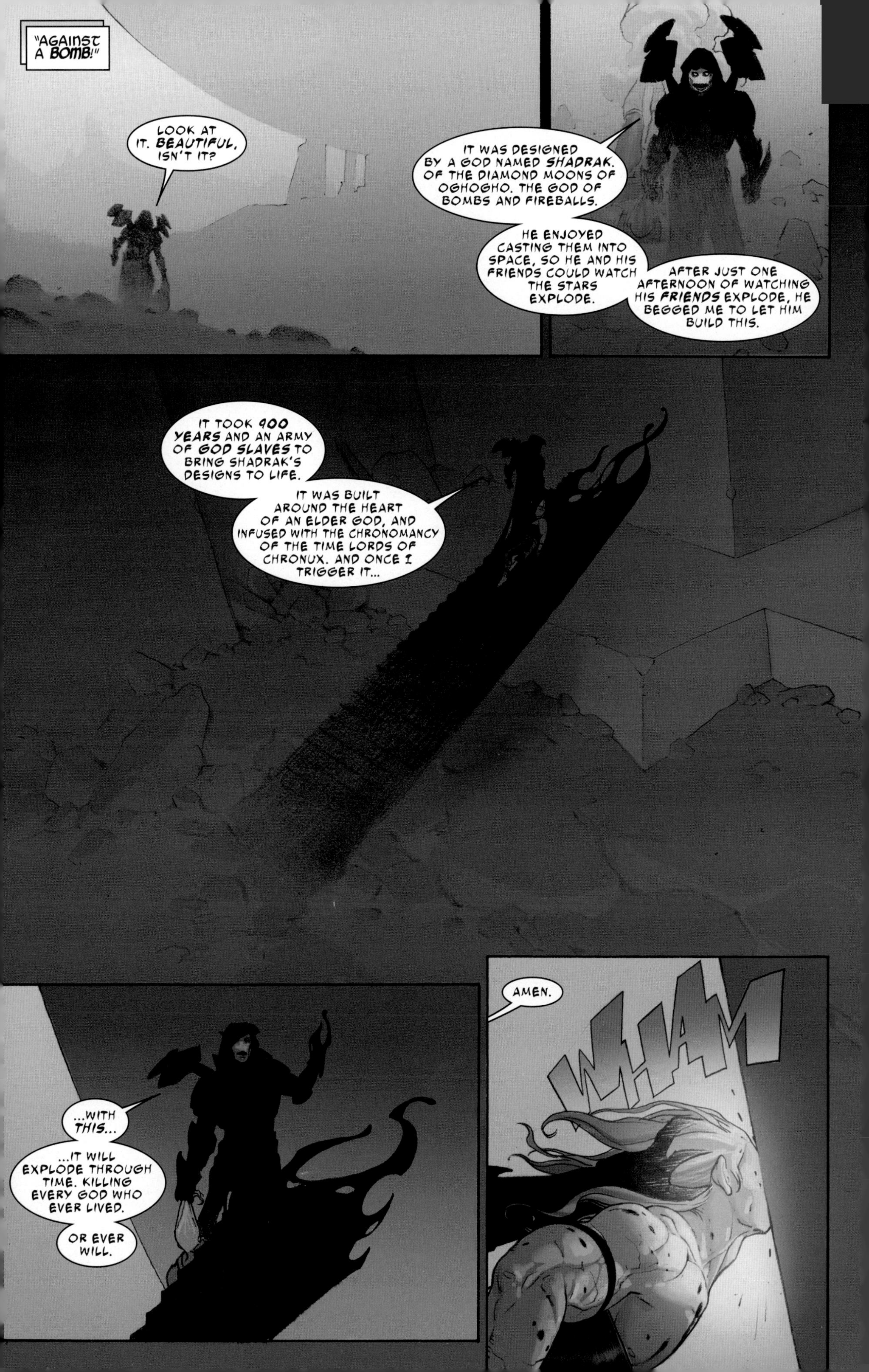
"AGAINST A BOMB!"
LOOK AT IT. BEAUTIFUL, ISN'T IT?
IT WAS DESIGNED BY A GOD NAMED SHADRAK. OF THE DIAMOND MOONS OF OGHOGHO. THE GOD OF BOMBS AND FIREBALLS.
HE ENJOYED CASTING THEM INTO SPACE, SO HE AND HIS FRIENDS COULD WATCH THE STARS EXPLODE.
AFTER JUST ONE AFTERNOON OF WATCHING HIS FRIENDS EXPLODE, HE BEGGED ME TO LET HIM BUILD THIS.
IT TOOK 900 YEARS AND AN ARMY OF GOD SLAVES TO BRING SHADRAK'S DESIGNS TO LIFE.
IT WAS BUILT AROUND THE HEART OF AN ELDER GOD, AND INFUSED WITH THE CHRONOMANCY OF THE TIME LORDS OF CHRONUX. AND ONCE I TRIGGER IT...
...WITH THIS...
...IT WILL EXPLODE THROUGH TIME. KILLING EVERY GOD WHO EVER LIVED.
OR EVER WILL.
AMEN.
WHAM

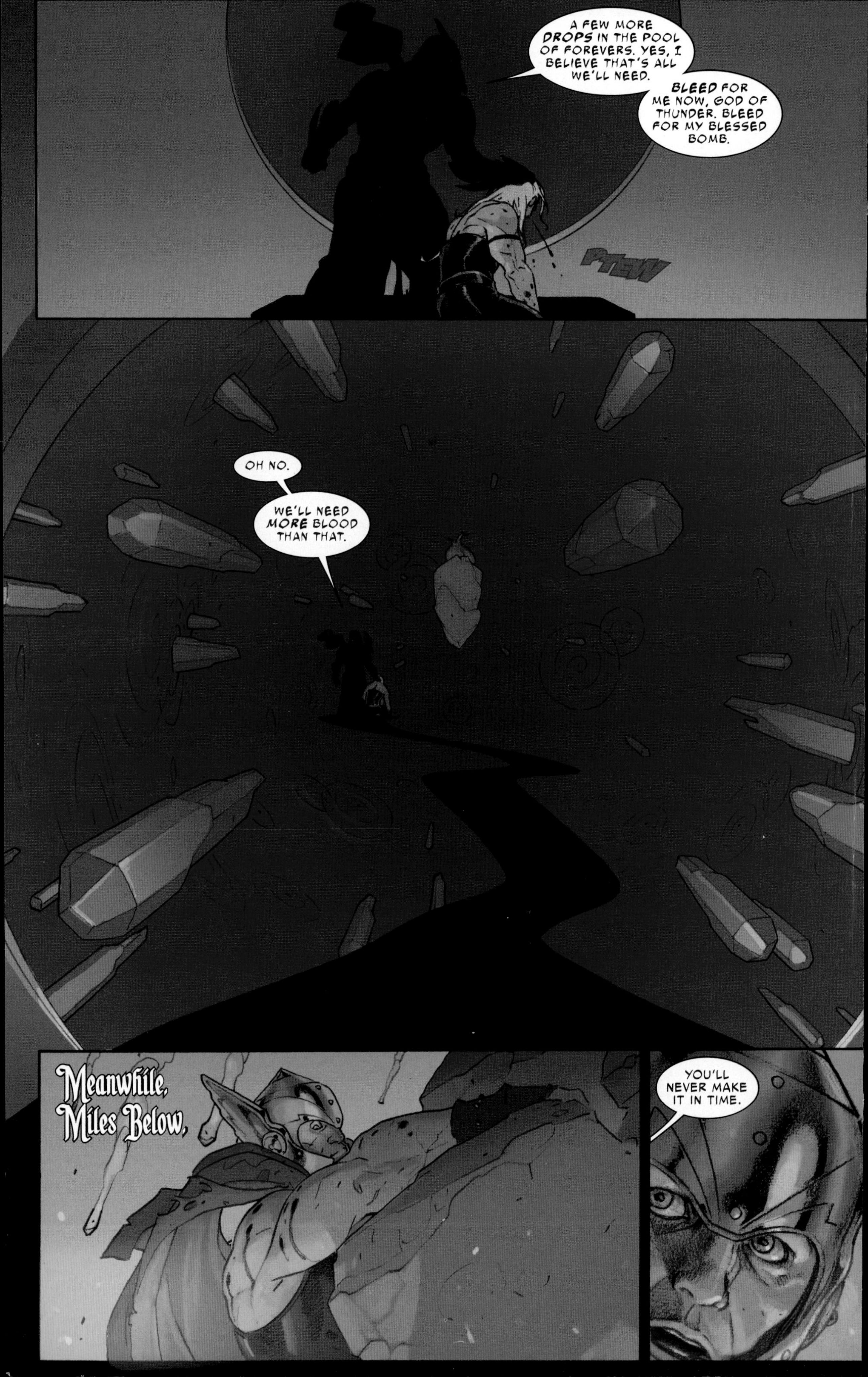
A FEW MORE DROPS IN THE POOL OF FOREVERS. YES, I BELIEVE THAT'S ALL WE'LL NEED.
BLEED FOR ME NOW, GOD OF THUNDER. BLEED FOR MY BLESSED BOMB.
PTEW
OH NO.
WE'LL NEED MORE BLOOD THAN THAT.
Meanwhile, Miles Below,
YOU'LL NEVER MAKE IT IN TIME.

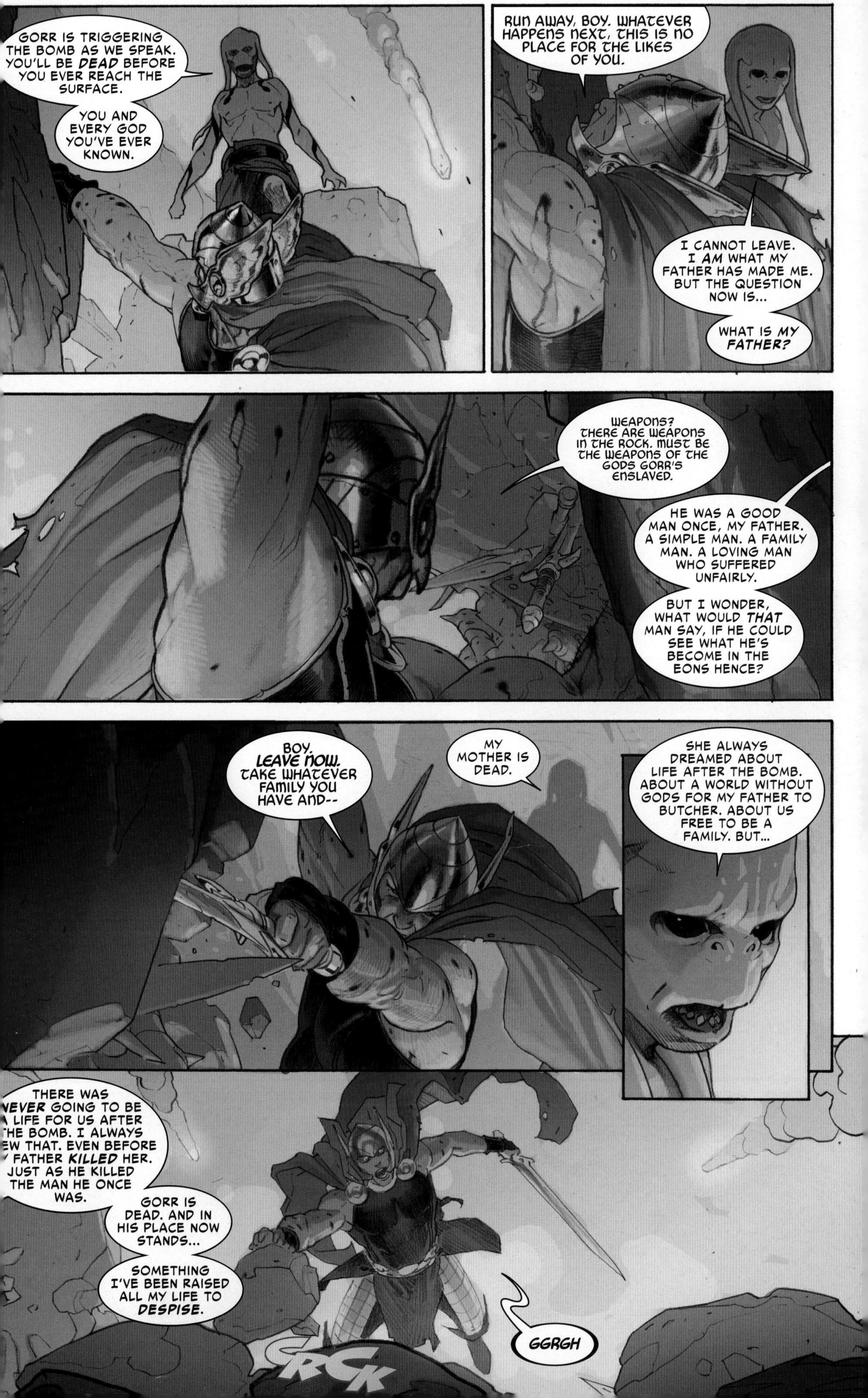

GORR IS TRIGGERING THE BOMB AS WE SPEAK. YOU'LL BE *DEAD* BEFORE YOU EVER REACH THE SURFACE.
YOU AND EVERY GOD YOU'VE EVER KNOWN.
RUN AWAY, BOY. WHATEVER HAPPENS NEXT, THIS IS NO PLACE FOR THE LIKES OF YOU.
I CANNOT LEAVE. I *AM* WHAT MY FATHER HAS MADE ME. BUT THE QUESTION NOW IS...
WHAT IS *MY FATHER?*
WEAPONS? THERE ARE WEAPONS IN THE ROCK. MUST BE THE WEAPONS OF THE GODS GORR'S ENSLAVED.
HE WAS A GOOD MAN ONCE, MY FATHER. A SIMPLE MAN. A FAMILY MAN. A LOVING MAN WHO SUFFERED UNFAIRLY.
BUT I WONDER, WHAT WOULD *THAT* MAN SAY, IF HE COULD SEE WHAT HE'S BECOME IN THE EONS HENCE?
BOY. ***LEAVE NOW.*** TAKE WHATEVER FAMILY YOU HAVE AND--
MY MOTHER IS DEAD.
SHE ALWAYS DREAMED ABOUT LIFE AFTER THE BOMB. ABOUT A WORLD WITHOUT GODS FOR MY FATHER TO BUTCHER. ABOUT US FREE TO BE A FAMILY. BUT...
THERE WAS *NEVER* GOING TO BE A LIFE FOR US AFTER THE BOMB. I ALWAYS EW THAT. EVEN BEFORE FATHER *KILLED* HER. JUST AS HE KILLED THE MAN HE ONCE WAS.
GORR IS DEAD. AND IN HIS PLACE NOW STANDS...
SOMETHING I'VE BEEN RAISED ALL MY LIFE TO *DESPISE*.
GGRGH
CRCK

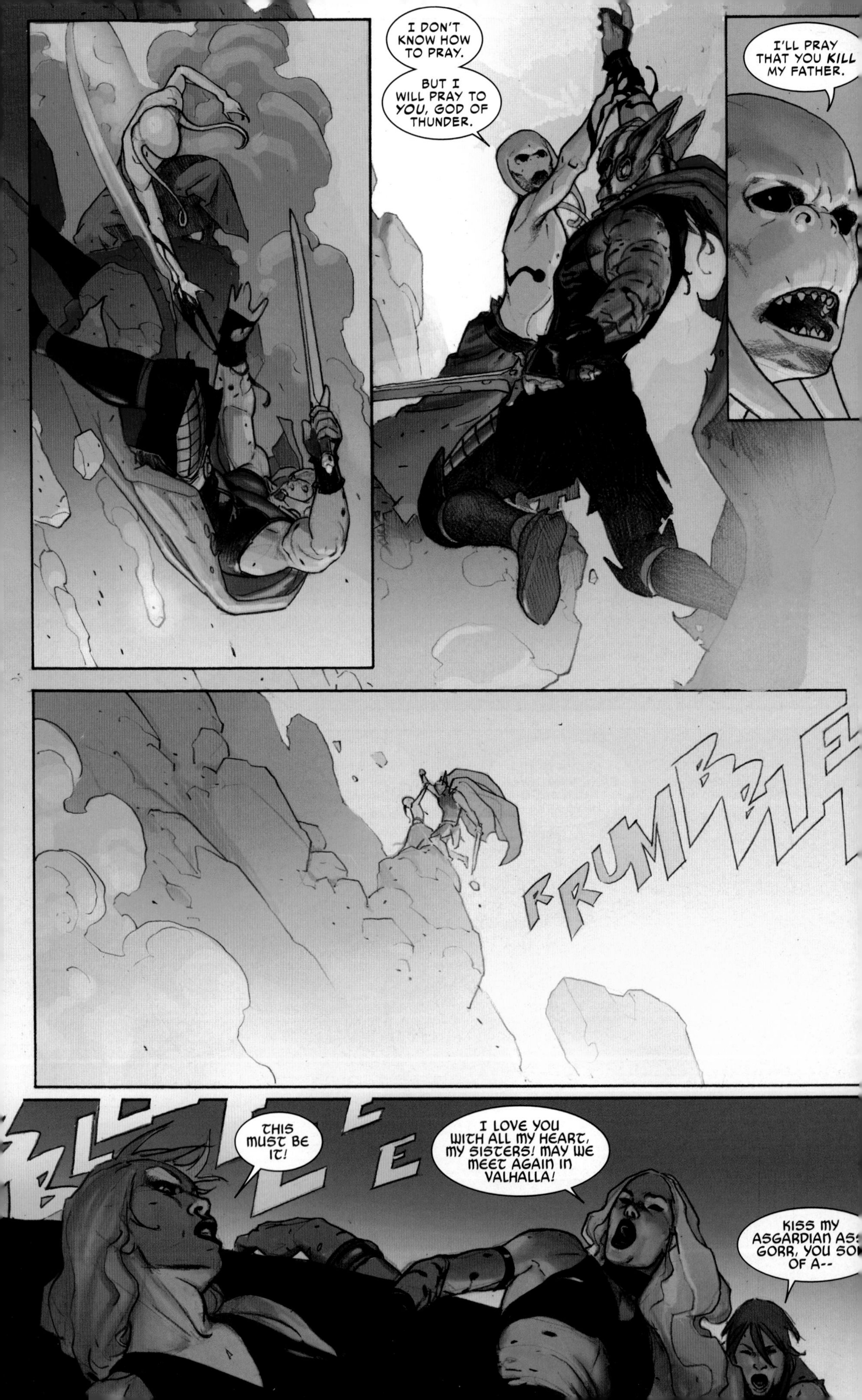

I DON'T KNOW HOW TO PRAY.
BUT I WILL PRAY TO *YOU*, GOD OF THUNDER.
I'LL PRAY THAT YOU **KILL** MY FATHER.
FRUMBLE
THIS MUST BE IT!
I LOVE YOU WITH ALL MY HEART, MY SISTERS! MAY WE MEET AGAIN IN VALHALLA!
KISS MY ASGARDIAN AS GORR, YOU SO OF A--

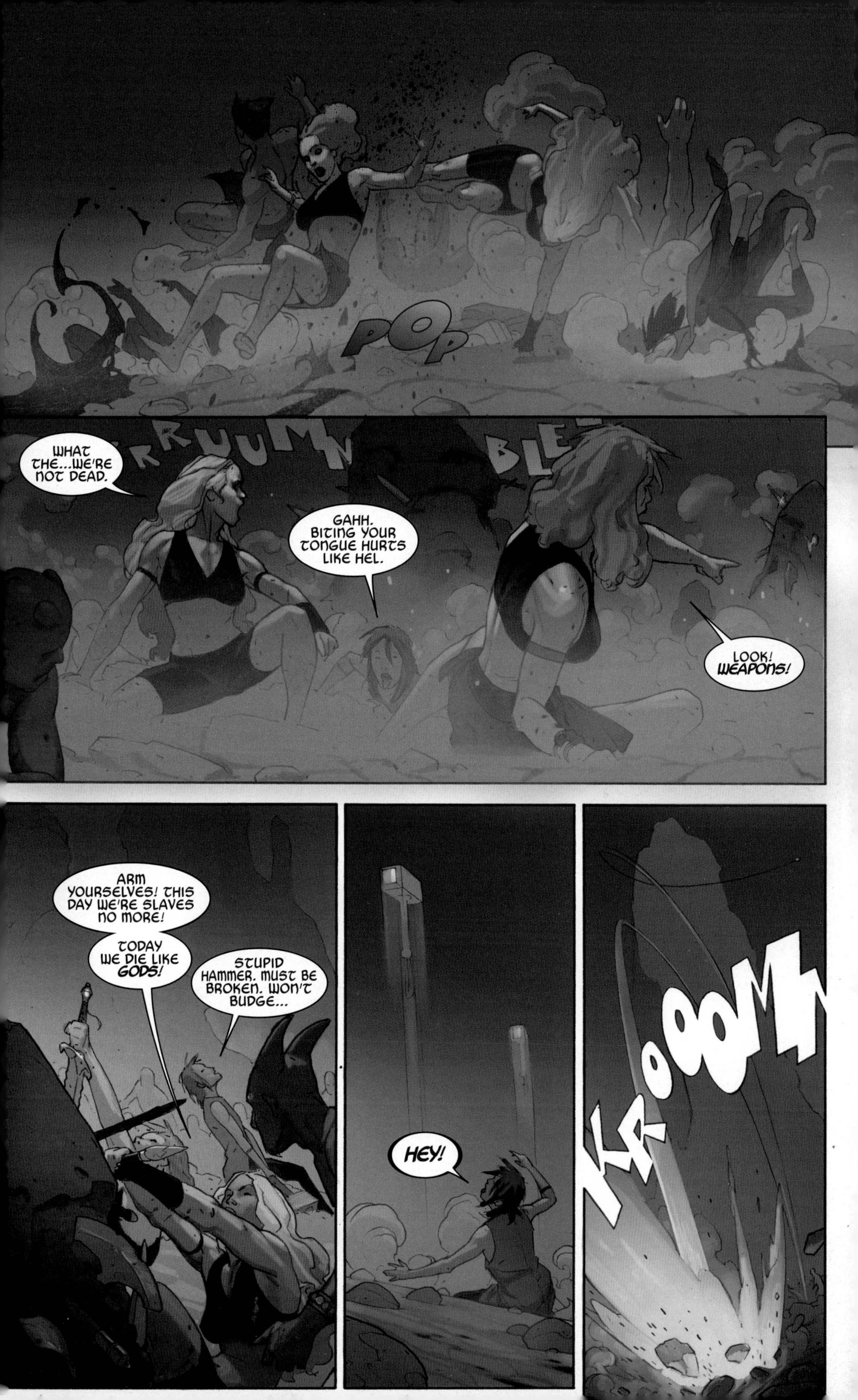
POP
WHAT THE...WE'RE NOT DEAD.
GAHH. BITING YOUR TONGUE HURTS LIKE HEL.
LOOK! WEAPONS!
ARM YOURSELVES! THIS DAY WE'RE SLAVES NO MORE!
TODAY WE DIE LIKE GODS!
STUPID HAMMER. MUST BE BROKEN. WON'T BUDGE...
HEY!
KROOOM

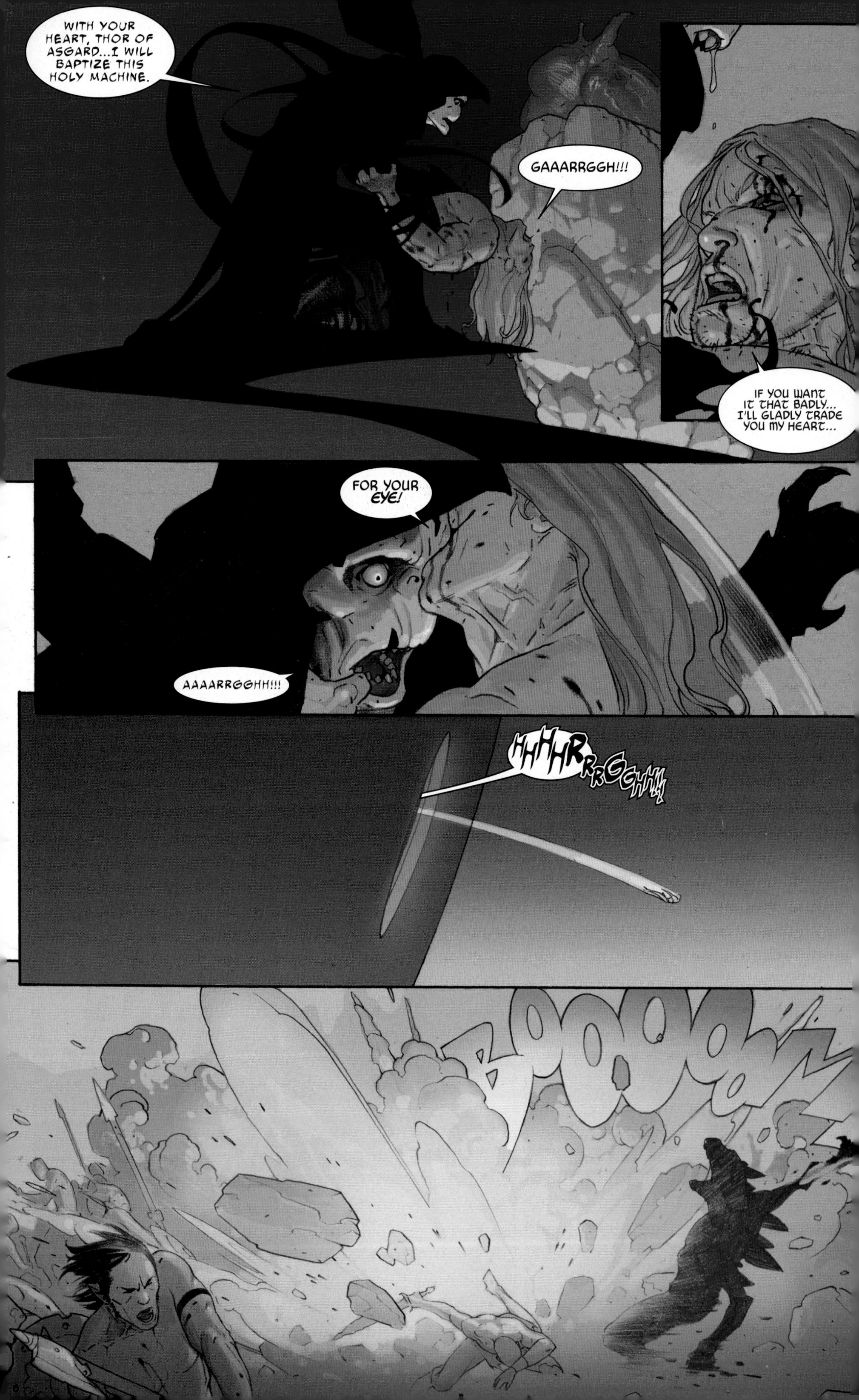
WITH YOUR HEART, THOR OF ASGARD...I WILL BAPTIZE THIS HOLY MACHINE.
GAAARRGGH!!!
IF YOU WANT IT THAT BADLY... I'LL GLADLY TRADE YOU MY HEART...
FOR YOUR EYE!
AAAARRGGHH!!!
HHHHRRRGGHH!!
BOOOOOM

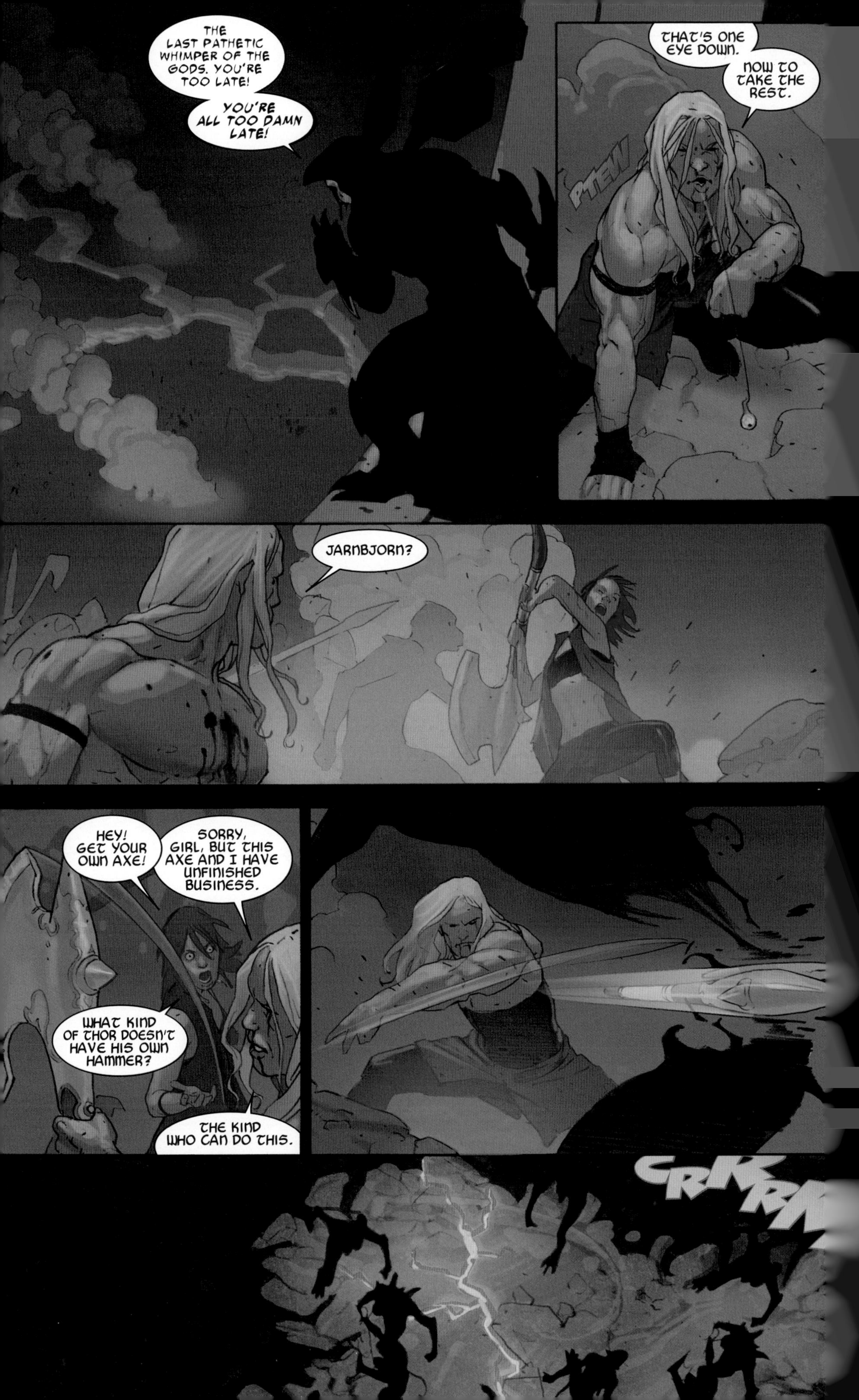
THE LAST PATHETIC WHIMPER OF THE GODS. YOU'RE TOO LATE!
YOU'RE ALL TOO DAMN LATE!
THAT'S ONE EYE DOWN.
NOW TO TAKE THE REST.
PTEW
JARNBJORN?
HEY! GET YOUR OWN AXE!
SORRY, GIRL, BUT THIS AXE AND I HAVE UNFINISHED BUSINESS.
WHAT KIND OF THOR DOESN'T HAVE HIS OWN HAMMER?
THE KIND WHO CAN DO THIS.
CRKRK

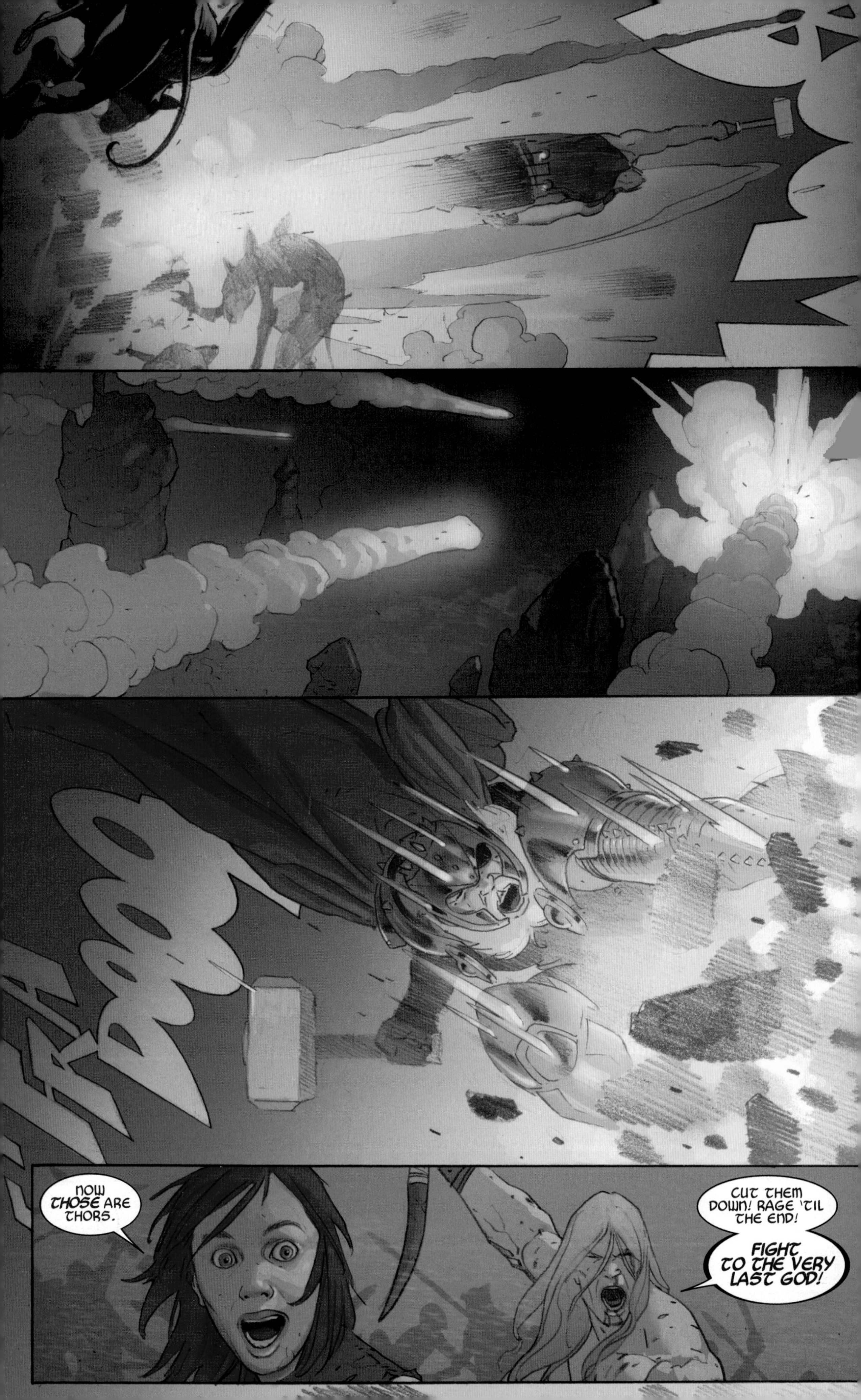
NOW THOSE ARE THORS.
CUT THEM DOWN! RAGE 'TIL THE END!
FIGHT TO THE VERY LAST GOD!

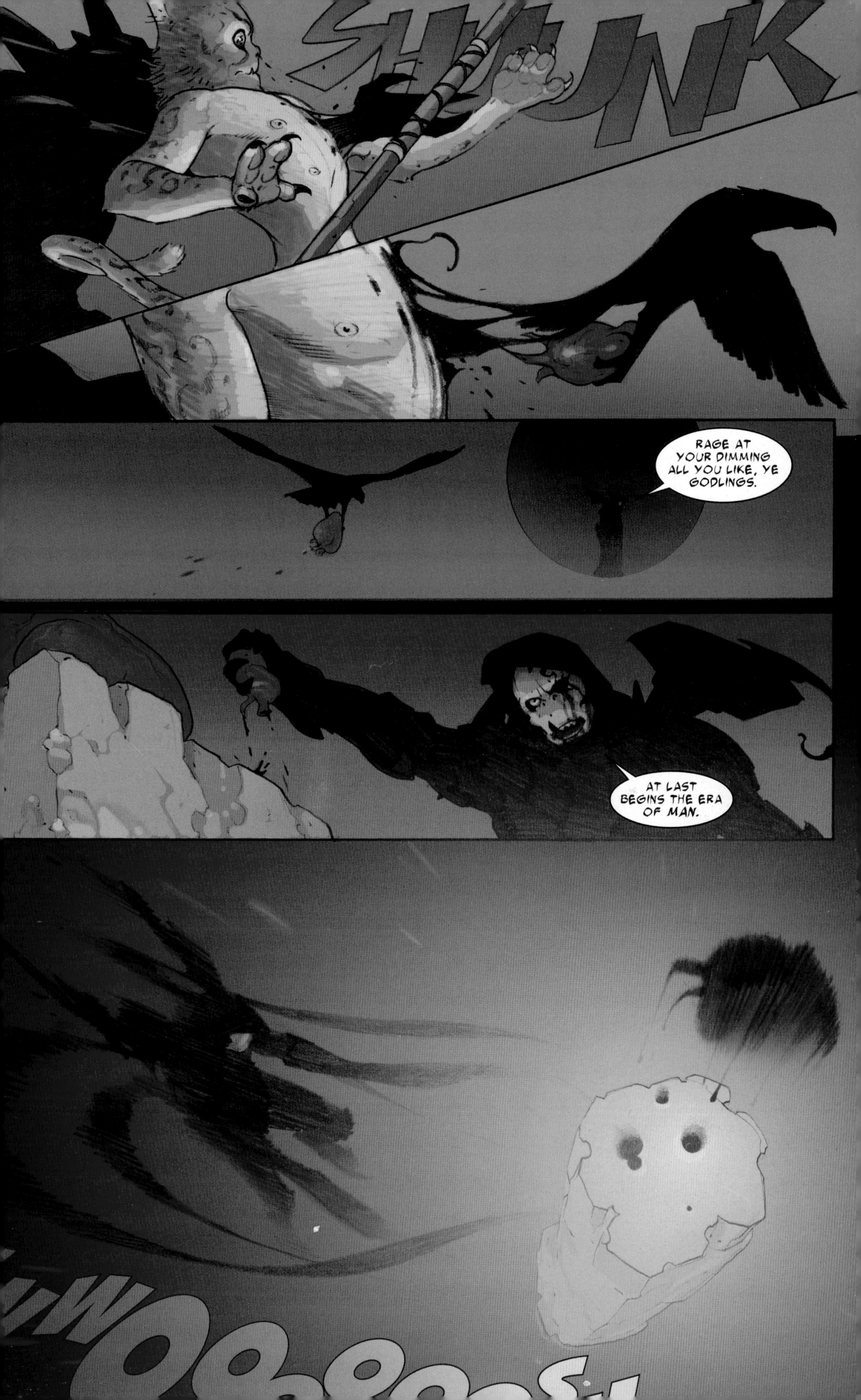
SHUNK
RAGE AT YOUR DIMMING ALL YOU LIKE, YE GODLINGS.
AT LAST BEGINS THE ERA OF MAN.

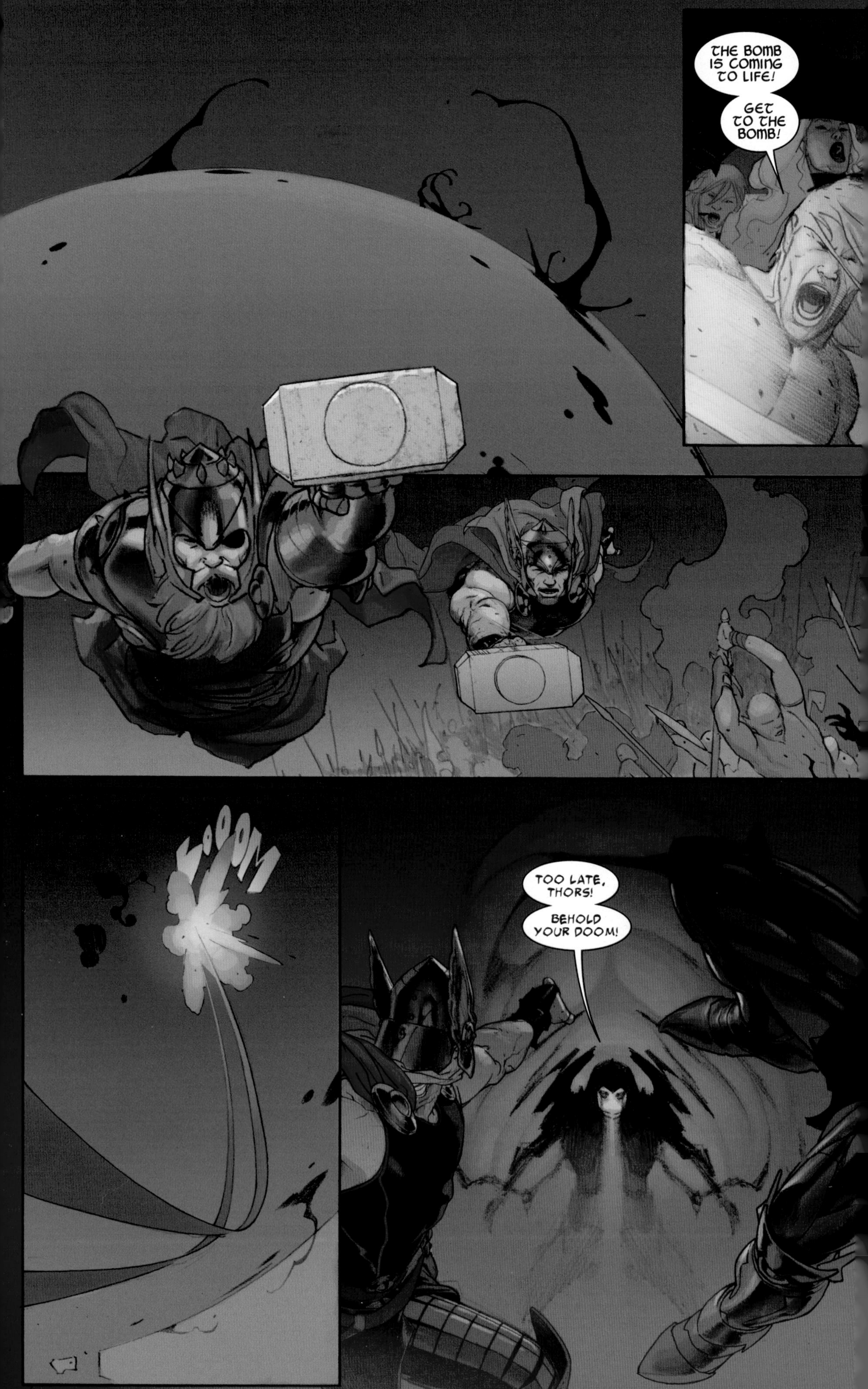
THE BOMB IS COMING TO LIFE!
GET TO THE BOMB!
VOOOM
TOO LATE, THORS!
BEHOLD YOUR DOOM!

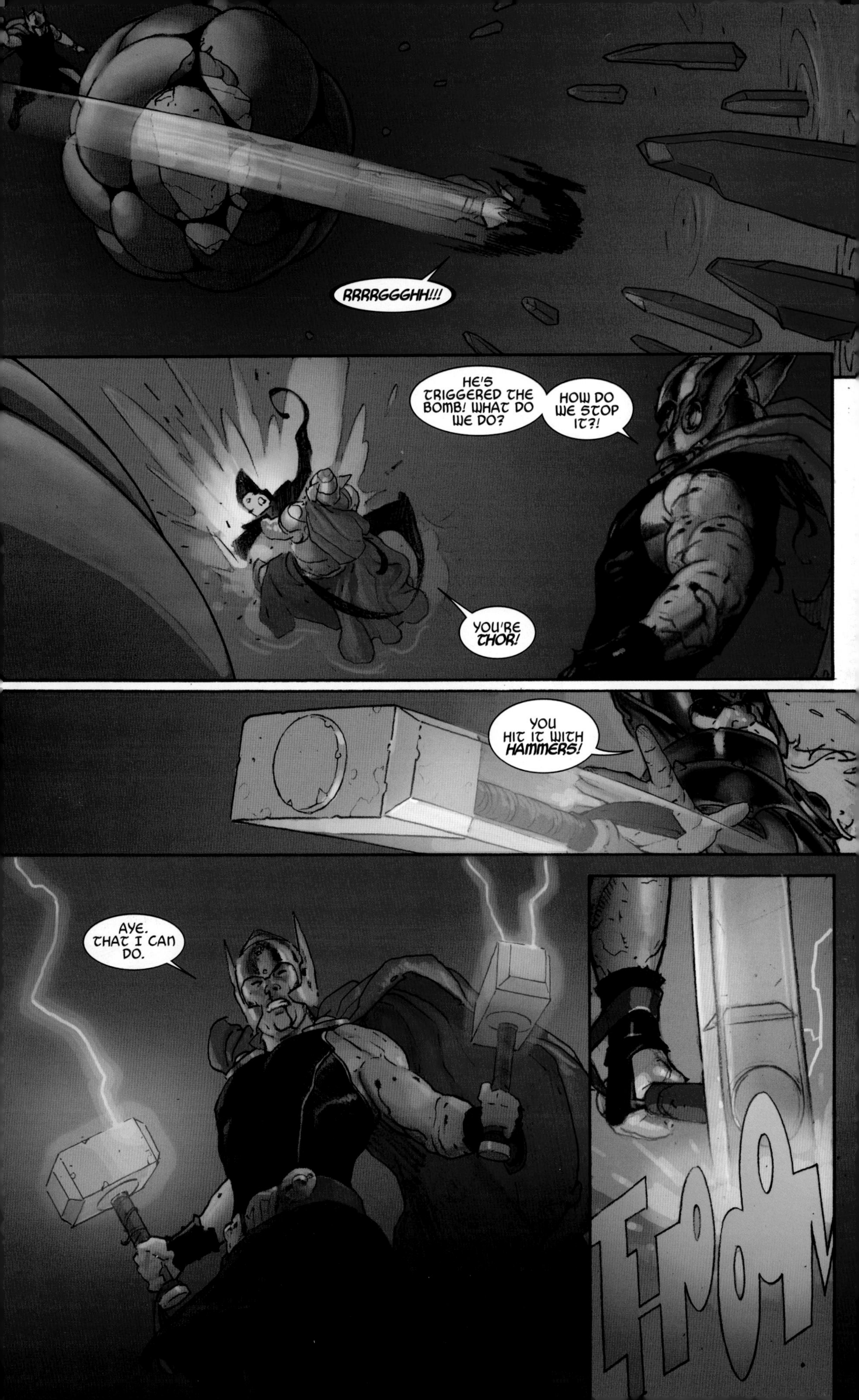
RRRRGGGHH!!!
HE'S TRIGGERED THE BOMB! WHAT DO WE DO?
HOW DO WE STOP IT?!
YOU'RE THOR!
YOU HIT IT WITH HAMMERS!
AYE. THAT I CAN DO.
TTOOM

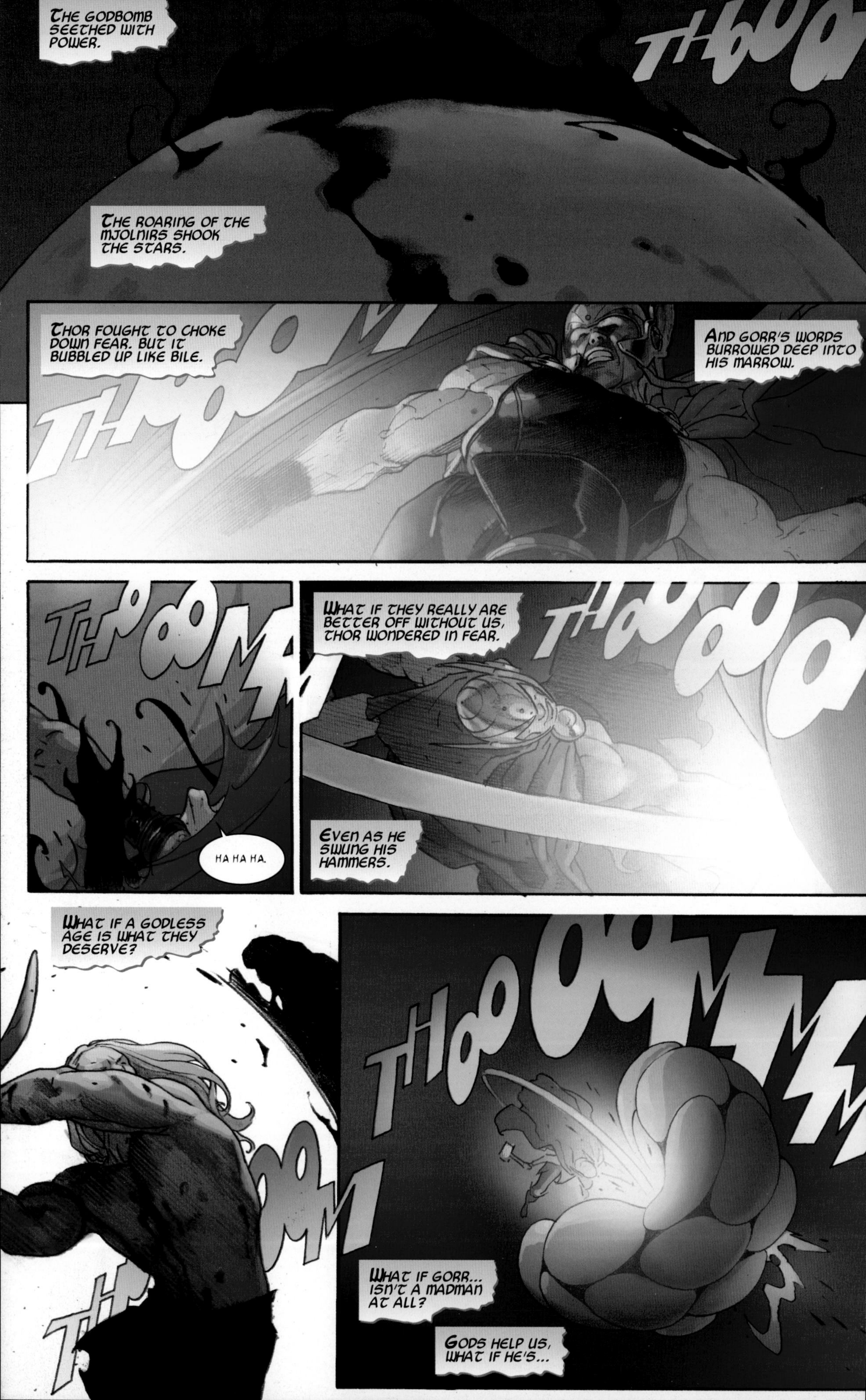

THE GODBOMB SEETHED WITH POWER.
THOOOM
THE ROARING OF THE MJOLNIRS SHOOK THE STARS.
THOR FOUGHT TO CHOKE DOWN FEAR. BUT IT BUBBLED UP LIKE BILE.
AND GORR'S WORDS BURROWED DEEP INTO HIS MARROW.
THOOOM
THOOOM
HA HA HA.
WHAT IF THEY REALLY ARE BETTER OFF WITHOUT US, THOR WONDERED IN FEAR.
THOOOOO
EVEN AS HE SWUNG HIS HAMMERS.
WHAT IF A GODLESS AGE IS WHAT THEY DESERVE?
THOOOM
THOOOOMMM
WHAT IF GORR... ISN'T A MADMAN AT ALL?
GODS HELP US, WHAT IF HE'S...

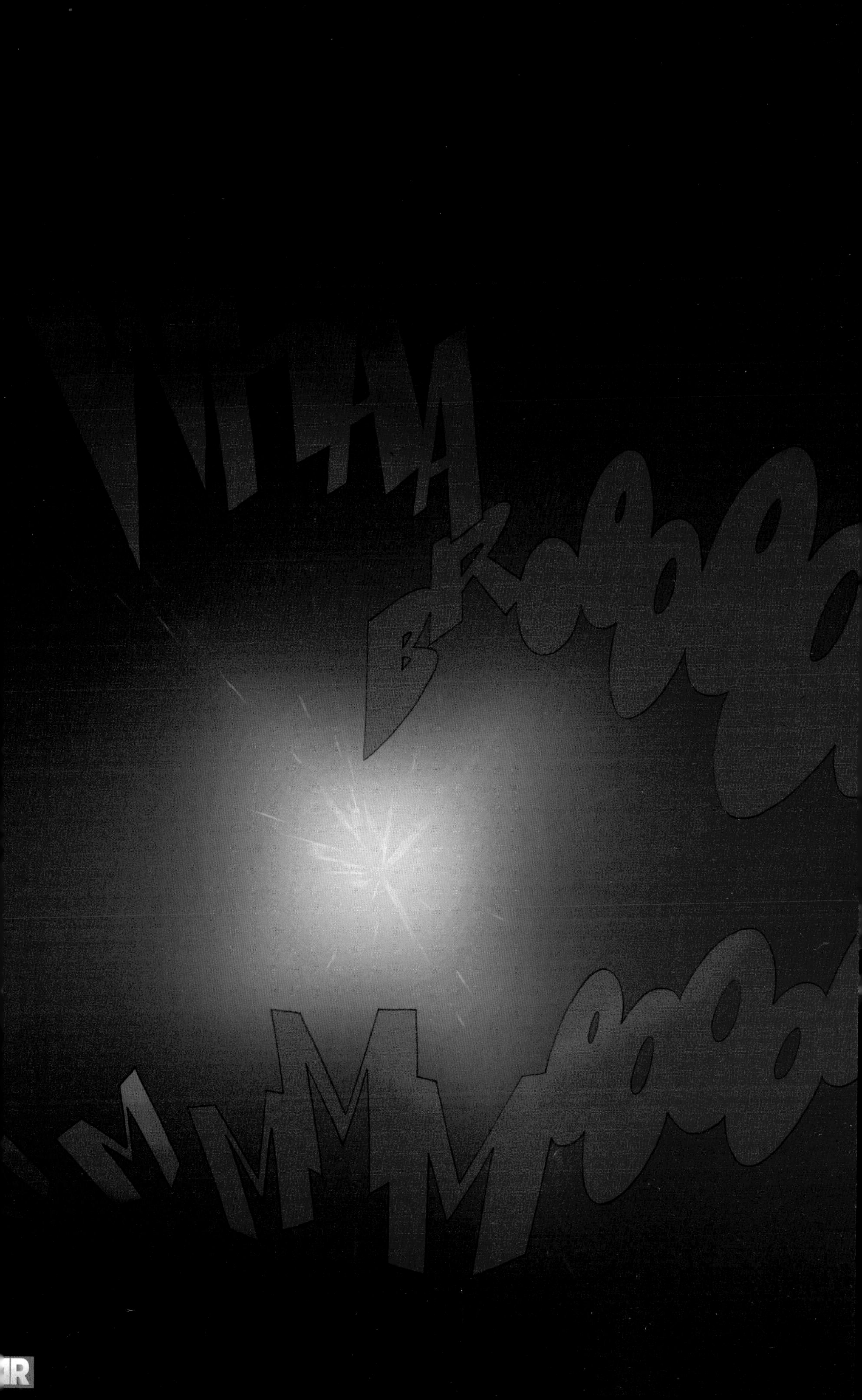

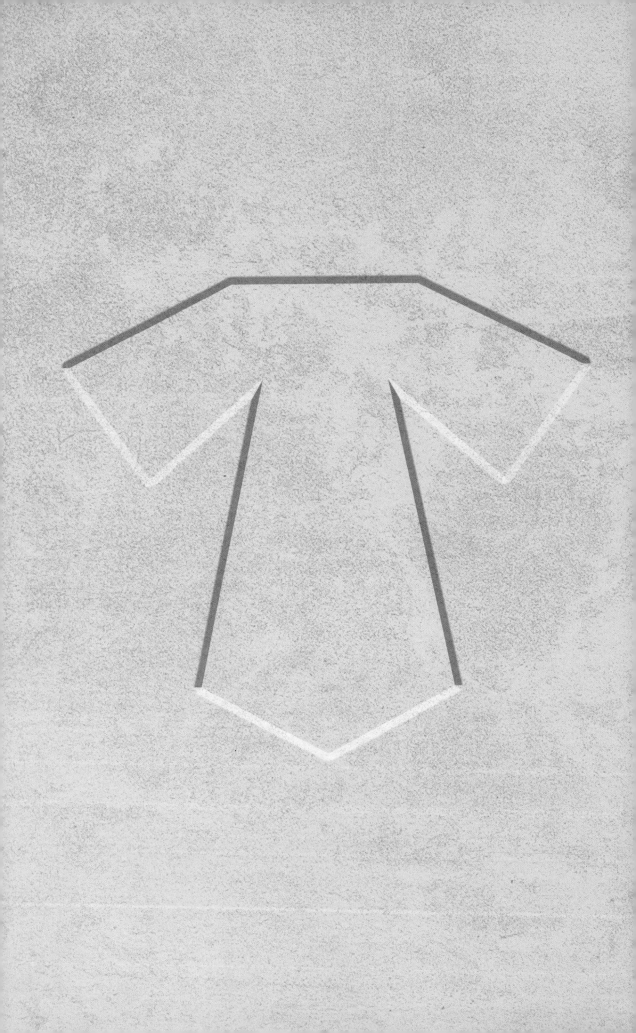

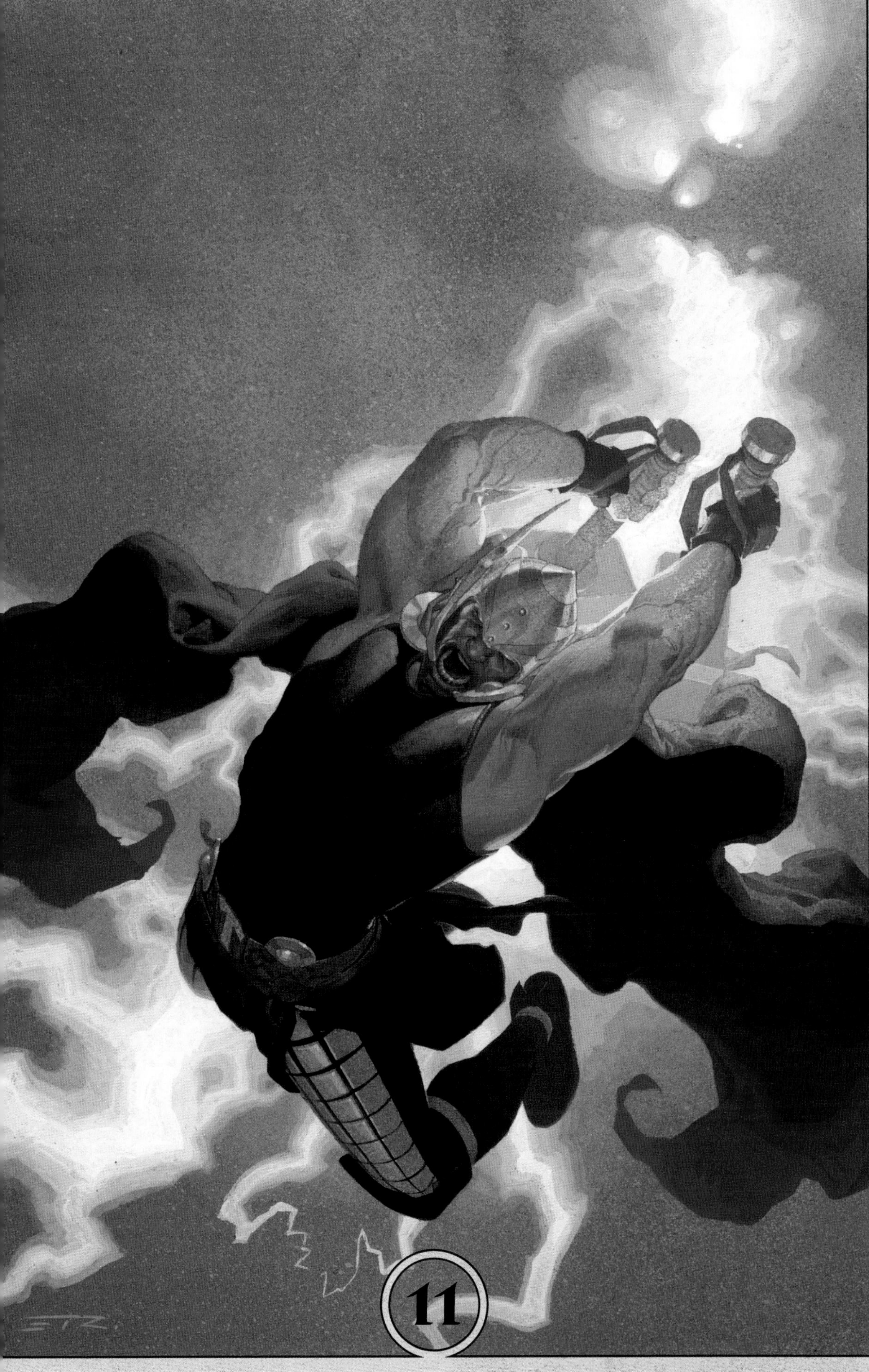
11

GODBOMB PART 5: THE LAST PRAYER

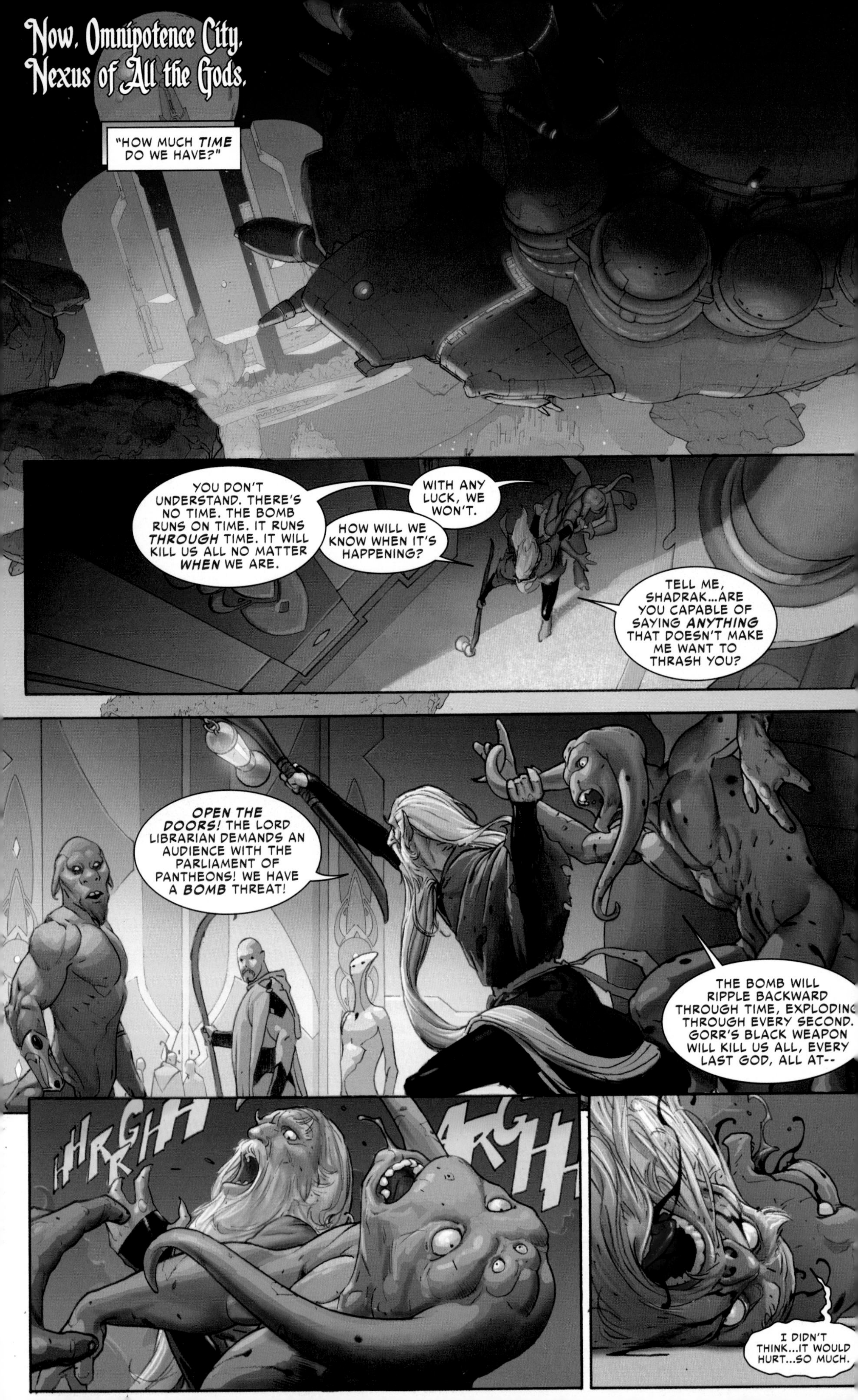
Now, Omnipotence City, Nexus of All the Gods.
"HOW MUCH TIME DO WE HAVE?"
YOU DON'T UNDERSTAND. THERE'S NO TIME. THE BOMB RUNS ON TIME. IT RUNS THROUGH TIME. IT WILL KILL US ALL NO MATTER WHEN WE ARE.
HOW WILL WE KNOW WHEN IT'S HAPPENING?
WITH ANY LUCK, WE WON'T.
TELL ME, SHADRAK...ARE YOU CAPABLE OF SAYING ANYTHING THAT DOESN'T MAKE ME WANT TO THRASH YOU?
OPEN THE DOORS! THE LORD LIBRARIAN DEMANDS AN AUDIENCE WITH THE PARLIAMENT OF PANTHEONS! WE HAVE A BOMB THREAT!
THE BOMB WILL RIPPLE BACKWARD THROUGH TIME, EXPLODING THROUGH EVERY SECOND. GORR'S BLACK WEAPON WILL KILL US ALL, EVERY LAST GOD, ALL AT--
HHRGH
ARGH
I DIDN'T THINK...IT WOULD HURT...SO MUCH.

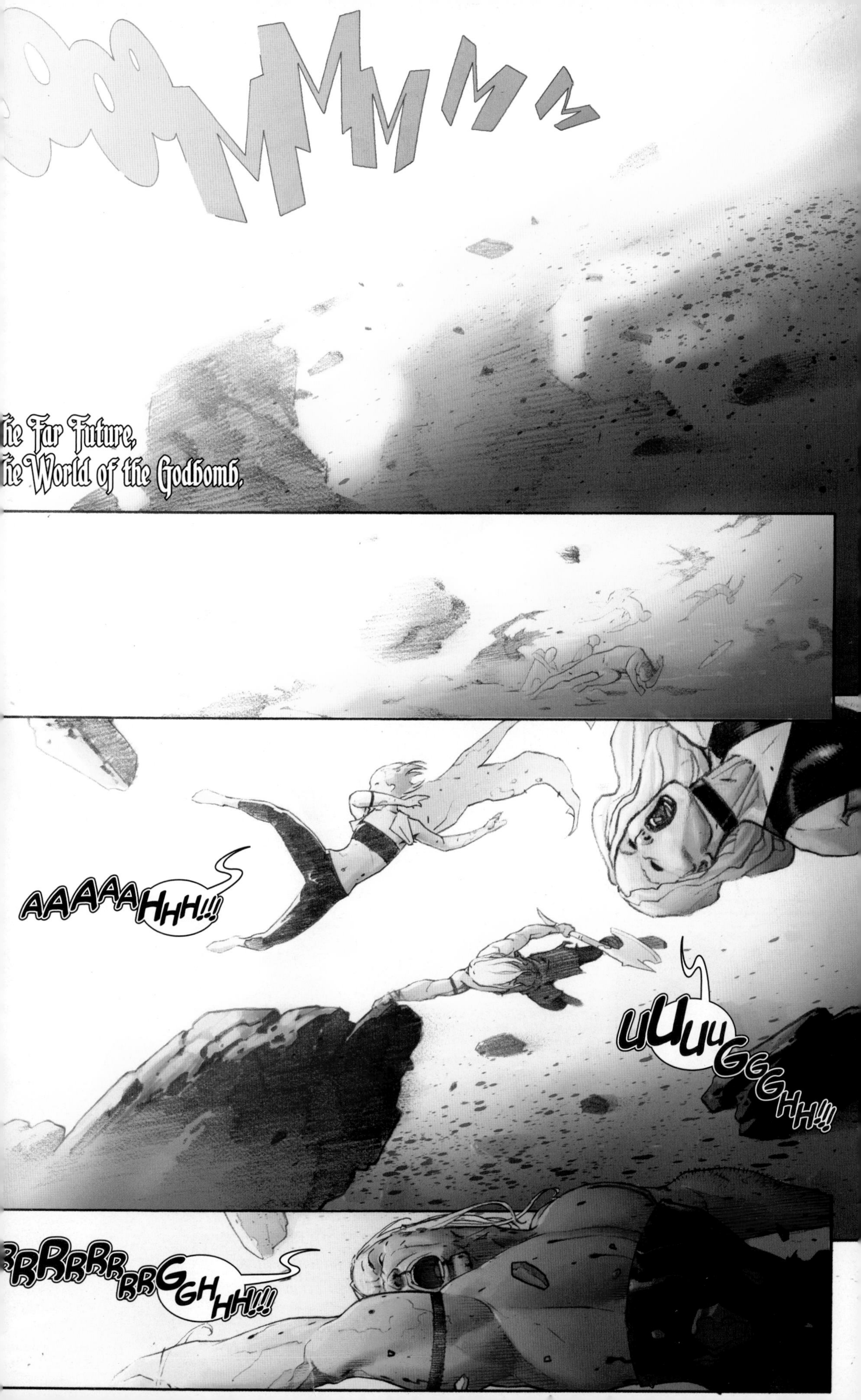
OOOOMMMMM
...he Far Future,
...he World of the Godbomb.
AAAAAAHHH!!!
UUUUGGGHH!!!
RRRRRRRRRGGHHH!!!

YOU'RE DYING.

AND YOU KNOW IT. DON'T YOU, KING THOR?

DYING OVER EVERY SECOND OF YOUR LIFE ALL AT ONCE. YOU AND TRILLIONS MORE JUST LIKE YOU.

I DO HOPE IT HURTS.

GGGRRRAAGGHHH!!!

*I*NSIDE THE HEART OF THE GODBOMB, TIME BECAME TAR.

ETERNITY ECHOED WITH WAILING AND THE GNASHING OF TEETH. WITH THE DYING OF THE GODS.

IF HE'D BEEN A LESSER GOD, THOR MIGHT HAVE ACCEPTED THAT GORR HAD WON. AND MORE SO, THAT GORR DESERVED TO WIN.

THAT GODS WERE CRUEL AND JEALOUS CREATURES. THAT IT WAS TIME FOR THEIR AGE TO PASS.

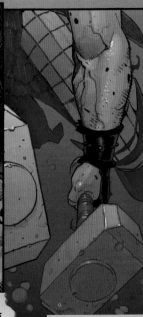

BUT THIS WAS NO LESSER GOD.

THIS WAS THE GOD OF ROARING THUNDER AND RAGING STORMS, AND EVEN IF HE HAD BEEN THE LAST GOD LEFT ALIVE IN ALL THE UNIVERSE...
KA
THUNG
HE STILL WOULD HAVE BEEN GOD ENOUGH.
HHHHRRRRRGGHH!!!
WHAT...IS HE DOING?
DYING.
LIKE A GOD.

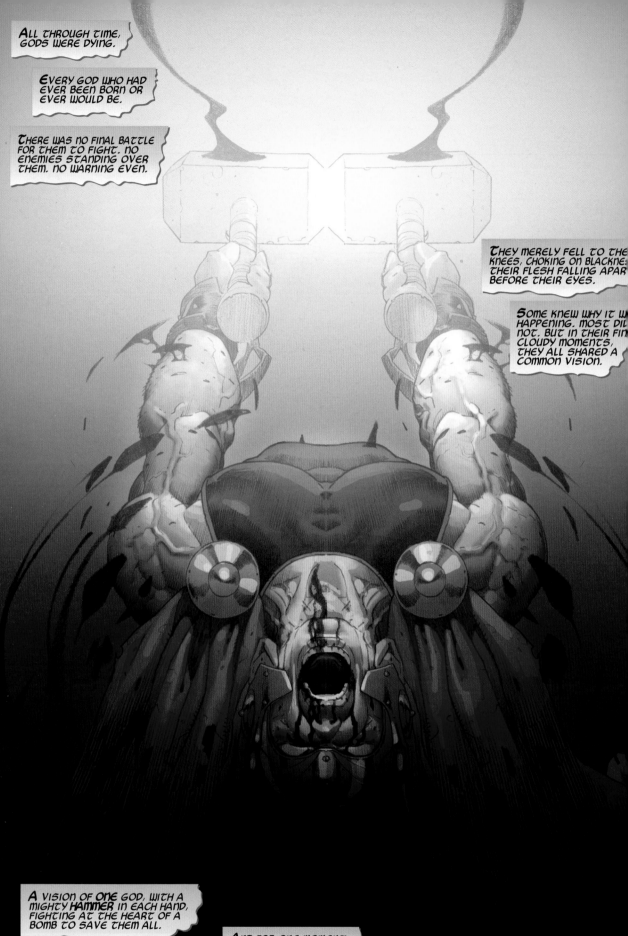

ALL THROUGH TIME, GODS WERE DYING.

EVERY GOD WHO HAD EVER BEEN BORN OR EVER WOULD BE.

THERE WAS NO FINAL BATTLE FOR THEM TO FIGHT. NO ENEMIES STANDING OVER THEM. NO WARNING EVEN.

THEY MERELY FELL TO THE KNEES, CHOKING ON BLACKNE: THEIR FLESH FALLING APAR BEFORE THEIR EYES.

SOME KNEW WHY IT W. HAPPENING. MOST DII NOT. BUT IN THEIR FIN CLOUDY MOMENTS, THEY ALL SHARED A COMMON VISION.

A VISION OF ONE GOD, WITH A MIGHTY HAMMER IN EACH HAND, FIGHTING AT THE HEART OF A BOMB TO SAVE THEM ALL.

AND FOR ONE MOMENT THAT STRETCHED ACROSS TIME...

...EVERY GOD IN ALL THE UNIVERSE CLOSED THEIR EYES...

AND PRAY TO THOR.

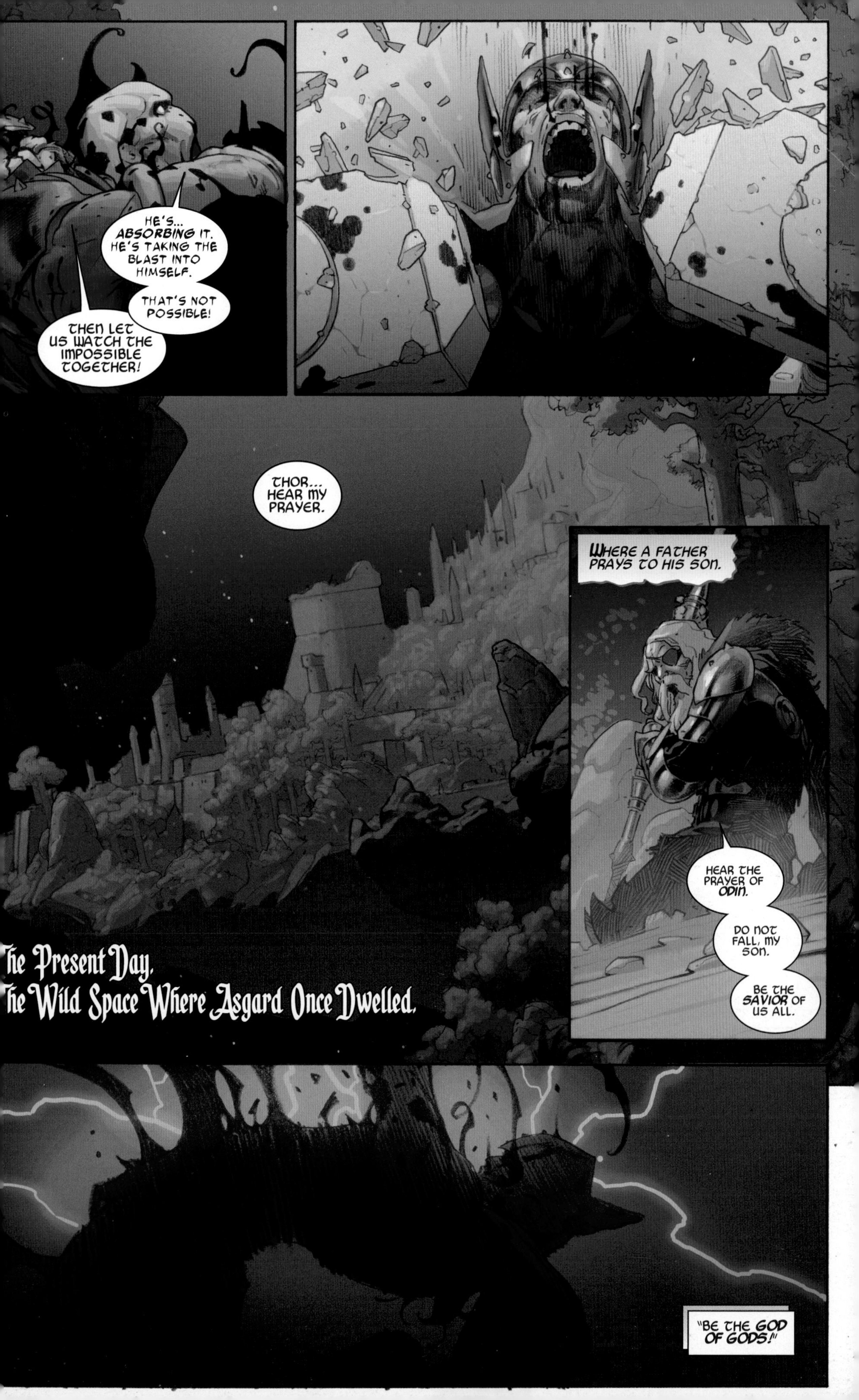
HE'S... ABSORBING IT. HE'S TAKING THE BLAST INTO HIMSELF.
THAT'S NOT POSSIBLE!
THEN LET US WATCH THE IMPOSSIBLE TOGETHER!
THOR... HEAR MY PRAYER.
The Present Day.
The Wild Space Where Asgard Once Dwelled.
WHERE A FATHER PRAYS TO HIS SON.
HEAR THE PRAYER OF ODIN.
DO NOT FALL, MY SON.
BE THE SAVIOR OF US ALL.
"BE THE GOD OF GODS!"

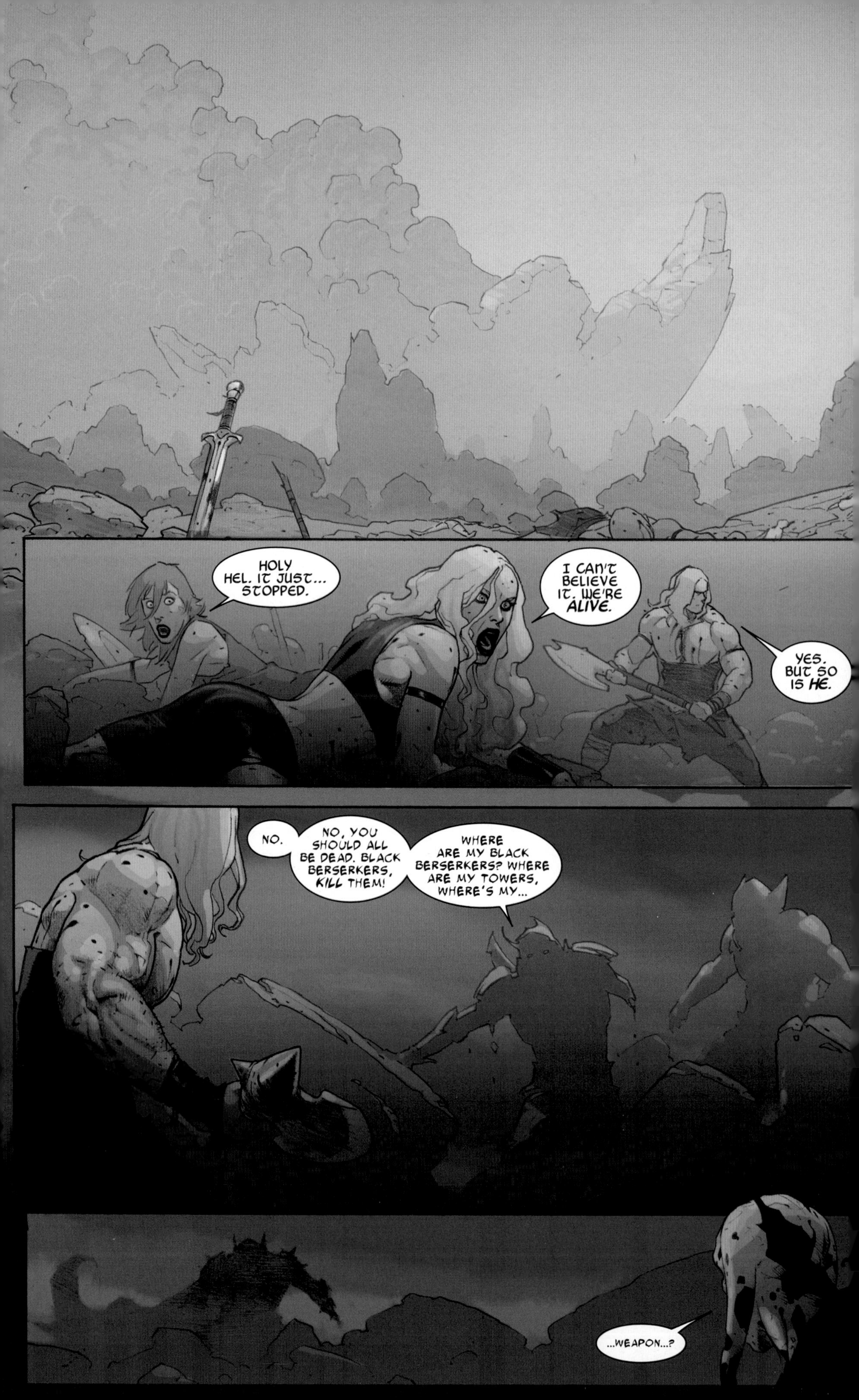
HOLY HEL. IT JUST... STOPPED.
I CAN'T BELIEVE IT. WE'RE ALIVE.
YES. BUT SO IS HE.
NO.
NO, YOU SHOULD ALL BE DEAD. BLACK BERSERKERS, KILL THEM!
WHERE ARE MY BLACK BERSERKERS? WHERE ARE MY TOWERS, WHERE'S MY...
...WEAPON...?

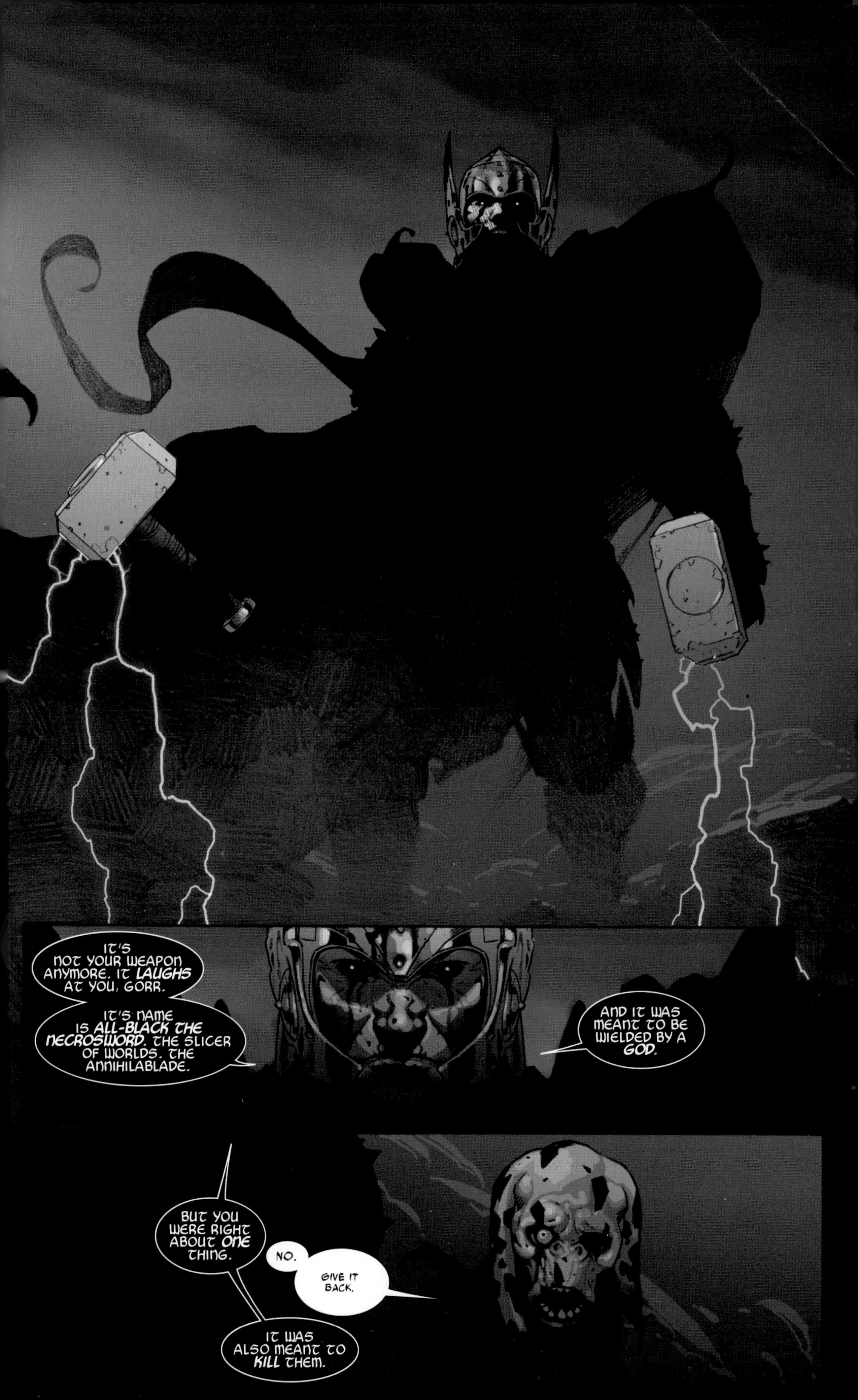

IT'S NOT YOUR WEAPON ANYMORE. IT LAUGHS AT YOU, GORR.
IT'S NAME IS ALL-BLACK THE NECROSWORD. THE SLICER OF WORLDS. THE ANNIHILABLADE.
AND IT WAS MEANT TO BE WIELDED BY A GOD.
BUT YOU WERE RIGHT ABOUT ONE THING.
NO.
GIVE IT BACK.
IT WAS ALSO MEANT TO KILL THEM.

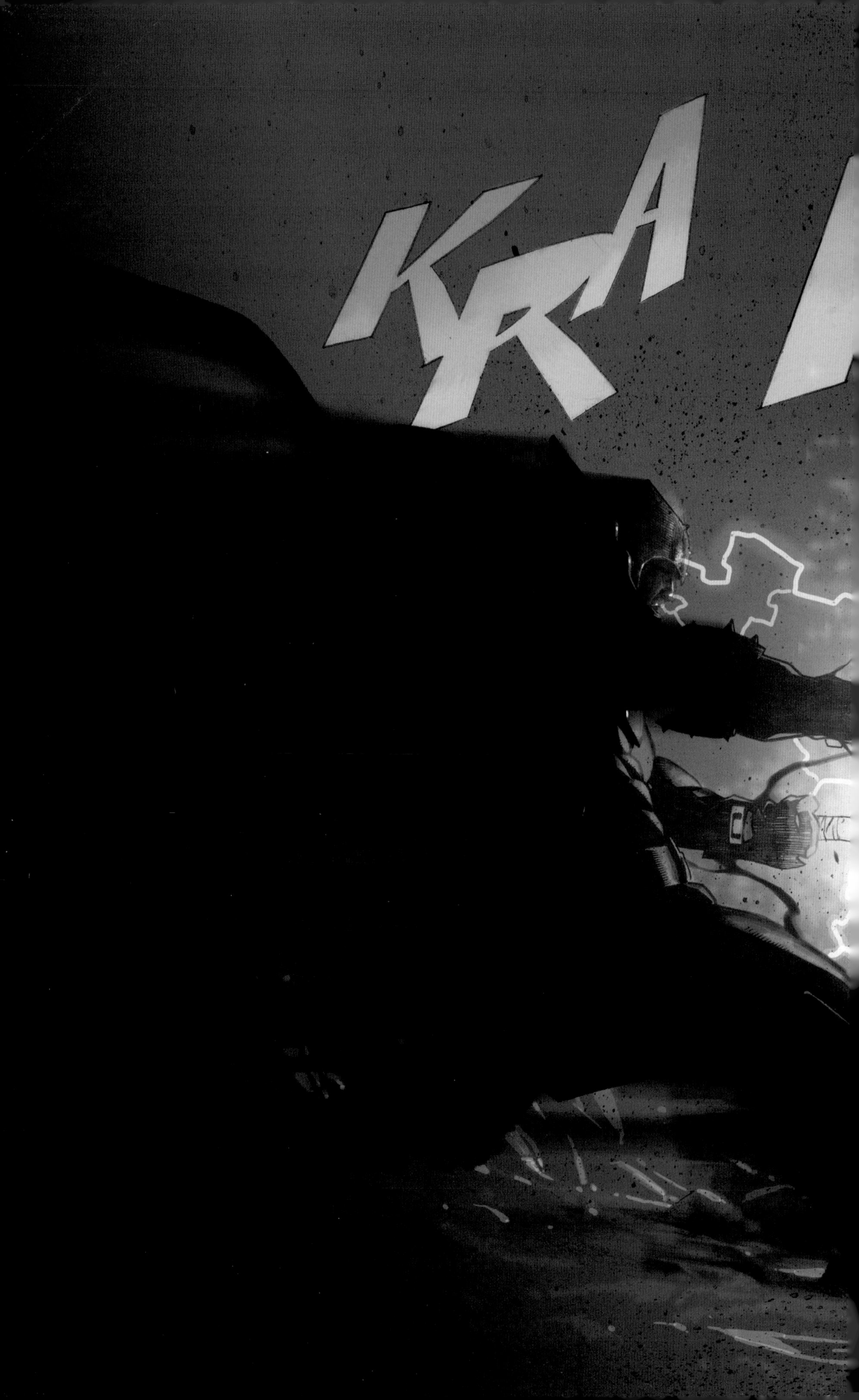
KRA

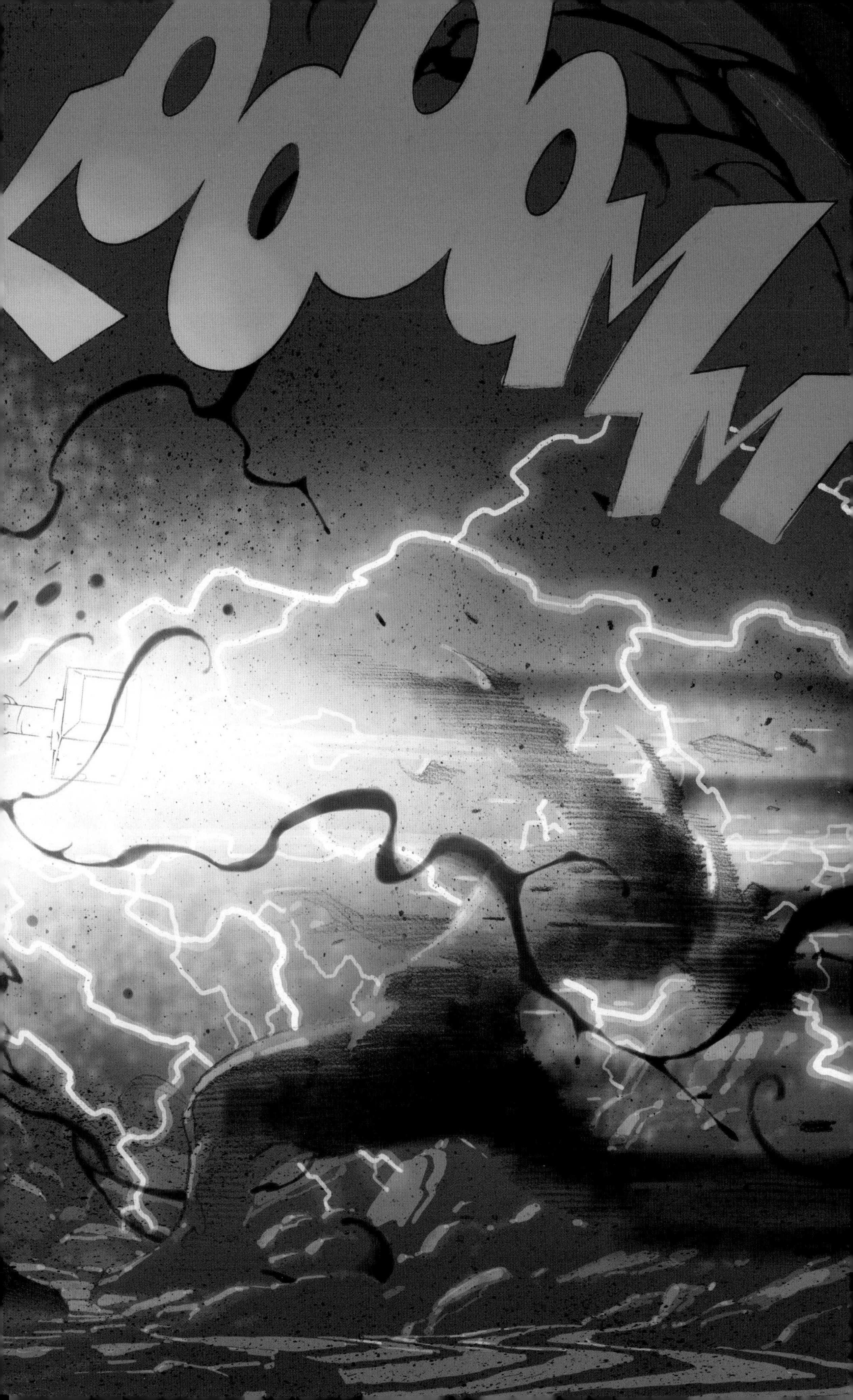

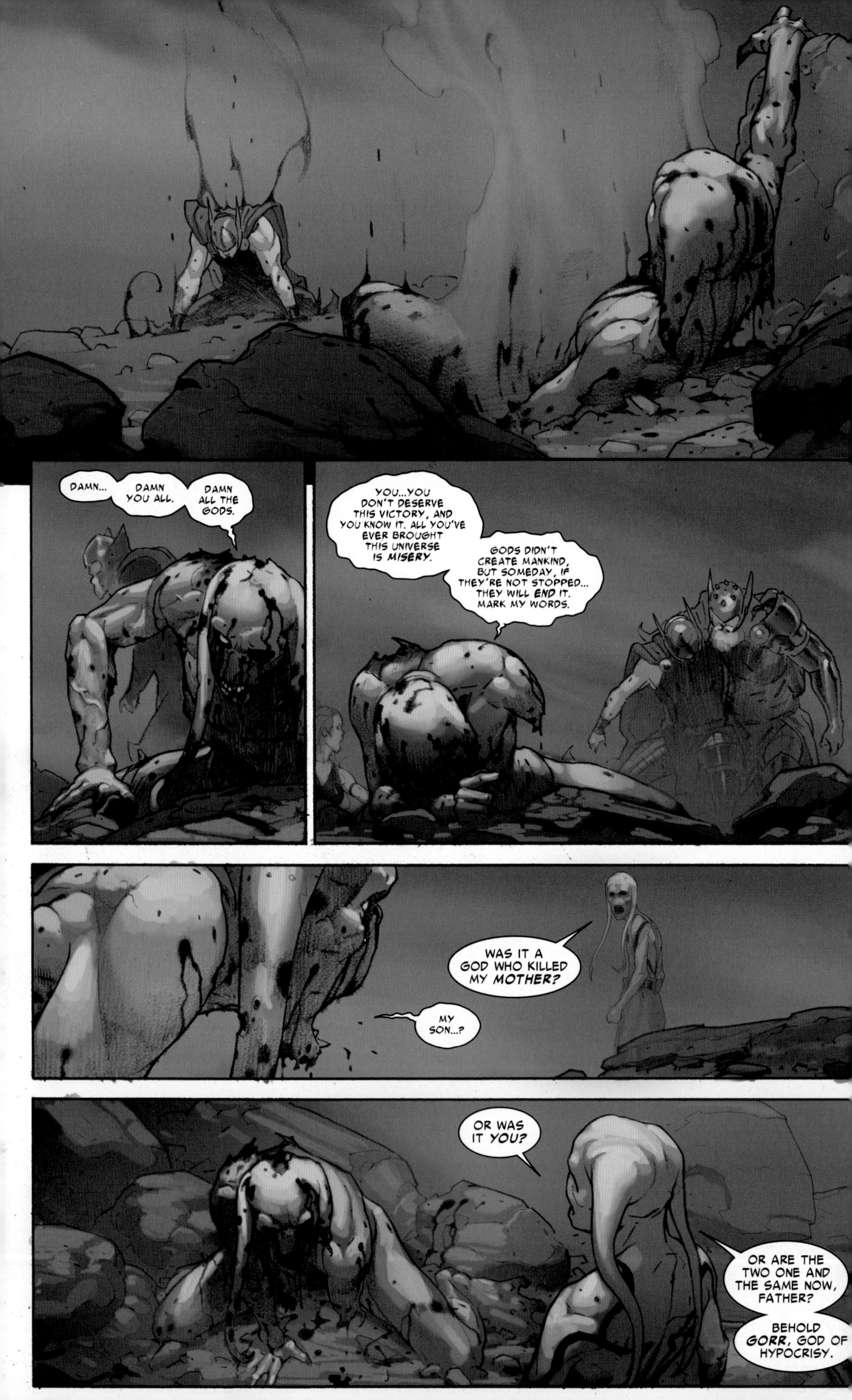
DAMN...
DAMN YOU ALL.
DAMN ALL THE GODS.
YOU...YOU DON'T DESERVE THIS VICTORY, AND YOU KNOW IT. ALL YOU'VE EVER BROUGHT THIS UNIVERSE IS MISERY.
GODS DIDN'T CREATE MANKIND, BUT SOMEDAY, IF THEY'RE NOT STOPPED... THEY WILL END IT. MARK MY WORDS.
WAS IT A GOD WHO KILLED MY MOTHER?
MY SON...?
OR WAS IT YOU?
OR ARE THE TWO ONE AND THE SAME NOW, FATHER?
BEHOLD GORR, GOD OF HYPOCRISY.

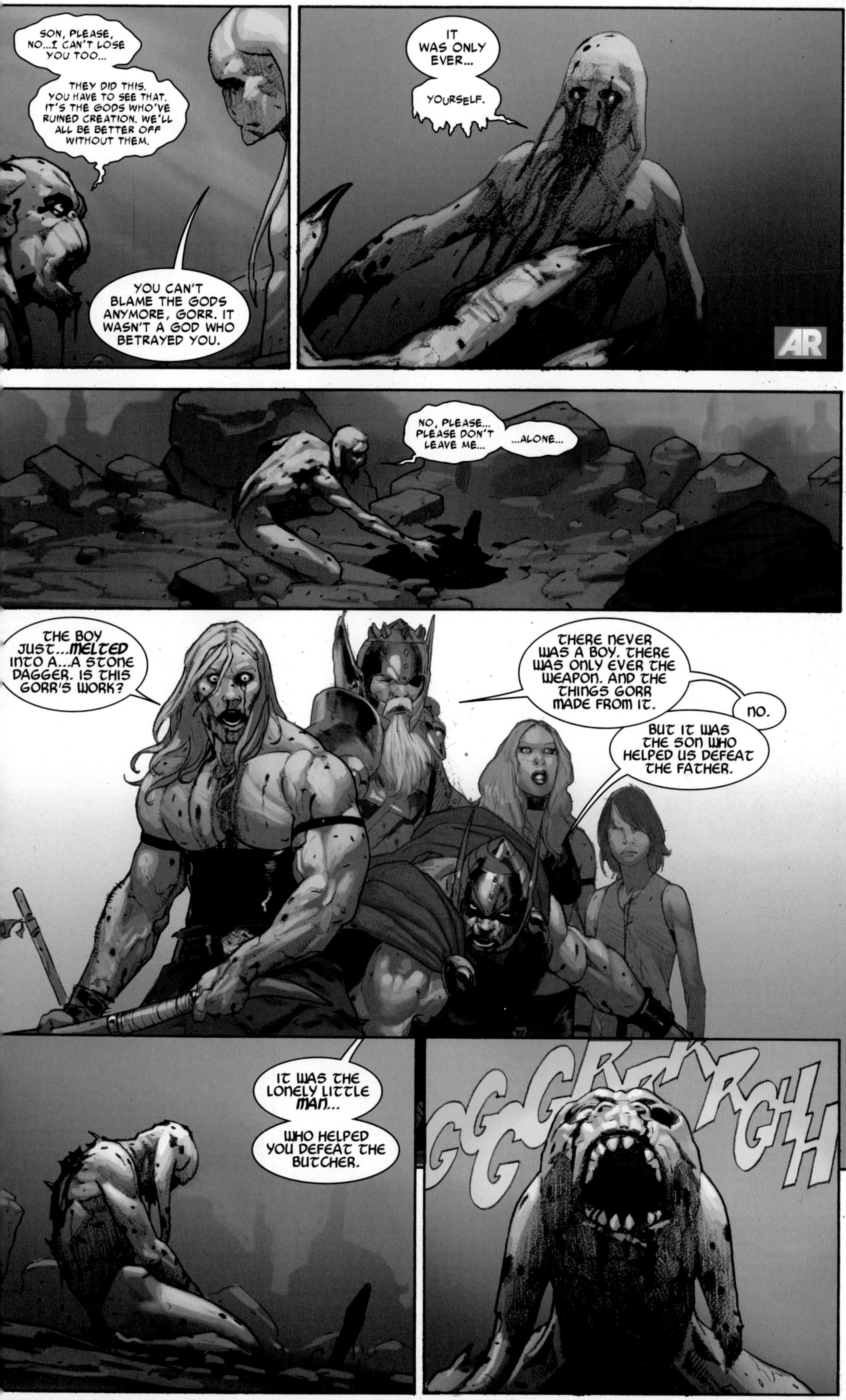
SON, PLEASE, NO...I CAN'T LOSE YOU TOO...
THEY DID THIS. YOU HAVE TO SEE THAT. IT'S THE GODS WHO'VE RUINED CREATION. WE'LL ALL BE BETTER OFF WITHOUT THEM.
YOU CAN'T BLAME THE GODS ANYMORE, GORR. IT WASN'T A GOD WHO BETRAYED YOU.
IT WAS ONLY EVER...
YOURSELF.
NO, PLEASE... PLEASE DON'T LEAVE ME...
...ALONE...
THE BOY JUST...MELTED INTO A...A STONE DAGGER. IS THIS GORR'S WORK?
THERE NEVER WAS A BOY. THERE WAS ONLY EVER THE WEAPON. AND THE THINGS GORR MADE FROM IT.
NO.
BUT IT WAS THE SON WHO HELPED US DEFEAT THE FATHER.
IT WAS THE LONELY LITTLE MAN...
WHO HELPED YOU DEFEAT THE BUTCHER.
GGGGRRKRGH

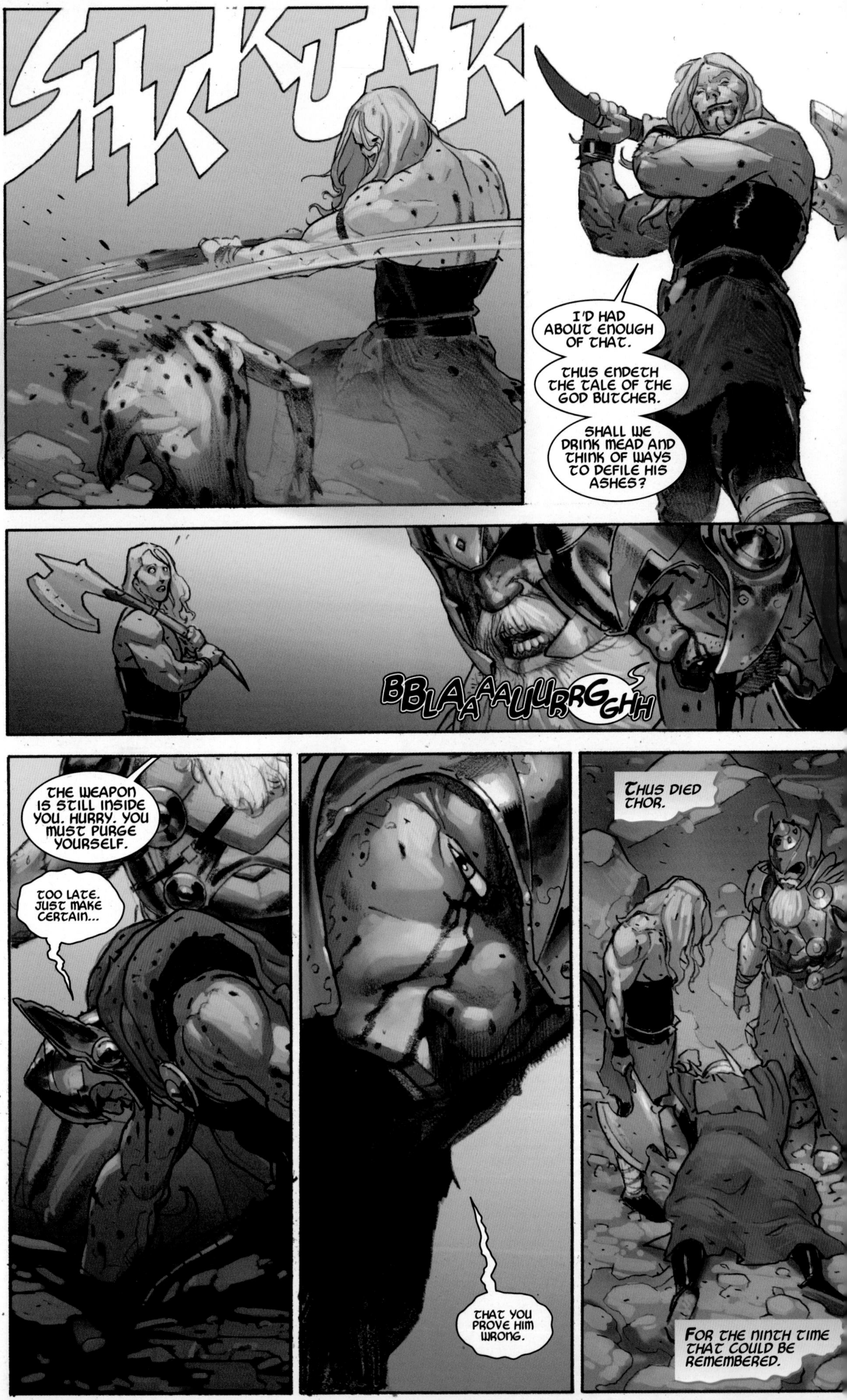
SHKTUNK
I'D HAD ABOUT ENOUGH OF THAT.
THUS ENDETH THE TALE OF THE GOD BUTCHER.
SHALL WE DRINK MEAD AND THINK OF WAYS TO DEFILE HIS ASHES?
BBLAAAAAUURRGGHH
THE WEAPON IS STILL INSIDE YOU. HURRY. YOU MUST PURGE YOURSELF.
TOO LATE. JUST MAKE CERTAIN...
THAT YOU PROVE HIM WRONG.
THUS DIED THOR.
FOR THE NINTH TIME THAT COULD BE REMEMBERED.

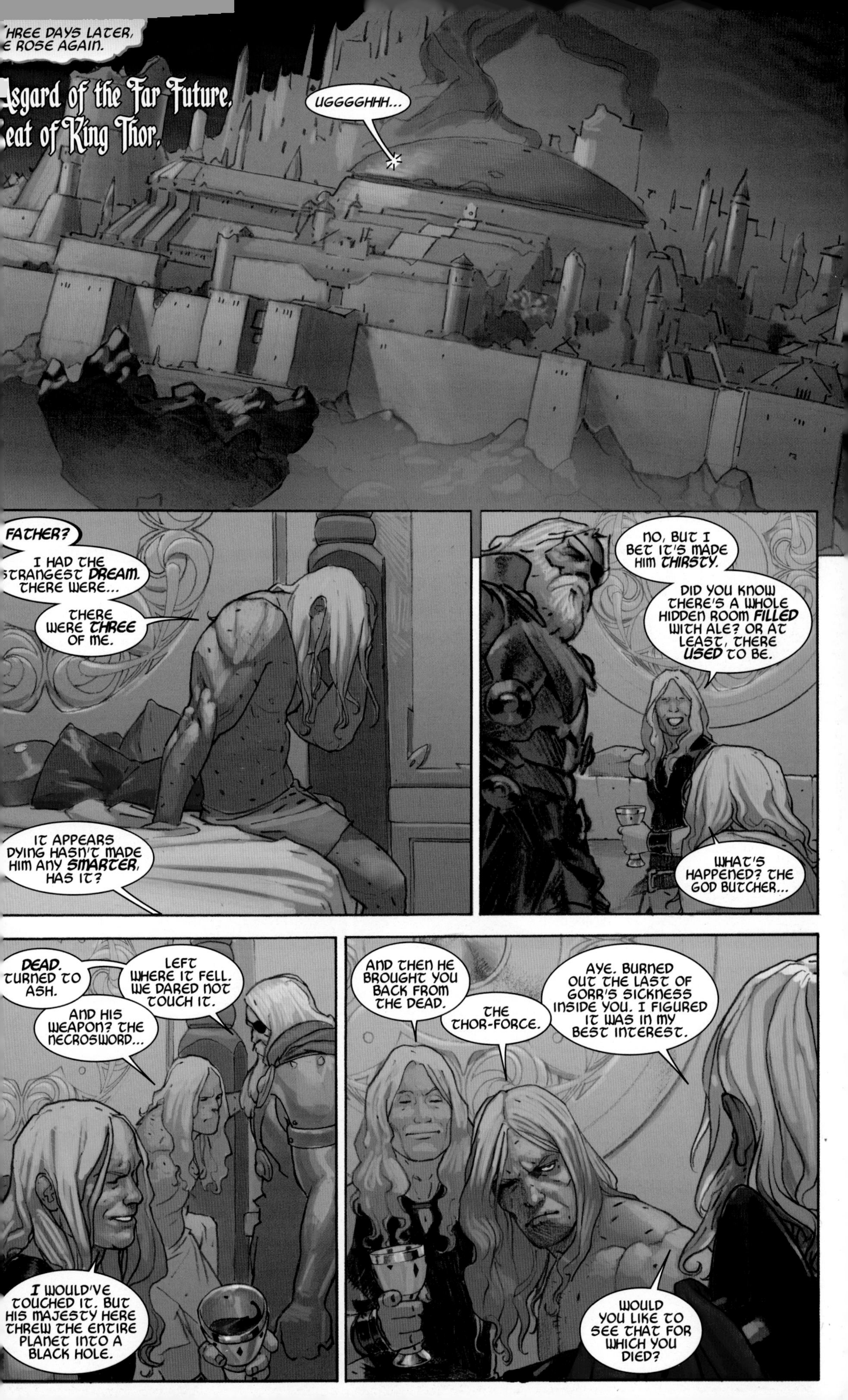

HREE DAYS LATER,
E ROSE AGAIN.
Asgard of the Far Future,
Seat of King Thor,
UGGGGHHH...
FATHER?
I HAD THE STRANGEST DREAM. THERE WERE...
THERE WERE THREE OF ME.
IT APPEARS DYING HASN'T MADE HIM ANY SMARTER, HAS IT?
NO, BUT I BET IT'S MADE HIM THIRSTY.
DID YOU KNOW THERE'S A WHOLE HIDDEN ROOM FILLED WITH ALE? OR AT LEAST, THERE USED TO BE.
WHAT'S HAPPENED? THE GOD BUTCHER...
DEAD. TURNED TO ASH.
AND HIS WEAPON? THE NECROSWORD...
LEFT WHERE IT FELL. WE DARED NOT TOUCH IT.
I WOULD'VE TOUCHED IT. BUT HIS MAJESTY HERE THREW THE ENTIRE PLANET INTO A BLACK HOLE.
AND THEN HE BROUGHT YOU BACK FROM THE DEAD.
THE THOR-FORCE.
AYE. BURNED OUT THE LAST OF GORR'S SICKNESS INSIDE YOU. I FIGURED IT WAS IN MY BEST INTEREST.
WOULD YOU LIKE TO SEE THAT FOR WHICH YOU DIED?

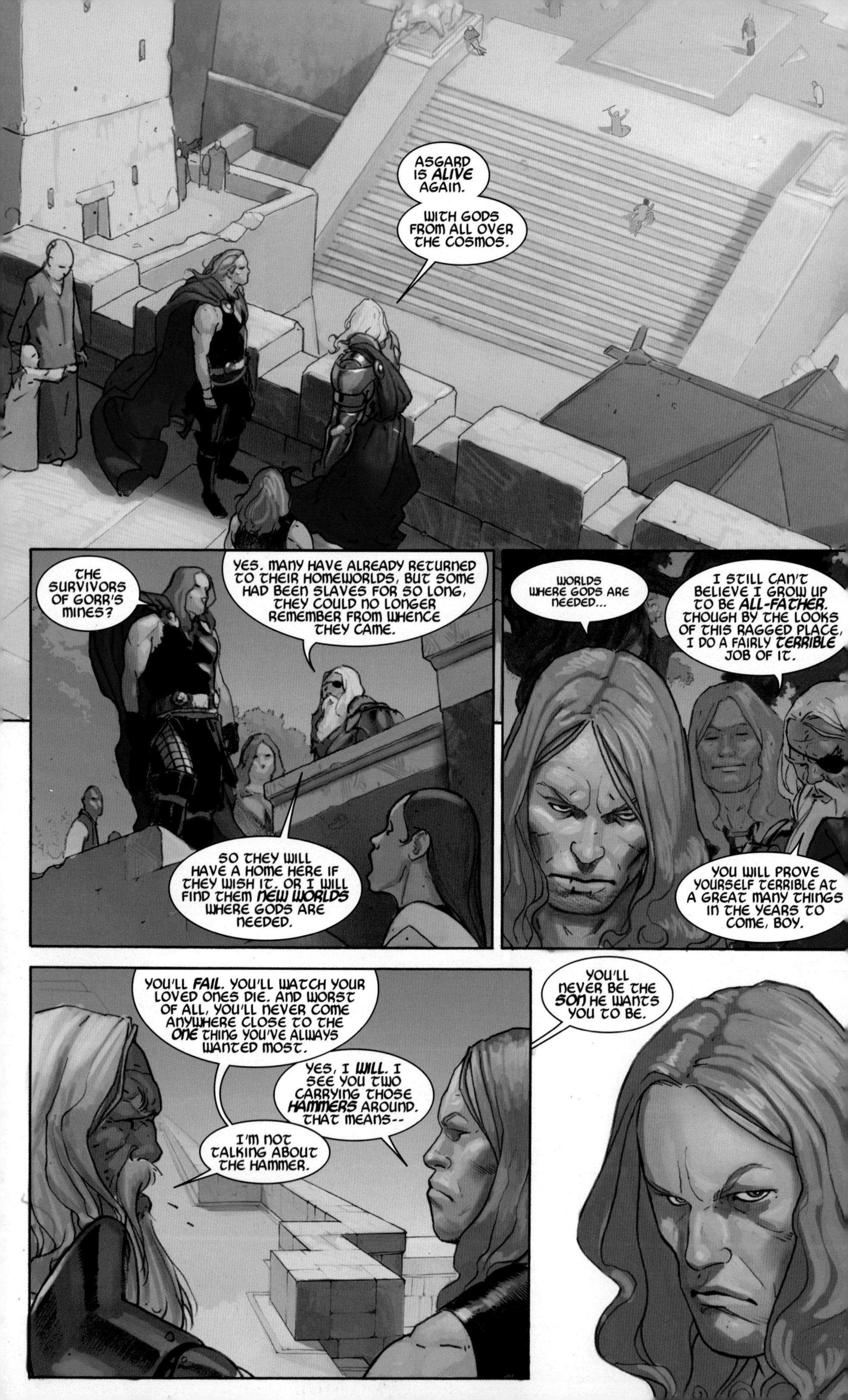
ASGARD IS ALIVE AGAIN.
WITH GODS FROM ALL OVER THE COSMOS.
THE SURVIVORS OF GORR'S MINES?
YES. MANY HAVE ALREADY RETURNED TO THEIR HOMEWORLDS, BUT SOME HAD BEEN SLAVES FOR SO LONG, THEY COULD NO LONGER REMEMBER FROM WHENCE THEY CAME.
SO THEY WILL HAVE A HOME HERE IF THEY WISH IT. OR I WILL FIND THEM NEW WORLDS WHERE GODS ARE NEEDED.
WORLDS WHERE GODS ARE NEEDED...
I STILL CAN'T BELIEVE I GROW UP TO BE ALL-FATHER. THOUGH BY THE LOOKS OF THIS RAGGED PLACE, I DO A FAIRLY TERRIBLE JOB OF IT.
YOU WILL PROVE YOURSELF TERRIBLE AT A GREAT MANY THINGS IN THE YEARS TO COME, BOY.
YOU'LL FAIL. YOU'LL WATCH YOUR LOVED ONES DIE. AND WORST OF ALL, YOU'LL NEVER COME ANYWHERE CLOSE TO THE ONE THING YOU'VE ALWAYS WANTED MOST.
YES, I WILL. I SEE YOU TWO CARRYING THOSE HAMMERS AROUND. THAT MEANS--
I'M NOT TALKING ABOUT THE HAMMER.
YOU'LL NEVER BE THE SON HE WANTS YOU TO BE.

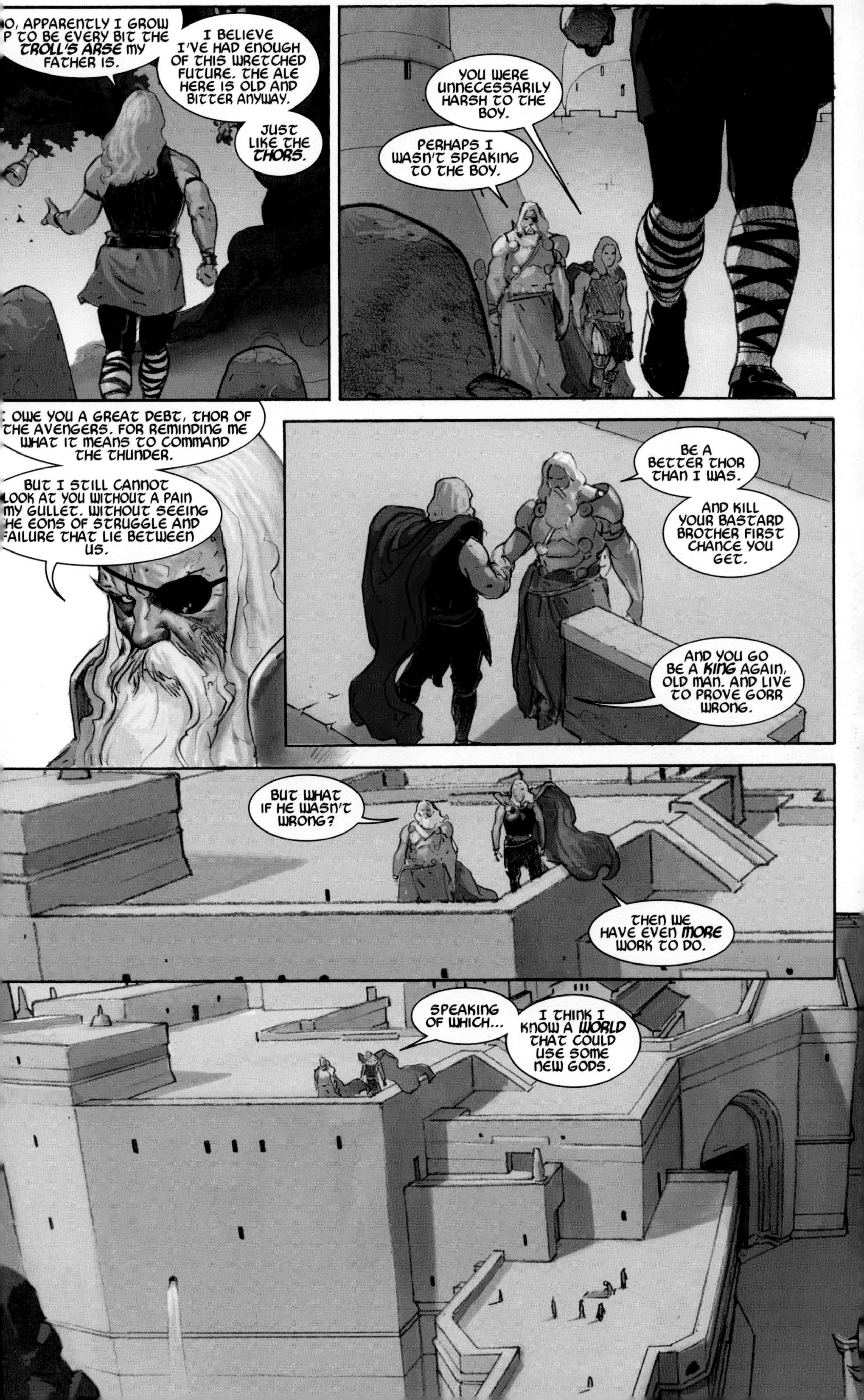
O, APPARENTLY I GROW
P TO BE EVERY BIT THE TROLL'S ARSE MY FATHER IS.
I BELIEVE I'VE HAD ENOUGH OF THIS WRETCHED FUTURE. THE ALE HERE IS OLD AND BITTER ANYWAY.
JUST LIKE THE THORS.
YOU WERE UNNECESSARILY HARSH TO THE BOY.
PERHAPS I WASN'T SPEAKING TO THE BOY.
I OWE YOU A GREAT DEBT, THOR OF THE AVENGERS. FOR REMINDING ME WHAT IT MEANS TO COMMAND THE THUNDER.
BUT I STILL CANNOT LOOK AT YOU WITHOUT A PAIN MY GULLET. WITHOUT SEEING HE EONS OF STRUGGLE AND FAILURE THAT LIE BETWEEN US.
BE A BETTER THOR THAN I WAS.
AND KILL YOUR BASTARD BROTHER FIRST CHANCE YOU GET.
AND YOU GO BE A KING AGAIN, OLD MAN. AND LIVE TO PROVE GORR WRONG.
BUT WHAT IF HE WASN'T WRONG?
THEN WE HAVE EVEN MORE WORK TO DO.
SPEAKING OF WHICH...
I THINK I KNOW A WORLD THAT COULD USE SOME NEW GODS.

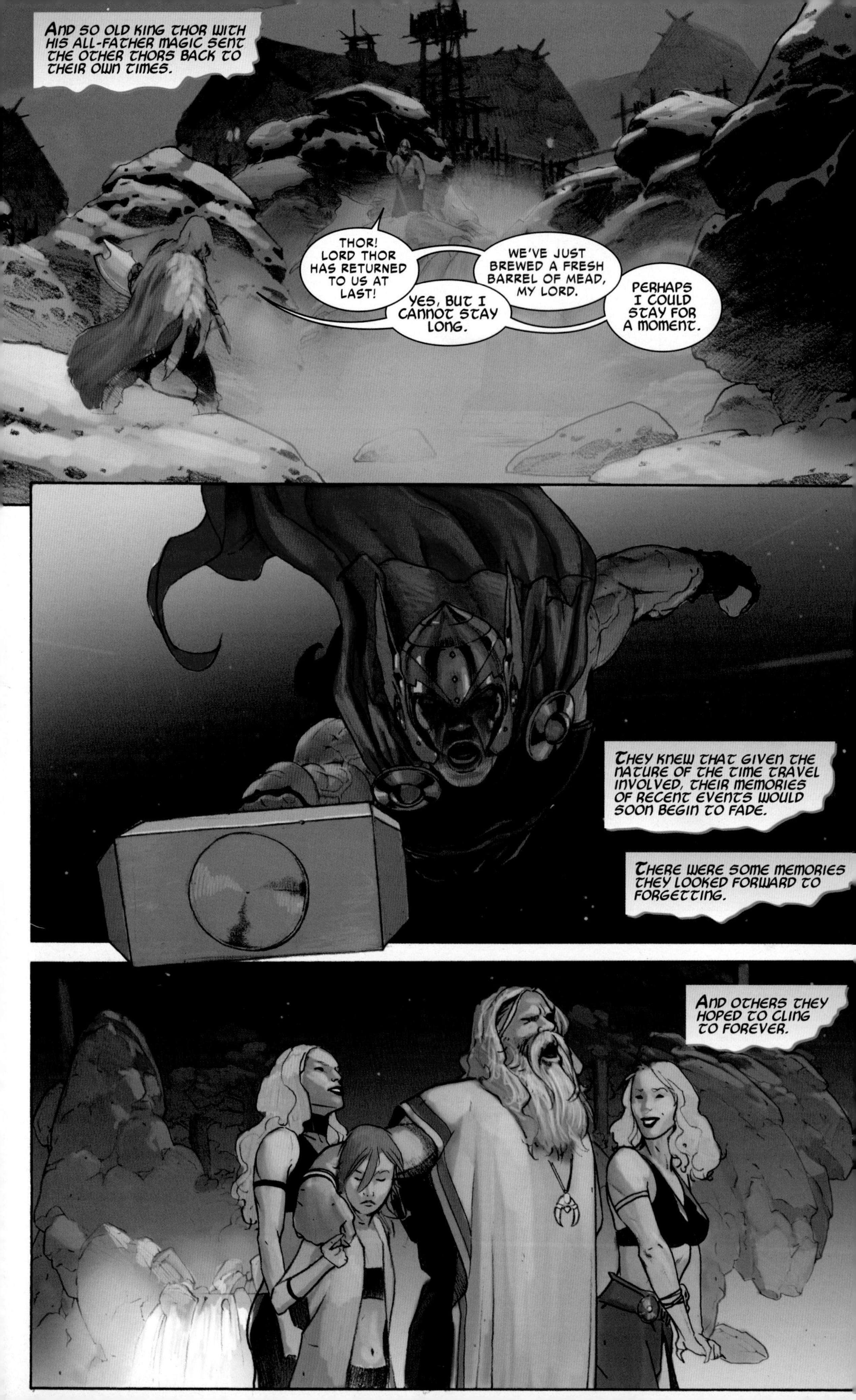
AND SO OLD KING THOR WITH HIS ALL-FATHER MAGIC SENT THE OTHER THORS BACK TO THEIR OWN TIMES.
THOR! LORD THOR HAS RETURNED TO US AT LAST!
YES, BUT I CANNOT STAY LONG.
WE'VE JUST BREWED A FRESH BARREL OF MEAD, MY LORD.
PERHAPS I COULD STAY FOR A MOMENT.
THEY KNEW THAT GIVEN THE NATURE OF THE TIME TRAVEL INVOLVED, THEIR MEMORIES OF RECENT EVENTS WOULD SOON BEGIN TO FADE.
THERE WERE SOME MEMORIES THEY LOOKED FORWARD TO FORGETTING.
AND OTHERS THEY HOPED TO CLING TO FOREVER.

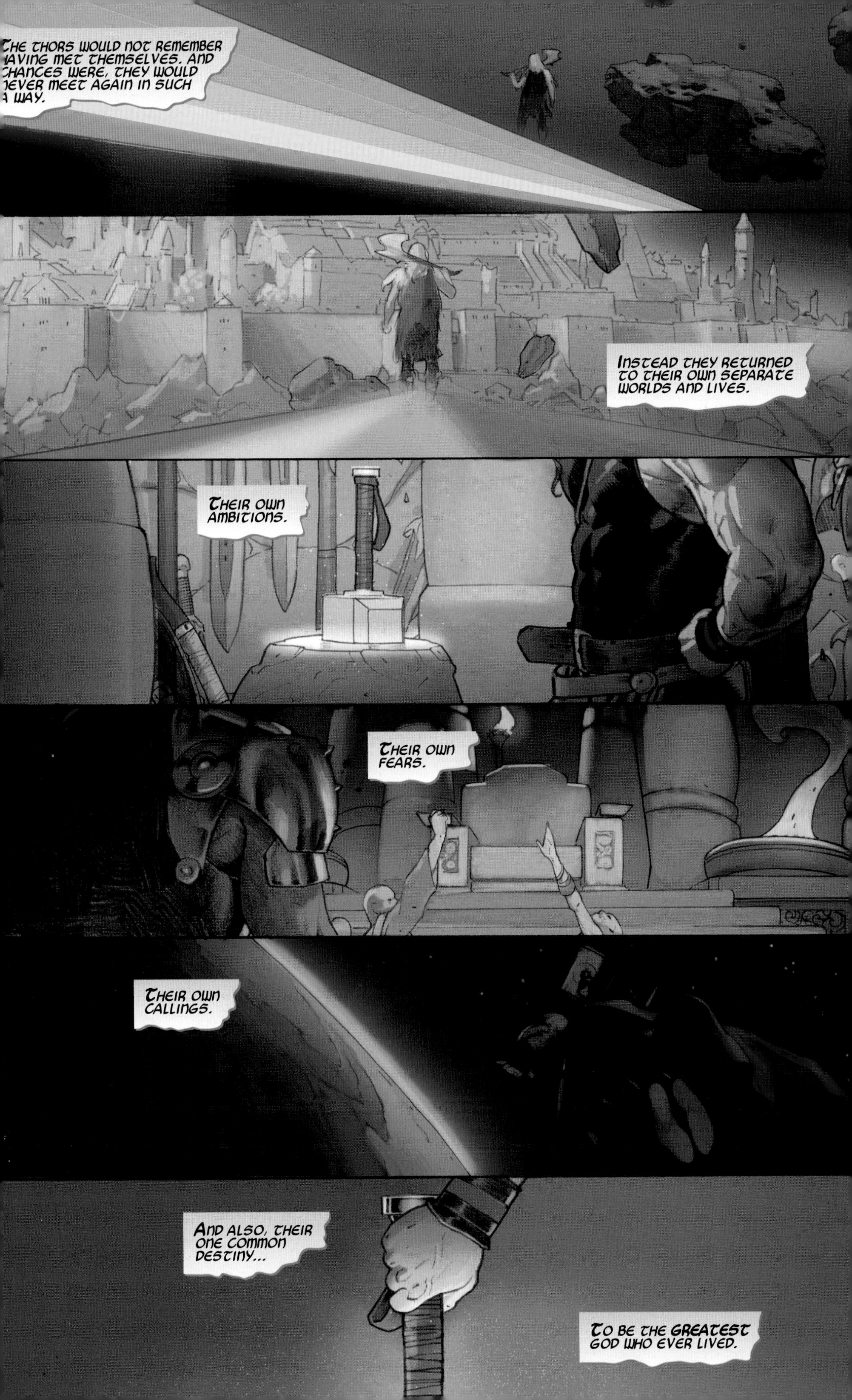

THE THORS WOULD NOT REMEMBER HAVING MET THEMSELVES. AND CHANCES WERE, THEY WOULD NEVER MEET AGAIN IN SUCH A WAY.
INSTEAD THEY RETURNED TO THEIR OWN SEPARATE WORLDS AND LIVES.
THEIR OWN AMBITIONS.
THEIR OWN FEARS.
THEIR OWN CALLINGS.
AND ALSO, THEIR ONE COMMON DESTINY...
TO BE THE GREATEST GOD WHO EVER LIVED.

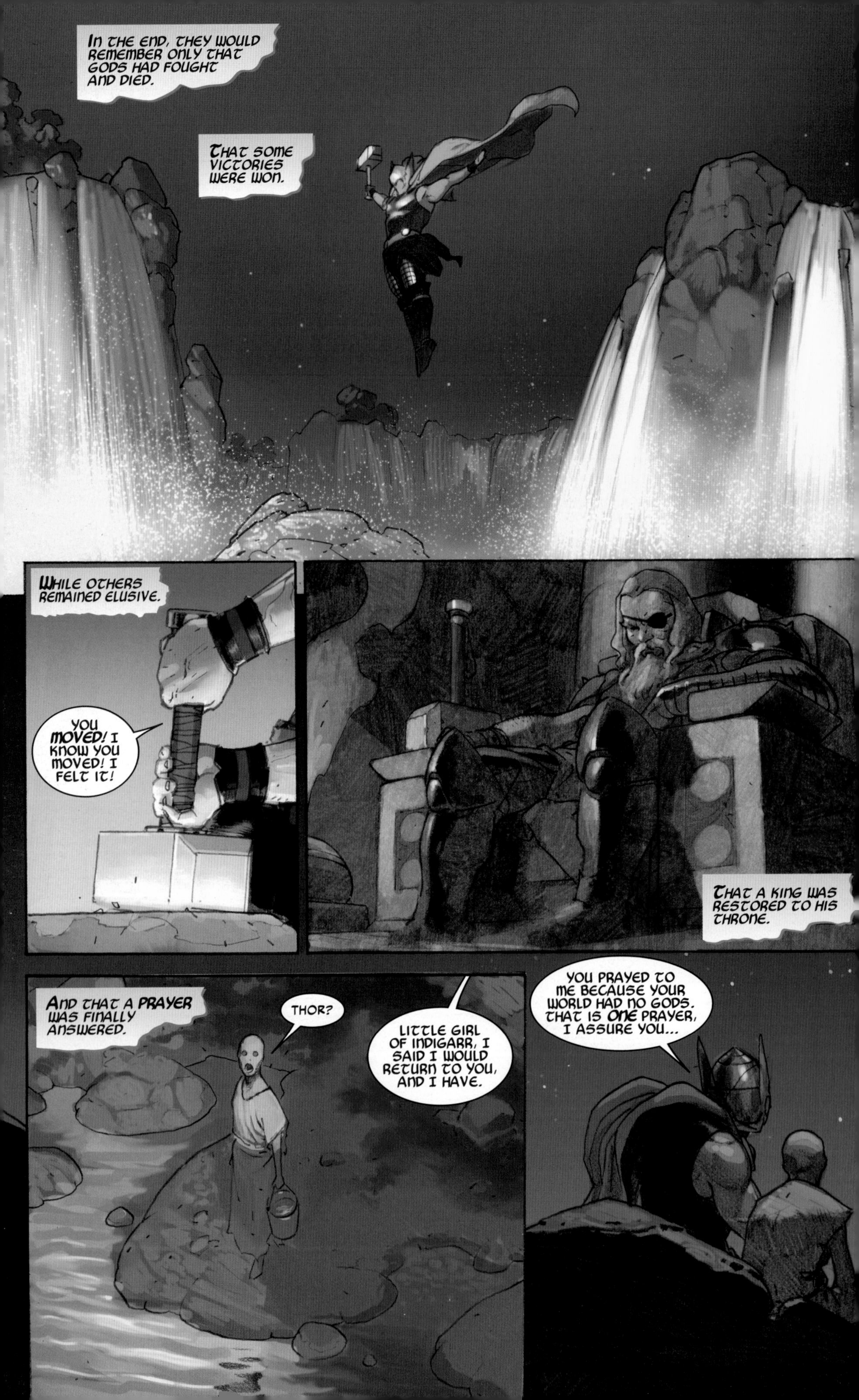
In the end, they would remember only that gods had fought and died.
That some victories were won.
While others remained elusive.
You MOVED! I know you moved! I felt it!
That a king was restored to his throne.
And that a PRAYER was finally answered.
Thor?
Little girl of Indigarr, I said I would return to you, and I have.
You prayed to me because your world had no gods. That is ONE prayer, I assure you...

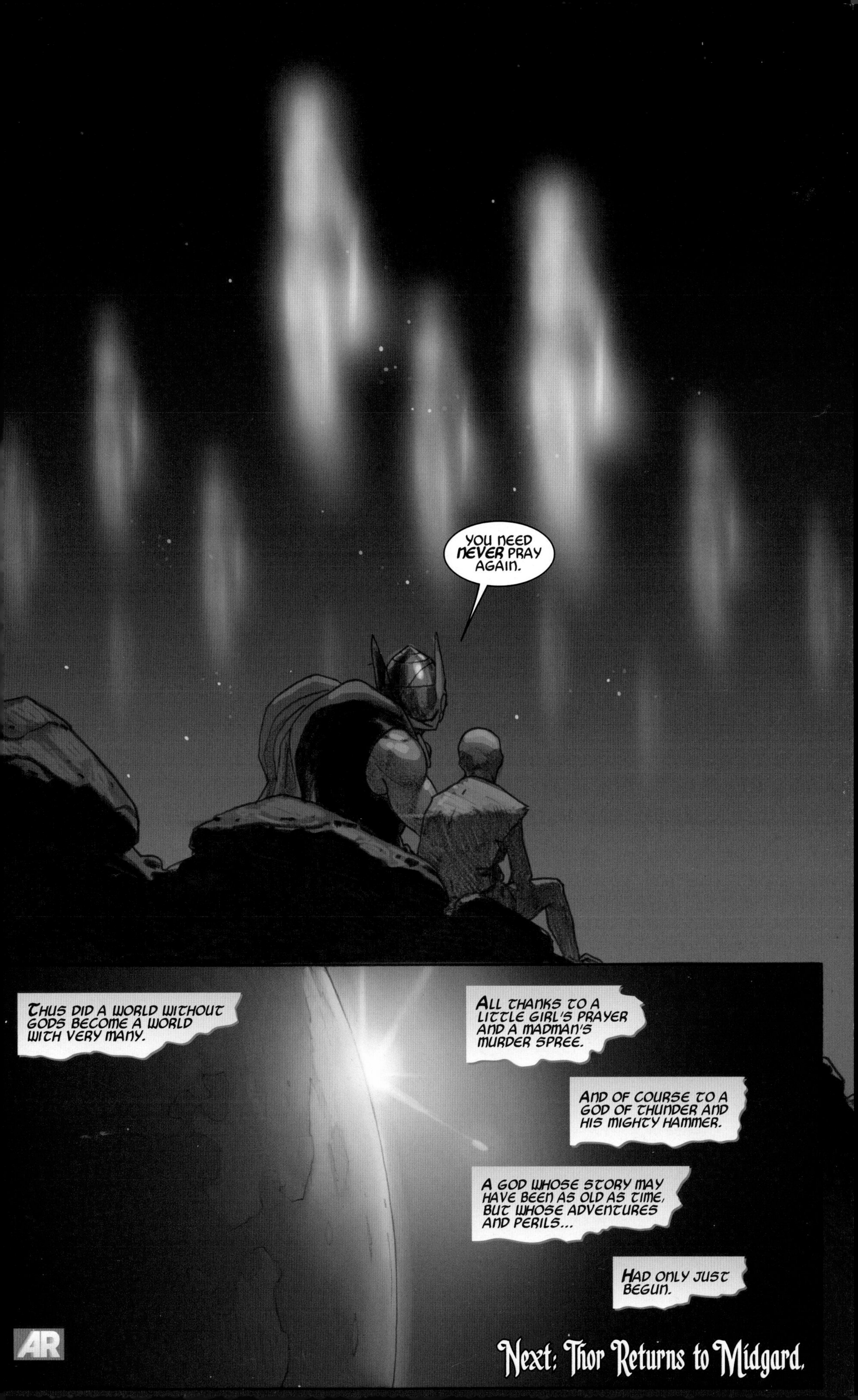
YOU NEED NEVER PRAY AGAIN.
THUS DID A WORLD WITHOUT GODS BECOME A WORLD WITH VERY MANY.
ALL THANKS TO A LITTLE GIRL'S PRAYER AND A MADMAN'S MURDER SPREE.
AND OF COURSE TO A GOD OF THUNDER AND HIS MIGHTY HAMMER.
A GOD WHOSE STORY MAY HAVE BEEN AS OLD AS TIME, BUT WHOSE ADVENTURES AND PERILS...
HAD ONLY JUST BEGUN.
AR
Next: Thor Returns to Midgard.

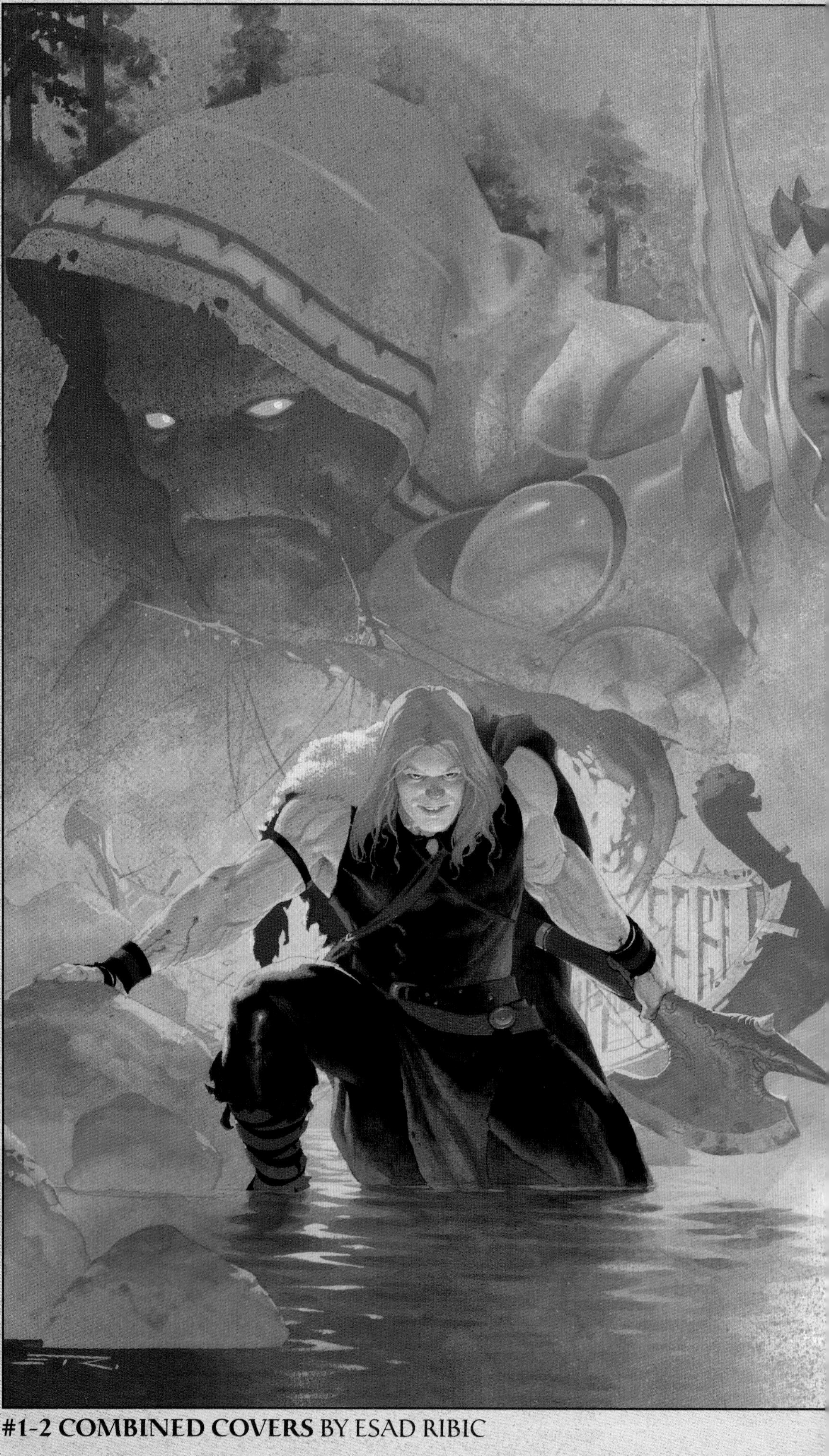

#1-2 COMBINED COVERS BY ESAD RIBIC

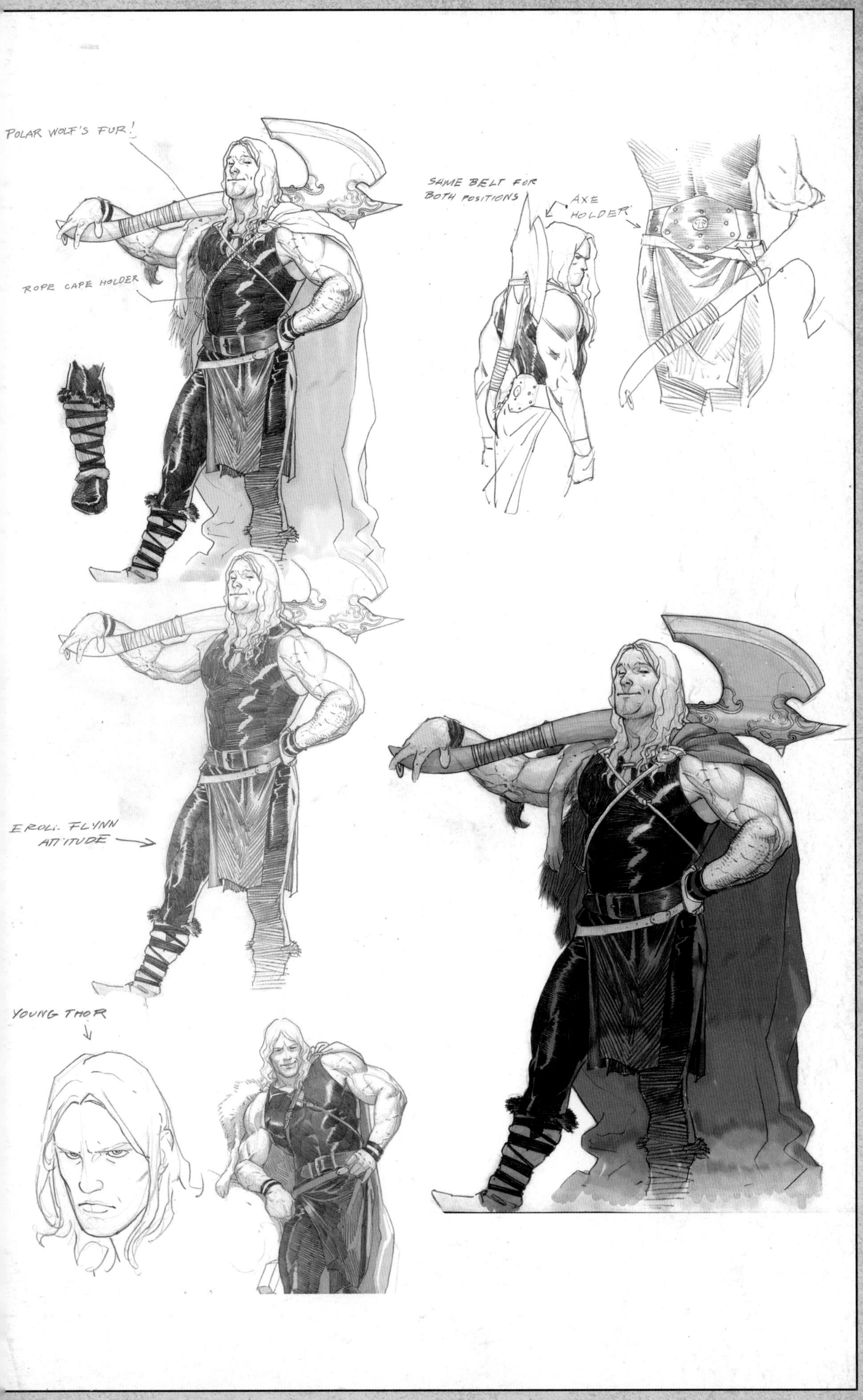

POLAR WOLF'S FUR!
ROPE CAPE HOLDER
SAME BELT FOR BOTH POSITIONS
AXE HOLDER
EROLL FLYNN ATTITUDE
YOUNG THOR

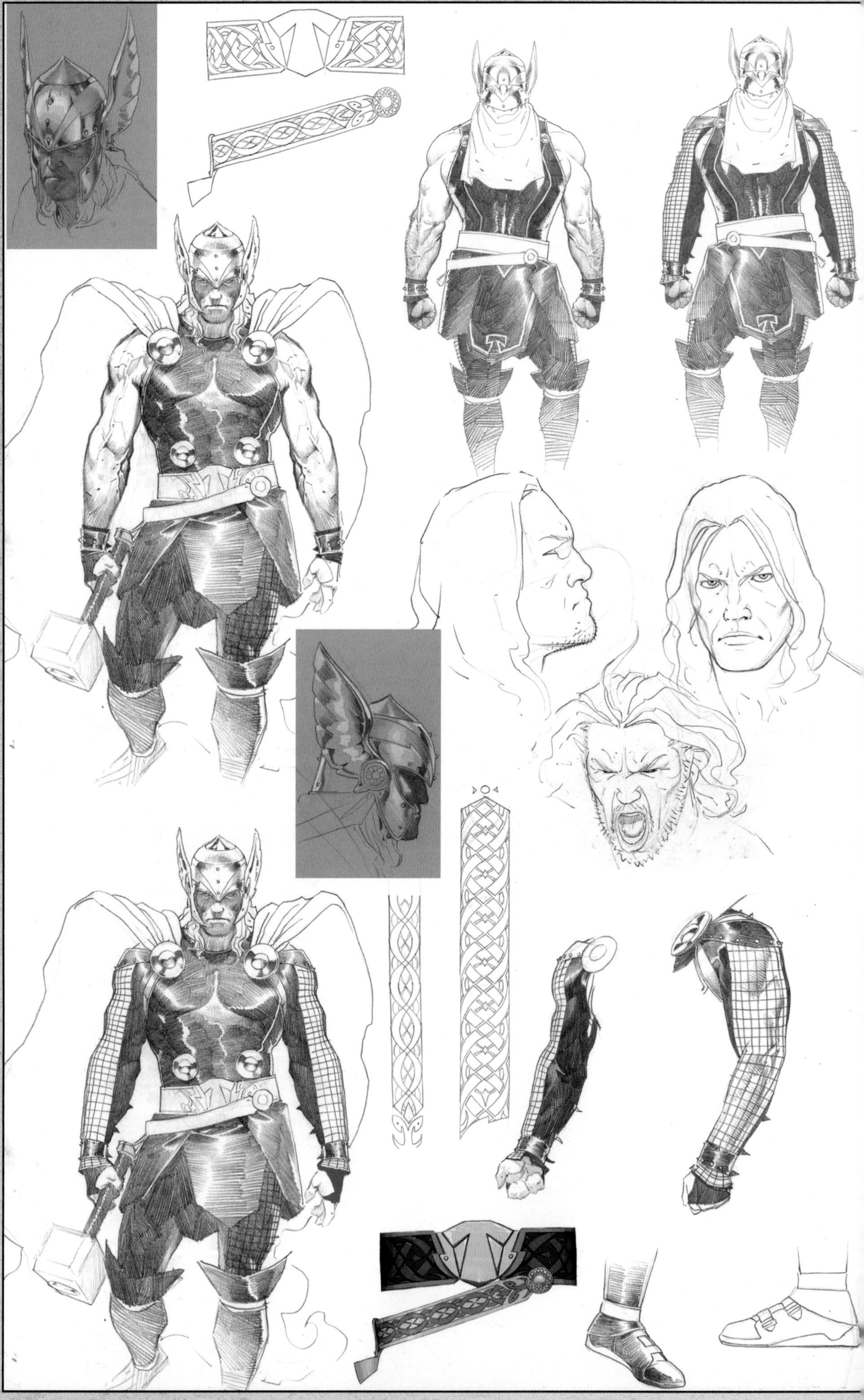

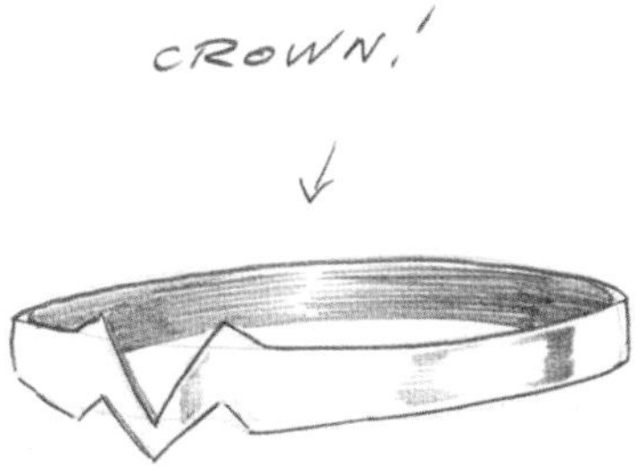
CROWN!
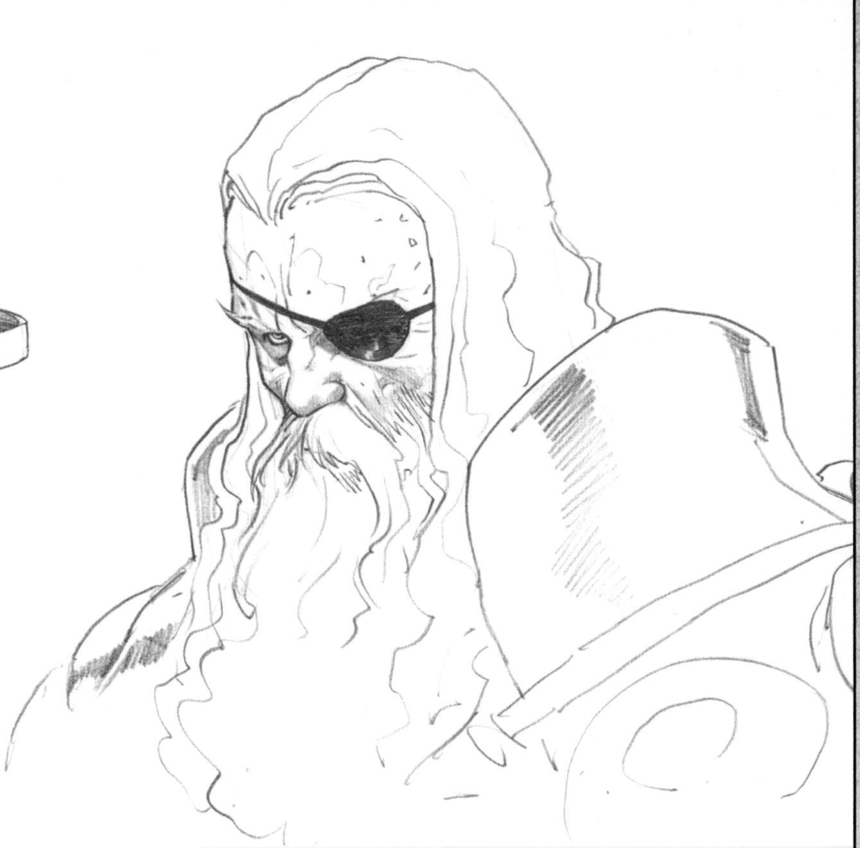
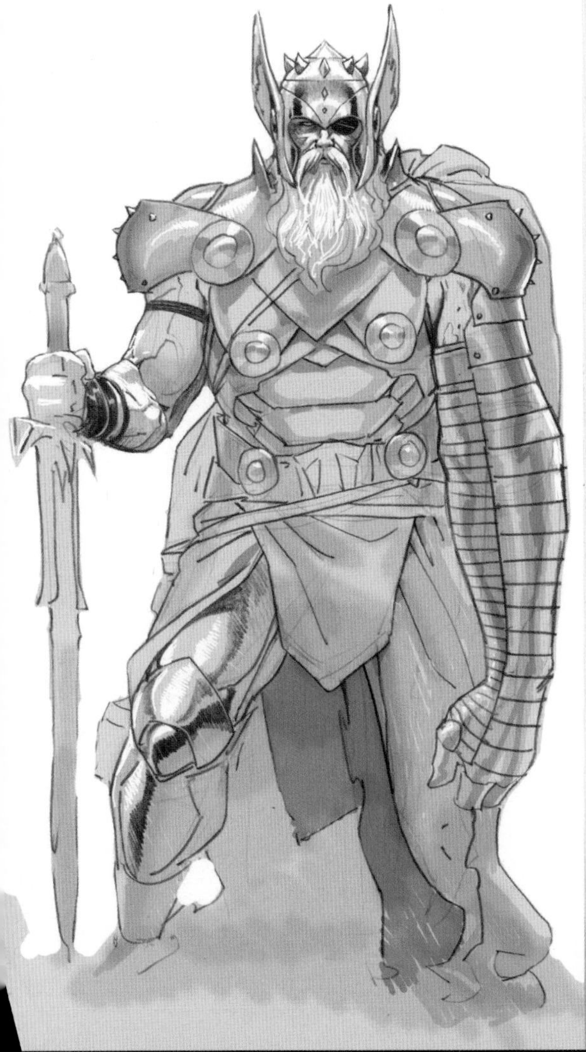
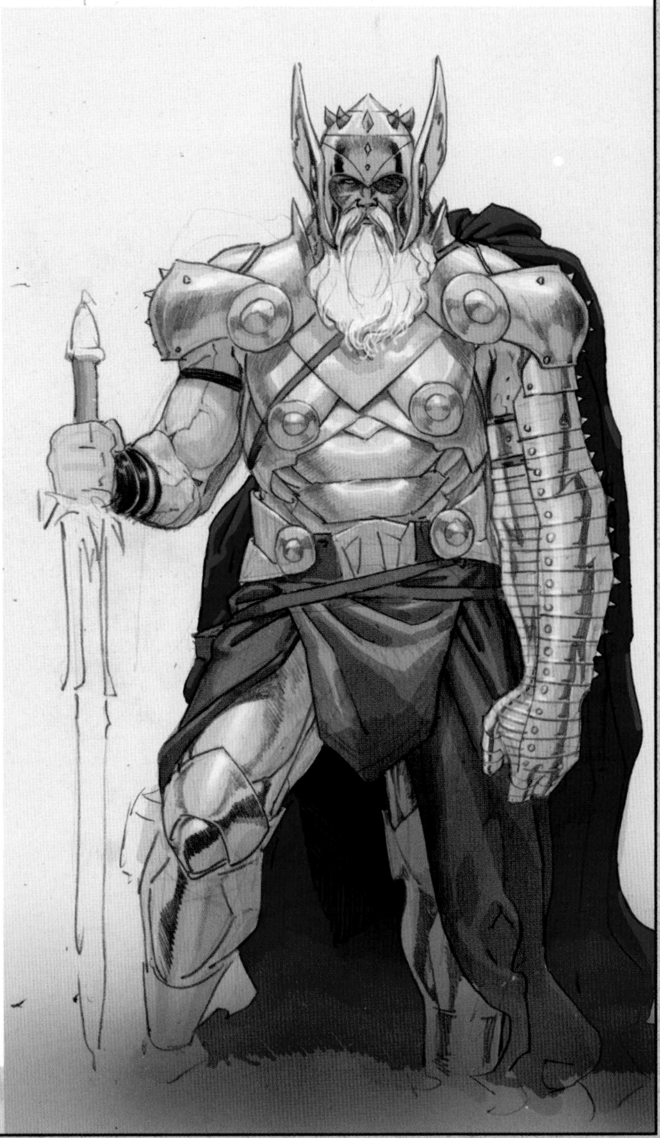

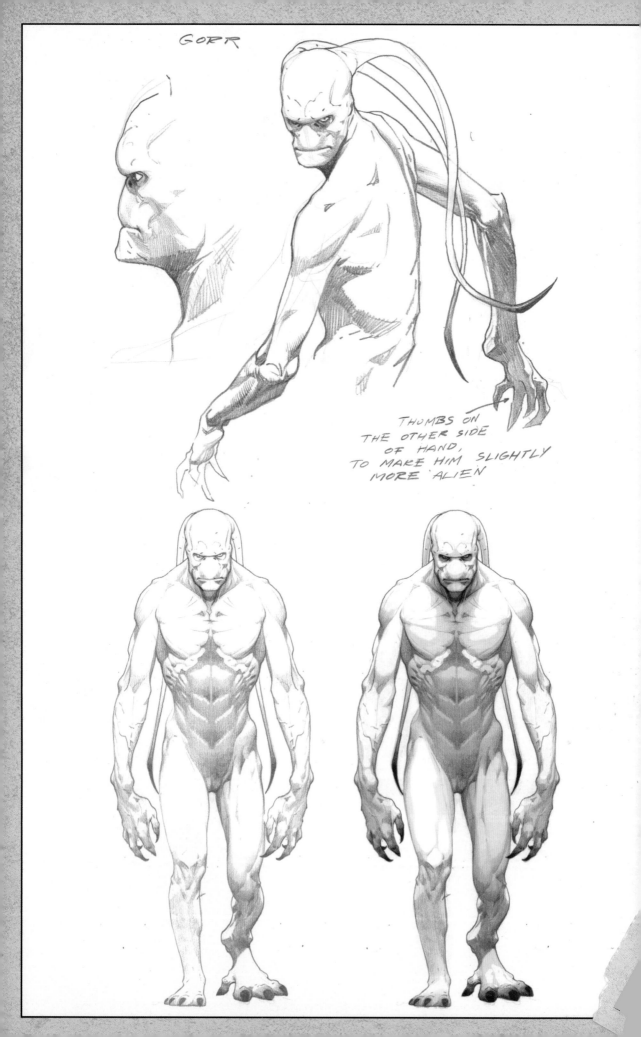

GORR

THUMBS ON
THE OTHER SIDE
OF HAND,
TO MAKE HIM SLIGHTLY
MORE 'ALIEN'

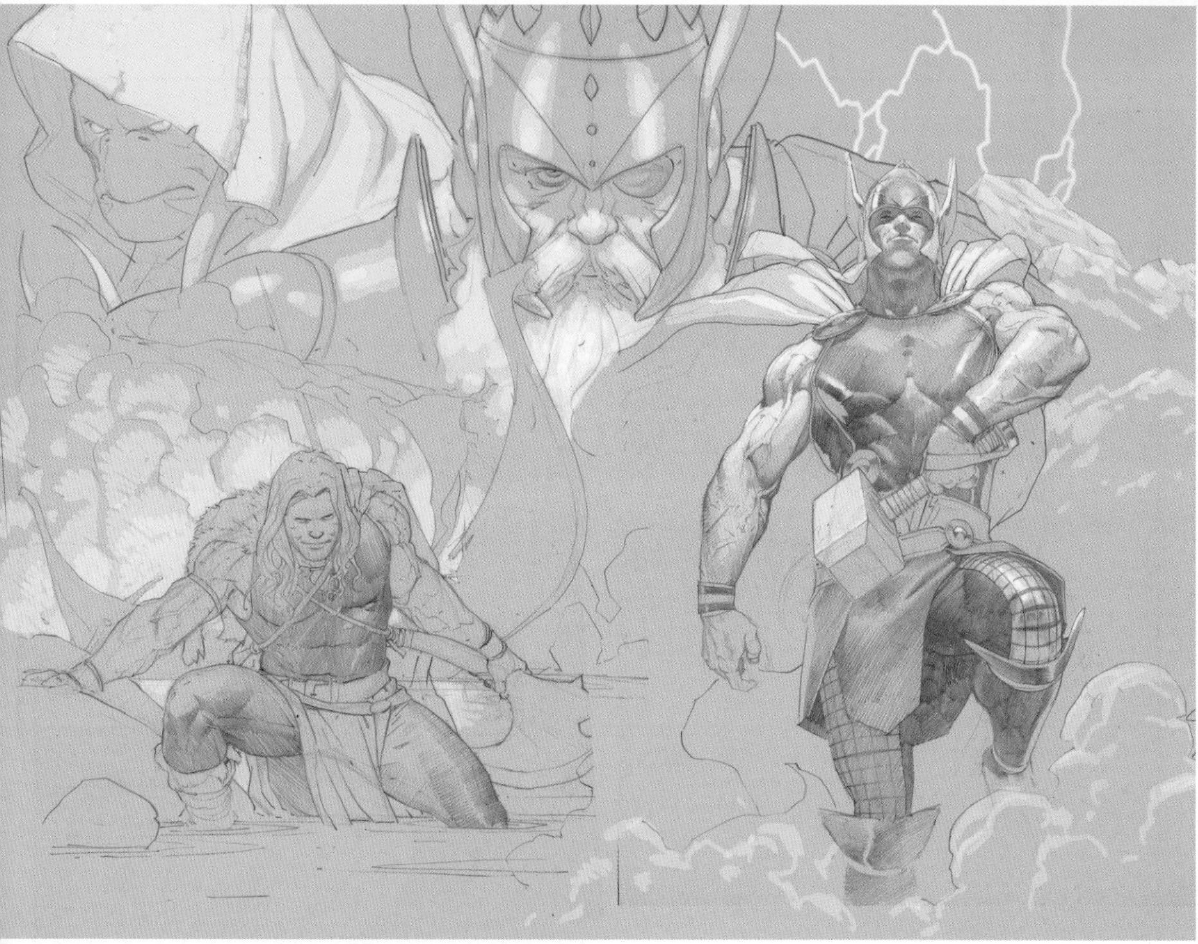

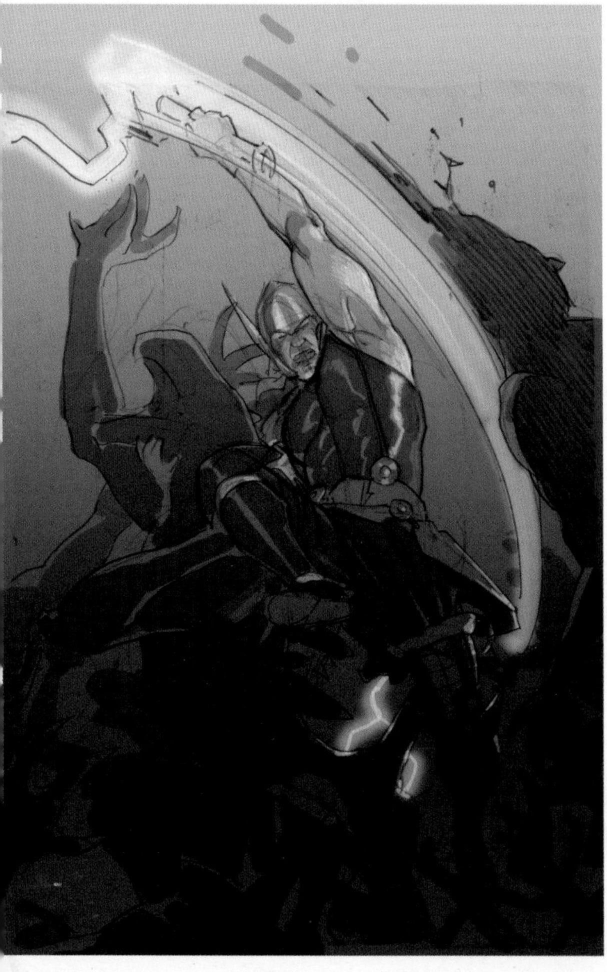

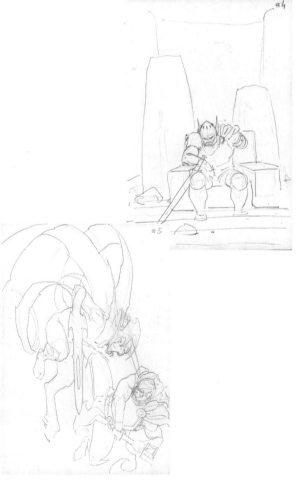

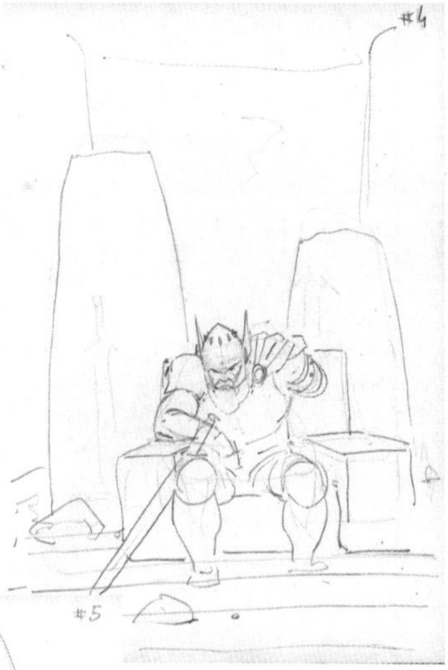
#4
#5

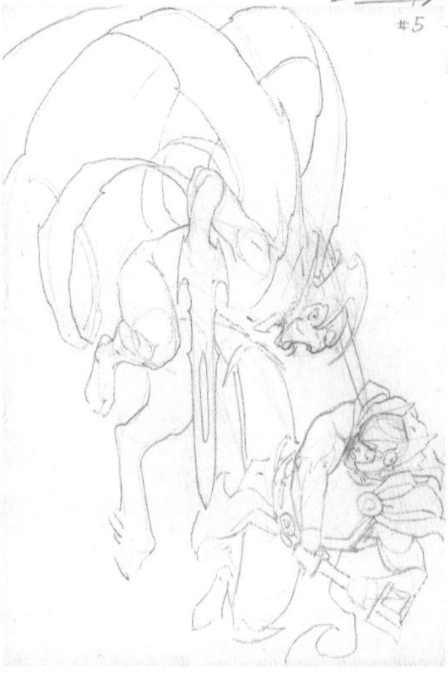

COVER SKETCHES

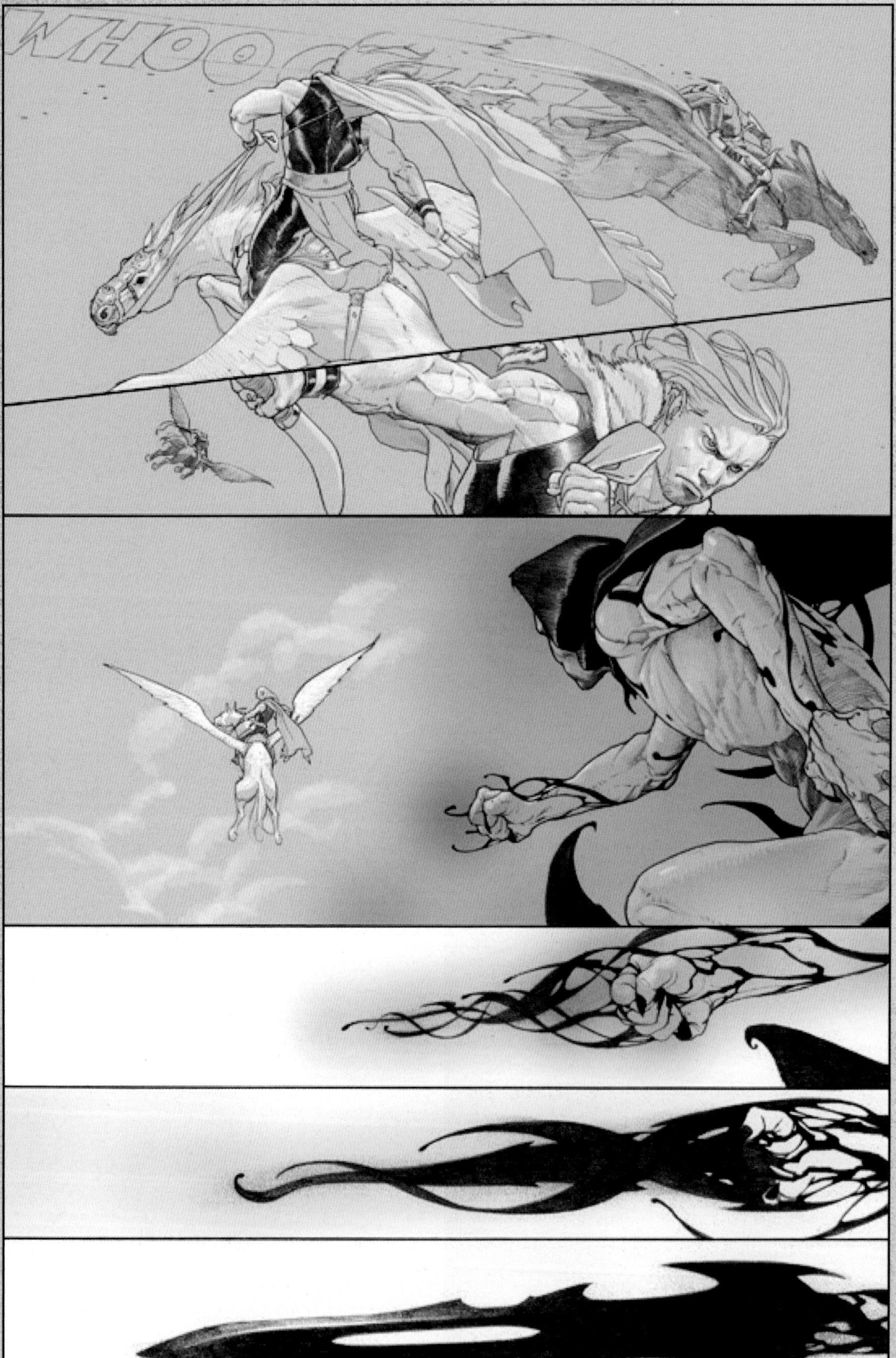
WHOO

#2, PAGE 9 PENCILS

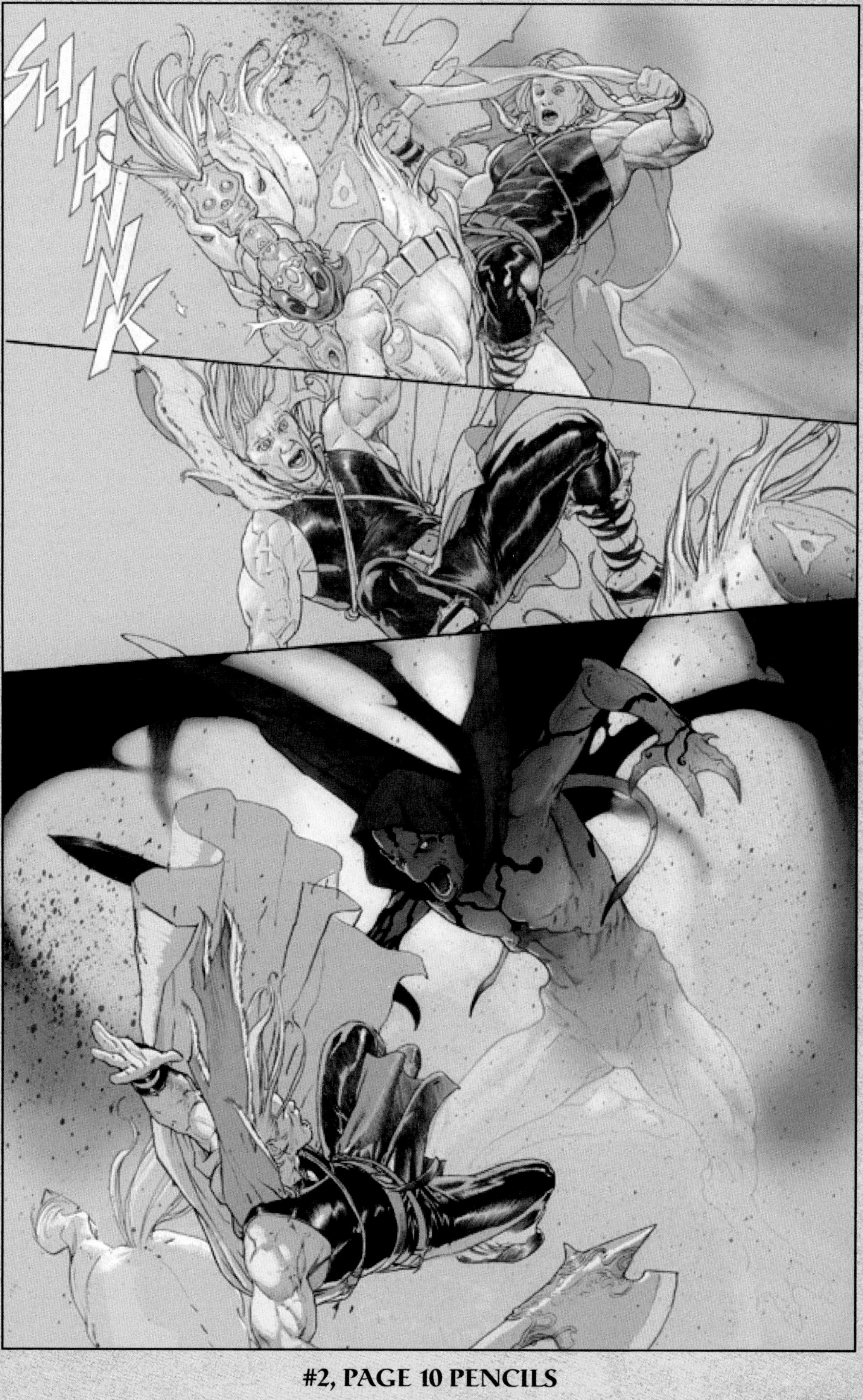
SHHHINNK

#2, PAGE 10 PENCILS

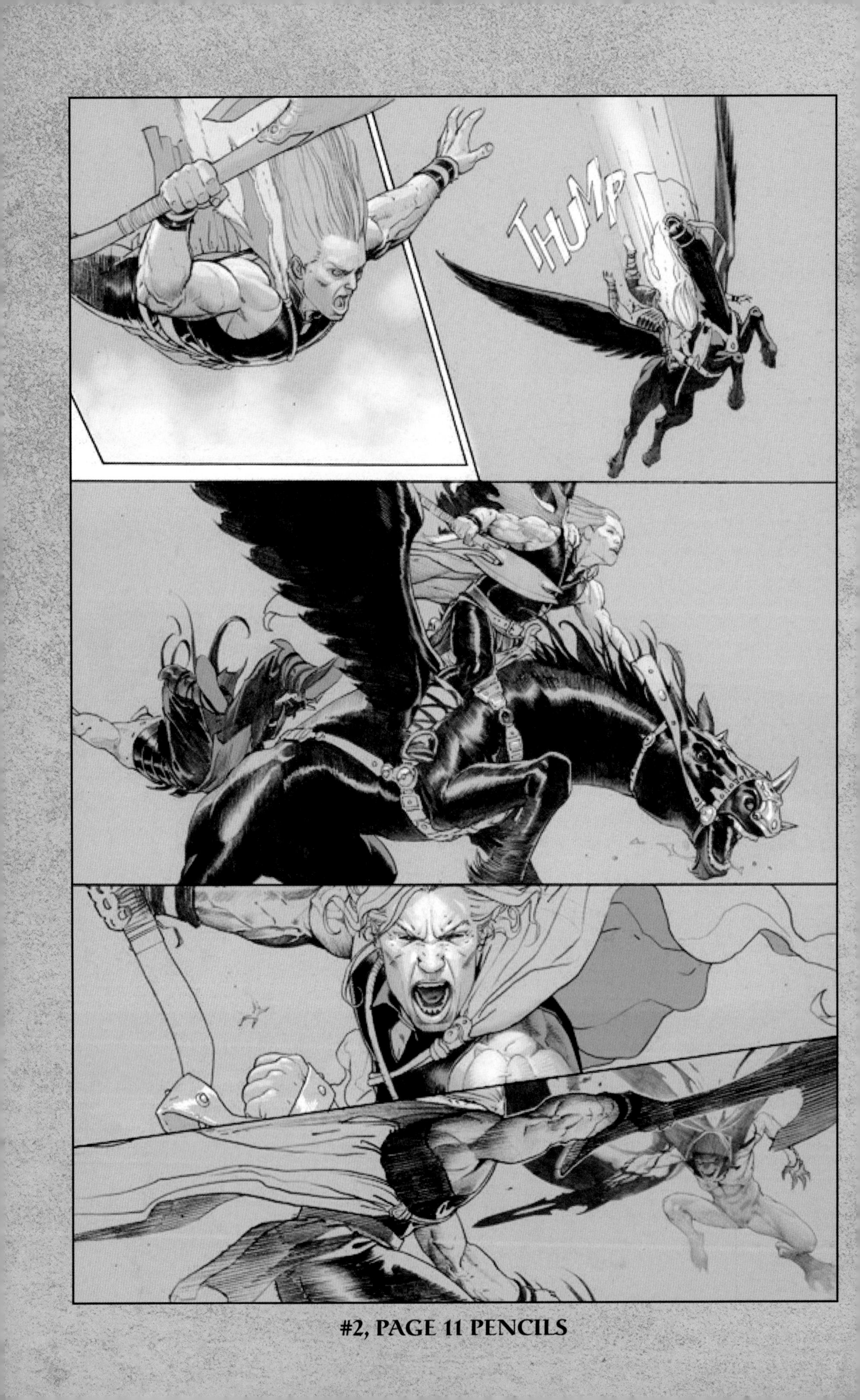
THUMP

#2, PAGE 11 PENCILS

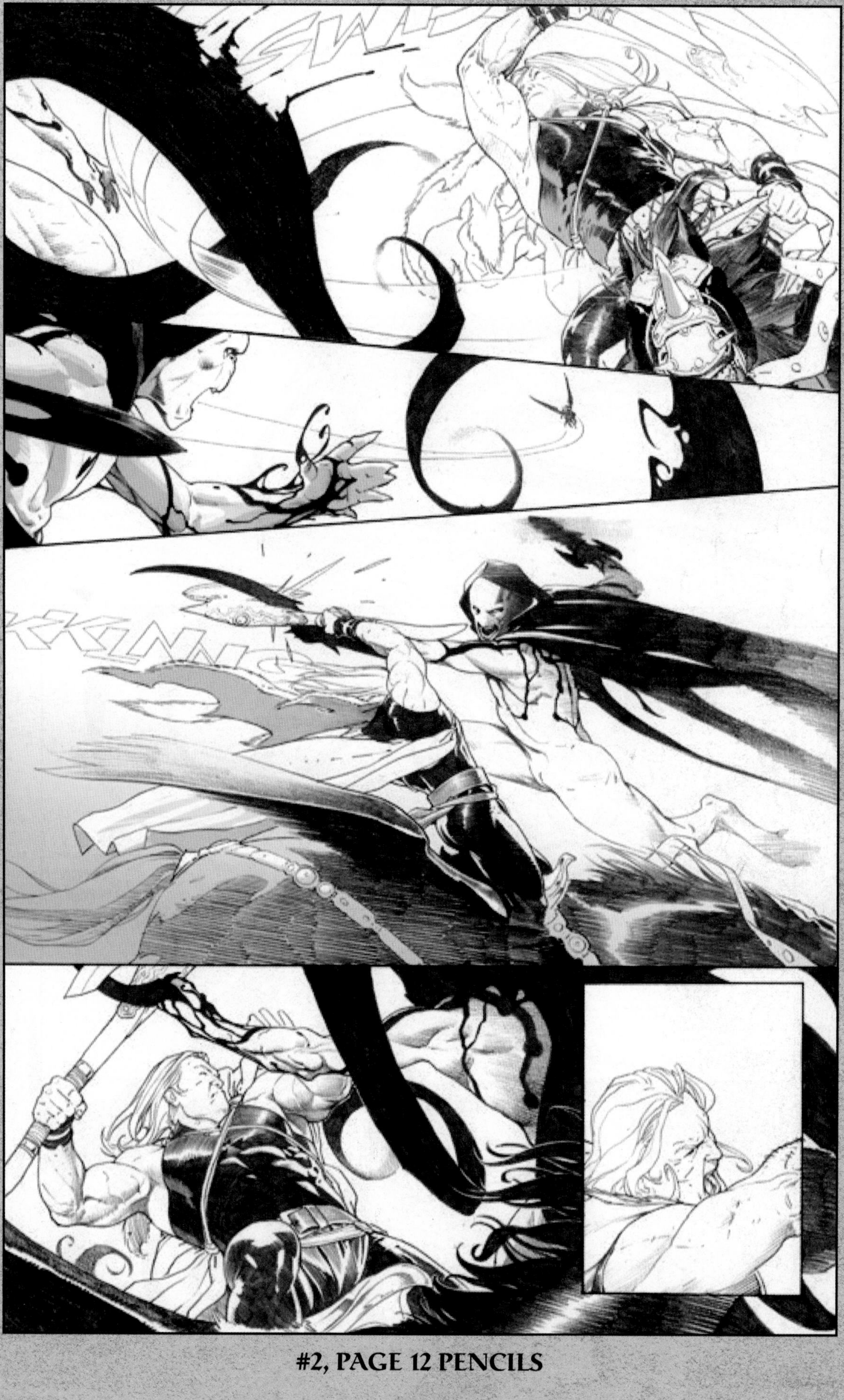

#2, PAGE 12 PENCILS

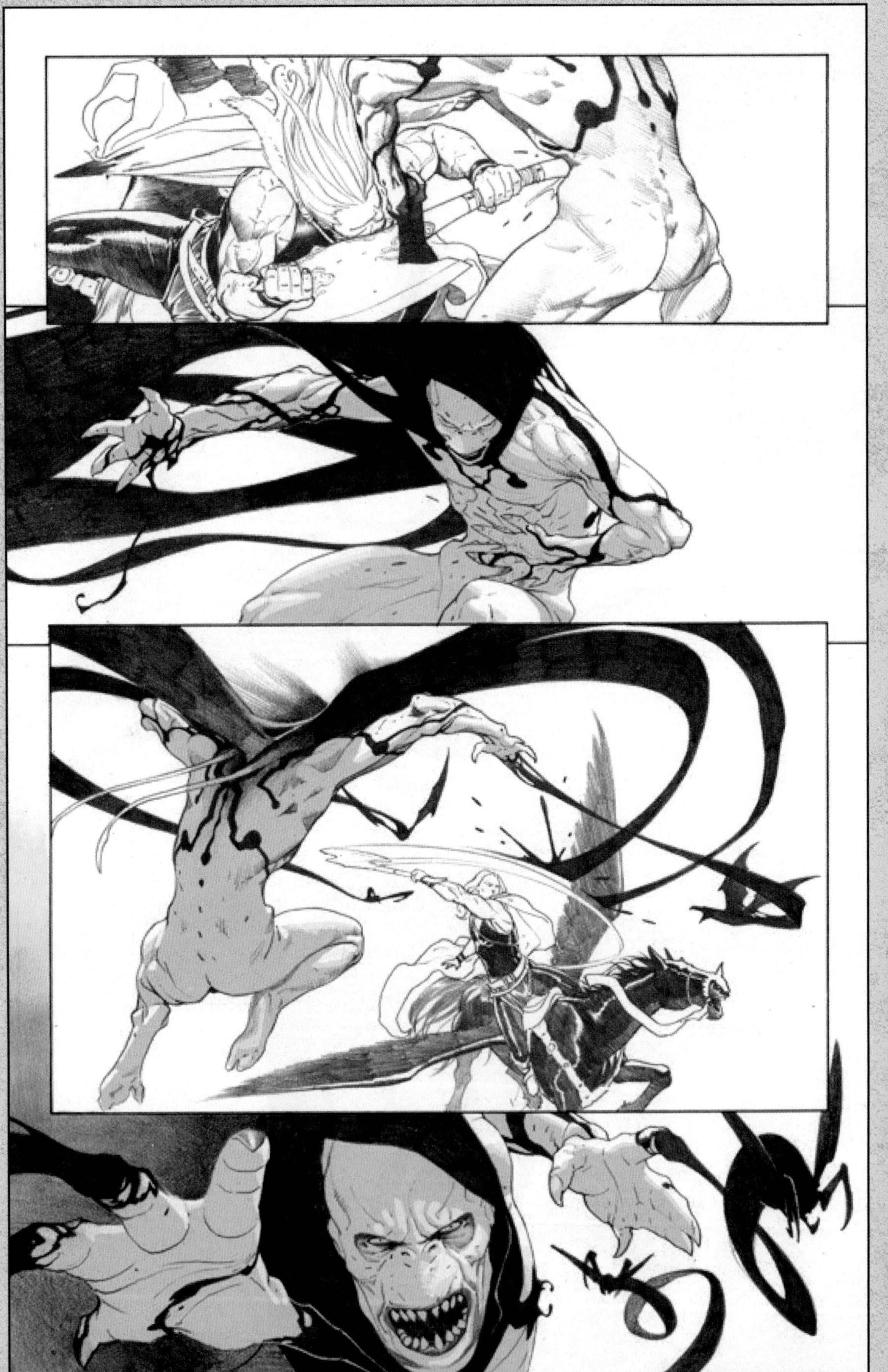

#2, PAGE 13 PENCILS

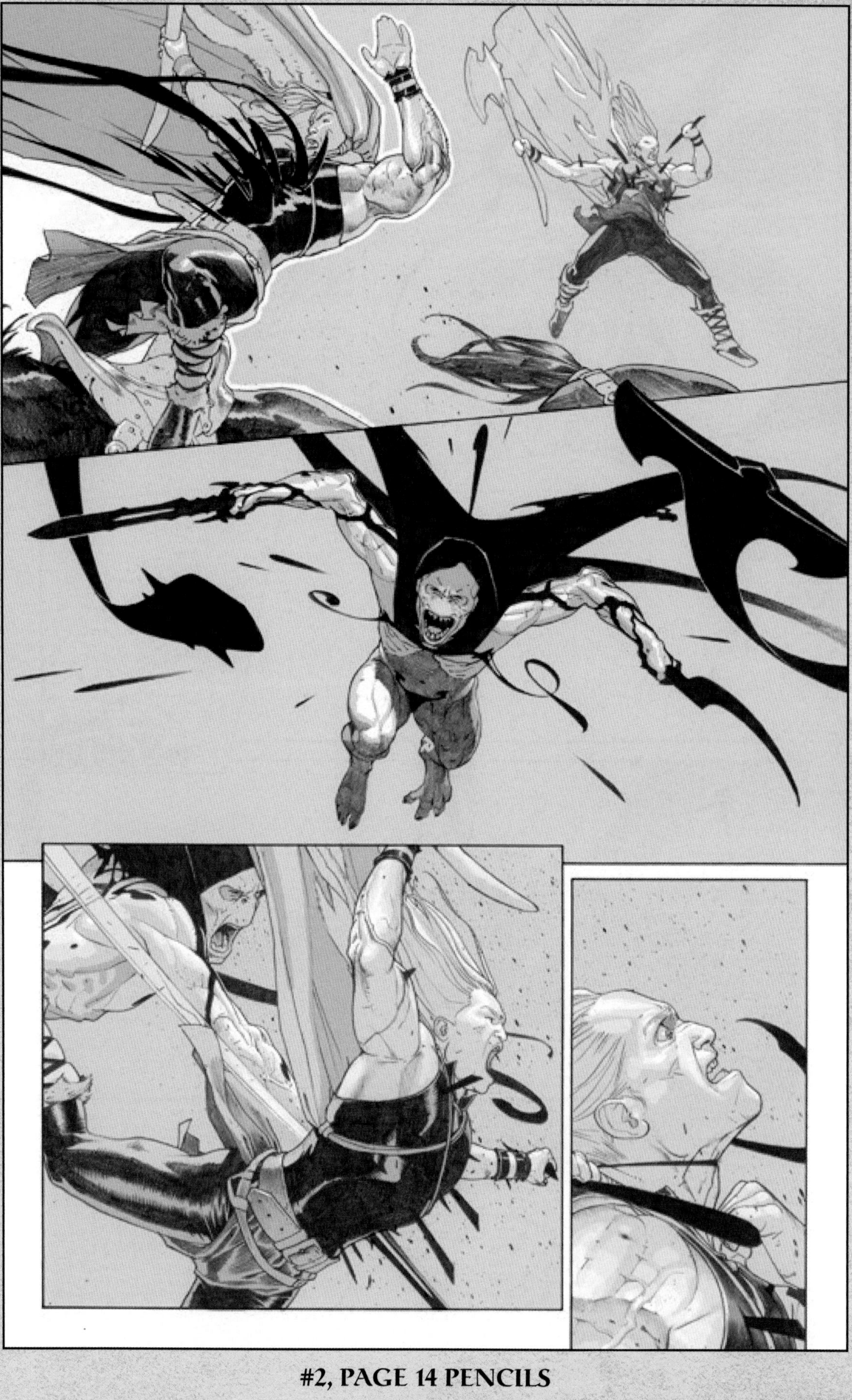

#2, PAGE 14 PENCILS

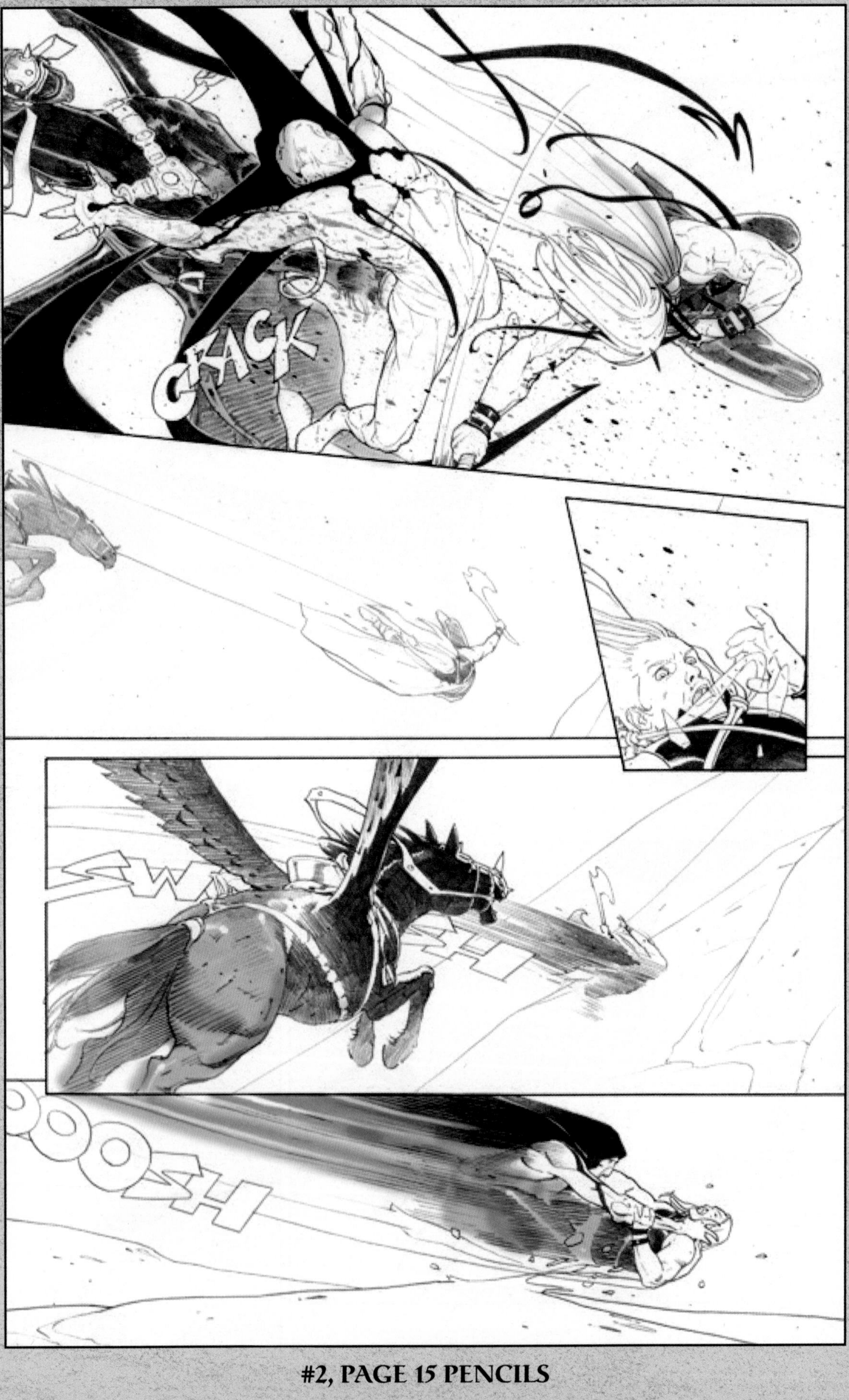
CRACK

#2, PAGE 15 PENCILS

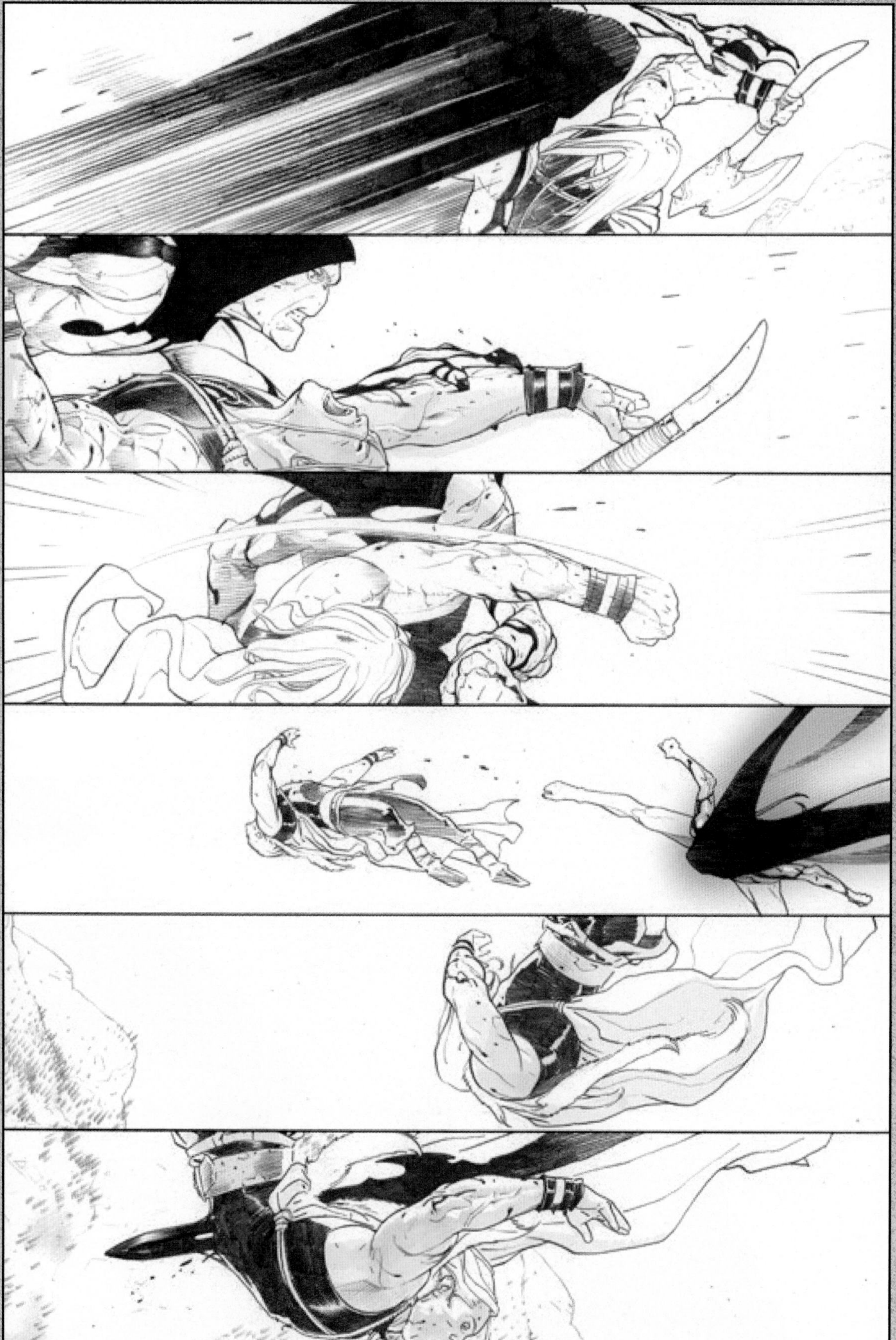

#2, PAGE 16 PENCILS

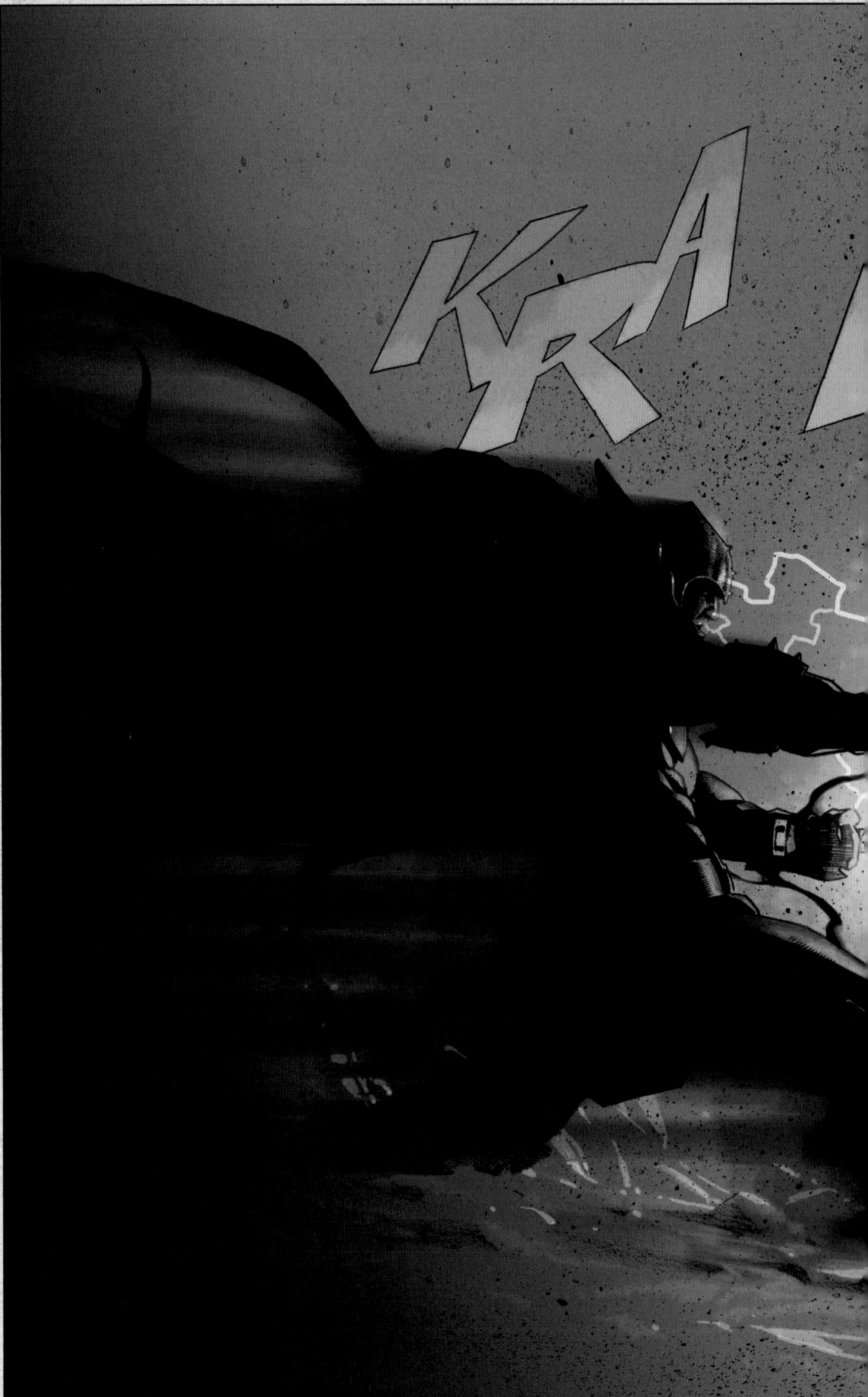
KRA

#11, PAGES 9-10 PENCILS

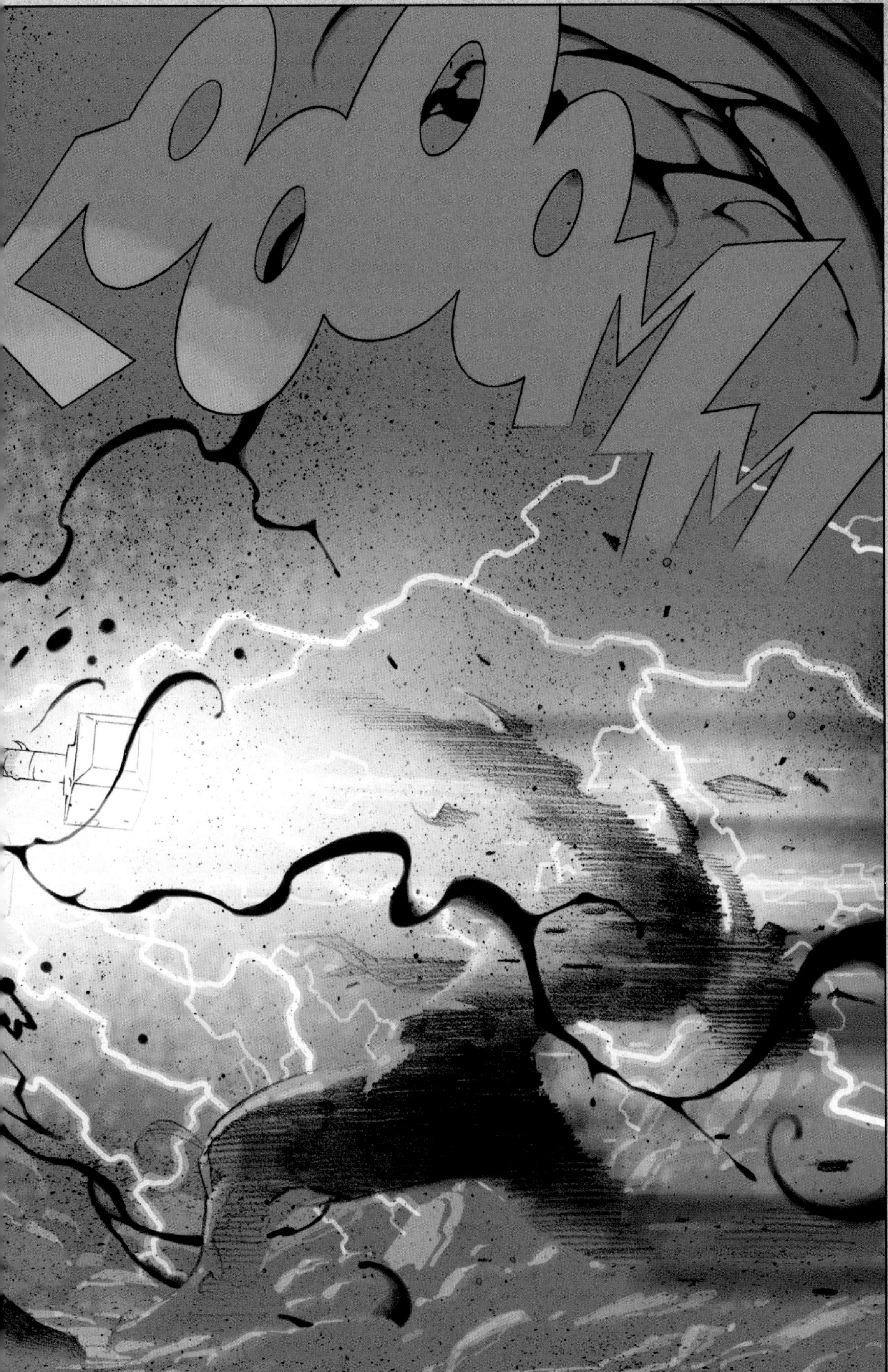

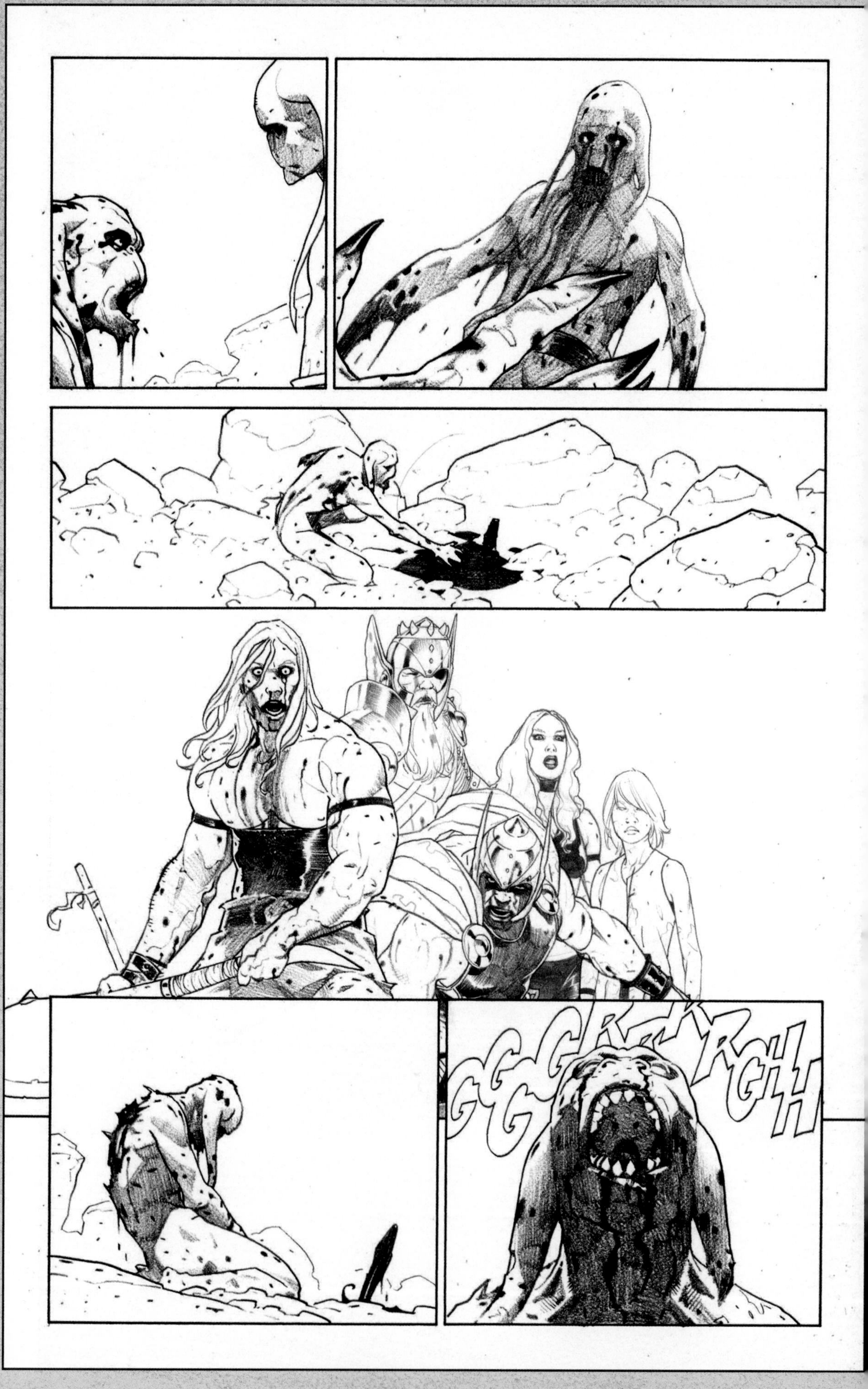

#11, PAGE 12 PENCILS

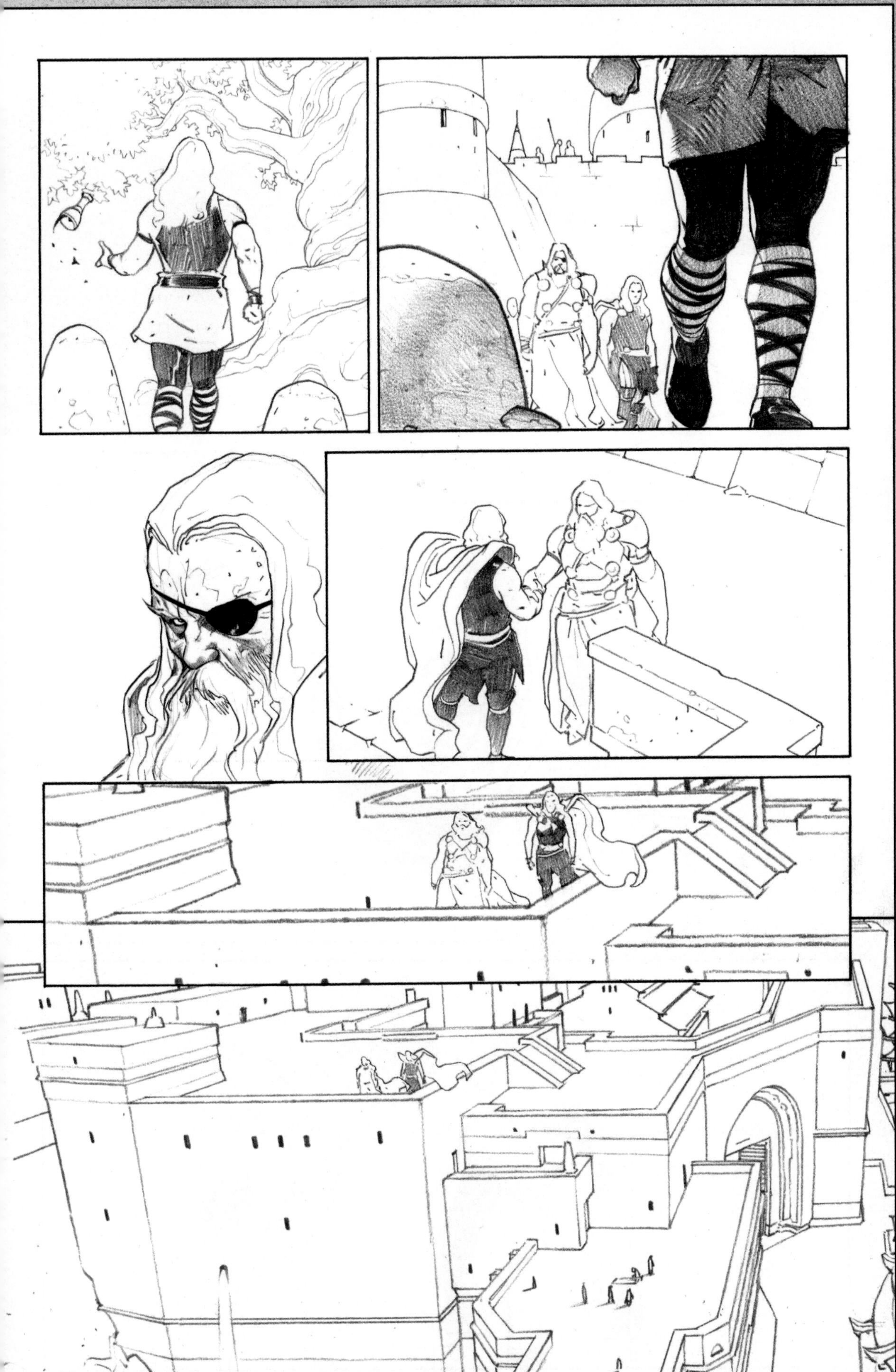

#11, PAGE 16 PENCILS

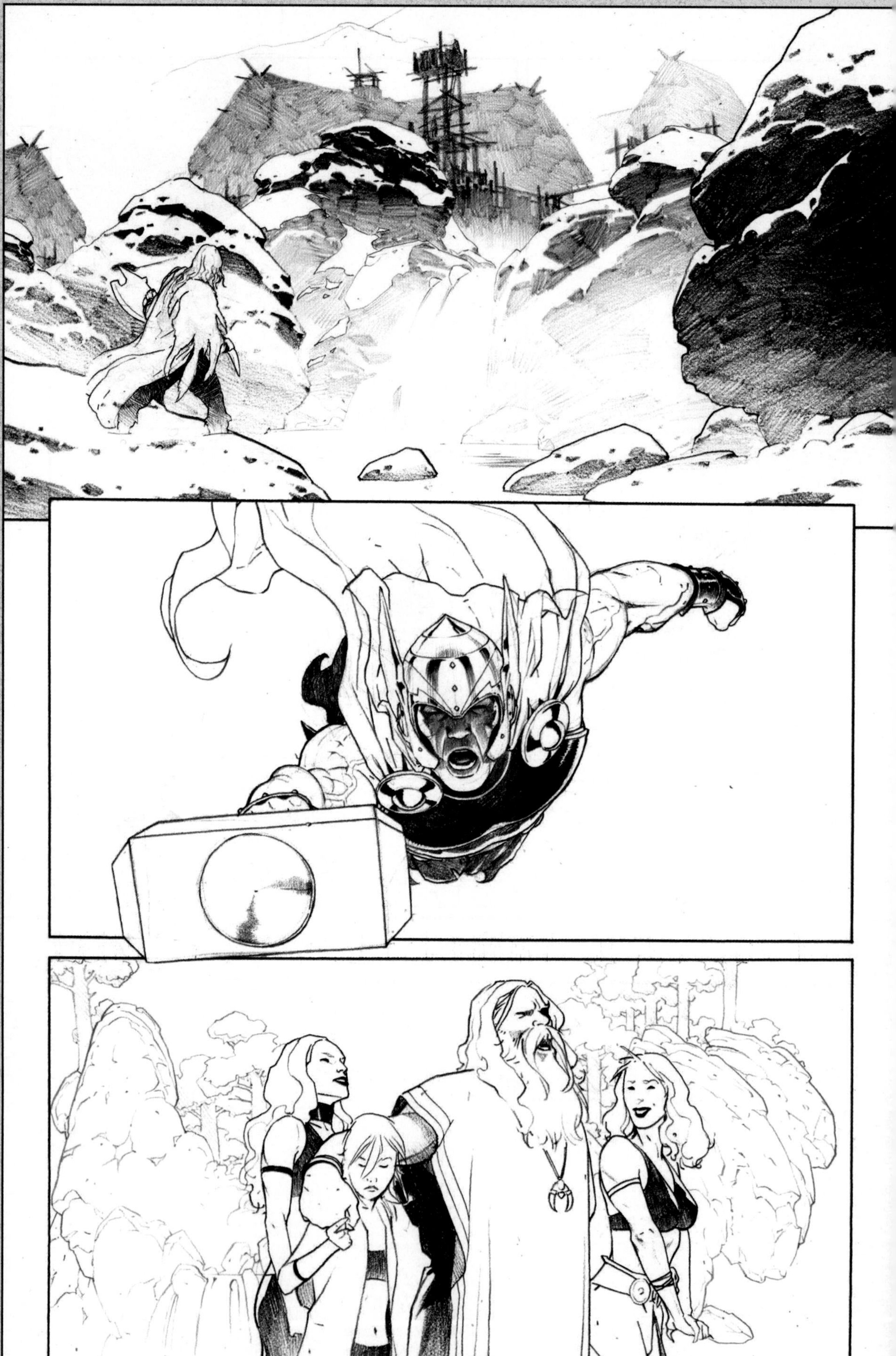

#11, PAGE 17 PENCILS

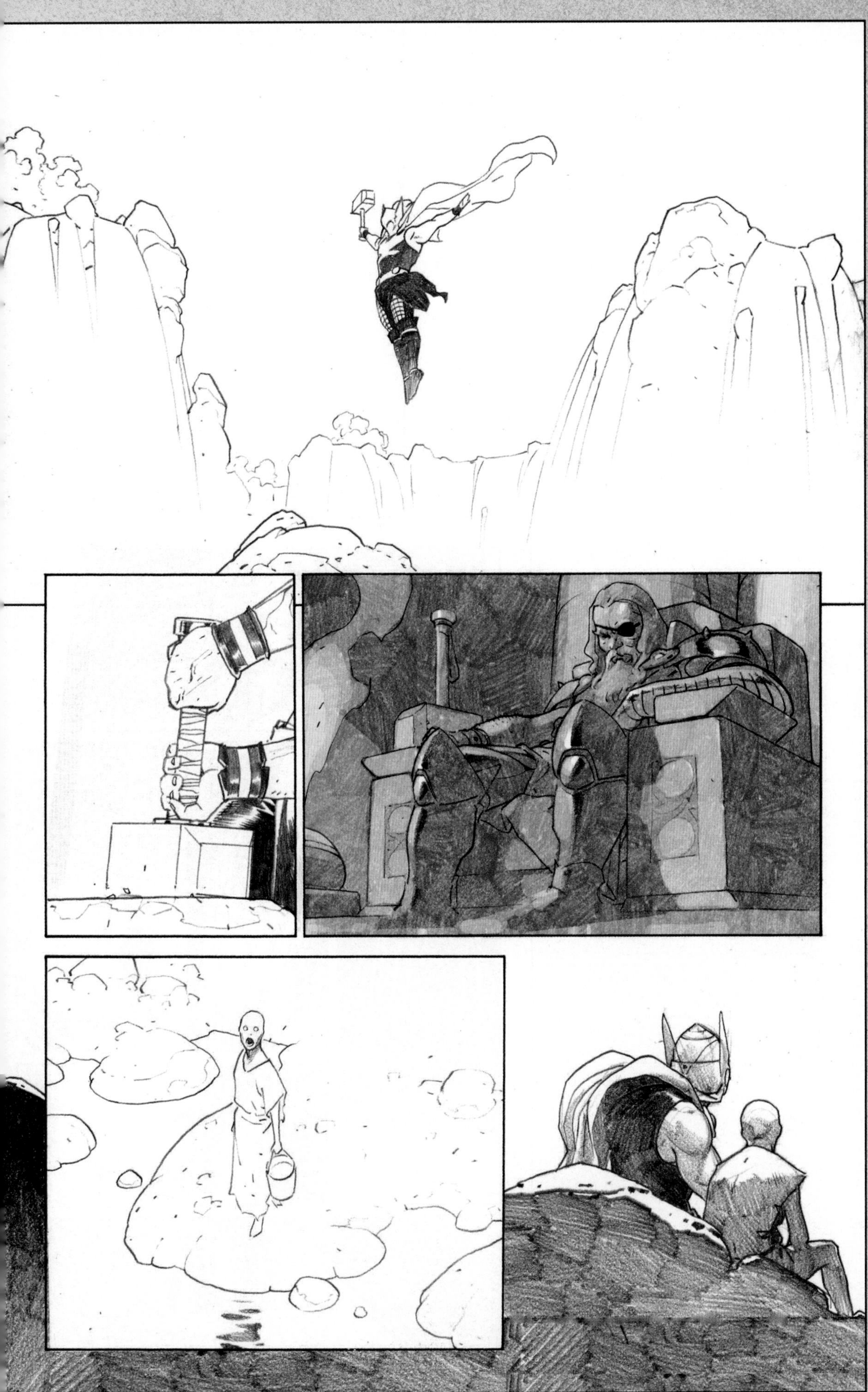

#11, PAGE 19 PENCILS

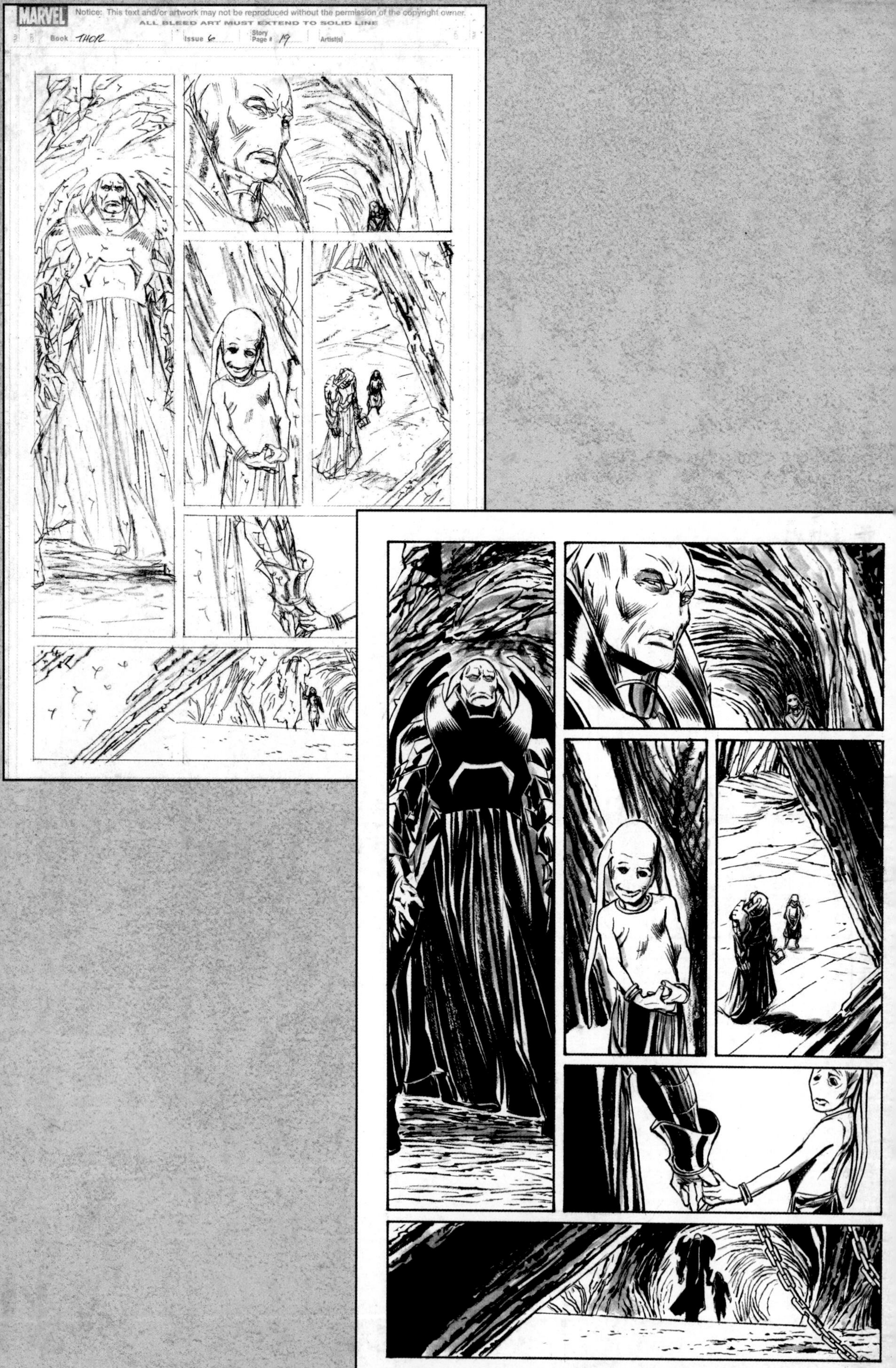
MARVEL
Notice: This text and/or artwork may not be reproduced without the permission of the copyright owner.
ALL BLEED ART MUST EXTEND TO SOLID LINE
Book THOR
Issue 6
Story Page # 19
Artist(s)

#6, PAGE 19 PENCILS & INKS
BY BUTCH GUICE & TOM PALMER

#6, PAGE 20 PENCILS & INKS
BY BUTCH GUICE & TOM PALMER

MARVEL AR AUGMENTED REALITY

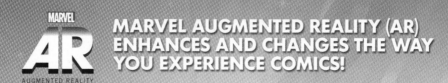

MARVEL AUGMENTED REALITY (AR) ENHANCES AND CHANGES THE WAY YOU EXPERIENCE COMICS!

TO ACCESS THE FREE MARVEL AR CONTENT IN THIS BOOK*:

1. Locate the AR logo within the comic.
2. Go to Marvel.com/AR in your web browser.
3. Search by series title to find the corresponding AR.
4. Enjoy Marvel AR!

*All AR content that appears in this book has been archived and will be available only at Marvel.com/AR – no longer in the Marvel AR App. Content subject to change and availability.

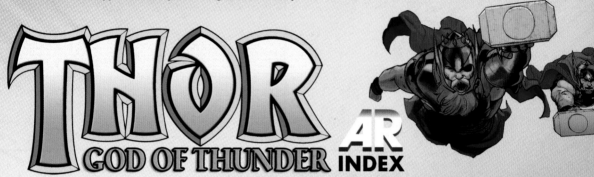

THOR GOD OF THUNDER AR INDEX